Handbook of Research on Remote Work and Worker Well-Being in the Post-COVID-19 Era

Daniel Wheatley
University of Birmingham, UK

Irene Hardill
Northumbria University, UK

Sarah Buglass
Nottingham Trent University, UK

A volume in the Advances in Human Resources Management and Organizational Development (AHRMOD) Book Series

IGI Global
PUBLISHER of TIMELY KNOWLEDGE

Published in the United States of America by
IGI Global
Business Science Reference (an imprint of IGI Global)
701 E. Chocolate Avenue
Hershey PA, USA 17033
Tel: 717-533-8845
Fax: 717-533-8661
E-mail: cust@igi-global.com
Web site: http://www.igi-global.com

Library of Congress Cataloging-in-Publication Data

Names: Wheatley, Daniel, 1982- editor. | Hardill, Irene, editor. | Buglass, Sarah, 1979- editor.
Title: Handbook of research on remote work and worker well-being in the post-COVID-19 era / Daniel Wheatley, Irene Hardill, and Sarah Buglass, editors.
Description: Hershey, PA : Business Science Reference, [2021] | Includes bibliographical references and index. | Summary: "This edited book presents an understanding of the impacts of the rapid expansion of remote working in response to the global COVID-19 pandemic with the intent to progress understanding and raise awareness of both the benefits and challenges faced from the large-scale adoption of remote working, considering the multiple dimensions in which this large-scale movement is impacting our working lives"-- Provided by publisher.
Identifiers: LCCN 2020052476 | ISBN 9781799867548 (hardcover) | ISBN 9781799867562 (ebook)
Subjects: LCSH: Telecommuting. | Quality of work life. | Well-being. | COVID-19 (Disease)
Classification: LCC HD2336.3 .R47 2021 | DDC 331.25/68--dc23
LC record available at https://lccn.loc.gov/2020052476

This book is published in the IGI Global book series Advances in Human Resources Management and Organizational Development (AHRMOD) (ISSN: 2327-3372; eISSN: 2327-3380)

British Cataloguing in Publication Data
A Cataloguing in Publication record for this book is available from the British Library.

Advances in Human Resources Management and Organizational Development (AHRMOD) Book Series

Patricia Ordóñez de Pablos
Universidad de Oviedo, Spain

ISSN:2327-3372
EISSN:2327-3380

Mission

A solid foundation is essential to the development and success of any organization and can be accomplished through the effective and careful management of an organization's human capital. Research in human resources management and organizational development is necessary in providing business leaders with the tools and methodologies which will assist in the development and maintenance of their organizational structure.

The **Advances in Human Resources Management and Organizational Development (AHRMOD) Book Series** aims to publish the latest research on all aspects of human resources as well as the latest methodologies, tools, and theories regarding organizational development and sustainability. The **AHRMOD Book Series** intends to provide business professionals, managers, researchers, and students with the necessary resources to effectively develop and implement organizational strategies.

Coverage

- Employee Communications
- Process Improvement
- Workplace Culture
- Worker Behavior and Engagement
- Upward Feedback
- Disputes Resolution
- Personnel Retention
- Employee Benefits
- Human Resources Development
- Work-Life Balance

IGI Global is currently accepting manuscripts for publication within this series. To submit a proposal for a volume in this series, please contact our Acquisition Editors at Acquisitions@igi-global.com or visit: http://www.igi-global.com/publish/.

The Advances in Human Resources Management and Organizational Development (AHRMOD) Book Series (ISSN 2327-3372) is published by IGI Global, 701 E. Chocolate Avenue, Hershey, PA 17033-1240, USA, www.igi-global.com. This series is composed of titles available for purchase individually; each title is edited to be contextually exclusive from any other title within the series. For pricing and ordering information please visit http://www.igi-global.com/book-series/advances-human-resources-management-organizational/73670. Postmaster: Send all address changes to above address.

Titles in this Series

For a list of additional titles in this series, please visit: http://www.igi-global.com/book-series/advances-human-resources-management-organizational/73670

Asian Women in Corporate America Emerging Research and Opportunities
Sambhavi Lakshminarayanan (Medgar Evers College, City University of New York, USA)
Business Science Reference • © 2021 • 263pp • H/C (ISBN: 9781799843849) • US $185.00

Critical Issues on Changing Dynamics in Employee Relations and Workforce Diversity
Radha Yadav (Dayananda Sagar University, India) Priyanka Panday (Doon Business School, India) and Naman Sharma (Indian Institute of Foreign Trade, India)
Business Science Reference • © 2021 • 326pp • H/C (ISBN: 9781799835158) • US $215.00

Handbook of Research on Autopoiesis and Self-Sustaining Processes for Organizational Success
Małgorzata Pańkowska (University of Economics in Katowice, Poland)
Business Science Reference • © 2021 • 432pp • H/C (ISBN: 9781799867135) • US $275.00

Designing and Implementing HR Management Systems in Family Businesses
Luca Gnan (University of Rome "Tor Vergata", Italy) and Giulia Flamini (University of Rome "Tor Vergata", Italy)
Business Science Reference • © 2021 • 368pp • H/C (ISBN: 9781799848141) • US $195.00

Transforming Human Resource Functions With Automation
Anchal Pathak (Bule Hora University, Ethiopia) and Shikha Rana (IMS Unison University, India)
Business Science Reference • © 2021 • 192pp • H/C (ISBN: 9781799841807) • US $195.00

Examining the Career Development Practices and Experiences of Immigrants
Jared Keengwe (University of North Dakota, USA) and Kenneth Kungu (Clayton State University, USA)
Business Science Reference • © 2021 • 362pp • H/C (ISBN: 9781799858119) • US $215.00

Future of Work, Work-Family Satisfaction, and Employee Well-Being in the Fourth Industrial Revolution
Ethel Ndidiamaka Abe (University of KwaZulu-Natal, South Africa)
Business Science Reference • © 2021 • 382pp • H/C (ISBN: 9781799833475) • US $215.00

Handbook of Research on Cyberbullying and Online Harassment in the Workplace
Leslie Ramos Salazar (West Texas A&M University, USA)
Business Science Reference • © 2021 • 717pp • H/C (ISBN: 9781799849124) • US $265.00

IGI Global
PUBLISHER of TIMELY KNOWLEDGE

701 East Chocolate Avenue, Hershey, PA 17033, USA
Tel: 717-533-8845 x100 • Fax: 717-533-8661
E-Mail: cust@igi-global.com • www.igi-global.com

List of Contributors

Table of Contents

Detailed Table of Contents

Section 1
Understanding the Impacts of Remote Working

The coronavirus (COVID-19) pandemic has resulted in a swift and dramatic global shift in the location of work for many employees. Organizations around the world have implemented remote work arrangements to allow continuity of service while conforming with social distancing requirements. As a result of ongoing uncertainty regarding the current and future pandemics, reduced costs associated with housing employees remotely, and survey results suggesting employees are reluctant to return to a primarily office-based work model, many organisations are implementing ongoing remote arrangements for their employees. This chapter provides a review of current research on the psychological effects of remote working. Recommendations are made regarding future research directions across various remote work environments that will enhance understanding of the psychological effects of remote work under social distancing.

Drawing from a questionnaire answered by 455 people during social distancing in Brazil, the chapter analyzes how individuals who worked remotely and those who did not cope with the increase in domestic and care work and how this extra work was divided in gender terms. The questionnaire indicates that the pandemic increased both domestic and care activities, with the former being more frequent for women and those under remote work. In general, this was not accompanied by a better division of these activities across sexes as women remained mainly responsible for them. Nevertheless, some improvements in the division of the domestic work were observed amongst those under remote work. However, when such a rebalance does not occur, remote work tends to be associated with an increase in women's overburdening.

Workplace sexual harassment is a serious occupational hazard, adversely affecting workers' employment trajectories, economic well-being, and mental and physical health. Prior to COVID-19, it was widespread and primarily perpetrated by men against women, both in the physical workplace and physical and virtual public spaces associated with work. This chapter examines how the transition to remote work has effected changes in the prevalence and types of sexual harassment, paying attention to its gendered nature. Remote work holds both promise and peril. While exposure to physical harassment has fallen, information and communications technology has increased the risk of sexual harassment in virtual spaces. The cases of the United States and India are explored in more detail to compare worker experiences across the Global North and Global South, in countries with vastly different socioeconomic structures. This chapter contributes to the understanding of the benefits and challenges of remote work in combatting sexual harassment.

Some might think that the COVID-19 pandemic changes little, because novelists have always worked from home and found isolation to be necessary for their creative process. But in fact, there is a spectrum in sites of production. Even in a novelist's solitary study, her task is to construct a narrative out of her past social experience. The pandemic has caused a drastic reduction in such face-to-face activities. Changes in the consumption of fiction during the pandemic can be tracked on Amazon and include a shift from print to Kindle, and also shifts in genres. The biggest gain in share on Kindle has been in children's books. Post-publication activities have become steadily more important, as promotion of a book is now integral to its production. The rise of self-publishing on Kindle Direct Publishing bypasses traditional gatekeepers. With KDP almost everyone now can have their own press, and the centres of gravity of publishing have moved from London and New York to Seattle. Post-apocalyptic fiction envisions life in the wake of natural disasters.

The suddenness of COVID-19 forced, literally overnight, a transformation in the higher education sector. Students and instructors were migrated to an online engagement and knowledge transfer process, which created unforeseen challenges to instruction and prompted the development of new delivery systems. Further, the transition merged private and academic life as home life converged with work and ultimately, albeit unintentionally, promoted a more human perspective through widespread use of video-based communication. This chapter will address how COVID-19 affected the teaching of Introductory Economics, highlighting a case study of a course offered at Northeastern University in Boston, Massachusetts. The discussion addresses both positive and negative outcomes related to instruction and the role that COVID-19 has potentially had on teaching beyond the pandemic.

This chapter presents a qualitative research project called "Oversight Points." Fifty-nine Italian teachers participated in in-depth semi-structured interviews focusing on their perceptions, grievances, and hopes about remote teaching during the COVID-19 lockdown. Interviewees belong to a national school network and share a longstanding cooperation in blended action research initiatives. The research was inspired by the teacher professional identity (TPI) theory, and dialogical self-theory (DST) was used as an analytic lens. Data was organised through Nuvolar, a software that can generate word-clouds and provide timestamps of related video-clips. Results suggest that teachers are peculiar smart-workers. For them freedom of space and time, self-improvement, and autonomy—distinctive aspects of smart-working—acquire specific meanings, implying both positive and negative aspects. A set of positionings was found. The authors discuss how they compete in determining the re-organisation of teacher identities' landscape. Finally, they indicate some possible developments and practical implications.

Job and work design are critical factors in the development and maintenance of a committed high-quality workforce. The pandemic has been the catalyst or global social experiment for people to work at home en masse encouraging employers and employees to think about how and why their jobs are being done, to develop new work and job design policies and practices. However, as well as significant benefits, there are potential pitfalls in moving 'on-line' that needs to be considered as many see this as a permanent feature of the new workplace post pandemic. This chapter explores these issues in the context of job crafting.

A rise in contingent work, the increasing real estate costs for organizations, technological advances, and more recently, restrictions on movement emerging from the COVID-19 pandemic have resulted in a sharp increase in the number of employees working from home. These have significant implications for individuals, organizations, and society. Yet the physical work environment within the home has received little attention from scholars. Research on traditional office settings indicates that the physical environment influences a range of well-being and performance outcomes, indicating a critical need for researchers to consider the impact of the physical work environment at home. To address this issue, the authors briefly summarize the effects of the physical work environment and review existing research on working from home. They then propose directions for future research and emerging methodologies to undertake this research. Finally, they detail the practical implications that these changes bring for individuals, organizations, and society.

This chapter examines the industrial relations and workplace challenges associated with increasing remote work in Australia. First, the chapter reports on responses obtained from 11 in-depth interviews with human resource and industrial relations practitioners to assess the support and barriers for continuing and or increasing the uptake of remote work post COVID-19. It then examines the Australian industrial relations framework to determine its support of extending flexible work arrangements for a wider scope of workers.

The COVID-19 pandemic forced many organizations to abruptly introduce remote working, without an accurate analysis of organizational processes and employees' expectations about work flexibility. Thus, remote working has been implemented without a rational plan of interventions based on remote work-enabling technologies, managerial practices, and resources. This chapter aims at understanding the role of "supporting" structures and practices in driving the effective implementation of remote working in the post-COVID era. The authors rely on a case study of a multi-national IT company with a long experience

The chapter highlights the social distance, i.e. lack of emotional connection, formed among individuals working remotely in a geographically distributed team. The virtuality and cultural diversity of such teams creates limited opportunities for dispersed members to build social ties with remote team members leading to formation of 'us' versus 'them' attitudes which corrode team effectiveness. Based on a survey of 482 Indian IT professionals working in distributed teams, we find that social distance negatively impacts team effectiveness. Further, the results of the study show that practices such as task interdependence, inclusive communication, contextual information and shared identity can moderate the negative relationship between social distance and team effectiveness at varying levels of perceived status equality among individuals working in geographically distributed teams. The chapter provides recommendations for the effective management of geographically distributed teams whereby managers act as a bridge between the team members to overcome social distance.

Chapter 17
The Post-COVID-19 Era: Impacts, Challenges, and Opportunities for Worker Representatives....... 308
Tatjana E. Byrne, Allianz, Germany
Rosa Maria Martins de Oliveira, Allianz, Germany

The repercussions of months of social distancing have affected workers and their representatives. Nearly 25% of workers in Europe had never teleworked before the pandemic. The accelerated adoption of digital technologies and continued remote working required workers' representatives to adapt their ways of working, as well as reassess priorities. By examining three key questions—1) What forms of governance were used to respond to the challenges of the COVID-19 crisis? 2) What topics will gain in importance and which ones may become less important? 3) How will the post-COVID-19 world affect the organization and ways of working of representative bodies?—the authors argue that post-COVID-19 it is imperative to revise governance arrangements to enable representatives to remain effective as the workers' voice. Normative considerations combined with practitioner insights also lead the authors to conclude that the pandemic has the potential to trigger a paradigm shift in organizational participation.

Chapter 18
Work, Family, and Identity: How Remote Work Will Challenge and Change Who We Are 329
Phil Lord, Faculty of Law, McGill University, Canada

The COVID-19 pandemic has accelerated the existing transition to remote work and, more broadly, flexible forms of work. Much energy and attention have been dedicated to analysing this transition and how governments and other actors can best respond to it. This chapter takes a step back and analyses the potential impacts of the transition to remote work on our individual and collective identities. Recognising that work is an important part of who we are and has historically been a microcosm and a catalyst of broader social change, this chapter analyses how remote work challenges gender roles, contemporary family structures, and our conceptualisation of the relationship between work and other commitments. The chapter admittedly offers more questions than it does answers. It complexifies our understanding of remote work and seeks to spark future discussions as to its consequences.

Preface: The Rapid Expansion of Remote Working

INTRODUCTION

This handbook explores the multifaceted realities of remote working in the context of the COVID-19 global pandemic, reflecting on working routines, impacts to worker and organizational performance and well-being, and with a specific focus on the ways in which the developments witnessed since early 2020 will change work in the post-COVID era. Historically, remote working has been more often the domain of the self-employed, for example those engaged in skilled trades and craft-based work, and highly skilled employees who have job autonomy, e.g. managers and professionals, and are able to blur the boundary between work and home (Hardill, 2012; Hardill & Green, 2003; Pyöriä, 2011; Wheatley, 2020). In the latter case, these employees have generally undertaken some work remotely but have not been 100% home-based. With the introduction of policies to combat COVID-19 far greater numbers of employees across the globe – including those with limited job autonomy – encountered significant shifts in their work routines to working remotely all of the time (Brynjolfsson et al., 2020; ILO, 2020; Milasi et al., 2020).

The chapters in this handbook present the latest research from a multidisciplinary and international authorship to reflect on the implications of the rapid expansion of remote working in response to the global pandemic. Contributions are drawn from practitioners and academics across multiple disciplines including economics, economic geography, education, human resource management, law, philosophy, psychology and social policy. As such, the handbook has global reach, providing insights from, and of relevance to, all continents and a diverse range of economies. A particular focus of this edited book is in exploring the practical challenges of maintaining job quality and well-being in the face of the rapid expansion of remote working for organizations, in all sectors of the economy, not fully prepared to operate elements, or all, of their business remotely.

The handbook explores the realities of the observed large-scale expansion of remote working with a particular focus on the impacts of remote working on physical and mental health including for different groups of workers and in differing international contexts. The chapters of the handbook consider the impacts of the expansion of remote working on the nature of work and job design, the physical work environment, notions of productivity, organizational processes and systems, use of Information and Communication Technologies (ICTs) including to manage relationships and trust within teams and organizations. Within the chapters of the handbook we also observe, and reflect upon, a strong gender dimension to the impact of remote working with women workers more adversely affected as they juggle 'work' and 'home' with care roles. The authors draw on the existing evidence base as well as reporting novel findings from the latest empirical studies, to explore both the benefits and challenges faced in the adoption of remote working.

REMOTE WORK IN CONTEXT

Remote working has gained significant traction as a term used to refer to the recent expansion of home-working in response to the COVID-19 global pandemic. While remote working can involve paid work taking place within or from the home, it is broader in meaning and has in the past often been defined in reference to paid work that takes place outside of the normal or main workplace (Green, 2017; Pyöriä, 2011). It should, therefore, be acknowledged at the outset of this handbook that the recent use of remote work employed is somewhat of a departure from some existing definitions which focus on mobile forms of work outside of the main workplace. Indeed the home has become the main workplace for many, at least in the short term, and this reflects an evolving understanding of the concept of remote work.

The focus in this handbook is on remote working as work taking place within the home, while acknowledging the broader use of the term in some chapters which touch upon forms of mobile and distributed work. A useful definition of remote working as employed in this handbook is a 'flexible work arrangement that affords employees the ability to periodically, regularly, or exclusively perform work for their employers from home or another remote location that is equipped with the appropriate computer based technology to transfer work to the central organization' (Caillier, 2012, 462). Remote working under this definition can be used interchangeably with other terms including teleworking or telecommuting, both of which are understood as flexible forms of work in which the tasks of employment take place within a range of locations including at home, at client sites, on the move, in hotels, airports, in a co-working location, smart centre or digital work hub (Bentley et al., 2016, 207). Definitions of teleworking describe it as a 'work arrangement in which employees perform their regular work at a site other than the ordinary workplace, supported by technological connections' (Fitzer, 1997, 65), or as 'remote work [that] involves the use of [ICT]' (Sullivan, 2003, 159). As such, a range of other terms can also be used to refer to these notions of remote work such as mobile work, distributed work, distance work and virtual work, all of which are themselves distinct to some degree in their meaning (see Hislop & Axtell, 2009; Pyöriä, 2011, 166; Bailey & Kurland, 2002).

Home-based teleworking, as a sub-form of teleworking, is a further term useful in defining remote working as employed in the chapters of this handbook. Home-based teleworking refers to teleworking which takes place within the home and is facilitated by ICTs. It includes workers whose main workplace is the home, but also extends to those whose main workplace is in a standard employer premise and who work at home on a more informal or fluid basis (Mokhtarian et al., 2004; Wheatley, 2020). As per the definitions of both remote work and teleworking more broadly, use of ICTs – broadband internet, wireless technologies, cloud computing, personal computers, tablets and Smartphones – is highlighted as an important component and facilitator of home-based teleworking (Bentley et al., 2016). These technologies enable work to be conducted without geographical limits, providing virtual and location-independent work potential and 24/7 connectivity (Moos & Skaburskis, 2007). The use of these technologies, however, does vary considerably and some workers will employ fairly basic ICTs in their remote working routines.

REMOTE WORK IMPACTS: THE EVIDENCE BASE

A substantive international evidence base has developed in recent decades which explores the range of impacts associated with remote working. A number of potential benefits have been identified. One of the most commonly cited potential benefits of working remotely at home is the greater control it enables workers to have over the timing and structure of the working day (Tietze et al., 2009; Wheatley, 2012). An associated benefit is the removal of the time and financial cost invested in the commute, an outcome that also offers wider societal benefits from reductions in the environmental impacts of cars and other modes of transportation. The commute has been shown to be one of the least appreciated activities among many workers, although this is primarily among those travelling by car (Wheatley & Bickerton, 2016). It should also be noted that the commute does offer an important spatial separation between work and home (life), and this separation is often desirable as it enables workers to prepare for work at the beginning, and equally to switch-off at the end, of the working day (Kurland & Bailey, 1999). An often-argued benefit arising from the other impacts of remote working is that it can result in higher levels of productivity (Bloom et al., 2015). Workers are able to better manage the tasks of employment alongside household responsibilities, and have an improved ability to focus where there are fewer distractions present in the home relative to a workplace (Sander et al., 2019).

Existing research, further, suggests that these impacts can offer well-being benefits that are reflected in subjective well-being i.e. self-reported measures of well-being consisting of emotional responses and experienced feelings which can be both positive and negative (Pavot & Diener, 2013). Remote working, and especially homeworking, have been found to have positive effects on job and leisure satisfaction (Felstead & Henseke, 2017; Morganson et al., 2010; Wheatley, 2012, 2017). However, the extent of these effects may be dependent on the personality type of the individual worker. For example, an individual who is more extroverted may find it difficult be gain satisfaction from work when there is physical distance from the workplace and their colleagues (Virick et al., 2010). The relative benefits may also differ between different occupations and sub-groups of workers. Some of the greatest benefits have been reported by highly skilled homeworkers, whose jobs exhibit a number of qualities of 'good work' and accompanying benefits for levels of satisfaction. In contrast, some part-time and self-employed remote workers report lower quality experiences (Wheatley, 2021). This is highly important given the recent expansion in remote working has included workers in occupations exhibiting lowers levels of job autonomy. Working remotely at home may also be more inclusive as it expands opportunities to engage in paid work, including for workers who may find employment in standard workplace environments challenging, such as individuals with substantive caring responsibilities or a disability (Green, 2017, 1646). A number of the aforementioned benefits not only impact the individual but also the organization. Enhanced productivity is a primary benefit felt by the organizations, as well as cost reduction through the ability to reduce or even close workplace locations (Bailey & Kurland, 2002; Moos & Skaburskis, 2008).

While there a range of benefits that can be realised, remote working is not without its challenges. One of the primary difficulties encountered is the loss, or reduction, of face-to-face contact with colleagues and clients. Workers can suffer negative well-being effects arising from the loss of professional and social networks where workers find it difficult to maintain regular contact, and associated feelings of isolation (Bentley et al., 2016; Tietze et al., 2009). Potential negative impacts have also been reported on career development as workers become less visible within the organization as they interact with a smaller pool of colleagues and receive less managerial support (Virick et al., 2010). At the wider team and organizational level associated challenges are faced in coordinating collaborative and team working tasks when teams are physically distant. While many of those working remotely adapt to the use of online platforms for meetings and socialising, relationships can be difficult to maintain virtually. Organizations have to consider these communication difficulties and, moreover, the loss of agglomeration benefits associated with informal knowledge sharing and idea development i.e. water cooler chat.

Another of the major challenges faced in the use of remote working is that of workers dividing time and space between work and the rest of their lives. Working in the home results in a blurring of boundaries potentially acting as a source of work-life conflict (Russell et al., 2009). Not all employees will find remote working a stress free experience. Difficulties are faced in combining work with other household responsibilities including childcare, lack of appropriate home space for a workstation, and potential domestic disharmony especially where more than one individual is working at home resulting in distractions or competition for space. These impacts also appear distinct across diversity characteristics including gender and social class, creating some concerns around the inclusivity of remote working, as explored within some of the chapters of this handbook. Overwork, i.e. working longer hours than those contracted, and more intense working patterns are a particular risk faced by many individuals when working remotely (Nätti et al., 2011). Recent analysis performed on the CIPD's 2019 UK Working Lives Survey, for example, identified the potential for significant overwork amongst those working at home (see Wheatley & Gifford, 2019). Expectations around workers always being available and difficulties in separating both time and space between work and home can act as drivers of these behaviours.

The physical remote working environment also poses a number of concerns, including around health and safety. Carrying out health and safety assessments and the obvious invasion of privacy that this could necessitate has historically acted as a considerable barrier to employee interest in working at home (Tietze et al., 2009). Where remote working reflects more of a cost reduction exercise by an organization it effectively shifts onto the worker the costs of workspace (Moos & Skaburskis, 2008, 336), but this could leave the worker with an unsuitable physical work environment and/or significant costs in adapting a workspace within the home. Provision of physical resources by employers including equipment e.g. laptops, Wi-Fi routers, workstations and others, not only provide a more comfortable environment and act as a source of job satisfaction, but can have health and safety implications that impact upon worker productivity (including via sickness absence rates). Investments in physical resources to enable and enhance remote working have to be weighed against relative benefits, but lack of investment can have detrimental impacts for worker and organization, as poor ergonomics and inadequate equipment can lead to health impacts including eyestrain and musculoskeletal disorders (MSDs) (Brand, 2008). In addition, working at home is often a sedentary activity, and this represents a further dimension with regard to health impacts. Even where resources are available, a range of other concerns may be present including the pressure of multiple people in the home requiring a workspace and/or equipment as already noted, and technical issues such as slow internet connections. The rapid expansion of remote working has tested the capacity of organization systems with regard to both the realities of ICTs being used so widely, but also due to historic lack of investment among some employers who have remained too strongly wedded to traditional work routines. Remote working has seen the repurposing of online tools, including social media for work tasks and the socialisation of remote colleagues (Davison et al., 2018; Forgren & Byström, 2018). Use of some of these tools has been controversial due, for example, to concerns over encryption and security, potential misuse by workers and vulnerabilities associated with contextual collapse (Buglass et al., 2016; Koch et al., 2013).

Fear of the loss of control over workers and malfeasance have acted as an organizational barrier to the application of remote working routines (Allen et al., 2015). Sato (2019) reports on this assertion in the context of the practice of teleworking in Japan where it was found that many, even larger, organizations do not provide formal teleworking opportunities for the majority of employees. Where employers lack trust in their workers, they often engage in high levels of micro-management using monitoring tools

(Wight & Raley, 2009). This can be enacted using technical control systems including software which records and monitors activity and task completion (Callaghan & Thompson, 2001). These systems provide a mechanism for work to be monitored and evaluated and do have the potential to be used effectively to promote task completion and productive work effort among remote workers through targets and deliverables, however this is not always the case.

Concerns around malfeasance drive the application of Taylorist 'low discretion' work organization and micro-management and monitoring and surveillance systems (Choi et al., 2008). These measures, though, reflect distrust and inflexibility around task completion which can result in high intensity and potentially demotivating working conditions. Employed in this manner, remote working creates an invasion of privacy and can cause work-related stress (Russell et al., 2009, 89), counteracting a number of the benefits from paid work being performed outside of the traditional workplace. Technical control systems can be exploited by workers as it is possible with the use of some of these systems to take advantage of limitations in the monitoring mechanisms such as asking others to occasionally log activity when not working. More intelligent systems continue to be developed, partly in response to these concerns, including those that incorporate facial recognition software to monitor time spent at the workstation. Concerns of this nature can, therefore, both reflect a risk to productivity and performance or a lack of trust dependent on the worker and other case-specific factors, but either way these concerns act to limit buy-in from some employers (Wight & Raley, 2009) and the realised benefits from remote work.

The existing evidence base reports a range of impacts from remote working, both positive and negative. However, much of the evidence base focuses on work taking place at home or in other locations outside of employer/business premises among workers who work at least some of the time in other locations (a main workplace, client sites etc.). Generating understanding of the specific impacts of the rapid expansion of remote working in response to the COVID-19 global pandemic and its longer term effects is, therefore, of high importance, as workers, organizations and policy-makers consider previous and current modes of work and make decisions regarding future application of remote work.

RAPID EXPANSION DURING THE GLOBAL PANDEMIC

The rapid expansion of the numbers of workers across the globe undertaking paid work at home all of the time or as the main place of work has been unprecedented. Proportions of workers reporting remote or home-based teleworking eclipsed the levels prior to the COVID-19 global pandemic as a result of lockdowns and other social distancing measures employed in many nations throughout 2020 and 2021. Estimates prior to the pandemic suggested a steady growth in workers who reported their home as their main or primary workplace (Wheatley, 2020). For example, across the EU-27 countries a relatively consistent figure was reported between 2009 and 2019 of around one-in-twenty employees usually working from home. More notable growth has occurred in more flexible applications of remote working involving homeworking being combined with time spent at the office, visiting clients or some other, often informal, flexible arrangement. This more hybrid model of remote working was reported across the EU-27 by 5.2% of employees in 2009, but had increased to 9% by 2019 (Milasi et al., 2020). Working from home has historically always been more prominent among the self-employed and recent UK data from 2018 suggests around one-third of the self-employed reported their home as their primary workplace (Wheatley, 2020).

An important distinction present in the rapid expansion of remote working is that it has been imposed in response to the external environment rather than it reflecting a more flexible working arrangement. Government guidance has influenced the short-term prevalence of remote working across a number of nations where workers have been asked to work from home where it is possible. Many employees, as a result, have during at least some of 2020 and 2021 reported the home as the sole location of work. This is reflected in substantive growth in remote working. For example, in the EU-27 and the UK it was estimated that around 40% of those who remained working shifted to homeworking at peak in 2020 (Milasi et al., 2020). In Brazil over one-third (35%) of workers reported working from home in mid-2020 (ILO, 2020). In the US the proportions reporting working remotely on a regular basis peaked at up to half of workers (Brynjolfsson et al., 2020). The expansion is, in principle, temporary and rates of homeworking have reduced in some nations from peak, for example to around one-in-three workers reporting exclusively homeworking in the UK and US by Autumn 2020 (Brenan, 2020; Milasi et al., 2020). The changes have, though, prompted wider debate regarding more permanent transformation of working routines toward greater application of remote working. In addition, it has led some high profile businesses to make the decision to close workplace locations and ask their employees to work at home on a permanent basis (Brownlee, 2020).

It is, however, necessary to contextualise the recent growth in remote work. Working at home has continued to reflect somewhat of a privilege that is most widely available in highly skilled managerial and professional occupations, although significant expansion has been reported in associate professional and other occupations such as sales which exhibit lower levels of job autonomy. Some of those unable to work at home, meanwhile, have been subject to furlough schemes or in some cases loss of employment. In addition, estimates from the International Labour Organisation (ILO) suggest that currently only around 18% of workers globally could work from home. There are significant variations present in current potential for home-based work between high and lower to middle income countries as summarized in Figure 1.1. For a far greater proportion of workers in some regions of the globe homeworking

Figure 1. Global home-based work potential
Source: data from ILO (2020)

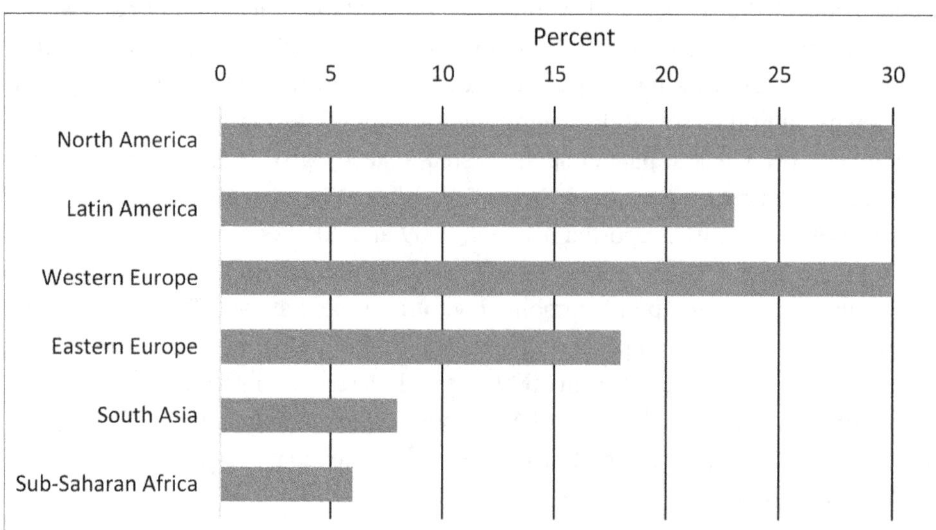

is not feasible due to: (1) the nature of jobs associated with the organization of production i.e. more jobs in primary and secondary sectors; (2) the size of the informal employment sector, and; (3) the limited availability of technology which facilitates work at home.

As such, the evidence identifies that currently there are quite considerable limits to the application of remote working geographically. There are jobs that cannot simply be converted to be performed in the home in their current design, including those involving mass production and highly divided labour, for example, machine operatives and assembly workers. Meanwhile, other occupations are heavily reliant on workers travelling to an employment centre including certain jobs in the hospitality sector. Further expansion of remote working may, therefore, result in significant structural change in the labour market. Returning to the main focus of this handbook, generating an understanding of the impacts of a more permanent application of remote working in those occupations where it can be applied is of significant relevance, both in relation to the well-being of workers and their organizations. Much of the existing evidence focuses on working remotely on a more flexible basis i.e. combining working at home and in the office, where more positive impacts have generally been reported (Wheatley, 2017, 2021). And despite the enforced nature of the expansion of remote working initial evidence has suggested that many workers do show a preference to continue to work at home at least some of the time (Eurofound, 2020).

In the aftermath of the pandemic organizations will need to consider how to manage the phased lifting of social distancing and other health and safety measures, and reorganization of work in potentially more space-limited physical working environments where workplaces have been rationalised. Organizations may choose to adopt hybrid working routines i.e. blending homeworking and office working, as social distancing would not allow all staff to be on site at the same time. As well as obvious impacts on workers, these considerations have implications for human resource management in organizations as challenges will be faced in managing employees where new working routines have been adopted. The impacts of the rapid expansion of remote working, are in many respects, still being revealed and the chapters of this handbook contribute to our understanding in this arena.

CONTRIBUTION OF THE HANDBOOK

This handbook explores a highly important area of recent change in paid work; the rapid expansion of remote working arising from the COVID-19 global pandemic. As such the handbook provides a significant contribution through generating understanding of the impacts, challenges, and opportunities presented by the large-scale move to remote working, including considering how the changes put in place in response to the global pandemic may have lasting impacts on the places and ways in which we work. The handbook is innovative in both its content and approach. It draws together the latest research from academics from across the globe, providing a wide range of contexts and cases to develop an early evidence base on this current and highly important area of research. The contributions in this handbook outline the findings from up-to-the-minute research into the impacts of the rapid expansion of remote working, providing novel evidence as well as setting debates and agendas for continued research. Within the handbook the authors consider a wide range of different dimensions of remote working. These include but are not limited to: how to design and redesign jobs for remote working; the skills essential for effective remote working; how to balance remote working with the rest of our lives; the physical remote working environment; the physical and psychological impacts of working from home; how to maintain relationships with colleagues and clients when working remotely; the role of trust in building and maintaining virtual teams, and; the impacts of remote working on industrial relations and labour market regulation.

As the handbook contains contributions from multiple disciplines it has relevance to a number of academic fields across the social sciences including economics, economic geography, human resource management, psychology and social policy. The handbook is global in its coverage, offering a comprehensive reference to inform scholars and practitioners of the ways in which remote working can be employed effectively as well as the range of challenges faced in its operation. This handbook draws together the latest research on remote working and its impacts, and as such has a clear relevance to academic audiences. However, the breadth of scope and accessibility of the chapters provide a resource of much wider relevance including for a range of practitioners, e.g. HR professionals, and policy-makers. It also has a wider relevance to workers given the highly relevant nature of the content included in the handbook to the quality of our working lives. The shift to remote working witnessed in response to the COVID-19 global pandemic offers a significant opportunity to critically reflect on labour mark structures and modes of work and this handbook offers an invaluable resource in informing research and practice surrounding remote work and worker well-being in the post-COVID era.

OVERVIEW OF THE HANDBOOK

This handbook comprises chapters reflecting on research conducted by the authors into the impacts, challenges, and opportunities presented by the large-scale move to remote working in response to the COVID-19 global pandemic. Following this introduction in Section 1 of the handbook, Chapters 1 to 6 report on the impacts of remote working in a range of contexts during the COVID-19 pandemic. In Section 2, Chapters 7 to 12 reflect on the structure of remote work in the post-COVID era, including implications for job design, careers, workplace, and the regulation of work. Finally, in Section 3, chapters 13 to 18 turn to consideration of the implications for managing and working remotely in the post COVID-19 era, offering insight into the potential lived realities of the future of work.

Section 1: Understanding the Impacts of Remote Working

In this part of the handbook, we begin with a chapter by Oliver Baumann and Elizabeth Sander, which uses self-determination theory (Ryan & Deci, 2017) as a foundation to assess the existing literature on the psychological impacts of remote work arrangements and outlines suggestions for future research. The chapter provides a number of important insights including highlighting the importance of autonomy, a key benefit, and social isolation, a key potential negative impact, as factors influencing experiences of remote work.

In Chapter 2, Lygia Sabbag Fares, Ana Luíza Matos de Oliveira and Lilian Nogueira Rolim explore the gender dynamics of remote working under social distancing restrictions in Brazil. They report on the findings of a survey receiving 455 responses, and outline the patterns of domestic and care work, comparing men and women, and remote and non-remote workers. The chapter highlights that remote work tends to be associated with an increase in the time spent on domestic work. This takes place in a continued uneven division of reproductive work and, despite individual improvements when men undertook remote work, the interplay between remote work and domestic and care work has important implications for gender inequality.

Jacqueline Strenio and Joyita Roy Chowdhury present a discussion of how the transition to remote work and increased reliance on ICTs have effected changes in the perpetration of sexual harassment in Chapter 3. Using a comparison of countries from the Global North (US) and Global South (India), they examine the benefits and challenges posed by remote work in combatting sexual harassment. They provide both cautions and policy recommendations and argue, importantly, that remote work provides an opportunity to challenge workplace cultures, to establish guidelines and set examples for an inclusive work environment where all workers can work with security and dignity.

In Chapter 4, Paul Delany offers an in-depth reflection on how the pandemic has affected writers and readers of literary fiction. The chapter uses this case to illustrate the importance of social settings in the production of literary works, how the structure of this market has changed in recent years, and the potential impacts of the pandemic for the future of the sector. While the chapter focuses on a specific case, it has a much broader relevance to sectors that are characterised by what the author describes as a 'winner-takes-all' labour market structure such as professional sports.

Madhavi Venkatesan, in Chapter 5, uses the case of teaching a Principles of Economics course in Higher Education to illustrate a number of the impacts of the adoption of remote working. The chapter considers the impacts on both instructor and learners of the adoption of remote and hybrid models of learning including increasing the inclusivity of Higher Education through offering a potentially more flexible, efficient and personalised approach, but also some of the difficulties associated with reduced human physical contact including social isolation and loss of motivation. The chapter also emphasizes the importance of investment in suitable communication technologies to facilitate remote working and learning arrangements.

Chapter 6, by Francesca Amenduni and colleagues, considers the impact of the move to remote education using the case of teachers in Schools in Italy. The chapter reports the findings from 59 interviews with teachers across levels of education. It reflects on the adoption of smart-working methods and ICTs in education, offering the perspectives of teachers including reflections on how they adapted to the change in their role and delivery of education, and how the experience of teaching in new ways online impacts their professional identity. The chapter reports on the self-efficacy gained from the process of learning-by-doing and having to adapt to new ways of working resulting from the pandemic.

Section 2: The Structure of Remote Work in the Post-COVID Era

This part of the handbook begins, in Chapter 7, with a discussion presented by Peter Holland and Chris Brewster focusing on the ways in which the rapid expansion of remote working can inform job (re)design in the post-pandemic era. Explored in the context of job crafting, they consider the good and not so good aspects of working from home, including relationships, workloads, the role of management, and impacts of technologies being deployed for the purpose of monitoring and surveillance of employees. They also reflect on the potential benefits of the widespread adoption of flexible and hybrid work routines, including those offered by the new Finnish model of flexible work that provides flexibility through recasting working time to focus on the work done, as opposed to the place or space in which it occurs.

Maria Kordowicz, in Chapter 8, reflects on the economic and societal focus on productivity, arguing that the dominant ideology of productivity, in reducing societal progress to a measure of input versus output, is problematic. The chapter highlights how enforced home-based remote working has increased tensions with productivity as workers encounter more intense routines, excessive monitoring, and work-life blurring, which increase risk of burnout. The chapter argues that through highlighting the problems of the current system, the pandemic provides a platform for social, political and economic change, toward a focus on human values such as the right to rest and secure meaningful employment over profits and the pervasive push for productivity.

In Chapter 9, the authors Navya Kumar and Swati Alok, apply a new cyclical model of career advancement, the Competence Career Advancement Model (CCAM), to consider career advancement in white-collar occupations engaged in working from home. The chapter uses the CCAM model to consider the range of impacts on career development and progression of working from home, and methods for employees to achieve career success, and employers to effectively manage talent when working remotely. They argue the importance of considering the suitability of the job, and support required for the employee (resources, training etc.), when making decisions regarding shifting to work from home. The chapter also highlights the role of communication and relationships in effectively applying work from home.

Chapter 10, by Anne Green and Rebecca Riley, traces the possible short- and medium-term implications for workplaces. Drawing on data for the UK, the chapter considers a number of important dimensions of potential spatial change in work, including: the changing attractiveness of different locations of work and related impacts for city centres, outer urban centres, market towns and rural areas. It also considers the potential implications for geographical segregation and inequalities as different sub-groups face different possibilities for remote working and highlights the importance of place-based policy. They emphasize that agglomeration benefits of centralised economic activity may still be realised, but in a different form, as workers adopting a hybrid home-workplace routine desire social interaction when visiting the workplace requiring offices to evolve to cater for such working patterns.

Elizabeth Sander, Alannah Rafferty then Peter Jordan explore the under-researched aspect of the physical work environment of the home in Chapter 11. It draws on existing understanding of the impacts of the physical work environment of the office and considers the potential impacts of the physical home working environment. The chapter emphasizes the impact of work entering the home in changing the relationship with space, as workers balance potentially conflicting demands and challenges of work and non-work activities. They further highlight the role of the organization both in providing the physical resources to enable work from home, but also in embedding safe working routines including breaks and hours of work.

Chapter 12, by Kantha Dayaram and John Burgess, considers the regulatory implications of the expansion of remote work using the case of Australia. Drawing on qualitative data collected during the pandemic through semi-structured interviews with human resource and industrial relations professionals, they argue that continued extensive use of remote working requires regulatory change. This includes revisiting/designing legislation regarding the right to request flexible working arrangements, the right to disconnect, associated monitoring of incidence of long hours and work intensification, employee privacy associated with monitoring and surveillance systems, and support for physical and psychological health and safety. They also highlight the complexities faced in providing appropriate regulation of casual workers, including gig workers.

Section 3: Informing the Future of Remote Work

The final section of the book considers how the rapid expansion of remote working will influence the future of work. We begin this part of the handbook with Chapter 13, by Luisa Errichiello and Tommasina Pianese, who draw on a case study of an IT multinational in Italy to explore how different forms of (perceived) organizational support – supervisor/manager, employee/co-worker, and technology-related – can facilitate the effective implementation of remote working. They categorize under seven themes the specific features that, individually and collectively, contribute to positively shaping employee perception of support through a set of recommended institutionalized practices and ICT tools. Importantly, the chapter notes that while these tools and practices facilitate effective remote work, too much emphasis on embedding a fully remote culture could result in an undervaluing of organizational support for hybrid (remote and office-based) routines.

In Chapter 14, Julia Ayache and colleagues, reflect on the role played by the workplace as a collective social space and in building a sense of belonging and the challenges faced in replicating these characteristics in virtual workspaces. Reviewing existing contributions, they suggest that media richness, co-temporality and visibility are key factors which can be employed to nurture the sense of social presence, build emotional connections and provide a sense of proximity and shared identity among virtual teams. They argue the benefits of the provision of virtual spaces that encourage informal congregations and casual conversations, and explore the potential use of virtual reality in enhancing virtual interactions.

Chapter 15, by Colin Hughes and Mark Saunders, explores the role of trust in virtual teams. As well as emphasizing the challenges faced in building trust when working remotely, the chapter highlights the behaviours of leaders that can both demonstrate their own trustworthiness to, and of, virtual team members. The evidence from an empirical study, which reveals the behaviours which signal a leader's own trustworthiness to virtual team members and their trust of team members, is used to develop a member-centric framework for enabling high trust virtual team leadership.

In Chapter 16, Vinita Seshadri and Elangovan N. consider factors affecting, and methods for effectively managing, geographically distributed teams (GDTs). Using data collected pre-pandemic in India they explore the challenges faced in GDTs associated with social distance i.e. 'us' vs 'them' attitudes where teams are geographically dispersed and there is status inequality. They outline a number of potential methods to enhance team effectiveness including alignment of tasks with, and increased awareness of, higher level objectives; increasing shared identity, creation of a more inclusiveness working environment, and increasing understanding around the context in which different teams work.

Tatjana Byrne and Rosa Martins de Oliveira, in Chapter 17, consider the implications of the rapid expansion of remote working for worker representation and worker rights using evidence from an empirical study of a multi-national financial organization in the EU. They consider the impacts of remote operation of meetings and consultations, relationships between workers, worker representatives and leaders, and how the learning from the pandemic may inform the future of worker representation. They argue that alternatives to existing forms of consultation and co-determination, in the form of adaptive governance, are necessary to ensure continued worker representation in the changing work environment. They also highlight the importance of re-instituting worker representation into decision making, following its loss where organizations responded to the short-term challenges faced by the pandemic.

In the final chapter of the handbook, author Phil Lord reflects on the impacts of the growth of remote work on our individual and collective identities. The chapter provides important insight into the tension between the expanded flexibility offered by homeworking and the lived reality in which greater flexibility in paid work can result in work and life competing at all times. The chapter also considers how remote working may challenge the gendered household division of labour. The chapter ends by proposing that the structural changes witnessed in relation to the growth in remote work will in turn likely lead to a long-term change in our identities, driving a positive transformation of gender roles and of the household which will make the spouses closer to equal partners.

Daniel Wheatley
University of Birmingham, UK

Irene Hardill
Northumbria University, UK

Sarah Buglass
Nottingham Trent University, UK

REFERENCES

Allen, T. D., Golden, T. D., & Shockley, K. M. (2015). How Effective Is Telecommuting? Assessing the Status of Our Scientific Findings. *Psychological Science in the Public Interest*, *16*(2), 40–68. doi:10.1177/1529100615593273 PMID:26403188

Bailey, D., & Kurland, N. (2002). A review of telework research: Findings, new directions, and lessons for the study of modern work. *Journal of Organizational Behavior*, *23*(4), 383–400. doi:10.1002/job.144

Bentley, T. A., Teo, S. T. T., McLeod, L., Tan, F., Bosua, R., & Gloet, M. (2016). The role of organisational support in teleworker wellbeing: A sociotechnical systems approach. *Applied Ergonomics*, *52*, 207–215. doi:10.1016/j.apergo.2015.07.019 PMID:26360212

Bloom, N., Liang, J., Roberts, J., & Ying, Z. J. (2015). Does working from home work? Evidence from a Chinese experiment. *The Quarterly Journal of Economics*, *130*(1), 165–218. doi:10.1093/qje/qju032

Brand, J. L. (2008). Office Ergonomics: A Review of Pertinent Research and Recent Developments. *Review of Human Factors and Ergonomics*, *4*(1), 245–282. doi:10.1518/155723408X342871

Brenan, M. (2020). *COVID-19 and remote work: an update*. Gallup. Available at: https://news.gallup.com/poll/321800/COVID-remote-work-update.aspx

Brownlee, D. (2020). Twitter, square announce work from home forever option: What are the risks? *Forbes*. Available at: https://www.forbes.com/sites/danabrownlee/2020/05/18/twitter-square-announce-work-from-home-forever-optionwhat-are-the-risks/?sh=437570402565

Brynjolfsson, E., Horton, J.J., Ozimek, A., Rock, D., Sharma, G. & TuYe, H.-Y. (2020). *COVID-19 and remote work: an early look at US data*. National Bureau of Economic Research Working Paper No. 27344. Available at: https://www.nber.org/papers/w27344

Buglass, S. L., Binder, J. F., Betts, L. R., & Underwood, J. D. (2016). When 'friends' collide: Social heterogeneity and user vulnerability on social network sites. *Computers in Human Behavior*, *54*, 62–72. doi:10.1016/j.chb.2015.07.039

Caillier, J. (2012). The impact of teleworking on work motivation in a U.S. federal government agency. *American Review of Public Administration*, *42*(4), 461–480. doi:10.1177/0275074011409394

Callaghan, G., & Thompson, P. (2001). Edwards Revisited: Technical Control and Call Centres. *Economic and Industrial Democracy*, *22*(1), 13–37. doi:10.1177/0143831X01221002

Choi, S., Leiter, J., & Tomaskovic-Devey, D. (2008). Contingent Autonomy Technology, Bureaucracy, and Relative Power in the Labor Process. *Work and Occupations*, *35*(4), 422–455. doi:10.1177/0730888408326766

Davison, R. M., Ou, C. X., Martinsons, M. G., Zhao, A. Y., & Du, R. (2014). The communicative ecology of web 2.0 at work: Social networking in the workspace. *Journal of the Association for Information Science and Technology*, *65*(10), 2035–2047. doi:10.1002/asi.23112

Eurofound. (2020). *Working during COVID-19*. Available at: https://www.eurofound.europa.eu/data/COVID-19/working-teleworking

Felstead, A., & Henseke, G. (2017). Assessing the growth of remote working and its consequences for effort, well-being and work-life balance. *New Technology, Work and Employment*, *32*(3), 195–212. doi:10.1111/ntwe.12097

Fitzer, M. M. (1997). Managing from afar: Performance and rewards in a telecommuting environment. *Compensation and Benefits Review*, *29*(1), 65–73. doi:10.1177/088636879702900110

Forsgren, E., & Byström, K. (2018). Multiple social media in the workplace: Contradictions and congruencies. *Information Systems Journal*, *28*(3), 442–464. doi:10.1111/isj.12156

Green, A. (2017). Implications of technological change and austerity for employability in urban labour markets. *Urban Studies (Edinburgh, Scotland)*, *54*(7), 1638–1654. doi:10.1177/0042098016631906

Hardill, I. (2012). Gender, Migration and the Dual Career Household. London: Routledge.

Hardill, I., & Green, A. E. (2003). Remote working-altering the spatial contours of work and home in the new economy. *New Technology, Work and Employment*, *18*(3), 212–222. doi:10.1111/1468-005X.00122

Hislop, D., & Axtell, C. (2009). To infinity and beyond? Workspace and the multi-location worker. *New Technology, Work and Employment*, *24*(1), 60–75. doi:10.1111/j.1468-005X.2008.00218.x

International Labour Organisation (ILO). (2020). *Working from Home: Estimating the worldwide potential*. Geneva, Switzerland: ILO. Available at: https://www.ilo.org/global/topics/non-standard-employment/publications/WCMS_743447/lang--en/index.htm

Koch, H., Leidner, D. E., & Gonzalez, E. S. (2013). Digitally Enabling Social Networks: Resolving IT–Culture Conflict. *Information Systems Journal*, *23*(6), 501–523. doi:10.1111/isj.12020

Kurland, N. B., & Bailey, D. E. (1999). Telework: The advantages and challenges of working here, there, anywhere, and anytime. *Organizational Dynamics*, *28*(2), 53–68. doi:10.1016/S0090-2616(00)80016-9

Milasi, S., González-Vázquez, I., & Fernández-Macías, E. (2020). *Telework in the EU before and after the COVID-19: where we were, where we head to*. European Commission: Science for Policy Briefs. Available at: https://ec.europa.eu/jrc/sites/jrcsh/files/jrc120945_policy_brief_-_covid_and_telework_final.pdf

Mokhtarian, P., Collantes, G., & Gertz, C. (2004). Telecommuting, residential location, and commute-distance traveled: Evidence from State of California employees. *Environment & Planning A*, *36*(10), 1877–1897. doi:10.1068/a36218

Moos, A., & Skaburskis, M. (2007). The Characteristics and Location of Home Workers in Montreal, Toronto and Vancouver. *Urban Studies (Edinburgh, Scotland), 44*(9), 1781–1808. doi:10.1080/00420980701507639

Moos, M., & Skaburskis, A. (2008). The probability of single-family dwelling occupancy: Comparing home workers and commuters in Canadian cities. *Journal of Planning Education and Research, 27*(3), 319–340. doi:10.1177/0739456X07311937

Morganson, V. J., Major, D. A., Oborn, K. L., Verive, J. M., & Heelan, M. P. (2010). Comparing telework locations and traditional work arrangements. *Journal of Managerial Psychology, 25*(6), 578–595. doi:10.1108/02683941011056941

Nätti, J., Tammelin, M., Anttila, T., & Ojala, S. (2011). Work at home and time use in Finland. *New Technology, Work and Employment, 26*(1), 68–77. doi:10.1111/j.1468-005X.2010.00258.x

Pavot, W., & Diener, E. (2013). Happiness Experienced: the Science of Subjective Well-being. In S. David, I. Boniwell, & A. Conley Ayers (Eds.), *The Oxford Handbook of Happiness* (pp. 134–154). Oxford University Press. doi:10.1093/oxfordhb/9780199557257.013.0010

Pyöriä, P. (2011). Managing telework: Risks, fears and rules. *Management Research Review, 34*(4), 386–399. doi:10.1108/01409171111117843

Russell, H., O'Connell, P., & McGinnity, F. (2009). The Impact of flexible working arrangements on work-life conflict and work pressure in Ireland. *Gender, Work and Organization, 16*(1), 73–97. doi:10.1111/j.1468-0432.2008.00431.x

Ryan, R. M., & Deci, E. L. (2017). *Self determination theory.* The Guildford Press.

Sander, E. L. J., Caza, A., & Jordan, P. J. (2019). Psychological perceptions matter: Developing the reactions to the physical work environment scale. *Building and Environment, 148*, 338–347. doi:10.1016/j.buildenv.2018.11.020

Sato, A. (2019). Telework and its effects in Japan. In J. Messenger (Ed.), *Telework in the 21st Century: An Evolutionary Perspective* (pp. 76–127). Edward Elgar Publishing. doi:10.4337/9781789903751.00008

Sullivan, C. (2003). What's in a Name? Definitions and Conceptualisations of Teleworking and Homeworking. *New Technology, Work and Employment, 18*(3), 158–165. doi:10.1111/1468-005X.00118

Tietze, S., Musson, G., & Scurry, T. (2009). Homebased work: A review of research into themes, directions and implications. *Personnel Review, 38*(6), 585–604. doi:10.1108/00483480910992229

Virick, M., DaSilva, N., & Arrington, K. (2010). Moderators of the curvilinear relation between extent of telecommuting and life satisfaction: The role of performance outcome orientation and worker type. *Human Relations, 63*(1), 137–154. doi:10.1177/0018726709349198

Wheatley, D. (2012b). Good to be home? Time-use and Satisfaction Levels among Home-based Teleworkers. *New Technology, Work and Employment, 27*(3), 224–241. doi:10.1111/j.1468-005X.2012.00289.x

Wheatley, D. (2017). Employee satisfaction and use of flexible working arrangements. *Work, Employment and Society, 31*(4), 567–585. doi:10.1177/0950017016631447

Wheatley, D. (2020). Changing places of work. In Contemporary Work and the Future of Employment in Developed Societies. London: Routledge. doi:10.4324/9781351034906-8

Wheatley, D. (2021). Workplace location and the quality of work: The case of urban-based workers in the UK. *Urban Studies (Edinburgh, Scotland).*

Wheatley, D., & Bickerton, C. (2016). Time-use and well-being impacts of travel-to-work and travel-for-work. *New Technology, Work and Employment, 31*(3), 238–254. doi:10.1111/ntwe.12074

Wheatley, D., & Gifford, J. (2019). *UK Working Lives Survey Report 2019.* London: Chartered Institute of Personnel and Development (CIPD). Available at: https://www.cipd.co.uk/knowledge/work/trends/uk-working-lives

Wight, V., & Raley, S. (2009). When Home Becomes Work: Work and Family Time among Workers at Home. *Social Indicators Research, 93*(1), 197–202. doi:10.100711205-008-9377-6

Acknowledgment

We would like to thank the authors who have contributed to this handbook for their efforts in researching and communicating remote home-based work while at the same time living the reality of the COVID-19 global pandemic. We would also like to thank the peer reviewers for the helpful comments and feedback they provided on the chapters of our contributors.

Section 1
Understanding the Impacts of Remote Working

Chapter 1
Psychological Impacts of Remote Working Under Social Distancing Restrictions

Oliver Baumann
Bond University, Australia

Elizabeth (Libby) J. Sander
Bond University, Australia

ABSTRACT

The coronavirus (COVID-19) pandemic has resulted in a swift and dramatic global shift in the location of work for many employees. Organizations around the world have implemented remote work arrangements to allow continuity of service while conforming with social distancing requirements. As a result of ongoing uncertainty regarding the current and future pandemics, reduced costs associated with housing employees remotely, and survey results suggesting employees are reluctant to return to a primarily office-based work model, many organisations are implementing ongoing remote arrangements for their employees. This chapter provides a review of current research on the psychological effects of remote working. Recommendations are made regarding future research directions across various remote work environments that will enhance understanding of the psychological effects of remote work under social distancing.

INTRODUCTION

The coronavirus (COVID-19) pandemic has forced a swift and dramatic shift in the way we work (Carnevale & Hatak, 2020) as organizations around the world have implemented working from home arrangements to allow continuity of service, while conforming with social distancing requirements. Remote work, which has previously been available to a limited group of employees (Allen et al., 2015), or as the privilege of the self-employed, has therefore become the new norm for many. Moreover, the uncertainty regarding the duration and impact of the pandemic (Altig et al. 2020) means that many organizations

DOI: 10.4018/978-1-7998-6754-8.ch001

are considering longer-term working from home arrangements. Finally, greater availability of technology to support remote working, combined with substantial reductions in direct costs for organizations (Manocheri & Pinkerton, 2003) suggest that work-from-home (or blended working) is likely to become much more common.

Work environments present both benefits and risks for mental health, and traditional work arrangements have been the centre of extensive investigations over the last century (Bliese et al., 2017; Cooper, 1976; Stansfeld & Candy, 2006; Thayer et al., 2010;). There is much less data, however, on the psychological impacts of remote work arrangements. A recent meta-analysis of the literature on home offices and telecommuters has identified a range of topics and issues that are at the centre of current research (de Macêdo, et al. 2020). Broadly, the dominant themes in the reviewed literature highlighted advantages of increased productivity, increased employee flexibility and reduced stress, and potential disadvantages of increased isolation, intensified work, and family-work conflicts. More research, however, is necessary, to provide a comprehensive understanding of the impacts of work-from-arrangements across a broad range of industries and employee demographics.

As a result of COVID-19, the number of employees working from home has increased dramatically around the world. For instance, in May 2020, 35% of the US workforce worked entirely from home, compared to just 8% in February 2020 (Bick et al., 2020). Even industries that traditionally do not rely much on work-from-home arrangements were forced to introduce them (Banerjee et al., 2020). The COVID-19 scenario presents a unique opportunity to evaluate the positive and negative psychological impacts of working from home on a large scale. Better knowledge about the psychological impacts of working from home will allow for informed decision-making and proactive interventions to ensure that work arrangements enhance well-being and performance, rather than impeding them. As mentioned above, there are several key outcome variables at the focus of research on work at-home-environments. However, rather than exploring those outcome measures in a bottom-up fashion, in this chapter we focus on the mediating inner mechanisms, namely motivation and the fulfilment of basic psychological needs, to provide structure for future research. We begin by presenting a model of how work arrangements might act via motivation and need satisfaction to influence performance and well-being utilising self-determination theory (Ryan & Deci, 2017). Subsequently, we assess the literature on remote work arrangements within this framework and outline suggestions for future research on the psychological impacts of remote work under social distancing restrictions.

Work Arrangements and Motivation

For an organization to be successful and profitable, it is crucial that it supports employees to achieve and maintain a high level of performance and well-being. Individual well-being has been shown to be an important precursor to both individual and organization performance (Ford, Cerasoli, Higgins & Decesare, 2011; Taris & Schreurs, 2009). Fundamentally, work performance is underpinned by motivation (Deci et al., 2017). Importantly, there are two types[1] of motivation, extrinsic motivation which is reliant on external rewards and pressures (such as pay and deadlines), and intrinsic motivation that derives both from within the individual and the task itself (i.e. fuelled by interest; Deci, 1971). While extrinsic motivation can lead to elevated performance, especially for tasks that are easily quantifiable and for which quality is less relevant, intrinsic motivation is useful for tasks in which qualitative excellence and creativity matters (Covington & Mueller, 2001). Extrinsic motives not only shift attention away from the task to the reward (Pittman et al., 1983), but may make behaviour dependent on external-regulation and inhibit independent thought (Ryan, 1993). More recent work has highlighted that the negative effect of external rewards on intrinsically rewarding tasks may be explained by a distractor effect, which may eventually wear off in real-life settings (Reiss, 2012). In any case, given that monetary remuneration is an integral part of employment, employers are less focussed on avoiding extrinsic motivators, and seek instead to enhance intrinsic motivators. In one study Kuvaas and colleagues (2017) surveyed thousands of employees in retail, finance, and technology organizations in Norway and found that intrinsic motivation (derived from their role and associated activities) was uniformly associated with positive employee outcomes such as performance and well-being, while extrinsic motivation (monetary rewards) was found to be negatively related, or unrelated to these outcomes. So, if intrinsic motivation is so important for work performance and well-being, how can we foster it? In the next section we propose a model of how work from home arrangements might act via motivation and need satisfaction to influence performance and well-being utilising self-determination theory (Ryan & Deci, 2017).

Self-determination Theory and Remote Work

According to Ryan's and Deci's self-determination theory (Ryan & Deci, 2017) intrinsic motivation is underpinned and promoted by three basic and universal psychological needs: *competence*, *autonomy*, and *relatedness*. These three needs are also referred to as organismic psychological needs, borrowing the name from the term organism, a living being that reacts to and is dependent on its environment. Ryan and Deci (2017) posit that in addition to biological needs, in order to thrive and grow, humans need to satisfy certain psychological requirements. According to self-determination theory, only activities and environments that fulfill these three basic needs will support individuals in developing the intrinsic motivation that is crucial for productivity and well-being (see Figure 1). Failing to satisfy those basic psychological needs is likely to lead not only to a lack of motivation, but ultimately poorer mental and physical health outcomes. In the following sections we will define these basic needs, and discuss how they can be conceptualised and explored as potential mediators of both positive and negative outcomes of work-from-home arrangements.

Competence

Competence refers to the psychological need of individuals to be successful in interactions with one's environment (White, 1959). Competence also reflects the drive to challenge and extend capabilities, and to seek out opportunities for personal growth (Steers & Spencer, 1977). To develop a sense of competence and a growth mindset it is important that the task provides an optimal level of challenge, i.e. avoiding boredom and frustration by matching the requirements of the task with the capabilities of the employee (Nakamura & Csikszentmihalyi, 2002). Further, and equally important, is the provision of timely and informative feedback, since obtaining feedback is vital for employees to develop a sense of competence (Butler & Nissan, 1986). Information about task performance opportunities for further development do not necessarily have to be provided by supervisors or co-workers but could also be intrinsic to the task (Anderson et al., 2001). Work-from-home arrangements typically lack many of the spontaneous opportunities for feedback that occur in classical office environments, such as during incidental conversations with co-workers and supervisors in the lift or at lunch breaks.

Figure 1. The self-determination model of motivation by Ryan & Deci (2017) applied to the workplace

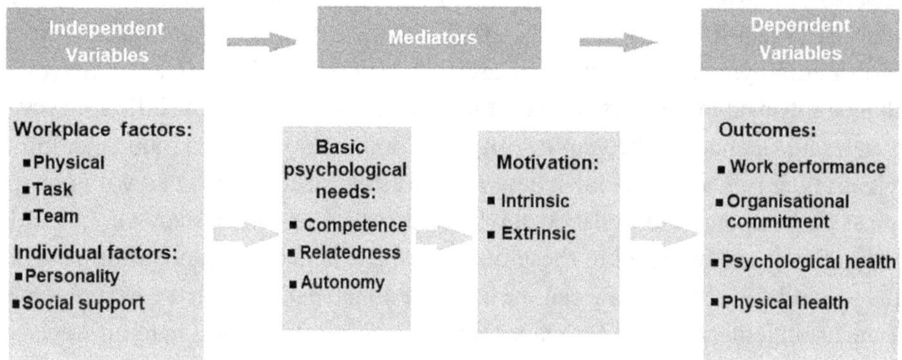

The effects of reduced opportunities for feedback became apparent in a study by Bloom and colleagues (2015). They conducted the first large scale long-term experimental study on the psychological effects of work-from-home arrangements, by sampling 16,000 call centre employees who were randomly assigned to work from home or in the office for 9 months. Bloom and colleagues (2015) found that overall the effect of working from home was positive, quantitative performance went up by 13% (mainly due to shorter break times and less sick leave) and qualitative performance stayed the same. Importantly, however, and relevant to the need for competence, the rate of promotions (to advanced functions or team leadership) was 50% lower in the work-from-home group. Follow-up interviews and focus-groups conducted by Bloom and colleagues (2015) further revealed that supervisors were less likely to notice good performance of work-at-home employees and were therefore also less likely to promote them, i.e. "out of sight, out of mind." Intriguingly, the increased productivity by the work-from-home group could potentially be partially explained by the lack of recognition, since the reduced visibility of achievements might lead to heightened desire by employees to appear productive, however, this effect may be extinguished over time if not successful. The negative effect of work-from-home arrangements on career development is likely to be even further compounded over time, with work-from-home employees losing out on developing interpersonal skills and relationships that are crucial for advancing to managerial positions (Mencl et al., 2016). Particularly for individuals with strong competence motivation, the reduced opportunity to receive performance feedback and recognition face-to-face may lead to reduced overall intrinsic motivation (Matsui et al., 1982), and subsequent lower levels of performance and well-being (Ryan & Deci, 2017). While doing overtime in the office might be a meaningful voluntary form of investment with the aim of achieving higher wages or promotions in the long run, extra hours at home do not seem to offer the same returns and have the additional potential to cause work-family conflicts (Song, 2009). It is therefore essential that work-at-home arrangements consider means to ensure that employees receive appropriate feedback on their performance. A current trend in delivering real-time performance feedback is to embed gamification elements to human-computer interfaces. This can be done by awarding automated achievements, such as batches, when employees meet pre-specified performance goals (Anderson et al., 2013, Grant & Betts, 2013). Gamification has generally been found to provide positive impacts on performance in a range of industries (Hamari, et al. 2014), and even increase the perceived meaningfulness of the task (Sailer et al. 2017). The evidence base, however, is still relatively limited, and long-term effects in particular will require further investigation. Furthermore, automated, real-time feedback is not an option for situations when objective indices of performance are not available, or on long-term projects where goals, metrics and personnel are likely to change with relative frequency. Furthermore, research has shown that employees may develop negative attitudes to gamification, since the inherent focus on extrinsic rewards may encourage competitive rather than cooperative behaviours (Hamari et al., 2014). Given the interindividual differences in motivation, it seems likely that gamification will be better suited to competence orientated individuals, than for individuals high in need of relatedness. In addition, individuals that have a high need for competence may become demotivated if the difficulty of the gamified challenges is perceived as too low or too high, therefore leading to boredom or anxiety (Csikzentmihalyi et al., 1993).

One strategy to support individuals who have a high need for relatedness, is to increase the frequency of short formal meetings, in both individual and group settings in order to compensate for the reduced opportunities for informal interactions in work-from home arrangements (Kello, 2015). However, more industry and task specific research will be necessary to develop evidence-based approaches to effectively manage performance for work-from-home arrangements.

Relatedness

Relatedness is the psychological need to connect emotionally with other people in reciprocal and meaningful relationships (Baumeister & Leary, 1995, Ryan & Powelson, 1991). This is a key benefit of the social environment that working with others can provide, and as such is essential for optimising work outcomes for both employees and organizations (Allen et al., 2015). Social psychology research has shown that sociable relationships can emerge seemingly spontaneously among groups of people, if individuals are given both sufficient proximity, and adequate time to build them (Wilder & Thomson, 1980). Importantly though, not all social interactions are able to satisfy relatedness needs. A key condition for developing satisfying relationships is perceived partner responsiveness (Reis, 2014). Work-from-home environments are clearly distinct to office environments in regard to the opportunities they provide to build and engage in responsive social interactions, since they offer reduced opportunities to engage socially with co-workers. In the aforementioned study by Bloom and colleagues (2015) the experimental work-from-home group was offered the choice to permanently switch to this arrangement, however half of the workers refused the offer, citing the lack of social contacts as a key reason. This finding dovetails with a study by Ozcelik and Barsade (2011), which investigated the links between perceived loneliness (i.e. the deprivation of close relationships) and work performance. The study measured loneliness in employees by using self-reports (i.e. UCLA Loneliness scale, Russel, 1996) as well as observations of co-workers and supervisors. The researchers assessed a range of demographic (e.g., education level, age, and organizational tenure) and psychological variables (e.g., extraversion, positive and negative affectivity) in their analysis, finding that loneliness was a significant negative predictor for task performance, team role performance, and affective commitment (Ozcelik & Barsade, 2011). Further, the effect of loneliness on performance was facilitated by lowered affective commitment to the organization. In other words, the findings indicate that work loneliness leads to emotional withdrawal, which ultimately leads to deteriorating performance and well-being (Ozcelik & Barsade, 2011). Importantly, a recent meta-analysis (Holt-Lunstad et al., 2015) highlighted that the negative effects of loneliness are not only psycho-behavioural, but that loneliness can have negative health implications. More specifically, this analysis indicated the effects of loneliness on mortality is comparable to smoking 15 cigarettes a day and that, somewhat surprisingly, loneliness is more predictive of premature death in those under 65 than in older age groups (Holt-Lunstad et al., 2015). Given concerns over the effects of the pandemic restrictions on the career development of younger employees, including developing networks and receiving social support, these findings are particularly significant.

Achor and colleagues (2018) followed up on these findings by investigating the demographic and professional profile that is most strongly associated with loneliness in a longitudinal survey of US full-time workers. Firstly, they found that several basic demographic factors such as age, gender, ethnicity, and even salary or job security, did not have much bearing on the severity of loneliness. In contrast, the nature of work had a robust effect, showing that professions that require less frequent social contact due to conducting more work on an individual basis (e.g., legal work, science and engineering) were more prone to high levels of loneliness than occupations that demand a high degree of social interaction (e.g. social work, marketing and sales). The most significant predictors of loneliness, however, were demographic factors related to an individual's private social life. Specifically, the smaller the private social support network, e.g., due to childlessness or the absence of a life partner or close friendships, the more prone to loneliness workers were at work. The results by Achor and colleagues (2018) further highlighted that, while any type of social support provided by an organization significantly improved well-being and performance, the most effective predictor on all human resource metrics was the presence of shared meaning across co-workers. The notion that shared meaning, or shared mental-models relating to how to carry out work, or the objectives of the organization for example, are crucial predictors or team processes and performance are not new (e.g. Mathieu et al., 2000). However, this newly discovered relationship with loneliness further highlights how important it is to provide employees with opportunities to fulfill their need for relatedness. The question remains though as to how to achieve this in work-from-home arrangements?

Video conferencing technologies provide a convenient and cost-effective means to facilitate remote work-related communication, but its use is limited for social interactions. As highlighted by Sander and Baumann (2020), teleconferencing has its side-effects and can reduce psychological well-being. Key factors are that teleconferences omit and supress nonverbal social cues (i.e., subtle aspects of body-language) that people typically use to communicate their feelings (Mehrabian, 1972). Moreover, research has shown that also the heightened focus on facial cues and the ability to see oneself can act as a stressor (Vergallito, et al., 2020). Previous research has also shown that virtual teams tend to express less excitement, social support, and trust than real-world teams (Rice and Love, 1987), however building efficient and supportive virtual teams is possible (Jarvenpaa & Leidner, 1999). Hawisher and Moran (1993) pointed out that virtual teams require an "intense need for response', so that failing to acknowledge an individual's initiatives and actions can quickly lead to erosion of trust, and rapid disintegration of the cohesion of the virtual group. As such, the use of traditional videoconferencing tools might not be optimal to create social bonds and shared mental models among co-workers. One avenue to overcome these limitations may be the use of novel immersive virtual reality (VR) technology for team meetings. Recent research has indicated that compared to traditional video-conferencing methods, VR-based environments increase not only the sense of presence, but also of team membership (Oprean et al., 2017). This may be because the increased presence might be mediated by increased immersion afforded by the wider fields of view offered by VR technology compared to traditional computer displays. Research in this area is, however, still in its relative infancy, and larger more comprehensive studies will be necessary to fully evaluate the potential of VR technology in generating socially cohesive co-worker experiences.

Autonomy

Autonomy is the psychological need to voluntarily initiate, control, and regulate behaviour (Ryan & Deci, 2017). In other words, the need for autonomy relates to the innate drive to make decisions and behave in ways that are congruent with our personal preferences. In the study by Bloom and colleagues (2015), productivity in the randomly selected work-from-home group increased by 13% relative to the office control-group. More impressively yet, in the second part of the study, in which employees were permitted to choose whether they wanted to work from home or in the office, the positive productivity difference grew to 22%. This further dramatic increase in productivity can be attributed to a self-selection effect, which shows that increases in productivity are not a uniform effect, but that employees who choose to work from home also contribute the largest increases in productivity. Importantly this study also showed that, in addition to increases in productivity, employees in the work-at-home group also reported subjectively higher satisfaction with work, which was objectively expressed in a ~50% lower turnover rate. This clearly highlights the importance of satisfying employees' autonomy needs as a contributor to enhancing productivity and well-being.

Work Life Balance, Family Issues, and Harassment

Directly related to the issue of autonomy, and arguably one of the most significant benefits of work-at-home arrangements, is the increased degree of flexibility that it offers (Sanchez et al., 2007). With the percentage of full-time working parents steadily increasing (Australian Bureau of Statistics, 2017; Cantillon et al., 2017; Pew Research Center, 2015), flexibility of work hours and the location of work for employees has been identified as the most important factor to balance work-family demands (Advancing Parental Leave Equality Network, 2019; Troup & Rose, 2012). Dockery & Bawa (2014) analysed survey data from 14,000 individuals and confirmed a positive association between working from home and employees' satisfaction with the flexibility to balance work and non-work commitments. Importantly, this effect is positively moderated by the total number of hours worked from home, showing that the more experience employees have with working from home the more they tend to like it. These findings are supported by research by Song & Goa (2018), which showed that subjective well-being also increased, due to greater control over work schedules and overall better work-life balance (e.g., due to reduced commute times). Moreover, Troup and Rose (2012) found that the positive effects of flexible arrangements are amplified for working women. This is in line with earlier findings, which highlight that flexible work hours are generally related to higher organizational commitment and job satisfaction in workers with family responsibilities (Scandura & Lankau, 1997). Importantly though, work-at-home arrangements appear to not actually increase the amount of time that employees spend on family activities, but the increased flexibility means that they are better able to manage the dual obligations (Ransome, 2007). A potential downside from this increased flexibility is the blurring of work-life boundaries, leading to family-conflicts and working longer hours (Duxbury & Higgins, 2001). This potential for work-family conflict seems to be particularly high in the case of involuntary work-from home arrangements, which do not satisfy the employees need for autonomy (e.g. due to an organization's need to reduce cost associated with office space; Lapierre and colleagues, 2016). In the context of the COVID-19 pandemic there have also been several published reports that suggest increases in domestic violence (Das et al., 2020; Jetelina et al., 2020 Peterman et al., 2020). These studies, however, also highlight that the pandemic is a multifactorial issue which involves economic uncertainty, loss of income, food insecurity, curtailing of personal rights and freedom of movement, and loss of loved ones. So far there is no data that specifically indicates a direct causal relationship between work-from-home arrangements and increases or decreases in domestic violence. While lockdown requirements can equate to more time at home with an abusive partner, there might be also protective factors, such as increased observation by neighbours who are likewise at home. In line with this idea, a working paper by Miller and colleagues (2020), which investigated the effects of the pandemic on domestic violence in Los Angeles, reported ambiguous effects, which also highlight the difficulty and complexity of reliably measuring domestic violence. For instance, they reported an increase in domestic violence calls to the police, but the actual number of reported crimes and arrests went down. It remains unclear whether these results mean that the threshold for reporting domestic violence was reduced by the pandemic, which in turn might have prevented more severe crimes to occur, or whether police was just more reluctant to arrest individuals, due to fears of infection. Related to this topic is also the question of whether work-from-home arrangements have any effects on the occurrence of work-related harassment. Recent news reports have suggested that work-at-home arrangements might not have a beneficial effect regarding workplace harassment, and have even suggested a further increase, due to the lack of managerial oversight and the impersonal nature of telecommunication (Martinuzzi, 2020). It is, however, also possible that remote work offers several protective factors from workplace harassment such as the removal of physical intimidation and the opportunity to record any telecommunication. Reports on this topic are so far only anecdotal in nature, and a more comprehensive assessment of this topic will be required. In any case this issue highlights that managers should be aware of the social and domestic risks that mandatory work-from-home arrangements could entail and ensure that appropriate reporting and support mechanisms are in place and widely communicated to employees.

Remote Work and Interindividual Differences

The research reviewed here has highlighted that the suitability of work-at-home arrangements will vary based on both individual differences, and organizational requirements, both of which need to be considered to maximise positive outcomes and avoid negative outcomes for both individuals and organizations. Due to individual differences, a one-size-fits-all approach is not the best way to approach this issue. For example, Van Yperen and colleagues (2014) conducted a psychometric study on a sample from a wide range of occupations and organizations, finding that employees with a low need for autonomy and a strong need of relatedness are typically most negatively impacted by an absence of social contacts. In contrast, individuals that suffer from social anxiety feel more comfortable in remote, digitally mediated interactions (Prizant-Passal et al., 2016). Further, Clark et al. (2012) investigated the relationship between the classic Big Five personality dimensions (i.e. extraversion, agreeableness, conscientiousness, neuroticism, and openness; Digman, 1990) in relation to attitude towards telecommuting. Their study was based on quantitative self-reports and involved a sample of over 300 senior business students. The study highlighted a positive relationship between agreeableness and sympathetic attitudes towards telecommuting. Individuals with high levels of agreeableness are more likely to be empathetic, cooperative, and trusting (Digman, 1990), whereas disagreeable individuals may be more likely to display traits of self-centredness, competitiveness, and distrust. It is open for interpretation why this pattern emerged, but one interpretation is that employees who score lower on trust and empathy may find it more difficult to engage with virtual team structures. Another interesting finding by Clark and colleagues (2012) was that individuals high in neuroticism (i.e. more anxious and emotionally instable; Digman, 1990) prefer work-from-home arrangements. A possible interpretation of this finding is that remote working allows those individuals to avoid social situations that could trigger negative mood states and further allows them to avoid social stigma. Clark and colleagues did not observe significant relationships between the other three personality factors (i.e. extraversion, conscientiousness, and openness) and attitudes toward telework. In contrast, Smith et al. (2018), obtaining quantitative self-reports of a sample of over 300 U.S. teleworkers, found that the personality factor of openness predicted how comfortable workers were with using video and phone communications channels. This is particularly important since the same study reported that satisfaction with these remote communication styles was significantly associated with overall job satisfaction in teleworkers. Given that openness indicates the level to which individuals are adaptable to new situations and their preference for new experiences (Digman, 1990), it is not surprising that this factor is also related to the willingness and appreciation of engaging with technology. In line with the observation by Clark and colleagues (2012), Smith and colleagues also observed a correlation between agreeableness and employees' satisfaction with communication technologies used in remote working environments, which again emphasises the importance of this personality factor to predict potential challenges for some employees in undertaking remote work. Another relevant study on the topic of personality and telework employed a quantitative self-report method in over 700 U.S. public service employees (Anderson et al. 2015). The authors observed a more positive attitude towards telework in introverted versus extraverted individuals, which seems not surprising given that extraversion is associated with being highly sociable and assertive, for which remote work environments offer limited opportunities. Taken together, these studies suggest that it is critical therefore that organizations understand the interindividual differences in needs and personalities of their workforce in implementing work-from-home arrangements. It is likely to be the case that some individuals will do well under permanent work-from-home arrangements, while others may require a hybrid arrangement working both from home and from the office or other remote work locations during a typical work week.

SOLUTIONS AND RECOMMENDATIONS

Research suggests that remote work arrangements, across a range of industries, are generally related to increases in productivity (see Rupietta & Beckmann (2016) for a large panel dataset), indicating that there is no need for management to feel too concerned about the performance and reliability of employees. However, the effectiveness of remote work for employees and organizations will depend on both the nature of work, and individual differences amongst employees (see also Allen, et al., 2015 for a review). Considering the potential cost-savings offered by work-at-home arrangements this paints an overall positive picture. From the perspective of the employee, the most significant benefits of work-from-home environments derive from the satisfaction of autonomy needs flowing from increased flexibility, however, this may only apply to work-from-home arrangements that are voluntary (Deci et al., 2017). However, while employees may not have been happy to have been forced out of the office, on a daily basis, each employee can get up and decide how to approach tasks with greater freedom than in the office.

The most significant concern related to work-from-home arrangements for both employers and employees appears to be the risk of social isolation that may eventually lead to organizational disenfranchisement (Achor et al., 2018). In particular, employees with high needs for social relatedness and who lack social-support networks at home are at risk, whereas those with low needs for relatedness and robust social networks outside of the office are likely to benefit (Van Yperen et al., 2014; Holt-Lunstad et al., 2015). Research has also shown that it will be important to develop approaches to regularly appraise performance in work-from-home arrangements, to avoid a scenario where reduced visibility of achievements leads to decrements in intrinsic motivation, especially for employees high in competence needs (Matsui et al., 1982; Bloom et al., 2015).

Moreover, whereas work-from-home arrangements can benefit intrinsic motivation for employees through the fulfilment of basic psychological needs of competence, relatedness, and autonomy (Ryan & Deci, 2017), there are also more pragmatic determinants of performance and well-being in work from home environments. It is therefore important to consider the physical differences of work-from-home compared to office environments. The elimination of common distractors present in office environments, particularly the detrimental effects of noise and distraction in open plan offices (Sander et al., 2019), are likely to provide significant benefits for those working from home (see also chapter by Sander, Rafferty & Jordan in this book). In addition to social dimensions of work environments, the effects of some dimensions of the physical work environment have also been shown to be moderated by personality factors, making it important to note that there is no one-size-fits-all solution for employees and employers. For example, research has shown that the detrimental effects of noise on cognitive performance is exacerbated in introverted individuals (Morgenstern et al., 1974, Standing et al., 1990, Belojevic et al., 2001), where more extroverted employees may in fact seek out noisier working environments (Campbell & Hawley, 1982). In addition to taking into account physical differences between office and home environments, organizations must also pay attention to and adjust procedural and task related aspects of work. For instance, Microsoft has indicated that traditional meeting structures and schedules do not translate well into remote work environments (Miller, 2020). To address this, Microsoft reduced the duration of meetings from 1 hour to 30 minutes, and decreased the maximum number of participants in order to increase employee engagement and productivity.

Finally, it is important to emphasize that for a significant percentage of employees, work-from-home arrangements are preferred, however organizational limitations may present a barrier to this occurring. For instance, Mokhtarian & Salomon (1996) discovered that more than half of their surveyed employees indicated that they would prefer to work from home if they could, but that the most frequent impediment for this was manager disapproval. It is important for organizations to be aware of potential barriers to the take up of work from home arrangements, and to address these through policy intervention, education and awareness programs.

FUTURE RESEARCH DIRECTIONS

Future research could explore several different avenues, in particular examining the effects of individual differences on work-from-home outcomes, differences in both job type and tasks that are suitable for work-from-home arrangements, and lastly, the effects of broader changes on social interaction and well-being under the pandemic on psychological outcomes of work-from-home. Firstly, as noted earlier in the chapter, research has started to highlight the profound effect of individual differences (demographic factors as well as personality types) on whether work-from-home arrangements are beneficial or detrimental to performance and well-being. By better understanding the role of individual differences on well-being and performance outcomes in work-from-home arrangements, organizations will be better placed to make appropriate decisions for their workforce. Secondly, more research is needed to assess differences in job types and work tasks, to determine how well they lend themselves to be accomplished from home. For example, tasks that require long periods of uninterrupted concentration may be better suited to work-from-home than tasks that require exchanging ideas and building consensus with other co-workers. Secondly, home-offices avoid many of the well-researched environmental nuisances of open-office environments. On the flip side, however, home-offices may feature several potential threats to cognitive performance and psychological well-being that will require more systematic investigation. Depending on demographic and economic context factors, home-offices may lack privacy, and as mentioned above, bear the potential for work-role conflict with other residents of the home (Duxbury & Higgins, 2001; Lapierre et al., 2016). The COVID-19 pandemic presents an opportunity to evaluate cognitive-emotional distractors in home-offices across an unprecedentedly broad range of industries, roles and tasks. Finally, work-from-home arrangements under social-distancing requirements are likely to lead to even higher levels of loneliness than is typically the case, given that in many cities, private social contacts are being limited. This presents a new opportunity for researchers to understand how the limitations of the pandemic affect cognitive, emotional and relational outcomes for employees working from home. Without proper controls and rigorous empirical design, data acquired during social-distancing or lock down restrictions is likely to overestimate levels of loneliness associated with work-from-home environments. The physical and social well-being effects of working from home under pandemic restrictions have significant implications for both organizations and policy makers. As such, research to better understand these effects is important.

CONCLUSION

Though the long-term implications of COVID-19 are currently unknown, our review of the literature suggests that if individual differences and preferences are considered, work-from-home arrangements can both maintain, and potentially significantly increase productivity. While the pandemic and the restrictions on movement and work location present challenges, there is an opportunity for exploration and innovation in work-from-home arrangements. In this chapter we have made the case for structuring research findings and future efforts on work-from-home arrangements using the self-determination model of motivation (Ryan & Deci, 2017). Focussing on the process of basic psychological need fulfilment in work-from-home settings can provide a valuable explanatory framework for the systematic investigation of characteristics that influence productivity, well-being, and personal growth. Taken together, while the reviewed evidence highlights that work-from-home arrangements can have a profound positive impact on satisfying psychological needs, organizations should be aware that if work-from-home arrangements are not voluntary, the decreased sense of autonomy may reduce intrinsic motivation, and ultimately lead to reduced levels of performance and well-being.

REFERENCES

Achor, S., Kellerman, G. R., Reece, A., & Robichaux, A. (2018). America's loneliest workers, according to research. *Harvard Business Review.* https://hbr.org/2018/03/americas-loneliest-workers-according-to-research

Advancing Parental Leave Equality Network. (2019). *National working families report 2019.* https://aplen.pages.ontraport.net/WorkingFamiliesReport2019

Allen, T. D., Golden, T. D., & Shockley, K. M. (2015). How effective is telecommuting? Assessing the status of our scientific findings. *Psychological Science in the Public Interest: A Journal of the American Psychological Society, 16,* 40-68.

Altig, D., Baker, S. R., Barrero, J. M., Bloom, N., Bunn, P., Chen, S., Mizen, P., Parker, N., Renault, T., Smietanka, P., & Thwaites, G. (2020). Economic uncertainty before and during the COVID-19 pandemic. *Journal of Public Economics, 191*, 104274. doi:10.1016/j.jpubeco.2020.104274 PMID:32921841

Anderson, A., Huttenlocher, D., Kleinberg, J., & Leskovec, J. (2013). Steering user behavior with badges. *Proceedings of the 22nd international conference on World Wide Web*, 95-106. 10.1145/2488388.2488398

Anderson, A. J., Kaplan, S. A., & Vega, R. P. (2015). The impact of telework on emotional experience: When, and for whom, does telework improve daily affective well-being? *European Journal of Work and Organizational Psychology*, *24*(6), 882–897. doi:10.1080/1359432X.2014.966086

Anderson, D. I., Magill, R. A., & Sekiya, H. (2001). Motor learning as a function of KR schedule and characteristics of task-intrinsic feedback. *Journal of Motor Behavior*, *33*(1), 59–66. doi:10.1080/00222890109601903 PMID:11265058

Australian Bureau of Statistics. (2017). *Childhood Education and Care, Australia.* Cat no. 4402.0.

Banerjee, I., Jacobsen, R., Krivkovich, A., Libotte, G., & Rambachan, I. (2020). *Shaping and safeguarding the banking workforce after COVID-19*. McKinsey & Company. https://www.mckinsey.com/industries/financial-services/our-insights/shaping-and-safeguarding-the-banking-workforce-after-covid-19#

Baumeister, R., & Leary, M. R. (1995). The need to belong: Desire for interpersonal attachments as a fundamental human motivation. *Psychological Bulletin*, *117*(3), 497–529.

Belojevic, G., Slepcevic, V., & Jakovljevic, B. (2001). Mental performance in noise: The role of introversion. *Journal of Environmental Psychology*, *21*(2), 209–213. doi:10.1006/jevp.2000.0188

BickA.BlandinA.MertensK. (2020). *Work from Home after the Covid-19 Outbreak.* CEPR Discussion Paper No. DP15000. https://ssrn.com/abstract=3650114

Bliese, P. D., Edwards, J. R., & Sonnentag, S. (2017). Stress and well-being at work: A century of empirical trends reflecting theoretical and societal influences. *The Journal of Applied Psychology*, *102*(3), 389–402. doi:10.1037/apl0000109 PMID:28125263

Bloom, N., Liang, J., Roberts, J., & Ying, Z. J. (2015). Does working from home work? evidence from a Chinese experiment. *The Quarterly Journal of Economics*, *130*(1), 165–218. doi:10.1093/qje/qju032

Butler, R., & Nisan, M. (1986). Effects of no feedback, task-related comments, and grades on intrinsic motivation and performance. *Journal of Educational Psychology*, *78*(3), 210–216. doi:10.1037/0022-0663.78.3.210

Campbell, J. B., & Hawley, C. W. (1982). Study habits and Eysenck's theory of extraversion–introversion. *Journal of Research in Personality*, *16*(2), 139–146. doi:10.1016/0092-6566(82)90070-8

Cantillon, B., Chzhen, Y., Sudhanshu, H., & Nolan, B. (2017). *Children of Austerity: Impact of the Great Recession on Child Poverty in Rich Countries*. Oxford University Press. doi:10.1093/oso/9780198797968.001.0001

Carnevale, J. B., & Hatak, I. (2020). Employee adjustment and well-being in the era of COVID-19: Implications for human resource management. *Journal of Business Research*, *116*, 183–187. doi:10.1016/j.jbusres.2020.05.037 PMID:32501303

Clark, A. L., Karau, S. J., & Michalisin, M. D. (2012). Telecommuting Attitudes and the 'Big Five' Personality Dimensions. *Journal of Management Policy and Practice*, *13*(3), 31–46.

Cooper, C. L., & Marshall, J. (1976). Occupational sources of stress: A review of the literature relating to coronary heart disease and mental ill health. *Journal of Occupational Psychology*, *49*(1), 11–28. doi:10.1111/j.2044-8325.1976.tb00325.x

Covington, M. V., & Mueller, K. J. (2001). Intrinsic versus extrinsic motivation: An approach/avoidance reformulation. *Educational Psychology Review*, *13*(2), 157–182. doi:10.1023/A:1009009219144

Csiksentmihalyi, M., Rathunde, K., & Whalen, S. (1993). *Talented teenagers: The roots of success and failure*. Cambridge University Press.

Das, M., Das, A., & Mandal, A. (2020). Examining the impact of lockdown (due to COVID-19) on Domestic Violence (DV): An evidences from India. *Asian Journal of Psychiatry*, *54*, 102335. doi:10.1016/j.ajp.2020.102335 PMID:32801078

de Macêdo, T., Cabral, E., Silva Castro, W. R., de Souza, C. C. Junior, da Costa, J. F. Junior, Pedrosa, F. M., da Silva, A. B., de Medeiros, V., de Souza, R. P., Cabral, M., & Másculo, F. S. (2020). Ergonomics and telework: A systematic review. *Work (Reading, Mass.)*, *66*(4), 777–778. doi:10.3233/WOR-203224 PMID:32925139

Deci, E. L. (1971). Effects of externally mediated rewards on intrinsic motivation. *Journal of Personality and Social Psychology*, *18*(1), 105–115. doi:10.1037/h0030644

Deci, E. L., Olafsen, A. H., & Ryan, R. M. (2017). Self-determination theory in work organizations: State of the science. *Annual Review of Organizational Psychology and Organizational Behavior*, *4*(1), 19–43. doi:10.1146/annurev-orgpsych-032516-113108

Digman, J. M. (1990). Personality structure: Emergence of the five-factor model. *Annual Review of Psychology*, *41*(1), 417–440. doi:10.1146/annurev.ps.41.020190.002221

Dockery, A. M., & Bawa, S. (2014). Is working from home good work or bad work? Evidence from Australian employees. *Australian Journal of Labour Economics*, *17*(2), 163–190.

Duxbury, C. & Higgins, C. (2001). *The 2001 national work-life conflict study*. The Healthy Communities Division, Health Canada Report.

Ford, M. T., Cerasoli, C. P., Higgins, J. A., & Decesare, A. L. (2011). Relationships between psychological, physical, and behavioural health and work performance: A review and meta-analysis. *Work and Stress*, *25*(3), 185–204. doi:10.1080/02678373.2011.609035

Grant, S., & Betts, B. (2013). Encouraging user behaviour with achievements: An empirical study. *Proceedings of the 10th Working Conference on Mining Software Repositories*, 65-68 10.1109/MSR.2013.6624007

Hamari, J. Koivisto, J., & Sarsa, H. (2014). Does gamification work? A literature review of empirical studies on gamification. *System Sciences (HICSS)*, 3025-3034.

Hawisher, G. E., & Moran, C. (1993). Electronic mail and the writing instructor. *College English*, *55*(6), 627–643. doi:10.2307/378699

Holt-Lunstad, J., Smith, T. B., Baker, M., Harris, T., & Stephenson, D. (2015). Loneliness and social isolation as risk factors for mortality: A meta-analytic review. *Perspectives on Psychological Science*, *10*(2), 227–237. doi:10.1177/1745691614568352 PMID:25910392

Jarvenpaa, S. L., & Leidner, D. E. (1999). Communication and trust in global virtual teams. *Organization Science*, *10*(6), 791–815. doi:10.1287/orsc.10.6.791

Jetelina, K. K., Knell, G., & Molsberry, R. J. (2020). Changes in intimate partner violence during the early stages of the COVID-19 pandemic in the USA. *Injury Prevention: Journal of the International Society for Child and Adolescent Injury Prevention*. Advance online publication.

Kello, J. E. (2015). The science and practice of workplace meetings. In J. A. Allen, N. Lehmann-Willenbrock, & S. G. Rogelberg (Eds.), *Cambridge handbooks in psychology. The Cambridge handbook of meeting science* (pp. 709–734). Cambridge University Press. doi:10.1017/CBO9781107589735.030

Kuvaas, B., Buch, R., Weibel, A., Dysvik, A., & Nerstad, C. G. (2017). Do intrinsic and extrinsic motivation relate differently to employee outcomes? *Journal of Economic Psychology*, *61*, 244–258. doi:10.1016/j.joep.2017.05.004

Lapierre, L. M., Van Steenbergen, E. F., Peeters, M. C., & Kluwer, E. S. (2016). Juggling work and family responsibilities when involuntarily working more from home: A multiwave study of financial sales professionals. *Journal of Organizational Behavior*, *37*(6), 804–822. doi:10.1002/job.2075

Manochehri, G., & Pinkerton, T. (2003). Managing telecommuters: Opportunities and challenges. *American Business Review*, *21*(1), 9–16.

Martínez Sánchez, A., Pérez Pérez, M., de Luis Carnicer, P., & José Vela Jiménez, M. (2007). Teleworking and workplace flexibility: A study of impact on firm performance. *Personnel Review*, *36*(1), 42–64. doi:10.1108/00483480710716713

Martinuzzi, E. (2020, June 17). As Work Has Moved Home, So Has Harassment. *Bloomberg*. https://www.bloomberg.com/opinion/articles/2020-06-17/as-work-has-moved-home-so-has-online-bullying-harassment

Mathieu, J. E., Heffner, T. S., Goodwin, G. F., Salas, E., & Cannon-Bowers, J. A. (2000). The influence of shared mental models on team process and performance. *The Journal of Applied Psychology*, *85*(2), 273–283. doi:10.1037/0021-9010.85.2.273 PMID:10783543

Matsui, T., Okada, A., & Kakuyama, T. (1982). Influence of achievement need on goal setting, performance, and feedback effectiveness. *The Journal of Applied Psychology*, *67*(5), 645–648. doi:10.1037/0021-9010.67.5.645

Mehrabian, A. (1972). *Nonverbal communication*. Aldine- Atherton.

Mencl, J., Wefald, A. J., & van Ittersum, K. W. (2016). Transformational leader attributes: Interpersonal skills, engagement, and well-being. *Leadership and Organization Development Journal*, *37*(5), 635–657. doi:10.1108/LODJ-09-2014-0178

Miller, A. R., Segal, C., & Spencer, M. K. (2020). Effects of the COVID-19 Pandemic on Domestic Violence in Los Angeles. National Bureau of Economic Research, 28068.

Miller, C. C. (2020, July 31). Remote Work Isn't Working? Maybe Your Company Is Doing It Wrong. *The New York Times*. https://www.nytimes.com/2020/07/31/upshot/remote-work-tips.html

Mokhtarian, P. L., & Salomon, I. (1996). Modeling the choice of telecommuting: 2. A case of the preferred impossible alternative. *Environment & Planning*, *28*(10), 1859–1876. doi:10.1068/a281859

Morgenstern, S., Hodgson, R. J., & Law, L. (1974). Work efficiency and personality. *Ergonomics*, *17*(2), 211–220. doi:10.1080/00140137408931340 PMID:4845889

Nakamura, J., & Csikszentmihalyi, M. (2002). The concept of flow. In C. R. Snyder & S. J. Lopez (Eds.), *Handbook of positive psychology* (pp. 89–105). Oxford University Press.

Oprean, D., Simpson, M., & Klippel, A. (2017). Collaborating Remotely: An evaluation of immersive capabilities on spatial experiences and team membership. *International Journal of Digital Earth*, *11*(4), 1–17.

Ozcelik, H., & Barsade, S. (2011). Work loneliness and employee performance. *Academy of Management Annual Meeting Proceedings*, 1-6.

Peterman, A., Potts, A., O'Donnell, M., Thompson, K., Shah, N., Oertelt-Prigione, S., & van Gelder, N. (2020). *Pandemics and violence against women and children.* Center for Global Development Working Paper 528. Washington, DC: Centre for Global Development.

Pew Research Center (2015). *Raising Kids and Running a Household: How Working Parents Share the Load.* Technical Report.

Pittman, T. S., Boggiano, A. K., & Ruble, D. N. (1983). Intrinsic and extrinsic motivational orientations: Limiting conditions on the undermining ad enhancing effects of reward on intrinsic motivation. In J. Levine & M. Wang (Eds.), *Teacher and student perceptions: Implications for learning* (pp. 319–340). Erlbaum.

Prizant-Passal, S., Shechner, T., & Aderka, I. M. (2016). Social anxiety and Internet use–A meta-analysis: What do we know? What are we missing? *Computers in Human Behavior*, *62*, 221–229. doi:10.1016/j.chb.2016.04.003

Ransome, P. (2007). Conceptualizing boundaries between 'life' and 'work'. *International Journal of Human Resource Management*, *18*(3), 374–386. doi:10.1080/09585190601167425

Reis, H. T. (2014). Responsiveness: Affective interdependence in close relationships. In M. Mikulincer & P. R. Shaver (Eds.), *The Herzliya series on personality and social psychology. Mechanisms of social connection: From brain to group* (pp. 255–271). American Psychological Association.

Reiss, S. (2012). Intrinsic and extrinsic motivation. *Teaching of Psychology, 39*(2), 152–156. doi:10.1177/0098628312437704

Rice, R. E., & Love, G. (1987). Electronic emotion: Socioemotional content in a computer-mediated communication network. *Communication Research, 14*(1), 85–108. doi:10.1177/009365087014001005

Rupietta, K., & Beckmann, M. (2016). *Working from home: What is the effect on employees' effort?* University of Basel, Centre of Business and Economics.

Russell, D. W. (1996). The UCLA Loneliness Scale (Version 3): Reliability, validity, and factor structure. *Journal of Personality Assessment, 66*(1), 20–40. doi:10.120715327752jpa6601_2 PMID:8576833

Ryan, R. M. (1993). Agency and organization: Intrinsic motivation, autonomy, and the self in psychological development. In J.E. Jacobs (Ed.), *Nebraska Symposium on Motivation: Developmental perspectives on motivation* (pp. 397-427). Academic Press.

Ryan, R. M., & Deci, E. L. (2000). Self-determination theory and the facilitation of intrinsic motivation, social development, and well-being. *The American Psychologist, 55*(1), 68–78. doi:10.1037/0003-066X.55.1.68 PMID:11392867

Ryan, R. M., & Deci, E. L. (2017). *Self determination theory.* The Guildford Press.

Ryan, R. M., & Powelson, C. L. (1991). Autonomy and relatedness as fundamental to motivation and education. *Journal of Experimental Education, 60*(1), 49–66. doi:10.1080/00220973.1991.10806579

Sailer, M., Hense, J. U., Mayr, S. K., & Mandl, H. (2017). How gamification motivates: An experimental study of the effects of specific game design elements on psychological need satisfaction. *Computers in Human Behavior, 69*, 371–380. doi:10.1016/j.chb.2016.12.033

Sander, E. L. J., Caza, A., & Jordan, P. J. (2019). Psychological perceptions matter: Developing the reactions to the physical work environment scale. *Building and Environment, 148*, 338–347. doi:10.1016/j.buildenv.2018.11.020

Sander, L., & Bauman, O. (2020). Why Zoom Meetings are So Exhausting. In M. Glassey (Ed.). 2020: The year that changed us. Thames & Hudson.

Scandura, T., & Lankau, M. (1997). Relationships of Gender, Family Responsibility and Flexible Work Hours to Organizational Commitment and Job Satisfaction. *Journal of Organizational Behavior, 18*(4), 377–391. doi:10.1002/(SICI)1099-1379(199707)18:4<377::AID-JOB807>3.0.CO;2-1

Smith, S. A., Patmos, A., & Pitts, M. J. (2018). Communication and teleworking: A study of communication channel satisfaction, personality, and job satisfaction for teleworking employees. *International Journal of Business Communication, 55*(1), 44–68. doi:10.1177/2329488415589101

Song, Y. (2009). Unpaid Work at Home. *Industrial Relations, 48*(4), 578–588. doi:10.1111/j.1468-232X.2009.00576.x

Song, Y., & Gao, J. (2018). *Does telework stress employees out? A study on working at home and subjective well-being for wage/salary workers.* Institute of Labor Economics (IZA).

Standing, L., Lynn, D., & Moxness, K. (1990). Effects of noise upon introverts and extroverts. *Bulletin of the Psychonomic Society*, *28*(2), 138–140. doi:10.3758/BF03333987

Stansfeld, S., & Candy, B. (2006). Psychosocial work environment and mental health-a meta-analytic review. *Scandinavian Journal of Work, Environment & Health*, *32*(6), 443–462. doi:10.5271jweh.1050 PMID:17173201

Steers, R. M., & Spencer, D. G. (1977). The role of achievement motivation in job design. *The Journal of Applied Psychology*, *62*(4), 472–479. doi:10.1037/0021-9010.62.4.472

Taris, T. W., & Schreurs, P. J. G. (2009). Well-being and organizational performance: An organizational-level test of the happy-productive worker hypothesis. *Work and Stress*, *23*(2), 120–136. doi:10.1080/02678370903072555

Thayer, J. F., Verkuil, B., Brosschot, J. F., Kampschroer, K., West, A., Sterling, C., ... Sternberg, E. M. (2010). Effects of the physical work environment on physiological measures of stress. *European Journal of Cardiovascular Prevention and Rehabilitation*, *17*(4), 431–439. doi:10.1097/HJR.0b013e328336923a PMID:20404733

Troup, C., & Rose, J. (2012). Working from home: Do formal or informal telework arrangements provide better work-family outcomes? *Community Work & Family*, *15*(4), 471–486. doi:10.1080/13668803.2012.724220

Van Yperen, N. W., Rietzschel, E. F., & De Jonge, K. M. (2014). Blended working: For whom it may (not) work. *PLoS One*, *9*(7), e102921. doi:10.1371/journal.pone.0102921 PMID:25033202

Vergallito, A., Mattavelli, G., Gerfo, E. L., Anzani, S., Rovagnati, V., Speciale, M., Vinai, P., Vinai, P., Vinai, L., & Lauro, L. (2020). Explicit and Implicit Responses of Seeing Own vs. Others' Emotions: An Electromyographic Study on the Neurophysiological and Cognitive Basis of the Self-Mirroring Technique. *Frontiers in Psychology*, *11*, 433. doi:10.3389/fpsyg.2020.00433 PMID:32296363

White, R. W. (1959). Motivation reconsidered: The concept of competence. *Psychological Review*, *66*(5), 297–333. doi:10.1037/h0040934 PMID:13844397

Wilder, D. A., & Thompson, J. E. (1980). Intergroup contact with independent manipulations of in-group and out-group interaction. *Journal of Personality and Social Psychology*, *38*(4), 589–603. doi:10.1037/0022-3514.38.4.589

ENDNOTE

1 Deci & Ryan (2000) proposed four different types of extrinsic motivation, ranging from fully externally regulated to a state that is supposedly indistinguishable from intrinsic motivation. The full model has, however received so far only limited empirical support.

Chapter 2
Working, Caring, Surviving: The Gender Dynamics of Remote Work in Brazil Under COVID-19

Lygia Sabbag Fares
Brooklyn Institute for Social Research, USA

Ana Luíza Matos de Oliveira
https://orcid.org/0000-0002-9623-3305
FLACSO, Brazil

Lílian Nogueira Rolim
https://orcid.org/0000-0002-9880-2823
University of Campinas, Brazil

ABSTRACT

Drawing from a questionnaire answered by 455 people during social distancing in Brazil, the chapter analyzes how individuals who worked remotely and those who did not cope with the increase in domestic and care work and how this extra work was divided in gender terms. The questionnaire indicates that the pandemic increased both domestic and care activities, with the former being more frequent for women and those under remote work. In general, this was not accompanied by a better division of these activities across sexes as women remained mainly responsible for them. Nevertheless, some improvements in the division of the domestic work were observed amongst those under remote work. However, when such a rebalance does not occur, remote work tends to be associated with an increase in women's overburdening.

INTRODUCTION

Remote work, teleworking, working at home, home-based work and their effects on workers, and especially on women, have long been discussed in the literature (Huws et al, 1996; Lyttelton, Zang & Musick, 2020). Indeed, working from home potentially increases women's total (paid and domestic) working time and blurs the boundaries between the two. Despite not being a new phenomenon, remote work became

DOI: 10.4018/978-1-7998-6754-8.ch002

widespread in 2020 due to the COVID-19 pandemic (ILO, 2020). In this context, the relation between remote work, domestic work and gender inequality became even more relevant, as the consequences of such drastic increases in remote work on workers is subject to the already existing sexual division of labor. This chapter focuses on the impact of remote work in Brazil considering the gender dynamics of social distancing during the COVID-19 pandemic and contributes to the literature and to this book by addressing how remote work imposed by social-distancing measures impacts unpaid work and women. It discusses the sexual division of labor in the Brazilian society (in which women are socially responsible for domestic work) and the consequences of remote work for women. In this sense, it proposes a framework for discussing the challenges of remote work for women during and post pandemic, highlighting the lessons from the pandemic period. The chapter contributes to understanding the effects of remote work on society in general and on the sexual division of labor.

It is important to provide some context to the Brazilian situation when this study took place. The response to the pandemic by the Brazilian government in 2020 was controversial, with strong economic implications. The President dismissed the gravity of the disease, the need for social distancing and the use of masks, and even pushed for the use of Hydroxychloroquine, a drug with no proven effect against COVID-19. By October 2020, Brazil had reached 5 million infections and 150,000 deaths from the disease, a number which is likely to be underreported. According to Worldometers (2020), by October 2020, Brazil, the third country in absolute number of infections, was at the 91st place in COVID-19 tests per million inhabitants. At the same time, the country's economy suffered, first in early 2020 as a reflection of the crisis in Europe and in China; then from March 2020 onwards, when the virus reached Brazil and social distancing measures were initiated. Social distancing measures varied in time and between regions, with very few going into full lockdown and for very short periods of time. In most regions, economic activities which require interaction were prohibited in the beginning of the pandemic (March 2020) and there was a social awareness of the need for social distance. Yet, the lack of national coordination in this process is an important feature of Brazil's response to the crisis. Particularly exposed to the crisis are those in vulnerable groups and informal workers.

In social and economic terms, the effects of the pandemic are likely to be long lasting, as it adds to the already unequal structure of the Brazilian society, characterized by vulnerability, informality, and various forms of inequality. According to Oliveira & Emídio (2021), inequality is set to worsen as in this moment of crisis, those with monetary savings, support and social capital are in better positions to move forward. Indeed, the authors argue that the pandemic affects not only economic variables per se but also life trajectories. In this sense, the pandemic may reinforce existing economic and geographic divides.

There is also a relevant gender dimension to this process, as social distancing and the related increase in remote work affected a society already marked by significant gender inequalities. National statistics show that in 2019, women dedicated 21.4 hours per week on average for domestic labor, while men spent 11 hours per week (IBGE, 2020a). Being primarily responsible for reproductive labor entails numerous and long-lasting implications for women, such as reduced available time for paid work and various discrimination experiences in the labor market. Adding to this context, the pandemic of COVID-19 has disrupted the world of work in many ways, one of which being the increase of domestic work, as social distancing imposed the closure of workplaces, schools, restaurants, and governmental services that aid the reproduction of the workforce.

Therefore, the chapter seeks to answer the following questions: How did individuals, especially those working remotely, coped with the increase in domestic work? How was this extra work divided in terms of gender? The authors' hypothesis is that although the pandemic of COVID-19 might have opened an opportunity to question the sexual division of domestic and care work, it augmented the time spent by women in domestic work in an uneven manner, therefore increasing gender inequality. Given the analysis on remote work under the world's "largest work-from-home experiment" (Williamson, Colley & Hanna-Osborne, 2020) during COVID-19, the chapter also sheds light on the potential reality post-COVID-19, if remote work were to become more widespread in Brazilian society.

The chapter is organized as follows. It discusses the sexual division of labor in Brazil before the pandemic and performs a literature review on this topic during the pandemic in Brazil and in other countries and on the impacts of remote working. Then, it analyses data from a questionnaire answered by 455 people during social distancing in Brazil, between 26 May 2020 and 15 June 2020. The respondents who declared to be working remotely due to social distancing measures are brought under special focus, as those who did not do remote work form a "control group" for the study. Then, a discussion of solutions and recommendations is presented and a conclusion section closes the chapter.

BACKGROUND

This chapter is based on the concept of the sexual division of labor, which relegates roles of care and domestic work—paid or not—to women. Folbre & Nelson (2000) argue that traditionally, the "public" world of markets and government was the realm of men, while the "private" realm of family and social relationships was entrusted to women. In this sense, the sexual division of labor relies on women to perform unpaid domestic work and those who perform paid and unpaid work suffer from what the literature calls a "double burden".

Unpaid care and domestic work are fundamental for the reproduction of the workforce and can be considered "subsidies" that women provide to the capitalist system (Folbre, 2006). In Brazil, where the public provision of such activities is very low, the unpaid work women perform at home is even more fundamental, though not socially valued. Also, when there are jobs that provide market substitutes for services women once provided at home (such as health and education), these occupations tend to also be dominated by women and are associated with lower wages when compared to jobs with otherwise similar characteristics (Folbre, 2006).

Thus, the sexual division of labor relates to the concepts of gender and gender roles. Gender, for the purpose of this chapter, is defined as a social and cultural relation between sexes. Around the world, women spend two to ten times more time on unpaid care work than men due to discriminatory social institutions and stereotypes on gender roles. In Brazil, the sexual division of labor imposes lower wages for women (Baltar, Rolim & Leone, 2020), combined or not with lower working hours and more precarious jobs. Labor flexibility measures theoretically give them the possibility of reconciling their productive and reproductive labor, but in most cases, it just means more work for women (Oliveira, 2013; Gibb, 2017). This also keeps them out of the labor market, given the high opportunity cost resulting from the low remuneration of women's productive work. By doing so, women act as a reserve army, exercising both the function of reducing the price of labor and available labor power, when necessary. Finally, the sexual division of labor imposes free reproductive work on women, who subsidize the reproduction of the workforce and reduce wages, and, at the same time, legitimizes the underutilization of this contingent of workers (Saffioti, 2013).

As Folbre (2006), Gibb & Oliveira (2015) and Fares & Oliveira (2020) argue, it is important to understand care and domestic activities as work, adding them to the total working time. Esquivel et al.

(2012) argue that although care and the domestic economy have an undeniable importance, they still occupy a marginal role in the analysis of the "real economy" and at best are only tangentially present in research on social and labor policy. However, all welfare regimes are associated, by definition, with a combined arrangement of work and care. For the case of Brazil, women work less hours than men on paid work, but have a higher total working time if unpaid work is also considered.

The phenomena of the "feminization of poverty" (Folbre, 2006; Costa et al., 2005) can be observed in Brazil and reflects the complex reality women face in the labor market, connected with the gender roles and the sexual division of labor previously presented. In Brazil, women have lower income and formality rate (Baltar, Rolim & Leone, 2020). Depending on their race, social status and region, Brazilian women take on different paths. Women from more affluent classes can "outsource" domestic labor to domestic workers (women of lower income) (Folbre, 2006; Gibb, 2017).

Adding to this context, the pandemic of COVID-19 has disrupted the world of work in many ways. One of which is by increasing domestic and care work as social distancing has imposed the closure of workplaces, schools, restaurants, and governmental services that aid social reproduction. In this scenario, some workers have been allowed to perform remote work, but faced an increase in their unpaid work. ILO (2020a) argues that under normal circumstances (non-pandemic), remote working may disadvantage women, as they typically must shoulder both childcare and household chores as well as paid employment; it may also, alternatively, help to facilitate work-life balance. However, one observation must be made regarding remote working: during the pandemic this was only an option for some highly skilled workers in the services/industry sector, whose occupation allowed for their work to be performed from home and who possessed the means and skills to use technology to perform their work. ILO (2020b) estimated that approximately one in six occupations can be done at home at the global level and just over one in four in advanced countries, but that the potential to do so requires, at a minimum, that countries make the necessary investments in improving telecommunications infrastructure.

In Brazil, in 2017, less than 20% of the population had access to broadband internet connection (Eclac, 2020). For a part of the informal sector (40% of the occupied population) home-base work was already a reality (Gibb, 2017), however, for a sensible parcel of the informal sector (street vendors, for example) and for many in the formal sector this was not an option. In this sense, the population which the authors investigate in this chapter – Brazilians under remote work — are in a sense privileged for being among those who have been able to protect themselves and their families while maintaining their occupation. Nevertheless, the study of this privileged group, and the comparison with those who could not do remote work during the pandemic (for various reasons) bespeaks important effects that remote work can have on workers in general and, more specifically, on women and sheds light on the potential benefits and risks of making remote work a generally accepted practice.

In this sense, this chapter is related to the emerging literature concerning the effects of the pandemic on the sexual division of labor and its relation to the increase in remote work. Research on remote working under COVID-19 and its impacts on the sexual division of labor in the household is still limited. The emerging research presents different findings concerning the impact of remote work. Manzo & Minello (2020), Nash & Churchill (2020) and Van Eck & Jammaers (2020) find that under remote work regimes during the COVID-19 pandemic there is a reinforcement of the sexual division of labor in the household in line with the present work's hypothesis, as presented in the introduction. On the other hand, Raišienė et al. (2020) argue that remote work and mixing personal and professional life challenges traditional masculine roles, refuting this hypothesis for the case of Lithuania. The authors' literature review also did not find studies on this topic specifically focusing on Brazil. Therefore, following the studies of

Manzo & Minello (2020), Nash & Churchill (2020), Raišienė et al (2020), Van Eck & Jammaers (2020) and Oliveira, Rolim & Fares (2021), this chapter contributes to the literature by filling a gap on this important matter in Brazil and by analyzing how remote work imposed by social-distancing measures impacts women.

THE GENDER DYNAMICS OF REMOTE WORK IN BRAZIL UNDER COVID-19

Methodology

The chapter analyses new data from a questionnaire administered during part of the social distancing period in Brazil, between 26 May 2020 and 15 June 2020, using a snowball technique (Alloatti, 2014). Accordingly, the authors shared the questionnaire with an initial group of people and every respondent was asked to share it with other people to increase the questionnaires' reach. The questionnaire received 455 responses. In the period of data collection, Brazil was under different types of restrictions associated with the pandemic, as there were no mandatory restrictions put in place by the federal government. This means that most of the measures were taken by the state level administrations and, although there was no national lockdown as in other countries, the degree of restrictions varied according to the situation in each state. Indeed, after the World Health Organization recognized that the situation could be characterized as a pandemic in mid-March 2020, a number of measures were undertaken by the private and public sectors: while many companies closed their offices and factories and started moving to remote work, state level administrations declared quarantines and/or implemented restrictions to limit (or prohibit) stores, schools, restaurants, bars and parks from opening and to allow only essential services to function. In the period analyzed by this survey, most of these restrictions were still in place - in the state of São Paulo, for instance, most regions were still classified as either "red" or "orange", which are the most restrictive levels (out of five levels). The situation was similar in other regions of the country and, overall, around 8.8 million people were working remotely in Brazil when the questionnaire circulated (IBGE, 2020b).

Main Characteristics of Participants

The questionnaire sample comprised 288 (63.3%) women and 167 (36.7%) men. Also, 346 (76.0%) respondents declared to be white, 99 (21.8%) black,[1] 8 (1.8%) Asian descendants,[2] and 2 (0.4%) indigenous. In terms of age, 104 (22.9%) respondents were between 18 and 29 years old, 237 (52.1%) between 30 and 49, 107 (23.5%) between 50 and 69 and 7 (1.5%) between 70 and 79. Most of the respondents resided in three Brazilian states located in the southeast region:[3] 237 (52.1%) in São Paulo, 69 (15.2%) in Minas Gerais and 46 (10.1%) in Rio de Janeiro. The remaining 103 (22.6%) respondents resided in 17 Brazilian states and the federal district.

At the time of the survey, 453 (99.6%) respondents declared to be under at least some degree of social distancing. With respect to their employment situation before the pandemic, 370 (81.3%) respondents were working (employees, employers, self-employment, or internship), 36 (7.9%) respondents did not work or were students, 25 (5.5%) respondents were retired, and 24 (5.3%) respondents were unemployed. Most of the respondents declared they have performed at least a period[4] of remote work after the pandemic started (348 respondents, equivalent to 76.5%).[5] While 213 (74.0%) women said they did some amount of remote work, 135 (80.8%) men declared having done so. It is worthwhile mentioning that 96

(21.1%) respondents did at least a period of office work during the pandemic. In terms of gender, 57 (19.8%) women and 39 (23.4%) men said they did at least a period of office work during the pandemic. Thus, a larger percentage of men declared doing at least a period of office work, while a larger percentage of men also declared doing remote work; hence, a combination of office and remote work was more relevant for men than for women. Indeed, the data indicates that 28 (9.7%) women did both types of work, while 27 (16.2%) men did so.

To analyze how domestic and care work affected people who did remote work during the pandemic, the questionnaire asked the participants their perception on how these activities changed with the pandemic. In the analysis presented in the next section, the information for those who did at least a period of remote work is compared with those who did not do any remote work to assess the difference in the amount of time dedicated to domestic and care work and the division of these activities between partners.

Remote Work and Domestic and Care Work

The analysis of the responses concerning domestic work suggests the existence of some patterns related to sex and the type of work (remote work or not). The responses from the questionnaire show that 278 (79.9%) of the 348 participants who did remote work declared that the amount of domestic work increased with the onset of the pandemic. This contrasts with 73 (68.2%) of the 107 respondents who did not do any amount of remote work and declared that the amount of domestic work increased. In other words, those under some sort of remote work regime reported more frequently an increase in domestic work. In terms of gender, considering all participants, 228 (79.2%) women and 123 (73.7%) men declared that their amount of domestic work increased with the pandemic. As expected, the proportion of each gender that declared an increase in their domestic work was higher for those who did remote work: 175 (82.2%) women and 103 (76.3%) men who did remote work confirmed that their domestic work increased, while 53 (70.7%) women and 20 (62.5%) men who did not do remote work observed that their domestic work increased as well. While these figures suggest that gender and the category of work (remote or not remote) were linked with the reported increase in domestic work, which was more expressive for women and for those who did remote work, the comparison between each category of work within each sex was rather similar: the percentage of women who reported an increase in domestic work was 11.5 percentage points (p.p.) higher for women who did remote work than for those who did not, while this difference was equal to 13.8 p.p. in the case of men. This suggests that remote work had a similar impact for both genders, although women tended to declare more frequently than men an increase in their domestic work within each group.

Overall, without considering gender or remote work, the type of domestic work that increased the most was grocery cleaning (379 respondents or 83.3% of the total declared an increase), dishwashing (342 respondents or 75.2% of the total declared an increase), house cleaning (337 respondents or 74.1% of the total declared an increase) and cooking (320 respondents or 70.3% of the total declared an increase). Importantly, a larger percentage of people engaged in remote work than those who did not do this type of work reported an increase in the time dedicated to each type of domestic work. The only exceptions were grocery cleaning, whose increase was directly linked to the official COVID-19 prevention recommendations and thus increased expressively in both categories (increased to 291 respondents or 83.6% of those who did remote work and 88 respondents or 82.2% of those who did not do remote work), and ironing, which increased more for people who did not do remote work (increased to 66 respondents or 19.0% of those who did remote work and 24 respondents or 22.4% of those who did not do remote work).

Thus, the activities that had a more expressive increase for those doing remote work than those who did not do this type of work were dishwashing (274 respondents or 78.7% and 68 respondents or 63.6% respectively), cooking (253 respondents or 72.7% and 67 respondents or 62.6% respectively), grocery shopping (210 respondents or 60.3% and 51 respondents or 47.7% respectively), house cleaning (266 respondents or 76.4% and 71 respondents or 66.4% respectively), and doing laundry (191 respondents or 54.9% and 48 respondents or 44.9% respectively).

As with the overall time dedicated to domestic work, a larger percentage of women than men declared an increase in the time devoted towards each type of domestic work. This pattern was also observed in the gender comparison within each category of workers (remote work or no remote work). Yet, there are a few remarkable differences in the gender patterns within each category. For those who did remote work, the percentage of women and men who reported an increase in dishwashing (80.3% and 76.3% respectively), house cleaning (77.5% and 74.8% respectively), and ironing (20.2% and 17.0% respectively) was closer than in the case of the other activities, in which the percentage of women who reported an increase was much higher, as in the case of cooking (77.0% and 65.9% respectively), grocery cleaning (86.9% and 78.5% respectively), grocery shopping (64.3% and 54.1% respectively), and doing the laundry (59.6% and 47.4% respectively). While this pattern is similar among those who did not do remote work for activities such as dishwashing (65.3% and 59.4% respectively) and grocery cleaning (84.0% and 78.1% respectively), the difference between women and men who did not do remote work and reported an increase in the time dedicated to activities such as house cleaning (72.0% and 53.1% respectively) and ironing (25.3% and 15.6% respectively) were much larger and in activities such as cooking (64.0% and 59.4% respectively) and doing laundry (46.7% and 40.6% respectively) were lower than among those who did remote work. An exception to the pattern identified so far is that the increase in the time spent in grocery shopping was more relevant for men who did not do remote work than for women in this category (45.3% women and 53.1% men in this category).

While there is a clear pattern in the comparison between men and women and remote work or not in the case of domestic work, the picture is less clear when it comes to care work. Before proceeding, it is important to mention that only a portion of the respondents declared doing care work:[6] 189 (41.5%) respondents declared to do at least one type of care activity. The percentages for each sex and type of work are rather similar as 117 (40.6%) women, 72 (43.1%) men, 149 (42.8%) people doing remote work, and 40 (37.4%) people not doing remote work declared they did at least one type of care activity. Therefore, the analysis below focuses only on those who did engage in each specific activity, which reduces considerably the size of the sample.

With respect to the activities related to childcare (watching over children, supervising their homework and online classes, or playing with them), they were performed by 153 (33.6%) respondents. Among those who performed each type of activity, 97 (63.4% of a total of 153) reported an increase in the time dedicated to childcare, 67 (55.4% of a total of 121) reported an increase in the time dedicated to helping children with their homework, and 83 (59.7% of a total of 139) reported an increase in the time spent playing with their children.[7] In all cases, those under remote work reported more frequently an increase than those not involved with remote work. However, within each group there is no clear pattern in terms of gender, as in some cases women reported more frequently an increase in the time spent on the activity, and in others less frequently. Consequently, the percentage of men and women who declared an increase in these activities is overall very similar (in all cases, the difference reported is less than 2.5 p.p.).

As for the elderly and sick care activity, which was undertaken by 108 (23.7%) respondents, 43 (39.8%) respondents reported an increase in the time dedicated to this activity. As an exception to the previous pattern, the increase with the pandemic was considerably more expressive for those who did not do remote work (51.9% of those who did not do remote work) than to those who did (35.8% of those who did remote work). In terms of gender, the increase in the time dedicated to elderly care was slightly more frequent for men than women who did remote work (39.4% and 33.3% respectively), while the opposite applies to the comparison between men and women who did not do remote work (42.9% and 55.0% respectively) - in both cases, however, this comparison should take into consideration the small number of respondents who were involved with this activity. Also, in this case, if the category of work is not considered, the percentage of women and men who declared an increase in the time dedicated to this activity is consistent (39.7% and 40.0% respectively).

Remote Work and the Sexual Division of Domestic and Care Work

While the previous section presents important aspects concerning the sexual division of domestic and care work, there is little information on how these activities are shared. Therefore, this section assesses whether the pandemic brought a change in the way domestic and care work is shared between partners and verifies if remote work played any role in this process. This analysis has the advantage of capturing more precisely whether the reported increase in the time dedicated to care and domestic work brought about a change in the sexual division of labor.[8] As this analysis is aimed to capture the sexual division of labor within the household, only heterosexual respondents who live with their partners were selected. This subsample is equal to 230 respondents for domestic work and 100 respondents for care work.[9]

Overall, the division of the domestic and care work did not change considerably during the pandemic. If only gender differences are considered, a similar pattern, before and after the pandemic started, is verified. There was an increase from 64 to 67 women (48.5% and 50.8% respectively) who declared to either do alone or do more domestic work than others, while these figures are equal to 13 and 17 for men (13.3% and 17.3% respectively). For both men and women, there is an increase in the percentage of respondents who declared that the domestic work is equally divided, going from 41 (31.1%) to 53 (40.2%) women and 36 (36.7%) to 50 (51%) of men, but in the case of women this was mostly due to a decrease in the percentage who declared not to do domestic work (from 13 or 9.8% to 1 or 0.8%) and in the case of men it was due to both a decrease in the percentage who declared not to do domestic work (from 10 or 10.2% to 3 or 3.1%) and that another person does more than others (from 39 or 39.8% to 28 or 28.6%). In the case of care work, the number of women who reported doing alone or doing more care work than others increased from 25 to 27 (47.2% and 50.9% respectively), while for men these figures remained marginal, increasing from 1 to 4 (2.1% and 8.5% respectively). Also, slightly fewer women declared that care work is equally divided during (23 (43.4%)) compared to before (25 (47.2%)) the pandemic, whereas the figure remained static at 27 (57.4%) for men. Therefore, taking into consideration both domestic and care activities, the previous pattern of sexual division of labor does not appear to have been greatly altered by the pandemic, and this pattern can be characterized by an unequal division of domestic and care activities, with the overburden of these activities continuing to fall on women.

However, remote work did seem to play a role in the sexual division of labor between partners. The most relevant changes in the information concerning domestic work sharing indicate an improvement in the division of this type of work within the household for both men and women who declared to do remote work and whose partner also undertook remote work. This is reflected in the comparison between the period before and after the pandemic started, as there was an increase in the number of men and women in this group who declared to equally share their domestic work with others (increase from

33.3% to 46.7% for women and increase from 42.6% to 63.0% for men)[10] and a reduction of the number of men in this category who declared that another person did more care work than them (reduction from 40.7% to 27.8%). There was also an increase in the number of men who did remote work and declared doing more domestic work than others when their partner did not do remote work (increase from 0% to 23%). In line with the previous analysis on care work, there were no significant changes in the way this type of work was divided.

Issues, Controversies, Problems

The information collected in the questionnaire provides insight into the increase in domestic and care work and how this affected, in particular, women and those under remote work, as well as on how this extra work was divided between men and women. First, with respect to domestic work, two clear patterns seem to have emerged with the pandemic: while domestic work increased more frequently for women in the sample, its increase was also more relevant for those (men and women) doing remote work. The former aspect reflects the previous sexual division of labor, in which women bear the greatest responsibility for this activity. The latter aspect suggests that remote work was accompanied by more domestic work than otherwise, and this was particularly relevant in the activities related to nurturing, house cleaning and laundry, the activities affected by social distancing.

Second, a more diverse scenario with respect to care work was observed. As in the case of domestic work, the authors observed that the increase in the time dedicated to these activities was more expressive for those who did remote work than for those who did not. The only exception to this pattern was the elderly and sick care, which increased more for those who did not do remote work. However, in terms of gender, the differences in how remote work affected care work were less clear, and, in general, a similar percentage of each sex declared an increase in the time dedicated to care work. This suggests that the pandemic had a more homogeneous impact across groups of individuals who were already involved with care work before the pandemic.

Finally, the information concerning the division of labor for heterosexual individuals who live with their partner provides additional considerations. While the authors observed that a significant number of men and women declared to have faced an increase in their domestic and care activities, this was not met, overall, by an improvement in the sexual division of labor, meaning that the time spent by women in domestic and care work increased in an uneven manner. However, the analysis shows some improvements in the division of domestic work associated with remote work, which can be explained by the idea that men under remote work were more available to participate in these activities. This observation suggests two possible effects of remote work. Firstly, for those who observed an improvement in how the domestic work is shared, the increase in domestic work with the pandemic was at least partially counterbalanced by an increase in men's participation. Secondly, for those who did not experience an improvement in the division of domestic work, which is still a relevant part of this subsample, the more expressive increase in domestic work for those under remote work meant an even more significant increase of unpaid work for women. As there was no clear change in how care work was divided, its increase also tended to worsen women's situation because they tend to be primarily responsible for it. Consequently, this observed increase in the amount of domestic and care work, if not accompanied by a change in the division of work, could have important implications for gender inequality in the longer term.

SOLUTIONS AND RECOMMENDATIONS

While the COVID-19 virus is still spreading in Brazil and workers' lives are disrupted, it is essential to include women and the gender dimension in COVID-19 responses and task forces, to address women's increasing vulnerability in the labor market (Alloatti & Oliveira, 2021). Further research is required to explore these issues regarding time use, gender, and domestic work under the COVID-19 pandemic. This, however, is a controversial topic in President Jair Bolsonaro's government, which "naturalizes" gender roles (Orrico, 2019). Nonetheless, it is fundamental that policies and campaigns around this issue are implemented at the national, state, and municipal levels, while the country is still under the effects of the pandemic.

Firms are also confronted, in the short term, with the profound challenges that workers and especially women are facing regarding balancing their paid work and caring responsibilities during the pandemic. The ILO (2020a) argues that employers should not prioritize only those workers who were able to continue working at full capacity during the pandemic for promotions or penalize those who could not do so because of personal challenges; they should also promote family-friendly measures, with a particular focus on encouraging men to more equally share the responsibilities of unpaid care and domestic chores. The ILO (2020a) stresses that continuing with remote work should not become a significant setback for previous gender equality achievements. Although this research contains elements specific to the pandemic, such as the increase in care work for many of the respondents due to the closure of schools and daycare centers, it sheds light on what could be the reality post-COVID-19, if remote work were to become more widespread in Brazilian society.

The Brazilian economy must be rebuilt considering gender differences in terms of unpaid work and the amplified double burden that some women have faced during the pandemic. The public apparatus to assist in social reproduction needs investment to allow families to reduce the time spent performing these activities, as they impose costs in the form of financial obligations, lost opportunities, and foregone wages. Finally, policies should be aimed at encouraging men to participate more actively in family care. As remote work seems to be associated with an increase in both care and domestic work, if its adoption increases in the long term, these policies will be even more fundamental for achieving gender equality.

CONCLUSION

Remote work during the COVID-19 pandemic brought significant changes to the world of work. This chapter discussed the Brazilian experience and focused on how remote work affected domestic and care activities and its implications for gender inequality. Traditionally, these activities have been associated with the "private" or "women's" spheres. Indeed, previous studies have shown that this means an increased workload for women, who suffer an overburden due to their paid and unpaid work. However, remote work can break down these boundaries as men are spending more time at home and potentially become more available to engage in domestic activities and, as such, it can be an opportunity for questioning previously established gender roles. The findings based on the questionnaire answered by 455 people suggest that remote work was associated with an increase in unpaid work (except for elderly and sick care, which is undertaken by a relatively small portion of the sample). In addition, while this increase was more frequently reported by women than men (in both remote work and in-person work), the results suggest that a portion of heterosexual men who live with their partners and who worked remotely became more engaged with domestic work, as an improvement in the division of this activity was identified.

However, it is not possible to affirm that this means an improvement for women, as remote work increases unpaid work, so, even if it is better shared with their partners, women's situation may not improve in absolute terms. Also, in those cases where a better division is not observed, which were relevant in the sample, women must cope with the increase in domestic work associated with remote work in an uneven manner. This possibility is supported by this chapter's data also through the relatively more frequent increase in domestic work for women than men under remote work. If care work is also considered, remote work becomes even more clearly associated with an increase in women's unpaid work, as the authors could not associate remote work to any change in care work division. Concerning the future of work, if remote work becomes more disseminated after the pandemic and the pre-pandemic gendered segregation in remote work is maintained (i.e., more women performing remote work to conciliate productive and reproductive work) or gender roles in the division of domestic and care work are not broadly questioned, this chapter's findings suggest that the increase in unpaid work associated with remote work may further deepen gender inequality.

ACKNOWLEDGMENT

This research received no specific grant from any funding agency in the public, commercial, or not-for-profit sectors. The authors declare no conflict of interest.

REFERENCES

Alloatti, M. (2014) *Una discusión sobre la técnica de bola de nieve a partir de la experiencia de investigación en migraciones internacionales*. Paper presented at IV Encuentro Latinoamericano de Metodología de las Ciencias Sociales, La Plata.

Alloatti, M., & Oliveira, A. L. M. (2021). *Deepening and widening the gap: the impacts of Covid-19 pandemic on gender and racial inequalities in the labor market, domestic work and domestic violence in Brazil*. Manuscript in preparation.

Baltar, C. T., Rolim, L. N., & Leone, E. T. (2020). The effects of the Brazilian recession on wage inequality between men and women. RBEST: Revista Brasileira de Economia Social e do Trabalho, 2.

Costa, J. S., Pinheiro, L., Medeiros, M., & Queiroz, C. (2005). *A Face Feminina da Pobreza: Sobre-Representação e Feminização da Pobreza no Brasil* (TD 1137). Retrieved from https://www.ipea.gov.br/portal/index.php?option=com_content&view=article&id=4726

Eclac. (2020). *América Latina y el Caribe ante la pandemia del COVID-19. Efectos económicos y sociales* (Informe Especial COVID-19 N1). Retrieved from: https://bit.ly/3gzeHWJ

Esquivel, V., Faur, E., & Jelin, E. (2012). Hacia la conceptualización del cuidado: familia, mercado y estado. In Las lógicas del cuidado infantil. Entre las familias, el estado y el mercado (pp. 11-45). Buenos Aires: IDES, UNFPA, Unicef.

Fares, L. S.; Oliveira, A. L. M. (2020) Increasing inequality in working time: An international trend. *Revista da Sociedade Brasileira de Economia Política*, 57.

Folbre, N. (2006, July). Measuring Care: Gender, Empowerment, and the Care Economy. *Journal of Human Development*, *7*(2), 183–199. Advance online publication. doi:10.1080/14649880600768512

Folbre, N., & Nelson, J. A. (2000). For love or money—Or both? *The Journal of Economic Perspectives*, *14*(4), 123–140. doi:10.1257/jep.14.4.123

Gibb, L. S. F. (2017). *A tendência de despadronização da jornada de trabalho: configuração no brasil e impacto nas mulheres* [Unpublished PhD Thesis]. UNICAMP.

Gibb, L. S. F., & Oliveira, A. L. M. (2015) A Desigualdade na Distribuição do Trabalho Total no Brasil: A Quem Favorece? Pesquisa & Debate, 26, 87-104.

Huws, U., Podro, S., Gunnarsson, E., Weijers, T. A., & Trova, V. (1996). Teleworking and Gender. Institute for Employment Studies. Report 317. Sussex University.

Instituto Brasileiro de Geografia e Estatística (IBGE). (2020a) *Outras formas de trabalho: 2019*. Retrieved from https://biblioteca.ibge.gov.br/visualizacao/livros/liv101722_informativo.pdf

Instituto Brasileiro de Geografia e Estatística (IBGE). (2020b) *PNAD COVID-19*. Retrieved from https://covid19.ibge.gov.br/pnad-covid/trabalho.php

International Labour Organization (ILO). (2020a). *Teleworking during the COVID-19 pandemic and beyond: a Practical Guide*. Retrieved from https://www.ilo.org/wcmsp5/groups/public/---ed_protect/---protrav/---travail/documents/publication/wcms_751232.pdf

International Labour Organization (ILO). (2020b). *Working from Home: Estimating the worldwide potential* (Policy Brief April 2020). Retrieved from https://www.ilo.org/wcmsp5/groups/public/---ed_protect/---protrav/---travail/documents/briefingnote/wcms_743447.pdf

Lyttelton, T., Zang, E., & Musick, K. (n.d.). *Gender Differences in Telecommuting and Implications for Inequality at Home and Work*. 10.31235/ doi:osf.io/tdf8c

Manzo, L. K. C., & Minello, A. (2020). Mothers, childcare duties, and remote working under COVID-19 lockdown in Italy: Cultivating communities of care. *Dialogues in Human Geography*, *10*(2), 120–123. doi:10.1177/2043820620934268

Nash, M., & Churchill, B. (2020). Caring during COVID-19: A gendered analysis of Australian university responses to managing remote working and caring responsibilities. *Gender, Work and Organization*, *27*(5), 833–846. Advance online publication. doi:10.1111/gwao.12484 PMID:32837013

Oliveira, A. L. M. (2013). *Regulação estatal das relações de trabalho no capitalismo contemporâneo: uma crítica ao discurso da flexibilização e desregulamentação* [Unpublished Master Dissertation]. Unicamp.

Oliveira, A. L. M., & Emídio, A. P. (2021). *"The great equalizer"? The long-lasting effects of the COVID-19 pandemic on poverty and inequality in Latin America*. Manuscript in preparation.

Oliveira, A. L. M., Rolim, L. N., & Fares, L. S. (2021). *Who cares? Gender, unpaid domestic and care work in Brazil during the pandemic*. Manuscript in preparation.

Orrico, A. (2019, January 3). An Official In Brazil's New Right-Wing Government Said "Boys Wear Blue And Girls Wear Pink". *BuzzFeed*. Retrieved from https://www.buzzfeednews.com/article/alexandreorrico/brazil-boys-wear-blue-girls-wear-pink-damares-alves

Raišienė, A. G., Rapuano, V., Varkulevičiūtė, K., & Stachová, K. (2020). Working from Home—Who Is Happy? A Survey of Lithuania's Employees during the COVID-19 Quarantine Period. *Sustainability, 12*(13), 1-21. doi:10.3390u12135332

Saffioti, H. (2013). *A mulher na sociedade de classe: mito e realidade* (3rd ed.). Expressão Popular.

Van Eck, D., & Jammaers, E. (2020). Chronicles of conflicting care in confinement: Documenting the work experiences of seven 'patient zeros'. *Gender, Work and Organization, 2020*, 1–14. doi:10.1111/gwao.12532

Williamson, S., Colley, L., & Hanna-Osborne, S. (2020). Will working from home become the 'new normal' in the public sector? *Australian Journal of Public Administration, 2020*(4), 1–7. doi:10.1111/1467-8500.12444

Worldometers. (2020). https://www.worldometers.info/coronavirus/

ADDITIONAL READING

Baltar, C. T., & Omizzolo, J. A. (2019). Participação da mulher no mercado de trabalho brasileiro de 2014 a 2019. *Textos de Economia, 23*(1), 1–17. Advance online publication. doi:10.5007/2175-8085.2020.e71522

Braunstein, E., & Seguino, S. (2018). The impact of economic policy and structural change on gender employment inequality in Latin America, 1990–2010. *Review of Keynesian Economics, 6*(3), 307–332. doi:10.4337/roke.2018.03.02

Dweck, E., Rossi, P., & Oliveira, A. L. M. (Eds.). (2020). *Economia pós-pandemia: desmontando os mitos da austeridade fiscal e construindo um novo paradigma econômico no Brasil* (1st ed.). Autonomia Literária.

KEY TERMS AND DEFINITIONS

Care Work: Caring for children, elderly or sick and other dependents.

Domestic Work: The activities regarding household cleaning and maintenance, preparation of meals for the consumption of household and family members, household budgeting, caring for family members and a variety of other tasks. Domestic work may be performed for pay or in an unpaid regime (for the individual him/herself or those in the household, friends, and neighbors).

Gender: A social construction which stipulates gender roles and implicitly and explicitly categorizes people and social behaviors.

"Gender Ideology": An expression used to reject the sex and gender distinction, arguing that gender roles and inequalities are "natural".

Labor Flexibility: Labor flexibility is defined as an elimination, dilution, loosening or adaptation of classical labor protection (Oliveira 2013; Gibb 2017). It is frequently connected to a precarization of labor conditions, increasing the employer's freedom to dispose of the worker's time, while presenting itself as an alternative for women to reconcile paid and unpaid work.

Reproduction of the Workforce: The worker's reproduction of his/her own labor power (or of future generations of workers), which consist of care and domestic work. Women "subsidize" the capitalist system by performing these activities.

Sexual Division of Labor: The delegation of different tasks between men and women. In the Brazilian society, women are responsible for domestic and care work.

Total Working Time: The total amount of time spent in paid work and in care/domestic activities (unpaid). As women are usually responsible for these unpaid activities, combining paid and unpaid work leads to women's overburden.

Unpaid Work: Work that produces goods and/or services with no direct remuneration or payment for the individual performing it. In the household, unpaid work is visible through domestic and care work.

ENDNOTES

1 Black is composed by *Preto* and *Pardo*, according to the terms used by the Brazilian Institute of Geography and Statistics (IBGE).

2 *Amarelo*, according to the terms used by the IBGE.

3 The Southeast of Brazil is the region with the highest Human Development Index in the country.

4 The questionnaire asked if the respondent was conducting a certain activity during the whole social distancing period, from March 2020 to when the questionnaire was answered, during most of the period, during less than half of it or if the question did not apply.

5 All respondents who answered that they were doing both office and remote work, that they started doing remote work during the pandemic, or that they already did and continued to do remote work are included in this subgroup.

6 Care work was presented in the questionnaire as comprising caring for children (including assisting in school activities and playing with them) and caring for the elderly or sick.

7 From March 2020 to when the questionnaire was answered, most schools and daycare centers were closed in Brazil. Some people resorted to online learning, depending on the children's age and the availability of internet and hardware to do so.

8 In the previous analysis, when respondents answered that the time dedicated to an activity increased, this may be due to either a general increase in the amount of time required for the activity or a change in how this activity was divided between men and women.

9 In this case, care work comprises only childcare and only those who did this activity are considered.

10 In the case of women, this increase was mostly determined by a decrease in the number of respondents who declared not to do domestic work, while in the case of men it was also determined by a reduction in the number of respondents who declared that another person does more domestic work than others. Thus, the overall pattern identified in the comparison between men and women is mostly due to the changes in this subgroup.

Chapter 3
Remote Work, Sexual Harassment, and Worker Well-Being:
A Study of the United States and India

Jacqueline Strenio
Southern Oregon University, USA

Joyita Roy Chowdhury
FLAME University, India

ABSTRACT

Workplace sexual harassment is a serious occupational hazard, adversely affecting workers' employment trajectories, economic well-being, and mental and physical health. Prior to COVID-19, it was widespread and primarily perpetrated by men against women, both in the physical workplace and physical and virtual public spaces associated with work. This chapter examines how the transition to remote work has effected changes in the prevalence and types of sexual harassment, paying attention to its gendered nature. Remote work holds both promise and peril. While exposure to physical harassment has fallen, information and communications technology has increased the risk of sexual harassment in virtual spaces. The cases of the United States and India are explored in more detail to compare worker experiences across the Global North and Global South, in countries with vastly different socioeconomic structures. This chapter contributes to the understanding of the benefits and challenges of remote work in combatting sexual harassment.

INTRODUCTION

Crises are often associated with an increased incidence of crime and violence, including violence against women (VAW) (Fraser, 2020; Palermo & Peterman, 2011). The COVID-19 crisis is no exception. It has created significant challenges in the global economy, including increasing all types of VAW. Despite

DOI: 10.4018/978-1-7998-6754-8.ch003

international consensus and country-level efforts to eradicate VAW and promote gender equality, there are still various forms of discrimination which do not allow women to enjoy a safe and secure workplace (International Labour Organization [ILO], 2013). One widespread form of discrimination is workplace sexual harassment. As the vast majority of cases involve men harassing women, sexual harassment is also considered a form of VAW and is the most widespread form of VAW worldwide (Morgan & Gruber, 2010). The ILO defines sexual harassment as:

unwelcome sexual advances or verbal or physical conduct of a sexual nature which has effect of unreasonably interfering with the individual's work performance or creating an intimidating, hostile, abusive or offensive working environment. (2013, 6)

Sexual harassment also includes harassment that is not sexual in nature but rather based on a person's sex or gender, such as gender-based insults. This includes any "unwanted sexual, homophobic, transphobic, and/or sexist experiences" (Stop Street Harassment, 2018). When considering *workplace* sexual harassment, in particular, this chapter takes a broad view of the 'workplace', similar to that defined in the UN's Working Group on Discrimination Against Women and Girls [UN WG], which includes:

...formal and informal work, public and private spaces of work, the commute to and from work, work taking place online or work enabled through information and communications technology, and work-related trips and events. (2020, 4)

Workplace sexual harassment is an occupational hazard and a substantial public health concern that adversely affects worker well-being (Sarkar et al., 2020). It is associated with mental and physical health issues, reduced productivity, impeded career progression, and financial distress. In many countries, it is classified as a form of sex discrimination and, therefore, illegal. Internationally, it is considered a human rights violation (UN WG, 2020). Despite all this, workplace sexual harassment is common. About 40% of women and 16% of men in the United States have experienced workplace sexual harassment. Even among humanitarian organizations, sexual harassment is rampant. One in three respondents in a United Nations (UN) sexual harassment survey reported experiencing sexual harassment in the past two years while working at the UN (Deloitte, 2019). In India, the prevalence is even higher. According to a survey conducted in 80 organizations across India's major cities, more than 50% of women have experienced multiple forms of sexual harassment at the workplace (Sarkar, 2019).

There is no single, simple cause of sexual harassment nor one unified theory; however, multiple theories highlight the importance of power and status differentials in the perpetration of sexual harassment (Pina et al., 2009). For example, feminist theories view sexual harassment as a means of maintaining male dominance. Organizational theories focus on the role of sexual harassment in enforcing, challenging, or equalizing more general power hierarchies, rather than gender-specific ones (Pina et al., 2009). It is not surprising, then, that workplace sexual harassment disproportionately affects women. Although women bear the brunt of harassment, it is not just a women's issue. Sexual harassment affects the physical, mental, and occupational well-being of workers of all genders globally, not to mention the 'bottom line' for firms and society (Cortina & Berdahl, 2008).

The high prevalence rates have changed little over the past four decades despite increased awareness and training. The widespread transition to remote work in the wake of COVID-19 provides an interesting point to reflect on workplace sexual harassment and worker well-being and consider more radical changes. This chapter examines how the transition to remote work and increased reliance on information and communications technologies (ICTs) have effected changes in the perpetration of sexual harassment. It examines the benefits and challenges of remote work when it comes to combatting sexual harassment and offers both cautions and policy recommendations for reducing sexual harassment in an era of remote work. As most prominent research on sexual harassment focuses on white women from the Global North (Cortina & Berdahl, 2008), this chapter consciously extends the analysis to women from other ethnic and cultural backgrounds by focusing on the case of India in addition to the United States. The different economic and social structures of these two countries allow for a brief comparison of workplace sexual harassment in the Global North and Global South.

BACKGROUND

Overview of Sexual Harassment in the United States

The term "sexual harassment" was coined in the 1970s in the United States, which has been referred to as "ground zero" in the global movement against sexual harassment (Morgan & Gruber, 2010). The phrase gained traction after legal scholar Catharine MacKinnon published her book *Sexual Harassment of Working Women* in 1979, which additionally provided the framework for the legal argument that sexual harassment constituted sex discrimination.

In the United States, workplace sexual harassment encompasses both quid pro quo and hostile environment harassment. It is considered a form of sex discrimination and, therefore, illegal under Title VII of the Civil Rights Act of 1964. It is legally defined by the Equal Employment Opportunity Commission (EEOC) to include:

unwelcome sexual advances, requests for sexual favors, and other verbal or physical conduct of a sexual nature constitute sexual harassment when this conduct explicitly or implicitly affects an individual's employment, unreasonably interferes with an individual's work performance, or create an intimidating, hostile, or offensive work environment. (EEOC, 1997)

The forty years after the publication of MacKinnon's book witnessed increased awareness, training, and a growing body of case law supporting the constitutionality of the EEOC's definition. However, it was ultimately the #MeToo social media movement, founded by Tarana Burke in 2007 and reignited by U.S. actress Alyssa Milano a decade later, that brought widespread public attention back to the issue of workplace sexual harassment. Starting in October 2017, women came forward with stories of sexual harassment, assault, and abuse by prominent and powerful men, beginning in Hollywood with allegations against Harvey Weinstein. The #MeToo movement gained momentum, spurring women across the world to share their own experiences of workplace sexual harassment.

The extent of workplace sexual harassment is difficult to pinpoint. In the United States, recent estimates come from several nationally-representative surveys that present similar findings: 38-40% of women and 14-16% of men have reported experiencing sexual harassment in a professional work setting (Graf, 2018; Kearl et al., 2019). A quarter of women and 10% of men reported experiencing sexual harassment on mass transportation and many more in public spaces, such as streets or parks (68% of women and 23% of men). Additionally, nearly 25% of women and 12% of men reported changing their route or routine as a result of sexual harassment (Kearl et al., 2019). Although the survey did not assess whether or not respondents were indeed commuting to work, it highlights the prevalence of sexual harassment in other spaces that individuals might be required to access for work.

Lower-bound estimates come from data on new charges filed with the EEOC. In fiscal year 2019, there were 7,514 new charges filed with the EEOC, the vast majority of which were filed by women (83.2%) (EEOC, 2020). However, only a small percentage of those who are harassed file a formal complaint or grievance (Cortina & Berdahl, 2008). A 2019 national survey found that only one in eight women reported filing an official complaint or reporting the harassment to an authority figure, while only about one in twenty men did so (Kearl et al., 2019). Additionally, these labor protections only apply to employers with 15 or more employees and most likely represent only the most serious cases of sexual harassment.

In the United States, as elsewhere, gender is the most important risk factor for sexual harassment, with harassment primarily committed by men against women (Morgan & Gruber, 2010). Women that defy conventional gender expectations are at elevated risk for sexual harassment (McLaughlin et al., 2012). Other marginalized populations also face increased risk, including those in poverty (Morgan, 1999) and migrant workers, especially those that are undocumented (Morgan & Gruber, 2010). Additional risk factors are occupation- and workplace-specific. These include working in men-dominated domains, those in which masculine norms are important to stereotypes about the type of work being done (Morgan & Gruber, 2010), those where men hold a disproportionate share of supervisor roles (DuBois et al., 1998), or more generally, settings that have a significant power differential (Shaw et al., 2018). Recent nationally-representative data from Sweden shows that being in the gender-minority in terms of occupation or workplace is associated with more self-reported sexual harassment among both women and men (Rickne & Folke, 2020). Isolated spaces and decentralized workplaces are also risk factors as a lack of witnesses might embolden potential harassers (Shaw et al., 2018).

These risk factors are supported by results from surveys examining the experiences of U.S. workers as disparate as corporate women to Mexican immigrant women working on farms. Among corporate women workers, the prevalence of self-reported sexual harassment was higher for women with senior-level positions, women in technical roles, and lesbian and bisexual women, all identities which defy conventional gender roles in some way (LeanIn.org & McKinsey & Company, 2019). The precarious socioeconomic position and isolated working conditions of immigrant farmworkers may help explain the high, 80%, prevalence rate of workplace sexual harassment they report (Waugh, 2010).

Although the movement against workplace sexual harassment started in the United States, it quickly spread worldwide. Now, more than 75 countries have laws that make sexual harassment illegal, including a large majority of high-income OECD countries, with the exception of Japan. In the Middle East and North Africa, Algeria and Morocco have laws against workplace sexual harassment, while in South Asia, India, Bangladesh, Pakistan, and Sri Lanka (although not Nepal) also have such laws (Hersch, 2015). In the present chapter, the United States is used as an example of the experiences of a high-income country. Among the group of developing countries, the situation of sexual harassment in India is highlighted, including an overview of its legal definition, prevalence, and risk factors.

Overview of Sexual Harassment in India

The Indian Supreme Court defines sexual harassment as any unwelcome, sexually-determined physical, verbal, or non-verbal conduct. Examples included sexually suggestive remarks about women, demands for sexual favors, and sexually offensive visuals in the workplace. The definition also covers situations where a woman could be disadvantaged in her workplace due to threats relating to employment decisions that could negatively affect her working life (Government of India, 2015).

In India, sexual harassment is also primarily perpetrated by men against women as women are more vulnerable due to their low status in the patriarchal social structure. Nearly 9 out of 10 women employed in Information Technology and Business Process Outsourcing companies reported experiencing sexual harassment at their workplace (Sharma, 2010). Media reports found that many private sector organizations did not have policies to address the problem of sexual harassment (Satpodar, 2013). The National Commission for Women in India took some revolutionary steps to ensure women's rights and equal status, including advocating for a law to prevent all forms of sexual harassment at the workplace. Eventually, the Sexual Harassment of Women at Workplace (Prevention, Prohibition and Redressal) Bill 2013 was enacted on April 22, 2013 to protect women from verbal and physical abuse at workplaces and ensure equality of status and opportunities for them.

In India, the workplace is defined as "any place visited by the employee arising out of or during the course of employment, including transportation provided by the employer for undertaking such a journey" (Varma, 2020). The Sexual Harassment Act covers employees in formal and informal sectors, including self-employed workers. In the formal sector, the law sanctioned the formation of an internal committee and an independent external expert to address all complaints related to sexual harassment. In the informal sector, the responsibility was handed over to the local committees at the district level (Gartenberg & Harikumar, 2019). While the law was designed to address the problem of sexual harassment, in actual practice, it has failed to protect women's rights to work with dignity in the formal private sector. As highlighted by Satpodar (2013), the national press reported that multinational companies were defying the Supreme Court's Vishaka guidelines, the set of guidelines in place for sexual harassment before the new Sexual Harassment of Women at Workplace (Prevention, Prohibition and Redressal) Act was enacted.

Despite being underreported (Shukla, 2002), sexual harassment is one of the most prevalent forms of gender discrimination in India. Several factors may be contributing to these high prevalence rates. First, employers may not be paying enough attention to implementing sexual harassment guidelines in the workplace (Satpodar, 2013). In some cases, there is also a lack of trained staff to handle cases of sexual harassment (Sharma, 2010). Internationally, there is strict compliance with anti-harassment policies; however, such policies are only gradually developing in Indian companies (Ghosh et al., 2010). In recent years, private sector companies became legally mandated to emphasize corporate social responsibility and provide a safe working environment for their employees (Satpodar, 2013). For instance, an Indian fast-moving consumer goods (FMCG) company incorporated gender diversity in its strategic plan by ensuring that more women are hired and retained in the company (Gartenberg & Harikumar, 2019). This policy has a clear focus on gender-inclusiveness in its business plan. However, this recent awareness of sexual harassment is primarily limited to the educated urban class employed in the formal sector.

In India, around 90% of women workers are employed in the informal sector, defined by the ILO (2020) as unregistered small-scale units employing less than ten workers, including unpaid family workers. These women primarily work as domestic workers, street vendors, construction workers, home-based producers, and artisans. Although women constitute a vast majority of the informal workforce, their workplace safety and security remain largely ignored. According to a study conducted jointly by Oxfam India and the Social and Rural Research Institute, the women most vulnerable to workplace sexual harassment are laborers (29%), followed by domestic workers (23%), and workers employed at small scale manufacturing units (16%) (Kumar, 2018). Case studies from Gartenberg and Harikumar (2019), presented below, provide examples of the type of workplace sexual harassment faced by women in the informal sector:

1) A seven-year-old street vendor selling vegetables in a busy market is frequently grabbed and fondled by the male street vendors in full public view. She is too afraid to scream or ask for help. Her elder brother, all of nine years old, understands her helplessness and informs their mother. The mother tells her daughter that such instances will keep happening and she will have to learn to ignore it, be brave and focus on her work.

2) A 33-year-old new mother is a helper at a construction site. She and her entire family live and work at the site. A contractor known to her family has brought them from the village to the city. Her work is hard; she is also nursing her newborn daughter; and cooking, cleaning, and washing for her family. The contractor knows her family has multiple debts. He and the site supervisor frequently whistle and sing songs when she passes by and touch her inappropriately. She has come to expect and accept this kind of behaviour by powerful men. She does not utter a word to her husband or other family members. Other women do the same.

3) A 47-year-old widow works in a tiny garment unit in a slum, snipping threads off the rims of readymade garments, neatly folding and packaging them. She works 10 hours every day, her work is considered unskilled, her wages are low and irrespective of the work volume she is paid the same amount each month. Her supervisor, masterji (the fabric cutter, the most powerful man there) offers to increase her salary and reduce her working time, provided she agrees to having sexual intercourse with him whenever he demands. She refuses and faces intimidation.

4) A 65-year-old domestic worker, working in an affluent household, is forced to see pornographic films by one of the younger men in the family. She is scared and embarrassed, but does not know what to say and to whom.

As seen in the above-cited instances, the power differential between men and women is an important determinant in the risk for sexual harassment. Under a patriarchal system, where women are forced to follow traditional gender roles, patriarchal values create the biggest obstacle to the prohibition and prevention of sexual harassment (Government of India, 2015). Most of the time, women remain silent and do not seek justice for fear of being socially stigmatized and losing their jobs or a lack of awareness about the presence of a redressal mechanism (Kumar, 2018). Moreover, informal sector jobs provide no protection against arbitrary dismissal from work, access to paid sick leave, or other social protection measures (Roy Chowdhury, 2014). Furthermore, the Prohibition of Sexual Harassment Act's implementation in the informal sector is severely constrained due to the nature of the employer-employee relationship. The absence of a work contract in most informal sector jobs makes it difficult to trace employers, employees, and workplace activities (Sharma, 2020). Therefore, perpetrators often go unnoticed after their criminal activities.

The Effects of Sexual Harassment on Worker Well-Being

The detrimental effects of sexual harassment on worker well-being are extensive and multi-dimensional. Sexual harassment has been associated with adverse mental and physical health outcomes, including depression, anxiety, post-traumatic stress disorder, and sickness absence from work (Cortina & Berdahl, 2008). In the United States, about 30% of women and 18% of men that reported sexual harassment also reported anxiety or depression (Kearl et al., 2019). Harassment has also been associated with low self-esteem and life satisfaction (Cortina & Berdahl, 2008; Morgan & Gruber, 2010). At the most extreme, sexual harassment is a significant risk factor for suicide attempts and deaths among both men and women even after controlling for a variety of demographic variables, baseline health, and work characteristics (Hanson et al., 2020).

Sexual harassment can also negatively affect job performance and labor market attachment and, ultimately, disrupt career trajectories. Specifically, sexual harassment is associated with work withdrawal and reduced productivity and performance (Cortina & Berdahl, 2008). One in seven women and one in 17 men reported seeking a new job assignment, changing jobs, or quitting a job as a result of sexual harassment (Kearl et al., 2019). Even after controlling for a wide breadth of variables, including the sex-ratio of the workplace and other forms of workplace incivility, workers in Sweden who reported sexual harassment had twice the rate of job dissatisfaction and quit intentions than those who did not. However, only women workers were more likely to actually leave their job as a result of sexual harassment, primarily moving to more women-dominated workplaces (Rickne & Folke, 2020). This same research quantifies the dissatisfaction associated with workplace sexual harassment; both men and women in Sweden were found to have a dislike of sexual harassment equivalent to a 10-percentage point wage cut (Rickne & Folke, 2020).

Not only is sexual harassment itself detrimental, but the reporting and grievance processes in many countries can cause additional harm to workers' well-being. Evidence from the United States has found worse career and health outcomes for women workers who file complaints compared to those who do not (McLaughlin et al., 2017). Among U.S. federal workers, this included subsequent assault and harassment, demotion, and job loss, which were reported by two-thirds of the women workers (U.S. Merit Systems Protection Board, 1995).

These negative individual-level effects add up to costly consequences for firms by reducing productivity and increasing absenteeism and turnover. Society also pays for sexual harassment in the form of reduced diversity among the upper levels of management. Sexual harassment has been shown to disrupt career trajectories and limit the advancement opportunities of women and minority groups, who are disproportionately at risk for harassment.

REMOTE WORK AND SEXUAL HARASSMENT

The country-specific overviews both support the theories of power differentials and patriarchal norms as risk factors for sexual harassment. If the perpetration of sexual harassment is not solely a result of physical access to individuals to harass, but rather a result of power differentials and workplace culture, remote work in and of itself will not reduce workplace sexual harassment. In fact, men-dominated virtual spaces with limited bystanders and an appearance of anonymity may exacerbate technology-facilitated workplace sexual harassment.

The exposure reduction hypothesis (Dugan et al., 2003) comes from the criminology literature on intimate partner violence. Applied to sexual harassment, it would predict that any change that reduces an individual's exposure to potential harassers will reduce sexual harassment. Since remote work means no commuting and no physical time in an office space, it is logical to assume that it is reducing opportunities for physical sexual harassment to occur. Therefore, remote work is predicted to reduce instances of sexual harassment in physical workplaces and while commuting to and from work. However, the transition to remote work means that workers' digital activity and use of ICTs, such as email, social media, video conferencing software, and cell phones, has surged. Individuals are now *virtually* exposed to potential harassers – coworkers, bosses, and customers – 24/7 through these remote-working technologies.

Technology has also enabled sexual harassment to take on new forms, many of which may be harder to identify as sexual harassment, and in fact, may be exacerbating its prevalence (Holland, 2020). Workplace sexual harassment is already notoriously difficult to identify and measure (Hersch, 2015), which contributes to the difficulty of combatting it. As it moves online, this identification problem is amplified. In research about harassment on social media and in social virtual reality, a common challenge even among those that experienced such harassment was the difficulty of defining it. Researchers found that what people considered to be harassment was highly subjective (Blackwell et al., 2019; Duggan, 2017).

Remote work may increase the risk of sexual harassment in several ways. First, virtual communication provides a degree, or at least the appearance of a degree, of anonymity that may embolden potential harassers as there are fewer bystanders to witness and intervene. There are also more channels of communication, including more one-on-one exchanges, which can make it more difficult for managers to observe everything that happens. For example, Microsoft has reported an 18% increase in one-on-one meetings among their employees since the move to remote work (Miller, 2020). These virtual work environments fit the definitions of isolated and decentralized workplaces, both contributing factors to workplace sexual harassment. Secondly, the combination of the pandemic and mobile technology has created a 24/7 employee experience for many workers, blurring the lines between work and life. Glimpses into coworkers' homes and less direct oversight can make work feel more informal and intimate, facilitating harassment. Finally, the stressful conditions of the pandemic, including increased economic vulnerability, could exacerbate incivility and harassment, as seen during the Great Recession (Martinuzzi, 2020).

The increased risk for sexual harassment is detrimental to worker well-being. The negative effects of sexual harassment in remote workplaces can be longer lasting and more broadly amplified than more traditional forms of workplace sexual harassment (Franks, 2012). Since perpetrators of online harassment have direct digital access to individuals through computers and phones, it can make workers feel as if nowhere is safe from their harassers. Recent research on online harassment also shows that it can change future technology use, and it is significantly associated with emotional and physical distress (Duggan, 2017). As working from home becomes the new normal, remote work may also inadvertently increase workers' risk of domestic violence.

Lastly, it should also be noted that technologies associated with remote work can be a force for good in the fight against workplace sexual harassment. For example, social media contributed to worldwide connection and organizing around combatting workplace sexual harassment in the #MeToo movement. Technology can also make it easier to document and report sexual harassment. For example, emails can be forwarded, and exchanges over social media can be documented using screen capture. Additionally, a variety of apps and reporting software facilitate new and easier methods for formal and informal reporting.

Remote Work and Sexual Harassment: The Case of the United States

Despite growing in popularity in the United States over the past decade, remote work was still relatively rare prior to the coronavirus pandemic. Only 7% of civilian workers reported flexible workplace benefits, predominately those in management, business and finance, or professional and related occupational groups, and even fewer state and local government workers, at about 4% (Desilver, 2020). However, COVID-19 rapidly altered workplace arrangements. The majority of changes to remote work occurred by early

April 2020 in the United States (Brynjolfsson et al., 2020), at the peak of the first wave of restrictions. Nationally-representative survey results from that month estimate that about half of all Americans that were employed before the pandemic were now working from home (Brynjolfsson et al., 2020). However, when including workers who said they were working remotely always *or sometimes*, that number increases to 69%, according to a Gallup poll from the same month (Brenan, 2020).

The likelihood of transitioning to remote work did not significantly vary by gender, although it did vary by geographic region, age, and occupation. Specifically, younger workers, those in the Northeast, and those working in management, professional, and related occupations were more likely to report switching to remote work (Brynjolfsson et al., 2020). While the number of remote workers has declined somewhat in subsequent months to 33% of workers reporting always working remotely and another 25% sometimes working remotely in October 2020, hybrid work arrangements, including some amount of remote work, seem to be the new normal. In fact, the majority of workers surveyed said they would prefer to continue remote work (Brenan, 2020).

Sexual harassment is still illegal under these new work arrangements. Legally, sexual harassment can violate U.S. antidiscrimination laws regardless of whether it is face-to-face or online (Phillips & Associates, 2020). Nevertheless, online sexual harassment was already common in the United States before the mass transition to remote work. In a 2019 survey, 40% of women and 21% of men reported virtual sexual harassment (Kearl et al., 2019). Examples of such online sexual harassment include bosses soliciting explicit photos by email or jokes that are demeaning to women during a Zoom meeting. Perhaps the most prominent example from the United States during the pandemic was when CNN's chief legal analyst, Jeffrey Toobin, exposed himself to coworkers over Zoom (Darcy, 2020).

Such cases are rife and not constrained to Zoom. Early anecdotal evidence from the financial services industry amid remote work conditions shows that sexual harassment is up and has found a new space in other forms of communication technology such as WhatsApp and text messages (Martinuzzi, 2020). U.S. workers are working longer hours during the pandemic (*The Economist,* 2020), and these work hours often extend into the evening, creating further opportunity for harassment. For example, Microsoft reported a 52% increase in their employees' online chats between 6 pm and 10 pm (Miller, 2020). Longer workdays and the extension of the workday into evening hours increase the risk for virtual workplace sexual harassment by increasing exposure. Evening work hours can have a more informal and casual feel and may occur in bedrooms or on couches, in which potential harassers are invited into private spaces via video calls. These situations can embolden potential harassers by seemingly removing the "wall" between an employee's work and personal life (Schaefer, 2020), creating situations that feel more intimate than those that occurred in the physical workplace.

Further, virtual teambuilding trends that take place in the evening hours or on weekends, such as Zoom happy hours or virtual escape rooms, facilitate the use of remote work technologies and communications streams for more personal conversations. They also often include side channels that are difficult to monitor, thus replicating workplace conditions previously identified as risk factors for sexual harassment – decentralized and isolated spaces, with little oversight and no bystanders. These situations may specifically increase the risk for women workers. Women have disproportionately taken over childcare and schooling responsibilities meaning remote work is pushed to evening hours. Additionally, more women-dominated jobs have been lost due to COVID-19, enhancing power differentials between employers and those employees that have retained their jobs.

A related challenge for worker well-being associated with remote work is the increased risk for domestic violence. Remote work, which is predominantly work done at the worker's home, can increase exposure to an abusive partner, exacerbating the risk for domestic violence (DV) (Dugan et al., 2003). Current evidence from the United States on the prevalence of DV during the pandemic is mixed, with different indicators often providing conflicting evidence. For example, in Los Angeles, the initial shutdown resulted in increased DV calls to the police and DV hotlines, but a decrease in DV crimes (Miller et al., 2020). Similar conflicting evidence is found in Chicago, with an increase in DV-related calls for police service, but a decrease in official reports and arrests (Bullinger et al. 2020). The authors hypothesize a significant underreporting of DV cases. Another study using 911 call records and mobile phone location data from 14 large U.S. cities finds an initial surge in DV calls from mid-March to early April 2020. Interestingly, the largest increases in DV calls occurred during weekday work hours, when many individuals under pre-COVID conditions would likely have been at work rather than working remotely at home (Sanga & McCrary, 2020).

Domestic violence and workplace sexual harassment may intersect in ways that are important to consider. Women that experience workplace sexual harassment are more likely to leave their job and, in many cases (but not all), employment is protective with respect to DV through its ability to increase a woman's bargaining power. Therefore, losing (or quitting) a job may exacerbate a woman's risk for DV (Strenio, 2019). The potential for these forms of violence to compound has serious implications for remote worker well-being, especially for women who are most at risk for both workplace sexual harassment and domestic violence.

This early evidence from the United States highlights that perpetrators of workplace sexual harassment are able to adapt to various work settings and conditions. Combined with the increase in work hours and overall online activity, workers are also increasingly exposed to the risk of sexual harassment. Ultimately, it is workplace culture that allows for the continued perpetration of harassment (Dobbin & Kalev, 2020) regardless of whether that workplace is remote or physical. Research shows that solutions to sexual harassment involve changing culture from the top down. One way to do that is by changing who's at the top—moving more women into management positions and core jobs (Dobbin & Kalev, 2017). In a recent survey of U.S. human resources leaders, more than half indicated that one of the major challenges of pandemic recovery will be establishing a workplace culture that supports remote workers (AP News, 2020).

Remote Work and Sexual Harassment: The Case of India

In India, the work-from-home arrangements arising from COVID-19 did not extend to all workers. A survey of around 3000 workers over 100 Indian occupations, as listed in the 2004 National Classification of Occupations, showed that occupations that require closer human proximity are less suitable for remote work. These occupations include drivers, shop sales professionals, and domestic help. Occupations found suitable for remote work include professions like directors, computing professionals, and general managers. In all of these professions, the need for human proximity is minimal (Mani & Tomar, 2020). Many big IT firms, such as Cognizant and Tata Consultancy Services, shifted to remote work as coronavirus cases increased. Software companies, including Infosys, HCL Technologies, Wipro, and Tech Mahindra, also asked their employees to work from home. Overall, 4 million IT workers started to work remotely after the national lockdown on March 24, 2020 (Sangani & Chandrasekhar, 2020).

While COVID-19 changed the nature of work with many working from home, it has also exposed them to online privacy threats. While companies have been active in resolving issues related to cybersecurity and data privacy, they also need to ensure that the new remote workplace is free from online harassment

(Varma, 2020). Online harassment can include "online bullying, trolling, cyberstalking, defamation and hate speech, public shaming, and identity theft and hacking, amongst other offences" (UN Women, 2020). Section 354D of the Indian Penal Code (IPC) deals with cyberstalking. Per this law,

if a man continues his attempt to pursue a woman via the internet, email, or any other form of electronic communication without her consent. In that case, he can be jailed for three years if the offense is being committed for the first time. On repeating the crime, he can be awarded a five-year jail sentence. He may be liable to pay a fine regardless of whether it is his first or second offense (Matta, 2020)

The Center for Advanced Research in Digital Forensics and Cyber Security (ARDC) states that most cyber defamation victims in India are women. Under the Information Technology Act, 2000, individuals found conducting sexual harassment in cyberspace are penalized under sections 354A, 354D, or 509 of the Indian Penal Code, 1860 (Chhabaria & Tripathi, 2020). However, many of these online crimes are severely underreported due to the social stigma associated with them.

The pandemic and subsequent transition to remote work have increased telecommuting in the formal sector, leading to a considerable rise in digital activity. Cybercriminals have taken advantage of this work situation to send malicious emails to hack confidential information resulting in a rise in online crimes against women. Collaborative research conducted by the International Center for Research on Women (ICRW) and Quilt.AI examined online violence across rural and urban India before and during the COVID-19 outbreak (Fortson et al., 2020). Their findings show an increase in conversations around doxing (i.e. searching for and publishing private and/or identifying information on the internet), online stalking, and hacking during COVID-19. Technology-facilitated gender-based violence remains concentrated in urban cities, like Delhi and Mumbai, and Kolkata, as opposed to rural India. It is often the case that women lack sufficient information and awareness on whom to seek assistance from when such incidents occur. Ritesh Bhatia, a cyber expert, stated that the rise in cybercrimes could be attributed to other factors such as easy access to internet services, availability of cheap smartphones, and data packages (Narayan, 2020).

In particular, the cases of sextortion have increased during the COVID-19 lockdown (Pakrasi, 2020). Sextortion is a form of corruption where a person in authority uses his power to demand sexual favors from others in subordinate positions or electronically distribute private and sensitive material (Amin, 2020). The National Commission for Women reported a considerable rise in sextortion cases during the COVID-19 lockdown when remote work was prevalent (Amin, 2020). They reported 54 cases of cybercrime in April compared to 37 cases in March and only 21 cases in February (The Economic Times, 2020). The Akancha Srivastava Foundation reportedly received 412 cyber abuse complaints from March 25 to April 25. Of these, 396 complaints were received from women complaining about "abuse, indecent exposure, unsolicited obscene pictures, threats, malicious emails claiming their account was hacked, ransom demands, blackmail and more" (The Economic Times, 2020). Despite this, India does not have a strict law to prevent sextortion.

The threat of sexual harassment at work still continues in India. However, now it has turned digital as most employees who are able to work remotely are working under work-from-home arrangements in the midst of COVID-19. A number of companies in India have started to provide training to employees to identify unwanted gestures and unwelcome behaviors in a remote working environment. Some companies, such as Phonepe, Natwest Group India, Razorpay, and Wakefit Co., have prohibited some behaviors containing sexual undertones, such as using inappropriate language or gestures during virtual meetings, making sexual colored remarks, and placing unwarranted requests for video calls after normal office hours (Sarkar & Basu, 2020). For instance, Santhosh KT, founder of elearnPOSH.com, stated that the companies are also implementing virtual conferencing rules which include requiring sufficient notice for a video call and not requiring employees to switch on their video.

While these new protocols and awareness offer important protections for remote workers in the formal sector, the workers that reported the highest workplace sexual harassment rates prior to COVID-19 were women workers in the informal sector. In India, 90% of people are engaged in the informal sector meaning that nearly 400 million workers are at risk of falling into poverty during the pandemic (ILO, 2020). In the same report, the ILO called India's COVID lockdown measures some of the strictest according to the University of Oxford's COVID-19 Government Stringency Index. These stringent measures have negatively impacted informal workers by costing them their jobs and forcing them to return to rural areas. Therefore, although they may no longer be exposed to workplace sexual harassment, their well-being has drastically declined. In the first place, informal sector workers are excluded from all forms of work-related securities, and most of them cannot depend on alternate sources of income or savings. In addition, women informal workers cannot receive benefits covered under the Maternity Benefit Act, 1961. Due to low productivity and minimal capital accumulation in the informal sector, these workers are highly vulnerable to economic shocks and are excluded from COVID-associated short term financial benefits for businesses (ILO, 2020). Additionally troubling, the lack of employment opportunities may elevate their risk for experiencing sexual violence.

As the pandemic continues, the rate of gender-based violence and harassment has also gone up. Statistics suggest a 50% rise in domestic violence in India from the start of the national COVID-lockdown on March 25 to May 15 (Nandan, 2020). Per the data provided by the National Legal Services Authority (NALSA), in northern India, a total of 144 cases of violence against women were reported in Uttarakhand, followed by a high prevalence of cases in Haryana and New Delhi (Times of India, 2020). The National Commission for Women received 315 complaints across various crime categories, out of which 47.2% of cases were related to DV (Pandit, 2020). The economic disruption and the lack of social protection measures, and psychological stress due to lockdown and other COVID containment measures contributed to increasing the risk of violence against women (Samantrov & Sarkar, 2020). Therefore, women bear the dual threat of victimization. The current pandemic has enhanced the risk of technology-facilitated violence against women in a virtual working environment. During the COVID-19 institutional lockdown, women and girls are stranded at home with their abusers and the higher stress over health and financial issues have contributed to increasing offline violence against women and girls (Fortson et al., 2020). With the sinking economy and employment cuts for women workers in the informal sector, women's bargaining power has further deteriorated, providing perpetrators an opportunity to instigate sexual violence against women (Samantrov & Sarkar, 2020).

A Comparative Analysis of India and the United States

The experiences of both India and the United States highlight the stark gender dimension to workplace sexual harassment. Despite significant differences in employment type and sector, women were much more likely to experience workplace sexual harassment before the shift to remote work in both countries. The new, virtual workspaces and communication technologies that have become increasingly central in workers' lives do not seem to have changed these gendered patterns in either country. Instead, new forms of virtual sexual harassment, such as sextortion and inappropriate messages, have increased. In both cases, patriarchal norms that result in power asymmetries between men and women and perpetuate tolerance of workplace sexual harassment appear to be major contributing factors. However, women in both countries have also benefited from increased access to technology in terms of awareness building and organizing. The #MeToo movement that began in the United States quickly become international, including spreading to India, amplifying women workers' voices, and providing a global platform to speak out against harassment.

India and the United States primarily differ in terms of the size of their informal workforce and the strength and scope of the laws that protect workers. A key policy recommendation is the extension of labor rights and protections, including antidiscrimination policies that prohibit workplace sexual harassment, to cover more workers. However, the case of the United States also provides a cautionary tale for India. Anti-harassment policies, training, and formal reporting mechanisms are not panaceas for sexual harassment. In fact, as previously mentioned, such training can make potential perpetrators more likely to harass, and reporting can worsen worker well-being.

Ultimately, sexual harassment is a workplace culture and power issue. Intolerance for sexual harassment, be it in the formal or informal sector, must be clear and communicated from the those with the most power: politicians, managers, and CEOs. Improving women's power, through educational and career opportunities and especially moving more women into management and leadership positions will help eradicate workplace sexual harassment.

SOLUTIONS AND RECOMMENDATIONS

Strategies aimed at improving worker well-being by preventing virtual sexual harassment can be drawn from the literature on offline workplace sexual harassment. These solutions primarily fall into three categories: laws and regulation, workplace culture, and training programs (Barak, 2005). At the macro level, a coordinated approach is necessary. For instance, NGOs and local governments should work closely together to ensure women's safety, both in the physical and virtual workplace. Labor rights and protections should be expanded to cover more people in both the formal and informal sectors, including independent contractors and domestic workers. Stricter laws in many countries, such as India, may also be necessary. More generally, the expansion of labor policies that reduce power differentials and strengthen workers' rights, especially those of women, will be instrumental in combatting sexual harassment.

The most promising, but challenging, solution is the need to disrupt the masculine norms dominating workplace culture. Although this seems like a daunting undertaking, the rapid responses by firms and employees to adapt to remote work is evidence of the malleability of workplace norms. In the interim, updating workplace anti-harassment policies and procedures to reflect these new work conditions is imperative. Employers should clearly identify forms of online harassment, clarify that anti-harassment policies apply in virtual workspaces, and emphasize zero-tolerance policies. There is also a need for regulation and accountability when it comes to new and emerging work technology, such as WhatsApp, Slack, Zoom, Microsoft Teams, and Google Meet. Companies should be proactive in setting up safe and anti-discriminatory virtual workspaces. This may include allowing for audio-only calls and considering accountability measures for behavior in one-on-one calls and informal 'watercooler' channels on Slack or other messaging apps.

Increased familiarity with virtual technology can also improve the ease of implementing virtual training, especially for smaller businesses. In addition, workplaces may consider special training on sexual harassment in remote environments. However, the recent history of training programs and grievance procedures provide some cautions. Both have been found to increase employee disaffection and turnover (Dobbin & Kalev, 2019). One of the few exceptions is bystander training, shown to be successful pre-COVID (Dobbin & Kalev, 2020). A modified (virtual) bystander intervention training may be considered to adjust for the online world of work.

Many of these strategies are only effective if sexual harassment is reported. However, underreporting is rampant because of fear of backlash and lack of confidence in how the report will be dealt with (UN WG, 2020). In a survey of women workers in the corporate sector in the United States, only 50% of women said that they thought reporting sexual harassment would be effective, and 38% said they kept it to themselves because they were worried that it would have negative effects on their career. (LeanIn.org & McKinsey & Company, 2019). In a survey of organizations across India's major cities, about 30% of women said that they were hesitant to complain to the internal committee about sexual harassment (Sarkar, 2019). Providing informal, in addition to formal, reporting options, should be considered. Such informal, and anonymous or confidential, reporting options, such as an Ombuds office, can help reduce retaliation faced by victims who report (Dobbin & Kalev, 2020). Remote work and increased use of technology could help facilitate and scale the implementation of such programs. A variety of start-up options and apps already offer online complaint submission systems in the United States. Some even offer virtual Ombuds offices that operate confidentially online. To further encourage reporting, it is helpful to clarify the procedures for the different types of reporting and restate zero tolerances policies that extend to virtual work.

Implementing solutions to remote workplace sexual harassment are vital for protecting worker well-being. Employees are more likely to report that they recommend their company, plan to stay at their company, and that they feel happy with their career when their company emphasizes accountability for sexual harassment (LeanIn.org & McKinsey & Company, 2019).

FUTURE RESEARCH DIRECTIONS

Future research and data collection on workplace sexual harassment is imperative and should not be delayed in the wake of the pandemic and social distancing. If anything, data collection is more imperative in order to understand how sexual harassment has manifested in remote and virtual workspaces. In parallel to calls for swift and continued college campus climate surveys of sexual harassment, continued monitoring and collection of worker experiences is crucial (Holland et al. 2020).

CONCLUSION

Workplace sexual harassment is a human rights violation, a form of both violence against women and sex discrimination, and a public health epidemic in its own right. Yet, it is pervasive in countries in the Global North and Global South, in offices and over email, on mass transportation and work-related apps. Even the coronavirus pandemic, which rapidly shut down social gatherings, businesses, and travel, proved unsuccessful in eliminating workplace sexual harassment.

When it comes to sexual harassment, the impacts of remote work bring both protection and risk. Exposure to physical forms of workplace sexual harassment has largely been eliminated with remote work. The exception is for informal workers who have been left out of the work-from-home arrangements, finding themselves in increasingly precarious positions. For those that have shifted to remote work, however, many of the same risk factors still exist. The early evidence presented in this chapter from India and the United States suggests that sexual harassment is on the rise and has taken on new forms. The move to virtual workplaces has increased the channels of communication, including the prevalence of one-on-one meetings and reduced the ability of managers to monitor all forms of communication. Factors such as increased time online, the more informal feel of work-from-home situations, and the relative sense of anonymity that comes from working behind a screen have also contributed to increasing workplace sexual harassment.

The challenges of workplace sexual harassment in a post-COVID world continue much the same as they did before the coronavirus pandemic. Namely, how to define, identify, and monitor it? How to disrupt the existing norms regarding workplace culture that have long enabled and protected harassers? An additional, but inadvertent challenge, associated with the primary manifestation of remote work as "work-from-home" is the increased risk for domestic violence suggested by some, but not all, early research findings. As mobility is restored, employers may consider alternative remote work solutions that are not a worker's home.

Remote work has also brought many opportunities to improve worker well-being. Most importantly, it has provided protection against direct exposure to the virus. It has also presented the opportunity to harness technology for good, including expanding access to virtual training and increasing the ease of reporting. These nascent virtual workplaces provide the perfect opportunity to establish new *remote* workplace norms instead of replicating those steeped in patriarchy and rigid hierarchies. Those at the top must help in establishing an inclusive culture, emphasizing a zero-tolerance policy for discrimination. Such radical workplace culture change is possible. The world has already witnessed the incredible adaptability of workers and firms, as they rapidly adjusted to remote work. The time has never been better to focus on disrupting other norms, which just a year ago, seemed impossibly stubborn. Remote work has brought the opportunity to challenge workplace cultures globally, establishing guidelines and setting examples of what inclusive virtual workspaces can look like, where all workers can work with security and dignity.

REFERENCES

Amin, T. (2020, June 26). Laws related to sextortion. *Lawyered*. https://www.lawyered.in/legaldisrupt/articles/laws-related-sextortion/

Barak, A. (2005). Sexual harassment on the internet. *Social Science Computer Review*, *23*(1), 77–92. doi:10.1177/0894439304271540

Blackwell, L., Ellison, N., Elliot-Deflo, N, & Schwartz, R. (2019). Harassment in social virtual reality: challenges for platform governance. *PACM on Human-Computer Interaction, 3*(CSCW).

Brenan, M. (2020, October 13). COVID-19 and remote work: an update. *Gallup*. https://news.gallup.com/poll/321800/covid-remote-work-update.aspx

Brynjolfsson, E., Horton, J.J., Ozimek, A., Rock, D., Sharma, G., & TuYe, H.-Y. (2020). *COVID-19 and remote work: an early look at US data.* National Bureau of Economic Research Working Paper No. 27344. https://www.nber.org/papers/w27344

Bullinger, L. R., Carr, J., & Packham, A. (2020). *COVID-19 and crime: effects of stay-at-home orders on domestic violence.* National Bureau of Economic Research Working Paper No. 27667. doi:10.3386/w27667

Chhabaria, R., & Tripathi, A. (2020, June 4). Prevention of Sexual Harassment at 'Online' Workplace. *The Leaflet.* https://www.theleaflet.in/prevention-of-sexual-harassment-at-online-workplace/#

Cortina, L. M., & Berdahal, J. L. (2008). Sexual harassment in organizations: a decade of research in review. In J. Barling & C. L. Cooper (Eds.), SAGE handbook of organizational behavior: volume 1 – micro approaches (pp. 469–497). SAGE Publications. doi:10.4135/9781849200448.n26

Darcy, O. (2020, November 11). Jeffrey Toobin fired from The New Yorker after exposing himself on a Zoom call. *CNN Business.* https://www.cnn.com/2020/11/11/media/jeffrey-toobin-fired-new-yorker/index.html

Deloitte. (2019). *Safe Space Survey Report.* Author.

Desilver, D. (2020, March 20). Before the coronavirus, telework was an optional benefit, mostly for the affluent few. *Pew Research Center.* https://www.pewresearch.org/fact-tank/2020/03/20/before-the-coronavirus-telework-was-an-optional-benefit-mostly-for-the-affluent-few/

Dobbin, F., & Kalev, A. (2017, November 15). Training programs and reporting systems won't end sexual harassment. Promoting more women will. *Harvard Business Review.* https://hbr.org/2017/11/training-programs-and-reporting-systems-wont-end-sexual-harassment-promoting-more-women-will

Dobbin, F., & Kalev, A. (2019, June 18). The promise and peril of sexual harassment programs. *Proceedings of the National Academy of Sciences of the United States of America, 116*(25), 12255–12260. doi:10.1073/pnas.1818477116 PMID:31160444

Dobbin, F. & Kalev, A. (2020, May). Why sexual harassment programs backfire. *Harvard Business Review Magazine.*

Dugan, L., Nagin, D. S., & Rosenfeld, R. (2003). Exposure reduction or retaliation? The effects of domestic violence resources on intimate-partner homicide. *Law & Society Review, 37*(1), 169–198. doi:10.1111/1540-5893.3701005

Duggan, M. (2017, July 11). Online harassment 2017. *Pew Research Center.* https://www.pewresearch.org/internet/2017/07/11/online-harassment-2017/

Folke, O., & Rickne, J. (2020). *Sexual harassment and gender inequality in the labor market.* Stockholm University, Swedish Institute for Social Research Working Paper Series.

Fortson, J., Hinson, L., Rajbhandari, B., & Bhalla, P. (2020, December 8). Technology facilitated gender-based violence in the time of Covid-19. *International Center for Research on Women.* https://www.icrw.org/technology-facilitated-gender-based-violence-in-the-time-of-covid-19/

Franks, M. A. (2012). Sexual harassment 2.0. *Maryland Law Review (Baltimore, Md.)*, *71*(3), 655–704.

Fraser, E. (2020). *Impact of COVID-19 pandemic on violence against women and girls.* VAWG Helpdesk Research Report No. 284.

Gartenberg, I., & Harikumar, N. (2019, October 2). How do we combat rampant sexual harassment in the workplace? *The Wire.* https://thewire.in/women/how-do-we-combat-rampant-sexual-harassment-in-the-workplace

Ghosh, A., Puri, M., & Dewan, N. (2010, August 22). India inc Is waking up to the menace of sexual harassment. *The Economic Times.* https://economictimes.indiatimes.com/special-report/india-inc-is-waking-up-to-the-menace-of-sexual-harassment/articleshow/6389463.cms

Government of India. (2015). *Handbook on sexual harassment of women at workplace.* Ministry of Women and Child Development.

Hersch, J. (2015). Sexual harassment in the workplace. *IZA World of Labor: Evidence-Based Policy Making*, *188*, 1–10.

Holland, K. J., Cortina, L. M., Magley, V. J., Baker, A. L., & Benya, F. F. (2020, October 6). Do not let COVID-19 disrupt campus climate surveys of sexual harassment. *Proceedings of the National Academy of Sciences of the United States of America*, *117*(40), 24606–24608. doi:10.1073/pnas.2018098117 PMID:32948693

International Labour Organization. (2013). *Preventing and responding to sexual harassment at work: guide to the Sexual Harassment of Women at Workplace (Prevention, Prohibition and Redressal) Act, 2013.* International Labour Organization. https://www.ilo.org/newdelhi/whatwedo/publications/WCMS_630227/lang--en/index.htm

International Labour Organization. (2020). *COVID-19 crisis and the informal economy Immediate responses and policy challenges.* International Labour Organization.

Kearl, H., Johns, N. E., & Raj, A. (2019). *Measuring #MeToo: a national study on sexual harassment and assault.* UC San Diego Center on Gender Equity and Health.

Kumar, S. (2018, September 22). What keeps women from the workforce: the invisible scourge of sexual harassment at informal workplaces. *Times of India.* https://timesofindia.indiatimes.com/blogs/toi-edit-page/what-keeps-women-from-the-workforce-the-invisible-scourge-of-sexual-harassment-at-informal-workplaces/?source=app

LeanIn.org & McKinsey & Company. (2019). *Women in the Workplace 2019 Report.* https://wiw-report.s3.amazonaws.com/Women_in_the_Workplace_2019.pdf

Magnusson Hanson, L. L., Nyberg, A., Mittendorfer-Rutz, E., Bondestam, F., & Madsen, I. E. H. (2020). Work related sexual harassment and risk of suicide and suicide attempts: Prospective cohort study. *BMJ (Clinical Research Ed.)*, *2020*(370), m2984. doi:10.1136/bmj.m2984 PMID:32878868

Mani, D., & Tomar, S. (2020, March 30). Work from home in the time of COVID-19. *The Hindu.* https://www.thehindu.com/opinion/op-ed/work-from-home-in-the-time-of-covid-19/article31207008.ece

Martinuzzi, E. (2020, June 17). As work has moved home, so has harassment. *Bloomberg*. https://www.bloomberg.com/opinion/articles/2020-06-17/as-work-has-moved-home-so-has-online-bullying-harassment

Matt, A. (2020, February 14). Know your rights: online harassment. *The Swaddle*. https://theswaddle.com/know-your-rights-protection-against-online-harassment/

McLaughlin, H., Uggen, C., & Blackstone, A. (2017). The economic and career effects of sexual harassment on working women. *Gender & Society*, *31*(3), 333–358. doi:10.1177/0891243217704631 PMID:29056822

Miller, A. R., Segal, C., & Spencer, M. K. (2020). *Effects of the COVID-19 pandemic on domestic violence in Los Angeles*. National Bureau of Economic Research Working Paper No. 28068. https://www.nber.org/papers/w28068

Miller, C. (2020, July 31). Remote work isn't working? Maybe your company is doing it wrong. *The New York Times*. https://www.nytimes.com/2020/07/31/upshot/remote-work-tips.html

Morgan, P., & Gruber, J. E. (2010). Sexual harassment: violence against women at work and in schools. In C. M. Renzetti, J. L. Edleson, & R. K. Bergen (Eds.), *Sourcebook on Violence Against Women* (2nd ed.). SAGE Publications.

Nandan, A. (2020, May 21). Is domestic violence the next pandemic in India? *The Times of India*. https://timesofindia.indiatimes.com/blogs/voices/is-domestic-violence-the-next-pandemic-in-india/

Narayan, V. (2020, October 1). Mumbai second in cybercrimes for third consecutive year. *The Times of India*. https://timesofindia.indiatimes.com/city/mumbai/mumbai-second-in-cybercrimes-for-third-consecutive-year/articleshow/78419492.cms

News, A. P. (2020, October 29). New workforce challenges emerge as remote work expands, according to new SAP SuccessFactors report. *AP News*. https://apnews.com/article/business-technology-lifestyle-virus-outbreak-government-business-and-finance-f1bf3e9e9d111088c0484aa8c92f9ded

Pakrasi, S. (2020, May 3). Significant' increase in cybercrime against women during lockdown: experts. *Hindustan Times*. https://www.hindustantimes.com/india-news/significant-increase-in-cybercrime-against-women-during-lockdown-experts/story-QNPwq5Jr1iAkAXzacLnc5K.html

Palermo, T. & Peterman, A. (2011). Undercounting, overcounting, and the longevity of flawed estimates: Statistics on sexual violence in conflict. *World Health Organization, 89*(853), 924-926.

Pandit, A. (2020, June 2). Domestic violence accounts for over 47% complaints to NCW in lockdown. *The Times of India*. https://timesofindia.indiatimes.com/articleshow/76161829.cms?utm_source=contentofinterest&utm_medium=text&utm_campaign=cppst

Phillips & Associates. (2020). Amid coronavirus quarantines, workplace sexual harassment in New York goes virtual. *New York Employment Attorney Blog*. https://www.newyorkemploymentattorney-blog.com/amid-coronavirus-quarantines-workplace-sexual-harassment-in-new-york-goes-virtual/

Pina, A., Gannon, T. A., & Saunders, B. (2009). An overview of the literature on sexual harassment: Perpetrator, theory, and treatment issues. *Aggression and Violent Behavior*, *14*(2), 126–138. doi:10.1016/j.avb.2009.01.002

Roy Chowdhury, J. (2014). Insecurities of the workers in the informal enterprises: A study of West Bengal in comparison to Kerala. *Research in Applied Economics*, *6*(3), 220–252. doi:10.5296/rae.v6i3.6005

Samantrov, E., & Sarkar, K. (2020). Violence in times of COVID-19 lack of legal protection for women informal workers. *Economic and Political Weekly*.

SangaS.McCraryJ. (2020). The impact of the coronavirus lockdown on domestic violence SSRN. https://ssrn.com/abstract=3612491 doi:10.2139srn.3612491

Sangani, P., & Chandrasekhar, A. (2020, April 22). IT campuses will never be the same: how India's 4 million IT workers shifted to working from home overnight. *The Economic Times*. https://economictimes.indiatimes.com/tech/ites/it-campuses-will-never-be-the-same-how-indias-4-million-it-workers-shifted-to-working-from-home-overnight/articleshow/75290054.cms

Sarkar, B. (2019, June 19). More than 50% women professionals believe sexual harassment at the workplace has increased over the years: survey. *The Economic Times*. https://economictimes.indiatimes.com/news/politics-and-nation/more-than-50-women-professionals-believe-sexual-harassment-at-the-workplace-has-increased-over-the-years-survey/articleshow/69855500.cms?utm_source=contentofinterest&utm_medium=text&utm_campaign=cppst

Sarkar, B., & Basu, S. (2020, August 26). Companies now look to check harassment during work from home. *The Economic Times*. https://economictimes.indiatimes.com/news/company/corporate-trends/companies-now-look-to-check-harassment-during-work-from-home/articleshow/77725397.cms?utm_source=contentofinterest&utm_medium=text&utm_campaign=cppst

Sarkar, U., Hemmat, S., & Linos, E. (2020). Sexual harassment and suicide. *BMJ (Clinical Research Ed.)*, *2020*(370), m3330. doi:10.1136/bmj.m3330 PMID:32878861

Satpodar, A. (2013). Sexual Harassment of Women: Reflections on the Private Sector. *Economic and Political Weekly*, 18–23.

Schaefer, I. C. (2020, November 18). Rule 10: Don't be creepy. *The National Law Review*. https://www.natlawreview.com/article/rule-10-don-t-be-creepy

Sharma, H. (2020, April 9). Sexual harassment at workplace: a closer look at ILO Convention 190. *Intersectional Feminism*. https://feminisminindia.com/2020/04/09/sexual-harassment-workplace-ilo-convention-190/

Sharma, P. (2010). *India's first workplace sexual harassment survey reveals startling revelations*. http://www.releasenews.com/

Shaw, E., Hegewisch, A. & Hess, C. (2018, October). *Sexual harassment and assault at work: understanding the costs*. Institute for Women's Policy Research, IWPR Briefing Paper #B376.

Shukla, S. (2002, September 1). Indecent proposal. *Business Today*. http://archives.digitaltoday.in/businesstoday/20020901/cover1.html

Stop Street Harassment. (2018). *Study on sexual harassment and assault: the facts behind the #MeToo movement: A national study on sexual harassment and assault.* http://www.stopstreetharassment.org/resources/2018-national-sexual-abuse-report/

Strenio, J. (2019). Economic considerations of intimate partner violence. In R. Geffner, J. W. White, L. K. Hamberger, A. Rosenbaum, V. Vaughan-Eden, & V. I. Vieth (Eds.), *Handbook of interpersonal violence and abuse across the lifespan: a project of the National Partnership to End Interpersonal Violence Across the Lifespan (NPEIV)*. Springer Nature. doi:10.1007/978-3-319-62122-7_167-1

The Economist. (2020, November 24). People are working longer hours during the pandemic. *The Economist*. https://www.economist.com/graphic-detail/2020/11/24/people-are-working-longer-hours-during-the-pandemic

Times of India. (2020, May 18). Domestic violence cases in India on the rise during lockdown. *Times of India*. https://timesofindia.indiatimes.com/life-style/relationships/love-sex/domestic-violence-cases-in-india-on-the-rise-during-lockdown-says-report/articleshow/75801752.cms

United Nations Working Group on Discrimination Against Women and Girls. (2020) *Discrimination against women and girls: women's human rights in the changing world of work (A/HRC/44/51)*. https://unworkinggroupwomenandgirls.org/wp-context/uploads/2020/07/G2009480.pdf

U.S. Equal Employment Opportunity Commission. (1997). *Facts about sexual harassment.* Retrieved from: https://www.eeoc.gov/publications/facts-about-sexual-harassment

U.S. Merit Systems Protection Board. (1995). *Sexual harassment in the federal workplace: trends, progress, continuing challenges*. U.S. Merits System Protection Board.

Varma, A. (2020, April 22). Dealing with sexual harassment in the virtual workplace. *The Hindu Business Line*. https://www.thehindubusinessline.com/opinion/dealing-with-sexual-harassment-in-the-virtual-workplace/article31403719.ece

Waugh, I. M. (2010). Examining the sexual harassment experiences of Mexican immigrant farmworking women. *Violence Against Women*, *16*(3), 237–261. doi:10.1177/1077801209360857 PMID:20093433

Women, U. N. (2020, July 21). Take five: Why we should take online violence against women and girls seriously during and beyond COVID-19. *UN Women*. https://www.unwomen.org/en/news/stories/2020/7/take-five-cecilia-mwende-maundu-online-violence

KEY TERMS AND DEFINITIONS

#MeToo: An international social movement against sexual harassment and assault that encouraged the sharing of experiences of sexual harassment committed by powerful men, primarily over social media.

Domestic Violence: Abusive behavior within the home, usually perpetrated by intimate partners. It can include physical and sexual violence, psychological violence, emotional and verbal abuse, neglect, and economic abuse.

Information and Communications Technology: All forms of communication technology, which includes Wi-Fi and the internet, cell phones, computers, and tablets, social media and networking platforms, email, and videoconferencing, among others.

Sextortion: A form of sexual exploitation in which one person uses their power to extort sexual favors from another. Sextortion also refers to coercion that occurs through the threat of releasing sexual images of a person.

Sexual Harassment: Includes harassment that is sexual in nature, such as a request for a sexual favor, as well as harassment based on a person's sex or gender, such as gender-based insults. In many countries, it is considered a form of sex discrimination and illegal in the workplace.

Violence Against Women: Gender-based violence perpetrated against women and girls. It includes any acts or threats that result in harm to women, including sexual harassment and assault, domestic violence, and intimate partner homicide.

Workplace: The workplace is broadly envisioned to include public and private workspaces in the formal and informal sector. This includes both physical and virtual spaces, including work-related travel, commuting to and from work, and work that happens online.

Chapter 4
Home Alone:
Writers and Readers Respond to the Pandemic

Paul Delany
Simon Fraser University, Canada

ABSTRACT

Some might think that the COVID-19 pandemic changes little, because novelists have always worked from home and found isolation to be necessary for their creative process. But in fact, there is a spectrum in sites of production. Even in a novelist's solitary study, her task is to construct a narrative out of her past social experience. The pandemic has caused a drastic reduction in such face-to-face activities. Changes in the consumption of fiction during the pandemic can be tracked on Amazon and include a shift from print to Kindle, and also shifts in genres. The biggest gain in share on Kindle has been in children's books. Post-publication activities have become steadily more important, as promotion of a book is now integral to its production. The rise of self-publishing on Kindle Direct Publishing bypasses traditional gatekeepers. With KDP almost everyone now can have their own press, and the centres of gravity of publishing have moved from London and New York to Seattle. Post-apocalyptic fiction envisions life in the wake of natural disasters.

THE WRITER'S WORKPLACE

To speak of writers being "Home Alone" during the COVID-19 pandemic might provoke the response: "haven't they always been there, pursuing their solitary trade?" Yet a self-chosen solitude is experienced differently from one that is inflicted by some catastrophic outside event. Being locked down is not the same as wanting to lock other people out to focus on a creative task. A lockdown forces awareness of events in the wider world that have placed you in confinement. The isolation imposed by a pandemic is neither solitude nor loneliness but a condition different from either, and associated with an idea of punishment. In a Canadian prison visited by the author, the cell for solitary confinement had written

DOI: 10.4018/978-1-7998-6754-8.ch004

over the door: "Dissociation." In greater or lesser degree, everyone living with the pandemic has been dissociated.

The focus of this chapter will be on how the pandemic has affected writers and readers of fiction. For playwrights, and largely for non-fiction writers, the pandemic has abruptly shut down most of their usual activities. Theaters have been closed for the duration, access to archives and research travel have been blocked. For novelists, though, the situation has been more mixed. There is a mythology of their working in radical isolation: Dickens's Swiss chalet at Gad's Hill, Proust's cork-lined bedroom, Henry James's garden shed, have established the popular idea of novelists' preferred workspaces. Yet the writer's cell has always been in dialogue with its opposite: the need for social engagement, from which the novelist gathers material to be transformed into art. Balzac said that he was "by turns a hermit and a vagrant"; Henry James went to two hundred dinner parties in a single year; Proust's *A la Recherche du Temps Perdu* was a distillation of rich memories of previous social life.

Virginia Woolf made it a truth universally acknowledged that a writer must have "A Room of One's Own." (V. Woolf, 1929) But after her nervous breakdown in 1913-1914 she suffered acutely from her husband's determination to shield her from almost all social contact:

When we got back to London in the middle of September the problem arose of where we should live. Virginia had barely recovered and it was obvious that any strain, mental or physical, was dangerous to her. I was convinced that she could not possibly, in her present state, stand the strain of London life, but she herself was always in favor of living in London. (L. Woolf, 1964, p. 170)

The tension between engagement and retreat, immersion and seclusion, is a constant theme in Woolf's creative life, and is most fully expressed in *Mrs Dalloway* (V. Woolf, 1925). The novelist acquires her material through social observation and participation. She then needs to cast it into what Henry James called "the crucible," the mystic process that converts life into art:

We can surely account for nothing in the novelist's work that hasn't passed through the crucible of his imagination, hasn't, in that perpetually simmering cauldron his intellectual pot-au-feu, been reduced to savoury fusion. (James, 2011, p. 230)

Fictional transformation is not just something practised by realists like Balzac or high modernists like Virginia Woolf. From the English novel's beginnings with Daniel Defoe and Samuel Richardson, one of its defining missions has been social documentation. Whether it be the battle of Waterloo in Thackeray's *Vanity Fair*, or an unkind remark at a Box Hill picnic in Jane Austen's *Emma*, the novelist is one who observes, judges, and makes an event part of a story. More vividly than historians or social scientists, novelists show us what it was like to be alive in some particular place or time. In doing so, the novelist can work across the whole gamut of human experience, from battles to picnics and everything in between (and Waterloo and the Box Hill picnic were happening at close to the same time).

To consider only the cork-lined room as a site of production gives us too narrow a view of the creative process. Many novelists, whether by choice or by necessity, have written in spaces that were far from secluded. Jane Austen had a writing desk little larger than an open book, next to the kitchen of her house at Chawton. A sentimental view might see her as victimized by having such an exiguous space: despite her genius, she was not granted "a room of her own." Left at the mercy of trivial domestic interruptions, she suffered a specifically female devaluation. But Austen had a bedroom (shared with her sister Cassandra), and the house had other spaces where she might have written. Perhaps she liked being in the middle of her household's daily activities. That might have provided the best inspiration for, as she famously put it, "the little bit (two inches wide) of ivory on which I work with so fine a brush, as produces little effect after much labour." (Austen, 1959, p. 469)

In our own time, J. K. Rowling prefers crowded anonymity over privileged solitude:

It's no secret that the best place to write, in my opinion, is in a café. You don't have to make your own coffee, you don't have to feel like you're in solitary confinement and if you have writer's block, you can get up and walk to the next café while giving your batteries time to recharge and brain time to think. The best writing café is crowded enough to allow you to blend in, but not too crowded that you have to share a table with someone else.

The Harry Potter books may have limited value as social documentation, but Rowling still describes herself as a social being in her café workplace, "happily anonymous and free to people-watch" (Norah, 2019). George Steiner has also spoken up for the literary café:

From western Portugal to St. Petersburg, you have cafés, places where you can come in the morning, order a cup of coffee or a glass of wine, spend the day reading the world's newspapers, playing chess and writing. The bibliography of magnificent books written in cafés is enormous. There are people who have always worked that way and preferred to. (Steiner, 1995)

Keats is said to have written the "Ode to a Nightingale" in the garden of the Spaniards pub in Hampstead; the French existentialists wrote in the café *Les Deux Magots* after World War II. Such cases challenge the generalization that writers need isolation to ignite their creative process. If some writers do prefer to work in a social, rather than a secluded setting, then the pandemic has made this much more difficult. But all novelists are now hampered in doing their "field work": the social observation and participation that precedes the time of actual composition. Some might experience a period of sterility, just as ordinary folk might find themselves at a loss when unable to spend evenings at their local pub. For others, the changed world of the pandemic may provide the stimulus for a growing new mode of fiction, the "pandemic novel."

The Book Market in the Pandemic

How have consumers of fiction responded to the arrival of the pandemic in March 2020? Lockdowns have increased opportunities for reading, and sales of printed books have risen by 8.2 % in 2020 over 2019 (NPD, 2021). Sales of ebooks surely increased by more than this. People are also consuming more of other kinds of home entertainment. The closing of cinemas and theaters has contributed to a steep increase in viewing of movies on Netflix and other streaming services. There has been a similar increase in time spent on video games.[1] Netflix shares have gone from about $375 in March 2020 to about $540 in January 2021; Amazon has risen from $2100 to $3200. Streaming services and distributors have more money than ever before; this will lead to increases in the commissioning of new content, and in the purchase of rights to adapt existing works of fiction. Movie production was shut down in March 2020, though in September it started to resume. Already there is more work for script-writers, who can do most of their work at home. Lastly, the pandemic is causing people to spend more on home renovations for work, comfort and entertainment. When the castle is under siege, it is time to give the castle a makeover.

The closing of movie theaters during the pandemic finds a parallel in the closing of bookstores. When they do re-open, many customers may be wary about browsing and prefer to stay out of public spaces. Overall sales of printed books in the U.S. were about seven % lower in March 2020 than in March 2019. Yet by May they had recovered and were up 8 – 10 % year-on-year (Newton, 2020a). Bricks and mortar bookstores are still suffering closures and bankruptcies because even if customers are still buying books, they prefer to have them delivered by courier or as ebooks. Isolation gives people more time to read, but also a preference for home delivery.

It might be expected that the pandemic would set up a zero-sum shift: each sale lost by a bricks and mortar bookstore means a sales gain for Amazon. But anecdotal evidence suggests a less uniform outcome. Some publishers and bookstores have been able to increase their direct sales to readers by shifting their focus to digital marketing. Arsenal Pulp Press, a British Columbia publisher, reported a 60% decline in sales in the first three months of the pandemic. The publisher blamed this decline on the closing of bookstores and the cancelling of author events. Yet within this gloomy prospect, direct sales were up "400-plus %" year-on-year (Gee, 2020a, C1). Mosaic, a bookstore in Kelowna, BC, upgraded its website to emphasize its ties with local readers. It had 6,000 online orders in the second quarter of 2020, versus 800 orders in the same period the year before (Gee, 2020b). If they can get equivalent service, many readers would prefer to support a store they know, rather than the looming behemoth Amazon.

Digital retailing may be a successful gesture of local resistance, but distribution by ebook is intrinsically monopolistic. There is one dominant reading device, the Kindle, and one dominant provider, Amazon. Buying an ebook avoids any danger of exposure to the COVID virus. Kindle editions are usually cheaper than the paperback version, and much cheaper than hardback.[2] They can be delivered instantly, and available selections vastly exceed what any bookstore could have in stock. An 8GB Kindle can store roughly 6,000 books, at no cost; in printed form that would require about 600 ft of shelving. The pandemic may reinforce a long-term shift towards Kindle, in spite of any residual fetishism for ink and paper. One unwelcome consequence may be to solidify the advantages of "brand-name" authors, especially those who specialize in series titles. Browsing in a bookstore may lead to random discoveries; on Kindle there is only pseudo-browsing, where an algorithm recommends titles related to ones already purchased.

The publishers Simon and Schuster report that ebook sales in Q2 2020 were up by 25-50% year on year (Newton, 2020a). In November 2019, 65% of "Literature and Fiction" bestsellers were delivered by Kindle; by April 2020 the Kindle share had reached 80%. For "Romance" it was 94% (Newton 2020a). Within ebook genres the biggest gain, not surprisingly, has been in childrens' books. Shut out from school and from libraries, children have become a captive market for reading at home. Many of their favorites have ranked high on bestseller lists. This success has come even though illustrations are often important in childrens' books, and they do not display well in the Kindle format. Teen-oriented science fiction has also done well, perhaps as an extension of the childrens' book genre. Among genres that have lost popularity one stands out: post-apocalyptic fiction. Has experiencing the pandemic reduced the desire to read about it?

The Writer's Mode of Production

People who are suffering lockdown have shifted their book purchases from visiting bookstores to delivery by courier or by Kindle. That is an obvious effect of the pandemic. However, the Kindle format has three elements, and two of them are promoting a true revolution in publishing. Kindle appeared first as a new and steadily growing channel for traditional publishers to deliver books to buyers. So, just before the pandemic, Harper Collins registered 21% of total sales by Kindle in Q1 2019 and 23% in Q1 2020 (Newton, 2020a). But such a shift in the mode of delivery does not entail any radical change in the literary marketplace. That comes from two evolutionary changes in the Kindle space.

First is the arrival of Kindle Unlimited in 2014. For a monthly fee of $9.99 (unchanged since the inception), subscribers can read up to ten books at a time on their device, chosen from more than a million titles. This resembles the "all you can eat" model introduced by Netflix for streaming video in 2007. Yet neither service is truly unlimited, because their libraries include only a fraction of all books or movies that have ever been published or released.[3] The main weakness of Kindle Unlimited is that although it does include more than a million titles, there are relatively few mainstream bestsellers, and most of its titles are self-published—what used to be called the output of vanity presses.

Amazon's own vehicle for self-publishing—its vanity press, in a sense—is Kindle Direct Publishing (KDP). Two other self-publishing websites—Wattpad and Scribd—also are growing rapidly; but they do not have the scale of KDP, so we will focus here on the latter service. KDP is now by far the world's biggest publisher, except that it has given up the defining role of mainstream publishers up to now: that of being a gatekeeper. Vanity presses have usually published almost all manuscripts submitted to them, printing a token number of copies and charging a fee for doing so. Vanity publishing has been a massive yet largely invisible enterprise. In 2007, 73% of all titles published in the U.S. were from vanity presses. But since then Amazon has come to dominate self-publishing, with 92% of all titles in 2018 (Wogahn, 2019). Amazon does not disclose how many ebook titles it publishes on KDP, but in 2018 it published 1.4 million print titles—that is, books that in principle could be supplied in hard copy by print on demand. The total of print plus ebook must be significantly more.[4]

In terms of sheer volume, the world capital of publishing is no longer London or New York, but Seattle. KDP does not perform any of the "higher" cultural functions, however. It loads books onto the internet, tracks who is reading them, then pays out royalties proportionately. KDP does not commission manuscripts, sign contracts, negotiate advances, make editorial suggestions, or promote the work after publication.[5] When Gutenberg started his press, some 570 years ago, he combined all these functions, from selecting titles to advertising the printed result. Yet with his single invented machine he set off a cultural and religious revolution. With KDP, another revolution is under way in which anyone with an internet connection—about 4.8 billion people—has their own virtual press.[6] One should note a major exception: the 860 million internet users in China are blocked from publishing on KDP (and 25 million North Koreans are blocked from the internet altogether).[7]

The COVID pandemic has increased incentives for self-publishing, because dealings with conventional publishers have become more difficult. There has always been the problem of "the $1,000 cup of coffee": the cost of travelling to New York for a face-to-face meeting with a publisher or literary agent. At the height of the pandemic, such travel has been either impossible or unacceptably dangerous. All publishers have been under financial pressure, and wary of taking on new obligations. But authors who self-publish with KDP can bypass established gatekeepers altogether.

It might be argued that KDP remains a marginal initiative because only books from mainstream publishers can get reviewed, achieve mass sales, or make serious money for their authors. However, this is far from being the case. In 2017, 284 of the 1,000 top-selling ebooks in the U.S. were self-published (Spatz, 2018). The best-known case of success beginning with self-publishing has been E. L. James's *50 Shades of Grey* trilogy, with more than 125 million copies sold. Such success is rare, to be sure, and is typically due to an author's skill and commitment to self-promotion. Self-publishing is a "winner take all" market, like many others in this century and specially in sports and entertainment (Frank & Cook, 1995). There are vast numbers of authors who offer work in the market, but few successes. KDP will publish any book without charge or restriction, the author sets the price, and if it is between $2.99 and $9.99 the royalty received by the author will be 70% of the proceeds (35% if the price is higher or lower).[8]

Amazon limits information on KDP results, but the total amount paid out in KDP royalties has been steadily increasing, reaching $33.2 million in November 2020, a year-on-year increase of 27 % (Noblit, 2020). If there are about 1.5 million titles on KDP, the average royalty received would be about 22c per month. But clearly most authors get nothing, and only a select few get a living wage. One blogger asserts that it is "widely known in the industry" that any KDP title in the top-selling 10,000 will make at least $10,000 a year in royalties (Conrad, 2019). We can only guess at the actual distribution. Suppose that half the titles earn nothing, and that the remainder follow a Pareto distribution: the power law that says twenty % of titles (150,000) would receive eighty % of the current $33 million in monthly proceeds. Further, power laws are recursive: of the $26 million received by the top twenty %, eighty % would go to the top twenty % of the twenty %. And so on. Indeed, many power laws are more extreme than 80-20. For example, out of millions of basketball players worldwide only 450 have contracts to play in the NBA, with a median salary of $2.6 million (Basketball, 2020). The odds of having a lucrative self-published book are at least better than that.

KDP gives writers an unlimited ability to circulate texts with no interference from the COVID pandemic, even as many bookstores have been forced to shut down. Does it matter that most KDP authors will not gain any economic return from their work? That is just the nature of winner-take-all markets. Authors who use traditional publishers also have very unequal returns. Bowker has estimated that about 50,000 works of fiction were published in print in the U.S. in 2013 (Bowker, 2014). Most of them will have paid very little to their authors. A survey by the Authors Guild in 2017 found that 23% of "full-time" authors reported no income from their books. For all authors, whether full- or part-time, the median income from books was $2560 (Larson, 2020). As with other fields, such as sports or entertainment, the failure of the many only emphasizes the success of the few. The highest paid author in 2019 was J. K. Rowling, with earnings from all sources of $92 million (Cuccinello, 2019).

The Authors Guild laments that writers' incomes have suffered a steady decline through the 2010s (Larson, 2020). This may be blamed on the rise of Amazon, diminished interest in reading relative to other pastimes, or unknown causes. What is certain is that authors now succeed by establishing a "brand" that underpins continuing demand for their work. This is most evident in genre fiction: crime writers, for example, produce not individual books, but a series linked by a quirky detective protagonist. Each book may focus on a different crime, but the detective remains satisfyingly the same. This seems to be a deep law of crime fiction, going back to Sherlock Holmes, Hercule Poirot, and their innumerable successors.

Once a crime series has been established, readers experience each new title as a sequel to what has gone before. The same principle applies to movies: between 2010 and 2019, nine out of the ten highest-grossing movies each year were sequels—items in a series. Beyond the series is the "franchise," where familiar characters appear in an endless string of movies, video games, and other media. Each item in a franchise has the virtue, from the producer's point of view, of being "pre-sold" to a known audience (*Economist,* 2011). Readers, or movie-goers, no longer purchase individual items; rather, they want "the new Harry Potter" or "the new James Bond."

In the case of branded book authors, one might be more accurate in saying that people choose the name of the author rather than the title of the book. Martin Amis's *The Information* has an exchange between Gal Abplanalp, a literary agent, and the novelist Richard Tull:

"Writers need definition," Gal says, "The public can only keep in mind one thing per writer. Like a signature. Drunk, young, mad, fat, sick: you know. It's better if you pick it rather than letting them pick it. . . .

People are very interested in writers. Successful ones. More interested in the writers than the writing. In the writers' lives. For some reason. You and I both know they mainly sit at home all day." (Amis, 1995, pp. 130-31)

When Gal speaks of "successful" writers, she means ones who have built their brand. The brand may have, as a necessary condition, a certain volume of sales; but this is not sufficient. Some writers have massive sales, but no one has heard of them except for their hardcore fans. For others, their brand may be based on being a recluse, or even not publishing at all: Thomas Pynchon and J. D. Salinger are prominent examples. Don DeLillo had a business card that said: "I don't want to talk about it."

The book sections of newspapers are frequently exercises in branding. Three-quarters of a page may be devoted to an interview with a novelist, telling us how she got started, where she finds inspiration, what her domestic routine is, and so forth. At the bottom of the page someone else reviews the author's new book, literally as an afterthought, perhaps saying that the book is not as good as some of its predecessors. The mediocre review scarcely matters, because the author has occupied some new ground in the trench warfare of celebrity culture, where all publicity is good publicity. Or, as the saying goes: "Everyone has two businesses: their own, and show business."

Show business, for a writer, used to mean book tours: media interviews, doing readings and signing copies in bookstores. There might also be appearances at book festivals, or connecting with groups of readers in book clubs. In an earlier age, publicity was assigned to publishers' representatives, who made the rounds of provincial bookstores taking orders, and puffing the titles in their employers' current list.[9] Now, publishers all have marketing departments, who also have a say in which books are contracted. But, as with movie actors, authors are now often under contract to do some of their own promotion. Such commitments fill the gap left by the decline of book review sections in newspapers, and of the associated book advertising. Most important for recruiting authors to do such tasks is the publisher's need to build a stable of branded authors with consistent sales.

How many authors can achieve such name recognition? As a first estimate, perhaps the few hundred who, in pre-COVID days, might be invited to read at one of the four major UK book festivals: Hay, Oxford, Cheltenham, Edinburgh. In 2019 there were 278,000 tickets sold for the Hay Festival, for events spread over eleven days (Studemann, 2020). Has the pandemic crippled this machinery of authors' self-promotion? It might have, ten years ago; but virtual media can now do much to fill the gap. A self-publishing author who makes her debut on Kindle Direct Publishing has no chance of getting a radio interview or an invitation to a bookfest. But she may be instructed on how to build a profile on social media, by having a presence on Goodreads, a website, a Twitter following, or other means. All can be done from home, separately from a publisher's promotional machine. Once an author begins to get traction on social media, her profile can be reinforced by Amazon's algorithms serving up recommendations for her work. To some extent, the traditional business model of publishing can be stood on its head. Instead of contracting an author, paying an advance, and hoping that sales will justify the investment, a publisher may prefer to wait for her results on KDP. If her romance or thriller has sold 50,000 copies on KDP, the publisher can safely offer her a conventional contract.

The Location of Writing: Centers and Peripheries

Nicholas Bloom has touted the benefits of a blended workweek: three productive days at home, say, then two days in the office for companionship and intellectual stimulation (Bloom, 2020). The office still seems to have an essential role for most enterprises, even when much of its work may be decentralized. Bloom does predict an increased role for remote working in a post-pandemic world, due to fear of crowds, improvements in communications, and removal of the charge that remote work is an excuse for laziness. Yet for most writers the prospect of a physically blended week is a mirage, because their home is the only workspace they have. They may be able to blend writing and various kinds of self-promotion, but only over the internet.

Edholm's Law posits that bandwidth—roughly, the capacity of digital networks—has been doubling every 18 months since the 1970s (Cherry, 2004). That kind of exponential growth has made possible a revolution in remote working, comparable to the spread of railways in nineteenth century England. Writers then could live in the country, but also do business in London for one or two days of a typical week.[10] Most writing would still be done at home, but in London a writer could visit publishers, edit a journal, or get commissions for short pieces. He could also pick up material through lunch at his club, or random encounters in pubs. These activities represented a new mode of engagement with the literary marketplace. George Gissing portrays one such literary opportunist, Jasper Milvain, in *New Grub Street*:

"my intuition is so strong," [Milvain boasts], "that I can make a little experience go an immense way. Most people would imagine I had been wasting my time these last few years, just sauntering about, reading nothing but periodicals, making acquaintance with loafers of every description. The truth is, I have been collecting ideas and ideas that are convertible into coin of the realm, my boy; I have the special faculty of an extempore writer. Never in my life shall I do anything of solid literary value; I shall always despise the people I write for. But my path will be that of success. (Gissing, 1997, pp. 67-68)

There has been much debate about the decentralizing effects of digital communications, as opposed to the continuing vitality of cities (Florida, 2002; Glaeser, 2011; Cairncross, 2001). One side argues that innovation thrives in urban centers where people in the same trade can benefit from random encounters with each other. So New York is the most fertile place for finance and media, Los Angeles for entertainment, the Bay Area for technology; in the UK, everything converges on London. The other side, under the rubric of "The Death of Distance," argues that new communications media enable individuals to live anywhere and do business everywhere. In this debate, where do writers enduring the pandemic fit in? We have argued that writers need to strike a balance between their need for a creative refuge, and for the social and economic benefits typically provided by urban life. At present, the balance has swung towards an enforced seclusion. But after the pandemic we can expect a structural shift towards deeper reliance on social media, even after things have supposedly gone back to normal.

For writers, will measures adopted during the crisis—such as Zooming or posting videos on YouTube—become standard practice? Will it become evident that book tours are more expensive and less effective than self-promotion on social media? If central cities become less attractive, will the biggest cluster of U.S. writers—currently in Brooklyn—gradually disperse? Up to the present, experience suggests that new modes of communication have not been responsible for any hollowing-out of urban centers. Email, Facebook and WhatsApp have connected most of the world's population, at nominal cost, but that has not prevented—until this year—relentless growth in air travel. People still endure arduous commutes to work in the center of London or New York. Urban growth may moderate, and the relative status of cities may shift, but network effects ensure that centers will retain unique strengths. In the U.S., the U.K. and France the periphery suffers from more chronic ailments than the center. Globally, 30% of the population lived in cities in 1950. It is 55% now, and is projected to reach 68% in 2050 (UN, 2019).

Until the nineteenth century, infectious diseases caused a higher mortality rate in cities than in the countryside. Cities still managed to grow, thanks to immigration from rural areas. The pandemic crisis of today was, in earlier times, a more or less chronic condition. London's population seems to have shrunk by about eight % in 2020, largely because 700,000 migrants have returned to their home countries (Hammond, 2021). Yet in the long run, fear of infection has never prevented writers and publishers from clustering in cities. Clusters are innovative and productive, in most forms of human endeavor. Improved communications may increase interaction between center and periphery, but much of their effect may be to reinforce the strategic position of centralized services. When it took six days by stagecoach from Edinburgh to London, Scotland had a thriving publishing industry. By the end of the nineteenth century, the railway journey took 8 ½ hours and London completely dominated publishing (in part with firms founded by expatriate Scots like John Murray and the Macmillan brothers).

Pandemic Novels

Pandemic fiction has a long history, beginning with Boccaccio's 14th-century *Decameron* (Boccaccio 1995). Such novels come under the heading of "post-apocalyptic," where some catastrophe has destroyed the social structure of developed societies. Cormac McCarthy's *The Road* (2006) is a well-known example. The actual catastrophe is not named, just its effects: the world is covered in ash and bands of cannibals roam the wasteland. An asteroid strike, volcanic eruption, or nuclear war (Shute, 1957) can motivate the post-apocalyptic novel. Universal sterility is the premise of P. D. James's *The Children of Men* (1992). Post-apocalyptic novels about a pandemic include Albert Camus' *The Plague* (1948), George R. Stewart's *Earth Abides* (1949) and Emily St John Mandel's *Station Eleven* (2014). Diane Cook's *The New Wilderness* (2020) follows a group of survivalists, refugees from cities poisoned by pollution. The first of these novels, *The Plague*, is the most distinguished; it contributed to Camus winning the Nobel Prize in 1957. But it is not post-apocalyptic, strictly speaking. The novel focuses on a few days when the plague is at its height, ending with the expectation that life will go back to normal when the disease recedes. Stewart and Mandel, however, focus on the pandemic's aftermath: most of the world's population has died, and the survivors have regressed to tribalism.

Up to now, at least, the COVID pandemic does not qualify as an apocalyptic interruption of history. By January 2021 more than two million people had died of COVID-19, about one in 4,000 of the world population of 7.8 billion (CSSE, 2020). A conservative estimate of deaths from the Spanish flu of 1918 would be about 40 times as high (Spreeuwenberg, 2018). Even so, that pandemic had relatively little effect on the writing of fiction: two works by prominent authors can be cited, but they are autobiographical rather than speculative (Porter, 1939; O'Hara, 1963). Post-apocalyptic novels are related to science fiction, in that they imagine a radical change in the laws of everyday life. Such writing resembles fable or allegory, as opposed to standard novels that seek to document "the way we live now." COVID-19 fiction may emphasize adaptation to new social conditions, rather than a transformed world. This is, after all, the regular business of the novel: to examine the current state of the society, while also registering how it has changed, and is changing. Part of that mission would be the creation of "internet novels" about how the internet has affected the current pandemic—in remote working, certainly, but also in much else.

When connecting fictional representations with contemporary social history, a distinction should be made between the dystopian and the post-apocalyptic genres. Dystopian novels—like Aldous Huxley's *Brave New World* or George Orwell's *Nineteen Eighty-Four*—are about oppressive societies produced by human intention. Post-apocalyptic novels begin with the premise of a catastrophe either unintended, or beyond human control. Causes might include the escape of a toxin, pandemics, volcanic eruptions, pollution, asteroid strikes, or a miscalculation that leads to nuclear war. James's *The Children of Men* is a hybrid. The originating catastrophe is universal sterility, of unknown origin; the response is one of increased order, imposed by a Big Brother type of dictatorship. But most post-apocalyptic novels imagine a collapse of the state and of its infrastructure. The survivors are faced with Hobbesian anarchy, and they can only revert to tribalism and primitive technologies (Stewart, McCarthy, Mandel, Cook).

Perhaps the first post-apocalyptic novel is Defoe's *Robinson Crusoe*, though unlike most later versions it has a positive theme, of reconstruction. With an informal sense of economic rationality, Crusoe applies opportunity cost and the division of labor to make a small-scale replica of European civilization. Anarchy appears as an external threat, when his island is invaded by cannibals. The dark counterpart to *Crusoe* is William Golding's *Lord of the Flies*, where the boy survivors of a plane crash revert to a savage state. Both are "what if?" novels where readers can explore their own fears and hopes about the consequences of disaster.

Don DeLillo's *White Noise* offers a "before," "during," and "after" vision of catastrophe. The first section examines, not without irony, small-town American life as a consumerist idyll. Then comes the Airborne Toxic Event, when people flee their town to avoid a poisonous cloud of obscure origin.[11] In the final section, things seem to have returned to normal except that the novel's protagonist, Jack Gladney, has become haunted by the fear of his own death. The supposed antidote to the Airborne Toxic Event is Dylar, a pill that targets the area in the brain that generates fear of death. Whether the pill is effective, or a false hope, is left unresolved as the novel ends.

White Noise was influenced by the anthropologist Ernest Becker's *The Denial of Death* (1973). To live with the knowledge of one's own mortality demands recourse to literal or symbolic remedies: drugs, religion, and everything in between. Human life is thus an exercise in "terror management" (Solomon, 2015). For the surplus of terror inflicted by the COVID pandemic the only reliable means of defense—while waiting for the vaccine—is the avoidance of social contact, even though we need contact in order to keep terror at bay. Writers, suffering in lockdown, do their best to define the meaning of what we individually and collectively are facing.

Post-apocalyptic novels are cautionary tales, whether the social end-state is one of dictatorship, or of anarchy. The one outcome not represented is a moderate policy of reconstruction, accompanied by a reaffirmation of liberal values. In time we will have conventional novels that show the impact of the pandemic on everyday life, without overtones of world-ending catastrophe. Anthony Trollope's *Framley Parsonage*, to take an earlier example, provides down-to-earth details about how one Victorian family survives infection with typhus (Trollope, 1861: Chs. 36, 43, 46). Post-apocalyptic novels claim to reveal the dark side of human nature, once people are faced with the imperatives of survival. Conventional novels assume that the default state of social life is going to be "business as usual." Between them, the two kinds of novels cover the range of outcomes, whether "what might happen" or "what is most likely to happen." In due course, science will tell one story about COVID-19; fiction will tell many stories about many people, as it has always done.

REFERENCES

Amis, M. (1995). *The Information.* Flamingo.

Austen, J. (1959). *Jane Austen's Letters to the Sister Cassandra and Others* (R. W. Chapman, Ed.). Oxford UP.

Basketball. (2020). basketball-reference.com/contracts/players.html

Becker, E. (1973). *The Denial of Death.* Free Press.

Bloom, N. (2020). *The Bright Future of Working From Home.* SIEPR, Stanford. siepr.stanford.edu/research/publications/bright-future-working-home

Boccaccio. (1995). *The Decameron* (G. H. McWilliam, Trans.). Penguin.

Bowker. (2014). bowker.com/news/2014/Traditional-Print-Book-Production-Dipped-Slightly-in-2013.html

Cairncross, F. (2001). *The Death of Distance: How the Communications Revolution is Changing our Lives.* Harvard Business Review Press.

Camus, A. (1948). *The Plague.* Hamish Hamilton.

Center for Systems Science and Engineering. (2020). *COVID-19 Dashboard.* Johns Hopkins University.

Cherry, S. (2004). Edholm's Law of Bandwidth. *IEEE Spectrum, 41*(7), 58-60.

Conrad, J. (2019). *How Much Does the Average Kindle Direct Publishing Book Make?* quora.com/How-much-does-the-average-Kindle-Direct-Publishing-book-make

Cook, D. (2020). *The New Wilderness.* HarperCollins.

Cuccinello, H. C. (2019). World's Highest Paid Authors 2019. *Forbes, 20*(December).

Defoe, D. (1719). *Robinson Crusoe.* Taylor.

DeLillo, D. (1986). White Noise. Penguin.

Economist. (2011). *Pottering On, and On.* https://www.economist.com/blogs/dailychart/2011/07/film-franchises

Florida, R. (2002). *The Rise of the Creative Class.* Basic Books.

Frank, R., & Cook, P. (1995). *The Winner-take-all Society.* Free Press.

Gee, D. (2020a). An Uphill Battle. *Vancouver Sun, 1*(August), C1.

Gee, D. (2020b). A New Chapter. *Vancouver Sun, 5*(August), C1.

Gissing, G. (1997). *New Grub Street*. J. M. Dent.

Glaeser, E. (2011). *Triumph of the City: How Our Greatest Invention Makes Us Richer, Smarter, Greener, Healthier, and Happier*. Penguin.

Golding, W. (1954). *Lord of the Flies*. Faber & Faber.

Group, N. P. D. (2021). *After a Slow Start, U.S. Print Book Sales Rose 8.2 % in 2020*. https://www.npd.com/wps/portal/npd/us/news/press-releases/2021/after-a-slow-start--u-s--print-book-sales-rose-8-2-%-in-2020--the-npd-group-says/

Hammond, G. (2021, Jan. 23). London Falling? *Financial Times*.

James, H. (2011). *The Art of the Novel: Critical Prefaces*. Chicago UP.

James, P. D. (1992). *The Children of Men*. Faber & Faber.

Kennedy, R. (1978). *A Boy at the Hogarth Press*. Penguin.

Larson, C. (2020). *The Profession of Author in the 21st Century*. The Authors Guild.

Mandel, E. S. J. (2014). *Station Eleven*. Knopf.

McCarthy, C. (2006). *The Road*. Knopf.

Milliot, J. (2019, October). Number of Self-published Titles Jumped 40% in 2018. *Publishers Weekly*, 15.

Newton, A. (2020a). *Coronavirus Impact on Book Market – Part I*. K-lytics.com/coronavirus-impact-on-book-market-2020-part-1/

Newton, A. (2020b). *Coronavirus Impact on Book Market – Part #2*. K-lytics.com/coronavirus-impact-on-book-market-2020-part-2/

Noblit, C. (2020). *KDP Global Fund Payouts* [November 2020 Update]. WrittenWord Media. writtenwordmedia.com/kdp-global-fund-payouts/

Norah, J. (2019). *Where J. K. Rowling Wrote Harry Potter in Edinburgh*. independenttravelcats.com/cafes-where-jk-rowling-wrote-harry-potter-in-edinburgh/

O'Hara, J. (1969). The Doctor's Son. In *The O'Hara Generation*. Random House.

Porter, K. A. (1939). *Pale Horse, Pale Rider*. Harcourt, Brace.

Shute, N. (1957). *On the Beach*. Heinemann.

Solomon, S., Greenberg, J., & Pyszczynski, T. (2015). *The Worm at the Core: On the Role of Death in Life*. Random House.

Spatz, S. (2018). *3 Self-Published Authors Who Went On to Have Mainstream Success – And How They Did It.* https://writingcooperative.com/3-self-published-authors-who-went-on-to-have-mainstream-success-and-how-they-did-it-36ce6dc4512f

Spreeuwenberg, P. (2018). Reassessing the Global Mortality Burden of the 1918 Influenza Pandemic. *American Journal of Epidemiology, 187*(2), 2561-2567.

Steiner, G. (1995). Interview. *Paris Review, 137.*

Stewart, G. R. (1949). *Earth Abides.* Random House.

Studemann, F. (2020, May 23). Brave New World for the Bookfests. *Financial Times.*

Trollope, A. (1861). *Framley Parsonage.* George Smith.

United Nations Department of Economic and Social Affairs. (2019). *World Urbanization Prospects: The 2018 Revision.* Author.

Wogahn, D. (2019). *Bowker Self-Publishing Report Analysis – 5 Surprising Findings for 2019.* authorimprints.com/bowker-self-publishing-report/

Woolf, L. (1964). *Beginning Again: An Autobiography of the Years 1911-1918.* Hogarth Press.

Woolf, V. (1925). *Mrs Dalloway.* Hogarth Press.

Woolf, V. (1929). *A Room of One's Own.* Hogarth Press.

ENDNOTES

1 Nintendo sales income was up 108% in Q2 2020, year-on-year; number of consoles sold was up 167%.

2 Hardback sales are concentrated in November and December, when most are given as presents.

3 Netflix is also limited chronologically: very few movies made before about 2000 are included.

4 Milliot 2019. Before 2019 Amazon's self-publishing division was called CreateSpace; now it is Kindle Direct Publishing. KDP assigns its own book identifying numbers, which many of its authors prefer to use because in 2020 a single ISBN costs $125. KDP does not charge for identifying numbers.

5 However, there are many agencies that, for a fee, will give advice on manuscript preparation and on promotion.

6 Estimate is for July 2020, when internet users are 62% of the world population of 7.8 billion. 52% of internet users are in Asia, followed by 11.7% in Africa. internetworldstats.com/stats.htm

7 One might recall, also, that in the former Soviet Union there could be a seven-year prison term for misuse of a xerox machine.

8 In the UK, the price band for the 70% royalty is £1.77 to £9.99.

9 Richard Kennedy has described such a tour for the Hogarth Press in 1929. (Kennedy 1978, pp. 68-74)

[10] Railways also contributed to dramatic improvements in the speed and frequency of postal delivery, another key service for authors.

[11] Até is also the name of the Greek goddess of vengeance and disorder.

Chapter 5
Engagement and Efficiency of Remote Higher Education:
An Economics Perspective

Madhavi Venkatesan
Northeastern University, USA

ABSTRACT

The suddenness of COVID-19 forced, literally overnight, a transformation in the higher education sector. Students and instructors were migrated to an online engagement and knowledge transfer process, which created unforeseen challenges to instruction and prompted the development of new delivery systems. Further, the transition merged private and academic life as home life converged with work and ultimately, albeit unintentionally, promoted a more human perspective through widespread use of video-based communication. This chapter will address how COVID-19 affected the teaching of Introductory Economics, highlighting a case study of a course offered at Northeastern University in Boston, Massachusetts. The discussion addresses both positive and negative outcomes related to instruction and the role that COVID-19 has potentially had on teaching beyond the pandemic.

INTRODUCTION

Teaching is in itself an occupation that is challenging. There are many aspects that are beyond the control, or independent, of the instructor. Some are physical, such as classroom set-up including communication technologies, white/black boards and desk configuration, while others are related to students, and still others are specific to the subject of engagement. With respect to the aspects of teaching that are dependent on the instructor, depending on the level of desired engagement between the instructor and his or her class, these may evolve over time based on experience as well as be modified to meet the (perceived) needs of specific course dynamics. The latter being related to the culture of the classroom established by student engagement and interaction with the course.

The challenges of teaching in Higher Education involve an additional aspect of instructor stress in that both university solicited course teaching evaluations and "Rate My Professor" (in the U.S.) provide

DOI: 10.4018/978-1-7998-6754-8.ch005

students an opportunity to critique a professor's course instruction. Given that tenure and contract renewals include perceptions of teaching provided from, at minimum, the former of these channels, all academics can have their reputations attacked anonymously. However, the potential for harm is greater for junior tenure-track and contract faculty who do not have the job security provided by tenure (Flaherty, 2017). As a result, there is evidence that instructional quality has deteriorated to simply reflect a by-product of student evaluation. Instructors are essentially incentivized to default to satisfying the grade and ease of learning demands of students rather than promoting educational rigor (Becker and Watts, 1999).

As a final challenge, most graduate programs do not provide adequate support in developing an acumen related to teaching. Instead, for the same reason that the dissertation stage determines the validation of having a PhD designation, graduate programs focus on developing researchers because research promotes credibility and legitimacy (Sheridan, 2014). This inherently echoes the disconnect between classroom instruction and academic advancement, as research is often used as the primary basis for promotion, while teaching is a secondary but necessary function. From a living wage perspective, teaching essentially is the funding mechanism for baseline salary but research is the building of reputation. This trade-off affects the perception of teaching, by both the academic staff (employee) and the institution (employer), resulting in a diminishing of its significance. The irony of the hierarchy afforded to teaching is that instruction has the ability to affect a larger number of people than a given research project, though publication and a research agenda is granted greater value (Rai and Sharma, 2016).

In the teaching of economics, the discounting of the value of teaching has arguably led to the commoditization of introductory economics courses. These courses typically have the highest enrolments because at most U.S. institutions 'Principles' courses (i.e. introductory Microeconomics and Macroeconomics) satisfy distributional requirements for baccalaureate completion. This has presented a limitation to the promotion of economic literacy as large class sizes affect assessments, which have defaulted in the majority of institutions to multiple choice tests often supported by publishers, as collateral instructor materials available gratis with a professor's adoption of a textbook. The textbook adoption secures revenue for the publisher; the PowerPoint presentations, text banks and media reduce the workload on the professor, but the reduced instructor connection to both curriculum and student engagement limits the learning experience of the student. Given the significance of economic literacy, the costs of limited tangibility exceed the period of classroom instruction and stretch into the lifetime experience of the former student. Though the same may be said of other introductory courses across disciplinary areas, there is a direct and universal relationship between the teaching of economics and daily lifetime interaction in the economic system. Economic literacy is fostered by introductory economics and may be satisfied with these courses as well depending on the tangibility established by instruction. As early as 1938 Beach noted,

It has been the policy of many teachers of economics that beginners in economic theory should be taught only one theoretical explanation of each phenomenon. These teachers feel that the acquaintance of the student with other explanations can be postponed until the student has become more familiar with economics in general and therefore has a better sense of judgment... Perhaps the most important job of the teacher in social sciences is to develop the students' power of discernment. The students must learn that one idea does not contain the whole truth; and when this is learned, the students' progress will be more rapid (515).

This chapter highlights the pre and post COVID-19 teaching experience related to the teaching of introductory Economics. The discussion focuses on the immediate change in education delivery and its impact on instructor time demands. Related to this is the shift in the scrutiny of instruction as well impact to tenure and promotion. Further, given the breadth of educational delivery as well as the forced legitimacy now conveyed to distance learning, addressed is the potential for a more permanent shift in the role of the instructor that can include both remote and hybrid platform teaching. Though there is a significant push on the part of some university administrations to re-engage in traditional classroom instruction, COVID-19 may have established a permanent risk, as well as highlighted an opportunity, that may affect longer-term instructional delivery and perceptions of teaching in Higher Education.

TEACHING PRINCIPLES OF ECONOMICS: A BRIEF HISTORICAL REVIEW

The teaching of Principles of Economics from the instructor perspective offers the benefit of both guaranteed enrolment and consistency in course preparation. For most universities and colleges Principles courses are typically associated with distribution requirements for graduation. Given that Principles involves a standardized curriculum, there is limited preparation time for a routinely assigned instructor. Further, as enrolments establish profit in servicing the course, instructors have the benefit of receiving routine communications from textbook representatives offering products to assist in the noted limited preparation with additional perks such as lecture PowerPoint presentations, short tutorial videos for student study preparation, test question banks and interface with increasing standard use of educational delivery platforms such as Moodle, Blackboard, and Canvas.

The delivery of Principles courses has been heterogeneous due to enrolment caps and delivery variations across universities and colleges specific to enrolment limitations. As early as 1969, at the University of Illinois given high enrolments, course lectures were taped and delivered asynchronously as well as independent of directed instruction (Paden and Moyer, 1969; McConnell and Lamphear,1969). Though not necessarily an ideal learning vehicle for students, research highlighted student retention and performance in Principles was correlated with live course attendance (Schmidt, 1983; Romer, 1993; Durden and Ellis, 1995), the asynchronous format was congruous with a sensitivity to the workload of Principles on the instructor (Kelly, 1977).

With respect to the curriculum delivery side of instruction irrespective of live, taped, or instructor independent course offering (completely computerized), in 1988 Boskin noted that textbook dependence in Principles courses was leading to retention issues in students, as instructors defaulted to credible titles more readily than assessing the value of content. One example is specific to the increased use of graphs in texts, resulting in greater instruction with graphs, both of which were noted to not increase student understanding or retention of Principles curriculum (Cohn, Balch, and Bradley, 2001). For courses where course delivery was taped this attribution affected both student performance as well as student evaluation of the instructor (Becker and Watts, 1999). The latter of which impacted the instructor directly and highlights an incentive to increase tangibility of curriculum independent of a text.

In 1999, Vachris noted concern on the part of economics faculty given the introduction of online teaching. Discussing the experience at Christopher Newport University, where online instruction had been adopted in 1993, Vachris highlighted the challenges of online teaching:

Instead of developing a set of lectures that need only minor updating each semester, as in a classroom section, the online instructor must carefully devise new assignments each semester through which the students discover the concepts for themselves. The same assignments cannot be used over and over again, like successful lectures, because these assignments are graded. Just as a classroom instructor would not use the same midterm exam each semester, an online instructor would not use the same assignments (301).

Vachris' example addresses a situation where online instruction is not automated and the instructor provides a hands-on approach to the learning and engagement with students. The course, though asynchronous, includes assignment deadlines, course discussion with the instructor and fellow students, as well as tests but is accessible 24 hours a day and seven days a week. Allgood, Walstad, and Siegfried (2015) add to the discussion on the impact to instructors. Acknowledging that the instruction of economics has been significantly skewed to an assessment of students, the authors highlight the impact of online instruction on instructors is distributed from concerns related to job security in relation to fully automated online instruction, to heightened workload due to around the clock access and communication related to student engagement. Like Vachris there is an awareness that online instruction may lead to substitution from traditional full-time faculty to use of adjuncts, potentially modifying employment security within Higher Education.

PANDEMIC INITIATED UNIVERSAL REMOTE TEACHING

In March 2020, the COVID-19 pandemic created tremendous uncertainty and heightened health related risk and liability at U.S. universities and colleges. Literally overnight, these institutions required in-person instruction to migrate to remote learning. Depending on the institution, the channel of remote learning could have been synchronous or asynchronous with reliance on active instructor engagement dependent on the instructor's facility and interest in remote learning instruction. For many instructors who may not have used virtual learning platforms, such as Moodle, Blackboard, or Canvas, as part of their course delivery, the migration was a significant challenge. For others, the adjustment, at least with respect to content delivery was eased. The universal challenge, however, was in testing and deadline-based assessments. Further and related, for institutions with international students or students in different time zones, the instructor was now challenged to account for these variables.

Specific to Principles courses, where instruction may have involved low to no additional preparation in the past, remote learning required greater engagement with at minimum set-up of the delivery, along with the complexity of remote engagement with large classes. As noted by Leshchinskaya and Piani (2020), "Instructors spend a significant amount of time preparing for their courses well in advance of the start of instruction: they develop instructional materials, create student engagement activities, and construct course-appropriate assessments. According to online learning specialists, preparation of a semester-long course for online instruction using a learning management system takes at least three months; many instructors had just days to prepare." At the same time, instructors wishing to maintain an in-person style course were forced to revise the curriculum and add more interpersonal connection through the use of Zoom, Microsoft Teams or other video-conferencing based course meetings. Technology brought both the instructor and the student into a shared virtual environment that also included their living environments.

From a teaching perspective, the more intimate setting of remote engagement signaled an opportunity to align with Ramsett, Johnson, and Adams, who noted back in 1974 that a "primary course in economics cannot hope to teach students all they need to know about economics. It may make more sense to cover less subject matter and pursue more alternative learning activities, many of which may appear hazy for their immediate relevance to an economic principle, but might be very clear as to their effect" (83). Consistent with this reasoning, Zhang and Ramse (2021) highlight the potential for the pandemic to offer a real time engagement opportunity to increase the tangibility of the economics curriculum.

In spite of the potential opportunities, the stress of the migration on both students and faculty did affect learning outcomes and satisfaction. These were observed in student evaluations, which anecdotally and specific to Northeastern University were comparable on a mean basis to prior semesters but had a wider range, signaling a polarization between highly satisfactory and poor outcomes. As a result of the challenge faced by online migration, evaluations though collected were left to the discretion of the instructor with respect to use for tenure and promotion; similar actions were taken at other institutions (Lederman, 2020; Leshchinskaya and Piani, 2020).

Following the Spring of 2020, given the continuation of the pandemic, course offerings for Summer were also migrated online and this continued for a majority of institutions into the Fall, and then Spring of 2021. Presently given the flexibility and also the investment in the building-out of remote instruction, some institutions are considering the potential to maintain some proportion of course delivery through remote channels post COVID-19.

As in other business entities, remote instruction reduces overhead expenses, essentially shifting the cost to the instructor. To the extent that remote delivery does not adversely impact enrolment, the cost shifting could increase financial returns to institutions of Higher Education. However, this will likely not result in increases in instructor salary, as the remote environment may increase competition in instruction and further shift employment toward flexibilization in the form of adjuncts in lieu of full-time benefits paid instructors (Newton, 2018). This may further the divide in education quality as adjuncts may have high workloads in order to be able to create a living wage. Additionally, universities who have the financial capacity through endowments and enrolment may be able to maintain full-time instruction at a higher rate, increasing the divide in education quality across institutions and the quality of education based on access to income or income substitutes (i.e. scholarships, financial aid). There is some counter-speculation, however, that movement to remote teaching could increase the accessibility of Higher Education, independent of quality (Taparia, 2020), not least through providing a mechanism for individuals, such as those with caring responsibilities or disabilities, to engage in Higher Education without this necessitating availability at specific times or locations.

CASE STUDY: PANDEMIC REMOTE TEACHING

In March 2020, four weeks before the end of the Spring semester, Northeastern University made a decision to transition to fully online instruction delivery due to the emerging and uncertain health risks related to COVID-19. The transition was announced and simultaneously students were notified that University housing would be closed by the end of the week. The forced evacuation of the campus created challenges for all members of the campus community and as a result, class meetings were cancelled for two days in order to assist the transition for both students and instructors.

In the transition to the online environment it was assumed that courses would maintain synchronous delivery with original scheduled class meetings. Faculty were asked to set Zoom access links for the remainder of the semester for both class meeting times and office hours. This presented one of two significant technology and access hurdles as not all faculty were familiar with Zoom and not all faculty had access beyond the free access limited to 40 minutes by Zoom. The University had to quickly establish access to Zoom for faculty so that Zoom could be active for the duration of the class, which typically was 65 minutes or longer. However, with the movement of students to both off-campus housing, and as was more prevalent back to their family home, synchronous classes became increasingly challenging. This was due to both domestic time zone differences and the significant proportion of international students whose time zones limited active participation as a result of 5 to 14-hour time differences.

Instructors were provided the option of moving courses into an asynchronous format to accommodate students. Some instructors opted to record their synchronous class sessions, while others eliminated synchronous class meetings in lieu of more reading and assignments. In my case, I opted for a full asynchronous format and used additional documentary films to supplement the lack of lecture interaction. I maintained open office hours and sent daily emails to maintain my connection with my class. However, given that the course had started in an in-person format and transitioned abruptly to a completely remote learning environment, there was a significant challenge related to the uncertainty of the impact of the transition on the performance and assessment of performance from the instructor and student perspective, respectively. This challenge affected the class dynamic as did the lack of interaction resulting from the asynchronous delivery. Students were for the most part sympathetic to the challenges and refrained from commenting on these as negative course attributes in their course assessments.

During the same period, the University in recognition of the challenge in using Zoom and Blackboard as separate systems in the remote learning environment hastened a pre-existing transition to Canvas, which had Zoom as an integrated feature. By the end of the Spring 2020 semester, Summer courses were transitioning to Canvas but given the challenges noted in synchronous delivery were scheduled for asynchronous deployment. Though asynchronous delivery eliminated classroom teaching demands, it did not reduce course preparation time. Instead time spent on course development increased due to a need to ensure that standalone materials were understood and explained with the aid of written and taped explanations. Additionally, group work required additional facilitation and intervention to ensure participation of group members who may be distributed across time zones. To facilitate the learning experience and proactively limit these challenges, I set up one-on-one meetings with each student in my Summer classes to ensure their comfort in communicating with me. I then set up meetings for groups and weekly open office hours.

Summer classes are seven weeks in length compared to the 14-week duration of the standard semester. In effect, Summer term classes are compressed. My concern related to the asynchronous format was whether or not my students would be able to be sufficiently self-directed based on the revisions in the curriculum that made their learning independent from a live delivery from me. My concerns were eliminated by the exit surveys, which mimicked responses from pre-COVID-19 course administration. One student noted, "There are many takeaways that I can discuss in detail, but I believe one of the most important was how economic growth metrics do not account for pressing issues we face today." Another stated, "As mentioned above, my biggest takeaway is the flawed nature of our desire for GDP-based growth. This course has encouraged me to consider other factors that are more tightly correlated to a higher quality of life and sustainability." This was reinforced by another student who stated, "Our current economic system needs re-evaluation as to how it measures economic growth. Our education system should also re-evaluate how economics is taught to students. More schools of thought should be taught in the curriculum, and the economics of sustainability should be emphasized." The exit survey of yet another student reinforced the comments of Beach (1938), "In general, I never tend to question principles that I have been taught in school. But this course was eye opening in that not everything they teach you is necessarily 'right' or the best." Economics is not absolute, but a discipline based in context (Earle *et al.*, 2017).

Following the Summer session, the University devised a student-centric hybrid delivery system, which provided students with the option to attend live class sessions in the traditional classroom, opt for Zoom, or combine both. The University interpreted students' desire to be on campus as equatable to student desire to be in class. This perception was tested in the Fall as was the technology to enable a virtual classroom experience when the instructor was in the classroom and the student could be also in the classroom or remote on Zoom. Based on live class attendance, it became evident that students were more aligned to independence in living conditions in their desire to return to campus from their homes (Mishori, 2020). Though 90 percent of students were reported by University officials to have returned to Boston for the semester, significantly less than that proportion physically attended class. In other words, the overwhelming majority joined class via Zoom. Given the requirements to wear a mask at all times while on campus, instructors opting for on the ground delivery were observable to their students via classroom cameras that were physically distanced so as to be able to include the white board. Given that in-classroom computers did not have cameras, students were only able to view on-the-ground instructors in this limited manner. In the event that an instructor supplemented classroom video with personal laptop Zoom access, students were only able to see the instructor's head from above the portion covered by a mask, though they were able to fully see one another.

In my classes, less than 10 percent of students physically joined the classroom. The inefficiency of accommodating the duality of in-class and Zoom with the technology provided became evident fairly quickly. In addition, with the limited expression-based engagement with my students given my mask, I was limited in promoting class discussion; small group discussions were non-inclusive as Zoom breakout sessions challenged the randomized participation of in-classroom course members. All class member discussions were similarly challenged by having the two platforms. In an effort to promote efficiency, I moved my course delivery to online-only on Zoom. However, though I was now able to establish breakout rooms and interact with my students much more seamlessly in moving through different media from PowerPoint to video, I discovered how the video opt-out feature on Zoom could mask course participation. This latter aspect was extremely challenging initially and at the start of the term I thought that the issue could have been limited by a University mandate for cameras to be on if accessing classes remotely. As I started my one-on-one meetings with all my students based on the same process used in the Summer, I found that in many cases cameras remained off due to environmental reasons, such as younger siblings and limited privacy. It became clear that a mandatory rule may be discriminatory and even potentially an invasion of privacy.

As the semester progressed, I began to notice a polarization in my classes. Though the majority of students maintained a high operating standard, some started to fall behind in their assignments. In my outreach with those students, I found a common basis, depression (Czeisler et al., 2020). Students were increasingly noting that, much like the experience of many home-based remote workers discussed elsewhere in this book, the lack of physical interaction was resulting in a sense of isolation, loneliness, and uncertainty related to their future. Though I tried to increase my individual communications this did not assist. The desire to be around other students, though not witnessed in on the ground participation was stated in the course exit survey. Two students noted that though beyond my control, the class could have been better if it was in-person.

Whether the depression exhibited by a few students was brought on or exacerbated by COVID-19 requires an assessment of the baseline level of depression reported before COVID-19 compared to the incidence of depression reported following. The expectation would be for an increase in depression but with a rationale for the increase being different from that stated in the baseline group. In other words, the depression would be expected to be circumstantially driven rather than related to pre-existing conditions. Additionally, COVID-19 attributed depression would be expected to increase with successive semesters of forced remote learning. However, this speculation is limited without data to evaluate.

The remote learning experience has overall increased interaction with students, and increased time devoted to instruction, office hours, and Department meetings. Where I would have had an opportunity to travel and cancel class to attend a conference, I now go directly from a conference to class without a break. Overall, the work-life balance from remote teaching has increased work and only superficially added to "life" in that work is now performed at home where "life" previously had dominated. At the same time, uncertainty related to enrolment has resulted in a University freeze on wage increases for the past 18 months. Presently, faculty remain uncertain with respect to the future of course delivery and the University has signaled the potential to maintain remote course delivery in conjunction with in-class instruction going forward.

REMOTE LEARNING LESSONS

In the U.S. we are presently in the adjustment phase related to COVID-19. To some extent confusion related to risk resulting from COVID-19 stems from the inconsistency in domestic approach to COVID-19 safety protocols. While Massachusetts made it a requirement to wear a mask (NBC Boston, 2020), Georgia did not (CBS, 2020). Even on the national level, the sitting President did not wear a mask, even after contracting the virus, while the President-elect was not without it unless he was at a speaking engagement (BBC News, 2020). As a result, the convergence to a common perception and behavior toward pandemic precautions has taken a relatively long time and is presently speculated as being related to exercise of individual rights without responsibility to the greater society, incidence of COVID-19 transmission is expected to increase, along with death rates.

From a remote learning perspective, the continued unknowns related to COVD-19 signal that there is a need to develop technologies that are more learner focused than content access driven. In other words, access to information is a necessary but not sufficient learning mechanism. There is both a social element to learning as well as explanatory requirements that pre-taped, non-interactive media cannot address, which is also the case for written material. Studies related to distance and hybrid learning models were conducted pre-pandemic, meaning that participation in these learning environments has some aspect of choice. These same learning channels have ceased to be options as COVID-19 has limited the traditional course delivery on the ground, in-class meetings; making these past evaluations less relevant explanatory tools for the present situation.

Irrespective of the basis of the current remote and hybrid condition, content delivery needs to incorporate a multi-channel communication perspective. Some students can and do adjust due to their preference for independent learning experiences and similarly may be more comfortable writing on discussion forums than speaking in class (Tichavsky et al. 2015), others may not. Some students may struggle with self-motivation (Hunt, 2018). Research has correlated perceived teaching presence with greater student engagement with the curriculum as well as overall satisfaction from the learning experience (Maples and Taylor). Other studies have noted that increasing peer-to-peer opportunities can enhance the remote learning environment and enable stronger motivation (Clark-Ibáñez and Scott, 2008). And still other studies emphasize tailoring a learning environment to a learner's learning style (Xiao and Rahman, 2017). In all of these assessments there is a presumption that the learner is aligned to learning and is an active participant looking to maximize his or her learning. As a result, fostering the learning environment presupposes the desire to learn. To the extent that teaching and teaching evaluations are used in tenure and promotion, the complexity of education delivery needs to be considered by the instructor and is ultimately a new time-intensive challenge.

Perhaps in a live on-the-ground learning environment, the desire to learn, where weak, may be supplemented by classroom interaction and therefore not as easily discernable through a failure to participate as displayed in a COVID-19 prompted learning environment. Therefore, the issue related to remote delivery is in both ensuring engaging curriculum that provides simulated interaction and also routine peer-to-peer engagement that serves to motivate students at high-risk for depression or loss of motivation. To mitigate depression and loss of interest, there is a need to foster greater understanding of individual student learning motivations, which may actually enhance the direct contact between teacher and learner and directly enhance the learning experience for these individuals. Given that the future of instruction is inherently tied to the welfare of the student, issues related to course delivery are inherently issues related to instructor satisfaction, advancement, and job security.

CONCLUSION: HIGHER EDUCATION POST COVID-19

It remains unknown whether the post COVID-19 environment will see a return to previous routines or a new normal (Scudellari, 2020). Though some expectations are that an inherent risk aversion may become integrated in social interaction, others speculate that as long as personal contact increases, there should be limited long-term impact in social behavior as a result of pandemic precipitated social isolation. There will likely be a return to widespread use of in-person classes in Higher Education although the nature and frequency of these classes may well differ from pre-COVID-19 models. While there is ambiguity with respect to some aspects of COVID-19, there are aspects of the pandemic that have had universal appeal, including some of the benefits presented by working, and indeed learning, from home (Jones, 2020; O'Connor, 2020). People who are not burdened by the lack of livelihood security caused by the pandemic, have shared the benefits of not having a daily commute and the greater work-life balance, as a result (Farrer, 2020). Others, however, have reported increased workloads leading to work-life conflict. Benefits can also be realized by employers who can save in overhead, and in reported greenhouse gas emissions by increasing remote work opportunities. Further for some employers remote work environments staggered across employees can be included in longer term resiliency planning.

In summary, COVID-19 has created forced adoption of virtual interaction that has catalyzed the development of communications tools, promoted the social good in development of technologies that can adapt to individual needs, and reduced the greenhouse gas footprint while providing more people with the opportunity to engage with their environment both at home and with the world at large. This latter attribute may establish a stronger identification of work to well-being rather than income alone, and thereby transition the incorporation of qualitative attributes in assessment of economic status.

In the context of Higher Education, going forward, the capacity building resulting from COVID-19 is likely to drive teaching toward the adoption of a hybrid or selectively remote model, providing greater flexibility, efficiency, and a more personalized instruction process (Hill and Fitzgerald, 2020). Given that occupational work may also include remote attributes, use of a hybrid platform will be consistent with the use of this technology across the economic system. Therefore, students will not only have hybrid access as a tool for curricular instruction but also as a learning and preparatory tool for employment. In this manner as displayed in Figure 1, the technological advances in communication tools to promote virtual interaction, will themselves become a pervasive tool that in spite of limiting direct human contact may indeed increase the regularity and efficiency of human interaction, albeit virtual, due primarily to on-demand, real-time capacity (Vegas and Winthrop, 2020).

Figure 1. Technology Fostered Remote Engagement in Education
Source: Vegas and Winthrop, 2020

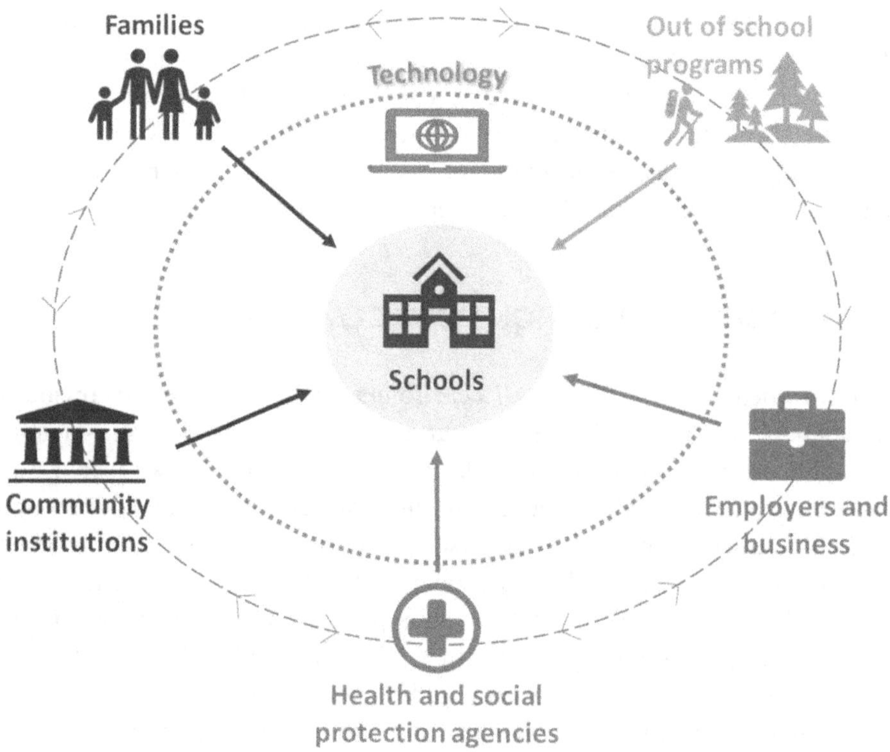

There are a number of questions which remain unanswered, including if human interaction will be reduced as a result of technology, and in this event, the impact of reduced human interaction on emotional well-being and health. As per the case study presented in this chapter, one of the greatest concerns of reduced face-to-face interaction remains around the potential for social isolation and associated impacts on mental health. This was reported by Higher Education students in my Principles of Economics course and has been a feature of much of the evidence on remote working generated since the beginning of the pandemic. A second concern relates to the impact on motivation and in turn, performance, whether it be the motivation of a student studying a Principles course, an instructor preparing and delivering the course, or indeed a worker engaged in all number of other occupations. In addition, if technology use further distances individuals from the natural environment, this may impact policies and protections related to environmental protection as the natural world is obscured by virtual delivery. Further, if the economic and social system does transition to having greater technological dependence (Jing et al., 2018), this may increase societal vulnerability due to a heightened dependence on energy and on an individual level may result in health related vulnerabilities resulting from the direct impact of technology on the functioning of the human body (Chang et al., 2015; Primack et al., 2017; Rosen et al., 2014).

REFERENCES

Allgood, S., Walstad, W., & Siegfried, J. (2015). Research on Teaching Economics to Undergraduates. *Journal of Economic Literature*, *53*(2), 285–325. doi:10.1257/jel.53.2.285

BBC News. (2020, May 27). *Trump and Biden trade barbs over wearing a mask*. Retrieved from https://www.bbc.com/news/av/world-us-canada-52828602

Beach, E. (1938). Teaching Economics. *The American Economic Review*, *28*(3), 515–515.

Becker, W., & Watts, M. (1999). How Departments of Economics Evaluate Teaching. *The American Economic Review*, *89*(2), 344–349. doi:10.1257/aer.89.2.344

Becker, W. E. (2000). Teaching Economics in the 21st Century. *The Journal of Economic Perspectives*, *14*(1), 109–119. doi:10.1257/jep.14.1.109

Boskin, M. (1988). Observations on the Use of Textbooks in the Teaching of Principles of Economics. *The Journal of Economic Education*, *19*(2), 157–164. doi:10.1080/00220485.1988.10845254

Boston, N. B. C. (2020 May 4). *What to Know About Massachusetts' Mandatory Mask Order*. Retrieved from https://www.nbcboston.com/news/local/what-to-know-about-massachusetts-mandatory-mask-order/2117445/

Bowles, S., & Carlin, W. (2020). What Students Learn in Economics 101: Time for a Change. *Journal of Economic Literature*, *58*(1), 176–214. doi:10.1257/jel.20191585

CBS. (2020 July 16). *Georgia governor bans cities from ordering people to wear face masks*. Retrieved from https://www.cbsnews.com/news/georgia-governor-brian-kemp-bans-city-face-mask-orders-coronavirus-pandemic/

Chang, A. M., Aeschbach, D., Duffy, J. F., & Czeisler, C. A. (2015). Evening use of light-emitting eReaders negatively affects sleep, circadian timing, and next-morning alertness. *Proceedings of the National Academy of Sciences of the United States of America*, *112*(4), 1232–1237. doi:10.1073/pnas.1418490112 PMID:25535358

Clark-Ibáñez, M., & Scott, M. (2008). Learning to Teach Online. *Teaching Sociology*, *36*(1), 34–41. doi:10.1177/0092055X0803600105

Cohn, E., Cohn, S., Balch, D., & Bradley, J. Jr. (2001). Do Graphs Promote Learning in Principles of Economics? *The Journal of Economic Education, 32*(4), 299–310. doi:10.1080/00220480109596110

Czeisler, M. E., Lane, R. I., Petrosky, E., Wiley, J. F., Christensen, A., Njai, R., Weaver, M. D., Robbins, R., Facer-Childs, E. R., Barger, L. K., Czeisler, C. A., Howard, M. E., & Rajaratnam, S. (2020). Mental Health, Substance Use, and Suicidal Ideation During the COVID-19 Pandemic — United States, June 24–30, 2020. *Weekly, 69*(32), 1049–1057. Retrieved from https://www.cdc.gov/mmwr/volumes/69/wr/mm6932a1.htm#suggestedcitation

Durden, G., & Ellis, L. (1995). The Effects of Attendance on Student Learning in Principles of Economics. *The American Economic Review, 85*(2), 343–346.

Earle, J., Moran, C., Ward-Perkins, Z., & Haldane, A. (2017). Economics as indoctrination. In *The econocracy: The perils of leaving economics to the experts* (pp. 34–59). Manchester University Press.

Farrer, L. (2020 May 12). The New Normal Isn't Remote Work. It's Better. *Forbes*. Retrieved from https://www.forbes.com/sites/laurelfarrer/2020/05/12/the-new-normal-isnt-remote-work-its-better/?sh=116d38c62405

Flaherty, C. (2017). What are students rating when they rate instructors? *Inside Higher Ed*. Retrieved from https://www.insidehighered.com/news/2017/05/10/study-student-ratings-instructors-dependent-discipline-quantitative-fields-are-most

Hill, K., & Fitzgerald, R. (2020). Student perspectives of the impact of COVID-19 on learning. *All Ireland Journal of Higher Education, 12*(2). Retrieved from https://ojs.aishe.org/index.php/aishe-j/article/view/459

Hunt, A. (2018). Pedagogical Techniques for Creating a Community of Inquiry in Online Learning Environments. In M. Kozimor-King & J. Chin (Eds.), *Learning from Each Other: Refining the Practice of Teaching in Higher Education* (pp. 27–39). University of California Press.

Jin, L., Duan, K., & Tang, X. (2018). What Is the Relationship between Technological Innovation and Energy Consumption? Empirical Analysis Based on Provincial Panel Data from China. *Sustainability, 10*(2), 145. doi:10.3390u10010145

Jones, S. (2020 March 31). Coronavirus forced me to slow down and spend more time with my family — and I'm grateful | Solomon Jones. *The Philadelphia Inquirer*. Retrieved from https://www.inquirer.com/health/coronavirus/coronavirus-covid-19-family-isolation-20200331.html

Kelly, A. (1977). Teaching Principles of Economics: The Joint Council Experimental Economics Course Project. *The American Economic Review, 67*(1), 105–109.

Lederman, D. (2020). Evaluating Teaching During the Pandemic. *Inside HigherEd*. Retrieved from https://www.insidehighered.com/digital-learning/article/2020/04/08/many-colleges-are-abandoning-or-downgrading-student-evaluations

Leshchinskaya, I., & Piani, C. (2020). *Student Evaluation of Teaching: COVID-19 Considerations for Validity and Fairness*. Liberal Education Blog. Association of American Colleges and Universities. Retrieved from https://www.aacu.org/blog/student-evaluation-teaching-covid-19-considerations-validity-and-fairness

Maples, J. N., & Taylor, W. V. (2013). Writing Children's Books in Sociology Class: An Innovative Approach to Teaching Social Problems to Undergraduate Students. *International Journal on Teaching and Learning in Higher Education*, *25*(3), 1–11.

McConnell, C., & Lamphear, C. (1969). Teaching Principles of Economics without Lectures. *The Journal of Economic Education*, *1*(1), 20–32. doi:10.1080/00220485.1969.10845293

Mishori, R. (2020 August 29). Despite pandemic, some college students want to be on or near campus. Here are ways for them to reduce their risks. *The Washington Post*. Retrieved from https://www.washingtonpost.com/health/covid-going-to-college/2020/08/28/517f18a0-e6ee-11ea-97e0-94d2e46e759b_story.html

Newton, D. (2018). Study: Online College Classes Cost Less To Deliver Because They Are Larger, Hire Cheaper Teachers. *Forbes*. Retrieved from https://www.forbes.com/sites/dereknewton/2018/05/23/study-online-college-classes-cost-less-to-deliver-because-they-are-larger-hire-cheaper-teachers/?sh=8a394ad53797

O'Connor, E. (2020 March 23). Yes, there is panic. But I'm embracing a slower life. *The Washington Post*. Retrieved from https://www.washingtonpost.com/lifestyle/2020/03/23/yes-there-is-panic-im-embracing-slower-life/

Paden, D., & Moyer, M. (1969). The Relative Effectiveness of Three Methods of Teaching Principles of Economics. *The Journal of Economic Education*, *1*(1), 33–45. doi:10.1080/00220485.1969.10845294

Primack, B. A., Shensa, A., Sidani, J. E., Colditz, J. B., Radovic, A., & Miller, E. (2017), Social Media Use and Perceived Social Isolation Among Young Adults in the U.S. *American Journal of Preventative Medicine*. Retrieved from https://www.ajpmonline.org/article/S0749-3797(17)30016-8/fulltext

Rai, A., & Sharma, N. (2016). Teaching versus research in higher education institutes: Revisiting the issue. *Current Science*, *111*(10), 1585–1586.

Ramsett, D., Johnson, J., & Adams, C. (1974). An Interinstitutional Study of Student Attitudes Towards Principles of Economics. *Journal of Experimental Education*, *42*(3), 78–85. doi:10.1080/00220973.1974.11011482

Romer, D. (1993). Do Students Go to Class? Should They? *The Journal of Economic Perspectives*, *7*(2), 167–174. doi:10.1257/jep.7.3.167

Rosen, L. D., Lim, A. F., Felt, J., Carrier, L. M., Cheever, N. A., Lara-Ruiz, J. M., Mendoza, J. S., & Rokkum, J. (2014). Media and technology use predict ill-being among children, preteens and teenagers independent of the negative health impacts of exercise and eating habits. *Computers in Human Behavior*, *35*, 364–375. doi:10.1016/j.chb.2014.01.036 PMID:25717216

Schmidt, R. M. (1983). Who Maximizes What? A Study in Student Time Allocation. *The American Economic Review*, *73*(2), 23–28.

Scudellari, M. (2020 August, 5). How the pandemic might play out in 2021 and beyond. *Nature*. Retrieved from https://www.nature.com/articles/d41586-020-02278-5

Sheridan, B., Hoyt, G., & Imazeki, J. (2014). A Primer for New Teachers of Economics. *Southern Economic Journal*, *80*(3), 839–854. doi:10.4284/0038-4038-2013.054

Taparia, H. (2020 March 25). The Future of College Is Online, and It's Cheaper. *The New York Times*. Retrieved from https://www.nytimes.com/2020/05/25/opinion/online-college-coronavirus.html

Tichavsky, L., Hunt, A. N., Jicha, K., & Driscoll, A. (2015). It's Just Nice Having a Real Teacher: Student Perceptions of Online Versus Face-to-face Instruction. *International Journal for the Scholarship of Teaching and Learning*, *9*(2). Advance online publication. doi:10.20429/ijsotl.2015.090202

Vachris, M. (1999). Teaching Principles of Economics without "Chalk and Talk": The Experience of CNU Online. *The Journal of Economic Education*, *30*(3), 292–303.

Vegas, E., & Winthrop, E. (2020). Beyond reopening school: How education can emerge stronger than before COVID-19. *Brookings*. Retrieved from https://www.brookings.edu/research/beyond-reopening-schools-how-education-can-emerge-stronger-than-before-covid-19/

Xiao, L., & Rahman, S. (2017). Predicting learning styles based on students' learning behaviour using correlation analysis. *Current Science*, *113*(11), 2090–2096. doi:10.18520/cs/v113/i11/2090-2096

Zhang, C., & Ramse, J. (2021). Teaching economics behind the global COVID-19 pandemic. *International Review of Economics Education*, *36*, 1–10. doi:10.1016/j.iree.2020.100206

Chapter 6
Teaching Remotely During a Pandemic:
Impact of Smart-Working on Teachers' Professional Identities

Francesca Amenduni
Swiss Federal Institute for Vocational Education and Training, Switzerland

Maria Beatrice Ligorio
University of Bari, Italy

Maria Grazia Chillemi
Department of Curriculum and Evaluation, Ministry of Education, Italy

Lorenzo Raffio
https://orcid.org/0000-0001-9499-8956
Tony Blair Institute for Global Change, UK

Patrizia Giaveri
ITCTS Vittorio Emanuele II, Bergamo, Italy

Dena Markudova
Polytechnic University of Turin, Italy

Giuseppe Giliberto
Nuvolar srl, Italy

Alberto Gritti
ITCTS Vittorio Emanuele II, Bergamo, Italy

Giovanna Barzanò
Ministry of Education, Italy

ABSTRACT

This chapter presents a qualitative research project called "Oversight Points." Fifty-nine Italian teachers participated in in-depth semi-structured interviews focusing on their perceptions, grievances, and hopes about remote teaching during the COVID-19 lockdown. Interviewees belong to a national school network and share a longstanding cooperation in blended action research initiatives. The research was inspired by the teacher professional identity (TPI) theory, and dialogical self-theory (DST) was used as an analytic lens. Data was organised through Nuvolar, a software that can generate word-clouds and provide timestamps of related video-clips. Results suggest that teachers are peculiar smart-workers. For them freedom of space and time, self-improvement, and autonomy—distinctive aspects of smart-working—acquire specific meanings, implying both positive and negative aspects. A set of positionings was found. The authors discuss how they compete in determining the re-organisation of teacher identities' landscape. Finally, they indicate some possible developments and practical implications.

DOI: 10.4018/978-1-7998-6754-8.ch006

INTRODUCTION

The COVID-19 crisis was a sudden and unexpected event. School disruptions due to the pandemic have consisted, in fact, in one of the longest breaks of formal education in modern times, in many countries. Carrillo and Flores (2020) highlighted how stressful it was for teachers to adapt their teaching style to meet the expectations of students, considering also the conditions in which schools had to operate. Schools often did not have an adequate online infrastructure, teachers did not have proper training, and the conditions students had at home in terms of quality of the internet connection were not clear (Zhang et al. 2020). Judd and colleagues (Judd et al. 2020) denounced also the lack of mentoring and support, which is recognised as essential.

Within the European context, Italy does not shine for its performance in digital development. The report "Educating Digital" (AGCOM 2019) indicated that only 47% of teachers use technology in their lessons daily, only 74% of schools have internet in all classes, and only 11.3% have high speed broadband access (30Mbps at least). Yet educational policy has not totally neglected digital issues. Starting from the 1990s the attention of policy makers has focused with increasing interest on the improvement of digital literacy among teachers and students. In 2007 an important national plan for digital school was launched aimed at changing learning environments and developing digital innovation in schools but most of these initiatives only concerned small groups of schools or teachers.

While this national plan was deeply criticised for its lack of impact, in 2015 a relevant reform occurred, embodied in the detailed and long discussed act, called "La buona scuola" (The Good School). This act introduced a new role, called "digital lead", with the appointment of 8,000 new experts that had to be both digitally skilled and internal to the school, therefore familiar with its culture. Despite its smarter strategies, this act could not be defined a success, probably due to the inadequate financial investments, weak training and monitoring settings The full disruption of schools occurring in Italy in March 2020 introduced the possibility of distance teaching, which became compulsory a month later. Technology came to the fore to play a crucial role never experienced before, in that it was the only means to concretely tackle the school disruption, allowing for the continuation of the educational mission.

As many commentators observe (Franchini, 2020; Giovannella et al., 2020), teachers found themselves confronted with an enormous effort; they became smart-workers without any specific preparation and the weaknesses of the system surrounding them made their tasks even harder. Of course, it is possible to teach at a distance, however this implies a surrogacy of physical presence that hides many challenges. With this study we intended to approach teachers' stories and experiences in this particular historical moment, to explore the opportunities and challenges they met, to make sense of their adventures, inventions, perceptions and emotions in performing a new, compelling role in a context affected by long standing weaknesses.

What Does it Mean to be a Smart-worker?

Many professions are currently changing to comply with social distancing rules, and most are adopting the so-called smart-working approach. Boorsma and Mitchell (2011) define smart working as the result of an evolutionary change taking place over several different dimensions in the world of work. These changing dimensions lead to a new approach to work, work cultures, business architectures, premises, decision making, communication, and collaboration (Bednar & Welch, 2019). These cultural changes are connected to some practical issues. For instance, the place where the work is performed becomes less relevant. Smart-workers should be able to collaborate remotely, to be autonomous in taking decisions and monitoring their outcomes, to introduce innovation in their practices (Hamel, 2007) and, finally, to be flexible in terms of time and objectives (Lake, 2013). McEwan (2013) conceptualises smart-working practices as agile, dynamic, and emergent. In other words, smart-workers are able to tailor their work to the customers' needs, valuing relationships that are good for all the agents involved.

Smart-workers are individuals who approach work in a very different way compared to traditional practices and processes. They work where they want and where it is needed, they do not usually follow fixed timetables and they make extensive use of information and communication technology (ICT). It is possible to identify the specific features of a smart-worker looking at data related to movement, location, speed and direction of workers, transportation and logistics, AI-augmented tracking. An attempt in this sense was made by Moore (2020). She argues that the algorithms treating the above-mentioned data sketch two dimensions featuring smart-workers as well as the machines used for smart-working: (a) self-improvement and (b) autonomy.

As machines are capable of self-improvement, similarly human workers should be able to self-improve in their workplace. This feature refers to the "wellness syndrome" (Cederström & Spicer, 2015) that, to some extent, could be improved by specific programmes, often strictly remaining under the worker's responsibility. Autonomous machines constitute a further actor with supposed agency and autonomy from the traditional employment relationship. This leads to a profound rethinking of what human autonomy means; it should in essence consider machines as partners in their work. Nowadays, a smart-worker is expected to work directly as well as in competition with new forms of intelligent machines (Moore, 2017). In short, the following dimensions appear most relevant to define a smart-worker:

1. Freedom of place. The activity composing the professional task can be performed anywhere;
2. Freedom of time. There are no strict limitations to when tasks should be performed;
3. Self-improvement. There should be the possibility to conduct the work in the way the worker considers most effective, aiming for the best possible results;
4. Autonomy. Although new initiatives should be discussed with colleagues and managers, smart-workers should be entitled to take initiative and use all resources available to maximise their results.

In this chapter, we analyse to what extent the dimensions pertaining to smart-working could be applied to teachers and how these dimensions may impact teachers' professional identity and their evolution as a result of the recent experience of enforced remote teaching.

Smart-teachers

Teachers and educators struggled with the adjustment to work and teach online (Donitsa-Schmidt, & Ramot, 2020), especially those who had always only taught in a traditional classroom setting and were asked to rapidly regroup and prepare for a longer period of educational "social distancing". Teachers and educators' difficult shift to online teaching/learning could have been predicted to some extent. For example, looking at the most recent OECD report (OECD, 2019), different issues can be observed concerning teachers' use of digital technologies in the classroom. Fewer than 60% of teachers were taught how to use ICT for teaching during their formal training, and fewer than 45% felt "well" or "very well prepared". Nevertheless, less than 20% of teachers reported a high need for professional development in ICT skills for teaching (OECD, 2019).

Teachers' perception of their needs in ICT professional development clearly changed during the first lockdown in Italy. According to INAPP (Ferritti, 2021) who surveyed a sample of 548 Italian teachers, 91% of participants think they would need a specific training in online education in the future. Teachers' attitudes toward ICT professional development is probably connected to a change in their actual behaviours. Only 8.1% of teachers received training about the use of educational platforms, video-lesson design, educational apps, cloud and storing services before March 2020. During the lockdown, the percentage of teachers using digital resources reached 91.9%.

The perceived digital skills gap required teachers to activate personal, social, and contextual resources. According to the INAPP report, teachers have resorted to non-formal and informal strategies such as self-directed training through webinars and tutorials (55%), asking support from colleagues with better digital skills (25%), and school "digital leads" (25%). The central role of "digital leads" during lockdown was also reported by INDIRE[1]; indeed 61.7% of teachers think that this figure provided the most relevant support, together with the class coordinator.

Besides the skills gap, teachers in Italy also experienced technological infrastructure issues. In some cases, teachers reported that the internet connection and the number of available devices for a family were not sufficient to allow them to do their job (Ferritti, 2021). Similar and, sometimes, worse issues were faced by students and their families. Low-income families could request new hardware (e.g. tablet) through loans. However, issues relating to internet access and speed, could not be tackled. This appeared to be the main reason for students' school dropout (Ferritti, 2021). The combination of these issues could have an impact on teachers' freedom, autonomy and processes of self-improvement, the key dimensions highlighted by Moore (2017) for smart workers. We found that a specific kind of resource employed by teachers was their professional identity.

Teachers Professional Identity and Dialogical Self

The Teachers' Professional Identity (TPI) approach (Beijaard et al., 2004) contends that teachers see their professional identity as consisting of a combination of distinct aspects, such as subject matter expertise, didactic and pedagogical knowledge. The ways these aspects are related to each other are flexible and dynamic. Years of experience, the nature of their subject areas, the school context, experiential and biographical factors might influence how teachers perceive their professional identity (Beijaard et al., 2000).

Recently, Beijard and his research group (Ping et al., 2020) showed how informal situations may represent a great opportunity to modify the perception of TPI. Informal learning initiatives range from personal interest to meeting job demands. In other words, teachers feed their professional identity not only based on their teaching, but also drawing from everyday experiences, even if loosely connected to teaching. A satisfying professional identity would help teachers to face professional changes, contributing to decreasing student dropout and teacher burnout (Alsup, 2006). Teachers proved to be able to overcome crises and turning points based on the re-configuration of their professional identities (Legrottaglie & Ligorio, 2017). Given this, it is quite compelling to wonder how a disruptive situation – such as the one caused by the pandemic – is impacting the TPI.

A further analytical lens in this respect is offered by the concepts of identity positions and positioning (Davies & Harré, 2001). The Dialogical Self Theory (DST) proposed by Hermans (2001) provides a definition of identity particularly useful for educational contexts: a flexible configuration of identity positions, relatively autonomous, dynamic and never stable, in perennial dialogue among themselves. For example, the positions a teacher assumes are dependent not only on the duties required by the job, but also on contextual elements, personal views, and the interpersonal relationships internally represented. The ensemble of positions composes an identity scenario, within which the positions are spatially organised and clustered into "internal" positions - extrapolated from the explicit declination of "I am" - and "external" positions that belong to the contextual dimensions, external to the individual but yet connected to the internal positions, inferred from the conceptualizations relating to people and objects defined as "mine". Any external position is connected to one or more internal positions. For instance, in the case of a teacher's identity mindscape, external positions such as "my students" are closely connected to internal positions such as "I-as-a student at their age" and "I-as-a parent with kids at school". In determining these dynamics, contextual elements play a relevant role. The current pandemic can be considered one of those elements capable of reconfiguring the set of positions and their relationship. At the same time, identity positionings are resources that teachers could activate to face this crisis.

Main Research Objectives

The main research objective is to describe the peculiarities of being a teacher in smart working in the Italian context during the first lockdown, showing how teachers activated personal, social and contextual resources. The disruptions caused by lockdown required devising rough and speedy solutions that deserve careful observation and a deep understanding to inform future decisions. Much data collection so far has involved mainly quantitative techniques through online questionnaires (Aliyyah, et al., 2020; Giovannella et al., 2020; Silva & Sousa, 2020; Sokal et al., 2020; UNESCO, 2020). To explore the effects of the changes, we set out a participatory qualitative study "on the move" through one-to-one video-recorded interviews. Beyond simple large overviews, we were interested in unravelling some crucial emergent issues through a deep exploration of teachers' lived experiences and feelings.

Therefore, the key research questions of our project are: To what extent are teachers becoming smart-workers? Can the new methods of communication with students and colleagues be considered a dimension of smart-working? How could this affect the daily practice of educational planning and professional development? Consequently, how is this interconnected with teachers' professional identity? To start answering these questions and capture their implications, we present our research project "Oversight Points", aimed at contributing to the understanding of how remote teaching during the COVID-19 pandemic affected some crucial aspects of teachers' professional identity.

THE "OVERSIGHT POINTS" PROJECT

The "Oversight Points" project was promoted by an Italian school network called Rete Dialogues (RD), together with the University of Bari (IT). The title "Oversight Points" was chosen to highlight that the health emergency led to 'lost sight' of consolidated references and, at the same time, brought to light what previously might have been considered a negligible, marginal element: an 'oversight'. The need to communicate remotely changed the perspective on what it means to teach, and highlighted a series of novel problems and questions, as well as unexpected opportunities.

RD is a professional learning community (PLC), launched in 2010 and clustering 30 schools located in different Italian regions. Its mission is to develop and implement initiatives that promote global citizenship education, intercultural and interreligious dialogue and sustainability among teachers and students, by offering innovative professional development opportunities and organising action-research projects with a variety of partners, including scholars, publishers, social actors, etc.

RD can be considered a "professional learning community" (PLC) as it is composed by a large group of teachers, continuously seeking and sharing practices and ideas (Brodie, 2013; Skinner et al., 2014).

When the COVID-19 lockdown started, several online initiatives were launched within RD. The longstanding relationships within RD, became a resource in the new scenario. It is in this context that the need emerged among teachers to understand more deeply what they were experiencing in their new life as smart-workers, challenged by the new request of remote teaching. Teachers started to share their concerns and ways to tackle the emergency. This was the very first step of the research "Oversight Points", from which the idea developed of creating a more structured research framework to collect and interpret teachers' experiences and perceptions. The research was further developed with the University of Bari, which had already been a major partner of RD.

We adopted the action-research methodology (Mills, 2003) to explore in-depth teachers' experiences, emotions and strategies enacted to face the sudden challenges of remote teaching. More precisely, we wanted a "joint action-research project", with practitioners working side to side with academics in a sort of "atelier" where academics/researchers are perceived as co-designers who shape the notions and concepts allowing practice to gain sense and meaning and enhancing the "reflective practitioner" culture.

Interview Strategy

Peer interviews have been at the core of our research, following a carefully designed participatory approach. A team of 15 volunteer interviewers (12 teachers and three researchers) was trained to pilot a semi-structured narrative interview with their colleagues. A first outline of the interview structure was drafted by a research team that included expert researchers and a few volunteer teachers. The final guidelines included questions enabling teachers report on their "points of view", both consolidated and new, developed during their experience of smart-working. Questions focused on what teachers had experienced during the pandemic and included several themes: grievances and fears, surprises and victories, emotions, and takeaways from the experience.

There were no predefined questions, but rather clear themes articulated in a "topic guide" (Seale, 1998) provided to the interviewers. We were inspired by Holstein and Gubrium's "active interview" (1995) and by the notion of "narrative inquiry and narrative learning" (Goodson, 2013) where the interviewer tries to unravel the stories of the interviewee with their embedded feelings and emotions. The guidelines prepared for the interviewers included the following list of themes:

- *School context*: families' social background; school culture and attitudes towards innovation;
- *Tools used for remote teaching:* the school's habits in supporting the use of educational technologies; teachers' reactions to the imposition of distance education; digital divide;
- *Teacher's professional challenge*: what they were able to learn from this experience, to what extent they had to reinvent and adapt their practices; how they saw their role; how they managed to receive and give support);
- *Time management*: the changes in the rhythm of life and work; how professional and private life cohabited;

- *Spaces:* how teachers experienced the change of scenery from the classroom (conceived as a formal space) to the private space from where they connected at home; the perception of the affordances of this new digital space;
- *Relationships and emotions:* how the relationship with pupils, colleagues, and families has changed; what emotional reactions have emerged; how the lack of physical contact impacted teaching;
- *Future expectations:* what effects are expected after the experience of remote teaching; advantages and disadvantages; the impact of the pandemic on the perception of teachers' professional identity; what expectations are emerging for the future.

Teachers-interviewers were instructed to adopt a non-inductive communication style during the interviews; nevertheless, they were flexible in formulating the right questions and deciding the order of the topics, following the flow of the interaction and establishing a constructive relationship with the interviewees. Both interviewers and interviewees were involved in meaning-making work on the issues tackled during the interviews. The "Oversight Points" project originated from the desire to enable teachers to share their stories and experiences in more structured ways rather than leaving it just to informal conversations. It was intended as an opportunity to exploit the difficulties confronted during the lockdown to elicit new perspectives, enhancing teachers' professional identity and expanding the awareness of what teaching means. All interviews were conducted online, video-recorded and later transcribed.

Our Sample

The team of 12 teachers and three researchers already trained to conduct interviews was integrated with other teachers available for online interviews. The final sample, spanning different regions, consisted of 59 teachers (54 female, 5 male), 12 of which were both interviewers and interviewees. In addition, three researchers participated only as interviewers. Interviewees had different years of experience and taught different subjects at various school levels (see Table 1).

We deemed it important to involve only motivated and committed teachers, already familiar with the action-research methodology through their experience in RD. This led to a purpose sample (Silverman, 2005) of teachers committed to providing an honest and deep account of their experiences and perceptions. With respect to the aims of our project, we considered them the most reliable informants to answer our research questions, since they were highly interested in the development of the research and in its results. Teachers involved in the first step recruited other colleagues, creating a snowball effect (Breakwell et al., 2000) that allowed us to reach a large group of participants.

Table 1. Breakdown of sample composition

Region	School level	Subject	Years of experience				Total
			1-9	10-19	20-29	30+	
Northern Italy	Lower secondary	Religious Education			2		2
		Science			1		1
		Humanities		2	1	4	7
	Upper secondary	Religious Education				1 (Male)	1
		Science			1	1	2
		Humanities	2 (Male)	3	1	2	8
	Primary	General education	1	1	4	6	12
	Total		**3**	**6**	**10**	**14**	**33**
Central Italy	Lower secondary	Religious Education			1		1
		Humanities		1	1 (Male)	2	4
	Upper secondary	Religious Education				1	1
		Humanities	1(Male)	3	1	2	7
	Primary	General education			2	2	4
	Total		**1**	**4**	**5**	**7**	**17**
Southern Italy	Lower secondary	Science			1		1
		Humanities	1			2	3
	Upper secondary	Humanities			4	1	5
	Total		**1**		**5**	**3**	**9**
Grand total			**5**	**10**	**20**	**24**	**59**

Collecting and Analysing Teachers' Video-interviews

59 video-interviews were recorded and held remotely on Google Meet. The data collection occurred between April and June 2020, which corresponded to the first wave of the pandemic in Italy. Interviews lasted from 36 minutes to 1 hour and 37 minutes, accounting for a total of 55 hours of video recordings. Recordings were then loaded in a software called Nuvolar that transcribes the videos and offers different research tools, including providing a list of the most relevant words, calculating correlations between words' frequencies, or providing timestamps of the minutes of the interviews. Nuvolar considers the frequency of words used in a document and across a set of documents. Words receive a rank based on their importance or correlation – and this is used to produce word clouds.

Videos were analysed through a two-step process. Firstly, patterns of how words are organised within the video recordings collected were plotted by Nuvolar, which was able to trace the main topics and the connections that emerged during the interviews by creating a word cloud. The second step involved organising the cloud and introducing specific words that could be connected to the four dimensions outlined by the literature and previously described. This way, we could see how those dimensions were perceived by the teachers.

Figure 1. Word cloud of the 50 most relevant words, as presented by Nuvolar

A "Cloudy" Overview

Figure 1 shows the word cloud generated by Nuvolar based on the 59 video-interviews. This is a dynamic cloud composed of the 50 most relevant words. The size of the font provides an indication of the relevance of the words in relation to the corpus of the video-interviews. As we can see in Figure 1, the word cloud puts two macro-groups of words in the foreground:

- words related to internal, external and collective *positioning* such as "Family" (Famiglia), "Colleague" (Collega), "Parent" (Genitore), "Learner/ Student" (Alunno/Studente), "Teacher" (Insegnante) and "Group" (Gruppo);
- words related to socio-material work conditions such as "Home" (Casa), "Space" (Spazio), "Platform" (Piattaforma) and "Digital" (Digitale).

Other important words are related to the challenging moments faced by teachers, such as "Difficulty" (Difficoltà) and "Problem" (Problema).

Analysing the Video-clips

Nuvolar allowed to quickly retrieve the clips where specific topics/words were mentioned by teachers during the interviews. Figure 2 displays an example of the visualisation offered by the software. On the right, the tab shows all the times the word "space" was mentioned in one of the interviews and the corresponding timestamps. This allowed to explore in detail teachers' conceptualisations of the most relevant words throughout the interviews.

Figure 2. A screenshot from Nuvolar

These preliminary analyses provide a general idea of how the corpus is structured and what are the most relevant themes for teachers. The cloud of words created by Nuvolar is explicative of both the internal and external positions. Table 2 presents a list of internal and external positionings mentioned by teachers throughout the interviews, accompanied by demonstrative excerpts. We identified two main dimensions for the internal position: the first as a person, where emotional and personal aspects are considered; the second as a teacher, where all aspects related to teaching are included. These internal positions were sometimes presented through a temporal continuum, in which the teachers compared their past, present and future Self, highlighting the trajectories of their identity development.

Concerning internal positions, several teachers felt challenged both as individuals and as professionals. For many, teaching remotely allowed them to reveal some personal weaknesses together with unexpected personal resources, and this underlined the relevance of personal relationships in teaching. When looking at internal positions, we attempt to single out words capable of telling something about how teachers felt regarding their self-efficacy and self-improvement, which is one of the distinctive dimensions characterising smart-working. For teachers in smart-working, self-improvement meant to fill their ICT and digital skills gap. In response to teachers' newly perceived learning needs, schools provided more or less structured professional opportunities. Besides formal training, teachers extensively reported that they learned from their peers and from more experienced teachers, mostly in informal contexts.

Words like "thinking", "talking", "feeling" were often mentioned in relation to an increased perception of self-efficacy, when considering the span of time in which they taught from home. For example, one of the teachers said that she felt completely unprepared at the start of lockdown. However, she reports how progressively her feelings toward her work became more and more positive. In several excerpts she signalled a growing sense of self-efficacy, so that she finally claims "I did my best things right at the moment when I didn't know what I was supposed to do".

In regard to external positions, colleagues are often mentioned. Teachers reported several experiences of mutual support. One teacher, for instance, reported to be "proud to be a member of this community". A key role was played by more experienced teachers, such as the "digital lead". Almost all teachers highlighted how the pandemic helped to know their students in a deeper way, to see aspects of their life they would have never been able to access otherwise. They also discovered more about private aspects related to the economic conditions and emotional fragilities of their students and their families. Having to connect from their homes, students' private, personal, and family life became visible to their teachers.

Table 2. Internal and external positioning reported by teachers

	POSITIONS	EXCERPTS
INTERNAL	I-as-person	*I started to disclose myself not anymore as an adult who knows everything but as a person with fragilities*
	I-as-teacher	*I am moved and surprised by myself when I look back at the lessons that I have prepared*
EXTERNAL	My-Colleagues	*I was surprised and inspired by one of my colleagues. She wasn't able to send even an email at the beginning. But she reacted and she became an example for me*
	My-expert colleagues in technologies	*We had amazing technical support. After the first day of lockdown, our expert has already prepared a video tutorial for us*
	Students' Parents	*Parents who previously defended their children now recognise more the work of teachers*
	My-Students	*I was scared because students from other schools posted parodies of the teachers' video lessons on YouTube*
	My-Classroom	*I see peer-learning among students. This happened also in the classroom but now it is more evident*
	My-headteacher	*The headteacher delegated a lot. This was both a good and a bad thing. Initially it caused disorientation, but later allowed to draw out the teachers' potential*
	My-school/community	*I'm proud to be a member of this community*

Interesting external positions are those that could be considered indicators revealing the socio-material conditions within which teachers experienced smart-working. One of the most reported socio-material aspects mentioned by teachers was *space*. This dimension is particularly relevant, in that it is heavily connected to the concept of "freedom of space" highlighted by Moore as crucial in smart-working. The cloud produced by Nuvolar (see Figure 1) shows how words such as home and platform – obviously referring to places involved in teaching – are often mentioned by our respondents. Finding a suitable space from which to perform their online lessons was an important concern voiced by teachers.

Excerpt n.1

I always connect from different points of the house, so as not to make them bored, sometimes I would wear sunglasses, it was a fun thing. My way of operating was validated by a rapporteur during a training course on how to manage remote teaching. She stressed how among the limits of this teaching there is the fact that we only use two senses, sight and hearing, everything else does not apply. Therefore, it is essential to speak from different locations. You might position yourself in the same room, but then you should change / add objects e.g. with a different painting behind you, standing near the balcony, from where you will probably see a flower. It will make the kids think that the flower will perfume. It is necessary to try and ensure that the other senses that cannot be directly activated, at least can be stimulated.

(Upper secondary, Mathematics, 38-years' experience, Northern Italy)

This teacher shows a lot of care in setting the scene the students will see. In her words the new space for her lessons looks indeed like a performance stage. She is aware of the communicative power of the environment shown in the background. The "phenomenology" of communication in post-COVID education is an important aspect of smart-working teachers. From a socio-material perspective, both real and virtual backgrounds become important non-human actors taking part in the lesson (Barzanò et al., 2020). In the excerpt 1, we also see the different I-positioning the teacher activates to make decisions about how to structure her working space. She relies on external "experts" she respects and validates her intuition concerning the video-lesson setting. At the same time, she takes in consideration her students' psychological states, their attention span and their sensorial experience. In other words, many external positions are computing in dictating how to organize the material setting for remote teaching.

Backgrounds can also become interesting means to mark the boundary between educational tasks and private life, i.e. to distinguish the "school" space from the "personal" space. Concerning the distinction between school and personal spaces, in the following excerpt the teacher is aware of her privilege with respect to the majority of students that cannot enjoy a room in their home from where to "feel" at school.

Excerpt n.2

"I feel I am privileged. I created my space with a table 1-meter x 1 meter. In my background, I have all my diplomas. From the window, I see the sunlight and the flowers from the garden. I have decided that on this table I will not have meals. This is the working table; this is the school. When I finish my work, I have other places to live: the couch, the kitchen, and so on. Outside the working table, there is my private life. Regarding students, I have noticed that not all of them attend the lessons from their room. I usually did a viva test at lunch time, but I had to anticipate it because I noticed that parents start to prepare lunch at that time. Students feel embarrassed when their parents walk in the same room. In those moments, I feel as an "infiltrator", I feel guilty because they have to lunch later because of me. But these are my working hours!"

(Lower secondary, Humanities, 28-years' experience, Southern Italy)

In excerpt 2, we see an example regarding how a teacher defines herself and her "privileged" condition through the comparison (and the contrast) with her students. Moreover, we retrieved an intense dialogue between her internal positions, as a teacher ("these are my working hours") and as a person ("I feel as an infiltrator, guilty") and her external positioning of the students' parents ("they have to lunch later because of me"). This internal dialogue concretely affected her professional position, so that she changed the schedule of the viva test.

As shown in this excerpt, both space and time overlap and constitute fields where the need is perceived to make clear distinctions between the private and the professional. Similarly, other teachers tried as much as possible to reproduce the school schedule and, as a consequence, they did not have the opportunity to experiment the so-called "freedom of time" that seems to be a distinctive feature of smart-working. Teachers needed to devote their time in real-time online meetings with students. Moreover, they not only had to design lessons as usual, but they also had to learn how to design and redesign their educational learning paths according to the new constraints. Therefore, most teachers experienced a perception of "time-dilation", as expressed in the following excerpt.

Excerpt n. 3

"Working hours are two or three times higher than usual. When we work from school, we have a different timing. The bell rings at 1.15 pm. Then we have lunch, we rest and then we go back to work. Now, the time seems to be dilated. There is no ring of the bell, there is no fixed time-schedule. You have your whole day at disposal since you work from home. Thus, you can manage it better. Personally, I worked much more than usual. I didn't pay attention to the time, I answered messages at 3 pm or even later in the evening. I worked much more to adapt to the new reality. It wasn't a burden; it was a need."

(Upper secondary, Humanities, 20-years' experience, Southern Italy)

In this excerpt, the teacher describes how the boundary between personal and professional positions changed during the crisis, by comparing her present internal position with her past position. If in the past the "ring of the bell" helped her to divide the personal from the professional dimension, now she "didn't pay attention to the time", if it is needed. Although the teacher declared that a better time-management was possible, this excerpt is a meaningful example of how teachers did not experience much flexibility and freedom of time. This limitation was probably due to the complex network of relationships which characterises the school system. Timetables needed to be negotiated with different actors: other colleagues, students and families. Moreover, even within a range of differences, the strategies adopted by headteachers granted teachers with a certain degree of autonomy to organise their work. Headteachers behaviours towards teachers' autonomy vary. It is interesting to learn how in some cases the headteacher may to some extent subvert their role and intervene to protect teachers from the intrusiveness of uninterrupted contacts.

Excerpt n. 4

"Work time was around the clock practically. Continuous contact with colleagues, with parents... until the headteacher intervened saying: "please do not write emails on Sunday", which instead went out anyway. She even wrote an official note asking parents, students and teachers not to write emails on Saturday afternoon and Sunday... For sure being at home you are continually tempted to say "well... let's do it: I have 10 minutes to mark or prepare the lesson". Distance invaded the private space very much"

(Lower secondary, Humanities, 20-years' experience, Northern Italy)

Similarly, other teachers reported an overload of communication from parents at any time. The teacher in Excerpt 4 feels supported by her headteacher's sensitivity to the problem and by her attempt to establish clear boundaries, limiting the times when messages can be sent. Usually, communication between school actors is promoted and now the official note mentioned by the teacher highlights the paradox of the situation, when instead an official note is required to curb the amount of messages. Moreover, the invasion of personal time is further underlined when this teacher admits her difficulties in restraining herself from working on school tasks at all times. The excerpt 4 highlights a reconfiguration of the dialogical relations among different external positions, which played emergent roles during the school closure: the headteacher as a "supportive" positioning and the parents from a periphery to a central role into the school community, marked by their growth presence in the school network communications. One of the teachers (Excerpt 5), started to reflect upon the possibility to rethink her freedom of time and space when schools reopen, and she will go back to school.

Excerpt n. 5

"I would like to do at least one video-lesson per week. I can't understand why I have to carry out lessons from 8am to 2pm. I could stay at school from 8am to 1pm and provide the last hour of teaching in the afternoon, after lunch, from home by sending out a video-lesson. Our current school schedule is insane, both for teachers and students".

(Lower secondary, Mathematics, 25-years' experience, Northern Italy)

The internal position as a teacher is critical; this teacher qualifies the school schedule as insane. Anyhow, she is projecting her position already in the future and she is trying to capitalise on some of the activities (video-lessons) implemented during smart-working by proposing a mix of in-presence teaching and video-lessons broadcasted from home. Ironically enough, while teachers' working patterns seem to have become dangerously intrusive with respect to private life, "contact time" with students suffers from a troubling shrinking, as an experienced primary school teacher observes:

Excerpt n.6

"There is a tremendous shortage of time… three online sessions in a week is very little. It is only 6 hours against the 40 hours we used to have in person. We try to make it as intensive as possible, but we will never be able to fill the gap. We have to cut a lot of proposals that we used to offer, we have to stick to the essentials if we want to make sure that our children can achieve at least the lowest expected level. Meanwhile we cannot take care of individual students in such a short time, and the students cannot socialise."

(Primary, General education, 30-years' experience, Northern Italy)

The uncontrolled extension of working time and parallel scarcity of time to spend with the students seems to be imbalanced. This mirrors the difficulty teachers are having in keeping up also a healthy balance between internal positions (as a person and as a teacher) and the external positions (care for the students). In this case the teacher, despite her commitment, seems astonished when faced by the need to narrow down to the "essential", giving up the complexity of the didactic activities she is used to providing. As we discover in other parts of her interview, she makes her best with technologies and she is eager to grasp any opportunity to improve the whole management, however the novelty of the situation makes her feel lost. Time management was probably complicated by the need to balance time devoted to work, self-improvement and professional learning. Learning took more time than usual because teachers perceived a digital skills gap when they tried to extricate themselves between the various digital tools available.

Excerpt n.7

"It was very disorienting… to face all these problems with software. However, in our school we set up a training course on ICT in a week. And it was not superficial, but very detailed. Some colleagues showed talents that I didn't even imagine could exist. There was also a lot of support. The other day I was almost going to cry: I did not know how to mark my students' homework on PDF. I was desperate and at 11 pm I sent an SOS message to a colleague. She replied! At 11 pm! She was very patient and sweet, and step by step she drove me in. I found it incredible. Would I have done it? I do not know… I was exhausted, I am not sure I would have been available at that time, in that way."

(Upper secondary, Humanities, 30-years' experience, Southern Italy)

Here we see an upper secondary teacher confronting the desperation of her lack of competence when faced by the impossibility of accomplishing an important task. We see the internal positions challenged by the external ones. She sincerely admits how unaware she was of her limits and how, at the same time, she was ready to accept and appreciate support. She was won over by her colleague's generosity and she wonders to what extent she could appropriate such an external position (the one taken by her colleagues). Evidence like this gave us precious insights into several teachers' internal positions that teachers may consider to better focalize and to newly include into their identity scenario; for instance as a teacher seeking and accepting generous help. Considerations like these may inspire how to plan more effective professional development initiatives concerning technologies.

In some cases, teachers felt they were left alone with their students in attempting to manage the complexity of the pandemic. In particular, help was needed to understand the potentialities and limits of the digital tools used to reconfigure the teaching strategies and to cope with the emotional background generated especially in those students located in regions most affected by COVID-19. It is difficult to offer support when structural constraints do not allow to plan activities and share know-how. At this point we detected an interconnection between internal positions and external material positions. One of the teachers responsible for the digital strategy at her school, reports the difficulties she faced in offering her digital know-how to support colleagues.

Excerpt n.8

"For my master's degree thesis I carried out a work on digital story-telling. From that experience, I developed skills to use technologies in education. However, when I entered the classroom I realised there were no tools nor resources that let me put these skills into practice. Even if I wanted to do it, I didn't have that opportunity. During this emergency, I had the tools to realise my ideas because I worked from home and I used my own resources. I really hope that this situation will increase awareness [about technology] and I hope we will have more resources to use technologies in schools".

(Primary, General education, 10-years' experience, Northern Italy)

Again external positions connected to the material conditions are influencing internal positions, in particular about being able to put in practice the competences acquired during the training. Technology as part of the external positions allow teachers to better tackle the current challenges of knowledge. However, we found that even teachers with a positive attitude toward digital technologies were, in this case, often unable to exploit their expertise in front of structural failures.

Discussion and Conclusions

In this chapter we undertook an initial analysis of 59 teachers' video-interviews to understand whether and to what extent teachers can be considered smart-workers. After identifying the main dimensions of a smart-worker – freedom of space and time, autonomy and self-improvement - we analysed the data against these dimensions. The conceptual framework we used to explore the emergent role of teachers as smart-workers was the "Teacher Professional Identity" theory and interviews were analysed through the analytical lens of the Dialogical Self Theory, which allowed us to differentiate and later interconnect internal and external positions teachers activated to face the challenges of "smart-working teaching".

Our data showed that teachers' emergent routines and practices as smart-workers can be deeply understood only within their complex network of internal and external positions which "dialogue" within the teachers' professional selves. Time, space, self-improvement and autonomy are considered the prominent aspects of smart-working (Moore, 2017). Our study suggests that in the distant teaching performance, these dimensions follow specific patterns, due to the challenges implied in the translation into the virtual setting of the teacher-student relationship which remains extremely relevant, still rich in expectations, emotions and unexpected events. Hereby, we will describe how the four dimensions proposed by Moore appeared in our interviews. In addition, we found a fifth dimension - the relational one - as crucial to contextualize teachers' practices in smart working.

Freedom of Time

In our sample, we saw that teachers did not have many opportunities to experiment with freedom of time. This is due to different factors. Firstly, in school contexts timetables need to be negotiated with different actors; such as other colleagues, students and families. For this reason, some teachers tried to reproduce the school schedule as much as they could, with a low level of flexibility. Secondly, teachers were expected to devote a certain amount of time in synchronous online meetings. Thirdly, teachers not only had to design lessons as usual, but they also had to learn how to redesign their educational learning paths trying to accommodate their usual lessons' pace, based on physical presence, in their online teaching, where the shorter attention span requires a shrinking of time. Consequently, most of the teachers experienced a perception of "time-dilation", as they actually had to spend more time planning, because the denser the lesson the longer the planning. The interconnection between internal and external positions lead toward a "time-dilation" based on the need/wish to make themselves available not only for their students but also for colleagues and parents, at any time. We also observed a few teachers that are already reflecting on the future, considering the possibility to organise their time in a more flexible way. A good example was the case of a teacher who started to reflect upon how to capitalise on some of the activities (video-lessons) by proposing a mix of in-presence teaching and video-lessons broadcasted from home. A reflection upon how to support teachers to better manage their time would be necessary in the near future.

Freedom of Space

One of the most common topics mentioned by teachers was space. The cloud produced by Nuvolar shows how words such as home and platform – obviously referring to places involved in teaching – are often mentioned by our respondents. Due to the lockdown restrictions, everyone had to connect from home, partially limiting the freedom to work from any place. Finding a suitable space from which to perform their online lessons was an important concern voiced by teachers. Interestingly, there is significant concern for the backgrounds framing the teacher's virtual presence. It is clear that the careful choice of backgrounds, the pictures and objects appearing behind the teacher are part of the lesson planning. The DST considers materiality as part of the external positions; therefore, we see a clear focus not only on tools used to teach but also the furniture and elements composing the scenario visible online. The place and its artifacts acquire a symbolic meaning, thus becoming non-human actors (Barzanò et al, 2020). However, working from home was not always suitable for different reasons. Both teachers and students experienced infrastructural constraints with their internet connection. Secondly, whilst most of the teachers managed to structure their working spaces, some students did not have the same privilege. Teachers expressed the need to mark the boundary between educational tasks and private life, i.e. to distinguish the "school" space from the "personal" space. However, teachers became aware that some students could not enjoy a room in their home from where to "feel" at school. The awareness of how relevant these aspects are cannot be conceived in terms of freedom but rather as enriching the interaction between internal and external positions.

Self-improvement

For teachers in smart-working, self-improvement meant to fill their ICT and digital skills gap. With regards to their digital competencies, our teachers were open in admitting their weaknesses and seemed worried for the difficulty in accomplishing essential tasks when based online. At the same time, they were proud to show their strategies to find support and improve their technical skills. Many teachers relied on more experienced colleagues to overcome their fears. In several contexts, the sense of community was strengthened. Yet, in some cases, teachers' confidence in their self-efficacy was threatened as they felt helpless dealing with emergencies. Finally, we noticed that when speaking about the future, many teachers mentioned their intention to use the competencies learned during this period not only to improve teaching, but also to rethink their classroom management strategies. Concerning this dimension, the external positions to which the teachers refer to are mainly colleagues with the subsequent reinforcement of the sense of community. A condition that could be considered as extremely internal as self-improvement, turns out to be strongly based on external positions. Furthermore, we found again the temporal projection in the future which surely enriches teachers mind-scape.

Autonomy

Autonomy is often perceived as a concession of the headteachers. Therefore, depending on them, teachers experience different degrees of autonomy in organising their work. Nevertheless, this freedom was twofold. On the one hand, it allowed teachers to choose the style of teaching they considered most appropriate; on the other hand, it caused a sense of urgency that transformed the "burden" to adapt to a new reality into an inescapable "need" (see Excerpt 3). Teachers with weak digital skills had to rely on their more expert peers. Only once they achieved the basic level of competency to perform online teaching tasks, they started to act in a more autonomous way. When teachers are confident in their mastery of digital tools, they showed how at ease they felt and they appreciated the autonomous working from home, where they had better facilities than at school. Once again, a dimension attributable to internal positions - such as autonomy - is now strongly affected not only by previous experiences and feeling competent but also by external positions, first the headteachers and tools available.

Relational Dimension

This is the extra-dimension we added as featuring in our teachers' smart work. For this dimension, external and internal positions seem to be strongly interconnected. Indeed, we witnessed how the opportunity to pop in each other's private spaces improved empathy and reciprocal knowledge. The care reserved to set up the scenario visible by video reveals how important it was for teachers to give concrete signs of attention to their students. Further important issues concern the school atmosphere. Teachers underlined how an open and supportive school culture, valuing informal learning opportunities and personal initiatives - e.g. fostering one-to-one relationships or providing support for sudden needs (effective helpdesks) - was playing an important role in improving their performance. This means that they are aware the quality of the relationships they entertain depends on the school culture.

Teachers also reported how belonging to the professional learning community (PLC) of Rete Dialogues, where they could experience a long-lasting culture of sharing, made an important difference. Firstly, it had allowed them to practice relational patterns that proved to be particularly useful in the emergency context. Secondly, it made possible to design and implement training activities tailored to their needs, to interact with renowned experts they were already familiar with, and to undertake action-research activities to better understand what was happening. The PLC enters the identity scenario as a further external position. The evidence gathered through the project "Oversight Points" brought us to cross some of the landscapes of the endemic uncertainty. The voices of our teachers suggest the need to understand how to move beyond a pre-active and pre-planned schooling, toward a more collective and cooperative pattern of learning (Goodson & Schostak, 2020).

Finally, an important aspect of the way in which teachers employ smart-working is their use and perception of digital tools. Too often, there has been a lack of effective support and sensitivity with respect to their social and psychological implications. The introduction of educational technologies is a longstanding priority of the European political agenda. The Digital Education Action Plan 2021-2027 recently published by the European Commission, calls for two interrelated aspects of digital education considered as priorities. Firstly, the intention to support the widest possible deployment of digital technologies (apps, platforms, software) to improve and extend education and training. Online, distance and blended learning are specific examples of how technology can be used to support teaching and learning processes. Our research pierced the veil on many problems underpinning schools' readiness for the use of technologies ranging from teachers' digital literacy to the availability of ICT infrastructure and the scarce employment of digital tools and resources in teaching. The evidence provided by our teacher-interviewees allows us to explore the details and the inherent paradoxes of these problems. The second priority identified by the plan of the European Commission, concerns the need to equip a growing number of students with digital competencies (knowledge, skills and attitudes) to live, work, learn and thrive in a world increasingly populated by digital technologies. Our data suggests that these actions need to be accompanied by an appropriate technology culture which is still to be implemented.

FUTURE RESEARCH DIRECTIONS

The data collected through the video-interviews is very rich because the teachers composing our sample were keen to narrate their experiences. This richness has not been fully exploited in this chapter, but we believe that this exploratory study will provide some hints for further developments in both the fields of research and policymaking. We have identified some paths for potential further research:

- a deeper diachronic analysis of how teachers see the changes during the first lockdown and how these could shed light on the perspectives influencing their professional identity;
- a closer look at students' reactions, in connection to teachers coping style. Many teachers observed how traditionally high-achieving students struggled during remote learning and, conversely, how students struggling before the pandemic are now flourishing. This opens the floor to many research questions about learning needs and how school strategies should tackle them by allowing different modes of engagement and participation.
- the relevance of teachers' reciprocal support. We found that many teachers were able to overcome their fears and struggles with ICT tools based on the support received from their colleagues. New support strategies are needed to make teachers more comfortable in their relationship with technologies and promote new means of teaching. How can these strategies be enacted and under which conditions are still issues to be clarified.

From a policy-making perspective, our study highlights the importance of:

- creating new patterns of professional development, valuing observations and awareness of processes, peer exchange, and participatory approaches, such as action-research;
- investing in strengthening and expand technological infrastructures, with particular attention to selecting the most appropriate software for remote teaching;
- ensuring that well-designed structures are in place to provide quick help at the right time, expanding teachers' opportunities for teachers to learn on the job;
- promoting new cultures of visual communication through the practice and understanding its mechanisms and functioning in real contexts;
- launching initiatives that engage teachers and students in the collaborative creation of knowledge through events and objects - also digital - that can be shared.

ACKNOWLEDGMENT

We want to thank all teachers who participated in this project, both as interviewers and interviewees. This research represented an opportunity for them to reflect on issues that are close to their everyday professional life, and we are truly grateful for their commitment. We would also like to thank the company producing Nuvolar, which allowed us to use the software for free. Having this tool enabled us to explore the data in ways that would not have been possible otherwise. We hope, in return, to have provided useful insights on how to adapt the software for educational contents.

REFERENCES

Aliyyah, R. R., Rachmadtullah, R., Samsudin, A., Syaodih, E., Nurtanto, M., & Tambunan, A. R. S. (2020). The perceptions of primary school teachers of online learning during the COVID-19 pandemic period: A case study in Indonesia. *Journal of Ethnic and Cultural Studies*, *7*(2), 90–109. doi:10.29333/ejecs/388

Alsup, J. (2006). *Teacher Identity Discourse. Negotiating Personal and Professional Spaces*. Lawrence Erlbaum Associates. doi:10.4324/9781410617286

Barzanò, G., Amenduni, F., Cutello, G., Lissoni, M., Pecorelli, C., Quarta, R., Raffio, L., Regazzini, C., Zacchilli, E., & Ligorio, M. B. (2020). When the place matters: Moving the classroom into a museum to re-design a public space. *Frontiers in Psychology*, *11*, 943. doi:10.3389/fpsyg.2020.00943 PMID:32581905

Bednar, P. M., & Welch, C. (2019). Socio-technical perspectives on smart working: Creating meaningful and sustainable systems. *Information Systems Frontiers*, 1–18. doi:10.100710796-019-09921-1

Beijaard, D., Meijer, P. C., & Verloop, N. (2004). Reconsidering research on teachers' professional identity. *Teaching and Teacher Education*, *20*(2), 107–128. doi:10.1016/j.tate.2003.07.001

Beijaard, D., Verloop, N., & Vermunt, J. D. (2000). Teachers' perceptions of professional identity: An exploratory study from a personal knowledge perspective. *Teaching and Teacher Education*, *16*(7), 749–764. doi:10.1016/S0742-051X(00)00023-8

Boorsma, B., & Mitchell, S. (2011). *Work-life innovation smart work—A paradigm shift transforming how, where, and when work gets done*. Cisco IBSG Point of View. Accessed December 5th 2020 at https://www.cisco.com/c/dam/en_us/about/ac79/docs/ps/Work-Life_Innovation_Smart_Work.pdf

Breakwell, G. M., Hammond, S. M., & Fife-Schaw, C. (2000). *Research Methods in Psychology* (2nd ed.). Sage Publications.

Brodie, K. (2013). The power of professional learning communities. *Education as Change*, *17*(1), 5–18. doi:10.1080/16823206.2013.773929

Carrillo, C., & Flores, M. A. (2020). COVID-19 and teacher education: A literature review of online teaching and learning practices. *European Journal of Teacher Education*, *43*(4), 466–487. doi:10.1080/02619768.2020.1821184

Cederström, C., & Spicer, A. (2015). *The wellness syndrome*. John Wiley & Sons.

Davies, B., & Harré, R. (2001). Positioning: the discursive production of selves. In M. Wetherell, S. Taylor, & S. Yates (Eds.), *Discourse theory and practice*. Sage.

Donitsa-Schmidt, S., & Ramot, R. (2020). Opportunities and challenges: Teacher education in Israel in the Covid-19 pandemic. *Journal of Education for Teaching*, *46*(4), 1–10. doi:10.1080/02607476.2020.1799708

Ferritti, M. (2021). *First evidence from the web survey: Closed Schools - Open Classes*. Speech by INAPP Public Policy Innovation, at the Convocation of the Council Commission "Education Culture Youth Communication."

Franchini, R. (2020). *Una crisi da non sprecare. L'educativo digitale prima, durante e dopo il Coronavirus* [A crisis not to be wasted. Digital education before, during and after Coronavirus]. RASSEGNA CNOS.

Giovannella, C., Passarelli, M., & Persico, D. (2020). The effects of the Covid-19 pandemic on Italian learning ecosystems: The school teachers' Perspective at the steady state. *Interact. Des. Archit., 45*, 264–286.

Goodson, I., & Schostak, J. (2020). Curriculum and coronavirus: New approaches to curriculum in the age of uncertainty. *Prospects*. PMID:33424039

Goodson, I. F. (2013). *Developing Narrative Theory, Developing Narrative Theory*. Routledge.

Hamel, G. (2007). *The future of management*. Harvard Business School Press.

Hermans, H. (2001). The dialogical self: Toward a theory of personal and cultural positioning. *Culture and Psychology, 7*(3), 323–366. doi:10.1177/1354067X0173005

Holstein, J. A., & Gubrium, J. F. (1995). *The active interview* (Vol. 37). Sage. doi:10.4135/9781412986120

Judd, J., Rember, B. A., Pellegrini, T., Ludlow, B., & Meisner, J. (2020). *"This is Not Teaching": The Effects of COVID-19 on Teachers*. Accessed 05 February 2021. https://www.socialpublishersfoundation.org/ knowledge_base/this-is-not-teaching-the-effects-of-covid-19-on-teachers/

Lake, A. (2013). *Smart flexibility: Moving smart and flexible working from theory to practice*. Routledge.

Legrottaglie, S., & Ligorio, M. B. (2017). The temporal dimension as a dialogical resource for teachers' professional development and fulfillment. *Teacher Development, 21*(1), 57–80. doi:10.1080/13664530.2016.1190783

McEwan, A. (2013). *Smart working: Creating the next wave*. Routledge.

Mills, G. (2003). *Action research: A guide for the teacher researcher* (2nd ed.). Merrill/Prentice Hall.

Moore, P. (2017). *The quantified self in precarity: Work, technology and what counts*. Routledge. doi:10.4324/9781315561523

Moore, P. (2020). Who is the" smart worker"? Who should she be? *Global Labour Journal, 11*(2), 164–167. doi:10.15173/glj.v11i2.4313

OECD. (2019). *Supporting and guiding novice teachers: Evidence from TALIS 2018, Teaching in Focus, No. 29*. OECD Publishing. doi:10.1787/fe6c9c0c-

Ping, C., Schellings, G., & Beijaard, D. (2020). Understanding What, How, and Why Teacher Educators Learn through Their Personal Examples of Learning. *Education Beyond Crisis*, •••, 249–276.

Silva, O., & Sousa, Á. (2020). Perception of teachers and students about teaching and learning in the period of Covid-19 pandemic. *Proceedings of ICERI2020 Conference*, 4832–4838.

Silverman, D. (2005). *Doing Qualitative Research: A Practical Handbook* (2nd ed.). Sage Publications.

Skinner, E. N., Hagood, M. C., & Provost, M. C. (2014). Creating a New Literacies Coaching Ethos. *Reading & Writing Quarterly, 30*(3), 215–232.

Sokal, L., Trudel, L. E., & Babb, J. (2020). Canadian teachers' attitudes toward change, efficacy, and burnout during the COVID-19 pandemic. *International Journal of Educational Research Open*.

Zhang, Wang, Yang, & Wang. (2020). Suspending Classes without Stopping Learning: China's Education Emergency Management Policy in the COVID-10 Outbreak. *Journal of Risk and Financial Management, 13*(58), 1–6.

ENDNOTE

1 https://www.indire.it/2020/12/10/online-il-report-integrativo-indire-sulle-pratiche-didattiche-durante-il-lockdown/

Section 2

The Structure of Remote Work in the Post-COVID Era

Chapter 7
Redesigning Work as a Response to the Global Pandemic:
Possibilities and Pitfalls

Peter J. Holland
Swinburne University of Technology, Australia

Chris Brewster
University of Reading, UK

ABSTRACT

Job and work design are critical factors in the development and maintenance of a committed high-quality workforce. The pandemic has been the catalyst or global social experiment for people to work at home en masse encouraging employers and employees to think about how and why their jobs are being done, to develop new work and job design policies and practices. However, as well as significant benefits, there are potential pitfalls in moving 'on-line' that needs to be considered as many see this as a permanent feature of the new workplace post pandemic. This chapter explores these issues in the context of job crafting.

INTRODUCTION

Advances in (smart) information communication technologies (ICT) symbiotically interacting with globalisation and neo-liberalism have had an increasingly profound effect on forms, meanings and importance of work in the 21st century. These changes have not (directly at least) impacted some work at all, but for an increasing number of people, particularly in the most developed market economies, they are increasing their ability to craft jobs and work more flexibly in terms of time, place and space (Holland & Brewster, 2020). Harvey (2005), channelling Schumpeter (1942), identifies these changes as substantial, using the term 'creative destruction' to describe the way technology (in this we also include artificial intelligence) is fundamentally changing traditional concepts of work as equal to employment

DOI: 10.4018/978-1-7998-6754-8.ch007

and re-focusing on wider interpretations of work and how work is done. Harvey argues these changes have created an intensive burst of 'time-space compression' in the organization of work. Reinforcing this point, Maitland and Thomson (2011, 32) note:

We are on the cusp of the next big transformation in the model of work..... technology allows us to work very differently than we did .... All this points to a fresh approach to work. We are poised for a revolution in work practices.

Writing in 2020, we would argue that the impact of the global coronavirus (or COVID-19) pandemic that year became the defining point of this transformation, creating what is increasingly being called the 'new normal'. In many situations this has led to making the 'place' of work incidental to the work itself and hugely expanding the phenomenon of 'working from home' or now in common language 'WFH'. We are also seeing not just the defined space of work (the workplace) but also the defined time during which people are 'at' work melting away. Indeed, countries like Finland had already moved, just prior to the COVID-19 pandemic outbreak, to pass laws allowing for more flexible location of work, giving employees the opportunity to negotiate a significant amount of their work time away from the office. Of course, we need a caveat: for many people their place of work has not changed – if you are constructing a building or caring for children or working in a hospital, then your work has to take place where the need is. For others, the time of work has not changed – if you are in retail or emergency services, then you have to be available when the needs arise. We also note that in many countries the technology is still behind where it is in the most advanced market economies (AMEs), limiting the opportunities ICT affords. However, for many in the developed economies, and for many kinds of workers, the place, space and time at which they can work have - through the catalyst of the pandemic - become much more flexible: people are working from home or the local café, they can work, to a much greater degree, at their own pace and around work-life issues. This kind of job redesign and flexibility is what we explore in this chapter.

Invoking one of the common terms used through the pandemic – 'never waste a crisis' - this (forced) social experiment conducted on millions of workers and managers moving *en masse* to the virtual workplace has created a new paradigm in how work can, and potentially will, be designed post the pandemic. However, the possibilities of this new normal are balanced by potential pitfalls. In this chapter we attempt to highlight these possibilities and pitfalls and outline a route-map for change.

Research continues to reinforce the fact that the foundation of good jobs and good work design remain fundamental to employee attraction, retention and motivation (Wang, Lui & Parker, 2020; Tims & Parker, 2020). As the dynamics of the 'new normal' challenge and push the boundaries of work organization, it is important to keep these concepts of quality work design central to our thinking. The technology underpinning the paradigm shift to the virtual workplace has the capacity to support and maintain fundamental changes in how work is and can be undertaken. Indeed, the terminology of 'Zoom' and 'Teams' describing the leading conferencing platforms used when working from home during the pandemic have entered the mainstream workplace language, as the terms 'Google it' and 'texting' did before them. As organizations embrace these new dynamics in work patterns and practices, new challenges emerge. We explore this emerging landscape of work in the context of quality job and work design.

Successful implementation of quality work design strategies can create high quality, high involvement work environments that are able to attract and retain high-quality employees and provide a bedrock to sustained competitive advantage for the organization (Boxall & Purcell, 2016). The flip side of this is a work environment where employees have little opportunity to be involved at a significant level in the work they do or how they do it, and where work intensification and increased electronic monitoring and surveillance are central to this new virtual workplace, creating a climate of oppression and control, and where isolation and lack of trust become sources of alienation (Holland & Tham, 2020). Job and work design are critical factors in the development and maintenance of a committed high-quality workforce. As we write, we expect that in the 'honeymoon' period as, with vaccines, the pandemic becomes better controlled and people start getting back to a more usual situation at work - and indeed in the months and years after that - the experience of working from home will have built in scope and expectation, even in highly structured work environments, encouraging employers and employees to think about how and why their jobs are being done. As Lepak and Snell (2007) note, human resource management systems need to reflect an environment characterised by continuous change and increased competition.

What's new?

Remote working is not a new concept. Indeed, the first industrial revolution was initially built on the 'putting-out' systems of outsourcing and the following industrial revolutions are linked to outsourcing of manufacturing and then offshoring of IT-based and other work (Mathews, 1989; Piore & Sabel, 1984; Holland, Brewster & Kougiannou, 2021). The technology to enable working from home is hardly new: some people (artists, writers, or the gender-defined 'needlewomen') worked at home for centuries (Berg, 1988; Mathews, 1989) and many still do. The Second World War and the technological developments that took place then accelerated working from home. Women who had become integral to the workforce found that the return of men from the war led to them being thrust out of traditional employment roles (Pahl, 1988). Many started working as sub-contractors, running their own businesses from home: holding 'tupperware' or 'personal finance' parties. The invention of the telephone had earlier enabled more people to do their job away from a workplace and the development of associated information technology led to a significant increase in the numbers of people 'working the phone' from home. Interestingly prescient government reports in many countries in the 1970s and 1980s discussed issues such as how working from home could save petrol during the oil embargo, or what the growth of working at home would do to central city office prices (see, e.g. Brady, 1984).

During this period influential futurists such as Alvin Toffler wrote of a technologically-enabled work environment where people would work like traditional artisans, as and when they needed, from their 'electronic' cottages (Tofler, 1980). Although technological development increasingly allowed for this vision to come true many, like Schon (1991), lamented the missed opportunity of this utopian leisure society as hours of work continued to rise. By the start of the twenty-first century the development of ICT had advanced to a point where working from home used the same levels of smart ICT as the office. Whilst technology-based conference-calling was well established, the growth in distance working stalled. Although gradually more people did work from home, many more could but did not.

The reasons for the failure of WFH to grow as the technology allowed seem to come from both sides of the employment relationship. For the employer, remote working offers clear benefits, such as reducing the need for expensive office space, and the associated heating, lighting and other costs. There are environmental benefits due to fewer CO_2 emissions related to commuting (Fuhr & Pociask, 2011) and potential increased organizational commitment from staff (Felstead & Henseke, 2017). There are also advantages of remote working for employees, such as greater control over time, less or no commuting, more time with the family, job satisfaction and job-related well-being (Felstead & Henseke, 2017). But there are also disadvantages: for employers these include extra investment in ICT systems and a loss of more traditional forms of control and, perhaps especially, managerial concern about loss of power and status (Errichiello & Pianese, 2016; Fleming, 2019; Graeber, 2018). For employees, the disadvantages include loneliness and stress (Crawford, Maccalman & Jackson, 2011) and the disadvantages of spending more time with the family – limited time to concentrate, uninterrupted, just on the work. These slowed the acceptance of working from home prior to 2020 (ONS, 2020).

There was certainly no sustained push from employees or their representative to follow the ideas of Toffler and others to an electronic cottage utopia. This could, in part, be related to the first major studies of work design after WWII, by the Tavistock Institute, highlighting the intrinsic aspects of work for the worker (Holland, 2017). Employed work is a social activity: people enjoy interacting with their work colleagues, they often develop extensive friendships there, some people even find their life partners at work. Putting these intrinsic values at risk for the saving of commuter time, the freedom to fit work around household activities and the dubious and potentially lonely practice of working from home did not appeal to many as a good bargain. Employers, or their representatives, the managers, were wary too. Some had well thought through reasons: for management, they might need to invest money that was not available to create these working patterns. They could perhaps find ways of outsourcing or off-shoring the work that were cheaper than any savings they could make in office space, however there might be information security issues. Others perhaps reflected a view of management that employees could not be trusted and would, if not immediately overseen by a superior in the evocatively named 'chain of command', reflecting a panopticon style of management, do as little work as possible. However, as Wheatley (2020) noted, with the increased digitisation and globalisation of work, the opportunity for greater diversity and flexibility has made the location of work increasingly fluid.

There had always been some people who worked from home. Authors, visual artists, and people living 'over the shop' had been around for generations. The internet enabled more people to do so: if you had a computer or in later years even a good mobile phone, the internet opened up opportunities for buying and selling, work on gaming and low-skilled computer-based crowdsourcing work that had never existed before. Over the years leading up to the 2020 pandemic, the numbers of people working from home expanded steadily (Wheatley, 2020). But, much to the chagrin of futurologists and management consultancies (Fried & Heinemeier-Hansson, 2013; Rifkin, 1995), and presumably because of that resistance by socially-minded workers and control-obsessed managers, the numbers grew steadily - but slowly.

Then everything changed. Suddenly, with the pandemic, overnight and with almost no planning, the numbers of people (primarily employees) trying to do their job from home expanded massively. Within the tensions of the debate, the coronavirus pandemic became a catalyst for remote working with governments across the developed world directing people to 'stay at home' and enforcing rules that only those for whom it was unavoidable should travel to a workplace. The pandemic period of 2020 resulted in a fundamental shift, *en masse*, to work at home, to work on-line wherever possible, and at all levels of the organization. What technologically had made possible, became the reality of what many people had to do.

Because the change was unplanned, there was very little investment by employers. Some brought subscriptions to mass conference calling facilities, but most relied on the money that had been spent by their employees to ensure everyone was connected. Significantly, during this period the technology not only sustained this massive change to on-line working, but many embraced it as the future of work (Liveris, 2020; Farrer, 2020).

The central question emerging out of the pandemic is: will these work patterns and practices continue as governments around the world begin to get a grip of the contagion, vaccination programmes begin to be effective and people are allowed to go back to their traditional working patterns and workplaces? As we emerge out of the pandemic, the initial consensus suggests that the work experience was a positive one for many employees and something many want to continue in one form or another (Liveris, 2020; Farrer, 2020). So, in re-adjusting to the post pandemic world what issues are likely to enhance or constrain the development of the new workplace? Clearly, the nature of how work will be organised and arranged is a critical issue.

Job-crafting: A Concept Whose Time has Come?

During the enforced shutdown of the physical workplace created by the pandemic, employees had to literally craft their own way of working at home, usually with very little advice from their employer, simply because the employer was also trying to address this dramatic and sudden change with no planning, and little tacit knowledge or 'road map' to the future. The notion of job crafting therefore provides a useful way of exploring the situation. The concept of job crafting is, in its simplest form defined by Wrzesniewski and Dutton (2001, 180) as "the actions employees take to shape, mould, and redefine their jobs". Of course, though rarely discussed in the literature, this is reshaping within severely curtailed limits: the employer still requires the same output and preferably at reduced costs. However, and importantly, research has shown that even within those limits there is a significant relationship between job crafting and engagement with work (Petrou, Demerouti, Peeters, Schaufeli & Hetland, 2012; Van Wingerdan, Derks & Bakker, 2017), based on the premise that when workers can shape jobs to fit their intrinsic needs, they are more satisfied (Bakker & Demerouti, 2007).

In practice, job crafting captures the ways in which workers can redesign their own job to enhance satisfaction and meaningful work, underpinned by the key aspects of the job and work design theory of autonomy and responsibility (Parker & Wall, 1998; Wrzesniewski & Dutton, 2001). Job crafting facilitates the customising of the role through three dimensions – task, relational and cognitive. Task refers to the elements making up the job, which means adjusting various tasks to enhance the motivational outcomes of the work. The relational dimension denotes the social aspects of the job and how it is experienced. This may include enhancing positive relationships, cultivating new ones, and minimising toxic relationships. Finally, the cognitive aspects of job crafting denote how an individual perceives their job in terms of the discrete parts that make up the whole, and what they want to emphasise within the role (Slemp, 2017). Research at the individual level has found a positive relationship between job crafting and several key outcome variables such as satisfaction, well-being and engagement (Berg, Grant, & Johnson, 2010; Demerouti, Bakker & Halbesleben, 2015) and organizational outcomes such as ability to adapt and change and, crucially for the employer, enhanced performance (Leana, Applebaum & Shevchuck, 2009). These outcomes are all increasingly critical factors through and post the pandemic.

A key feature that is increasingly being explored in job-crafting is that it can rarely if ever exist in a vacuum - other people are affected (Slemp, 2017). As with Newton's third law of motion - for every action, there is an equal and opposite reaction - most people work within a team and any changes in individual work design create ripples through the workplace and are likely to require negotiation, or what Leana et al (2009) describe as collective job crafting. Indeed, studies are increasingly exploring this and the potential downside of individualised job crafting (see Petrou, Demerouti & Schaufeli, 2015; Demerouti, et al, 2015). Research by Tims, Bakker and Derks (2011) found that the job crafting of one person could have a negative effect on colleagues' workloads and increase group conflict. Shin, Hur and Choi (2018), found that the emotional support of co-workers was a key factor in the success of job crafting. This is where the skill and knowledge of management comes into to play, to ensure the impact of job crafting is undertaken in a collective and collaborative context and in a fair and equitable way (Bizzi, 2017; Tims & Parker, 2020). Shin et al (2018) argue that managers need to promote a culture that nurtures team building. However, this is easier said than done, partly because some jobs are intrinsically individual and partly because, as Esteves and Lopez (2017) highlight, even where they are not, managements' general lack of understanding of job crafting and therefore its implications create problems. This matters for three reasons: firstly, it is management who creates the necessary conditions and environment for job crafting to be effective; secondly, managerial understanding and action can alleviate conflict; and, thirdly, without managerial support, resources and guidance in developing and maintaining it, job crafting is likely to be stifled and/ or to cause increased tension within the work group, and hence lead to its likely abandonment.

These are important issues. First, as noted (and proved), the technology for working remotely (both at a macro and micro level) during the pandemic period functioned exceptionally well given the sudden and dramatic increase in use. It remains available post pandemic. Secondly, we note that the catalyst for remote working was not initiated by the employer (nor by the employee) – it was determined by government, which in many Anglo-American countries, for example, is something of an irony as these countries (for example, USA, Australia and UK) were led during the pandemic by conservative neoliberalist governments with a strong preference for free markets and an avoidance of government intervention. Thirdly, the type and nature of the work undertaken means that some kinds of occupations and some kinds of tasks are best done this way (for example, writing this book chapter and this handbook). Other tasks may currently be more or less impossible to perform in such a manner because they are bound by place (construction, distribution, transport) or are services that cannot be offered that way (social work or elderly care) or that require access to customers or clients and others who may not have access to the internet (working with the homeless). Others may be possible but more difficult - for example, working on rapidly changing and complex issues (as our governments have had to do through the pandemic, with markedly varying success) or projects best carried via a virtual team of employees who can spark creative ideas off each other. Overall, however, the social experiment generated by the pandemic has proved that working away from the office is achievable with proper job crafting and negotiation.

As noted, a key issue is the available infrastructure. Working at home in these circumstances can be attractive when the technology works and frustrating when the technology does not work. Much of this is out of the hands of either employer or employee. However, with the use of systems and platforms such as Zoom, Microsoft Teams, Canvas and Skype which most organizations had available pre-pandemic, this appears to have worked reasonably well in most advanced economies. However, like the Tavistock research before it, assessment of the current situation needs to take a broader perspective and examine all aspects of the impact of these work patterns and practices. As well as the opportunities, there are pitfalls.

Work Life Balance or Work Life Collision?

One group of people that have traditionally worked from (or at) home are women: working as homemakers, cooks, cleaners and carers. The literature generally responded to this by implying that, as this was not 'employment', it did not count as work (Hill et al, 2019; Shelton, 2006). From the 1960s onward, there was a steady increase in the numbers and proportions of women in the (employed) workforce in the advanced societies, women 'going out' to work, even though the continuing gender stereotypes in most countries meant that women shoulder more of the burden of family responsibilities and non-paid work in the household. This has led to increased research interest in (and tension about) work-life balance (Gregory, 2015). It is potentially easier for single men, for example, to devote long hours to work, and more difficult for women with family caring responsibilities to devote even normal work hours to their job. The dramatic changes caused by the pandemic resulted in changes in work practices for the whole family, with partners (and grown children) negotiating work commitments at home, whilst those with school-aged children were required to take on a support-educator role to help and facilitate their children's education. Note too that some families were already coping with health-vulnerable family members, a problem made considerably more difficult by the pandemic and the lockdown, exacerbating these issues. In this context the situation might be better described as a spatial collision of work-life balance rather than spatial separation (Pocock, 2003; Wheatley, 2020). This has been reinforced by a family life and well-being study conducted under COVID-19 restrictions in the UK where the child-care and domestic responsibilities during lockdown were not shared equally, and indeed the burden actually increased for the majority of women. As Lacey et al (2020) note in their report:

- Of those who work, 73% of mothers report working from home as 'difficult' or 'very difficult'.
- A similar proportion of women reported being completely or mostly responsible for supporting children with home-learning, a task with considerable time costs.
- On average, seven weeks after lockdown, nearly half (48%) of female respondents with a male partner reported that his access to time, space, and equipment to work had been prioritised over her own. This compared with 34% of mothers who felt both partners' work had been balanced equally and 17% of mothers who felt their own work had been prioritised.

Although a preliminary report, the results highlight the potential for increasing the disadvantages of working from home for certain sectors of society. These findings were also borne out in our own research on the impact of the pandemic (see Walker, Brewster & Fontina and Holland, Ferrer & Newman, 2020) on academics. Typical quotes from the studies included:

Work-life balance has suffered owing to the increase in workload. Stress levels have been high.

The impact of home schooling two young children on a) ability to find the time to work and b) the ability to focus on work, to perform it to a high standard, it's near on impossible.

I love my work. But working from home, although I followed all of the advice, set standard work hours, have a home office, etc. - it zaps my motivation to work ...

This is supported by Pennington (2020), who emphasises the mounting unseen costs and risks of WFH including long work hours, increased pressure on employees with high caring demands, and the absence of national health and safety measures applied to the (private) home in most AMEs. Pennington notes that half of those working from home report increased stress, depression and self-harm. She also points to UK research indicating the likely significant increase in musculoskeletal workplace injuries as workers make do with dining and coffee tables, or desks which are ill-designed for eight or more hours of work. Added to this, workers facing increased isolation and the risk of work intensification from this 'new normal'.

Ironically, as Gregory (2015) and others (Henniger & Papouscheck, 2008) point out, the growth in interest in work-life balance in many AMEs was in part stimulated by trying to find working methods that did not disadvantage women and other disadvantaged groups such as the disabled or those with caring responsibilities.

Management or Leadership in Time of Crisis

Returning to an important theme of this chapter, the context and type of management also matters. The nature of the change to remote working and its associated pressures, be they work pressures, alienation, or anxiety in a time of uncertainty or increased familial pressures, puts leadership by employers and their representative managements under the spotlight. Teams of workers that may have existed before the lockdown had to be re-cast, re-created and re-energised, literally overnight. However, anecdotally at least, it seems that despite the technological infrastructure, management by and large showed little interest in developing these work patterns. In such situations, Wang, Demerouti and Le Blanc (2017) argue that transformational leadership is likely to be most effective in reframing threats as opportunities. Wang et al (2017) and others (eg Grant & Parker, 2009; Martin, Liao & Campbell, 2013; Piccolo & Colquitt, 2006) argue that transformational leadership encourages people to engage in job-crafting, acting as a catalyst for it. In the context of intensive and uncertain competition, Lu et al (2014: 142) argue that:

More than ever, organizations need their employees to be energetic, dedicated and fully engaged in their work because the quality of human resources is of vital importance to the success of the organization, especially in uncertain working contexts.

Lu et al (2014) and Grant and Ashford (2008) believe that in times of uncertainty and volatility, underpinned by job insecurity, employees are likely to exhibit more proactive behaviours. As such, where circumstances permit, there appears a growing potential to develop more proactive approaches to job-crafting, but equally these need to be crafted in the context of the 'new normal' in terms of work, relationships and technology. If management was reluctant, or did not have the necessary vision, capacity or trust, to develop these practices in less challenging times, is it realistic to think they will have the skill and ability to adopt them effectively now – let alone embrace these changes in a positive light? As one academic commented in our research:

It is literally impossible to look after small children full-time (with no childcare due to the pandemic) and work full-time. Universities have not addressed this issue in any way.

So, will employers accept these new work patterns forced upon them - but garnish them with traditional panoptical monitoring of work practices more reflective of 19th and 20th century control and coercive management styles?

The Dark Side of the new Normal

A word of caution is required. As people have the opportunity to return to the ways of working that they experienced pre-pandemic, things will change. Managers who were reluctant to avail themselves of the costs-savings that can come with working from home (saving car parking and office space, energy costs etc.) have been forced to confront the way it operates and may be less antagonistic. Employees who have experienced it may have enjoyed spending more time with their family, avoiding the daily commute and being able to manage their work more autonomously. For other managers, the loss of immediate control or their inability to interact socially with their workforce may have become increasingly frustrating; other employees may have found the noisy interrupted home-working experience as increasingly annoying. The loneliness of working at home and, especially perhaps for some cultures, the lack of physical contact may have been problematic. Mothers, (as noted above) especially of young children, seem to have borne the brunt of increased duties under lockdown (Lacey et al, 2020). Based on our research, and (as we write this chapter in the midst of online teaching, marking, etc.) living the experience, the pandemic seems likely to accelerate the pre-existing move towards distance working (and perhaps towards forms of work such as outsourcing and sub-contracting that avoid employment altogether). It appears that most people are going to continue to want to spend less time in the office each week. But that is not wanted by everyone and is not possible for many: it is going to be a complex tapestry - in which job crafting can provide an important role.

As Sparrow (2020), points out, for every person who wants to work from home, there is another who genuinely misses the community of the shared workplace, leading to the issues of alienation and social isolation. In Australia, for example, a third of the workforce acknowledged having symptoms of severe psychological distress during the pandemic (Patty, 2020). Research in the USA indicates that over 75% of the workforce had identified some signs of personal burnout, with 20% in the upper range, even before the pandemic hit (Braverman, 2020). Further social isolation could exacerbate this, creating a mental health pandemic if it is not managed correctly and/or a very dysfunctional work environment. In the years immediately before the pandemic, organizations such as Yahoo, Twitter and IBM, that had previously pushed for working at home as a way of reducing costs, encouraged employees to return to the office or at least develop a hybrid arrangement, for reasons of mental health. The opportunity to develop team cohesion and to generate those opportune creative conversations and 'light-bulb' moments may be missed in a virtual workplace. During the pandemic, several of these same organizations announced that, for many of their workers, they would no longer be offering any office space at all – they did not want their workers coming in to work.

Blanket 'one-size-fits-all' solutions are probably not likely to be the most effective way of dealing with these issues. Job-crafting is more likely to generate required results and, to be effective, there needs to be a detailed review of each role and how it interacts with others through collaborative job crafting. This will enable a balance to be achieved between the individual and collaborative work mode as well as combining the increased effectiveness of working at home with the socialising experience of meeting in the workplace to create the appropriate levels of cohesion, interactions and productive relationships. Sadly, rather than being the catalyst for a new approach to working based upon trust, there are already signs emerging of increased levels of electronic monitoring and surveillance by management during the pandemic that should be cause for concern. It seems that in many cases, managements who were forced into having to give up their visual control of employees (Errichiello & Pianese, 2016) tried to replace it not with trust and an assumption that employees would do their best, but with forms of surveillance based on the employees' computer or telephone use. We explore this particular pitfall below.

Home Working or Home Shirking?

As noted, one of the common sayings emerging out of the 'new normal' is never waste a crisis! And if you were selling IT software like Hubstaff or Time Doctor you will have seen your sales increase exponentially during this period. If these programmes are not familiar to you, they may be to your boss, as they are software designed to track people working remotely. Euphemistically called 'tattleware', during the pandemic lockdown evidence started to emerge of their increased use and impact. Research by Allyn (2020) identified one employee, quoted anonymously for fear of losing her job, who noted that employees at her organization were required to install Hubstaff on their personal computers two weeks into the pandemic-initiated remote working, so that their mouse movements could be monitored. This was followed by 'TSheets' on their phones to observe their whereabouts during working hours (Allyn, 2020). Another interviewee told Allyn her employer started using Time Doctor which downloads videos of the employees' screens as they work and enables the computer webcam to take pictures of the employee every 10 minutes (Allyn, 2020). She noted:

If you're idle for a few minutes, if you go to the bathroom or whatever, a pop-up will come up and it'll say, 'You have 60 seconds to start work again or we're going to pause your (paid) time' (cited in Allyn, 2020).

Further research noted the surveillance of working remotely during the pandemic:

My manager knows every single damn thing I do... I barely get to stand up and stretch, as opposed to when I am physically in the office. I feel like I have to constantly be in front of the computer and work because, if not, either the TeamViewer logs me out for being idle, or my manager randomly sends me a check-in email that I must reply to promptly (cited in Sparrow, 2020).

It was estimated that by the end of 2020, up to 80 per cent of companies were using some form of electronic surveillance to monitor remote working (Gartner cited in Martin, 2020). These facts highlight a further issue that has also emerged in the context of remote working with technology, the issue of work intensification summed up succinctly by the following comments including from our own research:

My employer realises I can be given more work now that he can monitor my screen directly (cited in Morrison, 2020).

It was horrible going into lockdown and working from home for months. I could never leave work and work never left me! Email and zoom meeting volume shot up drastically (cited in Holland et al, 2020).

Indeed, as Cook (2021) notes, the time previously lost to commuting is now used to catch up on administration. The commute 'downtime' (for reading or thinking) is being replaced by further work for the employee. Issues of electronic monitoring and surveillance are likely to emerge as key concerns in both the short and long-term with a move to remote working, under oppressive management cultures. Obviously, in the short-term overlaying these management practices on an insecure and anxious workforce suffering the pandemic raises deep concerns. Remote working almost invariable means working from home, where most people believe privacy should be at its strongest. This digitisation of the workspace highlights the tension not only of being electronic monitored and overseen by your boss at home but identifies the issues of boundaries when it comes to the concept of privacy for the employee (Determann & Sprague, 2011; Sewell & Barker, 2006). The seminal work on contemporary privacy developed by Westin (1967) and Altman (1975) is, as Margulis (2003) notes, as insightful today as it was when first proposed. Westin (1967) identified privacy as operating through individual, group, organizational and institutional levels, with tensions arising from intrusions into previously balanced relations between the public and private self. Altman (1975) introduced the dynamic and changing nature of the environment within which privacy operates i.e., the context (Altman, 1975, 1990; Marguis, 2003). In the context of working from home, Petronio (2002), and Watkins Allen et al. (2007), through the theory of communication privacy management (CPM), note that many see the home as a sanctuary from the demands of work, which, for homeworkers, creates tensions at and around setting the boundaries of monitoring and surveillance and the permeability or impermeability of these borders. Whilst deficiencies in these theories have been identified, what they do provide is the opportunity to reflect on and frame how privacy in the remote workplace can and should be managed by the individual employee and others (such as the employer).

Privacy is one area where we would argue job crafting has been blind-sided by the rush to remote working. Petronio et al. (1998) argue that individuals have a need and expectation for privacy. Even in the workspace, there needs to be boundaries on how much of oneself is revealed to the employer (Fairweather, 1999), especially in this era of intense and relentless electronic monitoring and surveillance: this is exacerbated when the workplace is also the home (Holland & Tham, 2019). This again raises the issue of the capacity of management to increase the level of trust needed in the employment relationship. Moving from a panopticon to a participatory model of management and leadership may be a particularly difficult change for some managers to adjust to in the 'new normal'. The sting in the tail for this increased intense electronic monitoring and surveillance is it could result not in increased work but, with the lack of trust creating morale issues, manifest itself in lower productivity and increased turnover (Martin, 2021); and damage to employer brand reputation (Holland & Jeske, 2019).

What Happens Next: A Road map to job Crafting?

Whilst we can anticipate that working at home is likely to increase on a permanent basis – even if not at the same levels as during the pandemic - there has been much discussion generated about how it will work. The nature of its imposition on management and workers means that there was no road map for organizations on how to turn this short-term necessity into a long-term strategy. In this context, maybe the new Finnish model of flexible work could provide both a template and a solution. The *New Working Hours Act of Finland*, came into force on January 1st 2020 – just before the world-wide pandemic emerged. The fundamental basis of the new act is to provide flexibility in how people can, want to and do work in this internet age – in other words craft their job. It is argued that replacing the concept of the 'workplace' with the notion of 'the current working space', changes the dynamic as to how work fits with the lifestyle, technology, and challenges facing 21st century workers. The Act allows for employees to independently decide on up to 50% of their daily and weekly working times and where they wish to work – in those situations where their duties allow such changes. The new act has additional provisions for employees to 'bank' hours and withdraw them when they want. The key economic change is that working time will focus on the work done, not the place or space in which it occurs. In the information age of the 21st century this approach directly challenges the 20th century paradigm of work – why do people still 'go' to work every day? In addition, the pandemic, with appropriate technological support, has shown that these more flexible work patterns are a viable solution - to maintaining and crafting work, and other aspects of life, to obtain work-life balance.

We reiterate that not all jobs can be set up remotely, but those that can are on the increase, and the pandemic has helped push and test the boundaries of jobs that may not initially have been considered able to be done remotely. Most organizations have failed to take advantage of the technological possibilities and one of the key reasons for that may be the issue of trust, as alluded to in our discussion on monitoring and surveillance. The Nordic nations have a culture underpinned by cooperation and trust – a core aspect of their corporatist industrial relations model; in Anglo-American countries, there is a more adversarial model which also translates into the culture of the workplace and potentially a less trusting employment relationship (Chahine, et al., 2020; Goergen, et al., 2012). Reactions to working remotely mirror these national level cultural distinctions.

Governmental responses to the coronavirus pandemic (lockdown and what followed) can be seen as a huge social experiment in forcing people to work from home or, in the Nordic terminology, adjusting the 'current working space'. It seems very likely that one outcome will be, for those who have been able to keep their jobs, a significant acceleration in this form of working in the future (Colvile, 2016). Many of these jobs can continue to be done at home or, more likely, be done partly from home – a hybrid model. Employees may find that working one or two days at home is beneficial, allowing them to concentrate on certain tasks in a way that they cannot do at the office, but to avoid loneliness and retain the social side of office working life. As Cook (2021) points out, in this context returning to the office might be considered a comfort for many as it helps to structure their day and not least because of 'Zoom' and 'Teams' fatigue. Employers may come to like the increased productivity and the office-costs savings. Others may prefer to only go into the office one day a week or for a few days each month. How receptive will managers be to employee job crafting that, perhaps, allows employees to do half their working week at home or wherever they chose, and only half in the employers' workspace? Or indeed, in line with high performance work teams, how far will managers allow the work group to become self-managing and decide how, where and when work is conducted? As Wheatley has noted (2012) on these issues, research continually shows that control, governance and trust remain restricting barriers to remote working despite the demands of increasingly higher-skilled workers. The answers will be instructive, given that survey after survey on this issue indicates increased productivity associated with the ability to have flexible work patterns and significant cost-savings from the reduced need to have office space. Will employers trust their employees, or will any such move be associated with increased electronic monitoring and surveillance? Reaction will probably vary around the world, but the impact of the pandemic may be the catalyst needed to change these 20th century workplace cultures and practices. Are managements in the Anglo-American countries, for example, forward thinking enough to see the economic benefits as well as the attraction and retention objectives in being such an employer, or are their concerns rooted in the origins of management as an overseer of the work and people who they don't trust? We look forward to discovering the answer.

CONCLUSION

It is not an exaggeration to say the world of work for many in the developed economies has been fundamentally changed by the pandemic of 2020. Whilst the long-term impact of this change is difficult to estimate, we argue, with Wheatley (2020), that hybrid work patterns and practices or what Bosch-

Sijtseme, Riuohomaki and Vartianen (2010) have described as 'drop in desks' will continue to evolve across the work-base: home, on the move and remotely. However, there will still be a need and demand from employer, employees, and clients for face-to face interaction. As such, the long-term impact of the pandemic may be to accelerate a new hybrid model. However, to make that work, management needs to move from a 20th century model of panopticon management to a 21st century participatory approach based upon trust and transformational leadership: we are trying to be optimistic.

REFERENCES

Allen, M. (2007). Workplace surveillance and managing privacy boundaries. *Management Communication Quarterly*, *21*(2), 172–200. doi:10.1177/0893318907306033

Allyn, B. (2020). *Your boss is watching you: Work from home boom leads to more surveillance.* NPR.org.

Altman, I. (1975). *The Environment and Social Behavior: Privacy, Personal Space, Territory, Crowding*. Brooks/Cole.

Altman, I. (1990). Towards a transactional perspective: a personal journey. In I. Altman & K. Christensen (Eds.), *Environment and behavior studies: emergence of intellectual traditions* (pp. 335–355). Plenum. doi:10.1007/978-1-4684-7944-7_10

Bakker, A., & Demerouti, E. (2007). The job demands-resources model: State of the art. *Journal of Managerial Psychology*, *22*(3), 309–328. doi:10.1108/02683940710733115

Berg, J. M., Grant, A. M., & Johnson, V. (2010). When callings are calling: Crafting work and leisure in pursuit of unanswered occupational callings. *Organization Science*, *21*(5), 973–994. doi:10.1287/orsc.1090.0497

Berg, M. (1988). Women's Work: Mechanization and the early phases of the industrialization of England. In On Work: Historical Comparative and Theoretical Approaches. Oxford: Blackwell.

Bizzi, L. (2017). Network characteristics: When an individual's job crafting depend on the job of others. *Human Relations*, *70*(4), 436–460. doi:10.1177/0018726716658963

Bosch-Sijtsema, P., Ruohomaki, V., & Vartianen, M. (2010). Multi-locational knowledge workers in the office: Navigation, disturbances and effectiveness. *New Technology, Work and Employment*, *25*(3), 183–195. doi:10.1111/j.1468-005X.2010.00247.x

Boxall, P., & Purcell, J. (2016). *Strategy and Human Resource Management* (4th ed.). Palgrave Macmillan. doi:10.1007/978-1-137-40765-8

Brady, T. (1984) *New Technology and Skills in British Industry.* A report prepared for the Manpower Services Commission (Research and development series).

Braverman, B. (2020). The coronavirus is taking a huge toll on workers' mental health across America. *CNBC Online*.

Chahine, S., Goergen, M., Wood, G. T., & Brewster, C. (2020). Context, governance, associational trust and HRM: Diversity and commonalities. *International Journal of Human Resource Management.*

Colvile, R. (2016). *The Great Acceleration.* Bloomsbury.

Cook. D. (2021, Jan. 5). How the pandemic will shape the workplace trends of 2021. *The Conversation.*

Crawford, J. O., Maccalman, L., & Jackson, C. A. (2011). The health and well-being of remote and mobile workers. *Occupational Medicine, 61*(6), 385–394. doi:10.1093/occmed/kqr071 PMID:21921124

Demerouti, E., Bakker, A. B., & Halbesleben, J. (2015). Productive and counterproductive job crafting: A daily diary study. *Journal of Occupational Health Psychology, 20*(4), 457–469. doi:10.1037/a0039002 PMID:25798721

Demerouti, E., Hetland, J., Peeters, M. C. W., Petrou, P., & Schaufeli, W. B. (2012). Crafting a job on a daily basis: Contextual correlates and the link to work engagement. *Journal of Organizational Behavior, 33*(8), 1120–1141. doi:10.1002/job.1783

Determann, L., & Sprague, R. (2011). Intrusive monitoring: Employee privacy expectations are reasonable in Europe, destroyed in the United States. *Berkeley Technology Law, 26*, 979–1036.

Errichiello, L., & Pianese, T. (2016). Organizational Control in the Context of Remote Work Arrangements: a Conceptual Framework. In Performance Measurement and Management Control: Contemporary Issues, vol. 31, Studies in Managerial and Financial Accounting, (pp. 273-305). Emerald Group Publishing.

Esteves, T., & Lopes, M. P. (2017). Leading to crafting: The relation between leadership perception and nurses' job crafting. *Western Journal of Nursing Research, 39*(6), 763–783. doi:10.1177/0193945916659507 PMID:27432346

Fairweather, N. (1999). Surveillance in employment – the case of teleworking. *Journal of Business Ethics, 22*(2), 39–49. doi:10.1023/A:1006104017646

Farrer, L. (2020). The new normal isn't remote work. It's better. *Forbes.com.*

Felstead, A., & Henseke, G. (2017). Assessing the growth of remote working and its consequences for effort, well-being and work-life balance. *New Technology, Work and Employment, 32*(3), 195–202. doi:10.1111/ntwe.12097

Fleming, P. (2019). Robots and organization studies: Why robots might not want to steal your job. *Organization Studies, 40*(1), 23–38. doi:10.1177/0170840618765568

Fried, J., & Heinemeier-Hansson, D. (2013). *Remote: Office not required.* Random House.

Fuhr, J. P., & Pociask, S. (2011). Broadband and telecommuting: Helping the U.S. environment and the economy. *Low Carbon Economy, 2*(01), 41–47. doi:10.4236/lce.2011.21007

Goergen, M., Chahine, S., Brewster, C., & Wood, G. T. (2012). Trust, owner rights, employees and firm performance. *Journal of Business Finance & Accounting, 40*(5-6), 589–619. doi:10.1111/jbfa.12033

Graeber, D. (2018). *Bullshit Jobs: a theory.* Simon and Schuster.

Grant, A. M., & Ashford, S. J. (2008). The dynamics of proactivity at work. *Research in Organizational Behavior, 28*, 3–34. doi:10.1016/j.riob.2008.04.002

Grant, A. M., & Parker, S. K. (2009). Redesigning work design theories: The rise of relational and proactive perspectives. *The Academy of Management Annals, 3*(1), 317–375. doi:10.5465/19416520903047327

Gregory, A. (2015). Work-life balance. In S. Edgell, H. Gottfried, & E. Granter (Eds.), *The Sage Handbook of Sociology of Work and Employment* (pp. 502–5519). Sage.

Harvey, D. (2005). *A Brief History of Neo-Liberalism*. OUP. doi:10.1093/oso/9780199283262.001.0001

Henniger, A., & Papouscheck, U. (2008). Occupation matters – blurring work-life boundaries in mobile care and media industry. In C. Warhurst, D. R. Eikhof, & A. Huanschild (Eds.), *Work Less, Live More? Critical analysis of the work-life boundary* (pp. 153–177). Palgrave. doi:10.1007/978-1-137-11537-9_9

Hill, E., Baird, M., Vromen, A., Cooper, R., Meers, Z., & Probyn, E. (2019). Young women and men: Imagined futures of work and family formation in Australia. *Journal of Sociology (Melbourne, Vic.), 55*(4), 778–798. doi:10.1177/1440783319877001

Holland, P., & Brewster, C. (Eds.). (2020). *Contemporary Work and the Future of Employment in Developed Countries*. Routledge. doi:10.4324/9781351034906

Holland, P., Brewster, C., & Kougiannou, N. (2021). Employment, work and industrial revolutions: A Faustian deal. In The Changing Face of Globalisation and its Effects on Risk at Work. Routledge.

Holland, P., Ferrer, J. & Newman, A. (2020). *Impact of COVID-19 on the Working Lives of Business Academics in Australia and New Zealand*. Unpublished.

Holland, P., & Tham, T. L. (2019). Working under electronic monitoring and surveillance. In Contemporary Work and the Future of Employment in Developed Societies. Routledge.

Holland, P., & Tham, T. L. (2020). Workplace biometric: Protecting employee privacy one fingerprint at a time. *Economic and Industrial Democracy*. doi:10.1177/0143831X20917453

Holland, P. J. (2017). Job and work design. In Human Resource Management (2nd ed). Palgrave Macmillan. doi:10.1057/978-1-137-52163-7_7

Jeske, D., & Holland, P. (2019). Employer and Employee Vetting: Reputation Management Challenges in the Information Age. In Contemporary HRM in the 21st Century. Emerald Publishing.

Lacey, A., Lester, K., Cartwright-Hatton, S., & Banerjee, R. (2020). *Coronavirus (COVID-19): Relationship, Emotional Well Being and Family Adjustment Study*. University of Sussex.

Leana, C., Appelbaum, E., & Shevchuk, I. (2009). Work process and quality of care in early childhood education: The role of job crafting. *Academy of Management Journal, 52*(6), 1169–1192. doi:10.5465/amj.2009.47084651

Lepak, D., & Snell, S. (2007) Employment subsystems and the 'HR architecture'. In The Oxford Handbook of Human Resource Management: A Critical Text. OUP.

Liveris, C. (2020, May 16). We proved we can work from home. Why do we need to go back to the office? *WA Today*.

Lu, C., Wang, H., Lu, J., Du, D., & Bakker, A. (2014). Does work engagement increase person- job fit? The role of job crafting and job insecurity. *Journal of Vocational Behavior*, *84*(2), 142–152. doi:10.1016/j.jvb.2013.12.004

Maitland, A., & Thomson, P. (2011). *Future Work*. Palgrave–Macmillan Hampshire. doi:10.1057/9780230354043

Margulis, S. (2003). On the status and contribution of Westin's and Altman's theories of privacy. *Social Issues*, *59*(2), 411–429. doi:10.1111/1540-4560.00071

MartinD. (2021). https://www.perthnow.com.au/business/workplace-matters/is-the-boss-watching-your-every-wfh-moment-ng-b881722997z

Martin, S. L., Liao, H., & Campbell, E. M. (2013). Directive versus empowering leadership: A field experiment comparing impacts on task proficiency and proactivity. *Academy of Management Journal*, *56*(5), 1372–1395. doi:10.5465/amj.2011.0113

Mathews, J. (1989b). *Tools of Change: New Technology and the Democratisations of Work*. Pluto Press.

Morrison, S. (2020, Apr. 2). Just because you are working from home doesn't mean your boss isn't watching. *Recode*.

Office for National Statistics. (2020). *Coronavirus and homeworking in the UK labour market*. https://www.ons.gov.uk/employmentandlabourmarket/peopleinwork/employmentandemployeetypes/articles/coronavirusandhomeworkingintheuklabourmarket/2019

Pahl, R. E. (1988). On Work: Historical Comparative and theoretical Approaches. Oxford: Blackwell.

Parker, S. K., & Wall, T. B. (1998). *Job and work Design: Organizing Work to promote Well-being and Effectiveness*. Sage Publications.

Patty, A. (2020). Employers prepare for return of mentally fragile workforce. *The Age Online*.

Pennington, A. (2020). *Working from home, once a novelty, is now wearing thin*. https://www.smh.com.au/business/workplace/-20201105-p56br1.html

Petronio, S. (2002). *Boundary of Privacy: Dialectics of Disclosure*. SUNY Press.

Petronio, S., Ellemers, N., Giles, H., & Gallois, C. (1998). (Mis)communicating across boundaries. *Communication Research*, *61*, 101–113.

Petrou, P., Demerouti, E., Peeters, M. C., Schaufeli, W. B., & Hetland, J. (2012). Crafting a job on a daily basis: Contextual correlates and the link to work engagement. *Journal of Organizational Behavior*, *33*(8), 1120–1141. doi:10.1002/job.1783

Petrou, P., Demerouti, E., & Schaufeli, W. B. (2015). Job crafting in changing organizations: Antecedents and implications for exhaustion and performance. *Journal of Occupational Health Psychology*, *20*(4), 470–480. doi:10.1037/a0039003 PMID:25798717

Piccolo, R., & Colquitt, J. (2006). Transformational leadership and job behaviors: The mMediating role of core job characteristics. *Academy of Management Journal, 49*(2), 327–340. doi:10.5465/amj.2006.20786079

Piore, M., & Sabel, C. (1984). *The Second Industrial Divide: Possibilities for Prosperity*. Basic Books.

Pocock, B. (2003). *The Work-life Collision*. Federation Press.

Rifkin, J. (1995). *The End of Work*. Putnam's Sons.

Schon, J. B. (1991). *The Overworked American: The unexpected decline in leisure*. Basic Books.

Schumpeter, J. (1942). *Capitalism, Socialism and Democracy*. Routledge.

Sewell, G., & Barker, J. R. (2006). Coercion versus care: Using irony to make sense of organizational surveillance. *Academy of Management Review, 31*(4), 934–961. doi:10.5465/amr.2006.22527466

Shelton, B. A. (2006). Gender and Unpaid Work. In J. S. Chafetz (Ed.), *Handbook of the Sociology of Gender* (pp. 375–390). doi:10.1007/0-387-36218-5_17

Shin, Y., Hur, W., & Choi, W. (2018). Coworker support as a double-edged sword: A moderated mediation model of job crafting, work engagement, and job performance. *International Journal of Human Resource Management, 31*(11), 1417–1438. doi:10.1080/09585192.2017.1407352

Slemp, G. R. (2017). Job crafting. In The Wiley Blackwell Handbook of the Psychology of Positivity and Strengths-Based Approaches at Work. Hoboken, NJ: John Wiley & Sons, Ltd.

Sparrow, J. (2020). Working from home has a long history – be careful what you wish for in not wanting to go back to the office. *The Guardian Online*.

Tims, M., Bakker, A. B., & Derks, D. (2011). Development and validation of the job crafting scale. *Journal of Vocational Behavior, 80*(1), 173–186. doi:10.1016/j.jvb.2011.05.009

Tims, M., & Parker, S. (2020). How co-workers attribute, react to, and shape job crafting. *Organizational Psychology Review, 10*(1), 29–54. doi:10.1177/2041386619896087

Toffler, A. (1980). *The Third Wave*. Pan Books Ltd.

Van Wingerden, J., Derks, D., & Bakker, A. B. (2017). The impact of personal resources and job crafting interventions on work engagement and performance. *Human Resource Management, 56*(1), 51–67. doi:10.1002/hrm.21758

Walker, J., Brewster, C. & Fontina. (2020). *Consultation on the Impact of Covid-19 on the working lives of business, management and economics' academics in UK – 2020*. International Business & Strategy, Henley Business School at the University of Reading.

Wang, B., Lui, Y., & Parker, S. (2020). How does the use of information communication technology affect individuals? A work design perspective. *The Academy of Management Annals, 14*(2), 695–725. doi:10.5465/annals.2018.0127

Wang, H.-J., Demerouti, E., & LeBlanc, P. (2017). Transformational leadership, adaptability, and job crafting: The moderating role of organizational identification. *Journal of Vocational Behavior, 100*, 185–195. doi:10.1016/j.jvb.2017.03.009

Watkins Allen, M., Coopman, S. J., Hart, J., & Walker, K. (2007). Workplace surveillance and managing privacy boundaries. *Management Communication Quarterly, 21*(2), 172–200. doi:10.1177/0893318907306033

Westin, A. F. (1967). *Privacy and Freedom*. Athenaeum Press.

Wheatley, D. (2012). Good to be home? Time use and satisfaction levels among home-based teleworkers. *New Technology, Work and Employment, 27*(3), 224–241. doi:10.1111/j.1468-005X.2012.00289.x

Wheatley, D. (2020). Changing places of work. In Contemporary Work: The Future of Employment in Developed Countries. Routledge. doi:10.4324/9781351034906-8

Wrzesniewski, A., & Dutton, J. E. (2001). Crafting a job: Revisioning employees as active crafters of their work. *Academy of Management Review, 26*(2), 179–201. doi:10.5465/amr.2001.4378011

Chapter 8
The Problem With Productivity:
Redefining Productivity and Meaning Post-COVID-19

Maria Kordowicz
https://orcid.org/0000-0002-1405-9607
University of Lincoln, UK

ABSTRACT

In this chapter, the author problematises and challenges the mantra of productivity as an occupational raison d'etre. She argues that equating an effective worker with their capacity for productive output over meaningful outcome undermines employee well-being and human-centred values. She explores the impact of neoliberalism on work and the individualisation of the worker and argues that productivity has gained the status of a value. Lastly, the author outlines a range of solutions in the second part of the chapter and explores the rise of recent socio-political movements which redefine rest and contemplative practices as tools of rebellion against the ruthless neoliberal push for productivity.

INTRODUCTION

In this chapter, I problematise and challenge the mantra of productivity as an occupational raison d'etre. I argue that equating an effective worker with their capacity for productive output over meaningful outcome undermines employee well-being and human values. I chart industrial and post-industrial conceptualisations of the worker in the Western 'developed' economic context as a) an extension of the production machine, and b) as a tool for neoliberal growth, along with their respective physical and mental health impacts.

Neoliberalism refers to market-oriented policy reform, favouring free markets and a reduction in state intervention in the economy. A neoliberal ideology predicts that with minimal government checks and balances, productivity growth should be accelerated. The impacts of this ideology are touched upon in this chapter in the context of the rapid expansion of remote working. With homeworking becoming commonplace in a range of industries as a result of the pandemic, the home has become increasingly

DOI: 10.4018/978-1-7998-6754-8.ch008

colonised by the extension of the productivity mantra into our personal sphere, affecting our capacity to demarcate our figurative and literal leisure and work spaces, as well as to rest and take stock. Literature emerging from the COVID-19 era, is increasingly recognising the negative consequences of enforced remote working such as increasing stress and impact on employee well-being, affected by constant connectivity and lack of work-life delineation.

After providing a rationale for the need to challenge and redefine productivity discourse, I outline a range of solutions in the second part of the chapter and explore the rise of recent socio-political movements which redefine rest and contemplative practices as tools of rebellion against the ruthless neoliberal push for productivity. I also call for a move away from the individualisation of the worker, in order to seek social, organizational and systems solutions to improving worker well-being. Lastly, the degrowth school of thought is explored, along with its potential impact on not only individual worker well-being, but also environmental and economic sustainability.

PRODUCTIVITY UBIQUITY

This chapter is an expansion of an opinion piece I wrote for The British Psychological Society's The Psychologist Magazine entitled "You are more than your productivity: discovering meaning post COVID-19". The original article was inspired by a meme entitled an "Anti-capitalist Love Note" with pushback against the status quo simply worded as 'you are more than your productivity (source unknown). Productivity as a value has become an inadequately contested, yet an accepted and embodied norm in neoliberal societies. My opinion piece has been the most read piece of my writing since the start of my academic career journey, and there were points when it was difficult to find the capacity to respond to all those who took the time to reach out to me over social media and email about how much the article had struck a chord with them. Many came forward stating how the article had helped them to make sense of the stress and burnout they were suffering and how it had given them the confidence to resist productivity pressures. Whilst these are my anecdotal reflections, I cannot help thinking that this reader response was further evidence of the existence of tangible malady resulting from the pervasiveness of the productivity dogma.

Productivity can be defined as the rate of output and the efficiency of production. We can think of it as the output one creates relative to the level of input over a period of time (Tangen, 2005). Therefore, productivity is typically understood to be doing lots in the shortest amount of time. Increasingly, productivity is conceptualised as a continuous reduction of input (for instance, decreased staffing and financial resource) whilst maximising gain, often without an upper limit. Productivity growth had seemingly reached a threshold in advanced economies pre-COVID-19, though productivity zeal continues in its ubiquity regardless.

Productivity assesses business operations in terms of allocated resources in relation to yield. Measuring productivity therefore allows business leaders to draw conclusions about whether these resources are effective in terms of achieving the desired business outcomes – usually driven by the bottom line, in other words, profitability. 'Resource allocation' also refers to the utilisation of human beings. The worth of workers is defined in dehumanising terms here – the extent to which they generate income for the business through maximum effort and minimal direct reward. This narrative of productivity sees the worker as collateral - of merit to their employer only when able to generate yield at pace.

A known malady resulting from a mandate to continuously do more with less in the work sphere is burnout. Burnout is defined by the World Health Organization (WHO) as a syndrome which results from chronic work stress (WHO, 2019). WHO identifies three facets of burnout: exhaustion, negativity towards one's employment and reduced professional efficacy. Burnout is listed in the International Classification of Diseases (ICD-11) as an occupational phenomenon, rather than as a medical condition, but nonetheless one that has a detrimental impact on our physical and mental health. Though conceptualised as a response to work, it is perhaps somewhat short-sighted to define burnout as distinct from life outside of it. No doubt, our home lives will impact on, and be influenced by, work stress as well our sense of inability to perform professionally, in particular with enforced remote working during the pandemic leading to a blurring of home/life boundaries.

And what do the statistics tell us about employee stress? My field of interest is health services research, having been a National Health Service (NHS) manager in the UK for over a decade before my academic career. The annual NHS staff survey has for several years indicated a burned-out workforce. Whilst surveys have their limitations around sampling and bias, as well as generalisability of findings, the 2019 survey (NHS Staff Surveys, 2019) garnered responses from 569,000 staff - a response rate of 48.5%. A notable portion of staff report experiencing stress as a result of their work, a phenomenon which has been steadily increasing since 2016 with 40.3% reporting feeling unwell as a result of work-related stress in the last 12 months. More widely, according to the Health and Safety Executive annual "Work-related Stress, Anxiety or Depression statistics in Great Britain" (HSE, 2020) up to March 2020 (the start of pandemic lockdown in England'), stress, depression or anxiety accounted for 51% of all work-related ill health cases and 55% of all working days lost due to work-related ill health. The causal factors for work stress identified by respondents overwhelmingly related to workload pressures, such as work volumes and the burden of having to complete work within tight deadlines. Notably, these productivity pressures may drive us to work longer hours and a positive correlation has been identified between working more than 40 hours per week and burnout (Hu et al, 2016). It can therefore be argued that the data indicate a problem with the push for work-based productivity – its detrimental impact on our physical and mental health.

For many of us, the pandemic has led to our work and home lives becoming increasingly intertwined due to the need to change our place of work to the home as part of national and global social distancing measures. The result has been the physical and metaphorical blurring of borders between our home spaces and work. For instance, Molino and others (2020) recently reported on the effects of technology use on employee well-being due to pandemic remote working. They defined this new phenomenon as 'technostress', namely 'the stress that users experience as a result of application multitasking, constant connectivity, information overload, frequent system upgrades and consequent uncertainty, continual relearning and consequent job-related insecurities, and technical problems associated with the organizational use of ICT', now permeating our work-life boundary.

A 'healthy' work-life balance is often identified as a key factor contributing to employee well-being. What constitutes a work-life balance and how one achieves it has been widely studied. The desire for this balance is a process in which employees seek to reorganise their lives in line with their own priorities (Byrne, 2005). These priorities may shift over time, influenced by contextual factors such as new technologies, task demands and family needs. No doubt, the pandemic has been a powerful re-prioritisation catalyst for some, prompted by unprecedented changes in working practices or situations, such as furlough or forced unemployment. However, the separation of life and work and the notion of work-life balance is somewhat of a false dichotomy, whereby a delineation of our work and home personas is unlikely to be truly achieved, given how much the two combine and influence one another to contribute to our sense of identity (e.g. Watson, 2008; Wiles, 2013). Notably, in a study conducted in China, high workload has been recognised as a factor during pandemic work-home life interference (Wang et al., 2020).

Nonetheless, with many of us changing where and how we work in the midst of a global pandemic, there is presently a proliferation of surveys and research in the area of what constitutes the occupational 'new normal', predominantly through the lens of productivity i.e. has the workforce become more or less productive due to home-working arrangements? At the time of writing we do not yet have a clear picture of this, media articles tend to convey extremes of either the disengaged and distracted unproductive worker or the anxious over-productive worker who forgets to take screen-breaks and works beyond even what would have been their commuting time. It seems however that responsibility for productivity and what is mandated as 'effective' work is viewed as resting largely with the individual. I begin to explore the pitfalls of individualisation later in the chapter.

Recent research indicates that productivity pressures are rife with employees utilising new technologies to demonstrate 'at work' presence, yet their sense of professional effectiveness has been challenged by contextual pressures such as home and familial responsibilities amalgamating much more extensively with their working lives (Sinclair et al., 2020). In addition a recent editorial (Hernandez, 2020) recognised that mandatory home working during the pandemic rests on an assumption that workers would not only have a means to set up a working space from home, but also adopt a 'work mindset' in their usual space of rest and family time. Whilst this editorial recognises the impact on socio-economic status and context on employees capacity to work from home, it nonetheless makes a case for 'an urgent need for data that can lead to tailoring and advocating for strategies to make remote work more productive while addressing well-being issues that may affect remote workers' productivity.' In this way, productivity remains a key prerogative at this globally challenging time, but also a justification for addressing well-being issues – namely that workers can continue to produce.

PRODUCTIVITY AS A VALUE

A value refers to standards of behaviour, worth and principle. Productivity has gained the status of a value, due to being intrinsically tied to neoliberal constructs of deregulated capital markets, maximising efficiencies and business and economic growth. Neoliberalism is a term given to economic market-driven reform policies, including deregulation and increased privatisation. Neoliberalism rooted in the Western Thatcher and Regan era, brought a resurgence of 19th century laissez-fairism and economic liberalisation in the late 1970s/early 1980s, and later a defunding of the welfare state. Under neoliberal oversight, through the removal of state restriction, business remains unhindered therefore maximising productivity – a core raison d'etre of industry.

Neoliberal ideas and ideals have endured. More recently, the introduction of austerity measures in 2009 as a response to the global economic crisis at that time, and packaged as a means of reducing government budget deficits typically through increased taxation and/or cuts in spending, have been a pronounced feature of a neoliberal economy in the UK. Productivity features highly in the government rhetoric sold as a moral responsibility of the individual to work one's way out of austerity through a mandated engagement in market and contractual competition. In his 2009 speech "The Age of Austerity", former Conservative Prime Minister David Cameron propagating key productivity values, emphasised that 'achieving more for less in this age of austerity is not just a technical question of managerial efficiency. It is a philosophical question too' (Conservative Party Speeches, 2020). Yet, paradoxically, an austere economic climate leads to a decrease in economic productivity and policymakers have been criticised for misinterpreting low productivity as the result of low capacity for output (TUC, 2015). Rather, the suppression of economic activity is the result of chronic under resourcing and the 'more for less' policy rhetoric.

A parallel development impacting on the experience of work, in particular in the public sector, was the proliferation of new public management philosophies and methods. New Public Management (Ferlie et al., 1996) is the term which refers to an era of public management based on Thatcherite neoliberal principles of the introduction of market incentives into the public sector in order to improve efficiency. As a result, performance and output management regimes became ubiquitous within the public sector.

Despite adopting a strategic approach to implementing improvements in line with pre-set top down standards, New Public Management is interesting in the ways through which it proposes to meet its aims. Unlike a traditional Weberian (Weberian refers to the work of Max Weber) bureaucracy structure typically associated with the public sector, namely a formal hierarchical structure and management by rules, New Public Management aims for flexible rather than hierarchical public sector organizations. The feature of these organizations is management through targets, which often become more challenging as performance improves. New Public Management thus assumes the responsiveness and flexibility of organizations, and staff within them, to be able to effectively engage with top-down productivity improvement measures, typically consisting of key performance indicators and working to mandated target frameworks.

These neoliberal narratives have permeated both private and public workplaces and spaces – the latter notably becoming infused with new public management rhetoric and control mechanisms, such as the proliferation of data reporting, metric-based performance standards, and the imposition of internal competition and output mandates. Training the populace to become obedient subjects of neoliberalism begins in early childhood – for instance, seven year old English primary schools pupils are coached to read quickly in order to perform well on a one-hour Government-set reading test which can be anywhere between 1,500 to 2,300 words in length. This significantly undermines the notion of reading for knowledge acquisition and/or simply enjoyment. Thus, the rhetoric suggests that this helps to achieve continuous quality improvement for tax-payer value, whereas the reality indicates that the on-going squeezing of the workforce for ever-greater productivity is of detriment to job satisfaction and well-being (e.g. Ratle et al., 2020).

Taking this further, it could be argued that managerialism resulting from New Public Management creates a negative culture of 'bureaucratic accountability', achieved through external surveillance. Indeed, the neoliberal goals of New Public Management are supported by an improved information technology infrastructure and increased computerisation to facilitate the collection and monitoring of performance data. The resulting bureaucracy and a feeling of being 'watched' can lead to workers' sense of professionalism and trust being undermined (Lorenz, 2012). Worryingly, homeworking during the pandemic resulted in a spate of media and guidance articles encouraging remote managerial monitoring and how this can be achieved in the home-based remote working environment.

Beyond the work sphere, the explosion of new technologies and unprecedented information exposure have challenged our capacity to interact with knowledge (and others) in a meaningful way. Daily, we are faced with volumes of information, and the resulting decisional burden that we simply do not have the resource to manage, not least in terms of length of our human lifespans. In her seminal book "The Age of Surveillance Capitalism: The Fight for a Human Future at the Frontier of Power" (2019), Shoshana

Zuboff powerfully argues that digital surveillance is the greatest threat to not only human values, but also our individual freedoms. Dependency on online interaction has been created, herding masses of users globally for data extraction for use in not only corporate marketing but also to influence and programme our intentions and principles (as in the case of Brexit and the Cambridge Analytica scandal for instance). In other words, we are programmed to engage in online productivity without depth of purpose, our data farmed for corporate gain and political exploitation.

Clearly, the mantra of productivity has entered both our personal and professional spheres. Additionally, home-based productivity pressures typically remain gendered, with unwaged social reproduction, such as home schooling in countries where school closures were mandated during lockdown and housework, largely the remit of women, wedged into personal and family time (e.g. Chung & van der Lippe, 2020). Moreover, we hear of pressures promoted by social media to embrace an 'ideal' of diet, exercise, interior design, external appearance, holiday destinations and the like. Things that appear to no longer be embraced simply due to their intrinsic value, but rather only hold worth if shared in the digital sphere and are only fleetingly bolstered by those physically remote from us clicking 'like'. Meanwhile, engagement with social media pervades our time, connecting us superficially, whilst disconnecting us from the physical world and those around us.

The constant squeezing of our routines for more output creates an illusion of productivity afforded to us through new technologies, paradoxically reducing our ability to move towards a longer-term vision, to embrace tasks requiring time and reflection. It may be our search for meaning and a value-based existence that conversely continues to drive the productivity fallacy – the self-help industry is booming with an estimated market value growth to $13.2 billion by 2022, with top sellers overwhelmingly focused on productivity 'improvement'. The productivity mantra has replaced the human search for meaning, and rather than a means to an end, it has become an end and a value in itself. 'Busy', a contemporary badge of honour, has become the accepted response to being asked how one is.

THE HARM OF INDUSTRIAL PRODUCTIVITY

Work is of course society's key mechanism for the distribution of income and resource, thus for most adult aged citizens and their dependents, work constitutes a means of survival. Moreover, work is often presented as not only the method for pecuniary income, but also as a way of individuals practicing autonomy in achieving fulfilment, along with professional, personal and spiritual development. The link between gratifying work and well-being has been well documented, usually studied through the interaction of job-satisfaction and employee well-being. Further, Bowling and colleagues (2011) found that a positive relationship between these two factors has a 'spillover' effect, leading to greater life satisfaction. However, ideologies surrounding the worth of work and individual employee autonomy at work also have more sinister uses as mechanisms of social control. Maravelias (2003) argued that there has been an increasing displacement of responsibility for setting limits between professional and non-professional concerns from the employing organizations to the individual. Through this move to individualisation, burnout resulting from productivity pressures becomes the fault of the employee and not their workplace.

The push for productivity may be one of the most significant contemporary threats to our mental health. Psychological harm can be defined as emotional damage which causes distress or undermines the ability of the individual to lead a fulfilled life (Echeburua, 2003). Occupational burnout, a state of mental and physical exhaustion, is on the rise across professional groups, with the HSE reporting over

600,000 workers suffering from work-related stress, depression or anxiety in 2018/2019. Improving Access to Psychological Therapies (IAPT) was launched as a result of the recommendations made by the economist Lord Richard Layard in "The Depression Report" (2006). IAPT interventions lend themselves well to metric-based assessment, and therefore are a good fit with New Public Management performance monitoring mechanisms. The premise of the report recommendations endures – that wider access to short-term psychological therapies (with the development of a parallel cheaper and faster IAPT practitioner career route) will improve our mental health, get us back to work, offer benefits and therefore help to engineer the population's economic productivity. Here lies a paradox. The on-going psychologisation of work 'performance' since the 2006 Layard Report has endorsed the notion of the unproductive burnt out worker as a mental pathology for which they themselves are culpable, thus creating a smokescreen for corporate exploitation of the workforce and its significant detriment to mental health.

The notion of 'industrial fatigue' – the reduced capacity for productive work - is not new. Blaney (2017) documents how by 1918 in the industrial era, the body and physical health were directly associated with productive capacity. The body was conceived of as being inextricably linked to industrial machinery and 'reimagined as a productive system'. Thus, medical approaches and social understandings conceptualised fatigue resulting from industry as a pathology to be eliminated in order to achieve peak performance. This reductionist view of the human body and the human purpose pervades our current working and personal lives. Downtime, relaxation, the natural bodily requirement to rest are viewed as barriers to industrial productivity - barriers to be overcome through continuous external and internal pressure for outputs. Daily, we push through bodily discomfort in order to deliver outputs to a cause that is not our own, rendering our bodies tools of neoliberal economies in a post-exhaustion era.

In this vein, even more so during the pandemic, we are bombarded with information about remaining resilient – as workers and for our personal mental well-being. Resilience can be defined as the capacity to recover from difficulty and challenge (CIPD, 2011; Windle, 1999). Also referred to in new pop-psychology lexicon as 'bouncebackability', resilience has increasingly become conflated with the ability to continue to produce within a challenging context. Individual resilience has become mandated as an extension of the neoliberal productivity lens. It can further be argued that resilience has become a weaponised construct towards individual workers – if they cannot cope with their workloads, the fault lies with their lack of resilience rather than with the relentless unrealistic systemic pressures that they are under. Individual resilience workshops and lunchtime mindfulness sessions (now delivered through online surveillance technologies) reign supreme, and whilst of some proven benefit to the individual, they are arguably an extension of the hyper-individualisation of the workforce. Employees bear the stress and sense of responsibility for their stress, whilst the stress-inducing corporate systems and structures remain unchanged.

Thus, the systemic issues which uphold productivity over people continue unresolved. Human beings are solely rendered as a standardised resource and the economic growth prerogative continues as the predominant ideology justifying our engagement with work. In "A Workplace Dignity Perspective on Resilience: Moving Beyond Individualized Instrumentalization to Dignified Resilience" (Bal et al., 2020), we argue that the presentation of resilience as self-directed and performative i.e. dependent on the individual rather than on the context and processes of which they are part neglects the social and relational role of organizations. We also recognise that multiple factors impact a person's agency to be resilient beyond the organization including genetic make-up, personality, life-events and socialisation among others. Instead of promoting resilience for organizational productivity gains, we position the notion of resilience within a dignity paradigm, namely by attributing an intrinsic meaning to resilience, through which it no longer has to be instrumental to economic value creation, but rather is enacted through collective social responsibility.

REST AND RESISTANCE

The current pandemic backdrop offers us an unprecedented opportunity to consign the unabating 'growth is good' ideology to history. Here, I begin to offer some solutions in line with a post-pandemic vision, which promote a reconnection with human values.

In terms of resilience, we argue for a shift away from the individualisation of employees towards a dignity perspective (Bal et al., 2020). We promote the concept of dignity as intrinsic worth of all that is part of the workplace, at the micro and external levels, including the environmental ecosystem within which it operates. Thus, we urge for a radical transformation concerning the role of work in society, addressing fundamental questions of today, including environmental destruction and rising inequality.

In relation to environmental sustainability, many of us may recall the photography of nature thriving and air pollution levels reducing due to pandemic lockdowns, demonstrating the progress achieved by humans leading lives which interact favourably with nature. In "Forces of Reproduction: Notes for a Counter-Hegemonic Anthropocene", Stefania Barca argues against the anthropocentric narrative which considers unrestrained production as a key enabler of human progress. Anthropocene is the name given to a geological era from the commencement of human impact on the planet's ecosystems, along with climate change resulting from industrialisation. Industrialisation is tied to constructs of maleness in the literature – as a feature and extension of hegemonic masculinity and male social and economic privilege (e.g. Elliott, 2019). Using Audre Lorde's aphorism, Barca views the Anthropocene epoch as 'the master's house'. She proposes that 'dismantling this master's house to liberate humanity and the earth requires formidable new tools.' Therefore, a powerful significant shift is needed in our thinking and how we understand the world. Barca promotes a feminist take, one which has the capacity to bring together 'ecological, decolonial, class and species perspectives' as a way of forging alternative knowledge with which to uphold environmental justice.

The push back against the pervasiveness of the productivity mantra is our conteporary call to arms, achieved by recognising alternative values in our search for meaning and self-improvement. For instance, the sociologist David Frayne (2019) proposes a 'post-work' society, whereby work is no longer the dominant moral imperative nor source of meaning, challenging the dogma of work productivity leading to a good life. In practical terms, and with many employers suffering from depleted teams during the pandemic, organizations ought to re-evaluate the workload their staff have to contend with, especially given that workload is seen as one of the greatest contributors to stress (e.g. MacDonald, 2013). It is imperative that workplaces do away with meaningless rituals which give a semblance of rationale for their existence (e.g. overly-bureaucratic 'tick-box' processes), and rather shift the design of their activity to that which benefits society, whilst affording plenty of scope for rest. A true, rather than condensed, four-day working week may be but one element of a solution to the productivity problem and is seen as a way of not only improving employment conditions, but also the environment through a resulting reduction in emissions and waste (Ashford & Kallis, 2013).

Through my academic work, I conceptualise contemplation, slow-living, and self-compassion as the powerful antitheses to productivity. Promoting space for rest and reflection is of utmost importance. In her article on contemplation and organization studies, Bartunek (2019) focuses on academic work, and how pressures to quantify research impact undermine the contemplative activities so necessary for knowledge generation. Indeed, Ratle (2020) argues for the benefits in early career academics learning how to collectively resist 'mechanisms of micro-terror' – i.e. neoliberal metricisation of performance. Bartunek also links contemplation as a means of practicing compassion to self and others. No doubt these are crucial skills not only for academics. Compassion is the term given to our expressions of empathy and concern for all sentient beings, along with a will to reduce the suffering of others. Compassion and care are presented by Bartunek as key features of contemplation, as through contemplation we develop to capacity to experience life and connect with all its facets in rich depth. A key example of the practice of contemplation embedded into the work sphere is "The Pause" – a pause at the bedside of a patient after their death, honouring their life and allowing for personal reflection through silence. This organizational intervention has been described by Ducar & Cunningham (2018) as not only a way for clinicians to regain a sense of meaning and authenticity in their work, but also as a grassroots egalitarian movement with a 'powerful systemic effect in fostering a culture of support.'

Along with a means of nurturing our desire to better our lives and those of others, contemplative time and space can simply be a way of taking time off. Due to the pervasiveness of the productivity agenda, many of us have to relearn how to participate in downtime and may lack the ability to know when to rest and recharge (Dunn et al., 2008). Arguably, the state apparatus benefits from us experiencing discomfort when taking time off. Rest of course has a multitude of physical benefits which may counter stress and burnout (e.g. Gundersen, 2001) – the maladies of productivity pressures and relentless work volumes. However, we must resist the main goal of treating burnout being the patient's return to work as presented in the medical literature (e.g. Maslach & Leiter, 2016). This can lead to the continuation of the vicious burnout/productivity pairing, whereby the only value in the employee regaining their well-being is to return to the context which caused the burnout in the first place.

A powerful example of rest as resistance, The Nap Ministry (2020) is a social movement founded on counter-productivity principles, endorsing rest as pushback against capitalism, white supremacy and patriarchy. Rest is conceptualised as a form of healing from the relentless pressures to do more within a 'grind' culture. The Nap Ministry upholds rest as a human right not a privilege. In a similar vein, we must challenge the notion of human economic prosperity being primarily attained by the utilisation of labour, along with the faceless standardisation and surveillance of human experience through technology. This is an opportunity to reflect on how intrusive new technologies and technostress have been to our working lives even before the current proliferation of connectivity undermining our work-life boundaries and intruding into our homes.

As indicated previously, as a shift away from individualisation, systemic social problems cannot go unaddressed. I made the point in my original article in The Psychologist that the pandemic highlighted how even the seemingly well off were living precariously from one payslip or invoice to the next. These were just some of the issues highlighted in the Taylor Review of Modern Working Practices (Taylor, 2017) commissioned by the British government to tackle exploitation and increase clarity in employment law. For the majority of us, our employment arrangements are not even affording us with mid-term security, with the 'uberisation' of the workforce and resulting precarity largely to blame. We have seen the richer getting richer (Amazon founder Jeff Bezos' profits are estimated to have at least doubled during the pandemic) and as many as 150 million additional 'extreme poor' will be created by COVID-19 within a year (The World Bank, 2020). However, at the time of writing this chapter, the UK's Supreme Court ruled that Uber drivers must be treated a workers, rather than as self-employed, potentially setting an important precedent, whereby previous 'gig' workers are afforded improved working conditions such as paid annual leave and the minimum wage.

Crucially, the degrowth movement and its ideals fit much of the discussion in this chapter. The movement advocates for the creation of societies which uphold social and ecological values and sustainability. Degrowth challenges the assumption that financial profits and economic growth are testament to human progress. Rather, it promotes indicators of human prosperity such as localism, resource sharing and happiness over gross domestic product. Degrowth living would also address a point made in a letter response published in The Psychologist in response to my original article (Stephens, 2020), which counter-argued that productivity as a value is intrinsically positive and that mass consumerism is the core of the problem. Whilst the premise of my work is in fact that productivity as a value is no longer intrinsically beneficial, indeed I support an alignment with the degrowth movement which upholds well-being over excess consumption and over-production. Importantly, in line with the work of Kallis and others (2018), through reduced resource exploitation and countering economic productivity principles, the movement signals a necessary social transformation, along with radical political and economic reorganization. The need for change can no longer be ignored.

CONCLUDING REMARKS

The intention of this chapter was to challenge enduring thinking and discourse surrounding work-based productivity, especially in light of the pressures many of us may face in a pandemic context having to work remotely from home and having to renegotiate our work volumes, household commitments and work-life balance. Predominantly spurred on by the detrimental effects of British neoliberal economic policy such as falling wages, poor working conditions and environmental impacts, the chapter as a 'think piece' has introduced the possibility of an alternative. Namely, a recognition of upholding human values such as the right to rest and secure meaningful employment over profits and the pervasive push for productivity. My aim was to urge the reader to consider the socio-economic, political and ideological factors which play into how we engage with our work. Enforced remote working has held up a mirror to structural inequality even more than before, with 'digital poverty' and housing issues becoming even more apparent. There is capacity for push back and resistance to the status quo as demonstrated by the thought and organised movements discussed in this chapter. The tragedy of the pandemic will only be eased by a new vision for how we live, how we care for others and for ourselves, and by promoting values of a world where humanity and the environment can fully thrive again. Critically, we need to be unambiguous in our resolve that it is not productivity, but our own mental and physical health along with that of those for whom we have a duty of care, which take utmost priority. Taking an in depth look at our work and employment and being courageous about its reconfiguration for a sustainable future is surely a step worth taking.

REFERENCES

Ashford, N., & Kallis, G. (2013). A Four-day Workweek: A Policy for Improving Employment and Environmental Conditions in Europe. *The European Financial Review*, 53–58.

Bal, M., Kordowicz, M., & Brookes, A. (2020). Workplace Dignity Perspective on Resilience: Moving Beyond Individualized Instrumentalization to Dignified Resilience. *Advances in Developing Human Resources*, *22*(4), 453–466. doi:10.1177/1523422320946115

Barca, S. (2020). *Forces of Reproduction: Notes for a Counter-Hegemonic Anthropocene*. Cambridge University Press. doi:10.1017/9781108878371

Bartunek, J. (2019). Contemplation and Organization Studies: Why contemplative activities are so crucial for our academic lives. *Organization Studies*, *40*(10), 1463–1479. doi:10.1177/0170840619867717

Blayney, S. (2017). Industrial fatigue and the productive body: the science of work in Britain, c. 1900–1918. *Social History of Medicine*.

Bowling, N. A., Eschleman, K. J., & Wang, Q. (2010). A meta-analytic examination of the relationship between job satisfaction and subjective well-being. *Journal of Occupational and Organizational Psychology*, *83*(4), 915–934. doi:10.1348/096317909X478557

Byrne, U. (2005). Work-life balance: Why are we talking about it at all? *Business Information Review*, *22*(1), 53–59. doi:10.1177/0266382105052268

Chung, H., & van der Lippe, T. (2020). Flexible Working, Work–Life Balance, and Gender Equality: Introduction. *Social Indicators Research*, *151*(2), 365–381. doi:10.100711205-018-2025-x PMID:33029036

CIPD. (2011). *Developing resilience: An evidence-based guide for practitioners* [online]. Available at: https://www.cipd.co.uk/Images/developing-resilience_2011-evidence-based_tcm18-10079.pdf

Conservative Party Speeches. (2020). Available: https://conservative-speeches.sayit.mysociety.org/speech/601367

Ducar, D. M., & Cunningham, T. (2019). Honoring Life After Death: Mapping the Spread of the Pause. *The American Journal of Hospice & Palliative Care*, *36*(5), 429–435. Advance online publication. doi:10.1177/1049909118813553 PMID:30482027

Dunn, L. B., Iglewicz, A., & Moutier, C. (2008). A Conceptual Model of Medical Student Well-Being: Promoting Resilience and Preventing Burnout. *Academic Psychiatry*, *32*(1), 44–53. doi:10.1176/appi.ap.32.1.44 PMID:18270280

Echeburua, E., de Corral, P., & Amor, P. J. (2003). Evaluation of Psychological Harm in the Victims of Violent Crime. *Psychology in Spain*, *7*(1), 10–18.

Elliott, K. (2019). Negotiations between progressive and 'traditional' expressions of masculinity among young Australian men. *Journal of Sociology (Melbourne, Vic.)*, *55*(1), 108–123. doi:10.1177/1440783318802996

Frayne, D. (2019). *The Work Cure: Critical Essays on Work and Wellness*. Monmouth: PCCS Books.

Gundersen, L. (2001). Physician Burnout. *Annals of Internal Medicine*, *135*, 145–148. doi:10.7326/0003-4819-135-2-200107170-00023

HSE. (2020). *Work-related Stress, Anxiety or Depression statistics in Great Britain*. Available: https://www.hse.gov.uk/statistics/causdis/stress.pdf

Hu, N. C., Chen, J. D., & Cheng, T. J. (2016). The Associations Between Long Working Hours, Physical Inactivity, and Burnout. *Journal of Occupational and Environmental Medicine*, *58*(5), 514–518. doi:10.1097/JOM.0000000000000715

Kallis, G., Kostakis, V., Lange, S., Muraca, B., Paulson, S., & Schmelzer, M. (2018). Research on degrowth. *Annual Review of Environment and Resources*, *43*(1), 291–316. doi:10.1146/annurev-environ-102017-025941

Layard, R. (2006). *The Depression Report: A New Deal for Depression and Anxiety Disorders*. London School of Economics.

Lorenz, C. (2012). If you're so smart, why are you under surveillance? Universities, Neoliberalism, and New Public Management. *Critical Inquiry*, *38*(3), 599–629. doi:10.1086/664553

MacDonald, W. (2003). The impact of job demands and workload on stress and fatigue. *Australian Psychologist*, *38*(2), 102–117. doi:10.1080/00050060310001707107

Maravelias, C. (2003). Post-bureaucracy – control through professional freedom. *Journal of Organizational Change Management*, *16*(5), 547–566. doi:10.1108/09534810310494937

Maslach, C., & Leiter, M. P. (2016). Understanding the burnout experience: Recent research and its implications for psychiatry. *World Psychiatry; Official Journal of the World Psychiatric Association (WPA)*, *15*(2), 103–111. doi:10.1002/wps.20311 PMID:27265691

Molino, M., Ingusci, E., Signore, F., Manuti, A., Giancaspro, M. L., Russo, V., Zito, M., & Cortese, C. G. (2020). Well-being costs of technology use during covid-19 remote working: An investigation using the italian translation of the technostress creators scale. *Sustainability*, *12*(15), 5911. doi:10.3390u12155911

Nap Ministry. (2020). Available: https://www.instagram.com/thenapministry

Ratle, O., Robinson, S., Bristow, A., & Kerr, R. (2020). Mechanisms of micro-terror? Early career CMS academics' experiences of 'targets and terror' in contemporary business schools. *Management Learning*, *51*(4), 452–471. doi:10.1177/1350507620913050

Sinclair, R. R., Allen, T., Barber, L., Bergman, M., Britt, T., Butler, A., Ford, M., Hammer, L., Kath, L., Probst, T., & Yuan, Z. (2020). Occupational Health Science in the Time of COVID-19: Now more than Ever. *Occupational Health Science*, *4*(1-2), 1–22. Advance online publication. doi:10.100741542-020-00064-3 PMID:32838031

Staff SurveysN. H. S. (2019). Available: https://www.nhsstaffsurveys.com/Page/1085/Latest-Results/NHS-Staff-Survey-Results/

Stephens, J. (2020). *The Psychologist Letters*. Available: https://thepsychologist.bps.org.uk/volume-34/january-2021/want-and-buy-less

Tangen, S. (2005). Demystifying productivity and performance. *International Journal of Productivity and Performance Management*, *54*(1), 34–46. doi:10.1108/17410400510571437

Taylor, M. (2017). *Good Work: The Taylor Review of Modern Working Practices*. Available: https://www.gov.uk/government/publications/good-work-the-taylor-review-of-modern-working-practices

The World Bank. (2020). *COVID-19 to Add as Many as 150 Million Extreme Poor by 2021*. Available: https://www.worldbank.org/en/news/press-release/2020/10/07/covid-19-to-add-as-many-as-150-million-extreme-poor-by-2021

Tronco-Hernandez, Y. (2020). Remote Workers During the COVID-19 Lockdown. What Are We Missing and Why Is Important. *JOEM, 62*(11).

TUC. (2015). *Report: The Price of Austerity*. Available: https://www.tuc.org.uk/sites/default/files/The-PriceofAusterity.pdf

Wang, B., Liu, Y., Qian, J., & Parker, S. K. (2020). Achieving Effective Remote Working During the COVID-19 Pandemic: A Work Design Perspective. *Applied psychology = Psychologie appliquee*. doi:10.1111/apps.12290

Watson, T. J. (2008). Managing Identity: Identity Work, Personal Predicaments and Structural Circumstances. *Organization, 15*(1), 121–143. doi:10.1177/1350508407084488

WHO. (2019). *Burn out an 'occupational phenomenon.'* Available: https://www.who.int/news/item/28-05-2019-burn-out-an-occupational-phenomenon-international-classification-of-diseases

Wiles, F. (2013). 'Not easily put into a box': Constructing professional identity. *Social Work Education, 32*(7), 854–866. doi:10.1080/02615479.2012.705273

Windle, G. (1999). Critical conceptual and measurement issues in the study of resilience. In M. Glantz & J. L. Johnston (Eds.), *Resilience and Development: Positive Life Adaptations*. Kluwer Academic/Plenum Publishers.

Zuboff, S. (2019). *The Age of Surveillance Capitalism: The Fight for a Human Future at the Frontier of Power*. Profile Books Limited.

ENDNOTE

1 Origin Unknown.

Chapter 9
White-Collar Career Advancement When Working From Home

Navya Kumar
https://orcid.org/0000-0002-1576-6629
Birla Institute of Technology and Science, India

Swati Alok
Birla Institute of Technology and Science, India

ABSTRACT

Across the world, COVID-19 has driven millions of white-collar employees to work from home (WFH). Anticipated business benefits of WFH will likely compel employers to extend the work practice for several employees post-pandemic. WFH, by affecting job task execution, as well as opportunities to enhance and demonstrate capabilities, will hold implications for employee career advancement. In this context, a new model for career advancement is proposed, the competence career advancement model, comprising three cyclical stages (achieving, improving, and proving competence) based on the self-determination theory's psychological need for competence. The chapter covers job demands and resources that influence each stage of career advancement, as well as how these demands and resources are themselves affected under WFH conditions. Also discussed are the consequences of satisfaction/frustration through the stages of career advancement for worker well-being and work attitudes/outcomes. Human resource and technology practices to enable employee career advancement under WFH are suggested as well.

INTRODUCTION

Physical distancing for COVID-19 urged the world towards teleworking, specifically work from home (WFH). Previous studies revealed several advantages of WFH for employees including schedule flexibility enabling work-life balance, saving on commute time and cost, and fewer distractions at work (e.g., Kurland & Bailey, 1999; Mello, 2007). Employers also benefit including from greater employee

DOI: 10.4018/978-1-7998-6754-8.ch009

productivity and motivation, access to a wider talent pool, along with lower absenteeism, turnover, and operating costs (e.g., Eurofound and International Labour Organization [ILO], 2017; Kurland & Bailey, 1999; Mello, 2007; Raghuram, 2014). Even under the pandemic-driven sudden shift, WFH has allowed most employees to retain or improve their productivity (e.g., Bernstein, Blunden, Brodsky, Sohn, & Waber, 2020; Dahik et al., 2020; Felstead & Reuschke, 2020), while promising cost savings (e.g., Hitachi Capital, 2020; ServiceNow, 2020). Hence, several organizations worldwide are contemplating extending WFH as the standard work mode for a substantial percentage of their workforce post-COVID (Gartner, 2020).

Many types of white-collar jobs, as defined by Heron & Unger (1999), appear most feasible for home-based working across developed and developing countries (Dingel & Neiman, 2020; Gottlieb, Grobovšek, & Poschke, 2020). Thus, white-collar employees may be most significantly affected by a perpetuation of WFH. And the effect of the shift to WFH on employees' daily job execution and opportunities to learn and demonstrate capabilities will likely accumulate into implications for their career advancement in the long run. Career advancement is significant for its impact on employee job satisfaction (Herzberg, Mausner, & Snyderman, 1959/2017), which influences job performance (Judge, Thoresen, Bono, & Patton, 2001). Therefore, this chapter focuses on white-collar employees' career advancement under conditions of WFH, with career advancement in this context reflecting the ascending of the organizational ladder or assuming next-level responsibilities.

The authors propose the Competence Career Advancement Model (CCAM), a new cyclical model of career advancement based on the Self-Determination Theory's (Deci & Ryan, 2000; Ryan & Deci, 2000a) psychological need for competence and comprising three steps: Achieving Competence, Improving Competence, and Proving Competence. For each step, career advancement determinants of task characteristics and job resources, along with WFH effects on those determinants will be explored. Further, the chapter discusses how need for competence satisfaction/frustration, along the path of career advancement, impacts employee well-being (e.g., exhaustion) and work attitudes (e.g., job satisfaction) and outcomes (e.g., job performance). Worker well-being, which is the core focus of this book, and work attitudes/outcomes determine employee career sustainability, without which talk of career advancement is moot. Next are recommendations on human resource and technology practices to support employee career advancement in the new world of work. The chapter focuses on full-time WFH; part-time (a day or so per week) or occasional WFH tend not to significantly affect career advancement (McCloskey & Igbaria, 2003). Further, white-collar workers under consideration are full-time employees and not independent professionals or contractors without career advancement possibilities within the organization. Figure 1 lays out the structure of the CCAM model and its coverage in the chapter.

Figure 1. Chapter Flow and Structure
Source: Authors

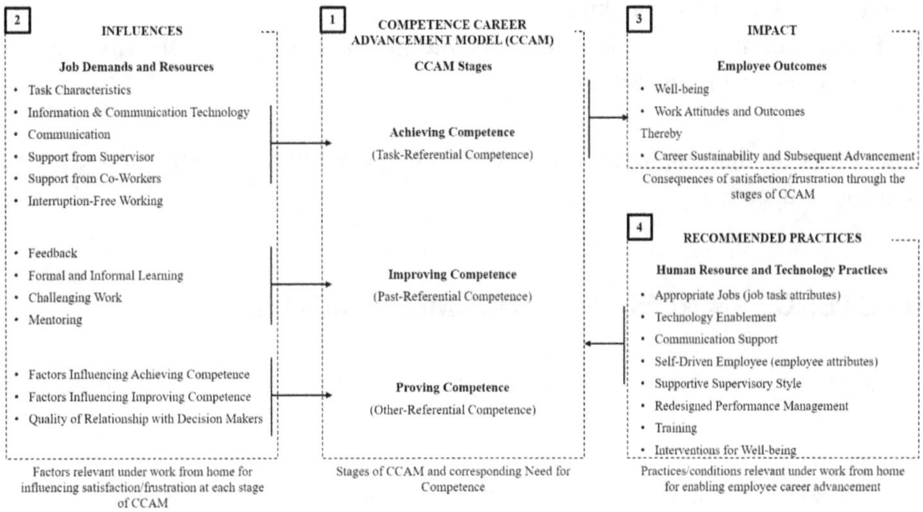

BACKGROUND

The Self-Determination Theory (SDT) aims to understand *motivation* or that which moves one to do something or persist at it (Deci & Ryan, 2000; Ryan & Deci, 2000a). SDT recognizes a continuum of motivation: from *amotivation* or no intention of doing something, *extrinsic motivation* or doing something because of external consequences such as rewards or punishments, to *intrinsic motivation* or doing something because it is inherently enjoyable (Gagné & Deci, 2005; Ryan & Deci, 2000a).

Regarding work/employment, extrinsic motivation likely dominates (Meyer & Gagné, 2008) and varies by the degree of *internalization* or imbibing an external behavioural regulation and its values (Gagné & Deci, 2005). With more deeply internalized extrinsic motivation or enhanced intrinsic motivation come well-being and positive work attitudes/outcomes, including job satisfaction and effective job performance (Gagné & Deci, 2005). In turn, intrinsic motivation is heightened, and extrinsic motivation increasingly internalized at the satisfaction of three basic psychological needs (Gagné & Deci, 2005). Namely the needs for autonomy or a sense of acting volitionally (Deci & Ryan, 2000); competence or feeling effective in interacting with one's environment (Legault, 2017); and relatedness or feeling connected with others (Ryan & Deci, 2000b). Through motivation, need satisfaction/frustration beget well-being/ill-being (Ryan & Deci, 2000b). Of the three needs, this chapter focuses on the need for competence or skills and mastery over the environment and the ability to "attain valued outcomes within it" (Deci & Ryan, 2000). Outcome attainment, or competence, is determined by evaluating one's performance against a referent; and on the basis of this referent type, competence takes three forms (Elliot & McGregor, 2001; Elliot, McGregor, & Thrash, 2002):

1. Task-referential competence: The referent is absolute or "the requirements of the task itself," and competence is task mastery.

2. Past-referential competence: The referent is intrapersonal or "one's own past attainment or maximum potential attainment," and competence is improving upon one's past performance or fully developing one's knowledge or skills.
3. Other-referential competence: The referent is interpersonal, i.e., "the performance of others," and competence is outperforming others.

This chapter proposes that employee career advancement involves three steps associated closely with the three forms of competence.

THE COMPETENCE CAREER ADVANCEMENT MODEL

According to career progress criteria, several career advancement models exist (Ishida, Su, & Spilerman, 2002):

- Seniority-based progression: Tenure with the organization affects promotions.
- Late-selection model: Employees entering the organization in the same cohort with the same education level progress similarly initially, but thereafter rise at varying rates on the basis of differentiating factors.
- Tournament model: Those who get promoted faster at junior levels are more likely to be promoted at later levels too.
- Sponsored model: Some are identified early in their careers as "destined for upper management," then given appropriate training and socialization.
- Gatekeeping model: The least competent workers are identified and promoted late in the initial and subsequent years.
- Contest mobility model: Promotion at every level is a contest among employees. Mobility is performance-based, and (dis)advantages of previous stages do not affect later stages.

The proposed Competence Career Advancement Model (CCAM) suggests that career advancement is determined by executing current tasks effectively, improving skills to better perform current tasks and prepare for next-level responsibilities, and demonstrating performance as superior to that of peers. The CCAM recognizes individual initiative and that each career level requires new effort. But it also acknowledges factors such as judgement and mentoring by seniors, whose influence can endure through several levels of an employee's career and imbalance the playing field between employees. Thus, the CCAM accommodates elements of both sponsored and contest mobility models (Turner, 1960). Career advancement, according to CCAM involves achieving, improving, then proving competence:

1. Achieving Competence: The first requirement for advancement is effectually delivering on tasks of the present role/level. For instance, job performance (e.g., timeliness and quality) significantly determines employee promotion prospects (Carmeli, Shalom, & Weisberg, 2007). Effective task accomplishment corresponds to the need for *task-referential competence* satisfaction.
2. Improving Competence: Developing and honing skills helps improve performance on current tasks and prepare for next-level responsibilities, thus determining career advancement. Increasing human capital or skill indeed "predicts" rise "through increasing productivity, and by establishing credentials

and credibility to provide signals on which advancement decisions are made" (Tharenou, 1997). These observations on managerial career advancement appear relevant to white-collar employees in general. Performance improvement and skill development correspond to the need for ***past-referential competence*** satisfaction. Notably, performance improvement under *past-referential competence* is similar to mastery attainment under *task-referential competence*, and the two forms of need for competence acknowledged as "intertwined" (Elliot & McGregor, 2001; Elliot et al., 2002).

3. Proving Competence: Every next rung of the organizational ladder accommodates fewer. Hence, advancement requires *being* competent, also *demonstrating* competence favourably vis-à-vis peers. Proving Competence thus involves interpersonal competition and external judgement in the form of performance appraisal (Grubb, 2007) and evaluations (Greenhaus, Parasuraman, & Wormley, 1990), respectively. Competitively outperforming others corresponds to the need for *other-referential competence* satisfaction.

After effectively Proving Competence and getting promoted, one starts anew with Achieving Competence at tasks of the new level, thus completing a turn of the cyclical CCAM (see Figure 2). Those not promoted must persist at achieving, improving, and proving competence where retained.

Figure 2. The Competence Career Advancement Model
Source: Authors

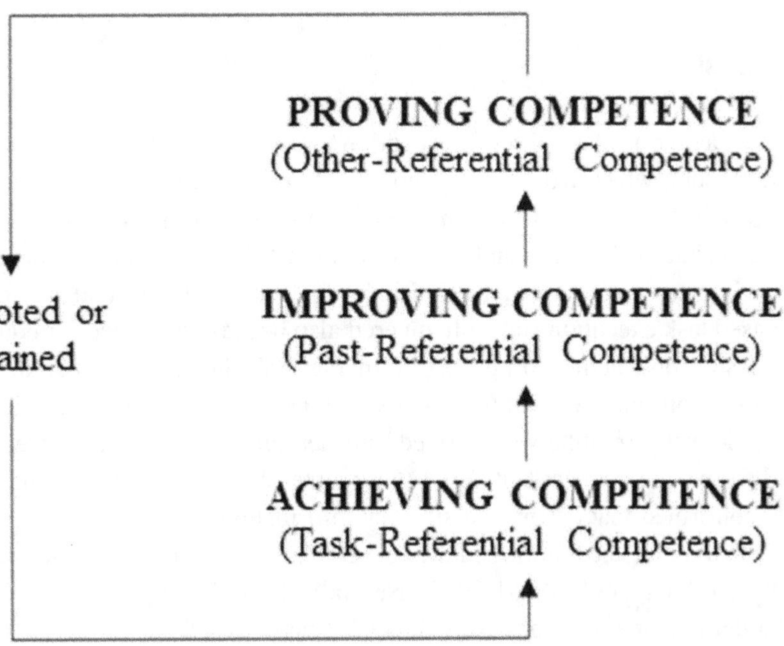

Meanwhile, the satisfaction of basic psychological needs, including the need for competence, is influenced "profound[ly]" by one's environment (Legault, 2017). For employees, the environment comprises of aspects of job design (e.g., challenge, variety, and potential for advancement) and work climate (e.g., manager and co-worker support) (Arnetz & Blomkvist, 2007; Baard, Deci, & Ryan, 2004; Deci, Connell, & Ryan, 1989; Gagné & Deci, 2005). This chapter examines work climate from the perspective of the Job Demands-Resource Model (JD-R). JD-R proposes that every job has "physical, psychological, social, or organizational" features that are *job demands* i.e., "things that have to be done" or *job resources* that help "get things done" (Schaufeli & Bakker, 2004). Job demands (e.g., time pressure) require effort hence impose physical and/or psychological costs (e.g., burnout). While job resources (e.g., manager support) reduce job demands and associated costs; are required to meet work goals; and stimulate personal growth, learning, and development (Schaufeli & Bakker, 2004). Job demands are not always negative: some (e.g., role ambiguity) are *hindrance stressors* that do hamper personal growth and achievement, but others (e.g., need for attention to detail) are *challenge stressors* that promote achievement (Podsakoff, LePine, & LePine 2007).

Job demands and resources affect psychological need fulfilment, thus linking JD-R and SDT (Gagné & Panaccio, 2014). WFH could frustrate or support psychological need satisfaction (Gagné & Panaccio, 2014; Gerdenitsch, 2017) by influencing job demands and resources. The subsequent sections cover how various job demands and resources are affected by WFH and influence each step of CCAM.

Achieving Competence

Achieving Competence or task mastery depends on how well if at all, a task can be performed in the given work setting. This achievability depends upon task characteristics and availability and/or adequacy of job resources.

Task Characteristics

Certain features of a task limit its effective execution under WFH's situational constraints, thus becoming hindrance stressors, which frustrate psychological needs (Van den Broeck, Cuyper, De Witte, & Vansteenkiste, 2010). High dependence on others' work, as well as complexity, ambiguity, or other requirements necessitating frequent and/or unscheduled face-to-face communication, are some task characteristics (Guimaraes & Dallow, 1999; Limburg, 1998) that can hinder effectual delivery from home. Home-based task execution can be hampered also because of a need for equipment, services, or other assets accessible only at the workplace (Guimaraes & Dallow, 1999), including due to contractual or regulatory stipulations on client confidentiality and data security (Raghuram, 2014).

Meanwhile, tasks that are routine, well-defined with measurable outcomes, and executable independently with little need for people-connect suit WFH (Guimaraes & Dallow, 1999; Limburg, 1998). COVID-enforced WFH confirmed that despite satisfactory information and communication technology (ICT) access, fewer were as connected, informed/aware, or collaborative as when at the workplace (Iometrics & Global Workplace Analytics [IGWA], 2020). Naturally, the *agile* way of rapid, collaboration-intensive working was harder to manage from home (Mancl & Fraser, 2020).

Information & Communication Technology

Working "away from the traditional office using computers and telecommunication facilities to maintain a link to the office" *defines* telework (Bélanger & Allport, 2008), making ICT core to Achieving Competence in WFH. ICT problems such as lost connectivity and system crash strain employees (Day, Paquet,

Scott, & Hambley, 2012), and as job hindrances hamper task achievement. Conversely, troubleshooting assistance, appropriate software, and high-speed internet are job resources that aid productivity (Bosua, Gloet, Kurnia, Mendoza, & Yong, 2013; Day et al., 2012). WFH may impede Achieving Competence by aggravating ICT problems and/or limiting resource access. For instance, poor home internet connectivity is a challenge across many countries, precluding teleworking for WFH-suitable jobs (Hatayama, Viollaz, & Winkler, 2020). Inadequate ICT resources hurt competence, also perhaps employees' need for autonomy by disallowing attending to tasks in a manner they deem fit and need for relatedness by preventing staying connected with colleagues.

Communication

Communication under WFH is limited largely to ICT-based interactions, such as emails or (video) phone calls. By not remaining face-to-face and spontaneous, communication may suffer under WFH (Bélanger & Allport, 2008; Kurland & Bailey, 1999). ICT as the communication channel can limit transmission of some informational cues, even leading to miscommunication (Day et al., 2012). But some found communication improving under WFH as formal, planned ICT-based exchanges brought structure, focus, and unambiguity (Duxbury & Neufeld, 2003). In either case, communication on task-related information is an important job resource. To the extent it impedes such communication, causing missed information or hindered problem resolution, WFH could harm productivity and performance (Bélanger & Allport, 2008; Orhan et al., 2016), i.e., hampers Achieving Competence. Obstructed communication under WFH can impede employees' need for relatedness too, by isolating them from colleagues. Isolation—feeling left out/separated—also inhibits job performance (Orhan et al., 2016).

Support from Supervisor

Albeit physically invisible, the supervisor is just as important under WFH, if not more so. Not all tasks are easily handled from home, especially ambiguous ones. Here, supervisory support becomes a job resource critical to Achieving Competence. By providing structure, guidance, and clear objectives (Guimaraes & Dallow, 1999; Orsini & Rodrigues, 2020) for tasks, supervisors extend the job resource of goal clarity (Richter, Tafvelin, & Sverke, 2018). Goal clarity eases the job hindrance of ambiguity (Podsakoff et al., 2007), which gets aggravated under WFH (Sardeshmukh, Sharma, & Golden, 2012). Furthermore, accommodating differences in employees' WFH coping abilities, supervisors could prudently allocate tasks and balance workloads (Orsini & Rodrigues, 2020), ensuring all have a chance at Achieving Competence. Of the many factors (e.g., individual personalities) affecting the seeking and giving of supervisor support, an important one is communication. Should WFH hamper communication, it would also limit supervisor support, hence restrict Achieving Competence. In COVID-triggered WFH, unfortunately, only 49% of employees received help and support from their managers (Eurofound, 2020), though *why* remains unclear.

Support from Co-Workers

With a rise in collaborative working (Harvard Business Review Analytic Services, 2017), the job resource of teammate support (Fernet, Austin, & Vallerand, 2013) in the form of information, advice, or assistance becomes crucial. For teleworkers, co-worker support can enable accomplishing tasks to Achieve

Competence, also overcoming the isolation that may thwart need for relatedness and impede job-related outcomes (Bentley et al., 2016; Orhan et al., 2016). But without face-to-face interaction under WFH, teammate aid and camaraderie may decline (Cooper & Kurland, 2002). Hearteningly though, during COVID-driven WFH, co-worker communication, help, and support did not fare poorly (Bernstein et al., 2020; Eurofound, 2020).

Interruption-Free Working

The office is rife with distractions, such as "the phones and the people walking in," (Kurland & Bailey, 1999), which can hinder Achieving Competence by preventing focus. WFH "fortuitous[ly]" helps avoid such interruptions, enabling productivity on tasks requiring concentration (Bailey & Kurland, 2002). But home may also present "a little more than a moderate amount of distractions" (Guimaraes and Dallow, 1999). "Children and spouses may not respect the sanctity and privacy of a home office" (Kurland & Bailey, 1999) and then WFH may inhibit Achieving Competence. For women especially, given the prevalence of traditional division of labour, WFH can add domestic distractions and burdens to work (Shamir & Salomon, 1985; United Nations, 2020). Thus, the particular conditions of one's home and their gender may determine whether WFH is an enabler for Achieving Competence.

Improving Competence

Developing and refining abilities to better perform current tasks and prepare for future responsibilities, i.e., Improving Competence, requires opportunities to learn, practice, and achieve.

Feedback

Performance feedback from supervisors, likely the first external reaction on task execution, is an important job resource, presenting developmental opportunities. It promotes learning and increases the likelihood of achieving work goals, thus enables competence (Bakker & Demerouti, 2007). Some contend that WFH constrains feedback: it becomes less frequent or regular and/or carries fewer informational cues due to being restricted to ICT-based interactions (Guimaraes & Dallow, 1999; Sardeshmukh et al., 2012). But others suggest that ICT-based collaborative tools can enable "greater feedback" (Bélanger & Allport, 2008). COVID WFH evidence has revealed that "providing advice and feedback" is possible virtually, but "much more" effective in-person (Lund, Madgavkar, Manyika, & Smit, 2020).

Formal and Informal Learning

Formal training and informal knowledge sharing by colleagues also help develop skills. WFH may curb learning, with organizations unable to "train, and share non-video based skills" with remote employees (Metzger & Von Glinow, 1988). Informal, spontaneous, interactive learning may especially be missed (Bailey & Kurland, 2002; Pérez, Sánchez, & Carnicer, 2002). Pandemic experiences confirmed that while "coaching, counselling" and "teaching and training" could occur remotely, they needed "significant rethinking" to make them as effective as when in-person (Lund et al., 2020). The loss of in-person interactions under WFH perhaps impedes the development of interpersonal skills the most. Interpersonal skills, not just technical abilities, are important for advancement to higher organizational levels (Tharenou, 1997).

Challenging Work

Challenging tasks as challenge stressors provide experiential learning that motivates employees to push themselves to meet demands due to the belief that such efforts will be effective and deliver valuable outcomes (LePine, Podsakoff, & LePine, 2005). Thus, challenging tasks enable personal development and achievement (Podsakoff et al., 2007) and satisfy the need for competence (Legault, 2017). Although ICT advancements make many tasks feasible from home (Pérez et al., 2002), it appears that to WFH is to compromise on challenging tasks. Raghuram, London, and Larsen (2001) relate telework with low masculinity, where masculinity means attaching greater importance to "earnings, recognition, advancement and challenging work." Almost two decades later, Beauregard, Canonico, and Basile (2019) find that for some employees, WFH benefits outweigh challenging work at the office. The takeaway: challenging work *still* means office, not WFH. This potential lack of access to challenging work at home may disadvantage women especially because among jobs expected to continue under WFH post-pandemic are those "commonly held by women" (Maurer, 2020; Shamir & Solomon, 1985).

Mentoring

Mentoring enables employee growth, learning, and development (Cooper & Kurland, 2002), hence it may be considered a job resource as per Schaufeli and Bakker's (2004) definition. Mentors extend various career and psychosocial development aids, including coaching, even challenging work (Kram, 1983). But access to mentoring is significantly reduced under WFH (Cooper & Kurland, 2002). During the pandemic, for instance, only 51% were satisfied with their performance at coaching/mentoring/managing others from home versus 81% when at the office (IGWA, 2020). WFH may worsen conditions for women particularly, given they already lack mentors (Noe, 1988).

Proving Competence

Proving Competence involves establishing the relative superiority of one's performance before external judges at performance appraisal. Chances at performance appraisal or advancement decisions are contingent on task performance (Tharenou, 1997), i.e., *being* competent or Achieving Competence, as well as on being *seen* as competent by decision-makers.

Being *seen* as competent is influenced by Improving Competence for "provid[ing] credential and credibility as signals" for advancement (Tharenou, 1997), also by interpersonal networking and mentor-facilitated visibility and sponsoring (Tharenou, 1997). Networking and mentoring benefits may be associated somewhat with the job resource of "quality of the relationship with the supervisor" (Schaufeli & Taris, 2014) or decision-makers. Thus WFH, which limits networking and mentoring (Cooper & Kurland, 2002), certainly appears unfavourable for Proving Competence, especially so perhaps for women, given they struggle with access to informal networks, mentors, and sponsors in general (Noe, 1988).

Visibility is particularly consequential for advancement and may diminish under WFH (Challenger, 1992), with women noting such decline more (Maruyama & Tietze, 2012). Bloom, Liang, Roberts, and Ying (2015) affirmed that invisibility may truly withhold advancement for WFH workers: "supervisors did not notice their performance as much and were less likely to promote them." But, when comparing WFH employees against at-office or even other WFH workers, one must consider the possibility of "previous relationships" (Wellman et al., 1996). These are informal communication networks formed at the office that employees may maintain even after shifting to teleworking (Wellman et al., 1996). Such relationships could enable visibility, sponsoring, and other dynamics that favourably influence appraisals. Thus, not all workers may fare as poorly at Proving Competence under WFH.

DISCUSSION: IMPACT OF WFH CAREER ADVANCEMENT CONDITIONS ON EMPLOYEE WELL-BEING

Achieving, Improving, and Proving Competence each relates to a form of the need for competence: i.e., task-referential, past-referential, and other-referential competence, respectively. Thus, facilitation/thwarting experienced at any stage of career advancement corresponds to satisfaction/frustration of a basic psychological need, thereby affecting employee well-being and work attitudes/outcomes (Ryan & Deci, 2000).

Need for competence satisfaction can reduce ill-being such as anxiety and burnout, and boost well-being and work attitudes/outcomes of work engagement, job satisfaction, organizational commitment, and job performance (Baard et al., 2004; Fernet et al., 2013; Van den Broeck, Vansteenkiste, De Witte, Soenens, & Lens, 2010). Under conditions of WFH, job demands and resources support/hinder Achieving, Improving, and Proving Competence, i.e., satisfy/frustrate the need for competence, thereby influence employee well-being and work attitudes/outcomes. For instance, WFH satisfies the need for autonomy (Gerdenitsch, 2017) by reducing supervisory oversight (Mello, 2007; Sardeshmukh et al., 2012). But it can hinder Achieving and Improving Competence, with WFH communication limitations increasing role ambiguity and reducing feedback, resulting in increased exhaustion and lower work engagement (Sardeshmukh et al., 2012).

WFH is also expected to boost autonomy by allowing flexibility to balance work-home responsibilities (e.g., Mello, 2007; Sardeshmukh et al., 2012). The pandemic confirmed that most WFH employees were satisfied with such flexibility (IGWA, 2020). However, some worked *longer* to complete job tasks alongside domestic chores (ILO, 2020). Also, more time was devoted to "one-on-one meetings or team check-ins" to compensate for physical separation (ILO, 2020). Some extended hours by over-working, over-communicating, or staying online to mark presence—all for visibility (Richter, 2020). Generally, under WFH, work hours lengthen and commute time savings and weekends also get diverted to work (ILO, 2020). The long-term effects of work hours extended to Achieve and Prove Competence in WFH remain unclear.

Furthermore, WFH can isolate workers from colleagues, thwarting needs for competence and relatedness. Telework isolation restricts access to task-related and social support from co-workers, thereby increasing exhaustion while lowering job performance, job satisfaction, and work engagement (Orhan et al., 2016; Sardeshmukh et al., 2012). Deficient ICT conditions compound WFH frustration and irritation (ILO, 2020), again thwarting needs for competence and relatedness—ICT being the sole means to work, learn, and connect with colleagues remotely.

Overall, during COVID WFH, most were satisfied with well-being (i.e., stress, sleep, and exercise) and flexibility to balance work/non-work (IGWA, 2020). However, about one-in-four WFH employees did feel emotionally drained from work and a similar number were physically exhausted (Eurofound, 2020). Leading WFH stressors included blurred work-home boundaries, isolation from co-workers, and unmanageable workloads/hours (Microsoft, 2020). On job performance, WFH was better for tasks requiring concentration, privacy, or creativity, but poorer for people-centric work, such as collaborating or coaching/mentoring (IGWA, 2020). Ultimately, employee well-being and work attitudes/outcomes relate to, even characterize, career sustainability (De Vos, Van der Heijden, & Akkermans, 2020; Van der Heijden & De Vos, 2015), the prerequisite for career *advancement*. Beyond individual careers, they also affect "long-term organizational health, customer satisfaction and loyalty, and financial success" (Deci, Olafsen, & Ryan, 2017).

SOLUTIONS AND RECOMMENDATIONS

On the surface, WFH may appear unfavourable for career advancement, hampering Achieving, Improving, and Proving Competence. Indeed, lower career advancement has often been a leading concern for employees when taking up teleworking (Maruyama & Tietze, 2012; Mokhtarian, Bagley & Salomon, 1998). However, such concerns and WFH reluctance may stem from doubts regarding organizations' human resource management (HRM) practices adapting suitably for telework (Illegems & Verbeke, 2004). Thus, appropriate HRM and technology practices *can* support employee career advancement under WFH.

Appropriate Jobs

First and foremost, organizations must judiciously select the jobs, hence teams, which may be moved to WFH. Job feasibility under home conditions should be the prime consideration and would ensure Achieving Competence. Baruch (2000) suggests that a telework-appropriate job is one "for which relevant technology is available, and is achievable without the necessity of physical presence in the workplace" and ICT is making a variety of jobs, even those involving some degree of client interaction, practicable from home. However, feasible-from-home need not mean the same ease or quality as at-office. For instance, the WFH-feasible "systems programmers" job (Guimaraes & Dallow, 1999) may involve collaborative agile work practices that are "harder to perform" virtually (Mancl & Fraser, 2020). Overall, for any job under WFH, Achieving Competence is better served if clear, measurable goals of what needs to be accomplished and by when are established through discussion between supervisors and employees (Guimaraes & Dallow, 1999).

Technology Enablement

Appropriate technology is critical for WFH employees to effectively deliver on task goals and Achieve Competence. Bosua et al. (2013) found that "[m]ultiple tools and devices" provided mostly by the employer can boost teleworker and team productivity. Suggested technology for seamless remote-working includes high-speed internet connection, laptops, smartphones, and a suite of cloud-based tools including email, file-share, chat, and videoconferencing apps (Bosua et al., 2013). Even "'Bring Your Own Devices' (BYOD) with some tools provided by the organisation" may "significantly facilitate productive telework" (Bosua et al., 2013). However, BYOD should not mean sub-par technology or shifting expenses onto employees. Employers should reimburse workers to afford office-quality equipment or provide it themselves (as per local laws) to prevent productivity loss, frustration, or disengagement (ILO, 2020). Further, employers must ensure requisite content is remotely available (Bosua et al., 2013). This may require becoming a "paperless organization," storing information digitally for anywhere, anytime access

(Akkirman & Harris, 2005). Going beyond digitizing content (e.g., scanning in papers) to digitizing workflows, organizations may discover more WFH-feasible functions.

Apart from tools and content for Achieving Competence, remote access to *training content* is also required for Improving Competence from home. The pandemic exposed that formal training was unavailable online for most (ServiceNow, 2020). Further, promptly available and helpful staff for ICT troubleshooting are important for strain-free, effectual digital working (Day et al., 2012). However, WFH access to equipment or content may first require appropriate regulatory and contractual waivers (e.g., TCS-NASSCOM: Choudhury, 2020; Mendonca & Pramanik, 2020). Client contractual waivers commonly relate to data security, privacy, and confidentiality concerns as WFH takes content out of safe, controlled environments. These concerns may be overcome with appropriate cybersecurity measures, such as preventing the use of personal accounts for sensitive emails (Borkovich & Skovira, 2020). Personal devices accessing enterprise assets under BYOD also call for care. However, overzealous security monitoring/curbs may hurt productivity (Achieving Competence) and are avoidable (Borkovich & Skovira, 2020). Overall, appropriate technology can help satisfy all three employee psychological needs: competence as discussed above, autonomy by allowing them to work as they choose (e.g., location/time/pace), and relatedness by connecting them with colleagues through communication.

Communication Support

Despite resources for effective task delivery or Achieving Competence, WFH may make employees feel relegated to what Shamir and Salomon (1985) call a "secondary" status lacking training and promotion opportunities, i.e., dissatisfied with Improving and Proving Competence. At first, WFH does appear to hamper Improving Competence by restricting access to supervisory feedback, informal learning, challenging work, and mentoring; and Proving Competence by limiting interpersonal networking, visibility, sponsoring, and other benefits of mentoring.

However, a closer look reveals that most enablers of Improving or Proving Competence are grounded in interpersonal communication; hence, the associated dissatisfaction may be remedied with appropriate communication mechanisms. Rich and varied communication media, from video-conferencing to chat apps, as also suggested by Bosua et al. (2013) may help WFH employees maintain robust and diverse interactions. A communication medium's richness is its ability to support multiple information cues, quick feedback, and personal focus (Lengel & Daft, 1988). Videoconferencing as an "interactive" medium is thus second only to in-person exchanges in richness (Lengel & Daft, 1988). Rich, real-time multimedia can enable emotional expression and social bonding to facilitate virtual mentoring (Hamilton & Scandura, 2003) and other sensitive interpersonal interactions. Another medium: chat/instant messaging, is useful for informal communication or "impromptu, brief, context-rich and dyadic" interactions that "support joint problem solving, coordination, social bonding, and social learning" (Nardi, Whittaker, & Bradner, 2000). Thus, with suitable communication media, organizations can support WFH employees to Achieve, Improve, and Prove Competence, as well as enable social bonding to overcome isolation and satisfy the need for relatedness.

Self-Driven Employee

While appropriate communication media may be provided, whether they will be effectively used remains to an extent the teleworker's choice, which in turn depends on personal characteristics. Some individual traits act as *personal resources* similar to job resources (Bakker & Demerouti, 2017) in enabling Achieving, Improving, and Proving Competence.

One personal resource especially significant for teleworkers is *proactive personality*, i.e., taking the initiative to identify opportunities, act, and persevere until the desired change is achieved (Vermooten, Boonzaier, & Kidd, 2019). Proactive teleworkers will leverage offered communication media to gather information and "remain 'in the loop'" (Greenberg, Ashton-James, & Ashkanasy, 2007), thus facilitate their career advancement, as well as combat isolation and satisfy their need for relatedness. As regards gender as a characteristic: to manage work-family conflicts under WFH and continue delivering effectively at job tasks, women may need to more strategically segment/structure work-home boundaries than men, as women tend to have greater domestic responsibilities but lesser "schedule control and job authority" (Fonner & Stache, 2012). Meanwhile, maturity, tenure, self-discipline, self-motivation, and the ability to work on one's own are other employee qualities that support successful WFH (Akkirman & Harris, 2005; Baruch, 2000). Organizations may evaluate individual characteristics when determining whom to shift to, or recruit for, WFH positions and the support they require.

Supportive Supervisory Style

WFH necessitates proactivity from managers (Lamond, 2000). Supervisors may proactively hold individual and group-level formal and informal virtual (occasionally in-person) interactions for social connect, information dissemination, and problem-solving (Lamond, 2000), which could aid employee career advancement and team effectiveness under today's increasingly collaborative work conditions. Such interactions could also satisfy employees' need for relatedness (Orsini & Rodrigues 2020). As Kotera et al. (2020) discovered, brief informal virtual team huddles held every morning during COVID helped beat isolation to enhance well-being and boost team cohesion.

A leading weakness of supervisors has been the "lack of regular feedback to telecommuters" (Guimaraes & Dallow, 1999). Thus, managers can proactively hold one-to-one feedback-sharing sessions to enable employees to Improve Competence. The sessions can be in-person occasionally, with virtual feedback found somewhat lacking (Lund et al., 2020). Yet, excess information and overly frequent communication are also inadvisable (Lamond, 2000)—it may frustrate employees' need for autonomy. Further on individual interactions, supervisors must eschew any discrimination: for instance, some women experienced less supervisor contact during the pandemic than men (The Economist, 2020).

Another major weakness of supervisors that teleworkers note is a "lack of trust" (Guimaraes & Dallow, 1999). Productive long-term WFH calls for trust in monitoring the physically invisible employee's performance. Under WFH, supervisors cannot make impromptu in-person status checks and must employ more disciplined and formal methods (Lamond, 2000). In this regard, ICT enables "considerably more" supervisory monitoring than possible in-person (Townsend, DeMarie, & Hendrickson, 1998). Employee activity tracking software sales surged during pandemic WFH (Morrison, 2020). However, supervision should not morph into invasive scrutiny (Lamond, 2000). Close observational monitoring breeds distrust (Liao & Chun, 2016) and thwarts employees' psychological need satisfaction (Mishra & Ghosh, 2020). COVID WFH confirmed that employees who self-reported their activities experienced autonomy and trust, while those under continuous digital surveillance felt forced/non-autonomous; such snooping also raising privacy-related legal concerns (Morrison, 2020). As such, managing based on trust and coaching not policing might be more effective (Lamond, 2000), and better support teleworker career advancement.

Further, supervisors can help teleworkers Prove Competence by bringing visibility and exposure to them before decision-makers (Lamond, 2000). Visibility may be enabled through "visits to the office to organise group presentations or participation in important project groups, or simply a lunch meeting with the boss" (Lamond, 2000). Virtual exposures may also be arranged. Overall, teleworkers would certainly benefit from supervisors providing task goal clarity and structure—elements of task-oriented leadership. However, the greater emphasis on communication, trust, and building advancement opportunities for employees indicate that WFH primarily requires relationship-oriented leadership (Dahlstrom, 2013).

Redesigned Performance Management

Although supervisor-facilitated visibility may enable one WFH employee's career advancement, a better enabler for all workers would be a result-oriented organizational culture. Specifically, "a culture of management where people are measured by results rather than by attendance" (Baruch, 2000) or "face time" (Bloom et al., 2015).

This culture would manifest through a "result-based performance management system" that evaluates employee performance, such as in terms of productivity and quality, against mutually agreed, clear, and specific goals (ILO, 2020; Kowalski & Swanson, 2005; Raghuram, 2014). Understandably, goals and performance may not be "easily quantified" for all jobs (Bloom et al., 2015), but qualitative goals may also be detailed, defined, and unambiguous. Evaluation criteria based on clear and specific goals (including what constitutes "fully satisfactory" or complete: ILO, 2020) would enable employees to autonomously track progress and adjust to "optimize performance," and build a "perception of procedural fairness" (Raghuram, 2014). Thus, clear and specific goals would help employees in *being* competent and perceive equity in being *seen* as competent.

After goals are set, supervisors should avoid micromanaging employee performance (impede autonomy) yet provide timely and useful feedback (support competence); and hold "sensitive performance conversations" over video-calls to support non-verbal cues (ILO, 2020). Note that teleworker "workload, performance measurement and evaluation, expectations, reporting, monitoring" must also align with local laws (ILO, 2020).

Training

WFH employees, as well as their at-office colleagues and supervisors would gain from telework fundamentals training, which could help everyone better adapt to the practice and may moreover be legally mandated (ILO, 2020). Training on the use of ICT (Akkirman & Harris, 2005), including cybersecurity practices (Borkovich & Skovira, 2020), would especially ensure undisrupted working. Learning about the importance and means of open and formal communication (Cooper & Kurland, 2002) would benefit too. Older employees may particularly require coaching on virtual communication (Choudhury, 2020). Training on "office organization and time management" (Guimaraes & Dallow, 1999) would also help operate effectively despite blurred work-home boundaries (ILO, 2020).

For supervisors, remote team management skills training would be beneficial, covering appropriate leadership skills, remote coaching and mentoring, role-modelling, proactive engagement, collaboration (ILO, 2020), also "techniques of results-based management, job analysis, work specification, and performance appraisal" (Guimaraes & Dallow, 1999). WFH and at-office workers should get equal access to training (Eurofound, 2020) in soft/domain skills, ensuring telework is not "secondary."

Interventions for Well-being

WFH's unique circumstances including blurred work-home boundaries, extended work hours, and separation from colleagues can impede well-being. Given its relevance for employee career sustainability, thereby advancement, employers must actively intervene to boost well-being. Coaching on mindfulness, healthy living (exercise, nutrition, and sleep), and handling stress (ILO, 2020; TechGig, 2020) would benefit well-being. And while training for work-life balance may be useful too, more effective will be policies empowering employees to disconnect without fear of career repercussions (e.g., company directive to end conference calls by 5:30 pm) and encouraging availing leaves (ILO, 2020; Natu & Ram, 2020; TechGig, 2020). The "right to disconnect" even finds reference in some teleworker laws (ILO, 2020). Also important are policies extending childcare support to teleworkers, such as parental leave (ILO, 2020) or childcare allowances. Challenges with combining work and childcare can hamper performance and trigger turnover (Metzger & Von Glinow, 1988). Virtual socialization sessions are also required to overcome isolation and boost team camaraderie (Choudhury, 2020), thus satisfying employee needs for relatedness and competence.

FUTURE RESEARCH DIRECTIONS

WFH will likely last for numerous white-collar employees and for some, irrespective of their personal preferences. Thus, research will need to examine favourable and unfavourable causes under WFH and their immediate and long-term implications. In this context, the new CCAM takes a psychological perspective of career advancement—a long-term phenomenon important for employee job satisfaction (Herzberg, Mausner, & Snyderman, 1959/2017) and significantly influenced by conditions of WFH.

While the CCAM was conceptualised amid mass pandemic-driven WFH, the model, its three stages, and the identified JD-R influences are generalizable beyond WFH. For instance, appropriate tools, supervisor and co-worker support, and opportunities to develop and demonstrate capabilities are as relevant to the advancement of an at-office white-collar worker of any industry. Thus, future research could focus on developing instruments to operationalize CCAM for application in varied work conditions. For this, researchers may leverage existing scales measuring need for competence satisfaction/frustration (e.g., Longo, Gunz, Curtis, & Farsides, 2016; Van den Broeck et al., 2010). However, from the CCAM perspective, current scales appear applicable primarily to task-referential competence, hence Achieving Competence. There remains an opportunity to gauge satisfaction/frustration of past-referential and other-referential competence as relevant to Improving and Proving Competence.

Further, training modules pertinent to each stage of the CCAM may be designed to aid career counselling. Additionally, the CCAM can help recognize gaps in job resources directly affecting competence to guide corporate policy, such as on technology asset access or performance management and appraisal. Meanwhile, transfer/recruitment for home-based work can benefit from the personal characteristics found WFH-suitable. The well-being impact identified under CCAM can inform policies on work hours and scheduling, employee health and wellness, employee engagement, leave, and childcare. The training modules and policy changes may be introduced and their impacts assessed through experimental research straddling academic and corporate worlds.

Research opportunities also exist in examining career advancement from the perspective of gender and regulations. Gender, for instance, has demonstrated its association with various relevant demands/

resources, such as family-work interference, access to networks and mentoring, and the nature of jobs likely to be retained at office versus shifted to home. Meanwhile, regulations such as those affecting equipment access/reimbursement, cybersecurity, work hours and overtime, performance appraisal, and mandatory training for teleworkers can all affect effectual working.

CONCLUSION

WFH is here and here to stay for several white-collar employees worldwide. Conditions of home-based working will likely profoundly affect executing job tasks, learning and development, also demonstrating capabilities in comparison to peers; all of which in turn hold implications for employee career advancement and organizational talent management in the long run.

In this context, the authors propose a new model for career advancement: the Competence Career Advancement Model. CCAM comprises three stages, each based on one form of the basic psychological need for competence or the need for effectance and attaining valued outcomes. The stages are: Achieving Competence or delivering effectively on current-level tasks (need for task-referential competence), Improving Competence or developing and improving skills to better perform at current tasks and prepare for next-level ones (past-referential competence), and Proving Competence or demonstrating competence vis-à-vis peers' at performance appraisal (other-referential competence). Further, the stages of CCAM are influenced by job demands—that which need to be done and job resources—that which help get things done and enable personal learning and development. In turn, the conditions of WFH affect job demands and resources, thereby impacting career advancement.

Looking at each stage of CCAM and relevant job demands and resources in the context of WFH: Achieving Competence depends on task characteristics/WFH-suitability, as also the job resources of ICT, communication, supervisor and co-worker support, and interruption-free working. Improving Competence depends on the job resources of feedback, formal and informal learning, challenging work, and mentoring. Finally, Proving Competence depends not only on having achieved and improved competence, but also the job resources of networking and mentor-facilitated visibility to show competence. Overall, WFH appears to constrain access to most job resources across stages.

The CCAM is linked to the need for competence and satisfaction/frustration of a basic psychological need driving well-being/ill-being. Therefore, WFH conditions supporting/thwarting the employee at any stage of CCAM positively/negatively affect well-being and work attitudes/outcomes. Overall, WFH can challenge need for competence satisfaction. Employees need to work longer and balance work-home boundaries while being isolated from colleagues among other issues, which can adversely affect job performance, job satisfaction, and work engagement. During COVID, many WFH employees were stressed, emotional drained, and physically exhausted. Employee well-being and work attitudes/outcomes affect career sustainability thus career advancement, and also organizational health. Therefore, employers must create job demand-resource conditions that enable employees to Achieve, Improve, and Prove Competence, hence satisfy their need for competence and experience well-being. Recommendations in this regard include shifting to WFH the most feasible jobs, providing sufficient ICT support, enabling unhindered and varied communication, considering employee characteristics to judge WFH suitability and required support, relationship-oriented supervising, managing by results, and training to cope with WFH. Organizations are also encouraged to take well-being-enhancing initiatives that facilitate work-life balance and overcome isolation under WFH.

Overall, the career advancement of the white-collar employee is a multi-stage process with numerous influences at each stage and implications for the employee, as well as the organization. Beyond tasks and tools, career advancement is also about communicating, relationship-building, and long-term well-being.

ACKNOWLEDGMENT

This work received no specific grant from any funding agency in the public, commercial, or not-for-profit sectors.

REFERENCES

Akkirman, A. D., & Harris, D. L. (2005). Organizational communication satisfaction in the virtual workplace. *Journal of Management Development*, *24*(5), 397–409. doi:10.1108/02621710510598427

Arnetz, B., & Blomkvist, V. (2007). Leadership, Mental Health, and Organizational Efficacy in Health Care Organizations: Psychosocial Predictors of Healthy Organizational Development Based on Prospective Data from Four Different Organizations. *Psychotherapy and Psychosomatics*, *76*(4), 242–248. doi:10.1159/000101503 PMID:17570963

Baard, P. P., Deci, E. L., & Ryan, R. M. (2004). Intrinsic Need Satisfaction: A Motivational Basis of Performance and Weil-Being in Two Work Settings. *Journal of Applied Social Psychology*, *34*(10), 2045–2068. doi:10.1111/j.1559-1816.2004.tb02690.x

Bailey, D. E., & Kurland, N. B. (2002). A review of telework research: Findings, new directions, and lessons for the study of modern work. *Journal of Organizational Behavior*, *23*(4), 383–400. doi:10.1002/job.144

Bakker, A. B., & Demerouti, E. (2017). Job Demands–Resources Theory: Taking Stock and Looking Forward. *Journal of Occupational Health Psychology*, *22*(3), 273–285. doi:10.1037/ocp0000056 PMID:27732008

Baruch, Y. (2000). Teleworking: Benefits and pitfalls as perceived by professionals and managers. *New Technology, Work and Employment*, *15*(1), 34–49. doi:10.1111/1468-005X.00063

Beauregard, T., Canonico, E., & Basile, K. A. (2019). "The Fur-Lined Rut": Telework and Career Ambition. In C. Kelliher & J. Richardson (Eds.), Work, Working and Work Relationships in a Changing World (pp. 17-36). Routledge.

Bélanger, F., & Allport, C. D. (2008). Collaborative technologies in knowledge telework: An exploratory study. *Information Systems Journal*, *18*(1), 101–121. doi:10.1111/j.1365-2575.2007.00252.x

Bentley, T., Teo, S., McLeod, L., Tan, F., & Bo, R. (2016). The role of organisational support in teleworker wellbeing: A sociotechnical systems approach. *Applied Ergonomics*, *52*, 207–215. doi:10.1016/j.apergo.2015.07.019 PMID:26360212

Bernstein, E., Blunden, H., Brodsky, A., Sohn, W., & Waber, B. (2020, July 15). The Implications of Working Without an Office. *Harvard Business Review*. Retrieved from https://hbr.org/2020/07/the-implications-of-working-without-an-office

Bloom, N., Liang, J., Roberts, J., & Ying, Z. J. (2015). Does Working from Home Work? Evidence from a Chinese Experiment. *The Quarterly Journal of Economics*, *130*(1), 165–218. doi:10.1093/qje/qju032

Borkovich, D. J., & Skovira, R. J. (2020). Working from home: Cybersecurity in the age of COVID-19. *Issues in Information Systems*, *21*(4), 234–246. doi:10.48009/4_iis_2020_234-246

Bosua, R., Gloet, M., Kurnia, S., Mendoza, A., & Yong, J. (2013). Telework, productivity and wellbeing: An Australian perspective. *Telecommunications Journal of Australia*, *63*(1), 11.1-11.12. doi:10.7790/tja.v63i1.390

Carmeli, A., Shalom, R., & Weisberg, J. (2007). Considerations in organizational career advancement: What really matters. *Personnel Review*, *36*(2), 190–205. doi:10.1108/00483480710726109

Challenger, J. E. (1992). Telecommuters Risk Becoming Invisible Workers. *Management World*, *20*(1), 8–10.

Choudhury, P. (2020). Our Work-from-Anywhere Future. *Harvard Business Review*, *98*(6), 58.

Cooper, C. D., & Kurland, N. B. (2002). Telecommuting, professional isolation, and employee development in public and private organizations. *Journal of Organizational Behavior*, *23*(4), 511–532. doi:10.1002/job.145

Dahik, A., Lovich, D., Kreafle, C., Bailey, A., Kilmann, J., Kennedy, D., . . . Wenstrup, J. (2020). *What 12,000 Employees Have to Say About the Future of Remote Work*. Boston Consulting Group. Retrieved from https://www.bcg.com/publications/2020/valuable-productivity-gains-covid-19

Dahlstrom, T. R. (2013). Telecommuting and Leadership Style. *Public Personnel Management*, *42*(3), 438–451. doi:10.1177/0091026013495731

Day, A., Paquet, S., Scott, N., & Hambley, L. (2012). Perceived Information and Communication Technology (ICT) Demands on Employee Outcomes: The Moderating Effect of Organizational ICT Support. *Journal of Occupational Health Psychology*, *17*(4), 473–491. doi:10.1037/a0029837 PMID:23066697

De Vos, A., Van der Heijden, B. I., & Akkermans, J. (2020). Sustainable careers: Towards a conceptual model. *Journal of Vocational Behavior*, *117*, 103196. Advance online publication. doi:10.1016/j.jvb.2018.06.011

Deci, E. L., Connell, J. E., & Ryan, R. M. (1989). Self-determination in a work organization. *The Journal of Applied Psychology*, *74*(4), 580–590. doi:10.1037/0021-9010.74.4.580

Deci, E. L., Olafsen, A. H., & Ryan, R. M. (2017). Self-determination theory in work organizations: The state of a science. *Annual Review of Organizational Psychology and Organizational Behavior*, *4*(1), 19–43. doi:10.1146/annurev-orgpsych-032516-113108

Deci, E. L., & Ryan, R. M. (2000). The "What" and "Why" of Goal Pursuits: Human Needs and the Self-Determination of Behavior. *Psychological Inquiry*, *11*(4), 227–268. doi:10.1207/S15327965PLI1104_01

Dingel, J. I., & Neiman, B. (2020). *How Many Jobs Can be Done at Home? NBER Working Paper Series: w26948*. National Bureau of Economic Research. Retrieved from https://www.nber.org/papers/w26948.pdf

Duxbury, L., & Neufeld, D. (1999). An empirical evaluation of the impacts of telecommuting on intra-organizational communication. *Journal of Engineering and Technology Management*, *16*(1), 1–28. doi:10.1016/S0923-4748(98)00026-5

Elliot, A. J., & McGregor, H. A. (2001). A 2×2 achievement goal framework. *Journal of Personality and Social Psychology*, *80*(3), 501–519. doi:10.1037/0022-3514.80.3.501 PMID:11300582

Elliot, A. J., McGregor, H. A., & Thrash, T. M. (2002). The Need for Competence. In E. L. Deci & R. M. Ryan (Eds.), *Handbook of Self-Determination Research* (pp. 361–388). The University of Rochester Press.

Eurofound. (2020). *Living, working and COVID-19*. Publications Office of the European Union. Retrieved from https://www.eurofound.europa.eu/sites/default/files/ef_publication/field_ef_document/ef20059en.pdf

Eurofound and International Labour Organization. (2017). *Working anytime, anywhere: The effects on the world of work. WCMS_544138*. Publications Office of the European Union and the International Labour Office., doi:10.2806/372726

Felstead, A., & Reuschke, D. (2020). *Homeworking in the UK: Before and During the 2020 Lockdown*. Wales Institute of Social and Economic Research.

Fernet, C., Austin, S., Trépanier, S.-G., & Dussault, M. (2013). How do job characteristics contribute to burnout? Exploring the distinct mediating roles of perceived autonomy, competence, and relatedness. *European Journal of Work and Organizational Psychology*, *22*(2), 123–137. doi:10.1080/1359432X.2011.632161

Fonner, K. L., & Stache, L. C. (2012). All in a day's work, at home: Teleworkers' management of micro role transitions and the work–home boundary. *New Technology, Work and Employment*, *27*(3), 242–257. doi:10.1111/j.1468-005X.2012.00290.x

Gagné, M., & Deci, E. L. (2005). Self-determination theory and work motivation. *Journal of Organizational Behavior*, *26*(4), 331–362. doi:10.1002/job.322

Gagné, M., & Panaccio, A. (2014). The Motivational Power of Job Design. In M. Gagné (Ed.), *The Oxford Handbook of Work Engagement, Motivation, and Self-Determination Theory* (pp. 165–180). Oxford University Press.

Gartner. (2020, April 3). Gartner CFO Survey Reveals 74% Intend to Shift Some Employees to Remote Work Permanently. *Gartner*. Retrieved from https://www.gartner.com/en/newsroom/press-releases/2020-04-03-gartner-cfo-surey-reveals-74-percent-of-organizations-to-shift-some-employees-to-remote-work-permanently2

Gerdenitsch, C. (2017). New Ways of Working and Satisfaction of Psychological Needs. In C. Korunka & B. Kubicek (Eds.), *Job Demands in a Changing World of Work* (pp. 91–109). Springer., doi:10.1007/978-3-319-54678-0_6

Gottlieb, C., Grobovšek, J., & Poschke, M. (2020). Working from home across countries. *CEPR Covid Economics: Vetted and Real-Time Papers, 8*, 71-91. Retrieved from https://cepr.org/sites/default/files/news/CovidEconomics8.pdf

Greenberg, J., Ashton-James, C. E., & Ashkanasy, N. M. (2007). Social comparison processes in organizations. *Organizational Behavior and Human Decision Processes*, *102*(1), 22–41. doi:10.1016/j.obhdp.2006.09.006

Greenhaus, J. H., Parasuraman, S., & Wormley, W. M. (1990). Effects of Race on Organizational Experiences, Job Performance Evaluations, and Career Outcomes. *Academy of Management Journal*, *33*(1), 64–86. doi:10.2307/256352

Grubb, T. (2007). Performance Appraisal Reappraised: It's Not All Positive. *Journal of Human Resource Education*, *1*(1), 1–22.

Guimaraes, T., & Dallow, P. (1999). Empirically testing the benefits, problems, and success factors for telecommuting programmes. *European Journal of Information Systems*, *8*(1), 40–54. doi:10.1057/palgrave.ejis.3000317

Hamilton, B. A., & Scandura, T. A. (2003). E-mentoring: Implications for organizational learning and development in a wired world. *Organizational Dynamics*, *31*(4), 388–402. doi:10.1016/S0090-2616(02)00128-6

Harvard Business Review Analytic Services. (2017). *How Collaboration Wins: Leadership, Benefits, and Best Practices.* Harvard Business School Publishing. Retrieved from https://hbr.org/resources/pdfs/comm/citrix/HowCollaborationWins.pdf

Hatayama, M., Viollaz, M., & Winkler, H. (2020). *Jobs' Amenability to Working from Home: Evidence from Skills Surveys for 53 Countries. Policy Research Working Paper 9241.* World Bank Group. Retrieved from https://openknowledge.worldbank.org/handle/10986/33753

Heron, R., & Unger, L. (1999). *Glossary of Labour Administration and Related Terms.* International Labour Organization. Retrieved from https://www.ilo.org/wcmsp5/groups/public/---ed_dialogue/---lab_admin/documents/publication/wcms_111331.pdf

Herzberg, F., Mausner, B., & Snyderman, B. B. (2017). *The Motivation to Work*. Routledge. (Original work published 1959) doi:10.4324/9781315124827

Hitachi Capital. (2020, July 29). *SME business cost savings from remote working*. Retrieved from https://www.hitachicapital.co.uk/business-finance/invoice-finance/invoice-finance-blog/sme-business-cost-savings-from-remote-working/

Illegems, V., & Verbeke, A. (2004). Telework: What Does it Mean for Management? *Long Range Planning*, *37*(4), 319–334. doi:10.1016/j.lrp.2004.03.004

International Labour Organization. (2020). *Teleworking during the COVID-19 pandemic and beyond: A Practical Guide*. International Labour Office.

Iometrics and Global Workplace Analytics. (2020). *Global Work-from-Home Experience Survey*. Iometrics and Global Workplace Analytics.

Ishida, H., Su, K.-H., & Spilerman, S. (2002). Models of Career Advancement in Organizations. *European Sociological Review*, *18*(2), 179–198. doi:10.1093/esr/18.2.179

Judge, T. A., Thoresen, C. J., Bono, J. E., & Patton, G. K. (2001). The Job Satisfaction-Job Performance Relationship: A Qualitative and Quantitative Review. *Psychological Bulletin*, *127*(3), 376–407. doi:10.1037/0033-2909.127.3.376 PMID:11393302

Kotera, Y., Green, P., Rhodes, C., Williams, A., Chircop, J., Spink, R., Rawson, R., & Okere, U. (2020). Dealing With Isolation Using Online Morning Huddles for University Lecturers During Physical Distancing by COVID-19: Field Notes. *International Review of Research in Open and Distributed*, *21*(4), 238–244. doi:10.19173/irrodl.v21i4.4843

Kowalski, K. B., & Swanson, J. A. (2005). Critical success factors in developing teleworking programs. *Benchmarking*, *12*(3), 236–249. doi:10.1108/14635770510600357

Kram, K. E. (1983). Phases of the mentor relationship. *Academy of Management Journal*, *26*(4), 608–625. doi:10.2307/255910

Kurland, N. B., & Bailey, D. E. (1999). Telework; The Advantages and Challenges of Working Here, There, Anywhere, and Anytime. *Organizational Dynamics*, *28*(2), 53–68. doi:10.1016/S0090-2616(00)80016-9

Lamond, D. (2000). Managerial Style and Telework. In K. Daniels, D. Lamond, & P. Standen (Eds.), *Managing Telework: Perspectives from Human Resource Management and Work Psychology* (1st ed., pp. 103–112). Thomson Learning.

Legault, L. (2017). Self-Determination Theory. In V. Zeigler-Hill & T. K. Shackelford (Eds.), *Encyclopedia of Personality and Individual Differences*. Springer. doi:10.1007/978-3-319-28099-8_1162-1

Lengel, R. H., & Daft, R. L. (1988). The Selection of Communication Media as an Executive Skill. *The Academy of Management Perspectives*, *2*(3), 225–232. doi:10.5465/ame.1988.4277259

LePine, J. A., Podsakoff, N. P., & LePine, M. A. (2005). A meta-analytic test of the challenge stressor-hindrance stressor framework: An explanation for inconsistent relationships among stressors and performance. *Academy of Management Journal*, *48*(5), 764–775. doi:10.5465/amj.2005.18803921

Liao, E. Y., & Chun, H. (2016). Supervisor monitoring and subordinate innovation. *Journal of Organizational Behavior*, *37*(2), 168–192. doi:10.1002/job.2035

Limburg, D. O. (1998). Teleworking in managerial context. In R. Suomi, P. Jackson, L. Hollmen, & M. Aspnas (Eds.), *Teleworking Environments: Proceedings of the Third International Workshop of Telework. TUCS General Publication No. 8*, (pp. 93-106). Turku, Finland: Turku Center for Computer Science.

Longo, Y., Gunz, A., Curtis, G. J., & Farsides, T. (2016). Measuring Need Satisfaction and Frustration in Educational and Work Contexts: The Need Satisfaction and Frustration Scale (NSFS). *Journal of Happiness Studies*, *17*(1), 295–317. doi:10.100710902-014-9595-3

Lund, S., Madgavkar, A., Manyika, J., & Smit, S. (2020). *What's next for remote work: An analysis of 2,000 tasks, 800 jobs, and nine countries*. McKinsey Global Institute. Retrieved from https://www.mckinsey.com/featured-insights/future-of-work/whats-next-for-remote-work-an-analysis-of-2000-tasks-800-jobs-and-nine-countries

Mancl, D., & Fraser, S. D. (2020). COVID-19's Influence on the Future of Agile. In M. Paasivaara & P. Kruchten (Eds.), *Agile Processes in Software Engineering and Extreme Programming – Workshops. XP 2020. Lecture Notes in Business Information Processing. 396* (pp. 309–316). Springer. doi:10.1007/978-3-030-58858-8_32

Maruyama, T., & Tietze, S. (2012). From anxiety to assurance: Concerns and outcomes of telework. *Personnel Review*, *41*(4), 450–469. doi:10.1108/00483481211229375

Maurer, R. (2020, July 30). *Admin Jobs Projected to Stay Remote After COVID-19*. Retrieved from SHRM: Society for Human Resource Management: https://www.shrm.org/resourcesandtools/hr-topics/talent-acquisition/pages/admin-jobs-projected-stay-remote-covid19.aspx

McCloskey, D. W., & Igbaria, M. (2003). Does "Out of Sight" Mean "Out of Mind"? An Empirical Investigation of the Career Advancement Prospects of Telecommuters. *Information Resources Management Journal*, *16*(2), 19–34. doi:10.4018/irmj.2003040102

Mello, J. A. (2007). Managing Telework Programs Effectively. *Employee Responsibilities and Rights Journal*, *19*(4), 247–261. doi:10.100710672-007-9051-1

Mendonca, J., & Pramanik, A. (2020, March 16). Covid-19 impact: IT firms seek client waivers so staff can work from home. *The Economic Times*. Retrieved from https://economictimes.indiatimes.com/tech/ites/covid-19-impact-it-firms-seek-client-waivers-so-staff-can-work-from-home/articleshow/74642447.cms

Metzger, R. O., & Von Glinow, M. A. (1988). Off-Site Workers: At Home and Abroad. *California Management Review*, *30*(3), 101–111. doi:10.2307/41166517

Meyer, J. P., & Gagné, M. (2008). Employee Engagement From a Self-Determination Theory Perspective. *Industrial and Organizational Psychology: Perspectives on Science and Practice*, *1*(1), 60–62. doi:10.1111/j.1754-9434.2007.00010.x

Microsoft. (2020, September 22). *Work Trend Index: A pulse on employees' wellbeing, six months into the pandemic*. Retrieved from https://www.microsoft.com/en-us/microsoft-365/blog/2020/09/22/pulse-employees-wellbeing-six-months-pandemic/

Mishra, M., & Ghosh, K. (2020). Supervisor monitoring and subordinate work attitudes: a need satisfaction and supervisory support perspective. Leadership & Organization Development Journal. doi:10.1108/LODJ-05-2019-0204

Mokhtarian, P. L., Bagley, M. N., & Salomon, I. (1998). The impact of gender, occupation, and presence of children on telecommuting motivations and constraints. *Journal of the American Society for Information Science*, *49*(12), 1115–1134. doi:10.1002/(SICI)1097-4571(1998)49:12<1115::AID-ASI7>3.0.CO;2-Y

Morrison, S. (2020, April 2). *Just because you're working from home doesn't mean your boss isn't watching you. Recode.* Retrieved from https://www.vox.com/recode/2020/4/2/21195584/coronavirus-remote-work-from-home-employee-monitoring

Nardi, B. A., Whittaker, S. J., & Bradner, E. M. (2000). Interaction and outeraction: instant messaging in action. In *Proceedings of the 2000 ACM conference on Computer supported cooperative work* (pp. 79–88). Philadelphia, PA: Association for Computing Machinery. doi:10.1145/358916.358975

Natu, N., & Ram, S. G. (2020, July 26). As WFH employees start burning out, companies rejig leave policies. *The Times of India.* Retrieved from https://timesofindia.indiatimes.com/city/mumbai/as-wfh-employees-start-burning-out-companies-rejig-leave-policies/articleshow/77176631.cms

Noe, R. A. (1988). Women and Mentoring: A Review and Research Agenda. *Academy of Management Review, 13*(1), 65–78. doi:10.5465/amr.1988.4306784

Orhan, M. A., Rijsman, J. B., & van Dijk, G. M. (2016). Invisible, therefore isolated: Comparative effects of team virtualitywith task virtuality on workplace isolation and work outcomes. *Journal of Work and Organizational Psychology, 32*(2), 109–122. doi:10.1016/j.rpto.2016.02.002

Orsini, C., & Rodrigues, V. (2020). Supporting motivation in teams working remotely: The role of basic psychological needs. *Medical Teacher, 42*(7), 828–829. Advance online publication. doi:10.1080/0142159X.2020.1758305 PMID:32366152

Pérez, M., Sánchez, A., & de Luis Carnicer, M. (2002). Benefits and barriers of telework: Perception differences of human resources managers according to company's operations strategy. *Technovation, 22*(12), 775–783. doi:10.1016/S0166-4972(01)00069-4

Podsakoff, N. P., LePine, J. A., & LePine, M. A. (2007). Differential Challenge Stressor–Hindrance Stressor Relationships With Job Attitudes, Turnover Intentions, Turnover, and Withdrawal Behavior: A Meta-Analysis. *The Journal of Applied Psychology, 92*(2), 438–454. doi:10.1037/0021-9010.92.2.438 PMID:17371090

Raghuram, S. (2014). Telecommuting in India: Pitfalls and Possibilities. *SA Journal of Human Resource Management, 1*(2), 207–220. doi:10.1177/2322093714549108

Raghuram, S., London, M., & Larsen, H. H. (2001). Flexible employment practices in Europe: Country versus culture. *International Journal of Human Resource Management, 12*(5), 738–753. doi:10.1080/09585190122083

Richter, A. (2020). Locked-down digital work. *International Journal of Information Management, 55*, 102157. doi:10.1016/j.ijinfomgt.2020.102157 PMID:32836629

Richter, A., Tafvelin, S., & Sverke, M. (2018). The Mediated Relationship of Leadership on Job Insecurity. *Scandinavian Journal of Work and Organizational Psychology, 3*(1), 2. doi:10.16993jwop.43

Ryan, R. M., & Deci, E. L. (2000a). Intrinsic and Extrinsic Motivations: Classic Definitions and New Directions. *Contemporary Educational Psychology, 25*(1), 54–67. doi:10.1006/ceps.1999.1020 PMID:10620381

Ryan, R. M., & Deci, E. L. (2000b). Self-determination theory and the facilitation of intrinsic motivation, social development, and well-being. *The American Psychologist, 55*(1), 68–78. doi:10.1037/0003-066X.55.1.68 PMID:11392867

Sardeshmukh, S. R., Sharma, D., & Golden, T. D. (2012). Impact of telework on exhaustion and job engagement: A job demands and job resources model. *New Technology, Work and Employment, 27*(3), 193–207. doi:10.1111/j.1468-005X.2012.00284.x

Schaufeli, W. B., & Bakker, A. B. (2004). Job demands, job resources, and their relationship with burnout and engagement: A multi-sample study. *Journal of Organizational Behavior*, *25*(3), 293–315. doi:10.1002/job.248

Schaufeli, W. B., & Taris, T. W. (2014). A Critical Review of the Job Demands-Resources Model: Implications for Improving Work and Health. In G. F. Bauer & O. Hämmig (Eds.), *Bridging occupational, organizational and public health: A transdisciplinary approach* (pp. 43–68). Springer. doi:10.1007/978-94-007-5640-3_4

ServiceNow. (2020). *The Work Survey.* ServiceNow. Retrieved from https://www.servicenow.com/content/dam/servicenow-assets/public/en-us/doc-type/other-document/the-work-survey-by-servicenow-research-summary.pdf

Shamir, B., & Salomon, I. (1985). Work-at-Home and the Quality of Working Life. *Academy of Management Review*, *10*(3), 455–464. doi:10.5465/amr.1985.4278957

TechGig. (2020, July 6). *Stress-free WFH: Accenture implements new rules for employees. TechGig*. Retrieved from https://content.techgig.com/stress-free-wfh-accenture-implements-new-rules-for-employees/articleshow/76810872.cms

Tharenou, P. (1997). Explanations of Managerial Career Advancement. *Australian Psychologist*, *32*(1), 19–28. doi:10.1080/00050069708259614

The Economist. (2020, December 3). How the pandemic is forcing managers to work harder. *The Economist*. Retrieved from https://www.economist.com/business/2020/12/03/how-the-pandemic-is-forcing-managers-to-work-harder

Townsend, A. M., DeMarie, S. M., & Hendrickson, A. R. (1998). Virtual Teams: Technology and the Workplace of the Future. *The Academy of Management Executive*, *12*(3), 17–29. doi:10.5465/ame.1998.1109047

Turner, R. H. (1960). Sponsored and Contest Mobility and the School System. *American Sociological Review*, *25*(6), 855–867. doi:10.2307/2089982

United Nations. (2020). *Policy Brief: The Impact of COVID-19 on Women.* United Nations. Retrieved from http://digitallibrary.in.one.un.org/TempPdfFiles/4896_1.pdf

Van den Broeck, A., De Cuyper, N., De Witte, H., & Vansteenkiste, M. (2010). Not all job demands are equal: Differentiating job hindrances and job challenges in the Job Demands-Resources model. *European Journal of Work and Organizational Psychology*, *19*(6), 735–759. doi:10.1080/13594320903223839

Van den Broeck, A., Vansteenkiste, M., De Witte, H., Soenens, B., & Lens, W. (2010). Capturing autonomy, competence, and relatedness at work: Construction and initial validation of the Work-related Basic Need Satisfaction scale. *Journal of Occupational and Organizational Psychology*, *83*(4), 981–1002. doi:10.1348/096317909X481382

Van der Heijden, B. I., & De Vos, A. (2015). Sustainable careers: introductory chapter. In A. De Vos & B. I. Van der Heijden (Eds.), *Handbook of Research on Sustainable Careers* (pp. 1–19). Edward Elgar., doi:10.4337/9781782547037.00006

Vermooten, N., Boonzaier, B., & Kidd, M. (2019). Job crafting, proactive personality and meaningful work: Implications for employee engagement and turnover intention. *SA Journal of Industrial Psychology, 45*, a1567. doi:10.4102ajip.v45i0.1567

Wellman, B., Salaff, J., Dimitrova, D., Garton, L., Gulia, M., & Haythornthwaite, C. (1996). Computer Networks as Social Networks: Collaborative Work, Telework, and Virtual Community. *Annual Review of Sociology, 22*(1), 213–238. doi:10.1146/annurev.soc.22.1.213

ADDITIONAL READING

Blackburn, R., Furst, S., & Rosen, B. (2003). Building a Winning Virtual Team: KSAs, Selection. In C. B. Gibson & S. G. Cohen (Eds.), *Virtual Teams That Work: Creating Conditions for Virtual Team Effectiveness* (pp. 95–120). Jossey-Bass.

Daniels, K., Lamond, D. A., & Standen, P. (Eds.). (2000). *Managing Telework: Perspectives from Human Resource Management and Work Psychology* (1st ed.). Thomson Learning.

Deci, E. L., & Ryan, R. M. (Eds.). (2002). *Handbook of self-determination research.* University of Rochester Press.

Gagné, M. (Ed.). (2014). *The Oxford Handbook of Work Engagement, Motivation, and Self-Determination Theory*. Oxford University Press. doi:10.1093/oxfordhb/9780199794911.001.0001

Gajendran, R. S., & Harrison, D. A. (2007). The Good, the Bad, and the Unknown About Telecommuting: MetaAnalysis of Psychological Mediators and Individual Consequences. *The Journal of Applied Psychology, 92*(6), 1524–1541. doi:10.1037/0021-9010.92.6.1524 PMID:18020794

KEY TERMS AND DEFINITIONS

Achieving Competence: The first stage of the Competence Career Advancement Model, it involves mastering and effectually delivering the job tasks at one's current career level.

Career Advancement: Progressing up the organizational hierarchy, with such progress usually bringing more decision-making responsibilities.

Competence Career Advancement Model: A model depicting three stages—Achieving Competence, Improving Competence, and Proving Competence—that are a precursor to career advancement. The model is cyclical in nature, i.e., whether a worker progresses to handling next-level responsibilities or is retained at the current level, they must yet repeat all three stages.

Improving Competence: The second stage of the Competence Career Advancement Model, it involves developing and improving skills to enhance performance on tasks of the current career level and prepare for next-level requirements.

Proving Competence: The third stage of the Competence Career Advancement Model, it involves demonstrating competence favourably versus peers at the interpersonal competition presented by performance appraisal.

White-Collar Employee: Those under contract of employment and required to perform mainly non-manual office work.

Work From Home: When workers, typically using information & communication technologies, perform from their place of residence the same job tasks as they were contracted to perform from their employers' or clients' place of operations.

Chapter 10
Implications for Places of Remote Working

Anne E. Green
University of Birmingham, UK

Rebecca Riley
University of Birmingham, UK

ABSTRACT

A shift to remote working raises important issues about the changing geography of work and the associated implications for places. It seems unlikely that a 'new normal' after the COVID-19 pandemic will replicate the pre-COVID-19 picture. This has implications for the geography of work, both directly and indirectly because remote working in some jobs has implications for the sustainability of other jobs previously reliant on them. This chapter traces the possible short- and medium-term implications for places of remote working, addressing important questions relating to (1) the changing attractiveness of places in the context of greater remote working; (2) the future for city centres; (3) a possible revival of outer urban centres, market towns, and rural areas; (4) implications for geographical segregation and inequalities as different sub-groups face different possibilities for remote working; and (5) the implications of remote working for place-based policy.

INTRODUCTION

An increase in remote working raises important issues about the changing geography of work and the associated implications for places. This chapter is written from a UK perspective, but many of the issues raised have wider international relevance. The contours of the shift to remote working at the height of the first wave of the COVID-19 pandemic in March-May 2020 in the UK were uneven by sector and by occupation. Infections and COVID-19 related deaths rose again later in 2020 and in January 2021 the nations of the UK were in lockdown once again. While at the time of writing in early 2021 the situation remains fluid, it seems likely that the process of a shift to a 'new normal' will involve the creation of a new and more flexible geography of work, with important implications for places. While it is possible

DOI: 10.4018/978-1-7998-6754-8.ch010

to undertake some jobs remotely – for all or at least some of the time on a shorter- and longer-term basis – there are other jobs that, of necessity, are undertaken at a fixed site. This has direct implications for the geography of work. There are indirect effects too. Remote working in some jobs has implications for the sustainability of other jobs. An example is sandwich shops in city centres that become less profitable as footfall reduces because more office workers are working at home, at least for some of the time.

This chapter traces the possible short- and medium-term implications for places of remote working. It has five key objectives:

Objective 1: To explore which types of places, where, and for whom, are most attractive in the context of greater remote working

Objective 2: To examine what city centres, which have thrived on the face-to-face interactions possible in an environment of proximity, will look like in future in the context of greater remote working and an associated acceleration of the trend towards online retailing

Objective 3: To question whether greater remote working will lead to a revival of outer urban centres, market towns and rural areas

Objective 4: To assess whether places are likely to become more segregated and more unequal as (often more affluent) workers exercise the possibility to work from home while (often poorer and younger) workers are unable to do so

Objective 5: To explore the implications of remote working for place-based policy

The chapter first sets out the background to the phenomenon of remote working and its longer-term impacts. Next it focuses on implications for place attractiveness and implications for cities and city centres, before turning to implications for outer urban areas, market towns and rural areas. Attention then turns to the possible accentuation of socio-spatial inequalities as a result of the trends outlined and implications for place-based policies.

BACKGROUND

Commuting Trends

Over time the tendency has been for journeys to work to become longer and more complex, so large urban centres expand their influence over time (Coombes & Bond, 2008; Rae, 2017). Given the changing composition of employment this is unsurprising. There are more professional and managerial jobs commanding higher rates of pay, so enabling more costly travel. A sustained increase in car use for travel-to-work over the long-term enables access to more workplaces in a wider range of geographical locations. The growth in two-earner households is an additional driver, as it is often not feasible for a household to live within close proximity of two workplaces when partners are working in specialist professional occupations. Conversely, part-time workers, low-paid workers and those who have to organize their journeys-to-work along with trips for other purposes tend to be much more restricted in their travel horizons. They are often restricted to jobs available in their local area (Green & Owen, 2006).

The increase in remote working and other changes in ways of working during the COVID-19 pandemic have uneven spatial impacts. There are implications for the evolving functional economic geography of local areas and wider regions and for the purpose of places - with consequences for competitiveness, inclusiveness and sustainability. From a supply-side perspective, some individuals may work from home more and travel to a workplace less frequently than formerly, perhaps leading to fewer longer journeys if they choose to live in a location further from their workplace. On the other hand, some may opt to live close to their place of work, so as to walk or cycle. Some might have no choice about where to live; hence they are dependent on opportunities available locally. On the demand-side, it remains to be seen whether city centre working will decline in the longer-term. This in turn has implications for the viability of public transport as worker behaviour and the spatial and temporal footprints of daily urban systems change.

Trends in Remote Working

In the early years of the 21st century Hardill & Green (2003) noted how the temporal pattern of work had and was changing in its daily, weekly and monthly rhythms, with implications for the 'spatiality' of work: for some individuals paid work is undertaken at home, or in cyberspace. The increase in remote working has been evident for several decades, but despite claims about teleworking presaging the 'death of distance' (Cairncross, 1997), the pace of change has been gradual in the UK until the COVID-19 pandemic: 1.5% of people in employment were working mainly from home in 1981 rising to 4.7% in 2019 (Felstead & Reuschke, 2020). This marks a slow detachment of workers from conventional 'spatially fixed' workplaces.

This emphasis on working mainly from home masks a potentially more important rise in spatially hybrid working. Felstead (2012) pointed to a growth in the range of places (whether in the office, at home, on the train, etc.) in which office workers worked, with the help of information and communications technologies. He also highlighted the growth in partial homeworking (often just one day per week): in 1997 11.3% of workers used their home for at least one day per week as a place of work, but by 2010 this had risen to 15.3%). Fast forward a decade, evidence on homeworking in the UK in the first half of 2020 is available from a study primarily examining data from three online surveys undertaken in April, May and June 2020 as part of the Understanding Society: COVID-19 Study. This shows that in the UK during the COVID-19 national lockdown in April 2020 43.1% of workers were working exclusively from home; by June 2020 this proportion had fallen back slightly to 36.5% (Felstead & Reuschke, 2020). In January/February 2020 5.7% of workers were working exclusively from home.

A clear occupational pattern of homeworking during the COVID-19 pandemic is evident. In April and May 2020, a majority of those in managerial, professional, associate professional and technical, and administrative and secretarial staff worked exclusively from home. During lockdown, those in associate professional and technical occupations and in administrative and secretarial occupations became more likely to be doing some of their work at home than managers. Only a small minority of those in elementary, operative and skilled trades occupations reported working exclusively from home at any stage during the lockdown. The proportion of graduates reporting that they worked exclusively at home rose from 8.0% before lockdown to 62.4% in the first month of lockdown. By contrast, for those with no qualifications, the proportion exclusively working from home remained below 10% throughout lockdown. Taking occupation and qualification as proxies for skill level, this points to a clear tendency for those with higher level skills being more likely to work from home than those with lower level skills. By sector, there were marked differences in the extent of homeworking: three-quarters or more of workers in manufacturing and construction were not working from home.

The highest paid, the better qualified, the higher skilled and those living in London and the South East led the surge in homeworking during the early months of the COVID-19 pandemic (Felstead & Reuschke, 2020). It is workers with these characteristics who are predominant amongst 'new home-centred workers' in the COVID-19 pandemic (i.e. those who did no work at home or did so only occasionally before the lockdown but reported working exclusively or often at home during the lockdown). 'New home-centred workers' comprise around a third of all workers. They are predominantly higher qualified and better paid and more likely to be located in London and the South East. By contrast 'established factory/office-centred workers' who both before and after lockdown hardly ever worked from home (accounting for around half of workers) are lower qualified, more poorly paid, lower-skilled and more likely than average to be located in the Midlands, the North and in Wales, Scotland and Northern Ireland. Table 1 shows the UK picture together with the extremes at regional level (i.e. London and the West Midlands).

Table 1. Use of home as a workplace in the UK, London and the West Midlands, April 2020

Use of home as a workplace	Country/ Region	Jan/Feb 2020	April 2020	May 2020	June 2020
No use of home as a workplace	UK London West Midlands	70.6% 61.8% 77.2%	39.5% 28.1% 48.4%	40.0% 32.0% 48.9%	45.3% 32.5% 54.6%
Use of home as a workplace - sometimes	UK London West Midlands	17.7% 21.8% 12.9%	9.1% 8.0% 6.9%	10.3% 7.5% 9.3%	9.6% 7.5% 7.6%
Use of home as a workplace - often	UK London West Midlands	6.1% 9.2% 5.3%	8.3% 6.5% 8.6%	8.9% 7.5% 7.6%	8.7% 7.6% 9.5%
Use of home as a workplace - always	UK London West Midlands	5.7% 7.3% 4.6%	43.1% 57.5% 36.2%	40.8% 53.0% 34.1%	36.5% 52.4% 28.4%

Source: data from Felstead & Reuschke (2020)

Such variations in the possibilities for, and extent of, homeworking are not unique to the UK. In a US study based on analysis of O*NET data on the nature of work and job behaviours by occupation, Dingel & Neiman (2020) estimated that 37% of all jobs could be performed entirely from home. That such jobs are higher paid on average is illustrated by the fact that these 37% of jobs account for 46% of all US wages. As in the UK, there are variations by place in possibilities of working from home, cities such as San Francisco, San Jose and Washington DC displaying amongst the highest proportions and Las Vegas amongst the lowest.

It is clear that the COVID-19 pandemic has brought marked changes to where work is undertaken. In terms of implications for place, the future behaviour of those who have used home as a workplace always or sometimes is key for thinking about implications for places going forward. At face value it appears that 'enforced' homeworking for some workers during lockdown has given many employees an appetite for continued homeworking. In June 2020 88% of employees who had worked at home during lockdown reported that they would like to continue working at home in some capacity, and 47% of employees wanted to work at home often or all of the time. Given that every business forms part of a local ecosystem comprising other businesses in the area, through the operation of multiplier effects changes in the behaviour of workers at one business affects others. Remote working on a large scale amongst employees at large businesses in a local area affects those businesses that serve them – especially in large office hubs. Lopez Vanlenzuela (2020) cites the example of Pret a Manger which closed 30 of its branches in summer 2020 and made nearly 3,000 members of staff redundant with continuing dramatically reduced footfall. This raises the issue of the responsibility of large employers to the local areas where their offices/factories are located.

Implications for Productivity

Increased remote working, alongside pressures in some quarters for a return to fixed workplaces – in part to help secure the fortunes of other businesses in their local ecosystem that depend upon them, raises the issue of the impact of remote working on productivity. There is evidence to suggest that working from home does not have large negative impacts on productivity. Results from a working at home experiment in 2013 amongst call centre employees at a Chinese travel agency, revealed a 13% performance increase amongst those working from home (Bloom et al., 2015). (The experiment involved 1,000 employees who volunteered to be assigned randomly to two teams: one team working from home four out of five days for nine months and the other team working exclusively from the office.). Of the 13% performance increase, 9% was attributed to working more minutes per shift (due to fewer breaks, less commuting and fewer days off sick) and 4% from more calls per minute (due to a quieter working environment). It is important to note that the experiment was restricted to a sub-group of employees who met three restrictive requirements: having no children, having a room at home to work in that was not their bedroom and possessing high-quality broadband internet (i.e. conditions conducive to homeworking with limited disruption). At the end of the experiment, the company rolled out a working from home option on a permanent basis. Interviews with those choosing to work from home at this stage revealed that half found working at home harder, as they became more isolated, while the other half were 22% more productive.

Given the state of the pandemic at the time of writing, the medium-term impact of the pandemic on productivity is unknown. Evidence from the Understanding Society: COVID-19 study in the UK found no significant reduction in productivity associated with homeworking during the lockdown; 41% of respondents working at home reported getting the same amount of work done in June 2020 as they did six months earlier. Similar proportions of homeworkers reported an increase (29%) and a decrease (30%) in productivity. Two-thirds of those reporting an increase in productivity wanted to work mainly at home in the future (Felstead & Reuschke, 2020). Workers who spent all (as opposed to some) of their time working at home were most likely to report improved productivity, so supporting a business case for continued homeworking. A study of how COVID-19 lockdowns changed knowledge workers' digital communication patterns in 16 large metropolitan areas in North America, Europe and the Middle East showed increases in the average working day (DeFilippis et al., 2020), but while work input increased capturing data on output is more difficult. Moreover, behaviours and preferences may change with the passage of time. Nathan & Overman (2020) argue that the length of the pandemic will influence both productivity and medium- and longer-term working patterns: the longer lockdowns and the need for social distancing last, the more that businesses and employees work out what works for them.

Longer-term Impacts

In the case of the COVID-19 pandemic a key issue is whether and for how long the trends towards remote working will be sustained and/or the manner in which they change. This has important implications for places in the longer-term. In the first ten months of the COVID-19 pandemic in the UK the primary urban areas that saw the biggest reduction in footfall and spend in the daytime on weekdays relative to the pre COVID-19 pandemic period were university cities and towns, urban areas with a high percentage of knowledge workers and those with a high percentage of employment in sectors where working from home was most prevalent. Conversely, seaside areas, places which are the only local significant centre with a relative lack of competition from elsewhere, and places with a relatively low percent of employment in sectors where working from home is most prevalent saw the smallest reductions in footfall (Centre for Cities, 2020). Businesses face difficult decisions going forward about when, and whether, to seek to reverse the remote working trend because homeworking can reduce costs and potentially increase productivity, the two biggest concerns especially in a recession.

PERSPECTIVES ON IMPLICATIONS FOR PLACES: SELECTED KEY ISSUES

Place Attractiveness in the Context of Increased Remote Working

What is Place Attractiveness: Why it Matters and What Matters for Whom?

Place attractiveness – which comprises the economic, housing, cultural and environmental offer of different places – is recognized as being increasingly important for local areas in retaining and attracting skilled people (Riley et al., 2020). This is especially the case in the context of a growth in remote working. Traditionally, all workers have had to live within easy reach of their workplace due to the need to travel there on a regular (usually daily) basis. Those with higher incomes have been in a position to exercise greater choice regarding their residential location decisions and commuting modes. A potential consequence of this is enhanced residential segregation.

As more people work remotely, either for some or all of the time, so the need for them to find a residential location within an easy daily commute of the workplace declines. As noted above, there has been a trend over time towards longer commutes, and also dual location household living arrangements, where some workers split their time over a main residence for long weekends and a secondary residence from which they commute during the week (Green et al., 1999). As the prevalence of remote working increases, so the geographical range of areas that are suitable residential locations grows. A longer (and more expensive) commute may be an acceptable trade-off for more residential space – that is becoming a requirement for those requiring a separate workspace when working from home - in a cheaper location.

Amongst the fastest-growing places for people commuting to London have been Peterborough, York, Somerset; all of which are beyond the traditional commuting belt (Hughes, 2020). Alongside this there is evidence that there has been greater interest in seaside resorts and rural locations as desirable residential environments, with estate agent Rightmove indicating that seaside resorts have seen the biggest rise in sales, as people sought more space during lockdown (Read & Espiner, 2020). Sellick (2020) points to intelligence from estate agents suggesting that more people – especially families with children - have been searching for, and looking at, rural properties online. They are seeking more bedrooms and particularly more outside space. Amongst landlords in urban areas there is some evidence of falling property prices in urban locations. An increased desire for rural living has further implications for housing affordability which is already a major problem in some rural areas, and also for investment in broadband access to other services.

Possible Longer-term Impacts for Geographical and Social Mobility

The developments outlined above relate to the short-term. However, they also raise important questions about how broader trends in geographical and social mobility will evolve going forward. There is evidence from the USA that internal migration is declining over the longer-term (Cooke, 2013), although broader international evidence on this is more circumspect (Champion et al., 2017). Technology-enabled home working for some people – particularly the highly qualified who drive geographical mobility for education and employment – has shown more people that they can work from home, at least for some of the time. This might suggest that the COVID-19 crisis acts as a further driver for less employment-related internal migration in Britain, so accentuating current trends. This means that family and amenity factors might then play a more important role in driving migration decisions and the choice of where to live and shifting residential preferences are relevant here.

Importantly for economy and society, a decline in employment-related geographical mobility could mean reduced social mobility (Papoutsaki, 2020). Resource constraints, given competing pressures on spending posed by the COVID-19 crisis and recession, at least in the short-term, may reduce prospects for targeted policies aimed at improving social mobility and the geographical distribution of opportunities over the short-term although the 'levelling up' agenda is important in this space. So, will the spatial mobility escalator that has operated to enhance social mobility of movers (Fielding, 1992) slow, stop or even go into reverse? Or will opportunity be less reliant on geography than in the past? Future trends in the movement of young people for higher education will be an important consideration here. Given that migration is not just a 'one off' event but rather shapes future behaviours of individuals, and of their families, over the life course, any COVID-19 induced downturn in the willingness of young people to move long distances away from home to pursue higher education and rather opting for local opportunities may have longer-term implications for lifetime mobility patterns and so for different places.

What Future for Cities and City Centres?

Urban Centres and Agglomeration

Urban centres, particularly the central business districts of wider metropolitan areas, provide advantages of agglomeration. Nathan (2020) notes the growth in employment in professional services and related services, together with technology-rich activities, in such urban centres. He suggests that the agglomeration effects they provide are beneficial in terms of staff interactions, idea exchange and innovation. With high early infection rates and subsequent lockdown many of these workers deserted their offices to work at home. The move to remote working has been particularly pronounced in the largest cities, notably London. The proximity that is important in harnessing agglomeration advantages "has become a friction" during the COVID-19 pandemic (Nathan, 2020).

Prior to, and during, the COVID-19 pandemic not all people who feasibly could work from home have done so – for all of the time. There is some evidence that interacting through video-conferencing is both more exhausting and a less rich experience than in-person interaction (Spicer, 2020). This chimes with research showing that proximity is an important factor in collaborative knowledge creation (Crescenzi, 2016). Florida (2020) suggests that because proximity is important in high value clusters like finance, high tech and media, big superstar cities where these activities are concentrated will recover. Similarly, Cheshire & Hilber (2020) speculate that higher-paid jobs may become even more concentrated in cities such as London and Edinburgh. Swinney (2020) postulates that because knowledge-based businesses are likely to become even more important in the years ahead, urban centres are likely to remain attractive locations, even if employees work remotely for part of the time. After all, there are some tasks that do work well remotely, suggesting that a combination of remote working and co-location may be beneficial for some jobs involving a range of different tasks and where remote working is feasible. Similarly, Duranton & Puga (2020), while emphasizing the strong link between physical proximity in cities and innovation and especially the subtle and unplanned in-person exchanges that cannot be replicated in online meetings, suggest that the inertia in cities is such that "the idea that this pandemic will change cities forever is likely an overstretch" (p. 22).

Estimates by PWC (2020) indicate that if office workers continue to work from home rather than return to pre COVID-19 patterns of workplace attendance, the loss of benefits of clustering in terms of reduced labour productivity could lead to a decrease in UK GDP of £3.2bn. The impacts of such a loss are geographically uneven. While suburban and rural areas are likely to gain from increased local spending and greater knowledge collaboration between local residents, leading to some levelling up of economic activity and outcomes at regional level, gains in these areas are unlikely to offset losses in city centres. These uneven geographical impacts are illustrated by analyses that show that the advantages of agglomeration would be diminished by between 10% and 30% in a belt from Central London, through West London to Heathrow if office workers were to work from home, while parts of South London, East London and North London would see an increase in agglomeration effects – but of insufficient magnitude to offset declines elsewhere.

The Role of big Businesses in Urban Economies

Large businesses with high proportions of office-based jobs in city centres have an important multiplier impact on central business districts. Workers spend money in local shops and attract other investment. Reduced footfall in city centres as those who can work remotely do so – at least for some of the time – leads in the short-term to lower economic activity with important implications for lower spend in hospitality and retail and less use of public transport. It also threatens the viability of the evening and night-time economy. In the medium-term possible consequences of reduced footfall and lower economic activity are job losses at the lower end of the wage spectrum (e.g. amongst cleaners and workers in hospitality) and decreasing investment in commercial real estate in city centres. Modelling by the Greater London Authority (Cook, 2020) focusing on London's Central Activities Zone (CAZ), suggests a £1.9 billion loss in expenditure from commuters to the CAZ from workplaces being closed; (£1.4 billion of this expenditure is from commuters from London and £0.5 billion is from commuters outside of London). Cook (2020) suggests that this estimate is conservative because it excludes expenditure on non-office related items, such as haircuts and gym memberships, ad hoc expenditure during lunch hours, or after-work activities that take place due to the concentration of workers. The key point is that it represents a considerable loss in expenditure in city centres.

Big businesses play an important role in the functioning of urban ecosystems. They have a responsibility to the local communities surrounding office hubs (with those surrounding Canary Wharf in London being an extreme example). In not supporting those local communities which have supported them prior to the COVID-19 pandemic, big businesses face a reputational risk – especially at a time when highly-skilled (prospective) employees are placing greater prominence on employers' values. At the same time employers have to consider the safety of their workers and the reluctance of some employees to return to work in central areas of large urban economies. Yet Lopez Valenzuela (2020) suggests that to rebuild their contract with society, maintaining a physical presence in urban centres is likely to remain important.

Offices of the Future

Prior to the COVID-19 pandemic commercial property sector trends pointed towards enhanced emphasis on health and safety issues, space for activity-based working, flexibility and improved space utilisation. Sustainability, smart buildings and developments in the digital workplace were already reshaping the nature of offices (Arup, 2020). Walker (2020), however, contends that organisations have continued scientific management office cost reduction strategies under the guise of innovative office designs. He suggests long-term historic trends will be tested by pandemic-induced radical changes to the office on safety grounds, at potentially significant cost. Nevertheless, the COVID-19 crisis seems likely to accentuate pre-existing trends so that in future the primary use of the office will be will be a multifunctional, flexible hub for meaningful interaction, rather than a mono-purpose 'get-things done' place (Arup, 2020), so changing the profile of office-based activities.

These trends mean that the nature of office space is likely to change. Traditionally offices have been organised around access to shared infrastructure, including printers and photocopiers. With the move to paperless offices, the focus shifts towards the office becoming a place to interact with colleagues and form social bonds, create corporate culture, host clients, and attract talent. If more of the work that requires an individual to concentrate in a quiet space on their own is done at home (or in some other remote location), there may be a reduced need for individual office space/cells in a main office, and more space for social interaction.

Nevertheless, a lack of space at home for effective remote working, especially for some young people in shared accommodation, means that there is likely to be continued demand for some quiet space in offices, However, the COVID-19 pandemic has heightened awareness about risks of physical proximity. This suggests a need for greater use of smart building technology to enhance building operating systems and also support optimal use of space, workplace allocation and physical distancing. In a reversal of trends over time towards greater density in offices, individual desks may require a large physical footprint, so increasing space requirements per person at a time when overall office occupancy is falling. Management strategies adopted will reflect prioritisation choices between occupational health and safety versus financial returns (Walker, 2020).

Urban Micro-mobility

Commuting to work has been a challenge for some workers during the COVID-19 pandemic, and for those who are able to work remotely the issue of transport availability and perceptions of safety of different transport modes have influenced the timing and frequency with which workers have travelled. For those who can walk or cycle to work, working from centrally located offices might seem more feasible, but for those who have longer journeys the situation is rather different. Some workers have the opportunity to switch mode from public transport to car, but this is not an option for all workers.

The COVID-19 crisis offers an opportunity to address old problems by focusing on new changes required to avoid the spread of the virus. For example, the problem of urban air pollution can be addressed to some degree by helping people to adopt new forms of sustainable green transport which will also have a positive impact on air quality. Incentivising active travel – walking and cycling – is key here. Urban micro-mobility options – i.e. single-user vehicles characterised by lightness, small size, often electric powered - have risen up the policy agenda (Cepeda Zorrilla, 2020). Electric scooters are one of the most common forms of urban micro-mobility with potential for implementation in a shared system; other forms include e-bicycles, folding bicycles, and mono wheels. In turn, urban micro-mobility options have implications for the use of urban space and may accelerate modal shift in some urban centres.

Implications for Outer Urban Areas, Market Towns and Rural Areas

New Opportunities Outside the Main Urban Centres

Proximity to the workplace could become less of a priority if a larger portion of the workforce works remotely, at least some of their time. This means that the geographical areas that come into consideration for residential decision-making become more spatially extensive. As noted in the section on commuting trends, longer commutes become more feasible if they are less frequent.

Real estate data on residential properties suggests that in 2020 demand was greatest in areas outside, but relatively close to, large cities. Suburbs also became increasingly attractive, offering more affordable space at lower density than in city centres. Workers who expect to work remotely for all or most of their time can contemplate living in more rural locations - broadband connectivity permitting - with greater access to outdoor amenities. A rise in homeworking could make suburbs, market towns and rural areas more vibrant as residents increase their expenditure locally. For rural areas in particular, there is a need to capture the value attached to those skilled incomers who have potential to be highly mobile (Bosworth & Venhorst, 2018). Corfe (2020) suggests that such a decentralisation of population and economic activity in the medium- and longer-term could contribute to the agenda of a greater levelling of economic activity across the country. However, whether this results in 'levelling up' or 'levelling down', given that movers are able to exercise choice and go to attractive destinations, while non-movers are left behind, remains an open question.

Remote working need not take place at home or in the office; the options are not binary, and this has important implications for places of work and places more generally. It is possible that local co-working hubs may develop in towns to meet the need for enhanced IT, some office services and for those working mainly at home to meet other people. Some employers might choose to invest in co-working spaces and shared low-cost operations for staff located away from city centres who do not have space at home that meets their work requirements (Arup, 2020).

Localized Living … and Working

The COVID-19 crisis has caused some individuals and families to rethink what they want from their local area. The experience of lockdown and working from home has led some people who commuted into large urban centres to re-evaluate what they want and need in their immediate local area and to reassess quality of life accordingly.

Urban planning initiatives such as 'complete neighbourhoods' are of relevance here. The term 'complete neighbourhood' refers to a neighbourhood where there is safe and convenient access to the goods and services needed in daily life. This includes a variety of housing options, grocery stores and other commercial services, schools, public open spaces and recreational facilities, connections to employment centres, affordable active transportation options and civic amenities. An important element of a complete neighbourhood is that it is built at a walkable and bikeable human scale. In Portland, Oregon, where the term originated, there is a focus in urban planning on creating such 'complete neighbourhoods' (Green et al., 2007). The concept has spread internationally. Melbourne, Australia, has developed '20-minute neighbourhoods' in which amenities and services are within 20 minutes, while in Paris the ideal of 'ville du quart d'heure' (the 'quarter hour city') has been promoted as a way of transforming the city into a collection of socially and economically mixed districts where people work near where they live (Hidalgo, 2020). These planning approaches are based on principles of proximity, diversity, density and ubiquity, with neighbourhoods fulfilling functions of living, working, supplying, caring, learning and enjoying. The rationale is that residents have safe and convenient access to the goods and services needed in daily life (Green et al., 2007).

Some outer urban areas and market towns in the UK already have many of these characteristics and their attractiveness as places to live has become increasingly evident during the COVID-19 crisis. This is where any revival of high streets following lockdown is likely to be most apparent, especially with changing customer sentiment towards increasing interest in buying locally. Nevertheless, how outer urban areas and market towns interact with larger urban centres remains important, given that it remains necessary for some workers to commute to such centres, albeit perhaps less frequently, and for residents to access high order goods and services beyond their immediate vicinity.

Accentuated Socio-spatial Inequalities

Who can Work Where?

The Office for National Statistics (2020) identified five factors that are associated with being less able to work from home (or otherwise remotely). The first is whether a job has to be carried out at a specific location because of its very nature. The second concerns the amount of face-to-face interaction required with other people. The third is exposure to hazards. Fourthly is whether it involves use of tools and protective equipment unsuitable for use in the home. Fifthly is whether the job requires physical activity. If these factors do not apply a worker is more able to work from home if they have access to the technology and environment they require to be able to do so.

The Office for National Statistics analysis shows that professional occupations like actuaries, economists and statisticians are most able to be done from home. Other management, technical and administrative jobs, involving relatively little face-to-face contact, physical activity or use of tools or equipment, are also more suited to home working. Amongst the job roles that are much less likely to be undertaken remotely are elementary occupations (such as cleaners, waiting staff and security guards) and process, plant and machine operatives. 'Key workers' such as carers, paramedics and the emergency services are also less able to work remotely.

Greater Polarization?

Trends towards labour market professionalization and polarization have been evident for some time (Jones & Green, 2009; Autor, 2019). Nathan (2020) distinguishes, in particular, between high-wage knowledge-intensive job roles and low-wage service roles, with the former having driven the latter. Traditionally, jobs in both groups have concentrated in cities, with the low-wage service roles depending on the knowledge-intensive roles (Moretti, 2012), but the scope for changes in the location of these jobs varies. Recent analysis shows that the median hourly earnings of employees in the quintile of the workforce most likely to be able to work from home is £19.01. This compares with median hourly earnings of £11.28 for workers in the quintile of jobs that are least adaptable to home working (Office for National Statistics, 2020). US evidence reveals a similar pattern: a study by Mongey et al. (2020) found that individuals in occupations where working from home is not possible are more likely to be lower-income, lack a college degree, rent their dwellings and be non-white.

The COVID-19 crisis could accelerate polarization between those on higher incomes who can work remotely and those on lower incomes who cannot, with important impacts for places. Regionally, more jobs based in workplaces in London and the South East are conducive to remote working than those in other regions, largely reflecting their higher than average proportion of professional and managerial jobs. At intra-regional scale, those local areas that are the origins and destinations of (pre COVID-19 crisis) commuting trips with higher than average shares of such jobs are likely to have seen the largest shifts in economic activity during the pandemic and are amongst those where greatest change is possible going forward.

Economic Vulnerability and Spatial Inequalities in the COVID-19 Crisis

Office-based knowledge workers in big businesses in large urban centres drive high-contact low-wage jobs that service them. Moretti (2012) estimates that each high-skilled job creates several less-skilled jobs within large cities. Some of these low-wage jobs are in the gig economy and these workers face particular vulnerable in the face of economic downturn since they may not be covered by employment rights.

Analyses by Sandher & Innes (2020) estimated that around 40% of employees on the minimum wage face a high or very high risk of losing their job because of the economic impacts of COVID-19 compared to less than 1% of those earning more than £41,500 per year (pro-rata). Groups that historically have been vulnerable in the face of labour market change are again amongst the most vulnerable during the COVID-19 crisis, with young people and some ethnic minorities – most notably those from Bangladeshi and Pakistani communities given the occupational and sectoral employment profile - at highest risk of losing their jobs. Those who are less qualified are amongst the most likely to lose their jobs and also face greatest difficulty in finding new employment ceteris paribus. When they do find employment, it is often in low-paid jobs. The analyses also suggested that a large number of jobs are at risk in major urban centres.

Many of those working remotely have adapted to doing so and to date the experience has not had negative implications for productivity. Bloom (2020) expects that a more hybrid way of working will emerge for those whose jobs will enable them to do so. As a result, he expects spending in city-centre bars, restaurants and shops to reduce by more than half as economic activity shifts away from city centres to suburbs and rural areas. He suggests that city centres will no longer be as attractive as formerly as places to live for young, highly educated people, and that demand for office space will shift towards suburban industrial parks and low-rise buildings. Those workers adopting a hybrid working style will likely want larger residential accommodation to facilitate remote working and are likely to be willing to substitute longer for less frequent commutes (Cheshire & Hilber, 2020). Quality of life for the highly-paid is likely to become more important.

There is no consensus amongst commentators about prospects for the larger high-cost cities, although some work in the USA suggests that remote working offers opportunities to spread economic opportunity, particularly in tech sectors, away from cities such as New York, San Francisco and Seattle. With a greater spread of activity away from high-cost areas disparities in wages might lessen, so reducing territorial polarisation (Muro, 2020; Wittenberg, 2020). However, as noted above, not everyone in a job that is conducive to remote working can work from home efficiently. Moreover, some do not want the social isolation of the lack of face-to-face contacts. Some jobs cannot be undertaken remotely. This suggests that a trend towards greater hybrid working for some will lead to greater socio-economic inequalities, which in turn will have a spatial expression.

Implications for Place-based Policies

How Places Work and Understanding Assets

The COVID-19 pandemic and a shift to greater remote working has triggered enhanced emphasis on how places work and how they relate to each other in a complex interacting system. Within this system each place needs to understand its purpose, role and unique selling point. Understanding a place's current offer, opportunities and potential futures, relative to other places, has always been key to successful local areas. This is likely to become even more important following the COVID-19 pandemic. The smart specialisation approach, whose origins are linked with the European Commission's Europe 2020 Strategy for smart, sustainable and inclusive growth, aims to find ways to develop local and regional indigenous potential. It rests on a clear understanding of the local asset base – including technology, people, culture, environment, innovation and business – and building this into a place offer (European Commission, 2020), so ensuring jobs growth around local assets and opportunities.

With a shift to remote and/or greater hybrid working there is a greater need to ensure that places provide a holistic offer to local residents. In the context of the COVID-19 crisis this needs to incorporate an understanding of how the foundational economy that meets every day needs (Bentham et al., 2013) operates at a local level and how it fits in as an element of place attractiveness alongside other local assets in place-based economic strategies.

Green Infrastructure

The COVID-19 pandemic has raised the issue of the viability of public transport that is largely reliant on revenue from fares at a time when social distances are in place and more people are working remotely (Day, 2020). This has implications for those who cannot work remotely and who are reliant on public transport for travel-to-work. As noted above, travel by car is an option for some people, but not for everyone, and in turn increased conventional car usage raises air quality and other environmental issues. A shift to remote and/or greater hybrid working emphasises the need for investment in green infrastructure, including in wider forms of transport enabling safe and clean travel.

Creating places which are safe, green, clean and open will enable those who are remote working to have an enhanced quality of life. It may also mean, in turn, that some may trade less remote working with more office-based interaction, albeit perhaps on a smaller scale than previously. In turn, this also depends in part on supporting opportunities for personalised, clean and safe mobility.

Prior to the pandemic a lack of good spaces for interaction and of open green infrastructure was already seen as a disadvantage. Green infrastructure is lacking most in post-industrial towns and dense urban areas. Parks, waterways and access to clean air and light are at a premium but are increasingly seen as core basic needs. To ensure places are attractive, to help drive consumer spend and support local businesses, there needs to be investment and adaption in the public realm that improves the environment, clean transport, walking and cycle paths, good integrated public transport, investment in green space and waterways. This adds to the social fabric of places and calls for engagement with both business and communities on the use of space in place. Debates on rethinking how high street spaces are used - including in terms of the balance between commercial, retail, community and residential spaces – are pertinent here too, with implications for sustainability, resilience and attractiveness (Wicks, 2020).

Institutional Structures and Approaches to Place-based Policies

The changes brought about by remote working underscore the importance of investing in local institutions so that they can respond in a place-specific way to demand for change, including through investment in new local infrastructure, and to react when crisis happens. The broader COVID-19 crisis, left behind places and the levelling up agenda also point in the direction of greater emphasis on place-shaping (Walker & Diamond, 2020).

There is an important role for public policy to invest in creating places where positive change is enabled and lasts. The centralized governance structure in the UK means that foremost emphasis tends to be on central rather than local priorities. Previous austerity has weakened local government capacity and this makes it harder to manage change. Creative leadership, vision setting for the future, gathering and analyzing trends, developing action plans to address change, investment in community engagement and policy delivery are more difficult in the context of weak local institutions. Yet in post the COVID-19 pandemic era they are even more important.

SOLUTIONS AND RECOMMENDATIONS

It is important to reflect that often crises accelerate the changes which were already evident and the 'next normal' arrivals sooner than expected. However, it is important to be aware of the idea that while in the main 'our tomorrows will be like our yesterdays' the tendency is to disregard the events in the tails of a distribution curve. Yet they often contribute most to changes in outcomes (Avishai, 2020). Hence it is important at a time of economic change to consider a range of scenarios regarding trends in remote working and possible implications for place.

Overall, the short- and longer-term trends highlighted above suggest that local and regional economies need to take place-shaping policies seriously given that place attractiveness – encompassing the economic, housing, cultural and environmental offer – is becoming more important. Places need to consider how they can be attractive for people at all stages of the life course. This involves looking outwards to consider their role vis-à-vis other places in the urban and regional system as well as inwards to the details of neighbourhood planning.

The changes brought about by remote working underscore the importance of investing in local institutions so that they can respond in a place-specific way to demand for change, including through investment in new local infrastructure, and to react when crisis happens (Walker & Diamond, 2020). Greater devolution to enable local places to invest in place development for residents and businesses is likely to be required.

FUTURE RESEARCH DIRECTIONS

Looking forward it is important that academics and policy analysts continue to monitor trends in remote working and their implications for places. Such monitoring is not as straightforward as it might seem. The COVID-19 crisis has brought to the fore the paucity of real time data. Yet it has also seen the emergence on new data sources – for example on footfall in city centres - to fill the gap. Conventional data sources have long been inadequate for capturing trends in non-standard/ less predictable patterns of behaviour, such as variable spatial and temporal patterns of travel-to-work – and yet these have important implications for place. Survey sources may provide some insights but sample sizes are often too small to permit spatial disaggregation to the scale desired.

Detailed place-based studies - focusing on different sizes and types of place – are needed to understand in more depth the choices and constraints surrounding decision-making around remote working, by employers and by workers, and their locational implications. Such studies need to encompass both those who are exercising remote (or hybrid) working patterns and those who are not doing so or cannot do so, since the interactions between the two have important implications for places.

There is also scope for more research on place-making in practice – on both the processes involved and the outcomes. This would benefit from insights from different disciplinary perspectives – including geography, planning, economics, sociology and psychology – alongside those of policy makers and practitioners.

CONCLUSION

Many workers in professional and administrative occupations, especially those with high qualifications and with higher than average earnings, have demonstrated to themselves and to their employers over the course of the COVID-19 crisis in 2020 that they are able to work remotely relatively effectively (Felstead & Reuschke, 2020). This has led to a shift in economic activity away from centres of the largest cities towards suburbs, towns and more rural areas – i.e. away from 'workplaces' towards 'residences'. Some workers who are able to exercise choice, and who wish to continue to work remotely or adopt a pattern of hybrid working, have begun to reassess what place attractiveness means to them. While the specifics of place attractiveness vary at different stages of the life course and between individuals, it seems that movers are placing a premium on increased residential space and outdoor space. Current trends suggest that attractive residential environments with good accessibility to enable longer distance commutes are at a premium. This may presage a revival of suburbs, outer urban centres and accessible rural areas. Peripheral rural areas may benefit from those choosing to work (nearly) entirely remotely.

Traditionally the centres of the largest cities have seen the benefits of agglomeration economies. Looking ahead these benefits of agglomeration may take a somewhat different form, at least in detail, from before. Kleinman (2020) suggests that polycentric mega-region structures may have advantages over a traditional urban pattern of a dense centre of concentrated economic activity surrounded by rings of urban development. Those workers who are able to work remotely and who choose a hybrid working pattern may want greater social interaction than formerly on their days in the office – perhaps extending their time in cities after working hours to partake in city-based cultural activities. In turn offices will need to evolve to cater for such working patterns (Jude & Fuchs, 2020). In this way the benefits of agglomeration may be maintained. On other days they may work from home or from a local co-working space and so be more embedded than formerly in their residential location (Farruggia et al., 2020).

The implication of those who can exercise choice doing so, while others do not have that option, is greater inequality and spatial segregation. In theory the prospect of greater remote working could lead to the revival of 'left behind' areas and an economic levelling as economic activity shifts away from the largest and most prosperous urban centres. But in the absence of planning policies to counter prevailing trends, greater socio-spatial polarization is likely to ensue (Ferguson, 2020). Levelling up is all the more difficult a goal to attain in the context of COVID-19 related recession (Centre for Cities, 2021). What is clear is that place-based policy is likely to become more important to address spatial disparities. In an era of greater remote working place still matters.

ACKNOWLEDGMENT

This research was supported by the Research England Development Fund and UKRI as part of the West Midlands Regional Economic Development Institute [grant number 724390].

REFERENCES

Arup. (2020). *Future of offices: in a post-pandemic world.* Arup.

Autor, D. H. (2019). Work of the Past, Work of the Future. *AEA Papers and Proceedings. American Economic Association, 109*, 1–32. doi:10.1257/pandp.20191110

Avishai, B. (2020, June 21). The pandemic isn't a black swan but a portent of a more fragile global system, *The New Yorker.*

Bentham, J., Bowman, A., de la Cuesta, M., Ertürk, I., Folkman, P., Froud, J., Johal, S., Law, J., Leaver, A., Moran, M., & Williams, K. (2013) Manifesto for the Foundational Economy. Centre for Research on Socio-Cultural Change, University of Manchester.

Bloom, N. (2020, June 29). Stanford research provides a snapshot of a new working from home economy, *Stanford News.*

Bloom, N., Liang, J., Roberts, J., & Ying, Z. J. (2015). Does working from home work? Evidence from a Chinese experiment. *The Quarterly Journal of Economics, 130*(1), 165–218. doi:10.1093/qje/qju032

Bosworth, G., & Venhorst, V. (2018). Economic linkages between urban and rural regions – what's in it for the rural? *Regional Studies*, *52*(8), 1075–1085. doi:10.1080/00343404.2017.1339868

Cairncross, F. (1997). *The Death of Distance: How the Communications Revolution Will Change Our Lives*. Harvard Business School.

Centre for Cities. (2020). *High streets recovery tracker: How are cities and large towns recovering from coronavirus?* Centre for Cities.

Centre for Cities. (2021). *Cities Outlook 2021*. Centre for Cities.

Cepeda Zorrilla, M. (2020, June 9). COVID-19 in the West Midlands: An opportunity for fostering urban micro-mobility. *West Midlands Economic Impact Monitor*.

Champion, T., Cooke, T., & Shuttleworth, I. (2017). *Internal Migration in the Developed World: Are we becoming less mobile?* Routledge. doi:10.4324/9781315589282

Cheshire, P., & Hilber, C. (2020). *COVID-19: Crashing the Economy so what will it do for the housing market?* Centre for Economic Performance, London School of Economics.

Cook, C. (2020). *Lost worker vs. tourism expenditure in the Central Activities Zone (CAZ)*. Greater London Authority.

Cooke, T. J. (2011). It is not just the economy: Declining migration and the rise of secular rootedness. *Population Space and Place*, *17*(3), 193–203. doi:10.1002/psp.670

Coombes, M., & Bond, S. (2008). *Travel-To-Work Areas: the 2007 Review*. Office of National Statistics.

Corfe, S. (2020). *A new life for the high street*. Social Market Foundation.

Crescenzi, R., Nathan, M., & Rodríguez-Pose, A. (2016). Do inventors talk to strangers? On proximity and collaborative knowledge creation. *Research Policy*, *45*(1), 177–194. doi:10.1016/j.respol.2015.07.003

Day, K. (2020). The impossible journey. *Public Finance*, (September/October), 37–40.

DeFilippis, E., Impink, S. M., Singell, M., Polzer, J. T., & Sadun, R. (2020). *Collaborating during coronavirus: the impact of COVID-19 on the nature of work*. Harvard Business School Organizational Behavior Unit Working Paper No. 21-006.

Dingel, J. I., & Neiman, B. (2020). How many jobs can be done at home? *Journal of Public Economics*, *189*, 104235. doi:10.1016/j.jpubeco.2020.104235 PMID:32834177

Duranton, G., & Puga, D. (2020). The economics of urban density. *The Journal of Economic Perspectives*, *34*(3), 3–26. doi:10.1257/jep.34.3.3

European Commission. (2020). *What is Smart Specialisation?* https://s3platform.jrc.ec.europa.eu/what-is-smart-specialisation-

Farruggia, F., Jones, P., & Siravo, J. (2020). The new normal: A blueprint for remote working. *Autonomy (Birmingham, England)*.

Felstead, A. (2012). Rapid change or slow evolution? Changing places of work and their consequences in the UK. *Journal of Transport Geography*, *21*(C), 31–38. doi:10.1016/j.jtrangeo.2011.10.002

Felstead, A., & Reuschke, D. (2020). *Homeworking in the UK: before and during the 2020 lockdown*. Wales Institute of Social and Economic Research.

Ferguson, K. (2020). *All in this together? The impact of COVID-19 on different places*. Local Government Information Unit.

Fielding, A. J. (1992). Migration and social mobility: South East England as an escalator region. *Regional Studies*, *26*(1), 1–15. doi:10.1080/00343409212331346741 PMID:12285048

Florida, R. (2020). *Cities and the COVID-19 Crisis*. Centre for Cities.

Green, A., Froy, F., Kispeter, E., & Sissons, P. (2017). *How do cities lead an inclusive growth agenda*. Joseph Rowntree Foundation.

Green, A. E., Hogarth, T., & Shackleton, R. E. (1999). *Long Distance Living: Dual Location Households*. Policy Press.

Green, A. E., & Owen, D. W. (2006). *The geography of poor skills and access to work*. Joseph Rowntree Foundation.

Hardill, I., & Green, A. (2003). Remote working—Altering the spatial contours of work and home in the new economy. *New Technology, Work and Employment*, *18*(3), 212–222. doi:10.1111/1468-005X.00122

Hidalgo, A. (2020, Feb. 7). Paris mayor unveils '15 minute city' plan in re-election campaign. *The Guardian*.

Hughes, R. (2020, May 31). Remote working: How cities might change if we worked at home more. *BBC*.

Jones, P. S., & Green, A. E. (2009). The quantity and quality of jobs: Changes in UK regions. *Environment & Planning A*, *41*(10), 2474–2495. doi:10.1068/a41228

Jude, S., & Fuchs, N. (2020). The office is not dead. It's evolving. *Property Week*, *87*(37), 26–27.

Kleinman, M. (2020). Policy challenges for the post-pandemic city. *Environment and Planning. B, Urban Analytics and City Science*, *47*(7), 1136–1139. doi:10.1177/2399808320950252

Lopez Valenzuela, A. (2020, Sept. 2). Can office workers save the day for local businesses ravaged by COVID-19? *City A.M.*

Mongey, S., Pilossoph, L., & Weinberg, A. (2020). *Which workers share the burden of social distancing policies?* NBER Working Paper 27085, National Bureau of Economic Research.

Moretti, E. (2012). *The new geography of jobs*. Houghton Mifflin Harcourt.

Muro, M. (2020). *Could Big Tech's move to permanent remote work save the American Heartland?* The Brookings Institution.

Nathan, M. (2020). *The city and the virus*. https://maxnathan.medium.com/the-city-and-the-virus-db8f4a68e404

Nathan, M., & Overman, H. (2020). Will coronavirus cause a big city exodus? *Environment and Planning. B, Urban Analytics and City Science*, *47*(9), 1537–1542. doi:10.1177/2399808320971910

Office for National Statistics. (2020). *What jobs can be done from home?* Office for National Statistics.

Papoutsaki, D., Buzzeo, J., Gray, H., Williams, M., Cockett, J., Akehurst, G., Alexander, K., Newton, B., & Pollard, E. (2020). *Moving out to move on: Understanding the link between migration, disadvantage and social mobility*. Social Mobility Commission.

PWC. (2020). *The Economic Impact of Returning to the Office*. PWC.

Rae, A. (2017). The Geography of Travel to Work in England and Wales: Extracts from the 2011 Census. *Applied Spatial Analysis and Policy*, *10*(4), 457–473. doi:10.100712061-016-9196-0

Read, S. & Espiner, T. (2020, Oct. 8). Lockdown city living 'wasn't the best idea'. *BBC*.

Riley, R., Billing, C., Bramley, G., Green, A., Hoole, C., & Taylor, A. (2020). *Professional & Business Services Sector: Creating Further Demand and Growth Outside London*. BEIS Research Paper Number 2020/006.

Sandher, J., & Innes, D. (2020). *Storm ready - how to keep us afloat as unemployment hits*. Joseph Rowntree Foundation.

Sellick, J. (2020, July 27). Are more people looking to escape to the countryside? *Rural Services Network*.

Spicer, A. (2020). *Finding endless video calls exhausting? You're not along*. The Conversation.

Swinney, P. (2020). Why our city centres will survive COVID. *New Statesman Spotlight – Regional Development: "Levelling Up" Post-COVID*, 16-17.

Walker, L. D. (2020). The COVID-19 office in transition: Cost, efficiency and the social responsibility business case. *Accounting, Auditing & Accountability Journal*, *33*(8), 1943–1967. doi:10.1108/AAAJ-06-2020-4609

Wicks, S. (2020). High street heart beat (regenerating town centres). *The Planner*, (August), 20–24.

Wittenberg, A. (2020). *The Economics of Remote Work*. Bloomberg CityLab.

ADDITIONAL READING

Brown, D., Champion, T., Coombes, M., & Wymer, C. (2015). The migration-commuting nexus in rural England: A longitudinal analysis. *Journal of Rural Studies*, *41*, 118–218. doi:10.1016/j.jrurstud.2015.06.005

Burchell, B., Reuschke, D., & Zhang, M. (2020). Spatial and temporal segmenting of urban workplaces: The gendering of multi-locational working. *Urban Studies (Edinburgh, Scotland)*. Advance online publication. doi:10.1177/0042098020903248

Champion, T., Cooke, T., & Shuttleworth, I. (2018). *Internal Migration in the Developed World: Are we becoming less mobile?* Routledge.

Felstead, A., Jewson, N., & Walters, S. (2005). *Changing places of work*. Palgrave Macmillan.

Glaeser, E. (2011). *Triumph of the City*. Macmillan.

Green, A. E. (1997). A question of compromise? Case study evidence on the location and mobility strategies of dual career households. *Regional Studies*, *31*(7), 641–657. doi:10.1080/00343409750130731

KEY TERMS AND DEFINITIONS

Agglomeration Economies: The benefits from concentrating activity in particular area.

Central Business District: The commercial and business district of a city.

Footfall: The number of people entering a particular area in a particular time period.

Hybrid Working: A working pattern combining remote working with working from an office or other fixed workplace.

Levelling Up: Reducing spatial disparities by boosting economic performance outside the most prosperous areas.

Place Attractiveness: The economic, housing, cultural, and environmental offer of different places.

Place Shaping: Ways in which local players collectively use their influence, powers, creativity and abilities to create attractive, prosperous and safe communities, places where people want to live, work and do business.

Chapter 11
Escaping the Cubicle:
Exploring the Physical Work Environment of the Home

Elizabeth (Libby) J. Sander
Bond University, Australia

Alannah Rafferty
Griffith University, Australia

Peter J. Jordan
Griffith University, Australia

ABSTRACT

A rise in contingent work, the increasing real estate costs for organizations, technological advances, and more recently, restrictions on movement emerging from the COVID-19 pandemic have resulted in a sharp increase in the number of employees working from home. These have significant implications for individuals, organizations, and society. Yet the physical work environment within the home has received little attention from scholars. Research on traditional office settings indicates that the physical environment influences a range of well-being and performance outcomes, indicating a critical need for researchers to consider the impact of the physical work environment at home. To address this issue, the authors briefly summarize the effects of the physical work environment and review existing research on working from home. They then propose directions for future research and emerging methodologies to undertake this research. Finally, they detail the practical implications that these changes bring for individuals, organizations, and society.

INTRODUCTION

The advent of the industrial revolution and the introduction of a centralized means of production has meant that factories or offices have been the primary setting for work for billions of people since the 1900s (Haigh, 2012). While work from home (WFH) arrangements have been in place in modern orga-

DOI: 10.4018/978-1-7998-6754-8.ch011

nizations since the 1970's, this has been considered by many managers as a tangential way of organizing work. While the technology to support remote work (Pérez, Sánchez, de Luis Carnicer, & Jiménez, 2004), and the desire of employees to WFH has been long established (Bloom, 2014), the willingness of organizations to embrace these work arrangements has lagged significantly. Researchers have identified several barriers to WFH including managerial concerns over supervision of employees, how to maintain productivity and how to effectively co-ordinate work (see Allen, Golden & Shockley, 2015 for a review).

The arrival of the COVID-19 pandemic and the subsequent waves of government initiated lockdowns have resulted in WFH becoming a global, overnight reality for millions of workers. This shift has brought the benefits and costs of WFH into sharp focus. Images rapidly emerged on social media of a wide array of make-shift workspaces, including the kitchen table, lounges, and even upturned laundry baskets as employees struggled to find both the space and equipment to undertake their work effectively. It has become apparent that while technology and a laptop can facilitate the completion of work tasks, many people do not appear to currently have the physical work environment to be able to WFH effectively and safely.

Despite the inherent challenges of sharing spaces with others who may be working in different jobs (e.g. call centre work with a partner who is doing accounting work) or doing online school, and the difficulties of not having an ergonomically safe work desk or chair, recent surveys in several countries have indicated that staff are reluctant to return to spending most of their work week in the office (Ziffer, 2020). Seeking to capitalize on the interest in WFH, companies including Facebook, Twitter, Microsoft, REI, and Mastercard have stated that they will allow their employees to continue working at home on a permanent basis (Brownlee, 2020). However, although the physical work environment of the office has been the focus of study across a broad range of disciplines for many decades, academic research tells us very little about the physical work environment of the home. This topic has received virtually no attention from scholars. Furthermore, a broad adoption of WFH may have significant implications for not only employees and their organizations but for the wider communities in which individuals live, and for policy makers and housing designers.

In this chapter, we briefly consider existing theory and research on WFH to identify potential issues related to the physical work environment of the home. Given that very little research has been undertaken from any discipline on the physical work environment of the home, we describe the existing multidisciplinary literature on the physical work environment before proceeding to propose suggestions for future research. Next, we consider relevant theoretical perspectives that may be applied to the physical work environment of the home, and then suggest directions for future research. Finally, we discuss the practical implications of the shift to WFH for individuals, organizations, designers and policy makers.

OVERVIEW OF RESEARCH ON WORK FROM HOME

The ability to WFH, also known as teleworking or telecommuting, has been enabled by developments in technology and flexible work practices (Eurofound & ILO, 2017; Nilles, 1997; Perez, 2004). As a result of technological developments, many formerly office-based employees can work outside of the traditional office setting. Prior to the COVID-19 pandemic, and in spite of numerous benefits in terms of cost-savings through reducing the need to situate employees in shared offices, environmental benefits from reduced commuting, and improved employee well-being and productivity (see Allen, Golden & Shockley, 2015 for review; Golden & Gajendran, 2019), WFH was not as common as might be imagined.

Impediments to implementing WFH include managers' perceptions that employees may 'slack off' (Allen, Golden & Shockley, 2015) and employee concerns that WFH may harm their career (Baruch, 2003). Although many companies state that they offer flexible work arrangements, including greater autonomy over employees' hours and conduct of work, this does not necessarily extend to support for employees to WFH (Allen, Johnson, Kiburz & Shockley, 2013). Even those permitted to work from home may only be allowed to do so on a limited basis despite reports suggesting that up to 40% of employees in developed economies are able to do their job from home (Travers, 2020).

Benefits of Work From Home

Research suggests that most employees highly value being able to work from home. In fact, research has shown that employees valued the option to WFH at about 8% of their wages (Alexandre & Pallais, 2017). Extant research has highlighted a number of benefits of working from home at both the organizational and individual level, which are briefly considered below.

Improved Organization Level Performance

Recent evidence suggests that there are generally positive benefits of WFH in terms of organizational level performance (Allen at al., 2015). Analysis of data from 156 Spanish companies using CEO's ratings, found that organizations who had higher percentages of employees who worked from home demonstrated the strongest innovation, financial and relational performance (Martínez-Sánchez, Pérez-Pérez, de-Luis-Carnicer, & Vela-Jiménez, 2007; Martínez-Sánchez, Pérez-Pérez, Vela-Jiménez, & de-Luis-Carnicer, 2008). This may be due to the increased autonomy associated with working from home leading to higher levels of satisfaction and commitment (Ryan & Deci, 2017). Additionally, organizations can make significant savings by implementing WFH arrangements. For example, Bloom et al. (2015) reported that a company they studied saved around US$2,000 (A$2,784) per employee on lease costs.

Increased Employee Productivity and Satisfaction

A meta-analytic review of studies highlights that there is a positive association between WFH and objective job performance (Gajendran & Harrison, 2007). Specifically, supervisor-rated task and contextual performance were higher for telecommuters than for non-telecommuters (Gajendran, Harrison & Delaney-Klinger, 2015). In one of the few controlled experimental studies on WFH, a two-year study using randomly assigned groups found a 13% productivity increase occurred after WFH was introduced to one of the groups. In this study, turnover decreased by 50% among the WFH group with individuals in this group taking shorter breaks and fewer sick days (Bloom, Liang, Roberts & Ying, 2015). The positive impact of WFH may be partially explained by an increased ability to focus and fewer distractions at home when the employee is away from co-workers (Sander, Caza & Jordan, 2019).

In their review of telecommuting, Allen et al. (2015) note that the extent of telecommuting influences a wide range of outcomes including employee well-being, satisfaction and productivity. However, the extent of telecommuting is insufficiently considered in many existing studies. Some research suggests that employees who WFH a moderate amount of time are the most satisfied (Golden & Veiga, 2005; martin & MacDonnell, 2012; Virick et al., 2010). However, individuals who telecommuted extensively, but also had high-quality supervisory relationships, had the highest levels of commitment, job satisfaction and job performance (Golden & Veiga, 2008). These findings highlight the importance of considering a range of contextual factors such as leadership quality, when establishing WFH arrangements.

Improved Employee Well-being and Health

WFH cuts commuting times and associated fatigue, transport congestion, and environmental impacts (Houghton, Foth & Hearn, 2018). Employees value WFH as a way to maintain a work-life balance, and this has been found to be especially important for the millennial work cohort (Allen et al., 2015). Additionally, some studies have found reductions in stress associated with work when individuals WFH as a result of increased autonomy and greater flexibility in their lives (see Gajendran & Harrison, 2007 for a review). Surprisingly, however, there is very little research in the field (Allen et al., 2015).

Challenges of WFH

Although there are clear benefits when employees WFH, there also are challenges for both individuals and organizations. Examples of potential negative effects of WFH at the individual level include social and professional isolation (Maruyama & Tietze, 2012) and the blurring of work and life boundaries (Kelliher & Anderson, 2009; Standen, Daniels & Lamond, 1999). At the organizational level, there can be difficulties in establishing and maintaining team cohesion and innovation (Allen et al., 2015) when work from home practices are in effect. These issues are discussed in more detail below.

Employee Social and Professional Isolation

Working from home for extended periods can leave employees feeling socially and professionally isolated (Maruyama & Tietze, 2012). When individuals work from home, they have fewer opportunities to interact and acquire information, which may explain why remote workers report feeling less confident than their office-based counterparts (Golden, Veiga & Dino, 2008). More than half of the volunteers who WFH full-time in one study felt so isolated that they changed their minds about wanting to work from home all the time (Bloom et al., 2015). According to a meta-analysis of 46 studies involving more than 12,000 employees, working from home more than 2.5 days a week can negatively affect relationships with co-workers as well as knowledge transfer (Gajendran & Harrison, 2007). Further, resentment can arise between co-workers if teleworking is not widely available (Collins, Hislop & Cartwright, 2016).

Blurred Work and Life Boundaries

Another significant issue that has been identified is that it can be hard for employees who are working from home to switch off, particularly when those individuals don't have a dedicated home office space (Kelliher & Anderson, 2009; Standen, Daniels & Lamond, 1999). Telecommuters often work longer hours, with 48% of employees increasing their work hours when WFH (Baruch, 2000). Another study from 15 countries found that 42% of individuals WFH had trouble sleeping and woke up repeatedly in the night, compared to only 29% of individuals who always worked in the office (Eurofound & ILO, 2017). Further, research showed that 41% of highly mobile workers felt stress "always or most of the time" compared to only 25% of those individuals who always worked at the office (Eurofound & ILO, 2017).

Reduced Team Cohesion and Innovation

WFH can have negative consequences for team cohesion and innovation compared to working in the office (Allen et al., 2015). Research supports the idea that as the availability of laptops and other remote work devices increases, proximity in face-to-face interaction is becoming more important. One study showed that engineers who shared a physical office were 20% more likely to stay in touch digitally when compared to those who worked remotely (Waber, Magnolfi & Lindsay, 2014). Employees who were in the same office emailed each other four times as often to collaborate on shared projects compared to staff who weren't in the office. In addition, performance benefits included 32% faster project completion times when employees were in the same office. Other research finds that face-to-face interaction is essential for identifying opportunities for collaboration, innovation and developing relationships and networks (Coenen & Kok, 2014).

THE PHYSICAL WORK ENVIRONMENT

The physical work environment in an organization incorporates the material objects and stimuli that people encounter in their day-today work life, as well as the nature and arrangement of these objects and stimuli (Davis, 1984; Davis et al., 2011; Elsbach and Pratt, 2007; Hedge, 1982; Sundstrom, Bell, Busby, and Asmus, 1996). Research on the physical work environment of the office has expanded significantly over the past decade, highlighting the effects of different functional aspects of the workspace, including privacy, layout, ergonomics, materials, noise, lighting, greenery and furniture, and examining the impact of these on, amongst other factors, employee performance and well-being (see Colenberg, Jylhä, & Arkesteijn, 2020; Davis, Leach & Clegg, 2011; Elsbach & Pratt, 2007, Zhong & House, 2012 for reviews).

Research on the Physical Work Environment of the Home

The physical work environment of the home has received virtually no scholarly attention. This presents both challenges and opportunities for researchers and practitioners. Although it may be possible that specific dimensions of the physical work environment of the office will influence similar outcomes in the home environment, these factors need to be investigated. In this section, we discuss dimensions of the physical work environment of the office and consider their potential relevance to the physical work environment of the home.

Drawing on research on workspaces within the office (see Davis, Leach & Clegg, 2011; Elsbach & Pratt, 2007; Kim & de Dear, 2013; Zhong & House, 2012 for reviews) the dimensions of the physical work environment of the home are likely to have both direct and indirect effects on employee and organizational outcomes. Aspects of the physical environment such as air quality, lighting, access to daylight, noise, views, and ergonomics have direct effects on employees. For example, poor air quality has been shown to reduce cognitive performance (MacNaughton et al., 2014), poor ergonomics can result in musculo-skeletal problems (Brand, 2008), and background noise in office settings has been shown to increase physiological stress (Evans & Johnson, 2000; Jahncke, Halin, Hygge, Green & Dimberg, 2011). The dimensions of the physical work environment, however, can also have indirect effects on employees. For example, a lack of privacy can result in negative affective and psychological reactions (Sander et al., 2019). Shared desk ownership has been shown to reduce perceptions of supervisory support, as well as to be associated with employees reporting that they feel indifferent to their colleagues (Brown & Robinson, 2011; Morrison & Macky, 2017). We anticipate that some of these findings in the workplace will be replicated when the impact of the physical WFH environment is investigated. For instance, at home, individuals also are likely to experience negative impacts from a lack of privacy and sharing desks or rooms with partners and children.

Although the physical work environment of the office is usually comprised of clearly defined spaces, defining workspaces in one's home can be much more difficult as the physical boundary between work and home will inevitably include shared private space. The reality of working and living in the same space means that the physical work environment of the home presents challenges not seen in office settings both in terms of fixed physical boundaries, and more fluid dynamic boundaries that arise in the conduct of the employee's work. In the office, employees are not distracted by private spaces and the responsibilities associated with those spaces. For example, when WFH an individual may see a load of laundry piling up as they make their way to the kitchen to get a cup of coffee. As such, WFH presents additional challenges in terms of navigating the separation of one's work and personal life, while having to manage the effects of WFH on other residents in the space, and concerns about a lack of separation of one's private life from one's work life (Wapshott & Mallett, 2012). Complicating matters, the constructs and objects of the physical work environment in the work setting, including an appropriate desk and chair, visual and auditory privacy, and the sensemaking role that an office plays may be much more challenging to recreate in the home.

Potential challenges the physical environment of the home present include visual and auditory privacy, ergonomic concerns, and creation of a defined workspace that is separate from home life. At present, though, our understanding of the effects of these issues when WFH is very limited. The role and importance of the physical work environment in the home and how work and private spaces overlap cannot be understated. Past research suggests that a third of respondents reported that work became more intrusive in their personal lives when they took up homeworking (Harris, 2003).

A range of interventions have been identified to manage issues related to the physical work environment of the office including the provision of healthy food and water, mindfulness or yoga spaces and exercise equipment. Such activities are now commonplace in organizations to encourage employees to take physical and mental breaks from their work (MMK, 2014). Further, the physical layout of modern offices is increasingly intentionally designed to encourage employees to move around the office to connect with others and undertake physical activity (Hess, 2017), elements that are dramatically altered when employees WFH. Other research suggests that there are increased tensions between the public (work) roles and private (domestic) roles for those who work from home (Marsh & Musson, 2008). Employees struggle to keep work and domestic roles such as parenting separate as technology makes it difficult to escape from "pings" on teamwork platforms, phone calls and email. These issues are complicated by differences in individual circumstances (e.g., single or living with others) (Berke, 2003), different personality types (e.g., introverts and extraverts) (O'Neill, Hambley, Greidanus, MacDonnell, & Kline, 2009) or institutional environments and sub-cultures (e.g. outcome or people focused cultures) (Peters and Heusinkveld, 2010).

Surman (2002) has highlighted the importance of the perceptions of not just the employee, but others around them as antecedents of the successful implementation of moving work into the home. Other researchers have argued that a successful transition to work from home is contingent on individual choice and control (Lee and Brand, 2005; Maruyama et al., 2009; Mirchandani, 1998), as autonomy has been found to be significantly correlated with satisfaction with the physical work environment (Elsbach &

Pratt, 2007). Knowledge workers commonly attempt to replicate familiar aspects of their office in the home environment, using similar desks, computers, and creating separate workspaces (Ng, 2010; Tietze and Musson, 2005). These actions transform private spaces to work areas with technology, files and other artefacts of traditional office environments (Halford, 2005; Maruyama et al., 2009). Since many organizations utilize the physical environment of their offices to convey messages about culture, a sense of belonging and desired behaviours, this presents a significant challenge as to how these elements can be recreated in virtual platforms or in the employee's home workspace.

Finally, it is important to note that while not having to dress for the office, and the reduction in commuting time are often cited as positive aspects of WFH in terms of time saved (Allen et al., 2015), research has highlighted a potential negative impact of losing the 'transition time' involved in travelling from home to the office (Kurland and Bailey, 1999). Often this transition time is used in separating private home issues from work issues or in preparing for the day by thinking through issues to be addressed in the day ahead. In working from home this opportunity is often lost.

FRAMEWORKS FOR THE PHYSICAL ENVIRONMENT AT HOME

Beginning with Taylor (1911), early theoretical approaches to the physical work environment have taken a practical view, examining instrumental features such as layout, privacy, lighting or spatial efficiency (Davis, 1984; Elsbach & Pratt, 2007. An extensive stream of research on disparate dimensions of the physical environment followed with a focus on spatial layout (Backhouse and Drew, 1992; Brennan et al., 2002; Zalesney and Farace, 1987), building materials (McCoy and Evans, 2002), decorations (Bringslimark et al., 2009), noise (Yadav, Kim, Cabrera, and de Dear, 2017; Zaglauer, Drotleff, and Lieble, 2017), lighting (Zhong and House, 2012) and opportunities for personalization (Elsbach, 2004). Gagliardi (1990) notes that this focus on features and layouts that could be replicated across contexts meant that the reactions of the employee to the physical work environment, and their experience at work took a back seat until researchers began to take a more subjective view based on employees' experiences of work. The importance of the individual *employee's subjective* reactions to the physical environment, rather than the objective (practical) characteristics of the environment are now well established (see Hackman and Oldham, 1975; Salancik and Pfeffer, 1978; Roethlisberger and Dixon, 1939; Sander et al., 2019).

Giving employees control over aspects of their physical work environment such as their seating arrangements, the lighting and temperature of work and the setting of work, mediates the effects of environmental characteristics that have otherwise been shown to have detrimental effects (Lee and Brand, 2005). Theoretical approaches have incorporated this perspective, recognising the link between employees' cognitive and affective reactions to their work environment and their impact on employee mood, behaviour and performance (see Ashkanasy et al., 2014; Bitner, 1992; Brown and Robinson, 2011; Sander et al., 2019 for examples).

In the last decade, a number of criticisms of existing theories have emerged suggesting that theorists have taken a fixed view of space and fail to account for spatial dynamics. Researchers have argued that there is a need to incorporate movement into the physicality of work, by examining how dynamic features can create and alter spatial arrangements (Stephenson et al., 2020; Wapshott & Mallett, 2012). For example, Wapshott and Mallett (2012) suggest that homeworkers explicitly control or demarcate the spaces of their home by replicating what they might have in the office. These authors argue that it is important to consider other significant aspects of work within the home including spatial practices, that is the cohesive practices and patterns of social activity, and representational space, that is spaces that we seek to change and appropriate and our passive experiences of the space (Lefebvre, 1991) which may not be conducive to becoming a work environment.

We suggest that theoretical frameworks of the physical environment in the home need to consider a wide range of factors to adequately capture the complex dynamics of the setting. For example, in order to maintain psychological anchors and associations for effective sleep behaviours, research suggests a range of factors need to be addressed in the physical environment. Potential interventions include reducing clutter (Thacher & Reinheimer, 2015), lighting and darkness control measures such as blinds or curtains (Blume, Garbazza & Spitschan, 2019), the choice of bed and linen (Jacobson, Boolani & Smith, 2009), use of scent (Sowndhararajan & Kim, 2016), the use of music which has been shown to reduce anxiety and alleviate physical pain (Trahan, Durant, Müllensiefen, & Williamson, 2018). Simarly, not using technology devices before bed can help with sleep as exposure to artificial light in the evenings can interrupt circadian rhythm and delay sleep onset (Tosini, Ferguson & Tsubota, 2016). Researchers have argued that addressing these factors, which directly and indirectly affect the brain's physiological process of producing melatonin, and signalling sleep (Irish et al., 2015), are critical when considering and managing the impacts of the physical workspace in the home. What is not clear is the impact of adding work requirements that fit with these recommendations, particularly for some employees who may not have spacious living space.

Rather than just identifying the spatial features and aspects of the physical work environment of the home, researchers need to consider the dynamics of movement and process (Stephenson et al., 2020; Wapshott & Mallett, 2012). For example, in addition to practical considerations such as closing technology programmes and finalising tasks, employees may use an end of day ritual to achieve psychological detachment, emotional regulation of the nervous system and the reduction of physiological stress (Sonnentag, Binnewies, & Mojza, 2010). Techniques such as meditation, journaling, listening to music, engaging in hobbies or pleasurable activities, or undertaking exercise may be useful in promoting effective end of day rituals (Zucker, 2019). Theories of the physical work environment of the home also need to consider how space can be utilised to create boundaries and support rituals that promote behaviours such as stopping work, reducing work spill over, rumination, visual distraction, and to support planning for the next day as a restorative physical environment has been shown to support detachment from work (Kaplan, 1995; Sonnentag, 2012). Potential frameworks that may be useful when considering managing the impacts of WFH that arise from the physical environment include those from emerging research on the use of circadian lighting to support biorhythms and melatonin production for sleep (Dai, Huang, Hao, Lin, & Chen, 2018), soundscaping using artificial noise of printers and other office equipment to create anchors to workplace behaviours (Acun & Yilmazer, 2018), as well as physical design elements such as tactile materials and the use of scent to promote cognitive and affective responses that support effective work (Bitner, 1992).

FRAMEWORK FOR FUTURE RESEARCH

Given the limited existing understanding of the impacts of the physical work environment of the home, there is a wide scope for scholars to build a body of knowledge in this emerging field. Below, we outline four areas of potential research into the physical work environment of the home.

Understanding the Dimensions of the Physical Work Environment

A first consideration should be to investigate to what extent the dimensions of the physical work environment of the office - layout, materials, lighting, temperature, colour, and privacy (as examples) are relevant in WFH settings. At present, no guidance exists for employees or organizations on how to create WFH environments to optimise well-being and performance. Areas that future researchers could investigate include the effects of different layouts of the workspace within the home on outcomes such as attention and the employee's ability to focus, engagement in high performance work behaviours, and well-being. Research could also investigate how work from home arrangements and the design of the physical environment of the home facilitate or hinder team cohesion and performance, creativity and innovation, career progression and co-worker relationships.

Another topic of interest arises from research on visual and auditory privacy, which have been found to be significant predictors of satisfaction and performance in office settings (Kim & de Dear, 2013). At present, we have no understanding of whether, how or when such dimensions are relevant in the home setting. Similarly, the beneficial effects of greenery, air quality and biophilic design have been demonstrated in office settings (see Colenberg, Jylhä, & Arkesteijn, 2020 for a review). In the WFH setting, it would also make sense to investigate the role that these factors play as antecedents of cognitive, affective and physiological outcomes.

In office settings, researchers have found that clutter influences employees' cognition, emotions and behaviours, affecting decision making and relationships with others, stress, eating choices and even sleep (see Sander, 2019 for review). Research shows disorganization and clutter have a cumulative effect on our cognitive functioning (McCains & Kastner, 2011). To think clearly individuals like order, and constant visual reminders of disorganization drain our cognitive resources, reducing our ability to focus as well as our working memory. That is, the visual distraction of clutter increases cognitive overload and can reduce our working memory (Gaspar, Christie, Prime, Jolicœur, & McDonald, 2016). Given the established body of research highlighting the effects of clutter across a wide range of outcomes, we suggest that future research could investigate the role of clutter in the home workplace and its potential influence on individual detachment and rumination, factors which will have important consequences for employee well-being (Sonnentag & Bayer, 2005; Mache, Servaty & Harth, 2020).

As outlined earlier in the chapter, ergonomics is a vitally important area for future research on the physical work environment of the home. Ergonomics has been highlighted as an important issue and a potential barrier in effective WFH implementation, and as such further understanding of this field in the home setting is essential. Research has shown that a "proper" ergonomic setup includes a minimum of a separate work desk with a flat surface, ergonomic chair, and suitable lighting. Such a setup can reduce problems such as muscle strain, lower back injuries and tendonitis, as well as decreasing muscle fatigue and enhancing productivity (Brand, 2008). Finally, we suggest that researchers should investigate how to utilize physical environment design for boundary setting for employees. For example, researchers may consider the use of barriers to separate workspaces from living areas thereby avoiding the cognitive distraction of work related materials and clutter, or the use of wind down practices such as work task review and filing of work materials to signal the end of the work day.

Objective Measurement to Assess the Impact of WFH on Employee Well-being and Performance

A significant body of research on both the physical work environment of the office, and on WFH arrangements, has utilized self-report methodologies (Allen, Golden & Shockley, 2015; Davis, Leach & Clegg, 2011). However, recent advances in technology and also the reduced cost of objective measurement tools such as heart rate monitoring and mobile EEG scans, has meant that objective measurement is now being used far more widely in research on the physical work environment (Ganster, Crain & Broissit, 2018). These tools allow researchers to assess psychophysiological effects of the physical work environment on outcomes such as employee stress, attention, and sleep. Using objective data, alongside traditional self-report surveys and more granular approaches such as experience sampling methodologies (Fisher, 2008), will allow researchers to track the effects of the physical work environment in the home. This offers the possibility that research also can assess temporal and process influences of the physical work environment of the home on employee physical and psychological well-being, work life balance, mood, performance and detachment.

Developing Process Approaches to the Physical work Environment

The physical work environment has traditionally been viewed as a fixed, physical workspace (Davis, Leach & Clegg, 2011; Elsbach & Pratt, 2007). However, a growing body of research has begun to take into account spatial dynamics and the incorporation of movement into the physicality of work (Kingma, Dale & Wasserman, 2018; Kornberger & Clegg, 2004, Wapshott & Mallett, 2012). This is particularly relevant to the changing dynamic of WFH, where boundaries between work and home are diluted and traditional structures are missing. As such, process studies have emerged as a way to investigate dynamic features that create and alter spatial arrangements (Stephenson, Putnam, Kuismin, & Sivunen, 2018). Situating work in the home changes the focus of the home environment from one of predominantly recreation, rest, and leisure to a setting where work occurs. By adding work as a significant feature within this context, WFH is likely to influence the relationships of the inhabitants of that space as they try to balance potentially conflicting demands and challenges of work and non-work activities (Wapshott & Mallett, 2012). Issues related to the separation of work, work/family conflict, work spill over and multiple role juggling are likely to be significantly heightened when work is occurring for some or all of the time within the home.

In the office environment, symbols and objects play important roles in communicating culture (Elsbach & Pratt, 2007). The layout of space designates the type of activities intended to take place there, acting as a container for spatial dynamics and different work processes (Stephenson et al, 2018). For example, a lunchroom or social eating space provides a separation from tasks, and the chance to interact with other colleagues. Furthermore, the physical work environment in the office acts as a signal for different activities. For example, water cooler discussions, printing, eating lunch, and meeting spaces. These activities constitute important rituals in our work, providing comfort, putting us at ease, and in building and maintaining rapport (Smith & Stewart, 2011). When these activities occur in one space, important elements of the work process are removed. For example, when working in an office with others, we often meet people on the way to a meeting to catch up on issues or discuss our views before going in. We get coffee, and the simple act of relocating to a different room is energising. But at home, we might be just working on a task and then we begin a meeting using video-conferencing software, often without taking breaks. WFH also eliminates the opportunity for casual conversations and social interactions with colleagues and employees from other parts of the organization.

Overall, the physical environment acts as a cognitive scaffold (Sander, Caza & Jordan, 2019), whereby we attribute certain meanings to different spaces within the office, leading to subtle changes in our behaviour. This can include providing anchors for important issues such as creativity and problem solving. For example, walking is known to improve creativity (Oppezzo & Schwartz, 2014), highlighting the importance of discussions while walking to meetings, bumping into others, and moving around the office. Given the likely prominence of WFH going forward, understanding the spatial implications of the physical work environment of the home on process studies of organizational space is a vitally important area of research.

Creating Identity and Connection

Items such as memorabilia from an employee's favourite sporting team, or a collection of Star Wars figurines play a role in helping an employee to signal their identity to others at work (Elsbach & Pratt, 2007), while the display of qualifications, awards and photographs may be used to communicate status (Elsbach, 2004; Elsbach & Pratt, 2007). Research could investigate whether these concepts are transferable in the WFH space and how individuals create a space that allows them to signal their identity to work colleagues when at home. If everyone uses virtual backgrounds and prefers to hide their home identity, what role does this play in relationship development, cohesion, and other identity outcomes for employees and managers?

PRACTICAL IMPLICATIONS

In addition to research direction, there are numerous implications for individuals, organizations, policy makers, urban planners, and designers that will require focussed attention. We outline these separately below.

Individual

A shift to the home environment as the default setting for work, or the predominant setting, will have profound implications for individuals. Situating work in the home changes the environment of the home from one of predominantly recreation, rest and leisure (and recuperation from work stresses) to a setting where work occurs. By adding work as a significant feature within this context, WFH will influence the relationships of the inhabitants of that space as they try to balance potentially conflicting demands and challenges of work and non-work activities. Implications such as separation of work, work/family conflict, work spill over and juggling multiple conflicting roles are likely to be significantly heightened when work is occurring some or all of the time within the home. Such scenarios require careful management and ongoing discussion between employers and employees. The design and use of the physical work environment of the home needs to support separation of these differing activities as they occur, as well as facilitate the transition to differing roles within the home. Design that supports effective detachment from work is essential for employee well-being.

Organizational

A key factor in the planning of WFH arrangements for organizations is the duty of care they bear to provide a safe workplace for their employees, incorporating both physical and psychological well-being. As outlined in the review of research on WFH earlier in the chapter, ergonomic workstations and accessories will be imperative to ensure the safety of employees and their productivity, and the onus is likely to fall to the employer to pay for this in designating the home as a primary or significant place of work. This is an important consideration, as ergonomic work furniture and equipment is expensive, and many employees may be unable to afford what is needed to ensure an appropriate home workspace. This topic has received little consideration to date beyond general media discussion and some industry publications.

In addition to physical considerations such as the workstation and chair, computer, lighting, and acoustics, employers will have a heightened imperative to ensure safe work practices in the home, including taking appropriate breaks and monitoring hours of work to prevent burnout. Employees working from home have been shown to work longer hours than their office-based counterparts (Allen et al., 2015). The increased autonomy and flexibility in terms of when work hours are completed and how work is done may result in enhanced outcomes in productivity, engagement and well-being (Bloom et al., 2015) if care is taken to address the negative effects of WFH. The issue that remains is how these new arrangements may impact on ongoing remuneration and compensation decisions.

Management training, training in separating work and life, and consideration of human resource practices and processes such as no afterhours emails or video conferences, will also need to be undertaken to assist employees to optimise the set-up of their WFH environments for safety, productivity and well-being. The logistical and cost considerations of these initiatives require planning, and may result in the emergence of workplace wellness certification consultants engaged by organizations in the way that ergonomics consultants have been used in the past to monitor the work set up of employees both in the office, and more infrequently, in home settings. Finally, organizations may need to consider the use of satellite offices, or access to coworking spaces, where personal situations or preferences of the employee may not align with hybrid or full-time work from home arrangements.

Policy Makers and Designers

Governments and policy makers continue to discuss the impact of smaller head offices and WFH arrangements on the landscape of cities, and in particular, central business districts. These shifts are likely to have several far-reaching implications. First, the shift to permanent or hybrid WFH arrangements means that employees are reconsidering where they live. A significant motivation for many employees in determining their choice of home relates to the distance from their workplace. In addition, as opportunities continue to arise for employees to be located anywhere in the world, employees may choose to relocate to regional and rural areas driven by lifestyle considerations rather than distance to the office (see the chapter by Green in this handbook).

Second, in the past 15 years there has been a global trend toward smaller homes, driven primarily by the cost of real estate in urban areas (Urban Developer, 2020), as well as the rise of single person households (Snell, 2017). The pandemic, with its associated fears for health and safety, and the concurrent shift to WFH is likely to result in a new lens when viewing the home. Emerging research indicates an increasing trend towards the home being seen as a retreat, a space that provides a feeling of comfort, separation and restoration from noisy cities, crowded offices and health concerns that the pandemic has presented (Kolomatsky, 2020). The WFH shift is likely to mean that people will spend more time at home, and more than one person may be working (or studying) from home. Where the home office was something of a rarity, the WFH shift will require designated work and study spaces in the home that include auditory and visual privacy, technology infrastructure, and critically, spaces that allow for both physical and psychological separation, retreat and restoration. For example, physical separation may be achieved through walls, partitions, screening and acoustic treatment. As noted earlier in the chapter, psychological separation, where employees are able to switch off and detach from work is particularly critical in work from home environments. The deliberate design of spaces that promote psychological and emotional detachment from work are also important considerations. Restorative spaces have begun to emerge in office settings in recent years (Pochepan, 2018) and may include areas designated for specific activities such as sleep pods, meditation spaces, yoga rooms, and indoor and outdoor "rooms" where employees can immerse themselves in nature. Home designers may also draw increasingly on the Danish concept of hygge (Jensen, Strengers, Raptis, Nicholls, Kjeldskov, & Skov, 2018), the idea of designing homes and the activities that occur in them to promote a feeling of comfort, cosiness and connection. A part of this design may now include the separation of work and private spaces within the home.

CONCLUSION

The COVID-19 pandemic has brought the physical work environment of the home into sharp focus. Despite an established body of research examining the psychological and social impacts of WFH, research has largely ignored the physical setting in which it takes place. Scholarly attention on the physical work environment is burgeoning (see Colenberg, Jylhä, & Arkesteijn, 2020; Stephenson et al, 2020) in line with our growing understanding of the impact of the physical environment on cognition, affect, behaviour and well-being in individuals, and organizational performance (Colenberg, Jylhä, & Arkesteijn, 2020; Masterton et al., 2019). As WFH is predicted to be a permanent feature of work arrangements going forward for millions of employees (Hirschfeld et al., 2020), it is critical that we better understand the physical work environment of the home. In this chapter, we have briefly summarised the research on WFH and the physical work environment in organizations. We have recommended a framework for future research on the physical work environment of the home, suggesting directions for future research as well as the use of emerging methodologies to undertake this research.

REFERENCES

Access Economics. (2010). Accessed 1 September, 2020. http://ict-industryreports.com.au/wp-content/uploads/sites/4/2010/07/2010-Impacts-of-Teleworking-under-the-NBN-July-2010.pdf

Acun, V., & Yilmazer, S. (2018). A grounded theory approach to investigate the perceived soundscape of open-plan offices. *Applied Acoustics*, *131*, 28–37. doi:10.1016/j.apacoust.2017.09.018

Allen, T. D., Golden, T. D., & Shockley, K. M. (2015). How Effective Is Telecommuting? Assessing the Status of Our Scientific Findings. *Psychological Science in the Public Interest*, *16*(2), 40–68. doi:10.1177/1529100615593273 PMID:26403188

Allen, T. D., Johnson, R. C., Kiburz, K. M., & Shockley, K. M. (2013). Work–family conflict and flexible work arrangements: Deconstructing flexibility. *Personnel Psychology*, *66*(2), 345–376. doi:10.1111/peps.12012

Arthur, C. (2013). Yahoo chief bans working from home. *The Guardian*. Accessed 18 August 2020. https://www.theguardian.com/technology/2013/feb/25/yahoo-chief-bans-working-home

Ashkanasy, N. M., Humphrey, R. H., & Huy, Q. N. (2017). Integrating emotions and affect in theories of management. *Academy of Management Review*, *42*(2), 175–189. doi:10.5465/amr.2016.0474

Backhouse, A., & Drew, P. (1992). The design implications of social interaction in a workplace setting. *Environment & Planning B*, *19*(5), 573–584. doi:10.1068/b190573

Baruch, Y. (2000). Teleworking benefits and pitfalls as perceived by professionals and managers. *New Technology, Work and Employment*, *15*(1), 34–49. doi:10.1111/1468-005X.00063

Baruch, Y. (2003). The status of research on teleworking and an agenda for future research. *International Journal of Management Reviews*, *3*(2), 113–129. doi:10.1111/1468-2370.00058

Berke, D. L. (2003). Coming home again: The challenges and rewards of home-based self employment. *Journal of Family Issues*, *24*(4), 513–546. doi:10.1177/0192513X02250754

Bitner, M. J. (1992). Servicescapes: The impact of physical surroundings on customers and employees. *Journal of Marketing*, *56*(2), 57–71. doi:10.1177/002224299205600205

Bloom, N. (2014). Fluctuations of uncertainty. *The Journal of Economic Perspectives*, *28*(2), 153–175. doi:10.1257/jep.28.2.153

Blume, C., Garbazza, C., & Spitschan, M. (2019). Effects of light on human circadian rhythms, sleep and mood. *Somnologie: Schlafforschung und Schlafmedizin*, *23*(3), 147–156. doi:10.100711818-019-00215-x PMID:31534436

Brand, J. L. (2008). Office Ergonomics: A Review of Pertinent Research and Recent Developments. *Review of Human Factors and Ergonomics*, *4*(1), 245–282. doi:10.1518/155723408X342871

Brennan, A., Chugh, J. S., & Kline, T. (2002). Traditional versus open office design: A longitudinal field study. *Environment and Behavior*, *34*(3), 279–299. doi:10.1177/0013916502034003001

Bringslimark, T., Hartig, T., & Patil, G. G. (2007). Psychological benefits of indoor plants in workplaces: Putting experimental results into context. *HortScience*, *42*(3), 581–587. doi:10.21273/HORTSCI.42.3.581

Brown, G., & Robinson, S. L. (2011). Reactions to territorial infringement. *Organization Science*, *22*(1), 210–224. doi:10.1287/orsc.1090.0507

Brownlee, D. (2020). Twitter, square announce work from home forever option: What are the risks? *Forbes*. Retrieved from: https://www.forbes.com/sites/danabrownlee/2020/05/18/twitter-square-announce-work-from-home-forever-optionwhat-are-the-risks/?sh=437570402565

Coenen, M., & Kok, R. A. W. (2014). Workplace flexibility and new product development performance: The role of telework and flexible work schedules. *European Management Journal*, *32*(4), 564–576. doi:10.1016/j.emj.2013.12.003

Colenberg, S., Jylhä, T., & Arkesteijn, M. (2020). The relationship between interior office space and employee health and well-being–a literature review. *Building Research and Information*, 1–15. doi:10.1080/09613218.2019.1710098

Collins, A. M., Hislop, D., & Cartwright, S. (2016). Social support in the workplace between teleworkers, office-based colleagues and supervisors. *New Technology, Work and Employment*, *31*(2), 161–175. doi:10.1111/ntwe.12065

Dai, Q., Huang, Y., Hao, L., Lin, Y., & Chen, K. (2018). Spatial and spectral illumination design for energy-efficient circadian lighting. *Building and Environment*, *146*, 216–225. doi:10.1016/j.buildenv.2018.10.004

Davis, M. C., Leach, D. J., & Clegg, C. W. (2011). The physical environment of the office: Contemporary and emerging issues. In G. P. Hodgkinson & J. K. Ford (Eds.), *International Review of Industrial and Organizational Psychology* (Vol. 26, pp. 193–237). Wiley Blackwell.

Davis, T. R. V. (1984). The influence of the physical environment in offices. *Academy of Management Review*, *9*(2), 271–283. doi:10.5465/amr.1984.4277654 PMID:10266030

Elsbach, K., & Pratt, M. G. (2007). The physical environment in organizations. *The Academy of Management Annals*, *1*(1), 181–224. doi:10.5465/078559809

Elsbach, K. D. (2004). Interpreting workplace identities: The role of office décor. *Journal of Organizational Behavior*, *25*(1), 99–128. doi:10.1002/job.233

Eurofound and the International Labour Office. (2017). *Working anytime, anywhere: The effects on the world of work*. Publications Office of the European Union, Luxembourg, and the International Labour Office.

Evans, G. W., & Johnson, D. (2000). Stress and open-office noise. *The Journal of Applied Psychology*, *85*(5), 779–783. doi:10.1037/0021-9010.85.5.779 PMID:11055149

Fisher, C. D. (2008). Experience sampling methodology in organizational psychology. In I. Glendon, B. Myors, & B. Thompson (Eds.), *Advances in organizational psychology: An Asia-Pacific perspective* (pp. 403–425). Australian Academic Press.

Gagliardi, P. (1990). *Symbols and artifacts: Views of the corporate landscape*. W. de Gruyter. doi:10.1515/9783110874143

Gajendran, R. S., & Harrison, D. A. (2007). The good, the bad, and the unknown about telecommuting: Meta-analysis of psychological mediators and individual consequences. *The Journal of Applied Psychology*, *92*(6), 1524–1541. doi:10.1037/0021-9010.92.6.1524 PMID:18020794

Gajendran, R. S., Harrison, D. A., & Delaney-Klinger, K. (2015). Are telecommuters remotely good citizens? Unpacking telecommuting's effects on performance via i-deals and job resources. *Personnel Psychology*, *68*(2), 353–393. doi:10.1111/peps.12082

Ganster, D. C., Crain, T. L., & Brossoit, R. M. (2018). Physiological measurement in the organizational sciences: A review and recommendations for future use. *Annual Review of Organizational Psychology and Organizational Behavior*, *5*(1), 267–293. doi:10.1146/annurev-orgpsych-032117-104613

Gaspar, J. M., Christie, G. J., Prime, D. J., Jolicœur, P., & McDonald, J. J. (2016). Inability to suppress salient distractors predicts low visual working memory capacity. *Proceedings of the National Academy of Sciences of the United States of America, 113*(13), 3693–3698. doi:10.1073/pnas.1523471113 PMID:26903654

Gibson, J. W., Blackwell, C. W., Dominicis, P., & Demerath, N. (2002). Telecommuting in the 21st Century: Benefits, Issues, and a Leadership Model Which Will Work. *The Journal of Leadership Studies, 8*(4), 75–86. doi:10.1177/107179190200800407

Global Workplace Analytics. (2020). Accessed 1 September 2020. https://globalworkplaceanalytics.com/telecommuting-statistics

Golden, T. D., & Gajendran, R. S. (2019). Unpacking the role of a telecommuter's job in their performance: Examining job complexity, problem solving, interdependence, and social support. *Journal of Business and Psychology, 34*(1), 55–69. doi:10.100710869-018-9530-4

Golden, T. D., & Veiga, J. F. (2008). The impact of superior–subordinate relationships on the commitment, job satisfaction, and performance of virtual workers. *The Leadership Quarterly, 19*(1), 77–88. doi:10.1016/j.leaqua.2007.12.009

Golden, T. D., Veiga, J. F., & Dino, R. N. (2008). The impact of professional isolation on teleworker job performance and turnover intentions: Does time spent teleworking, interacting face-to-face, or having access to communication-enhancing technology matter? *The Journal of Applied Psychology, 93*(6), 1412–1421. doi:10.1037/a0012722 PMID:19025257

Hackman, J. R., & Oldham, G. R. (1975). Development of the job diagnostic survey. *The Journal of Applied Psychology, 60*(2), 159–170. doi:10.1037/h0076546

Haigh, G. (2012). *The office: A hardworking history*. The Miegunyah Press, Melbourne University Publishing.

Hakim, C. (1996). *Key issues in women's work: Female heterogeneity and the polarization of women's employment*. Oxford University Press.

Halford, S. (2005). Hybrid workspace: Re-spatialisations of work, organization and management. *New Technology, Work and Employment, 20*(1), 19–33. doi:10.1111/j.1468-005X.2005.00141.x

Harris, L. (2003). Home-based teleworking and the employment relationship managerial challenges and dilemmas. *Personnel Review, 32*(4), 422–437. doi:10.1108/00483480310477515

Hedge, A. (1982). The open-plan office: A systematic investigation of employee reactions to their work environment. *Environment and Behavior, 14*(5), 519–542. doi:10.1177/0013916582145002

Hess, A. (2017). *The science and design behind Apple's innovation obsessed new workplace*. Retrieved from https://www.cnbc.com/2017/09/13/the-science-and-design-behind-apples-innovation-obsessed-new-workspace.html

Hirschfeld. (2020). Coronavirus: How the world of work may change forever. *BBC*. Retrieved from https://www.bbc.com/worklife/article/20201023-coronavirus-how-will-the-pandemic-change-the-way-we-work

Irish, L. A., Kline, C. E., Gunn, H. E., Buysse, D. J., & Hall, M. H. (2015). The role of sleep hygiene in promoting public health: A review of empirical evidence. *Sleep Medicine Reviews*, *22*, 23–36. doi:10.1016/j.smrv.2014.10.001 PMID:25454674

Jacobson, B. H., Boolani, A., & Smith, D. B. (2009). Changes in back pain, sleep quality, and perceived stress after introduction of new bedding systems. *Journal of Chiropractic Medicine*, *8*(1), 1–8. doi:10.1016/j.jcm.2008.09.002 PMID:19646380

Jahncke, H., Hygge, S., Halin, N., Green, A. M., & Dimberg, K. (2011). Open-plan office noise: Cognitive performance and restoration. *Journal of Environmental Psychology*, *31*(4), 373–382. doi:10.1016/j.jenvp.2011.07.002

Jensen, R. H., Strengers, Y., Raptis, D., Nicholls, L., Kjeldskov, J., & Skov, M. B. (2018, June). Exploring Hygge as a desirable design vision for the sustainable smart home. In *Proceedings of the 2018 Designing Interactive Systems Conference* (pp. 355-360). 10.1145/3196709.3196804

Kaplan, S. (1995). The restorative benefits of nature: Toward an integrative framework. *Journal of Environmental Psychology*, *15*(3), 169–182. doi:10.1016/0272-4944(95)90001-2

Kingma, S., Dale, K., & Wasserman, V. (Eds.). (2018). *Organizational space and beyond: The significance of Henri Lefebvre for organization studies*. Routledge.

Kolomatsky. (2020). How Is the Pandemic Shaping Home Design? *New York Times*. https://www.nytimes.com/2020/10/22/realestate/pandemic-shaping-home-design.html

Kornberger, M., & Clegg, S. (2004). Bringing space back in: Organizing the generative building. *Organization Studies*, *25*(7), 1095–1114. doi:10.1177/0170840604046312

Kurland, N. B., & Bailey, D. E. (1999). Telework: The advantages and challenges of working here, there, anywhere, and anytime. *Organizational Dynamics*, *28*(2), 53–68. doi:10.1016/S0090-2616(00)80016-9

Lee, S. Y., & Brand, J. L. (2005). Effects of control over office workspace on perceptions of the work environment and work outcomes. *Journal of Environmental Psychology*, *25*(3), 323–333. doi:10.1016/j.jenvp.2005.08.001

Lefebvre, H. (1991). *The Production of Space* (D. Nicholson-Smith, Trans.). Blackwell.

Mache, S., Servaty, R., & Harth, V. (2020). Flexible work arrangements in open workspaces and relations to occupational stress, need for recovery and psychological detachment from work. *Journal of Occupational Medicine and Toxicology (London, England)*, *15*(1), 1–11. doi:10.118612995-020-00258-z PMID:32206078

MacNaughton, P., Satish, U., Laurent, J. G. C., Flanigan, S., Vallarino, J., Coull, B., Spengler, J. D., & Allen, J. G. (2017). The impact of working in a green certified building on cognitive function and health. *Building and Environment*, *114*, 178–186. doi:10.1016/j.buildenv.2016.11.041 PMID:28785124

Marsh, K., & Musson, G. (2008). Men at work and at home: Managing emotion in telework. *Gender, Work and Organization*, *15*(1), 31–48.

Martin, B., & MacDonnell, R. (2012). Is telework effective for organizations? A meta-analysis of empirical research on perceptions of telework and organizational outcomes. *Management Research Review*, *35*(7), 602–616. doi:10.1108/01409171211238820

Maruyama, T., Hopkinson, P. G., & James, P. W. (2009). A multivariate analysis of work–life balance outcomes from a large-scale telework programme. *New Technology, Work and Employment*, *24*(1), 76–88. doi:10.1111/j.1468-005X.2008.00219.x

Masterson, V. A., Enqvist, J. P., Stedman, R. C., & Tengö, M. (2019). Sense of place in social–ecological systems: From theory to empirics. *Sustainability Science*, *14*(3), 555–564. doi:10.100711625-019-00695-8

McCains, S., & Kastner, S. (2011). Interactions of top-down and bottom-up mechanisms in human visual cortex. *The Journal of Neuroscience: The Official Journal of the Society for Neuroscience*, *312*(2), 587–597. doi:10.1523/JNEUROSCI.3766-10.2011 PMID:21228167

McCoy, J. M., & Evans, G. W. (2002). The potential role of the physical environment in fostering creativity. *Creativity Research Journal*, *14*(3-4), 409–426. doi:10.1207/S15326934CRJ1434_11

McMains, S., & Kastner, S. (2011). Interactions of top-down and bottom-up mechanisms in human visual cortex. *The Journal of Neuroscience: The Official Journal of the Society for Neuroscience*, *31*(2), 587–597. doi:10.1523/JNEUROSCI.3766-10.2011 PMID:21228167

Mirchandani, K. (1998). Protecting the boundary: Teleworker insights on the expansive concept of "work". *Gender & Society*, *12*(2), 168–187. doi:10.1177/089124398012002004

MMK. (2014). *Google offices around the world*. Retrieved from https://www.architecturendesign.net/google-offices-googleplex-around-the-world/

Morrison, R. L., & Macky, K. A. (2017). The demands and resources arising from shared office spaces. *Applied Ergonomics*, *60*, 103–115. doi:10.1016/j.apergo.2016.11.007 PMID:28166868

Ng, C. F. (2010). Teleworker's home office: An extension of corporate office? *Facilities*, *28*(3/4), 137–155. doi:10.1108/02632771011023113

Nilles, J. M. (1997). Telework: Enabling distributed organizations. *Information Systems Management*, *14*(4), 7–14. doi:10.1080/10580539708907069

O'Neill, T. A., Hambley, L. A., Greidanus, N. S., MacDonnell, R., & Kline, T. J. B. (2009). Predicting teleworker success: An exploration of personality, motivational, situational, and job characteristics. *New Technology, Work and Employment*, *24*(2), 144–162. doi:10.1111/j.1468-005X.2009.00225.x

Oppezzo, M., & Schwartz, D. L. (2014). Give your ideas some legs: The positive effect of walking on creative thinking. *Journal of Experimental Psychology. Learning, Memory, and Cognition*, *40*(4), 1142–1152. doi:10.1037/a0036577 PMID:24749966

Pérez, M. P., Sánchez, A. M., de Luis Carnicer, P., & Jiménez, M. J. V. (2004). A technology acceptance model of innovation adoption: The case of teleworking. *European Journal of Innovation Management*, *7*(4), 280–291. doi:10.1108/14601060410565038

Peters, P., & Heusinkveld, H. S. (2010). Institutional explanations for managers' attitudes towards telehomeworking. *Human Relations (New York)*, *63*(1), 107–135. doi:10.1177/0018726709336025

Pochepan. (2018). 'Recharge Rooms' Are the Next Trend Your Employees Need in the Office and no, they're not for plugging in your tech. *Inc.* https://www.inc.com/jeff-pochepan/recharge-rooms-are-next-trend-your-employees-need-in-office.html

Reaney, P. (2012). About 20 percent of global workers telecommute: Poll. *Huff Post*. Retrieved from https://www.huffingtonpost.com/2012/01/24/workers-telecommute_n_1228004.html

Roethlisberger, F. J., & Dickson, W. J. (1939). *Management and the worker*. Harvard Univ. Press.

Salancik, G. R., & Pfeffer, J. (1978). A social information processing approach to job attitudes and task design. *Administrative Science Quarterly*, *23*(2), 224–253. doi:10.2307/2392563 PMID:10307892

Sander, E. L. J. (2019). The case for finally cleaning your desk. *Harvard Business Review*. Accessed 1 November 2020. https://hbr.org/2019/03/the-case-for-finally-cleaning-your-desk

Sander, E. L. J., Caza, A., & Jordan, P. J. (2019). Psychological perceptions matter: Developing the reactions to the physical work environment scale. *Building and Environment*, *148*, 338–347. doi:10.1016/j.buildenv.2018.11.020

Shockley, K. M., & Allen, T. D. (2007). When flexibility helps: Another look at the availability of flexible work arrangements and work–family conflict. *Journal of Vocational Behavior*, *71*(3), 479–493. doi:10.1016/j.jvb.2007.08.006

Smith, A. C. T., & Stewart, B. (2011). Organizational rituals: Features, functions and mechanisms: Organizational rituals. *International Journal of Management Reviews*, *13*(2), 113–133. doi:10.1111/j.1468-2370.2010.00288.x

Snell, K. D. M. (2017). The rise of living alone and loneliness in history. *Social History (London)*, *42*(1), 2–28. doi:10.1080/03071022.2017.1256093

Sonnentag, S. (2012). Psychological detachment from work during leisure time: The benefits of mentally disengaging from work. *Current Directions in Psychological Science*, *21*(2), 114–118. doi:10.1177/0963721411434979

Sonnentag, S., & Bayer, U. V. (2005). Switching off mentally: Predictors and consequences of psychological detachment from work during off-job time. *Journal of Occupational Health Psychology*, *10*(4), 393–414. doi:10.1037/1076-8998.10.4.393 PMID:16248688

Sonnentag, S., Binnewies, C., & Mojza, E. J. (2010). Staying well and engaged when demands are high: The role of psychological detachment. *The Journal of Applied Psychology*, *95*(5), 965–976. doi:10.1037/a0020032 PMID:20718528

Sowndhararajan, K., & Kim, S. (2016). Influence of Fragrances on Human Psychophysiological Activity: With Special Reference to Human Electroencephalographic Response. *Scientia Pharmaceutica*, *84*(4), 724–752. doi:10.3390cipharm84040724 PMID:27916830

Stephenson, K. A., Kuismin, A., Putnam, L. L., & Sivunen, A. (2020). Process Studies of Organizational Space. *The Academy of Management Annals*, *14*(2), 797–827. doi:10.5465/annals.2018.0146

Stephenson, K. A., Putnam, L. L., Kuismin, A., & Sivunen, A. (2018). Spacing and organizing: Process approaches to the study of organizational space. *Academy of Management Proceedings*, *2018*(1), 18025. doi:10.5465/AMBPP.2018.18025abstract

Sundstrom, E., Bell, P. A., Busby, P. L., & Asmus, C. (1996). Environmental psychology 1989–1994. *Annual Review of Psychology*, *47*(1), 485–512. doi:10.1146/annurev.psych.47.1.485 PMID:8624141

Surman, E. (2002). Dialectics of dualism: The symbolic importance of the home/work divide. *Ephemera*, *2*(3), 209–223.

Taylor, F. W. (1911). *The Principles of Scientific Management*. W.W. Norton & Company.

Thacher & Reinheimer. (2015). https://www.stlawu.edu/news/student-faculty-sleep-research-published-presented

Tietze, S., & Musson, G. (2005). Recasting the home-work relationship: A case of mutual adjustment? *Organization Studies*, *26*(9), 1331–1352. doi:10.1177/0170840605054619

Tosini, G., Ferguson, I., & Tsubota, K. (2016). Effects of blue light on the circadian system and eye physiology. *Molecular Vision: Biology and Genetics in Vision Research*, *22*, 61–72. PMID:26900325

Trahan, T., Durant, S., Müllensiefen, D., & Williamson, V. (2018). The music that helps people sleep and the reasons they believe it works: A mixed methods analysis of online survey reports. *PLoS One*, *13*(11), e0206531. doi:10.1371/journal.pone.0206531 PMID:30427881

Urban Developer. (2020). Accessed November, 2020. https://theurbandeveloper.com/articles/commsec-abs-australian-houses-largest-world

Virick, M., DaSilva, N., & Arrington, K. (2010). Moderators of the curvilinear relation between extent of telecommuting and job and life satisfaction: The role of performance outcome orientation and worker type. *Human Relations*, *63*(1), 137–154. doi:10.1177/0018726709349198

Waber, Magnolfi, & Lindsay. (2014). Work spaces that move people. *Harvard Business Review*. Accessed 21 August 2020. https://hbr.org/2014/10/workspaces-that-move-people

Wapshott, R., & Mallett, O. (2012). The spatial implications of homeworking: A Lefebvrian approach to the rewards and challenges of home-based work. *Organization*, *19*(1), 63–79. doi:10.1177/1350508411405376

White, M. (2017). IBM Tells Its Remote Employees to Get Back to the Office. *ABC News*. Retrieved at https://www.nbcnews.com/business/business-news/ibm-tells-its-remote-employees-get-back-office-n763441

Yadav, M., Kim, J., Cabrera, D., & de Dear, R. (2017). Auditory distraction in open-plan office environments: The effect of multi-talker acoustics. *Applied Acoustics*, *126*, 68–80. doi:10.1016/j.apacoust.2017.05.011

Zaglauer, M., Drotleff, H., & Liebl, A. (2017). Background babble in open-plan offices: A natural masker of disruptive speech? *Applied Acoustics*, *118*, 1–7. doi:10.1016/j.apacoust.2016.11.004

Zalesny, M. D., & Farace, R. V. (1987). Traditional versus open offices: A comparison of sociotechnical, social relations, and symbolic meaning perspectives. *Academy of Management Journal*, *30*(2), 240–259.

Zhong, C. B., & House, J. (2012). Hawthorne revisited: Organizational implications of the physical work environment. *Research in Organizational Behavior*, *32*, 3–22. doi:10.1016/j.riob.2012.10.004

Ziffer, D. (2020). Coronavirus work from home might become work done overseas. *ABC News*. Retrieved from: https://www.abc.net.au/news/2020-08-11/covid-work-from-home-might-become-work-done-overseas/12542354

Zucker, R. (2019, December). How to stop thinking about work at 3am. *Harvard Business Review*, *20*. https://hbr.org/2019/12/how-to-stop-thinking-about-work-at-3am

Chapter 12
Regulatory Challenges Facing Remote Working in Australia

Kantha Dayaram
https://orcid.org/0000-0003-2388-2598
Curtin University, Australia

John Burgess
Torrens University, Australia

ABSTRACT

This chapter examines the industrial relations and workplace challenges associated with increasing remote work in Australia. First, the chapter reports on responses obtained from 11 in-depth interviews with human resource and industrial relations practitioners to assess the support and barriers for continuing and or increasing the uptake of remote work post COVID-19. It then examines the Australian industrial relations framework to determine its support of extending flexible work arrangements for a wider scope of workers.

INTRODUCTION

Remote work encompasses working from home or working away from a central workplace at a range of locations, such as on a train, at an airport, or a café, and involving different types of work (Berg et al, 2018). There have been long standing remote work arrangements, especially involving isolated work sites and remote communities, and in industries involving extensive travel e.g., trucking, shipping, flying, guided and adventure tourism, and defence industries (Felstead and Henseke, 2017). It can involve commuting long distances and staying onsite at remote mining, agriculture harvesting, fisheries, and construction sites. With the development of online work, the nature of workplace has changed to include the office, the home, or any location that is close to a customer (Hoath and Haslam McKenzie, 2013). The rise of digitally enhanced platform work has been supported by global platforms such as Clickworker and Upwork and allows work to take place anywhere and at any time (deStefano, 2016). There is also distinction by employment status (employee, self-employed, contractor), by duration (full-time,

DOI: 10.4018/978-1-7998-6754-8.ch012

part-time, occasional), by payment (the week, the hour, the service) and by employer (customer, agent, digital platform owner). There is a global trend towards remote working especially given the capacity developments in the internet and the emergence of global platforms delivering work from fast food to online translations.

Data suggests that across Europe and North America, and before the forced working from home arrangements associated with the COVID-19 pandemic, that remote working arrangements were expanding in response to technological change (Crosbie and Moore, 2004; Eurofound, 2017; Felstead and Henseke, 2018; Berg et al, 2018). These include information technology, software and internet improvements that support remote work, structural changes that have supported the growth in service and knowledge-based work, as well as preferences for flexible working arrangements to support work-life balance. However, there was also evidence of work intensification, long hours, intrusiveness, insecurity, and under payment (Crosbie and Moore, 2004; Felstead and Henseke, 2017; Berg et al, 2018). The growth in remote work was found to be uneven across sectors, with certain occupations and industries being tied to physical location such as manufacturing and transport (Eurofound, 2017).

There is an extensive literature on assessing the extent and trends in remote work; the drivers of remote work; and the benefits and costs of remote work (Eurofound, 2017; Felstead and Henseke, 2017; Berg et al, 2018). There has been less consideration given to the regulatory consequences and challenges associated with remote work, with recent attention being on the emergence of gig work and its implications for labour regulation (Stanford, 2017). The COVID-19 pandemic provided an unexpected impetus for remote work, and at the same time it brought out many of the regulatory challenges associated with remote work. There are suggestions that the changes to work, especially remote and home working, will become embedded not only as a consequence of the technology demonstrating that work can be effectively undertaken away from a central (co-located) workplace, but as a result of workers seeing advantages in working away from a central workplace (Hern, 2020). Home and remote work will no longer be a minority arrangement. This chapter examines the transitional and regulatory challenges that have arisen in Australia.

THE EXTENT OF REMOTE WORKING IN AUSTRALIA

Prior to COVID-19 it was estimated that, in Australia, around one third of the workforce was engaged in some form of working from home. This covered full-time and part-time arrangements, primary and second job arrangements, and working from home in addition to working in a central workplace. Between 2015 and 2019 the share of the workforce engaged in some form of remote working had doubled from around one quarter to one half of the workforce (ABS, 2020b). The official labour force estimates were supported by consultants' surveys that reported a preference for greater access to homeworking arrangements prior to 2020 (McCrindle Research, 2020). Survey evidence suggested a preference for homeworking arrangements to achieve flexibility in hours for working and improve work-life balance, with the preference being stronger for females compared to males (McCrindle Research, 2020). Following the spread of COVID-19 homeworking arrangements increased in response to public health and safety regulations that required social distancing, placed limits on the number of persons in confined spaces (including workplaces and public transport), placed restrictions on physical movements within and between cities, and requested employers to support working from home arrangements where possible (NSW Government, 2020). As a result, working from home arrangements became institutionalised across many occupations and industries (ACTU, 2020). Findings also suggest that as the risks of COVID-19 decline in Australia and the state economies open up, there is a preference for homeworking to continue and that many of those who were forced into homeworking arrangements (up to 80 percent) would like to continue with these arrangements after the restrictions on travel, social distancing, and attending the workplace are lifted (Karp, 2020).

ADVANTAGES AND CHALLENGES OF REMOTE WORKING

Crosbie and Moore (2004) and Eurofound (2017) highlight the contextual importance of working from home in terms of whether workers had negative or positive experiences through homework. The positive factors included greater flexibility in allocating time, an improved ability to manage work-life and work-family balance, increased personal time away from the office and reduced commuting time. Offsetting these findings was tension and contestation over space between home and work activities, isolation from colleagues and co-workers and the intrusion of work beyond standard working hours. Contextually, age, gender, family composition and occupation all have an impact on the working from home experience. For women with families, the care responsibilities and the tensions remain. In contrast, men who have lesser care responsibilities, tend to find greater personal space an advantage of homework (Bateman and Ross, 2020). Kelliher and Anderson (2010) identified improvements in job satisfaction and productivity from engaging in flexible work practices, including working from home. However, there was an offset through increased work intensification – working longer hours, being on call for long hours, or being expected to do more over a given number of hours.

In the Australian context, a survey by the Australian Council of Trade Unions (ACTU, 2020) of 10,000 employees found that the positive effects of working from home included a reduction in commuting time, greater flexibility in the hours and times of work, and improved work-life balance. Offsetting the positive effects were findings of increased hours and a greater spread of hours, greater surveillance, problems with software and internet connections, not being able to disconnect from work and under payment for hours worked.

THE AUSTRALIAN INDUSTRIAL RELATIONS SYSTEM

The Australian industrial relations system is complex and hybrid, involving different jurisdictions and regulatory frameworks. There is both a state industrial relations system, and a federal industrial relations system. The long-term trend has been away from the state system towards a unified national or federal system. The other major long-term trend has been away from centralised, often industry bargaining, towards decentralised, workplace bargaining (Bray et al, 2017). The history and development of the regulatory framework in Australia can be found in Bray et al (2017). Within the workforce the broad allocation of workers is around 20 percent in unregulated work (the self-employed, family workers and independent contractors); 10 percent who are outside of the main regulatory framework (this group represents public sector workers), and; the largest group, 70 percent, who are regulated by the *Fair Work Act 2009* (Baird, 2011). In this latter group there are those who are covered by collective agreements with employers, and those who are covered by awards that set out minimum conditions in certain industries and occupations who are not covered by a collective agreement (Productivity Commission, 2015).

There are a multitude of institutions that are responsible for different aspects of work and employment. While the Fair Work Condition (*Fair Work Act, 2009* (Cth)) covers the negotiated and minimum conditions of employment, the State-based industrial relations commissions deal with conditions that are relevant to state jurisdiction and there is a national Fair Work Ombudsman who is responsible for settling disputes (Fair Work Ombudsman, 2020a). There are other statutory rights that apply to work including anti-discrimination legislation; workplace health and safety regulation; worker's compensation legislation; and superannuation (pension) legislation. The responsibility for these conditions can apply at both the state and federal levels (Productivity Commission, 2015).

Within the Australian system there are ten minimum conditions or national employment standards (NES) that underpin all awards and collective agreements (Fair Work Ombudsman, 2020a). These include minimum weekly hours; the right to request flexible work arrangements; parental leave; annual leave; personal/carers leave; paid public holidays; and notice of termination and redundancy payments. There is also a national minimum wage rate that is subject to an independent annual review (Fair Work Commission, 2020).

Since the regulatory system was designed for ongoing full-time employee status, there are ambiguities and gaps in the system linked to temporary employment, known as casual workers in Australia (Campbell and Burgess, 2018). Employment is short term and irregular, and without continuity in employment, casual workers do not qualify for leave and redundancy conditions (Productivity Commission, 2015). In lieu of its exclusion from minimum employment conditions those on casual work contracts qualify for a wage premium or leave loading (payment in lieu of leave). Other workers such as contractors and the emerging gig workforce have ambiguous employment status, so their access to minimum wages and entitlements is also contestable (de Ruyter et al, 2019). Within the COVID-19 economy there were a group of workers who could not work at home by reason of their industry and occupation – such as health workers, transport workers, the police and emergency services. There were also a group of workers who as a result of being on a casual (temporary) employment contract or who were working short hours, had to continue employment despite the health risks in order to sustain living standards. Such workers in the aged care sector, security services, and food delivery, were not only at risk but also responsible for transmitting the virus since they could not afford to stop work when they had virus symptoms (Dayaram, Burgess, Fitzgerald, 2020b).

REGULATORY CHANGES INTRODUCED POST COVID-19

In response to COVID-19 and restrictions on economic activity the Federal government implemented several stimulus measures to sustain jobs and incomes. These include an allowance or subsidy to retain workers (Jobkeeper Program), an increase in welfare payments, and a range of assistance measures for business (Markey, 2020). Working from home arrangements were encouraged, especially given the restrictions on travel, social distancing, and prohibition on group gatherings. Not all workers could work from home as essential services had to be maintained and, in some industries, workers had to be physically present to perform their work tasks (such as in construction, transport, manufacturing).

The working from home arrangements and the Jobkeeper scheme resulted in regulatory changes to accommodate the shift away from a fixed and co-located workplace, with set operating hours. Many of these changes were enforced by State health and safety regulations that required employers, employees, and workplaces to conform to public safety regulations. The Fair Work Ombudsman (2020a) identified several regulatory issues that employers and employees should consider before entering into work from home arrangements. These included:

a. Examining whether existing awards, employment contracts or agreements included details linked to working from home.
b. Enforceable government directives regarding working from home or other locations.
c. Ensuring that workplace health and safety conditions are adhered to.
d. Recording the hours worked from home.

Employers under the JobKeeper scheme can use the Fair Work Act JobKeeper provisions to reduce an employee's hours or days of work, change an employee's usual duties, and change an employee's location of work (Fair Work Ombudsman, 2020b). In addition, there was the option to temporarily negotiate changes to awards or agreements in response to the pandemic. Potentially all workplace conditions previously negotiated could be re-negotiated with the approval of Fair Work Australia (Fair Work Ombudsman, 2020b). Public sector employees, especially those working in essential services, were subject to changes in their employment conditions to meet surges in the demand for some public services such as health and policing (Government of Victoria, 2020). There were also many instances where employees accepted pay cuts and used accrued leave to protect their jobs during the economic downturn generated by COVID-19 (Markey, 2020).

One emerging trend was tripartism in seeking solutions to the challenges of COVID-19 with the Federal government, trade unions, and employers cooperating towards developing workable solutions for keeping workers in jobs and varying conditions of employment towards that end (Markey, 2020).

MANAGING THE WORKFORCE UNDER CHALLENGING CONDITIONS

While there is literature on managing crisis (Roche, 2014), such as occasioned by a recession or a plant closure, COVID-19 posed unique challenges in that its spread was rapid and unpredictable, it impacted on all regions, occupations and industries, and it involved developing responses on an ad hoc and continuing basis. The spread of COVID-19 was spatially uneven and the individual states that make up the Australian Commonwealth were responsible for developing their policy responses including travel restrictions, quarantine regulations, local curfews, controls over trading hours, crowd and social distancing regulations, schooling, public transport, and quarantine controls for interstate and international visitors (WA.gov, 2021). As a consequence, the policy responses differed across the States according to the perceived health risks of the pandemic in each state. This was not a one-off incident, such as a natural disaster, and its duration was unknown. Even without crisis, the Australian industrial relations system is complex (Baird, 2020). Added to this were additional layers of complexity associated with changed working conditions supported by regulatory changes occasioned by the pandemic (Markey, 2020). To understand the initial strategies and processes applied by human resource (HR) and industrial relations (IR) professionals, the chapter reports on a survey of how HR/IR professionals managed the changes in the initial stages of the COVID-19 crisis.

METHODS

Semi-structured interviews were conducted during April and May 2020 when most Australian organizations had made the transition to work from home. In-depth interviews were conducted online using technology platforms such as Zoom™, WebEx™ and MS Teams™. Semi-structured interviews were considered appropriate (Bell et al, 2018; Creswell, 2014) as they allow for adaptability (follow-up and probe responses) and flexibility to capture individual meaning.

Since the study's objective was to gauge the challenges and support that were needed for transitioning to remote work, sampling was purposive to include professionals who were tasked with the implementation process such as operational managers, human resource managers (HR) and Industrial Relations (IR) professionals. The researchers used a snowball technique to contact a range of organizations that represented private, public, and not-for-profit sectors (refer to Table 1). The organizations ranged in size from small businesses with five employees to large multi-national organizations with more than 1,000 employees.

Table 1. Profile of Interviewees

Interviewee	Interviewee Profession	Sector	Organization Size Number of employees	Australian State
1	Human Resource Advisor	Private Small Business – HR Consultancy	5	WA
2	Industrial relations Advisor	Private Education	50-100	WA
3	HR Business Partner	Not for Profit	150-200	WA
4	Human Resource Advisor	Not for Profit	150-200	Victoria
5	Human Resource Advisor	Federal Public Sector	>500	WA
6	Industrial relations Advisor	Federal Public Sector	100	WA
7	Operations Manager	State Public Sector	>500	WA
8	Human Resource Executive Director	Private Sector Multi-National	>1000	WA/ Global
9	Human Resource Advisor	Not for Profit	50-100	WA
10	Human Resource Advisor	State Public Sector	>500	WA
11	Senior Human Resource Advisor	Private Sector Multi-National	>500	WA/Global

The interview schedule included open ended questions on issues relating to human resource management during the pandemic and decisions that were made with respect to all elements of staffing, redeployment, stand-downs, leave and pay arrangements, and transitioning to remote work. The questions on remote work included:

a. Prior to the COVID-19 pandemic what (types of/if any) remote working arrangements were in place?
b. How has the HR division responded to support remote working? Was it proactive or reactive?
c. What challenges did staff, HR and IR personnel experience with transitioning to remote work?
d. Did the employment framework that was in place such as enterprise agreements (EA) and awards enable or hinder remote working arrangements?
e. For the future, what organizational or regulatory changes are required to support remote work arrangements?

While qualitative studies are appropriate where participant experiences provide a rich source of data, the number of interviews are dependent on the point at which data saturation occurs. Guest et al. (2006) note that basic elements in non-probability sampling can occur by the sixth interview with saturation occurring by the 12th interview. For this part of the study on remote work regulations, the researchers found that by the eighth interview no new information or themes were emerging. Three further interviews from each sector (not for profit, public and private) were undertaken to ensure reliability that data saturation had occurred. In total, 11 online semi-structured interviews were conducted. All interviews were conducted in English and audio-recorded with participant consent noted. Ethical approval was granted by the researcher's university. The online interviews were supplemented by note taking and document analyses.

The data analysis involved transcribing the audio files into verbatim text, using a software package, Otter.ai™. This method ensured that the transcription was done without recourse to the researchers' meaning and interpretations of the experiences of the interviewees. In addition, on completion of the interviews, the researcher together with an independent research assistant verified the interview notes with the transcribed data. The transcribed data was subsequently coded into main and sub themes using Nvivo™ software. During the coding process, a large volume of textual interview transcripts was reduced to capture critical information relevant to the research focus. To further familiarise themselves with the data, the researchers undertook detailed content analysis to double check that the themes aligned with the Nvivo™ coded themes. The final step involved the comparison of codes, concepts and categories with the existing literature and the Australian employment regulatory framework.

FINDINGS

The interview findings emerged around five key areas relating to a) post-COVID-19 increase in working remotely; b) increased work intensification; c) need to regulate working hours; d) impact of trust and dilemmas around managing performance, and; e) amending regulatory frameworks to support remote work.

Increased Uptake in Remote Work Arrangements

Within this major theme, issues emerged that were linked to prior flexible work arrangements, access, remote work resource support, and compliance. Although most organizations noted having had some form of flexible work arrangements in place, these arrangements did not extend to all employees.

'It was common within our HR department. Like certainly I noticed that when I joined our organization, I thought my goodness, this is flexible, like I really love the flexibility that was offered to me. And I think that managers had a degree of flexibility, but I don't believe that was extended to all the teams.' (Interview 3)

In addition to the rapid large-scale shift to remote work, resourcing the transition was a challenge for some organizations, with employees having to access their personal servers, home facilities, and procuring a dedicated workspace. The infrastructure supporting remote work (office facilities, hardware, software, and connectivity) was uneven across employees.

'The issue was that not every employee had access to a laptop that they could log in remotely. Staff had to use their own laptops with remote access but the server couldn't handle everyone. (Interview 6). There is also health and safety that's a big issue for people who don't have enough space for an office. I don't have a study. I use my dining table which I did set up. I didn't have a proper chair.' (Interview 1)

The quick transition to remote work was viewed as a '*big issue*' with '*lots of changes to ensure compliance*'. For some organizations, shifting systems, and ensuring internet access and policy compliance became major challenges: '*Since staff had laptops, the transition was easy with resources, but actual remote working was new*.' (Interview 2)

Other organizations felt there was a lack of '*consistent guidance*', while trade union representatives held concerns for workers' safety. Despite the challenges, with the majority of employees, apart from those in essential services, there was a sense that in having made the transition to working away from a central workplace, there would be an increased uptake in remote work, post the pandemic.

'Remote work will have a higher uptake, because people have seen it happen. Organizations are going to see substantial savings on real estate. There will be access to a broader talent pool, rather than having a limited central workplace.' (Interview 8)

Others were optimistic that there would be improved management support for increasing remote work arrangements following the experience of meeting the challenges of the pandemic. *'Now managers can see that it works, and can do work 100% they will support it.'* (Interview 11)

Work Intensification

Work intensification refers to the additional hours that are worked, with a recent Microsoft survey (TechRepublic, 2020) indicating that Australian employees on average worked 1.9 additional hours per day because of working from home. In this study the participants noted both from their personal experiences and that of their colleagues that because of working from home, their hours of work had increased. In part this was due to not having set commute times and the hours of work became much more fluid and open ended. This reduced the boundaries and delineation between work and home time and resulted in increased working time. In addition, many workers reported increases in workloads: *'I don't know what the proportion is but my workload increased. I worked more.'* (Interview 1). Similar findings were reported from the ACTU (2020), survey of employees working from home, with 30 percent of the survey participants reporting an increase in workloads.

The respondents also raised concerns around expectations regarding continuing to work whilst being ill because they worked from home: 'I have a concern with remote work and expectation to work whilst sick.' (Interview 1). Work signalling was a concern for HR practitioners, where working remotely translated to working harder to be 'seen', while others suggested the need to shift mindsets from 'how work was done rather than what work was being done.' (Interview 8).

Regulating Work Hours

In other instances, organizations that did not have prior remote work arrangements and had prescribed work time periods such as 9am to 5pm, found that they had to make some fundamental changes: *'We had to have two shifts to accommodate and change start and finish times.'* (Interview 4). Some organizations noted breaching policies although their employees complied with the 7.5-hour shifts which did not strictly adhere to the prescribed work periods. They also noted the challenges associated with simultaneously undertaking caring responsibilities whilst working from home.

'Under the legislation that says you can only work between seven and six Monday to Friday, basically, you have to work under that. And I said to my boss, that's not feasible. Anyone with young children at home is not getting the hours done between seven and six. They're doing a lot of the hours at night. And he said, Yeah, I noticed that you guys are doing your hours at night and I said, will you rise a challenge for us? Do we lie on our timesheets and put all that hours in seven, six to comply with the award and the agreement? Or do I actually put on our timesheet and breach the agreement. And his advice was put your actual hours on it, and I'll deal with it later.' (Interview 7)

'In all honesty, the kids would come into the team meetings as well. So, I think, you know, that compassion element has really come into play. But what's been interesting is that with that flexibility of knowing our leaders know that the kids are home and there are a few distractions, the workers are then logging on later at night to come back to, to work still getting done.' (Interview 3)

Other respondents were cautious about setting parameters and saw the need to exercise flexibility for future remote work arrangements: *'They have common meeting times but also ensure greater structure e.g. no emails/meetings before 9am and after 3pm.'* (Interview 1)

Trust and Dilemmas Around Managing Performance

Issues around creating a culture of trust were raised in the context of working away from a central regulated workplace. This in turn brought the focus to managing performance under remote working arrangements, an issue that was unclear in some organizations.

'My previous place of employment was very averse to working from home because they were worried that people were just sitting at home watching TV. In my experience, working from home was the most productive day of my week. Because I wasn't getting a cup of sugar every five seconds then I could concentrate without being annoying.' (Interview 1)

However, others were concerned how remote work could 'jeopardise' their career progression should they continue with this pattern of work post-pandemic: 'I mean, if you do your work, and if you get things done, I don't see why it would stop your career progression.' (Interview 4)

Aligning with these concerns, some HR managers noted a level of uncertainty with regard to being able to adequately manage performance of remote workers, and the need for effective remote work performance management mechanisms to be in place.

'We need to redesign work to reduce presenteeism. What they [workers] do at work they still will do at home and still be productive at their located space. About under-performers that needs managing.' (Interview 7)

Amending Regulatory Frameworks to Support Remote Work

The fifth major theme related to future changes that were needed to accommodate remote work focused on regulatory frameworks. Some of the challenges included balancing work with home life which were '*a big shift in culture*' and to supporting '*parents*' with working remotely. Some respondents suggested greater collaboration between employers and trade unions to develop a framework that embraced flexibility but also gave some certainty around working hours: '*Maybe have a lobby group and we're collaborating with the union for creative ways to support workers with work hours and developing a platform for training needs.'* (Interview 9)

A further common concern for the future was the need to have mechanisms in place to support employee psychological well-being.

'Okay, let's start to look at how we do this differently moving forward, because it is going to feel a lot different to how we've been acting in the past, or what we've been doing in the past. And certainly, when we talk about uncertainty, we were certainly connecting with our stakeholders regularly. But I don't feel that we've been able to assist greatly other than an ear to listen and certainly, to answer questions, I don't feel that we've been able to meaningfully roll out any programmes or have put true support in play.' (Interview 3)

DISCUSSION

The participants' responses indicate a willingness to pursue post COVID-19 working from home or remote work arrangements, however regulatory support is needed for broader access, protection against work overload and protection from privacy misuse. Moreover, there were concerns over employer expectations of being on call outside of the 38-40 hours work week and uncertainty around performance management of remote workers. In this section we highlight the regulatory gaps in the context of the Australian industrial relations framework that need adjusting to support a continued wider uptake of remote work.

National Employment Standards Supporting Flexible Work Arrangements

The NES (Fair Work Ombudsman, 2020a) includes the "right to request" flexible employment arrangements that comprise: changes to the hours of work (start and finish times); changes to the patterns of work (shifts); and changes to the location of work (working from home). The post COVID-19 arrangements involved the location of work, but also potentially could include the other dimensions. Employees eligible to access the right to request include those in ongoing employment (at least 12 months) who have any of the following grounds for requesting flexible work arrangements: are a carer; have a disability; are aged over 55 years; are experiencing family or domestic violence. However, the standard only supports the right to request flexible working arrangements; the employer can reject such requests if there is a "reasonable" business argument.

The COVID-19 pandemic has highlighted two key issues in this regard: first, the current NES framework appears to be limited in its breadth of application and second, in its ability to challenge 'reasonable business grounds' with respect to having access to flexible work arrangements (Dayaram, Burgess, Fitzgerald, 2020b). Notwithstanding the eligibility criteria for flexible work where employees must have worked for a 12-month continuous period, this provision excludes the majority of workers who do not meet any of the above six criteria or casual workers who are not deemed to be in long term casual employment. In Australia casual employees account for around one quarter of the workforce (Campbell and Burgess, 2018).

Additionally, although employees have the right to request flexible work arrangements, employers have a right to refuse these requests on 'reasonable business grounds'. Although the employer needs to respond in writing within 21 days, reasonable grounds can include, but are not limited to (Fair Work Ombudsman, 2020a):

a. The requested work arrangement would be too costly to the employer.
b. There is no capacity to change the working arrangements of other employees to accommodate the request.
c. It would not be practical to change the working arrangements of other employees or employ new employees to accommodate the request.
d. The requested arrangement will result in a significant loss of productivity.
e. Have a significant negative impact on customer service.

The pandemic reversed the right to request case for flexible work arrangements in that awards and agreements were amended to support working from home arrangements as the norm. Within this norm the challenges for workplace regulation were around flexibility with start and finish times, with shift patterns and in general over the control of working hours.

The Right to Disconnect

One issue is the extent to which employees should be on call where they work away from a central workplace that has set working hours. Flexibility of hours and being on call over long hours are distinct issues but are easily conflated. Often seen as an employees' responsibility to enforce work-life boundaries, the right to disconnect legislation is an essential component of the State protecting workers from overwork and resultant psychological, physical, and emotional health issues (ILO, 2017).

Associated with working from home are the blurred lines between paid work hours, homework, and the rest of our lives. An agentic lens is often adopted for dividing the boundaries between work and non-working hours, however employees' protection from overwork and resultant physical and psychological health consequences extend beyond the individual culpability to that of the State (ILO, 2017). Notwithstanding the fluidity of work-life balance, recent findings from Microsoft's survey (TechRepublic, 2020) point to 30% of Australian workers experiencing some form of burnout. Reasons for burnout have been linked to psychological well-being and work intensification (Larson, Vroman & Makarius, 2020). There is currently no legislation in Australia for workers' right to disconnect, instead the protection relies on 'reasonable additional hours' provisions in enterprise agreements to protect employees (Jervis. 2017). The challenge for working from home for many employees is the ability to control working hours and of being on call to meet organizational demands (ACTU, 2020).

Monitoring Longer Hours and Work Intensification

Alongside the rapid shift to remote work, there has been an upsurge in long work hours being reported by those working from home (TechRepublic, 2020; ACTU, 2020). Reported work intensification was also associated with longer hours, with the ACTU (2020) survey reporting that 40 percent of participants were working longer hours. Outside of the regulated workplace the evidence suggests that productivity improvements are achieved through either working longer hours or through undertaking more work in allocated hours. In the Australian regulatory system working longer hours or working at unsociable times such as evenings and weekends attracts a premium or a penalty rate of pay. However, penalty rates were not always paid for long hours or working unsociable hours, with 90 percent of those surveyed by the ACTU (2020) reporting that they were not paid penalty rates when they worked long or unsociable hours. While surveillance and online supervision has been enhanced through software applications, it appears not to have been used to monitor malfeasance, but not to track those hours that qualified for penalty payments.

Employee Surveillance and Performance Management

As organizations struggle with remote management and with a lack of people interaction, issues around worker and workplace trust/mistrust emerge. While traditional organizational beliefs are associated with physical supervision and efficient performance, a lack of supervision is associated with employee inefficiency and reduced work performance (Larson, Vroman and Makarius. 2020). Boddy (2020) and Larson et al. (2020) note issues around mistrust that result in an increased use of employee surveillance and monitoring technologies, heightened levels of micro-management, and the prevalence of employees' psychological stress.

Since the onset of the COVID-19 pandemic, there has been a surge in the uptake of employee surveillance using technology-based solutions (Aitken-Fox et, al. 2020). In Australia the sales of software that monitor employee computer activity have surged since May 2020, with some suppliers reporting a 300 per cent increase (Wood, ABC 2020). Common features of surveillance technology include (Wood, ABC 2020):

- Recording when an employee clocks in and out.
- Recording the time spent on a website or on using certain software programs.

- Taking screenshots of what is being viewed at regular intervals.
- Tracking the person's location by installing a complementary app on their phone.
- The ability to log in and view their computer live.
- The ability to monitor emails and search for key words.

Different technologies have the ability to review aspects of an employees' workspace, from keystrokes to information stored on a computer that is outside the scope of work, as well as video and audio surveillance of the remote work location (IT Wire. 2020). The legality of these levels of monitoring varies depending on the employees' location and the classification of the "workplace" (IT Wire. 2020). The use of surveillance technology highlights concerns around breaches in employee privacy, particularly since the *Australian Privacy Act* (1988) (Cth) does not specifically cover workplace monitoring (OAIC, N.d.).

However, the *Workplace Surveillance Act (2005)* makes provisions for workplace monitoring so long as formal notice is given, or if a 'covert surveillance authority' has been obtained (Suemo, 2020, NSW Government, 2005). Monitoring software can be enabled on devices the workplace has provided, and employees must be informed of this (Suemo, 2020). An employer may monitor an employee's personal device as long as they have sound work related policies regarding the use of personal devices for work (Suemo, 2020).

Health and Safety

Within the context of the regulatory responses to COVID-19 there were restrictions on personal movement, school closures, social distancing, restrictions on gatherings and social events, curfews and border closures. This placed pressures on employees and their families to accommodate both working from home and the restrictions imposed to suppress the pandemic. As a consequence, throughout the community there was an increase in anxiety and in mental health problems, with survey estimates suggesting that those suffering from stress and anxiety had increased from three percent to 25 percent of the population (Mannix, 2020). The ACTU employee survey reported that around one half of those surveyed experienced stress and anxiety (ACTU, 2020). Australia's Productivity Commission (2020:300) inquiry on mental health reported that employers face a number of requirements under work health and safety laws to ensure both the physical and psychological health and safety of their employees. Recent amendments to the Western Australian Work Health and Safety (WHS) Bill (2019) will bring consistency across Australia's workplace health and safety legislation. A radical change under the Western Australian WHS Bill is that health is defined to include psychological health and safety (Parliament of Western Australia, 2020), and therefore extends the coverage of issues in the workplace that are subject to the legislation.

The Excluded Workforce

Employees engaged in essential services did not have the opportunity to work from home, so their potential health risks increased through increased public exposure, commuting under risky conditions, and this was especially the case in the health sector. For those exposed public sector workers there was an increased duty of care required to support the increased risks that were experienced by employees. For other workers on short-term, temporary, and part-time contracts in the aged care sector, food delivery and retail sectors, they were forced to work under conditions of exposure to financially survive (Dayaram et al, 2020b). The NES entitlements include a 25 percent leave loading (pay in lieu of leave) for causal employees, however it excludes paid sick leave. The pandemic highlighted the choices vulnerable employees (those on casual contracts) made when they chose to work over taking unpaid sick leave. Currently the Government of Victoria has announced that it will introduce a pilot program in 2021 of a leave scheme for casual workers to access, and thus reduce the pressure on them to work when they are ill (ABC, News, 2020b).

CONCLUSION

Australia has had relative international success in managing and controlling the spread of the COVID-19 virus. As of January 2021, there were very few reported active cases (less than 10 nationally) and many states have been virus free for several months. The path to control involved extensive tracing and testing, lockdowns, social distancing, the closure of state borders, controls over crowds and travel, curfews, and enforced quarantine. Part of the public health response agenda was to promote working from home, where possible, as a supportive and essential public health policy. The evidence suggests a large uptake in working from home, and with acknowledged acceptance by employers and employees to the working from home experience. The ACTU (2020, 11) survey suggested that of those working from home that "81 percent of workers said that they would like to have the option of performing all or most of their work from home if they were provided with enough support". If working from home is to become "normalised" then there are regulatory and employee support issues to address post COVID-19.

For organizations the speed and spread of COVID-19 meant that organizations had no prior experience or planning linked to an imposed and mass movement of employees away from a central and regulated workplace to working from home. The interviews reported in this Chapter indicated that there were a number of challenges over time management, employee health and well-being, surveillance, performance management, and management of work-life balance. Other issues that have been reported, for example by the ACTU (2020) survey, include poor infrastructure support (hardware, software, and connectivity) and inadequate preparation and training of the workforce and managers.

In terms of regulation the problem is that working from home was previously seen as a minority option for workers with issues around work-life balance and disability management that were addressed through working from home with the consent of the employer after going through a formal application and review process. However, as a result of COVID-19, working from home became a compulsory and enforced working arrangement for many employees. One challenge is to extend the access to working from home arrangements beyond the restrictive conditions that are currently present under the national employment standard (Dayaram et al, 2020a). Other regulatory challenges are linked to time management away from a central workplace – start and finish times, shift arrangements, overtime and unsociable working hours – and to work intensification. Regulating working time arrangements to conform to the national employment standard will be an ongoing challenge. There is also the regulatory gap associated with insecure and irregular workers who do not have the option for working at home because of their occupation and industry, and because of their precarious incomes. Many of these workers have faced the choice to continue working, putting themselves at risk of both infection and of spreading infection, or to stop earning an income (Dayaram et al, 2020b). The regulatory gaps in the Australian employment system associated with insecure employment arrangements exposed both the community and the workers who were forced to work, despite the risks, due to their insecure employment conditions.

REFERENCES

ABS. (2020a). *Household Impacts of COVID-19 Survey*. https://www.abs.gov.au/statistics/people/people-and-communities/household-impacts-COVID-19-survey/latest-release#data-download

ABS. (2020b). *Labour Force*, May https://www.abs.gov.au/ausstats

Aitken-Fox, E., Coffey, J., Dayaram, K., Fitzgerald, S., Gupta, C., McKenna, S. & Tian, A. (2020). COVID-19 has put trust front and centre in human resources management. *LSE Business Review*.

Australian Council of Trade Unions (ACTU). (2020). *Working from Home Report*. ACTU.

Baird, M. (2011). The state, work and family in Australia. *International Journal of Human Resource Management, 22*(18), 3742–3754. doi:10.1080/09585192.2011.622922

Bateman, N., & Ross, M. (2020). *Why has COVID-19 been especially harmful for working women? Brookings Gender Equality Series*. The Brookings Institution.

Bell, E., Bryman, A., & Harley, B. (2018). *Business Research Methods*. Oxford University Press.

Berg, J., Furrer, M., Harmon, E., Rani, U., & Six Silberman, M. (2018). *Digital labour platforms and the future of work Towards decent work in the online world*. International Labour Organization.

Boddy, N. (2020). More stress, less trust: the truth about remote work. *Australian Financial Review*. https://www.afr.com/work-and-careers/careers/more-stress-less-trust-the-truth-about-remote-work-20200714-p55bv0

Bray, M., Waring, P., Cooper, R., & Macneil, J. (2017). *Employment Relations: Theory and Practice*. McGraw Hill Education.

Campbell, I., & Burgess, J. (2018). Patchy progress? Two decades of research on precariousness and precarious work in Australia. *Labour & Industry, 28*(1), 48–67. doi:10.1080/10301763.2018.1427424

Creswell, J. W. (2014). *Research design: Qualitative, Quantitative, and Mixed Methods Approaches*. Sage publications.

Crosbie, T., & Moore, J. (2004). Work–life Balance and Working from Home. *Social Policy and Society, 3*(3), 223–233. doi:10.1017/S1474746404001733

Dayaram, K., Burgess, J., & Fitzgerald, S. (2020b). Workplace transmissions: a predictable result of the class divide in worker rights. *The Conversation*. https://theconversation.com/workplace-transmissions-a-predictable-result-of-the-class-divide-in-worker-rights-143896

Dayaram, K., Fitzgerald, S., & McKenna, S. (2020a). Working from home remains a select privilege: it's time to fix our national employment standards. *The Conversation*. https://theconversation.com/working-from-home-remains-a-select-privilege-its-time-to-fix-our-national-employment-standards-139472

De Stefano, V. (2016). The Rise of the Just-in-Time Workforce: On-Demand Work, Crowdwork and Labor Protection in the Gig-Economy. *Comparative Labor Law & Policy Journal, 37*, 471–504.

Deruyter, A., Browne, M., & Burgess, J. (2019). Gig Work and the Fouth Industrial Revolution: Conceptual and Regulatory Challenges. *Journal of International Affairs*, *72*(1), 37–50.

Dye, J. (2020, Sept. 20). NSW Workers get Pandemic Leave as state records first COVID-19 death in five weeks. *Sydney Morning Herald.*

Eurofound and the International Labour Office. (2017). *Working anytime, anywhere: The effects on the world of work.* Publications Office of the European Union, Luxembourg, and the International Labour Office.

Fair Work Commission. (2020). *National Minimum Wage Order 2020.* https://www.fwc.gov.au/awards-and-agreements/minimum-wages-conditions/national-minimum-wage-orders

Fair Work Ombudsman. (2020a). *National Employment Standards.* https://www.fwc.gov.au/awards-and-agreements/minimum-wages-conditions/national-employment-standards

Fair Work Ombudsman. (2020b). *Alternative Working Arrangements During Coronavirus.* https://coronavirus.fairwork.gov.au/coronavirus-and-australian-workplace-laws/alternative-work-arrangements-during-coronavirus

Felstead, A., & Henseke, G. (2017). Assessing the growth of remote working and its consequences for effort, well-being And work-life balance. *New Technology, Work and Employment*, *32*(3), 193–212. doi:10.1111/ntwe.12097

Gartner Global Survey. (2020). *Gartner HR Survey Reveals 88% of Organizations Have Encouraged or Required Employees to Work From Home Due to Coronavirus.* https://www.gartner.com/en/newsroom/press-releases/2020-03-19-gartner-hr-survey-reveals-88--of-organizations-have-

Gov, W. A. (2021). *COVID-19 coronavirus: Western Australia Government response.* https://www.wa.gov.au/organization/department-of-the-premier-and-cabinet/COVID-19-coronavirus-western-australian-government-response

Government, N. S. W. (2005). *Workplace Surveillance Act 2005 No 47.* https://www.legislation.nsw.gov.au/view/html/inforce/current/act-2005-047#sec.19

Government, N. S. W. (2020), *What You Can and Can't do Under the Rules.* https://www.nsw.gov.au/COVID-19/what-you-can-and-cant-do-under-rules

Government of Victoria. (2020). *Industrial Relations Framework for Managing the Coronavirus Pandemic.* https://www.vic.gov.au/victorian-public-sector-workforce-industrial-relations-framework-managing-coronavirus-pandemic

Guest, G., Bunce, A., & Johnson, L. (2006). How Many Interviews Are Enough?: An Experiment with Data Saturation and Variability. *Field Methods*, *18*(1), 59–82. doi:10.1177/1525822X05279903

Hern, A. (2020). Covid19 could cause permanent shift towards home working. *The Guardian.* https://coronavirus.fairwork.gov.au/coronavirus-and-australian-workplace-laws/alternative-working-arrangements-during-coronavirus/working-from-home

Hoath, A., & Haslam McKenzie, F. (2013). *The socio-economic impacts of long distance commuting on source communities*. Co-operative Research Centre for Remote Economic Participation and Curtin Graduate School of Business.

International Labour Organization. (2011). *New report highlights opportunities and challenges of expanding telework*. https://www.ilo.org/global/about-the-ilo/newsroom/news/WCMS_544108/lang--en/index.htm

Jervis, E. (2017). *Do Australians have a right to disconnect?* Legalvision. https://legalvision.com.au/do-australians-have-a-right-to-disconnect/

Karp, P. (2020), Unions Push for Better Protections as 80 Percent of Employees Say They Want to Keep Working from Home. *The Guardian*. https://www.theguardian.com/australia-news/2020/nov/04/unions-push-for-better-protections-as-80-of-employees-say-they-want-to-keep-working-from-home

Kelliher, C., & Anderson, D. (2010). Doing more with less? Flexible working practices and the intensification of work. *Human Relations*, *63*(1), 83–106. doi:10.1177/0018726709349199

Larson, B. Z., Vroman, S., & Makarius, E. R. (2020). A Guide to Managing Your (Newly) Remote Workers. *Harvard Business Review*. Retrieved 25 October 2020. https://hbr.org/2020/03/a-guide-to-managing-your-newly-remote-workers

Mannix, L. (2020), Here comes the COVID-19 mental health surge. *Sydney Morning Herald*. https://www.smh.com.au/national/here-comes-the-COVID-19-mental-health-surge-20200614-p552g6.html

Markey, R. (2020). The Impact of the COVID-19 Virus on Industrial Relations. *Journal of Australian Political Economy*, *85*, 147–154.

McCrindle Research. (2020). *Teleworking in Australia*. https://mccrindle.com.au/wp-content/uploads/2018/04/Teleworking-in-Australia_McCrindle-Research.pdf

News, A. B. C. (2020a). *Coronavirus have forced Australians to work from home, but what are the impacts on CBDs?* August 18. https://www.abc.net.au/news/2020-08-18/coronavirus-working-from-home-impact-on-australian-cities/12435248

News, A. B. C. (2020b). *Victoria to Pilot Sick and Carers Leave for Casual and Insecure Workers.* https://www.abc.net.au/news/2020-11-23/victorian-pilot-to-provide-sick-carers-leave-for-casual-workers/12910374

OAIC. (n.d.). *Workplace monitoring and surveillance.* Australian Government. Office of the Australian Information Commissioner, (Cth). Retrieved 3 November 2020. https://www.oaic.gov.au/privacy/your-privacy-rights/employment/workplace-surveillance/

Parliament of Western Australia. (2020). *Work Health and Safety Bill, 2020.* https://www.parliament.wa.gov.au/parliament/bills.nsf/BillProgressPopup?openForm&ParentUNID=8F320741B83643A8482584BF000CF89B

Productivity Commission. (2015). *Workplace Framework Inquiry Report*. Australian Government, Canberra. https://www.pc.gov.au/inquiries/completed/workplace-relations/report

Productivity Commission. (2020). *Mental Health, Report.* Australian Government, Canberra. https://www.pc.gov.au/inquiries/completed/mental-health#report

Roche, W. K. (2014). HRM in the Recession: Managing People in the Private and Public Sectors. In *Strategic HRM Research and Practice in Ireland* (pp. 35–58). Open Press.

Russell, S. (2019). Remote working could harm your mental health. *World Economic Forum and Conversation.* https://www.weforum.org/agenda/2019/10/remote-working-from-home-increase-stress-anxiety-mental-health/

Stanford, J. (2017). The resurgence of gig work: Historical and theoretical perspectives. *Economic and Labour Relations Review, 28*(3), 382–401.

Stewart, A. (2020). *COVID-19 and the Future of Australian Industrial Relations.* CCEP-Labour-2020-Andrew-Stewart-Industrial-Relations.pdf

Suemo, J. (2020). 12 most asked questions on Australian employee monitoring laws. *Work Time.* Retrieved 3 November 2020. https://www.worktime.com/12-most-asked-questions-on-australian-employee-monitoring-laws

TechRepublic. (2020). Transitioning Asia-Pacific to a New Normal of Work. *Microsoft.* Retrieved 25 October 2020. https://news.microsoft.com/wp-content/uploads/prod/sites/43/2020/07/Whitepaper-Transitioning-Asia-to-a-New-Normal-of-Work.pdf

Wire, I. T. (2020). Employee Monitoring Software Relevance in All Working Environments. *IT Wire.* Retrieved 2 November 2020. https://www.itwire.com/sponsored-announcements/employee-monitoring-software-relevance-in-all-working-environments.html

Wood, P. (2020). *Employee monitoring software surges as companies send staff home.* Retrieved 18 November 2020. https://www.abc.net.au/news/2020-05-22/working-from-home-employee-monitoring-software-boom-coronavirus/12258198

Section 3

Managing and Working Remotely in the Post-COVID Era

Chapter 13
The Role of Organizational Support in Effective Remote Work Implementation in the Post-COVID Era

Luisa Errichiello
https://orcid.org/0000-0003-0410-0300
National Research Council - Institute for Studies on the Mediterranean (CNR ISMed), Italy

Tommasina Pianese
https://orcid.org/0000-0001-6668-4255
National Research Council - Institute for Studies on the Mediterranean (CNR ISMed), Italy

ABSTRACT

The COVID-19 pandemic forced many organizations to abruptly introduce remote working, without an accurate analysis of organizational processes and employees' expectations about work flexibility. Thus, remote working has been implemented without a rational plan of interventions based on remote work-enabling technologies, managerial practices, and resources. This chapter aims at understanding the role of "supporting" structures and practices in driving the effective implementation of remote working in the post-COVID era. The authors rely on a case study of a multi-national IT company with a long experience with remote work arrangements, focusing on mobile work and virtual teams and looking at expectations and actions of remote workers in relation to organizational support. Findings revealed the importance to adopt a holistic approach to organizational support to remote working based on formal procedures, adequate evaluation systems, tools for self-management, blended training programs, supportive leadership style, along with a collaborative work environment and a remote culture.

DOI: 10.4018/978-1-7998-6754-8.ch013

INTRODUCTION

As of February 2021, over 230 countries in the world have been affected by the Coronavirus pandemic with 110 million cases and 2.5 million deaths. The need to limit the contagion from COVID-19 through social distancing measures has forced many organizations to introduce remote work programs (Toniolo-Barrios & Pitt, 2020). Employees have thus embraced digital work tools, including videoconferencing, to keep working remotely (Richter, 2020). Although the pandemic facilitated digital work, by unhinging old mindsets and changing social norms related to ways of working (Richter, 2020), two major aspects are noteworthy. First, the lockdown, which has affected countries to different degrees at different times, has implied that remote working mostly resulted in a "forced" home-based telework, with employees physically away from the organization and colleagues all of the time. Second, remote working is a disruptive organizational change, requiring a well-planned intervention on levers for organizational change, notably remote work-enabling technologies, managerial practices and organizational resources (By, 2005; Errichiello & Pianese, 2016, 2018, 2019).

The health emergency has compelled organizations to innovate existing work arrangements, and many governments simplified the bureaucrat procedure by making remote working applicable without trade union negotiations and/or individual agreements (Toniolo-Barrios & Pitt, 2020). This urgency has prevented management from an accurate analysis of implications of remote working on existing organizational processes, and of employees' expectations about this way of working. Although remote working emphasizes individual autonomy, job control and self-management, it is essential that employees perceive that their well-being is valued by their organizations (Bentley et al., 2016; Kossek et al., 2006; Smith et al., 2019). In this regard, during the pandemic many companies have underestimated the importance (or lacked the time) to define practices and tools for 'supporting' employees at a distance, and in turn employee interpretations of this as a tangible manifestation of how much the organization values their contributions and well-being.

Organizational support has been revealed to be even more relevant during the COVID-19 emergency. Many people have approached remote working for the first time and were disoriented by novel work routines and virtual relationships. They felt enormous pressure and had no time to experiment with new tools, and change social norms and work practices (Richter, 2020). At the same time, they felt more sensitive, and experienced a fear of becoming infected with the virus and an amplified sense of anxiety and sadness, nurtured by discordant versions of the pandemic offered by the media and doctors themselves (Richter, 2020; Vera et al., 2020).

The technological tools and systems enable work-from-home. However, organizations do not always understand that their role is not limited to providing employees with the technological infrastructure. During the COVID-19 pandemic, employees have also needed organizations to provide them with technology-related support, i.e. opportunities and resources for learning new technologies, coping with multi-tasking and addressing the constant connectivity and permanent availability to supervisors and colleagues (De et al., 2020; Errichiello & Demarco, 2020; Richter, 2020).

Many remote workers were unprepared and needed support by supervisors for managing the blurred line between career and personal life (Toniolo-Barrios & Pitt, 2020; Richter, 2020). After schools closed, working parents had to supervise children with online learning. They were continuously distracted in improvised work setups in living rooms, kitchen, bedrooms. Although literature has extensively investigated the overlap between private and professional spheres, the exceptional conditions of the pandemic have prevented people from being able to take the measures that would allow them to effectively manage boundaries between the two roles under normal conditions (Fonner & Stache, 2012; Kossek et al., 2006). At the same time, the suddenness of remote working adoption made it difficult for organizations to adequately prepare managers to lead in a virtual work environment (Newman & Ford, 2019).

Despite these issues, many companies that adopted remote working during the COVID-19 pandemic have announced their intention to embrace it beyond the emergency. Hence, in order to realize the potential benefits of remote working and maintain a healthier and productive workforce, in the post-COVID era organizations should engage in a serious effort to manage the transition towards remote work arrangements. The goal of this chapter is to understand the role of 'supporting' structures and practices in driving the effective implementation of remote working and managing employee well-being. We draw on a case study carried out in an Italian unit of a multinational IT company considered worldwide to offer a best practice example in implementing remote work arrangements. While the data was collected before the pandemic, this case study offers valuable insights for companies intending to adopt remote working in the post-COVID era. Indeed, these data were enriched with further information to understand how the company reacted to the COVID-19 pandemic. Specifically, the case study highlights the continuous efforts made by the company to support remote workers in different domains – such as task accomplishment, personal development, social and professional relations – by leveraging resources and practices at organizational, supervisor/employee and technology level (Bentley et al., 2016; Rhoades & Eisenberger, 2002).

The chapter contributes to literature on organizational support in several ways. First, it advances existing knowledge on the topic by addressing the interplay between the ostensive level of organizational support, as formally framed by the organization and HR management, and the remote workers' perceptions about support. Additionally, it offers an original conceptualization of organizational support as a multi-faced construct, encompassing interrelated dimensions, notably organizational, supervisor, employee and technology-related support. The case study also offers practical implications. In detail, it identifies the value for firms of a number of practices and tools for supporting remote workers. They could be viewed as leading principles in implementing remote working in the post-COVID era in order to support employee well-being. The empirical findings also reveal the importance of adopting a formal and structured approach in planning activities for each dimension of support. In remote working, these dimensions should be inherently connected to a well-designed digital work strategy that also addresses the risks and paradox of an excessive emphasis on e-work and on a remote culture imbued with technology.

SUPPORTING REMOTE WORK: A MULTI-LEVEL PERSPECTIVE

This section offers a critical review of organizational research on support for remote working. To this goal, the construct is broken down into its main dimensions, notably organizational, supervisor, employee, and technology-related support (e.g. Bentley et al., 2016; Kurtessis et al., 2017; Rhoades & Eisenberger, 2002). Although we acknowledge interdependencies among these dimensions, we first present them individually, and following this evidence the value of adopting a comprehensive and integrated perspective to understand the organizational support for remote workers' well-being.

Organizational Support

Organizational support refers to the extent to which organizations compensate employees for their efforts, help them in case of need, make their work interesting, and provide them with adequate working conditions (Rhoades & Eisenberger, 2002). Employees interpret the perceived organizational support as a tangible manifestation of how much the organization values their contributions and cares about their well-being. According to social exchange theory, employees desire to recompense the favorable treatment they receive by acting to help the organization reach its objectives (Aubè et al. 2007; Eisenberger et al., 2001).

Organizational support has a symbolic value that contributes to employees' sense of worth and reflects in benefits for the organization. Employees who perceive to be supported declare themselves proud to belong to the organization, reflected in improved performance and reduced intention to leave it (Aubè et al. 2007, Panaccio & Vandenberghe, 2009; Riggle et al., 2009). Beside obligation, the organizational support may also inspire a positive mood which can increase employee enthusiasm, excitement, and desire to help others (Eisenberger et al., 2001). Organizational support contributes to employee commitment, improves their job satisfaction (Riggle et al., 2009) and builds resource reservoirs able to neutralize workplace stressors (i.e., role ambiguity, role conflict, role overload) (Panaccio & Vandenberghe, 2009).

However, literature evidences that personal disposition and work design affect employee need to receive support (Riggle et al., 2009). According to Aubé et al. (2007), for example, employees with an internal locus of control and high work autonomy are less dependent on their employers and show a lower level of gratitude and obligations towards the organization. Organizational support produces positive outcomes as long as no self-serving actions are carried out, that is no promoting organizational self-interest at the expense of reward for individual merit (organizational politics, Randall et al., 1999).

A key role in organizational support is played by 'fairness' with regard to the existence of norms and procedures for resource distribution, both in term of rules and decisions, and in ensuring procedural justice, i.e. that people are treated equally (Rhoades & Eisenberger, 2002). A further way of providing organizational support concerns reward and job conditions, that includes performance and reward systems, career development plans and training development programs (Aubè et al. 2007; Rhoades & Eisenberger, 2002). Beyond organizational-level procedures, plans, systems and programs, organizational support can be provided through managing relationships (DeConinck, 2010; Wayne et al., 1997). In this respect, 'supervisor support', i.e. the extent to which supervisors value the employees' contribution (Rhoades & Eisenberger, 2002), and 'employee support', i.e. favorable treatment received from colleagues (Kurtessis et al., 2017), are two important forms of organizational support.

The importance for employers to show to care employees is not confined to traditional office work. Rather it has emerged to be even more important in the context of remote working where we find the emergence of distinct managerial challenges and individual beliefs, concerns and behaviors. Research shows that organizational support improves remote workers' job satisfaction and reduces their psychological strain (Bentley et al., 2016). The belief concerning the extent to which the organization values individual contributions and cares about well-being serves to reduce remote workers' fear of being abandoned, to be professionally isolated, and to increase their identification with the organization (Baker et al., 2006; Wiesenfeld et al., 2001). Specifically, remote workers particularly appreciate the existence of organizational norms and procedures that ensure procedural justice, that is employees are treated with dignity and respect when working at a distance (Bartel et al., 2012).

Supervisor Support

As supervisors are seen as organizational agents, who act on the behalf of the organization (Kurtessis et al., 2017), employees view supervisors favorable orientation toward them as indicative of organizational support (Rhoades & Eisenberger, 2002). Supervisor support is a form of beneficial treatment strongly appreciated by employees (Rhoades & Eisenberger, 2002; Rhoades et al. 2001). It reflects positive perceptions about how much the supervisor cares about employee opinions and well-being and consider their values and goals. In line with the Leader-Member Exchange theory (LMX), supervisor support assumes mutual trust and respect, with the leader providing support and resources, and the subordinate reciprocating through commensurate work effort. This implies the beliefs for employees that they could count on leaders when they need to talk about job-related problems (Kurtessis et al. 2017; Wayne et al. 1997).

Favorable treatment from supervisors is important to show to remote workers that organizations care for them even when they work at a distance (Bentley et al., 2016, Collins et al., 2013; Munir et al., 2016; Wiesenfeld et al., 2001). As in traditional contexts, a supportive leadership style towards remote workers plays a key role (Kurtessis et al. 2017; Lautsch et al., 2009). The scope is even richer because it is associated also with supporting remote workers in their private sphere to manage the overlap between private and family roles (i.e., boundary management strategies, Kossek et al., 2006; Lautsch et al., 2009). However, remote workers show different expectations about flexibility and desired level of work-life balance. This means that supervisors should consider individual needs to ensure they achieve the desired equilibrium between work and private dimensions (Collins et al., 2013). With remote work practices, supervisors have to adopt a transformation leadership style and behave as a coach, assisting remote workers in developing their full potential to favor collaboration and helping behaviors (Dambrin, 2004; Han, 2006; Kurtessis et al. 2017). This has to be balanced with direction-giving language aimed at providing subordinates with information about objectives and activities through formal communication (Al-Ani et al., 2011; Malhotra et al., 2007).

Employee Support

Organizational members are seen as agents of the organization too. Employees interpret a favorable treatment by colleagues as a signal of care from the organization itself, even though this may have lesser significance than supervisor support (Kurtessis et al., 2017). Value congruence and fulfillment of reciprocal obligations are usually seen as the primary factors underlying positive interpretations of treatment from colleagues (Wiesenfeld et al., 2001). The distance from the organization makes even more important this form of social support, referring to the degree to which remote workers perceive that they have positive social relationships with others in the virtual workplace (Belanger et al. 2013; Bentley et al. 2016; Wiesenfeld et al., 2001). The more they feel socially integrated with other members, the more they perceive to be central, valued and respected within the organization. This results in greater effort toward the pursuit of organizational goals (Wiesenfeld et al., 2001).

However, empirical studies evidence that remote workers' intensity influences expected support from colleagues. Full-time remote workers attach more importance to be supported by other remote workers with whom they have pre-existing relationships (Collins et al., 2016), while low intensity remote workers highly value support by office-based colleagues (Sewell & Taskin, 2015). At the same time, the level of perceived and/or desired support may be variable even within the same group because of individual personalities and attitudes, e.g., there may be remote workers that suffer from the lack of contact with colleagues, while others appreciate it (Wiesenfeld et al., 2001).

Technology-related Support

Information and communication technologies (ICTs) have become a ubiquitous part of today's work world (Day et al., 2012). This is especially true in remote working arrangements, where technological tools and systems are the main enabler for 'everywhere work' given their ability to gather, store, and/or send information to central office and distant colleagues (e.g. Belanger at al., 2013; Bentley et al. 2016). This increases the importance of providing employees with supportive organizational ICT practices (Day et al., 2010).

Technological-related support encompasses both the provision of tools (e.g., hardware, software, laptops, high-speed internet access, cell phones), and training about working in blended workspaces with both physical and virtual interactions (i.e., competencies about how to use the tools) (Baker et al., 2006; Bentley et al., 2016; Drouin & Bourgault, 2013). Baker et al. (2006) propose a wider distinction between "technology-related support" directly related to the use of technology, i.e. IT support in terms of timely assistance for IT related problems and appropriateness of the technology; and 'somewhat technology-related support' including training about IT usage but also financial support for buying technology.

In remote work arrangements, ICT tools and systems have both work-related purposes, i.e. support individual and collective work, and relational-related purposes, i.e. support socio-emotional processes with remote colleagues (Al Ani et al., 2011; Baker et al., 2006; Limburg & Jackson, 2007). As for work-related purposes, Information Systems, notably Workflow Management Systems, could support different control mechanisms, like self-control and peer control, independent of the location of employees and managers (Limburg & Jackson, 2007). Likewise, Management Control Systems (MCS) could play both a decision-facilitating role and a decision-supporting role for virtual team members (Bisbe & Sivabalan, 2017). From a relational perspective, correctly designed ICT tools and systems enable effective interactions among remote employees essential for both personal and professional relationships (Kimble, 2011). They even support cognitive trust-building and trust-maintaining among virtual team members who have no face-to-face interactions (Kimble, 2011; Kirkman et al., 2004).

METHODS

Research Context

To explore organizational support as a lever for the effective implementation of remote working in the post-COVID era, a field study was conducted in High Tech (a pseudonym), an Italian unit of a multinational IT company, active in the fields of information technology and consultancy. The case company was chosen as it provides an example of a successful long-term implementation of remote work arrangements.

The focus of analysis was on the role of support for two remote work arrangements, i.e. mobile work and virtual teams. To this goal, the units of analysis were: 1) the sales activities carried out towards small and medium enterprises in Southern Italy by a sales manager, with a mobile work contract; 2) a project manager leading virtual teams whose members collaborate remotely to develop projects. An intrinsic mobility characterized the activities of the sales managers. A significant part of the work was carried out at client premises. Sales range encompassed 'off shelf' solutions (i.e., from a catalogue), 'one of kind' solutions (i.e., customized), and/or 'as a service' solutions (e.g., e-commerce platform). The sales manager was used to going once a week to the office organized with open spaces and shared desks, for example, to prepare offers and/or report visits. He interacted mainly by phone calls or email with colleagues located outside Italy assigned to support system (e.g., sales transaction). Personal ICT equipment included a laptop and a smartphone with voice and data connection services.

The project manager was in charge of two types of customer-oriented projects: a) 'time and material projects', i.e., including support and maintenance services; b) 'task project', i.e. aimed at the development of ad hoc solutions. The project manager coordinated a group of junior consultants selected based on their competences and skills who collaborated remotely on specific projects (i.e., virtual teams). Although virtual team members did not usually physically interact, they had the opportunity to interact with colleagues at their own office. As for personal ICT equipment, the project manager was endowed with a smartphone and a laptop with wi-fi and/or key connection.

Data Collection and Analysis

A variety of data sources were used to support the exploration of the multiple facets of the supportive role of organizations in driving the effective implementation of remote working (Baxter & Jack, 2008). In detail, the case study combined interviews, archival data and non-participant observations to understand the role played by organizational, supervisor, employee and technology-related support (Eisenhardt, 1989; Yin, 2003).

Semi-structured interviews were the primary source of data. A first exploratory interview was conducted with the head office manager at the office in Napoli (Italy), who provided information about the company's strategies and remote working programs. Considering the objectives of the study, he invited a group of employees to join the research. In-depth interviews were then conducted with a sales manager and a project manager. Looking at the features of their activities, two protocol guides were developed for interviewing them. Each protocol was articulated to understand the expectations and actions of employees involved in remote work in relation to organizational, supervisor, employee and technology-related support. Interviews were carried out face-to-face and lasted 420 minutes overall. Both researchers interviewed employees, taking accurate notes immediately afterwards.

Data from interviews were triangulated with field visits made by authors and aimed at observing employee behaviors (e.g., interactions in open spaces), environmental conditions (e.g., space layout), ICT tools and technologies (e.g., internal messaging system). Authors collected documents from the company website, press reviews, reports, etc. Document materials collected at the time of the interviews was integrated with recent information in the press, including interviews released by senior (C-level) executives, in order to understand how the company reacted to the COVID-19 pandemic through nurturing practices and tools aimed at providing organizational support.

Collected data were analyzed according to the principles of the thematic analysis, following a top-down approach. This enabled the conversion of raw, unstructured and disorderly data into the categories of organizational, supervisor, employee and technology-related support as identified in the literature. An interim report was drawn up and submitted to the participants who, during a following 150 minutes long-lasting meeting, suggested revisions and integrations.

FINDINGS

Our empirical findings identified seven key emergent themes relating to effective support for remote workers: (1) a rooted 'remote culture'; (2) a performance management system centered on remote workers; (3) 'blended' training development programs; (4) structured methodologies for remote task accomplishment; (5) supportive remote leadership styles; (6) feedback and collaboration with remote colleagues, and; (7) a smart organization: ubiquitous technology and connectivity.

A Rooted 'Remote Culture'

Organizational culture is shaped by values and beliefs shared by employees and reinforced through organizational routines (Brown, 1995; Shein, 1990). It is a dimension of organizational-level support, since corporate values and beliefs reflect the extent to which an organization cares about employees, provides them with a stimulating work environment and adequate work conditions (Rhoades & Eisenberger, 2002). In this regard, High Tech's organizational culture is important for its remote workforce since remote work arrangements are embedded in a vision of 'global resources in a global company', hinged on corporate values of flexibility, result-oriented culture and connectivity.

This 'remote culture' has been reinforced over time through a progressive pilot-based process of adoption of remote working starting in 1980. At the end of 2006, 75 percent of the workforce worldwide were engaged in a remote work arrangement. This has resulted in the set-up of a methodology used by the consultancy division to support clients with the introduction of remote working, to whom it also provides the enabling technological solutions.

Although office-less efficiency was the initial driver for remote working adoption, the company has always considered flexibility and a result-oriented culture as effectiveness-oriented options to improve employee productivity and work-life balance, and to attract, retain and motivate people worldwide.

A Performance Management System Centered on Remote Workers

High Tech has gradually recognized the importance of involving employees in the design of a result-based performance management system to grasp the expectations and needs of remote workers. Interviews released by C-level executives during the COVID-19 pandemic confirmed the role of an employee-centric performance management system for supporting employees at home and to avoid physical distance negatively affecting their performance and commitment.

In 2015, the performance management system Checkpoint – also in use during the pandemic – replaced the previous Personal Business Commitments (PBC) system. PBC was based on one mid-year check-in with the manager and a final performance assessment, but this was considered as not being reliable for personal growth. The negative effect on employee productivity and morale led to the decision to introduce a new performance management system designed with remote workers around their needs. A crowdsourcing strategy was adopted: 380,000 workers around the globe were invited to take part in the design of this performance management system. Their suggestions put into the foreground the importance for remote employees to receive regular feedback from their managers. This became the leading principle in the design of Checkpoint, which was designed around short-term goals and frequent feedback from managers on employee performance. Regular feedback enables employees to adjust job performance during the year and to update skills to achieve the assigned goals. Moreover, rather than on a single assessment score by which 'employees become obsessed' (Chief Human Resource Officer, press release, 2016), through the new system employees started to be evaluated based on multiple qualitative and quantitative criteria.

'Blended' Training Development Programs

Training development programs are viewed by employees as a form of caring by the organization (Aubé et al., 2007; Johlke et al., 2001; Tansky & Cohen, 2001). High Tech has always attached importance to sustaining employee personal and professional growth. Because of the geographical dispersion, the company relies on a 'blended' approach, where online training is combined with traditional classrooms that can be attended individually and/or collectively.

Training courses centered on job-related competences are available to all organization members, i.e. employees, managers, and business partners. The company also organizes courses on its technological solutions accessible to employees and clients who may wish to develop understanding of how to use these tools through online courses, mentoring, boot camps and classrooms.

Ad hoc programs are available for managers, newly hired employees, and salespeople. As for managers, advanced learning courses are oriented at providing them with abilities for managing remote employees (e.g., to motivate distant people) and cross-cultural virtual teams (e.g., stimulate a creative environment). A talent management system is available for newly hired employees. A multi-stage process of 'onboarding' is used to introduce corporate values, as well as enable workers to gain job-related knowledge and skills for remote working (Bauer and Erdogan, 1996; Bauer, 2010). After one year of 'onboarding', individual training continues through personalized programs, including computer-based courses, along with a web-based skills assessment tool supporting the achievement of professional goals. As for sales activities, an ad hoc portal provides a portfolio of learning modules on, e.g. business solutions, sales methods and skills.

Structured Methodologies for Remote Task Accomplishment

In High Tech, structured methodologies are designed for supporting employees' self-management and mutual coordination for remote task accomplishment. Interviewees provided insights about features of these methodologies, evidencing how much they are appreciated by employees, who perceive standard norms and procedures as a demonstration of fairness and care from the company (Rhoades & Eisenberg, 2002).

Beyond the annual sales targets, each sales professional periodically discusses with the manager and sales team members: a *business review*, i.e. actions done in the last three months; a *forecast*, i.e. actions for the following months; a *recovery plan*, i.e. actions to implement for recovering gaps between expected and achieved goals. Appropriate systems and tools support remotely sales activities, e.g. for planning customer visits, tracking orders, monitoring sales revenues. Beyond basic technological tools (e.g. Outlook Calendar), a Customer Relationship Management (CRM) system is used worldwide by sales professionals to support the accomplishment of remote activities. This CRM, even if designed to allow managers to monitor the salesforce, is perceived by salespeople as an effective tool for self-managing, as well as for collectively sharing information about clients and business opportunities.

A structured methodology is available also for project managers, who coordinate resources dispersed worldwide. The Project Management system supports in the identification of phases, activities, standard procedures and outcomes for each project. It facilitates decision-making and ensures that managers have remote access to project data, along with materials and templates from previous projects stored in a central repository. The availability of a structured methodology is valuable also for virtual team members. The Project Management system, indeed, favors team members' autonomy and enhances their sense of responsibility. Moreover, as the system allows a clear understanding of team members' expertise and skills as well as a clear distribution of roles and tasks, it contributes to avoiding misunderstandings or task misallocation.

Supportive Remote Leadership Style

Manager leadership styles play a more crucial role than in office-based work arrangements, significantly shaping remote workers' perceptions about organizational support. In High Tech, coaching activities are a key pillar of the relationship between managers and employees. Coaching behaviors aim at helping remote employees to deal with the greater work autonomy while ensuring resources to remotely handle their tasks. In this respect, Checkpoint empowers managers and enhances their capacity to sustain remote employees. This also contributes to fostering trusting relationships, thus reducing the need for electronic control-seeking behaviors and monitoring systems that are often identified as detrimental to employee motivation and commitment.

Given the need to interact with a dispersed workforce, the company supports the development of digital skills among leaders. Simulations about e.g. 'leading a brainstorming activity in virtual spaces' are often used to introduce leaders to effective actions in virtual contexts. Investments are also made to sustain effective leader virtual communication. As claimed by the project manager, these communication abilities, along with those for managing cross-cultural differences, are crucial in virtual teams, often composed of individuals with different backgrounds. In relation to his managerial role, the project manager supports team members through periodic virtual meetings, and frequent interactions exploiting different communication tools. The salesperson confirmed the importance of virtual meetings organized by the manager to discuss business reviews with colleagues. Remote managerial support is also received through daily phone calls during which the salesperson informs the supervisor about activities and talks about job-related problems.

Notwithstanding the value of a supportive remote leadership, interviews evidenced the role of onsite support. The project manager explained that face-to-face meetings with the clients and/or other virtual team members are important in the early stage of a new project to define activities, roles, deadlines, and outcomes. The salesperson reported that they appreciate visits at customer sites with his supervisor, believed to be important to support less experienced salespeople in developing commercial abilities (e.g. negotiation), but also to help senior representatives to maximize the success of sales actions.

Feedback and Collaboration With Remote Colleagues

High Tech nurtures the culture of constructive feedback among employees, seen as key agents for the company's success. Employees are required to provide feedback on colleague performance, that are seriously considered by managers for their annual assessment. From the employee perspective, evaluation by peers is not perceived as an intrusive peer control, but as a mechanism enabling self-awareness about his/her own strengths and weaknesses. A culture based on 'up, down, and across' feedback is also sustained through an internal application, where employees can give and/or ask for feedback on colleagues (e.g. employees they manage) to understand their performance (e.g. contribution to a project).

Interviews revealed other horizontal mechanisms favoring the perceptions of peer support. The salesperson underlined the importance of assistance from office-based technicians during client visits, as well as of goal sharing with salespeople operating in the same area. In this respect, it emerged that interactions by phone are functional to discuss activities and share knowledge on clients. Next to formal salesforce meetings, virtual meetings are regularly organized by the SME division on 'repeatable solutions' i.e. solutions already realized for larger clients in order to evaluate their replicability for smaller firms.

A Smart Organization: Ubiquitous Technology and Connectivity

The leading firm position in advanced systems, tools and applications has contributed to shape a 'smart' organizational culture, with technology and connectivity as ubiquitous elements. Technological-related support – i.e. portfolio of hardware and software solutions – is provided to support work-related activities and personal and professional relationships. Over 90 percent of the workforce have a laptop computer and can connect from any location to the internal system, email and instant messaging. Both interviewees were satisfied with the ICT equipment, that allows them to access the necessary resources to accomplish remotely daily work and to interact inside and outside the office. Beyond basic mobile technologies (i.e. smartphones, tablets and laptops), they claimed to appreciate the proprietary system that allows access to basic (e.g. e-mail, calendar, contacts and IM) and advanced functions (e.g. integrated collaboration tools). Employees can also access the company intranet to update business information, and materials selected based on job position and interests.

Technology is pervasive and transversal to all dimensions of support. Notably, e-learning activities are enabled by an integrated technology platform, including the company intranet, web-based applications, multi-media content, and collaborative tools. Also, training goes hand in hand with a state-of-art technological infrastructure, including an online coaching simulator, live virtual classrooms, interactive presentations and application sharing. Many of the mentioned tools are also used to support ordinary business, such as those designed for project management where virtual team members can rely on teaming solutions to share information and collaborate in virtual environments. Performance measurement is also supported by technology. Indeed, a web-based personal skills assessment tool helps employees in the achievement of performance objectives and to plan future career goals, while Checkpoints plays a key role in nurturing a feedback-based culture.

A portfolio of technology solutions supports social networking, both internally and across organizational boundaries. The company developed a social platform, accessible through an online application offering several functionalities, notably: individual profiling, blogs, social bookmarking, specialized communities, social forums and wiki-connections. Interviews confirmed the value attached to social networking tools. To the salesperson, in particular, 'communities' are useful to connect to professionals worldwide. For example, his membership to the community of the SME salespeople allows him to know about commercial approaches used by other salespeople. Also, the project manager underlined the effectiveness of blogs, forum and wiki functions as spaces for virtual asynchronous collaboration and knowledge exchange next to traditional tools for synchronous interaction, like phone calls and conference-calls.

Table 1. Summary of key findings of the case study

Dimensions of support	Key Findings
A rooted remote culture	- Corporate values imbued with flexibility, a result-oriented culture and connectivity. - Pilot-based approach for progressive remote work adoption. - Remote working as: a) a strategic lever for maintaining a competitive position; b) HR practices for motivating and improving employees' work-life balance.
A performance management system centered on remote workers	- Adoption of an IT participatory design approach to develop a performance management system centered on remote workers' needs. - The new performance management system is based on: a) regular feedback from managers; b) multiple criteria for evaluating performance of remote workers.
Blended training development programs	- Investment in training development programs centered on job-related and technology-related competences and skills for remote working. - Training programs available online and/or in traditional classrooms, attended individually or collectively, in many cases also on demand. - Ad hoc courses for e.g. managers, newly hired employees, salespeople.
Structured methodologies for remote task accomplishment	- Availability of methodologies supporting salespeople and project manager activities. - A Project Management system supports project managers in e.g., resource allocation, task assignment, remote access to a project repository. - The methodology for salespeople includes: annual sales targets, procedures and work schemes, along with supporting technological tools (e.g. Outlook, CRM).
Supportive remote leadership styles	- Importance attached to trusting relationships between managers and employees. - Investment in the development of managers' abilities e.g. virtual communication and management of cross-cultural virtual teams. - For the project manager, the supportive remote leadership includes frequent virtual meetings with team members. - For the salesperson, the supportive remote leadership encompasses virtual meetings with colleagues, and phone calls with the manager. - Acknowledgement of the importance of face-to-face managerial support (e.g. joint visits at client sites).
Feedback and collaboration with remote colleagues	- Nurturing a culture of constructive feedbacks by peers. - Sharing goals and informal discussion with colleagues. - Remote assistance from office-based colleagues. - 'Informal knowledge' exchange (e.g. about business opportunities), and 'formal knowledge' exchange about best practices (e.g. repeatable solutions).
A smart organization: ubiquitous technology and connectivity	- Technology as transversal to all forms of support. - Technology provision to all employees with ICT basic equipment (e.g. smartphone, tablets), along with a proprietary system with basic functions (e.g. calendar) and advanced (e.g. collaboration) tools. - Technological systems supporting training programs (e.g. e-learning in virtual classrooms), performance management (e.g. Checkpoint), task accomplishment (e.g. Project Management) and social interaction and networking (e.g. internal social platform).

Source: Authors' elaboration

DISCUSSION

In High Tech, organizational support results from a formal and structured approach already in use before the pandemic. This approach has resulted in a well-established remote culture, formal procedures, an employee-centered performance management system, blended training programs, supportive leadership styles and collaborative work environments. Within this architecture, ICT plays a transversal role, by enhancing all forms of support (see Table 1 for a synthesis of key empirical results). This vision of organizational support has enabled the organization to successfully face the transition to full-time home-based telework as COVID-19 spread across the globe, avoiding interruptions to organizational routines while ensuring employee well-being.

Data collected before and during the COVID-19 pandemic confirmed that organizational support is appreciated by High Tech's remote workers, whose perceptions fit with formal support as framed by top managers. This is consistent with previous studies that found that favorable job conditions (i.e. remote working) contribute to organizational support when employees consider them as the result of company voluntary decisions, rather than a reaction to external contingencies and threats (Rhoades & Eisenberg, 2002). This explains why the experience of remote working among High Tech's workforce is dissimilar to that of many employees, who may be disappointed by the support received by their organizations and managers. Recent studies performed since the onset of the pandemic have found that many employees are frightened by the economic uncertainty (Gòmez et al., 2020), and that remote working has further worsened their productivity and motivation due to increased stress (Toniolo-Barrios & Pitt, in press). In these circumstances, employees suddenly constrained to work at home have not perceived support from their employers (Menman & Ford, 2019; Richter, 2020), whose actions have been interpreted as part of a recovery plan, rather than the result of a structured approach to remote working.

However, previous research showed that not all employees attach the same importance to organizational support. Personal factors and work design variables influence the employee's need to receive support (Riggle et al., 2009). Some authors investigated the relationship between work autonomy and employees' expectations for organizational support (Aubè et al., 2007; Kurtessis et al. 2017; Rhoades & Eisenberger, 2002). They found that as work autonomy increases, employees are less dependent on their companies and supervisors. Our empirical findings are consistent with previous research, for example, salesperson expectations of managerial support are higher compared to the project manager, whose job activities rely on highly autonomous decision-making.

Work autonomy is a debated and controversial issue. The optimistic views about the capacity of working remotely to enhance worker autonomy has been gradually replaced with a more realistic perspective that pointed toward the threats produced by the 'constant connectivity' (e.g. Mazmanian et al., 2013; Wajcman & Rose, 2011). These threats have become more serious since the COVID-19 pandemic has constrained millions of people to work at home, reinforcing their need to maintain virtual connections with colleagues to re-affirm their work identity and sense of belonging to their organization (Demarco and Errichiello, 2021). Our findings did not explicitly suggest complaint about the continuous availability via ICTs. We could thus infer that High Tech is effective in taking care to address work-life balance issues, and that managers and colleagues do not exert pressure in terms of work expectations and availability from remote workers, positively contributing to their digital well-being (Vanden Abeele, 2020).

The comparison of jobs also offers insight into an under-investigated relationship existing between a social dimension of work design (i.e. task interdependences) and the nature (i.e. formal/informal) of expected organizational support for task accomplishment. We found that the salesperson, whose activities are less contingent on others' work, attaches more importance to informal mechanisms of self-control (e.g. an excel file reporting information about clients) and mutual coordination (e.g. daily phone calls). On the contrary, to the project manager whose tasks accomplishment is highly dependent on the activities of virtual team members, the availability of formal methodologies and tools for project management is crucial for teamwork coordination. Coherently, he claimed to usually rely on formal meeting and communication tools (e.g. web conferences), and rarely on informal calls and instant messaging. This evidence supports the hypothesis that there is a stronger association between low task interdependencies and expectations of informal organizational support; on the contrary, high task interdependencies are more associated to expectations of formal organizational support.

The case study showed that a rooted remote culture is a key pillar of organizational support. Such a 'smart' culture has been favored by an effective digital work strategy (Dittes et al., 2019; Richter et al., 2018), oriented to let employees fully take advantage of the potential of technological solutions for working anywhere and anytime. Checkpoint is a case in point, since the performance management system is centered on the needs of remote workers, who were actively involved in its early design (Bødker et al., 2009; Bratteteig & Wagner, 2016). This remote culture has enabled the company to effectively face the COVID-19 pandemic and to support its workforce 'to thrive outside the walls of any company through use of technologies like videoconferencing' (*Chief Information Office,* press release 2020). Distinct from High Tech, as the pandemic has spread across the globe many companies are still striving to understand how to build a culture that fits with most employees working remotely (Howard-Greenville, 2020). As underlined by Spicer (2020), over the past months we have already witnessed changes and loss in symbols and rituals of the traditional 'office-based' culture, such as open plan workplaces, people wearing suits and water cooler chats. These artefactual representations and shared routines have been replaced with Perspex screens, informal home-wear and zoom calls. These changes are tangible elements of a radical transition towards a remote culture. We thus expect that an increasing number of companies will significantly invest to create the foundations of a remote culture, aligned with pre-existing corporate values and contributing to shape positive perceptions of support among the employee base (Dittes et al., 2019).

Notwithstanding the importance of ICT tools (Baker et al. 2006; Bentley et al., 2016), our findings shed light on potential risks associated with too much emphasis on a remote culture imbued with technology. In High Tech, employees have access online to a huge amount of information and have several options concerning learning programs and social networking tools. The downside is that they could feel overwhelmed by such a volume of information and possibilities, find it difficult to orient their choices effectively and feel too much pressure towards individual proactive behavior. To interviewees, the company overestimates the value of a technological infrastructure, and relies too much on personal initiative in fueling virtual interactions and self-creating opportunities for collaboration. The project manager explained that it is hard to keep updated about organizational life; continuous top-down communications cause psychological pressure in relation to expectations towards the personal level of knowledge about the company. Likewise, the variety of learning options could exacerbate the worker's sense of responsibility and expected commitment towards updated competences. On the basis of this evidence, we can infer that a new paradox arises from the availability of too many ICT tools, online resources and communication flows: what are framed as rituals and symbols of organizational support actually could reduce the perceptions of support received by the organization. This is a new paradox concerning virtual connections that adds to those already identified in the literature on remote working, notably the connectivity paradox (e.g. Leonardi et al., 2010), the identity paradox (Demarco & Errichiello, 2021) and the control paradox (Cunha et al., 2020).

The case study also offered evidence of a potential risk produced by nurturing the values and practices of a remote culture (Howard-Greenville, 2020). Too much emphasis on fully remote or 'e-work', indeed, could lead companies to undervalue organizational support in 'hybrid work', i.e. mixed forms based on the co-existence of remote and office-based activities (e.g. Halford, 2005). Empirical findings showed that remote workers value physical interaction with managers and colleagues. Both interviewees agreed that, when on-site meetings are completely replaced by virtual interactions, remote culture can result in detrimental impacts on work effectiveness. This process can be quite subtle, thus risking it going unnoticed. As explained by the salesperson, until 2000 on-site regular sales meetings were perceived as an occasion for socializing and exchanging knowledge with colleagues. The frequency of these meetings has gradually decreased, however, causing the loss of opportunities for professional growth. Likewise, the project manager explained that problems for virtual collaboration could result from geographical distance and cultural diversity among team members. These results illustrate how undervaluing hybrid work and physical interactions could become a serious threat in the pandemic's aftermath: companies have been constrained to experiment with remote work in extreme conditions and to develop new work routines for full-time home-based teleworking. However, these routines can hinder an organizational culture oriented towards supporting hybrid work, that will probably become the 'new normal' instead of jobs made permanently remote (Sytch & Greer, 2020).

Findings highlight the importance of physical organizational spaces. The chance to work at the office is viewed by remote workers as a resource to avoid professional isolation, by maintaining informal relationships and exchanging knowledge with colleagues. As underlined by the salesperson, informal interactions with "sited" employees working in technical support result in opportunities for the identification of new business opportunities. Professional isolation has been historically identified as an obstacle to remote working (e.g. Golden et al., 2008; Kurland and Cooper, 2002). Surveys carried out during lockdown suggest that the COVID-19 context has exacerbated the negative relationship between professional isolation and telework adjustment (Karillo et al., 2020). Unveiling the importance of organizational workplaces in remote working, the case study pointed at the need to redesign offices in the post-COVID-19 era (Boland et al., 2020; de Lucas Ancillo et al., 2020; Errichiello & Demarco, 2020; Parker, 2020). In the past decade, many firms worldwide have applied principles of flexibility, blended collaboration and well-being to re-design workplaces as 'smart work centers' (Errichiello & Pianese, 2018; 2019) and 'smart offices' (Papagiannidis & Marikyan, 2020), providing workers with gathering places, common areas and amenities along with social distancing, occupational health and safety (e.g. Parker, 2020). This should be carefully designed to avoid COVID-19 restrictions inhibiting interactions and serendipitous collaboration (Boland et al., 2020; de Lucas Ancillo et al., 2020). As underlined by Errichiello and Demarco (2020), designers and managers should pay attention to avoid offices becoming 'not-places', i.e. mere logistical supports for workers who are deprived of an institutional workplace, and ensure that work environments meet the needs of employees, whether they work locally or remotely.

CONCLUSIONS

The COVID-19 pandemic is likely to leave a permanent imprint on work organization independent from remote work becoming the 'new normal' or, alternatively, from a return to 'normal'. The radical changes triggered by the pandemic at most levels (e.g. individual, institutional, etc.) are likely to prevent a proportion of office and remote work from returning to past values (Foss, 2020). This presents a number of challenges for managers (Kniffin et al., 2020), who will be required to adapt human resource practices (Carnevale & Hatack, 2020) and organizational support to the virtual environment in the post-COVID era (Karillo et al., 2020).

The case of an organization that has historically implemented remote working effectively offered insights about the interplay between the ostensive level of organizational support, as formally framed by the organization and the individual perceptions of support as expressed by remote employees. Although extensive research is available on organizational support (e.g., Rhoades and Eisenberger, 2002), studies have mostly looked at factors affecting perceptions of organizational support, along with its effects on employees. Scant attention has been paid to how each dimension of support is actually implemented in the organization and how specific actions are perceived by employees. Moreover, studies tend to focus on a single dimension, and do not provide a multi-level understanding of organizational support. Finally, only few studies have hitherto examined its role in the context of remote working (e.g. Bentley et al., 2016; Karillo et al., 2020).

Our findings highlight the value of a holistic approach to organizational support and provide knowledge to guide managers and employees in flexible work practices after the pandemic. The breakdown of organizational support in several dimensions enables a comprehensive understanding about features that contribute to positively shaping employee perceptions regarding the support received from managers, colleagues and the organization through a set of institutionalized practices and ICT equipment. The study has some limitations. First, interviews were carried out before the COVID-19 pandemic, so the perceptions of organizational support witnessed by workers during the crisis are not directly analyzed. However, secondary data documenting the experience of the firm during the pandemic showed that the organization's response in term of supporting its employees has been significantly shaped by the holistic approach adopted by the company before the emergency. This means that High Tech is an enlightening example and that lessons can be learnt about its approach to organizational support by other companies. Second, interviews were restricted to mobile work and virtual teams. Hence, we excluded the experience of full-time teleworkers, that could be valuable to understand the current situation. Third, we looked at a best practice case with long-standing experience in remote working, a rooted remote culture and high technology maturity.

Notwithstanding the value of our case study, it is worth highlighting that dimensions of support have to be adapted to each organization, considering a number of factors, including the state of remote working implementation, the technology maturity, available financial resources for digitalization projects, as well as dominant leadership models and broader organizational culture. Accordingly, future studies should be directed at investigating the challenges of providing organizational support to remote workers in smaller firms and/or firms operating in non-technological sectors. Further research should also examine the perceptions of organizational support witnessed by employees relying on different remote work arrangements according to the 'space' dimension, i.e. where they work remotely (e.g. home-based telework, smart working), as well as comparing the perceptions and behaviors of different categories of remote workers in relation to the "time" dimension, i.e. when they work remotely (e.g. full-time or part-time).

AUTHORS' CONTRIBUTION

Authors equally contributed to conceptualizing and carrying on the study. However, the first author wrote the sections 4, 5 and 6; The second author wrote the sections 1 and 2. Both authors wrote the abstract and section 3.

REFERENCES

Al-Ani, B., Horspool, A., & Bligh, M. C. (2011). Collaborating with "virtual strangers": Towards developing a framework for leadership in distributed teams. *Leadership*, *7*(3), 219–249. doi:10.1177/1742715011407382

Aube, C., Rousseau, V., & Morin, E. M. (2007). Perceived organizational support and organizational commitment. *Journal of Managerial Psychology*, *22*(5), 479–495. doi:10.1108/02683940710757209

Baker, E., Avery, G. C., & Crawford, J. (2006). Home alone: The role of technology in telecommuting. *Information Resources Management Journal*, *19*(4), 1–22. doi:10.4018/irmj.2006100101

Bartel, C. A., Wrzesniewski, A., & Wiesenfeld, B. M. (2012). Knowing Where You Stand: Physical Isolation, Perceived Respect, and Organizational Identification Among Virtual Employees. *Organization Science*, *23*(3), 743–757. doi:10.1287/orsc.1110.0661

Baxter, P., & Jack, S. (2008). Qualitative case study methodology: Study design and implementation for novice researchers. *Qualitative Report*, *13*(4), 544–559.

Bélanger, F., Watson-Manheim, M. B., & Swan, B. R. (2013). A multi-level socio-technical systems telecommuting framework. *Behaviour & Information Technology*, *32*(12), 1257–1279. doi:10.1080/0144929X.2012.705894

Bentley, T. A., Teo, S. T. T., McLeod, L., Tan, F., Bosua, R., & Gloet, M. (2016). The role of organisational support in teleworker well-being: A socio-technical systems approach. *Applied Ergonomics*, *52*, 207–215. doi:10.1016/j.apergo.2015.07.019 PMID:26360212

Bisbe, J., & Sivabalan, P. (2017). Management control and trust in virtual settings: A case study of a virtual new product development team. *Management Accounting Research*, *37*, 12–29. doi:10.1016/j.mar.2017.02.001

Bødker, K., Kensing, F., & Simonsen, J. (2009). *Participatory IT design: designing for business and workplace realities*. MIT Press.

Boland, B., De Smet, A., Palter, R., & Sanghvi, A. (2020). *Reimagining the office and work life after COVID-19*. McKinsey Report.

Bratteteig, T., & Wagner, I. (2016). Unpacking the notion of participation in participatory design. *Computer Supported Cooperative Work*, *25*(6), 425–475. doi:10.100710606-016-9259-4

Brown, A. (1995). *Organisational Culture*. Pitman Publishing.

By, R. T. (2005). Organisational change management: A critical review. *Journal of Change Management*, *5*(4), 369–380. doi:10.1080/14697010500359250

Carillo, K., Cachat-Rosset, G., Marsan, J., Saba, T., & Klarsfeld, A. (2020). Adjusting to epidemic-induced telework: Empirical insights from teleworkers in France. *European Journal of Information Systems*, 1–20. doi:10.1080/0960085X.2020.1829512

Carnevale, J. B., & Hatak, I. (2020). Employee adjustment and well-being in the era of COVID-19: Implications for human resource management. *Journal of Business Research*, *116*, 183–187. doi:10.1016/j.jbusres.2020.05.037 PMID:32501303

Collins, A. M., Cartwright, S., & Hislop, D. (2013). Homeworking: Negotiating the psychological contract. *Human Resource Management Journal*, *23*(2), 211–225. doi:10.1111/j.1748-8583.2012.00200.x

Collins, A. M., Hislop, D., & Cartwright, S. (2016). Social support in the workplace between teleworkers, office-based colleagues and supervisors. *New Technology, Work and Employment*, *31*(2), 161–175. doi:10.1111/ntwe.12065

Cunha, J., Pianese, T., & Errichiello, L. (2020). *Paradoxes of Control in Remote Work Arrangements*. 4th RGCS symposium "Designing the Commons: Collaborative spaces, Open communities, Smart Cities", Lyon, France.

Dambrin, C. (2004). How does telework influence the manager-employee relationship? *International Journal of Human Resources Development and Management*, *4*(4), 358–374. doi:10.1504/IJHRDM.2004.005044

Day, A., Paquet, S., Scott, N., & Hambley, L. (2012). Perceived information and communication technology (ICT) demands on employee outcomes: The moderating effect of organizational ICT support. *Journal of Occupational Health Psychology*, *17*(4), 473–491. doi:10.1037/a0029837 PMID:23066697

De, R., Pandey, N., & Pal, A. (2020). Impact of Digital Surge during Covid-19 Pandemic: A Viewpoint on Research and Practice. *International Journal of Information Management*, *55*, 102171. doi:10.1016/j.ijinfomgt.2020.102171 PMID:32836633

de Lucas Ancillo, A., del Val Núñez, M.T., & Gavrila, S.G. (2020). Workplace change within the COVID-19 context: a grounded theory approach. *Economic Research-Ekonomska Istraživanja*, 1-20.

DeConinck, J. B. (2010). The effect of organizational justice, perceived organizational support, and perceived supervisor support on marketing employees' level of trust. *Journal of Business Research*, *63*(12), 1349–1355. doi:10.1016/j.jbusres.2010.01.003

Demarco, D., & Errichiello, L. (2021). Smart working, states of connectivity and work identities in transition Bridging philosophy and management research. *Research Trends in Humanities- Education & Philosophy*, *8*, 126-137.

Dittes, S., Richter, S., Richter, A., & Smolnik, S. (2019). Toward the workplace of the future: How organizations can facilitate digital work. *Business Horizons*, *62*(5), 649–661. doi:10.1016/j.bushor.2019.05.004

Drouin, N., & Bourgault, M. (2013). How organizations support distributed project teams. *Journal of Management Development*, *32*(8), 865–885. doi:10.1108/JMD-07-2012-0091

Eisenberger, R., Armeli, S., Rexwinkel, B., Lynch, P. D., & Rhoades, L. (2001). Reciprocation of perceived organizational support. *The Journal of Applied Psychology*, *86*(1), 42–51. doi:10.1037/0021-9010.86.1.42 PMID:11302232

Eisenhardt, K. M. (1989). Building theories from case study research. *Academy of Management Review*, *14*(4), 532–550. doi:10.5465/amr.1989.4308385

Errichiello, L., & Demarco, D. (2020). From social distancing to virtual connections. *TeMA Journal of Land Use, Mobility and Environment*, 151-164.

Errichiello, L., & Pianese, T. (2016). Organizational control in the context of remote work arrangements: a conceptual framework. *Studies in Managerial and Financial Accounting, 31, 273-305*. doi:10.1108/S1479-351220160000031009

Errichiello, L., & Pianese, T. (2018). Smart Work Centers as "creative workspaces" for remote employees. *CERN ideaSquare Journal of Experimental Innovation*, *2*, 14–21.

Errichiello, L., & Pianese, T. (2019). Toward a theory on workplaces for smart workers. *Facilities*, *38*(3/4), 298–315. doi:10.1108/F-11-2018-0137

Fonner, K. L., & Stache, L. C. (2012). All in a days work, at home: Teleworkers management of micro role transitions and the work-home boundary. *New Technology, Work and Employment*, *27*(3), 242–257. doi:10.1111/j.1468-005X.2012.00290.x

Foss, N. J. (2020). The impact of The Covid-19 pandemic on firms' organizational designs. *Journal of Management Studies*, 57. doi:10.1111/joms.12643

Gómez, S. M., Mendoza, O. E. O., Ramírez, J., & Olivas-Luján, M. R. (2020). Stress and myths related to the COVID-19 pandemic's effects on remote work. Management Research. *Journal of the Iberoamerican Academy of Management*, *18*(4), 401–420.

Halford, S. (2005). Hybrid workspace: Re-spatialisations of work, organisation and management. *New Technology, Work and Employment*, *20*(1), 19–33. doi:10.1111/j.1468-005X.2005.00141.x

Han, G. (2006). Helping you out while Im away: Examining tenure diversity, leader support and ocb in global teams. *Academy of Management Proceedings: Knowledge, Action and the Public Concern*, 1-9.

Howard-Grenville, J. (2020). How to Sustain Your Organization's Culture When Everyone Is Remote. *MIT Sloan Management Review*, *61*(4), 1–4.

Johlke, M. C., Stamper, C. L., & Shoemaker, M. E. (2001). Antecedents to boundary-spanner perceived organizational support. *Journal of Managerial Psychology*, *17*(2), 116–128. doi:10.1108/02683940210417049

Kimble, C. (2011). Building effective virtual teams: How to overcome the problems of trust and identity in virtual teams. *Global Business and Organizational Excellence*, *30*(2), 6–15. doi:10.1002/joe.20364

Kirkman, B. L., Rosen, B., Tesluk, P. E., & Gibson, C. B. (2004). The impact of team empowerment on virtual team performance: The moderating role of face-to-face interaction. *Academy of Management Journal*, *47*(2), 175–192.

Kniffin, K. M., Narayanan, J., Anseel, F., Antonakis, J., Ashford, S. P., Bakker, A. B., Bamberger, P., Bapuji, H., Bhave, D. P., Choi, V. K., Creary, S. J., Demerouti, E., Flynn, F. J., Gelfand, M. J., Greer, L. L., Johns, G., Kesebir, S., Klein, P. G., Lee, S. Y., ... Vugt, M. V. (2021). COVID-19and the workplace: Implications, issues, and insights for future research and action. *The American Psychologist*, *76*(1), 63–77. doi:10.1037/amp0000716 PMID:32772537

Kossek, E. E., Lautsch, B. A., & Eaton, S. C. (2006). Telecommuting, control, and boundary management: Correlates of policy use and practice, job control, and work–family effectiveness. *Journal of Vocational Behavior*, *68*(2), 347–367. doi:10.1016/j.jvb.2005.07.002

Kurland, N. B., & Cooper, C. D. (2002). Manager control and employee isolation in telecommuting environments. *The Journal of High Technology Management Research*, *13*(1), 107–126. doi:10.1016/S1047-8310(01)00051-7

Kurtessis, J. N., Eisenberger, R., Ford, M. T., Buffardi, L. C., Stewart, K. A., & Adis, C. S. (2017). Perceived organizational support: A meta-analytic evaluation of organizational support theory. *Journal of Management*, *43*(6), 1854–1884. doi:10.1177/0149206315575554

Lautsch, B. A., Kossek, E. E., & Eaton, S. C. (2009). Supervisory approaches and paradoxes in managing telecommuting implementation. *Human Relations*, *62*(6), 795–827. doi:10.1177/0018726709104543

Leonardi, P. M., Treem, J. W., & Jackson, M. H. (2010). The connectivity paradox: Using technology to both decrease and increase perceptions of distance in distributed work arrangements. *Journal of Applied Communication Research*, *38*(1), 85–105. doi:10.1080/00909880903483599

Limburg, D., & Jackson, P. J. (2007). Teleworkflow: Supporting remote control with Workflow Management Systems. *New Technology, Work and Employment*, *22*(2), 146–167. doi:10.1111/j.1468-005X.2007.00190.x

Malhotra, A., Majchrzak, A., & Rosen, B. (2007). Leading virtual teams. *The Academy of Management Perspectives*, *21*(1), 60–70. doi:10.5465/amp.2007.24286164

Mazmanian, M., Orlikowski, W. J., & Yates, J. (2013). The autonomy paradox: The implications of mobile email devices for knowledge professionals. *Organization Science*, *24*(5), 1337–1357. doi:10.1287/orsc.1120.0806

Munir, Y., Sadiq, M., Ali, I., Hamdan, Y., & Munir, E. (2016). Workplace Isolation in Pharmaceutical Companies: Moderating Role of Self-Efficacy. *Social Indicators Research*, *126*(3), 1157–1174. doi:10.100711205-015-0940-7 PMID:29563661

Newman, S. A., & Ford, R. C. (2020). Five Steps to Leading Your Team in the Virtual COVID-19 Workplace. *Organizational Dynamics*, 100802. doi:10.1016/j.orgdyn.2020.100802

Panaccio, A., & Vandenberghe, C. (2009). Perceived organizational support, organizational commitment and psychological well-being: A longitudinal study. *Journal of Vocational Behavior*, *75*(2), 224–236. doi:10.1016/j.jvb.2009.06.002

Papagiannidis, S., & Davit, M. (2020). Smart offices: A productivity and well-being perspective. *International Journal of Information Management*, *5*, 102027. doi:10.1016/j.ijinfomgt.2019.10.012

Parker, L. D. (2020). The COVID-19 office in transition: Cost, efficiency and the social responsibility business case. *Accounting, Auditing & Accountability Journal*, *33*(8), 1943–1967. doi:10.1108/AAAJ-06-2020-4609

Randall, M. L., Cropanzano, R., Bormann, C. A., & Birjulin, A. (1999). Organizational politics and organizational support as predictors of work attitudes, job performance, and organizational citizenship behavior. *Journal of Organizational Behavior*, *20*(2), 159–174. doi:10.1002/(SICI)1099-1379(199903)20:2<159::AID-JOB881>3.0.CO;2-7

Rhoades, L., & Eisenberger, R. (2002). Perceived organizational support: A review of the literature. *The Journal of Applied Psychology*, *87*(4), 698–714. doi:10.1037/0021-9010.87.4.698 PMID:12184574

Rhoades, L., Eisenberger, R., & Armeli, S. (2001). Affective commitment to the organization: The contribution of perceived organizational support. *The Journal of Applied Psychology*, *86*(5), 825–836. doi:10.1037/0021-9010.86.5.825 PMID:11596800

Richter, A. (2020). Locked-down digital work. *International Journal of Information Management*, *55*, 102157. doi:10.1016/j.ijinfomgt.2020.102157 PMID:32836629

Richter, A., Heinrich, P., Stocker, A., & Schwabe, G. (2018). Digital work design. *Business & Information Systems Engineering*, *60*(3), 259–264. doi:10.100712599-018-0534-4

Riggle, R. J., Edmondson, D. R., & Hansen, J. D. (2009). A meta-analysis of the relationship between perceived organizational support and job outcomes: 20 years of research. *Journal of Business Research*, *62*(10), 1027–1030. doi:10.1016/j.jbusres.2008.05.003

Schein, E. H. (1990). Organizational culture. American Psychological Association, 45(2).

Smith, E. F., Gilmer, D. O., & Stockdale, M. S. (2019). Culture and support for workplace flexibility matter: An ecological framework for understanding flexibility support structures. *Business Horizons*, *62*, 557–566. doi:10.1016/j.bushor.2019.04.002

Spicer, A. (2020). Organizational Culture and COVID-19. *Journal of Management Studies*, *57*(8), 1737–1740. doi:10.1111/joms.12625

Sytch, M., & Greer, L. I. (2020). Is your organization ready for permanent WFH? *Harvard Business Review*. https://hbr.org/2020/08/is-your-organization-ready-for-permanent-wfh

Tansky, J. W., & Cohen, D. J. (2001). The relationship between organizational support, employee development, and organizational commitment: An empirical study. *Human Resource Development Quarterly*, *12*(3), 285–300. doi:10.1002/hrdq.15

Timms, C., Brough, P., O'Driscoll, M., Kalliath, T., Siu, O. L., Sit, C., & Lo, D. (2015). Flexible work arrangements, work engagement, turnover intentions and psychological health. *Asia Pacific Journal of Human Resources*, *53*(1), 83–103. doi:10.1111/1744-7941.12030

Toniolo-Barrios, M., & Pitt, L. (2020). Mindfulness and the challenges of working from home in times of crisis. *Business Horizons*. Advance online publication. doi:10.1016/j.bushor.2020.09.004 PMID:33041346

Vanden Abeele, M. M. (2020). Digital Well-being as a Dynamic Construct. *Communication Theory*, qtaa024. doi:10.1093/ct/qtaa024

Vera, D., Samba, C., Kong, D. T., & Maldonado, T. (2020). Resilience as thriving: The role of positive leadership practices. *Organizational Dynamics*, 100784. doi:10.1016/j.orgdyn.2020.100784 PMID:32836512

Wajcman, J., & Rose, E. (2011). Constant connectivity: Rethinking interruptions at work. *Organization Studies*, *32*(7), 941–961. doi:10.1177/0170840611410829

Wayne, S. J., Shore, L. M., & Liden, R. C. (1997). Perceived organizational support and leader-member exchange: A social exchange perspective. *Academy of Management Journal*, *40*(1), 82–111.

Wiesenfeld, B. M., Raghuram, S., & Garud, R. (2001). Organizational identification among virtual workers: The role of need for affiliation and perceived work-based social support. *Journal of Management*, *27*(2), 213–229. doi:10.1177/014920630102700205

Yin, R. K. (2003). *Case Study Research: Design and Methods*. Sage Publications.

Chapter 14
Feeling Closer Despite the Distance:
How to Cultivate Togetherness Within Digital Spaces

Julia Ayache
https://orcid.org/0000-0002-8587-5628
Nottingham Trent University, UK

Nadja Heym
https://orcid.org/0000-0003-2414-8854
Nottingham Trent University, UK

Alexander Sumich
Nottingham Trent University, UK

Darren Rhodes
Nottingham Trent University, UK

Andy M. Connor
Auckland University of Technology, New Zealand

Stefan Marks
Auckland University of Technology, New Zealand

ABSTRACT

In the framework of "togetherness" as a psychophysiological experience of social presence, the current chapter highlights the importance of work environments to socializing. The absence of such physical collective spaces impacts group-dynamics and team performance in online meetings, which also tend to prioritize task-solving discussions and limit non-verbal exchanges. Interpersonal coordination (or "social glue"), characterized by a spontaneous mutual attunement, both in speech and gestures, is classically observed during collective events where social-bonding and affiliation are promoted. This chapter will review the cognitive, behavioral, and physiological consequences of togetherness and integrate those in the context of recent technological advancements in computer-mediated interaction which have culminated in the advent of virtual and augmented reality. Given the potential of such methods to increase embodied interactions, they have been coined as "empathy machines" and could be seen as a technological solution to restore the experience of togetherness in the workplace.

DOI: 10.4018/978-1-7998-6754-8.ch014

INTRODUCTION

Since March 2020, the world has faced an unprecedented global crisis. In addition to impacting health services, the COVID-19 pandemic has put a strain on economic and social exchange, led to social division, and raised political and civil tension. Riva and Wiederhold (2020) note that the disappearance of collective spaces due to COVID-19 goes hand-in-hand with a fading sense of belonging to a community, due to the lack of opportunities to create and nurture social connections. One specific space where meaningful interactions arise is the workplace, which has undergone a rapid and extensive shift from onsite to fully remote-working conditions to minimise the spread of the virus. Remote (or tele-) working had been promoted for several decades, both for its environmental benefits (Hardill & Green, 2003) as well as promoting workforce mobility and flexibility (Gunter & van der Hoeven, 2004). Consequently, such a radical switch was possible due to the ongoing digitalization of society and the transition from manufacturing products to service-centric business models, culminating in the widespread introduction of personal computers and smartphones with constant access to the internet (Valenduc & Vendramin, 2017). Whilst Computer-Mediated-Communication (CMC) enhances media richness and facilitates instant access to remote interactions, the rapid intensification of online information exchange has also been associated with burn-out (Hakanen & Bakker, 2017), loneliness (Nowland et al., 2018) and dissemination of fake news (Del Vicario et al., 2016). In a series of news articles, Amanda Mull (2020, 2021) depicts the struggles encountered by remote workers: loneliness, lack of networking opportunities and loss of a sense of belonging to a community are just a few consequences resulting from the isolation experienced by those secluded at home. Incidents of 'social serendipity' usually occurring among colleagues in work settings reveal the richness of the workplace as a space for impromptu social interactions to foster diversity and inclusiveness.

This chapter explores how this rapid increase in online interaction challenges the way social connections are built, redefining the meaning of "togetherness" as a technological phenomenon. This chapter will address why, despite the inconvenience of commuting and its environmental impact, individuals continue to value traditional workplaces as a space to interact and socialise. It emphasizes how physical proximity to another human fundamentally shapes how we experience our interaction and the environment. This chapter will discuss how the lack of sensory and social cues during online interactions limits the experience of these phenomena, and finally, how technological advancements in virtual and augmented reality may offer innovative solutions to these issues.

THE NEED TO BELONG AND SENSE OF TOGETHERNESS

The study of social interaction has a long-standing history, located at the intersection between anthropology, sociology and social psychology. Ironically and despite decades of research, the conceptualisation and definition of togetherness have not reached consensus yet. For instance, Durlach and Slater (2000, p.214) define togetherness as "the sense of being with other people in a shared (virtual) environment", stressing the need for sharing the same space. On the other hand, Darwall (2011) states that "being with" someone is different from mere spatial co-location, emphasizing the sense of being together "with" and the need to be mutually aware of each other. These differing conceptualisations are reflected in the different theoretical approaches that explore the sense of togetherness and why humans treasure social interactions.

Grounded in evolutionary psychology, the belongingness hypothesis (Baumeister & Leary, 1995) emphasizes the role played by social connectedness as a prerequisite for an individual's survival, and thus, a basic psychological need. The most well-known illustration is John Bowlby's (1969; 1973) attachment theory, which stresses the importance of infant-parent emotional bonds in determining relationship experiences in adulthood. The belongingness hypothesis explores specifically the affective, cognitive and behavioural consequences associated with a need for relatedness. According to Baumeister and Leary, the fulfilment of our need for social connectedness is achieved only when social interactions occur, both frequently and with a certain degree of intimacy. Thus, meaningful and frequent interactions in terms of time and space predict the occurrence of successful social-bonding and fulfill our need to belong. In romantic couples, perceptions of mutual support and caring are strong predictors of perceived attractiveness and satisfaction in the relationship (Valentine et al., 2020). When intimacy is lacking in a relationship, individuals are more likely to consider reconnecting with ex-partners (Spielmann et al., 2012), or more likely to seek online interaction to satisfy their need for social support (He et al., 2013). This phenomenon can also occur among co-workers and affect team performance. For example, the feeling of belongingness directly influences workplace satisfaction in nurses, where teamwork is crucial to ensure patient safety (Mohamed et al., 2014). In this specific context, a lack of cohesiveness among colleagues can lead to medical errors, resulting in life-threatening situations (Gkorezis et al., 2016). In other professional contexts, perceiving social exclusion or ostracism is directly related to a decrease in productivity and an increased risk of staff turnover (O'Reilly & Robinson, 2009).

According to the 'socio-meter theory' suggested by Leary (1999), social integration is reflected in variations in self-esteem, conceptualized as a barometer of the beliefs about how someone is evaluated by others. Like a barometer responds to changes in atmospheric pressure, self-esteem will fluctuate in response to the perceived degree of social integration. Higher levels of self-esteem have been associated with job satisfaction and work or organizational commitment (Jelil Ladebo et al., 2008). On the other hand, low self-esteem, reflecting unsuccessful achievement of social integration, is often associated with negative consequences such as absenteeism and burn-out (Parker & Kulik, 1995). Thus, perceived social integration at the workplace is vital as it influences staff well-being and performance.

Considering the negative outcomes associated with a lack of social integration at work, it is not surprising that in many organizations staff hours and budget allocations are dedicated to strengthening group cohesiveness and promote the creation of organizational identity. Using uniforms or common language and rituals, establishes a joint organizational culture to facilitate the development of a 'group affective tone' (Humphrey et al., 2016). As suggested by van Kleef, Heerdink and Homan (2017), this group affective tone can be considered as an indicator capturing the social bonding that occurs between members of the group. When positive emotions (e.g. happiness, authentic pride) are expressed, group members tend to perceive greater levels of cohesiveness, eliciting an increase in effective teamwork, coordination and creativity, and a decrease of absenteeism. On the other hand, negative emotions (e.g. anger, anxiety) elicit a perception of exclusion, reducing prosocial behaviors and lowering team performance. Thus, fostering a healthy and positive group affective tone in workplace settings is paramount.

Moreover, according to Estlund (2003), workplaces are not just limited to professional activities, but need to be understood as a specific social space, where social and cultural integration occurs through the mixing of individuals who otherwise may be segregated by their socioeconomic background. This has been recently supported by a large-scale national survey conducted in 2019 in the United Kingdom, concluding that 76% of the workplaces were ethnically diverse, fostering inter-cultural and religious mixing (Farley & Dahlgreen, 2020). In an increasingly digitized world, remote working conditions that do not provide alternative spaces or opportunities for such social integration may greatly reduce mixing between different religious and ethnic groups, and potentially foster prejudice and isolation.

Over a century ago, social theorists Gustave Le Bon (1896) and Emile Durkheim (1912) referred to the concept of 'group mind'. Inspired by the emergence of psychoanalysis, Le Bon described the crowd as a psychological entity in itself that may foster a group mind, whilst Durkheim's analysis described the 'collective effervescence' generated through religious rituals in aboriginal tribes as a foundation of social entities. According to Durkheim, the shared enthusiasm elicited by social rituals, characterized by their codifications in terms of actions and frequencies, act as 'social glue', binding individuals together. More contemporary research exploring the 'group mind' concept differentiate between action and cognition involved in this process. Collective action has been described as a switch from a self-centric perspective to a 'we-mode' and can be illustrated by the concept of self-agency - a multidimensional construct of the sense of intentionality and body ownership. According to Pacherie (2014), the sense of self-agency, usually experienced by someone when acting alone, is disrupted during joint action, suggesting the existence of a form of 'we-agency'. Thus, encouraging collective action despite a remote work environment can facilitate the sense of belonging and togetherness.

From a cognitive perspective, the group can be considered as an extension of our cognitive system that integrates our social network. This theoretical approach can be illustrated by Wegner's (1987) 'transactive memory system', which suggests that group members become part of an external storage system, often reflecting the expertise of each member of the group. Recent investigations in organizational psychology have stressed the importance of media richness to facilitate the transactive memory system (Ge & Lang, 2020). In virtual teams, content restricted to audio or text is less effective in building this memory network than interactions involving video. Indeed, Ge and Lang (2020) propose that video allows more effective conveyance of verbal and non-verbal cues, easing the establishment of 'who knows what' through emotional connection and the reduction of uncertainty. Thus, providing the right virtual working conditions can enhance team performance through facilitation of joint cognition.

Taken together, the different theoretical approaches briefly reviewed here, attempt to capture the experience of togetherness at different levels and through different processes. These propositions explain why belongingness is a fundamental need and highlight that we are motivated to maintain proximity through social interaction with others. They emphasize the role played by our physical world, such as the workplace as a collective social space and its capacity for fostering a sense of belonging. In the next section we will look at the psychological and physical mechanisms involved in how proximity shapes our sense of belonging and experience of togetherness.

EXPLORING THE DARK MATTER OF SOCIAL INTERACTION

Traditional ways of thinking about social interaction in terms of either action or cognition have shown how as individuals we process social cues and togetherness. For example, how we process facial or verbal cues in communications with others and how they impact our emotional state (Jospe et al., 2020). However, these studies are typically limited by the observation of an individual's responses during an interaction or watching others who interact. This is problematic in that these observations do not allow capture of the mutual exchanges that occur between individuals, leaving the underlying mechanisms of dynamic social interactions unknown. This has been labelled as the "dark matter" of social neurosciences, stressing the need to reconsider human cognition not as isolated, but a continuous and active process of interactions between the organism and its (social) environment (Schilbach et al., 2013). In support of this view, human survival (from the earliest stage of our lives) is dependent on the quality of the social environment (Fotopoulou & Tsakiris, 2017). Therefore, it requires a mutual understanding and shared consciousness to self-regulate our internal emotional states (Tronick, 1998). By reframing social interaction as a dynamic process involving two or more interactants, the research field of interpersonal coordination has established novel research methods to explore the behavioural and physiological components of togetherness.

Bernieri and Rosenthal (1991) refer to 'interpersonal coordination' as an umbrella term defined as the degree to which the behaviours in an interaction are non-random, patterned or synchronized in both timing and form. Coined as 'chameleon effect' by Lakin et al. (2003), mimicry (or behavioural matching) is the spontaneous tendency to mimic someone else, underpinned neurologically by a network of 'mirror neurons'. These activate in response to observing and executing actions and are modulated by situational factors that trigger the desire to be affiliated (e.g. threat of social exclusion or need for group membership). Mimicry is believed to have played a crucial part in human evolution as social glue. On the other side, 'interactional synchrony' stresses the role played by shared co-temporality, occurring when behavioural and physiological rhythms of individuals are mutually aligned or 'resonate' during social interaction (Trevarthen, 1999). While mimicry has been mostly studied using experimental paradigms involving confederates or pre-recorded videos, interpersonal synchrony has been typically studied in dynamic social interactions, involving two or more individuals.

The phenomenon of interpersonal coordination was already noted by Kendon (1970) who reported a tendency for rhythmical coordination between speakers and listeners' movements; and by LaFrance (1979) who reported posture sharing between students and instructors as a predictor of their relationship quality. Bayram and Ta (2019) observed that linguistic style matching, referring to the tendency to use common vocabulary, tends to reflect higher levels of cooperation and agreement between individuals in a conversation. In a series of studies, Lakens (2010) demonstrated that movement synchronization can lead to perceived social unity and group cohesion, due to the requirement of mutual attentiveness to synchronize movements. Despite the different approaches to study mimicry and interactional synchrony, both are thought to facilitate some aspects of prosocial outcomes by promoting emotional alignment and social bonding (Vicaria and Dickens, 2016). In professional contexts, interpersonal coordination has been studied in negotiations, design processes and therapeutic contexts where closeness, likeability and trust are strong predictors of more positive outcomes. Here, the power of imitation can be beneficial for commercial interaction and negotiators, as mimicry increases interpersonal trust, mediating the effect of imitation on deal-making (Maddux et al., 2008). The shift from individual to collective processing is also observed in design processes (SonicRim, 2001), where new methods based on empathic training are developed, using synchrony as a cue to foster designers' empathy toward users-friendly products (Chang-Arana et al., 2020). In clinical contexts, Ramseyer and Tschacher (2011) reported a positive relationship between non-verbal synchrony and psychotherapeutic outcomes, suggesting an effect of motor coordination in the formation of therapeutic alliance - reflecting the collaborative bond occurring between patient and therapist. Therefore, at a psychological level, we can see how interpersonal coordination affects individual's behaviour related to bonding or affiliation.

Interpersonal coordination is not limited to individual subjective experiences and behavioural expressions, but also occurs at the physiological level. For example, Palmieri et al. (2018) report physiological coupling of skin conductance (i.e., an electrodermal response facilitated during physiological arousal) between therapist and volunteers. Beyond this physiological signature of emotional arousal and contagion, other markers of peripheral nervous system activity (e.g. heart-rate activity, pupil dilatation) can be used as an indicator of the quality of the interaction among individuals. More contemporary innovative methods even allow simultaneous recording of the brain activity of two or more individuals (i.e. hyperscanning) and facilitate exploration of cerebral mechanisms underpinning social interaction (Dumas, 2011). Hyperscanning has been used to investigate interbrain-synchrony between mother and infant (Nguyen et al., 2020), among friends during gift exchanges (Balconi et al., 2020), between lovers and strangers engaging in a creativity task (Duan et al., 2020) and during counselling (Zhang et al., 2018). For example, romantic relationships characterised by stronger emotional and physiological bonds elicit greater neural synchrony in couples than in strangers (Kinreich et al., 2017). Furthermore, this inter-brain coordination is modulated by the level of attachment, where perceived insecure relationships decrease neural coupling, highlighting the need for mutual and stable bonds to allow synchronization to occur. Increased inter-brain synchronization during psychological counselling compared to chatting sessions has been interpreted as a physiological indicator of therapeutic alliance (Zhang et al., 2018). Thus, even at a physiological level, we can see how individuals implicitly respond during synchronised interaction and use it as an indicator of bonding or affiliation.

Despite cumulative evidence, the exact psychological mechanisms linking interpersonal coordination to social bonding are still unclear and several co-existing hypotheses are proposed in the literature (for an in-depth review, see Hale & Hamilton, 2016). One interesting neurobiological explanation suggests a link between interpersonal coordination and the release of endorphins and oxytocin, two neurotransmitters involved in social-bonding, which might mediate the relationship between synchronization and the desire for affiliation (Tarr et al., 2014; Zilcha-Mano et al., 2020). Nevertheless, as foreseen by Durkheim a century ago, moving in synchrony is indeed the "social glue" binding us together, and conceived as a prerequisite for empathic processing.

INTERPERSONAL COORDINATION AND EMPATHY

Described by some as 'kinesthetic' or motor empathy, interpersonal coordination has been suggested as a precursor of empathic capacities, due to the spontaneous tendency of infants to mimic others underpinned by the mirror neurons activity (Decety & Meltzoff, 2011). Indeed, interpersonal coordination is the scaffolding sustaining parent-infant interactions. For example, Cirelli et al. (2014) reported that motor synchronization is used as a social cue to elicit prosocial behaviours in 14-month-old infants. Following the developmental trajectories of infants, from birth to adolescence, Feldman (2007) observed that early parent-infant interactions act as a bedrock of later competencies in social interactions, going hand-in-hand with empathic processing. However, the relationship between empathy and interpersonal coordination is not as simple as that. Whilst some research sees interpersonal coordination as a precursor, others propose that interpersonal coordination is facilitated by empathic capacities - in other words, those who are more empathic, are better at synchronising.

Historically, derived from the German word Einfühlung - translated as 'feeling into', empathy refers to the capacity to project oneself into another body or mind and has also been implicated in prosocial consequences (Ganczarek et al., 2018). Modern conceptions of empathy consider this capacity as a multidimensional construct where affective and cognitive components need to be distinguished. While affective empathy refers to the capacity to perceive "the emotions and feelings of others with a minimal distinction between self and other" (Decety, 2010, p. 258), cognitive empathy, also coined as 'Theory of mind', refers to "the ability to attribute independent mental states to self and others" (Frith & Happé, 1999, p. 2). As highlighted by Heym et al. (2020), these conceptualisations of empathy are often conflated, leading to a jingle-jangle conundrum, and consequently, mixed findings within the literature. This is also seen in organizational research, where the lack of consensus to define and delineate these constructs has led to scattered results, despite a general acknowledgement of the benefits associated with empathy in the workplace to foster diversity and improve leadership (Clark et al., 2019).

In terms of cognitive empathy, a number of studies have looked at the association with interpersonal coordination using self-report measures, showing a positive link with perspective-taking (Novembre et al., 2019), but also no association between the two (Preissmann et al., 2016). However, these studies tell us little about the likely impact of one on the other. Using a behavioural measurement of cognitive empathy, Koehne et al. (2016) observed an improvement in the ability to understand others' mental states following a simple motor synchronization task, both for healthy and autistic individuals, suggesting that interpersonal coordination facilitates cognitive empathy. On the other hand, Jospe et al. (2020) looked at physiological synchronisation during the recognition of emotional states of others, and found that while verbal information, including linguistic content and speech variation (e.g. speech rate and utterance), facilitated the recognition of emotional states of others, this did not impact physiological synchrony (e.g. heart-rate) - latter was elicited by non-verbal information instead. Thus, as verbal and non-verbal cues differentially influence empathic understanding and physiological synchrony, they appear to be separable processes rather than dependent on one another. In terms of affective empathy, interpersonal coordination has often been operationalised as physiological coupling - that is the sharing of similar emotional arousal among individuals. This is illustrated by the shared physiological arousal (e.g. synchronised skin conductance responses) among romantic couples during therapeutic counselling sessions (Coutinho et al. 2019). Also applied in therapeutic contexts, Lecchi et al. (2019) explored the role of mindfulness meditation training on neural synchronization and therapeutic bond. They showed that cultivating the specific cognitive state of 'being present' facilitates synchronisation, which in turn elicits greater levels of empathetic concern for others. Taken together, interpersonal coordination and both affective and cognitive empathy are interrelated but independent processes that can facilitate each other. Importantly, they are beneficially linked to various positive outcomes in organizational and therapeutic settings.

Emotional contagion (an affective empathy subcomponent) has been studied in much more depth in the organizational literature as it is argued to be a prerequisite for the group affective tone, and directly related to the propensity of co-workers to convey emotional states in the workplace. Emotional contagion manifests with the capacity of a 'sender' to transfer affective state to others, and by the susceptibility of the receiver to perceive this emotion (Hatfield et al., 1993). Emotional contagion is useful in task-oriented interactions, because it fosters group cohesion and the sharing of common values/norms that mediate successful group dynamics (Von Scheve & Ismer, 2013). Emotional contagion also facilitates informal interaction between individuals. Traditionally considered trivial and a source of distraction from work tasks, organizational management is now re-evaluating these casual interactions as they recognise them as an asset to promote mutual support, team collaboration and cohesion. For example, Fayard and Weeks (2007) note that the traditional photocopier room can provide a certain form of 'social affordance', where informal interactions are encouraged, as both its specific function and spatial location, offers privacy and physical proximity. Similarly, cafeterias and lunchrooms can also be considered as spaces where social affordance takes place, encouraging informal congregation and communication among workers to 'blow off steam', and promoting social bonding (Kniffin et al., 2015). As such shared spaces do not naturally exist in remote working conditions, limiting the occurrence of informal and emotional exchanges, it challenges the creation of our sense of proximity and co-presence among co-workers (Kraut et al., 2002). Virtual platforms such as Gather.town, CozyRoom.xyz or HighFidelity.com can offer interactive and innovative ways to recreate spaces with social affordances to facilitate emotional contagion - crucial in promoting our sense of belonging and togetherness, and general well-being.

However, some studies have also highlighted the detrimental effects of these processes. Firstly, interpersonal coordination can impair emotional processing - specifically in those who have problems regulating their emotions (Galbusera et al., 2019). Similarly, the susceptibility for emotional contagion can increase risk of burnout as the continuous (over-)exposure to others' negative emotions can lead to emotional exhaustion (Barsade et al., 2018). Finally, at a cognitive level, Vink et al. (2017) reported that interpersonal coordination can also increase conflicts during decision-making processes due to the incapacity to disentangle one's own view from the others. The origins of such effects are still unclear, but nevertheless, these exacerbating factors may need to be taken into account when promoting affect sharing among co-workers to foster group affective tone. Therefore, organizations might consider options for promoting mental health and well-being support, particularly in sectors dealing with highly stressful situations that might facilitate negative emotional overload to prevent potential harmful effects.

Taken together, there appears to be a complex relationship between interpersonal coordination and the multi-dimensional nature of empathy. Importantly, as with interpersonal synchronisation, affective and cognitive empathy capacities are linked to beneficial outcomes in workplace behaviours, though some mitigating factors need to be considered. Delineating their unique and interactive effects on psychological states and behaviour would further our understanding of the specific impact of synchronisation and empathy during dynamic social interactions. Whilst we considered how proximity shapes our experience of social interactions, mainly face-to-face, the next section will discuss how these mechanisms are currently challenged in CMC due to the disruption of social and sensory cues necessary for our sense of belonging and experience of togetherness. We will consider how this might affect the elicitation of empathic processes and mutual understanding underlying the experience of togetherness in digital spaces.

DIGITAL WORLDS, A THREAT FOR "AUTHENTIC" SOCIAL INTERACTIONS?

The previous sections of this chapter have highlighted the importance of physical proximity and intimacy as two key ingredients to foster interpersonal coordination and cultivate a sense of belongingness. We will see in this section how these two components are compromised in CMC.

In terms of physical proximity, sharing the same space matters to elicit interpersonal coordination. Wu et al. (2013) observed an increase of interpersonal coordination among participants located in the same room compared to those executing the same task in separated spaces. More importantly, sharing the same space is not sufficient to elicit spontaneous interpersonal synchronization but requires mutual awareness (Okazaki et al., 2015). Because classical CMC lacks sensory and social cues during online interactions, it limits us from feeling social presence to effectively build a sense of togetherness. The Social Presence Theory (Short et al., 1976) highlights that the reduction of sensory channels available during an interaction decreases the attention paid to the presence of others. Standard CMC is limited in sensory feedback (e.g., lack of touch or smell) and lacks spatial proximity – factors known to be crucial in conveying social cues necessary for fostering intimacy and prosociality (Haans & IJsselsteijn, 2009; Semin & De Groot, 2013). Besides, the lack of proximity and additional cues can also be considered from a global level, where cultural and linguistic backgrounds need to be taken into account, especially since teams of international co-workers are collaborating around the world through CMC. In a study investigating inter-brain synchronization, Pérez et al. (2019) reported a decrease of synchrony between native Spanish and native English, due to the lack of common linguistic background between speaker and listener. Consequently, our social interactions in CMC are deeply compromised.

Our ability to build intimacy is also challenged in CMC as our beliefs about others are more biased. For example, we are more likely to construct false beliefs and stereotypical views of others when interacting through CMC (Tait, 2020). At the same time we are also more likely to use 'hyperpersonal' communication (Walther, 1996), casting ourselves in more socially desirable ways in CMC than in face-to-face interaction. On the other hand, the lack of perceived social presence provides also a false belief of anonymity and alleviates concerns of evaluation anxiety (Dubrovsky et al., 1991). This promotes deindividuation, characterising the phenomenon of de-personalisation usually occurring in crowds and associated with greater polarization, self-centeredness and dysregulated behaviour (Le Bon, 1896; Postmes et al., 1998). Therefore, a paradoxical situation occurs in CMC, where, from one side, individuals tend to advertise a "public" self, compliant with social norms; but on the other side, nurture a anonymized "private" self, reflecting their personal beliefs and attitudes (Matheson & Zanna, 1988). This split between public and private self, hampers the opportunity for sharing intimacy and meaningful exchanges.

On the other hand, it is also important to highlight that successful and rich exchanges can occur in digital interactions and CMC has been linked to some beneficial outcomes. For example, the lack of social cues has been shown to increase task-oriented performance through more efficient communication, where fewer exchanges are required to reach consensus. Hiltz et al. (1986) observed a larger number of communication units in face-to-face settings compared to CMC, in particular those oriented towards clarification and the release of tension (e.g. joking, laughing). Whilst the lack of social cues may benefit faster and more qualitative decision making, it may simultaneously lead to poorer group consensus due to the lack of emotional exchanges necessary to build the 'group affective tone' (*c.f.*, van Kleef et al., 2017). Highlighting the current pitfalls encountered in CMC compared to face-to-face interactions, Rhoads (2010) stresses difficulties in building trust and cooperation due to the lack of synchronicity and limited media richness of CMC, but emphasises the possibility to mitigate these issues with time spent in online exchanges. This is further illustrated by Leechi et al. (2019), where the emotional connection between therapist and patients was not affected by the method of interaction, as face-to-face and video conference modes generated similar levels of neural synchronization. Consequently, and in spite of the challenges to convey non-verbal cues in CMC, social bonding remains possible through video consultation (for a review, see Geller, 2020). Moreover, Preece (1999) showed that empathy can arise in online communities, especially when individuals share similar experiences in real life, such as concerns around health conditions. This might be due to the effect of common or shared affective experiences on interpersonal bonding, and also reflects the prolonged and more frequent time spent in such online communities to express and share these feelings, which would lead to a greater sense of intimacy and belonging. In the context of virtual teams, the cultivation of a feeling of proximity is more challenging as contents exchanged are more often task-oriented rather than centered on emotional experiences. Thus, the cultivation of a shared identity or common goals could facilitate the creation of an emotional connection among co-workers (O'Leary et al., 2012).

Nevertheless, as shared experiences are often created through joint actions that are lacking in CMC, our capacity to build a sense of belonging in virtual communities is often compromised by the limited capacity to construct collective memories. As highlighted by Riva et al. (2021), the switch from on-site to remote-working conditions resulting in the disappearance of the physical place, challenges the usual phenomena occurring in face-to-face settings and calls for a 'smart' use of technology to tackle these current issues. We will see in the next section how virtual reality is nowadays seen as a promising way to recreate a sense of co-presence, opening new possibilities for CMC.

DO I NEED A VIRTUAL BODY TO FEEL (YOU)?

Classical theories in psychology have often separated mental phenomena from body sensations, leaving the brain-body axis as uncharted territory. Recent reconceptualizations of human cognition have highlighted its inherent grounding in the body and, by extension, in action. According to Damasio (2006), emotions and affective states arise as a consequence of the disruption of the internal state of our body, given that organisms are motivated to maintain a stable internal state to ensure optimal functioning. Therefore, a body is essential to fully experience the world and, by extension, to experience togetherness.

Considering the effective exclusion of our physical bodies in classical CMC, the development of immersive virtual environments that allow us to feel embodied has been seen as a solution to tackle the current limitations posed by CMC to restore social presence and build a sense of togetherness. By reintroducing body interaction and shared social spaces, VR provides the spatio-temporal scaffolding sustaining usual face-to-face interactions. Thus, within the workplace, this allows the creation of dedicated virtual environments fostering task-oriented interactions such as creativity or offering social affordance for informal conversations.

By introducing the ability to be 'virtually' present somewhere, virtual environments have not only provided a new way to interact but also opened up an entire research field, attempting to redefine the experience of 'being somewhere' virtually. According to Slater (2009), a greater sense of presence can be elicited in VR through: (1) greater immersion, induced through a combination of technical features, such as the visual quality of the rendered scene and its ability to reproduce valid sensorimotor actions; (2) a place illusion, referring to the sense of 'being there', in spite of the knowledge of not being there; and (3) a plausibility illusion, where individuals experience what is happening 'as if real'. With the latest technological advancements, it is now possible to recreate the sensory feedback loops usually occurring during face-to-face interaction by incorporating visual, auditory, as well as haptic feedback. This generates a greater sense of presence, and consequently facilitates perceptions of closeness and intimacy as illustrated by Kim et al.'s (2004) first 'transatlantic touch' between two users located in different continents. Adding 'social touch' in virtual interaction seems also promising to increase the perceived humanness of virtual agents (Hoppe et al., 2020). Furthermore, an increasing number of observations highlight the similarity between real and virtual worlds in social norms application. For instance, Iachini et al. (2014) observed that the intrusion of virtual agents within the peri-personal space of participants, i.e. the space immediately surrounding our body, created the same feeling of discomfort and avoidance as in real life, as this space is usually reserved for intimate interactions. Thus, virtual meetings with others can feel as realistic as face-to-face meetings and as such facilitate social interactions by recreating the spatio-temporal scaffolding usually lacking in classical CMC.

Similarly to its effect in real life, mimicry appears as a powerful effect to elicit likeability in virtual spaces. For example, Grynszpan et al. (2017) report that gaze following from a virtual avatar was associated with perceived pleasantness, trust and closeness. On the other hand, using a virtual avatar depicting a Palestinian mimicking Israeli participants, Hasler et al. (2014) observed an increasing feeling of closeness and empathetic concern among Israeli participants toward Palestinian avatars. Indeed, virtual agents that use algorithms to automatically mimic players are rated as more persuasive and likeable than those who do not show mimicry (Bailenson & Yee, 2005). More interestingly, these 'digital chameleons' are more efficient than real humans in passing the Turing Test, designed to discriminate artificial intelligence from human beings (Bailenson et al., 2008). Nonetheless, as observed in these experiments, a certain threshold of behavioural convergence should not be exceeded to avoid 'phony' interactions. Despite this potential backlash, digital chameleons offer a promising application for improving the interactions between users and virtual agents introduced in customer services and therapeutic interventions by increasing their humanness and persuasiveness.

Yet, digital chameleons are not the only option explored in virtual reality to recreate embodied social interactions - other technological properties have also been investigated, such as changes in body-ownership - coined as 'Proteus effect'. This ability is achieved by the remarkable plasticity of the mental representation of our body, well-illustrated by the rubber hand illusion, where by the application of a synchronous stimulation, a rubber hand is perceived as the real hand by participants (Moseley et al., 2012; Won et al., 2015). This phenomenon can also occur in virtual reality as illustrated by Hoyet et al. (2016) where participants displayed a greater sense of ownership and agency toward a 6th finger, using the same principles of synchronous stimulation. Far from being restricted to one limb, such phenomena can also take place with faces using the Enfacement Illusion and go up to a full 'body-transfer' in a virtual avatar (Slater et al., 2009). Being embodied in Einstein's body improved cognitive functions of participants, possibly due to a heightened sense of self-esteem, and consequently greater resilience to induced stress, which usually impairs cognitive performance (Banakou et al., 2018). Thus, changing our bodies does not only redefine our physical boundaries but also impact our minds, and by extension, our sense of self including our cognitive biases and social judgments (Maister et al., 2015). Therefore, body-illusion appears to be an interesting solution for improving worker performances, for example, by increasing self-confidence and reducing social anxiety or stereotypical awareness about one's own or others' social categories.

Experimental manipulations to change the perspective and viewpoint of users is starting to be widely used in virtual reality to elicit empathy. For example, studies have studied perpetrators of domestic violence embodied in victim bodies to facilitate perspective-taking (Seinfeld et al., 2018), or humans being embodied in animals or corals to get more sensitized about global warming and involved in nature conservation (Ahn et al., 2016). While we cannot deny that these initiatives are commendable, their effectiveness on a long-term basis needs still to be proven. A longitudinal study conducted by Barbot and Kaufman (2020) observed that virtual reality exposure increased perspective-taking only rather than empathic concern per se. Nevertheless, as perspective-taking is a key ingredient to foster empathy, virtual reality interventions can be an interesting tool in managerial and design processes, to increase the capacity to see the world through another's point of view.

Despite its potential wider usefulness, virtual reality applications remain restricted to experimental purposes or target specific areas such as well-being and gaming industries (Naylor et al., 2020). Several ethical and technical issues need to be addressed and are actually debated among scholars and tech industries. Whilst some enthusiasts celebrate VR as an "empathy machine" (Pozo, 2018), others express deep concerns about its ethics, pointing out a risk of 'dark tourism', where users can "feel good about feeling bad" (Nakamura, 2020). Consequently, it is necessary to call for a "reason-guided" use of virtual reality for empathic purposes (Rueda & Lara, 2020) where three main ethical principles are proposed: (1) the involvement of marginalized groups to prevent stereotypical representations; (2) the implementation of contextual cues to mitigate the lack of social structure; and (3) the implementation of necessary complementary interventions in addition of the sole virtual reality interventions. Moreover, from an ethical point of view, the ability of VR to create a strong sense of presence has generated some concerns about the possibility of getting 'trapped' in virtual worlds without being able to distinguish between fictional and real environments. Facing these concerns, Murray (2020) countered that in spite of the powerful illusion induced by virtual environments, this remains a transient state, which can be easily broken. Additionally, the current concerns regarding the technological ability of VR to reach such a state of conflated real and virtual worlds are far from being achievable given technological limitations, such as cybersickness and eye strain after prolonged exposure in virtual environments. More recent technological developments such as mixed reality are able to combine real and virtual elements in a more naturalistic way, overcoming the current limitations of virtual environments by providing a "seamless" experience of immersion and presence (Billinghurst & Kato, 2002). Therefore, despite technical limitations and ethical considerations that need to be considered, virtual or mixed environments appear promising tools to enhance social interactions and facilitate a sense of togetherness. How, and to what extent, this can be applied effectively to our working lives are questions that still remain unanswered.

CONCLUSION

In this chapter we have seen that the current crisis is impacting our ability to work and be together due to the disappearance of collective spaces and the loss of a sense of belonging to a community. Among those spaces, workplaces need to be considered as specific locations, where social mixing and inter-group interactions usually occur, ensuring the cohesiveness of our inclusive values in civil societies. Well before the present crisis, social interaction experienced in traditional workplaces has already been threatened by the longstanding digitalisation of our societies. A fully remote workforce renders it difficult to translate our capacity to convey non-verbal and social cues to promote bonding and social interaction in CMC. These factors are critical in building a "common ground" and are required to understand each other and work cooperatively.

As discussed in this chapter, interpersonal coordination, occurring at several levels of behavioural and physiological processes, is one of the key components implicated in empathic processing and social interaction, and can be viewed both as a result of pre-existing relational bonds or as a cue to elicit greater social affiliation. While the spatio-temporal mapping, usually taking place during social interaction and required for interpersonal coordination to arise, is threatened by CMC, several decades of research have paved the way for implementable solutions to help us to overcome the current situation. As pointed out in this chapter, media richness, synchronicity and visibility are key factors to nurture the sense of social presence and build an emotional connection among group members, crucial to develop a sense of proximity and shared identity. Virtual spaces where a sense of privacy and proximity is perceived to encourage informal congregations and casual conversations, need to be encouraged to provide "social affordance''.

The advantages of virtual reality in facilitating embodiment, and thus, its capacity to enrich our perceptual processing of social interactions has been highlighted. Nevertheless, the applications of immersive virtual environments are still restricted due to technical limitations and ethical considerations that need to be addressed. Therefore, despite these encouraging advances, the widespread use of classical CMC during the present crisis continues to compromise our ability to maintain togetherness. New technological solutions offering embodied interactions are presented as potential solutions to "fix" the current challenges faced by classical CMC; however, "being together with" is a process requiring "headspace" and time, and our ability to build a "common ground" is challenged in digital spaces where an overwhelming amount of information is exchanged, and time considered as an economic value. The response of organizations to the opportunities presented by these developments remains unclear and is likely to be mixed. While some may embrace new methods of virtual interaction, others are likely to focus on efficiency in communication using more traditional CMC, potentially at the cost of bonding and social interaction and its benefits in terms of well-being of the workforce.

ACKNOWLEDGMENT

This research project is supported by the Doctoral Alliance Training co-funded by the European Union's Horizon 2020 research and innovation programme under the Marie Skłodowska-Curie grant agreement [801604].

REFERENCES

Ahn, S. J., Bostick, J., Ogle, E., Nowak, K. L., McGillicuddy, K. T., & Bailenson, J. N. (2016). Experiencing nature: Embodying animals in immersive virtual environments increases inclusion of nature in self and involvement with nature. *Journal of Computer-Mediated Communication*, *21*(6), 399–419. doi:10.1111/jcc4.12173

Bailenson, J. N., & Yee, N. (2005). Digital chameleons: Automatic assimilation of nonverbal gestures in immersive virtual environments. *Psychological Science*, *16*(10), 814–819. doi:10.1111/j.1467-9280.2005.01619.x PMID:16181445

Bailenson, J. N., Yee, N., Patel, K., & Beall, A. C. (2008). Detecting digital chameleons. *Computers in Human Behavior*, *24*(1), 66–87. doi:10.1016/j.chb.2007.01.015

Balconi, M., Fronda, G., & Vanutelli, M. E. (2020). When gratitude and cooperation between friends affect inter-brain connectivity for EEG. *BMC Neuroscience*, *21*(1), 1–12. doi:10.118612868-020-00563-7 PMID:32264825

Banakou, D., Kishore, S., & Slater, M. (2018). Virtually being einstein results in an improvement in cognitive task performance and a decrease in age bias. *Frontiers in Psychology*, *9*, 917. doi:10.3389/fpsyg.2018.00917 PMID:29942270

Barbot, B., & Kaufman, J. C. (2020). What makes immersive virtual reality the ultimate empathy machine? Discerning the underlying mechanisms of change. *Computers in Human Behavior*, *111*, 106431. doi:10.1016/j.chb.2020.106431

Barsade, S. G., Coutifaris, C. G., & Pillemer, J. (2018). Emotional contagion in organizational life. *Research in Organizational Behavior*, *38*, 137–151. doi:10.1016/j.riob.2018.11.005

Baumeister, R. F., & Leary, M. R. (1995). The need to belong: Desire for interpersonal attachments as a fundamental human motivation. *Psychological Bulletin*, *117*(3), 497–529. doi:10.1037/0033-2909.117.3.497 PMID:7777651

Bayram, A. B., & Ta, V. P. (2019). Diplomatic chameleons: Language style matching and agreement in international diplomatic negotiations. *Negotiation and Conflict Management Research, 12*(1), 23–40. doi:10.1111/ncmr.12142

Bernieri, F. J., & Rosenthal, R. (1991). *Interpersonal coordination: Behavior matching and interactional synchrony*. Academic Press.

Bowlby, J. (1969). *Attachment and loss* (Vol. 3). Random House.

Bowlby, J. (1973). Attachment and loss: Volume II: Separation, anxiety and anger. London: The Hogarth Press and the Institute of Psycho-Analysis.

Chang-Arana, Á. M., Piispanen, M., Himberg, T., Surma-aho, A., Alho, J., Sams, M., & Hölttä-Otto, K. (2020). Empathic accuracy in design: Exploring design outcomes through empathic performance and physiology. *Design Science, 6*.

Cirelli, L. K., Einarson, K. M., & Trainor, L. J. (2014). Interpersonal synchrony increases prosocial behavior in infants. *Developmental Science, 17*(6), 1003–1011. doi:10.1111/desc.12193 PMID:25513669

Clark, M. A., Robertson, M. M., & Young, S. (2019). "I feel your pain": A critical review of organizational research on empathy. *Journal of Organizational Behavior, 40*(2), 166–192. doi:10.1002/job.2348

Coutinho, J., Oliveira-Silva, P., Fernandes, E., Gonçalves, O. F., Correia, D., Perrone Mc-Govern, K., & Tschacher, W. (2019). Psychophysiological synchrony during verbal interaction in romantic relationships. *Family Process, 58*(3), 716–733. doi:10.1111/famp.12371 PMID:29888517

Damasio, A. R. (2006). *Descartes' error*. Random House.

Darwall, S. (2011). Being with. *The Southern Journal of Philosophy, 49*, 4–24. doi:10.1111/j.2041-6962.2011.00054.x

Decety, J. (2010). The neurodevelopment of empathy in humans. *Developmental Neuroscience, 32*(4), 257–267. doi:10.1159/000317771 PMID:20805682

Decety, J., & Meltzoff, A. N. (2011). Empathy, imitation, and the social brain. *Empathy: Philosophical and psychological perspectives*, 58-81.

Del Vicario, M., Bessi, A., Zollo, F., Petroni, F., Scala, A., Caldarelli, G., Stanley, H. E., & Quattrociocchi, W. (2016). The spreading of misinformation online. *Proceedings of the National Academy of Sciences of the United States of America, 113*(3), 554–559. doi:10.1073/pnas.1517441113 PMID:26729863

Duan, H., Yang, T., Wang, X., Kan, Y., Zhao, H., Li, Y., & Hu, W. (2020). Is the creativity of lovers better? A behavioral and functional near-infrared spectroscopy hyperscanning study. *Current Psychology (New Brunswick, N.J.)*, 1–14. doi:10.100712144-020-01093-5

Dubrovsky, V. J., Kiesler, S., & Sethna, B. N. (1991). The equalization phenomenon: Status effects in computer-mediated and face-to-face decision-making groups. *Human-Computer Interaction, 6*(2), 119–146. doi:10.120715327051hci0602_2

Dumas, G. (2011). Towards a two-body neuroscience. *Communicative & Integrative Biology, 4*(3), 349–352. doi:10.4161/cib.4.3.15110 PMID:21980578

Durkheim, É. (1912). *Les formes élémentaires de la vie religieuse: le système totémique en Australie* (Vol. 4). Alcan.

Durlach, N., & Slater, M. (2000). Presence in shared virtual environments and virtual togetherness. *Presence (Cambridge, Mass.), 9*(2), 214–217. doi:10.1162/105474600566736

Estlund, C. (2003). *Working together: How workplace bonds strengthen a diverse democracy*. Oxford University Press.

Farley, H., & Dahlgreen, W. (2020, November 17). *Working from home could lead to more prejudice, report warns*. BBC News. https://www.bbc.co.uk/news/uk-54937713

Fayard, A. L., & Weeks, J. (2007). Photocopiers and water-coolers: The affordances of informal interaction. *Organization Studies, 28*(5), 605–634. doi:10.1177/0170840606068310

Feldman, R. (2007). Parent–infant synchrony and the construction of shared timing; physiological precursors, developmental outcomes, and risk conditions. *Journal of Child Psychology and Psychiatry, and Allied Disciplines, 48*(3-4), 329–354. doi:10.1111/j.1469-7610.2006.01701.x PMID:17355401

Fotopoulou, A., & Tsakiris, M. (2017). Mentalizing homeostasis: The social origins of interoceptive inference. *Neuro-psychoanalysis, 19*(1), 3–28. doi:10.1080/15294145.2017.1294031

Frith, U., & Happé, F. (1999). Theory of mind and self-consciousness: What is it like to be autistic? *Mind & Language, 14*(1), 1–22. doi:10.1111/1468-0017.00100

Furman, W., & Buhrmester, D. (2009). Methods and measures: The network of relationships inventory: Behavioral systems version. *International Journal of Behavioral Development, 33*, 470–478.

Galbusera, L., Finn, M. T., Tschacher, W., & Kyselo, M. (2019). Interpersonal synchrony feels good but impedes self-regulation of affect. *Scientific Reports, 9*(1), 1–12. doi:10.103841598-019-50960-0 PMID:31604966

Ganczarek, J., Hünefeldt, T., & Belardinelli, M. O. (2018). From "Einfühlung" to empathy: exploring the relationship between aesthetic and interpersonal experience. In *The Effect of Media Richness on Transactive Memory System in Virtual Teams: the Moderating Role of Team Identity*. Academic Press.

Geller, S. (2020). Cultivating online therapeutic presence: Strengthening therapeutic relationships in teletherapy sessions. *Counselling Psychology Quarterly*, 1–17. doi:10.1080/09515070.2020.1787348

Gkorezis, P., Panagiotou, M., & Theodorou, M. (2016). Workplace ostracism and employee silence in nursing: The mediating role of organizational identification. *Journal of Advanced Nursing, 72*(10), 2381–2388. doi:10.1111/jan.12992 PMID:27113971

Grynszpan, O., Martin, J. C., & Fossati, P. (2017). Gaze leading is associated with liking. *Acta Psychologica, 173*, 66–72. doi:10.1016/j.actpsy.2016.12.006 PMID:28013039

Gunter, B. G., & van der Hoeven, R. (2004). The social dimension of globalization: A review of the literature. *International Labour Review, 143*(1-2). Advance online publication. doi:10.1111/j.1564-913X.2004.tb00545.x

Haans, A., & IJsselsteijn, W. A. (2009). The virtual Midas touch: Helping behavior after a mediated social touch. *IEEE Transactions on Haptics*, *2*(3), 136–140. doi:10.1109/TOH.2009.20 PMID:27788077

Hakanen, J. J., & Bakker, A. B. (2017). Born and bred to burn out: A life-course view and reflections on job burnout. *Journal of Occupational Health Psychology*, *22*(3), 354–364. doi:10.1037/ocp0000053 PMID:27732007

Hale, J., & Hamilton, A. F. D. C. (2016). Cognitive mechanisms for responding to mimicry from others. *Neuroscience and Biobehavioral Reviews*, *63*, 106–123. doi:10.1016/j.neubiorev.2016.02.006 PMID:26877104

Hardill, I., & Green, A. (2003). Remote working—Altering the spatial contours of work and home in the new economy. *New Technology, Work and Employment*, *18*(3), 212–222. doi:10.1111/1468-005X.00122

Hasler, B. S., Hirschberger, G., Shani-Sherman, T., & Friedman, D. A. (2014). Virtual peacemakers: Mimicry increases empathy in simulated contact with virtual outgroup members. *Cyberpsychology, Behavior, and Social Networking*, *17*(12), 766–771. doi:10.1089/cyber.2014.0213 PMID:25343577

Hatfield, E., Cacioppo, J. T., & Rapson, R. L. (1993). Emotional contagion. *Current Directions in Psychological Science*, *2*(3), 96–100. doi:10.1111/1467-8721.ep10770953

He, Y., Kraus, K., & Preece, J. (2013, July). You are not alone online: a case study of a long distance romantic relationship online community. In *International Conference on Online Communities and Social Computing* (pp. 23-32). Springer. 10.1007/978-3-642-39371-6_3

Heym, N., Kibowski, F., Bloxsom, C. A., Blanchard, A., Harper, A., Wallace, L., ... Sumich, A. (2020). The Dark Empath: Characterising dark traits in the presence of empathy. *Personality and Individual Differences*, 110172.

Hiltz, S. R., Johnson, K., & Turoff, M. (1986). Experiments in group decision making communication process and outcome in face-to-face versus computerized conferences. *Human Communication Research*, *13*(2), 225–252. doi:10.1111/j.1468-2958.1986.tb00104.x

Hoppe, M., Rossmy, B., Neumann, D. P., Streuber, S., Schmidt, A., & Machulla, T. K. (2020, April). A Human Touch: Social Touch Increases the Perceived Human-likeness of Agents in Virtual Reality. In *Proceedings of the 2020 CHI Conference on Human Factors in Computing Systems* (pp. 1-11). 10.1145/3313831.3376719

Hoyet, L., Argelaguet, F., Nicole, C., & Lécuyer, A. (2016). "Wow! i have six Fingers!": Would You accept structural changes of Your hand in Vr? *Frontiers in Robotics and AI*, *3*, 27. doi:10.3389/frobt.2016.00027

Humphrey, R. H., Burch, G. F., & Adams, L. L. (2016). The benefits of merging leadership research and emotions research. *Frontiers in Psychology*, *7*, 1022. doi:10.3389/fpsyg.2016.01022 PMID:27458415

Iachini, T., Coello, Y., Frassinetti, F., & Ruggiero, G. (2014). Body space in social interactions: A comparison of reaching and comfort distance in immersive virtual reality. *PLoS One*, *9*(11), e111511. doi:10.1371/journal.pone.0111511 PMID:25405344

Jelil Ladebo, O., Jacob Olaoye, O., & Oyekale Adamu, C. (2008). Extension personnel's self-esteem and workplace relationships: Implications for job satisfaction and affective organizational commitment foci. *Journal of Agricultural Education and Extension*, *14*(3), 249–263. doi:10.1080/13892240802207692

Jospe, K., Genzer, S., Selle, N. K., Ong, D., Zaki, J., & Perry, A. (2020). The contribution of linguistic and visual cues to physiological synchrony and empathic accuracy. *Cortex*, *132*, 296–308. doi:10.1016/j.cortex.2020.09.001 PMID:33010739

Kendon, A. (1970). Movement coordination in social interaction: Some examples described. *Acta Psychologica*, *32*, 101–125. doi:10.1016/0001-6918(70)90094-6 PMID:5444439

Kim, J., Kim, H., Tay, B. K., Muniyandi, M., Srinivasan, M. A., Jordan, J., Mortensen, J., Oliveira, M., & Slater, M. (2004). Transatlantic touch: A study of haptic collaboration over long distance. *Presence (Cambridge, Mass.)*, *13*(3), 328–337. doi:10.1162/1054746041422370

Kinreich, S., Djalovski, A., Kraus, L., Louzoun, Y., & Feldman, R. (2017). Brain-to-brain synchrony during naturalistic social interactions. *Scientific Reports*, *7*(1), 17060. doi:10.103841598-017-17339-5 PMID:29213107

Kniffin, K. M., Wansink, B., Devine, C. M., & Sobal, J. (2015). Eating together at the firehouse: How workplace commensality relates to the performance of firefighters. *Human Performance*, *28*(4), 281–306. doi:10.1080/08959285.2015.1021049 PMID:27226698

Koehne, S., Hatri, A., Cacioppo, J. T., & Dziobek, I. (2016). Perceived interpersonal synchrony increases empathy: Insights from autism spectrum disorder. *Cognition*, *146*, 8–15. doi:10.1016/j.cognition.2015.09.007 PMID:26398860

Kraut, R. E., Fussell, S. R., Brennan, S. E., & Siegel, J. (2002). Understanding effects of proximity on collaboration: Implications for technologies to support remote collaborative work. *Distributed Work*, 137-162.

LaFrance, M. (1979). Nonverbal synchrony and rapport: Analysis by the cross-lag panel technique. *Social Psychology Quarterly*, *42*(1), 66–70. doi:10.2307/3033875

Lakens, D. (2010). Movement synchrony and perceived entitativity. *Journal of Experimental Social Psychology*, *46*(5), 701–708. doi:10.1016/j.jesp.2010.03.015

Lakin, J. L., Jefferis, V. E., Cheng, C. M., & Chartrand, T. L. (2003). The chameleon effect as social glue: Evidence for the evolutionary significance of nonconscious mimicry. *Journal of Nonverbal Behavior*, *27*(3), 145–162. doi:10.1023/A:1025389814290

Le Bon, G. (1896). *Psychologie des foules*. F. Alcan.

Leary, M. R. (1999). Making sense of self-esteem. *Current Directions in Psychological Science*, *8*(1), 32–35. doi:10.1111/1467-8721.00008

Lecchi, T., da Silva, K., Giommi, F., & Leong, V. (2019). *Using dual-EEG to explore therapist client interpersonal neural synchrony*. Academic Press.

Maddux, W. W., Mullen, E., & Galinsky, A. D. (2008). Chameleons bake bigger pies and take bigger pieces: Strategic behavioral mimicry facilitates negotiation outcomes. *Journal of Experimental Social Psychology*, *44*(2), 461–468. doi:10.1016/j.jesp.2007.02.003

Maister, L., Slater, M., Sanchez-Vives, M. V., & Tsakiris, M. (2015). Changing bodies changes minds: Owning another body affects social cognition. *Trends in Cognitive Sciences*, *19*(1), 6–12. doi:10.1016/j.tics.2014.11.001 PMID:25524273

Matheson, K., & Zanna, M. P. (1988). The impact of computer-mediated communication on self-awareness. *Computers in Human Behavior*, *4*(3), 221–233. doi:10.1016/0747-5632(88)90015-5

Mohamed, Z. N. J. M. M. L., Newton, J. M., & McKenna, L. (2014). Belongingness in the workplace: A study of Malaysian nurses' experiences. *International Nursing Review*, *61*(1), 124–130. doi:10.1111/inr.12078 PMID:24512262

Moseley, G. L., Gallace, A., & Spence, C. (2012). Bodily illusions in health and disease: Physiological and clinical perspectives and the concept of a cortical 'body matrix'. *Neuroscience and Biobehavioral Reviews*, *36*(1), 34–46. doi:10.1016/j.neubiorev.2011.03.013 PMID:21477616

Mull, A. (2020, October). Generation Work-From-Home May Never Recover. *The Atlantic*. https://www.theatlantic.com/magazine/archive/2020/10/career-costs-working-from-home/615472/

Mull, A. (2021, January 21). The Pandemic Has Erased Entire Categories of Friendship. *The Atlantic*. https://www.theatlantic.com/health/archive/2021/01/pandemic-goodbye-casual-friends/617839/

Murray, J. H. (2020). Virtual/reality: How to tell the difference. *Journal of Visual Culture*, *19*(1), 11–27. doi:10.1177/1470412920906253

Nakamura, L. (2020). Feeling good about feeling bad: Virtuous virtual reality and the automation of racial empathy. *Journal of Visual Culture*, *19*(1), 47–64. doi:10.1177/1470412920906259

Naylor, M., Ridout, B., & Campbell, A. (2020). A Scoping Review Identifying the Need for Quality Research on the Use of Virtual Reality in Workplace Settings for Stress Management. *Cyberpsychology, Behavior, and Social Networking*, *23*(8), 506–518. doi:10.1089/cyber.2019.0287 PMID:32486836

Nguyen, T., Schleihauf, H., Kayhan, E., Matthes, D., Vrtička, P., & Hoehl, S. (2020). Neural synchrony in mother-child conversation: Exploring the role of conversation patterns. *Social Cognitive and Affective Neuroscience*. PMID:32591781

Novembre, G., Mitsopoulos, Z., & Keller, P. E. (2019). Empathic perspective taking promotes interpersonal coordination through music. *Scientific Reports*, *9*(1), 1–12. doi:10.103841598-019-48556-9 PMID:31439866

Nowland, R., Necka, E. A., & Cacioppo, J. T. (2018). Loneliness and social internet use: Pathways to reconnection in a digital world? *Perspectives on Psychological Science*, *13*(1), 70–87. doi:10.1177/1745691617713052 PMID:28937910

O'Leary, M. B., Wilson, J. M., & Metiu, A. (2012). *Beyond being there: The symbolic role of communication and identification in the emergence of perceived proximity in geographically dispersed work.* Academic Press.

O'Reilly, J., & Robinson, S. L. (2009, August). The negative impact of ostracism on thwarted belongingness and workplace contributions. In Academy of management proceedings (Vol. 2009, No. 1, pp. 1-7). Briarcliff Manor, NY: Academy of Management. doi:10.5465/ambpp.2009.44243707

Okazaki, S., Hirotani, M., Koike, T., Bosch-Bayard, J., Takahashi, H. K., Hashiguchi, M., & Sadato, N. (2015). Unintentional interpersonal synchronization represented as a reciprocal visuo-postural feedback system: A multivariate autoregressive modeling approach. *PLoS One*, *10*(9), e0137126. doi:10.1371/journal.pone.0137126 PMID:26398768

Pacherie, E. (2014). How does it feel to act together? *Phenomenology and the Cognitive Sciences*, *13*(1), 25–46. doi:10.100711097-013-9329-8

Palmieri, A., Kleinbub, J. R., Calvo, V., Benelli, E., Messina, I., Sambin, M., & Voci, A. (2018). Attachment-security prime effect on skin-conductance synchronization in psychotherapists: An empirical study. *Journal of Counseling Psychology*, *65*(4), 490–499. doi:10.1037/cou0000273 PMID:29494169

Parker, P. A., & Kulik, J. A. (1995). Burnout, self-and supervisor-rated job performance, and absenteeism among nurses. *Journal of Behavioral Medicine*, *18*(6), 581–599. doi:10.1007/BF01857897 PMID:8749987

Pérez, A., Dumas, G., Karadag, M., & Duñabeitia, J. A. (2019). Differential brain-to-brain entrainment while speaking and listening in native and foreign languages. *Cortex*, *111*, 303–315. doi:10.1016/j.cortex.2018.11.026 PMID:30598230

Postmes, T., Spears, R., & Lea, M. (1998). Breaching or building social boundaries? SIDE-effects of computer-mediated communication. *Communication Research*, *25*(6), 689–715. doi:10.1177/009365098025006006

Pozo, T. (2018). Queer games after empathy: Feminism and haptic game design aesthetics from consent to cuteness to the radically soft. *Game Studies, 18*(3).

Preece, J. (1999). Empathy online. *Virtual Reality (Waltham Cross)*, *4*(1), 74–84. doi:10.1007/BF01434996

Preissmann, D., Charbonnier, C., Chagué, S., Antonietti, J. P., Llobera, J., Ansermet, F., & Magistretti, P. J. (2016). A motion capture study to measure the feeling of synchrony in romantic couples and in professional musicians. *Frontiers in Psychology*, *7*, 1673. doi:10.3389/fpsyg.2016.01673 PMID:27833580

Ramseyer, F., & Tschacher, W. (2011). Nonverbal synchrony in psychotherapy: Coordinated body movement reflects relationship quality and outcome. *Journal of Consulting and Clinical Psychology*, *79*(3), 284–295. doi:10.1037/a0023419 PMID:21639608

Rhoads, M. (2010). Face-to-face and computer-mediated communication: What does theory tell us and what have we learned so far? *Journal of Planning Literature*, *25*(2), 111–122. doi:10.1177/0885412210382984

Riva, G., & Wiederhold, B. K. (2020). *How Cyberpsychology and Virtual Reality Can Help Us to Overcome the Psychological Burden of Coronavirus*. Academic Press.

Riva, G., Wiederhold, B. K., & Mantovani, F. (2021). Surviving COVID-19: The Neuroscience of Smart Working and Distance Learning. *Cyberpsychology, Behavior, and Social Networking*, *24*(2), 79–85. doi:10.1089/cyber.2021.0009 PMID:33577414

Rueda, J., & Lara, F. (2020). Virtual Reality and Empathy Enhancement: Ethical Aspects. *Frontiers in Robotics and AI*, *7*, 160. doi:10.3389/frobt.2020.506984 PMID:33501297

Schilbach, L., Timmermans, B., Reddy, V., Costall, A., Bente, G., Schlicht, T., & Vogeley, K. (2013). Toward a second-person neuroscience 1. *Behavioral and Brain Sciences*, *36*(4), 393–414. doi:10.1017/S0140525X12000660 PMID:23883742

Seinfeld, S., Arroyo-Palacios, J., Iruretagoyena, G., Hortensius, R., Zapata, L. E., Borland, D., de Gelder, B., Slater, M., & Sanchez-Vives, M. V. (2018). Offenders become the victim in virtual reality: Impact of changing perspective in domestic violence. *Scientific Reports*, *8*(1), 2692. doi:10.103841598-018-19987-7 PMID:29426819

Semin, G. R., & De Groot, J. H. (2013). The chemical bases of human sociality. *Trends in Cognitive Sciences*, *17*(9), 427–429. doi:10.1016/j.tics.2013.05.008 PMID:23796879

Short, J., Williams, E., & Christie, B. (1976). *The social psychology of telecommunications*. John Wiley & Sons.

Slater, M. (2009). Place illusion and plausibility can lead to realistic behaviour in immersive virtual environments. *Philosophical Transactions of the Royal Society of London. Series B, Biological Sciences*, *364*(1535), 3549–3557. doi:10.1098/rstb.2009.0138 PMID:19884149

Slater, M., Pérez Marcos, D., Ehrsson, H., & Sanchez-Vives, M. V. (2009). Inducing illusory ownership of a virtual body. *Frontiers in Neuroscience*, *3*(2), 29. doi:10.3389/neuro.01.029.2009 PMID:20011144

SonicRim, L. S. (2001). Collective creativity. *Design*, *6*(3), 1–6.

Spielmann, S. S., MacDonald, G., & Tackett, J. L. (2012). Social threat, social reward, and regulation of investment in romantic relationships. *Personal Relationships*, *19*(4), 601–622. doi:10.1111/j.1475-6811.2011.01377.x

Tait, A. (2020, September 9). You met them on Zoom, now they're in the office freaking everyone out. *Wired*. https://www.wired.co.uk/article/meeting-colleagues-zoom-second-first-impressions

Tarr, B., Launay, J., & Dunbar, R. I. (2014). Music and social bonding:"self-other" merging and neurohormonal mechanisms. *Frontiers in Psychology*, *5*, 1096. doi:10.3389/fpsyg.2014.01096 PMID:25324805

Trevarthen, C. (1999). Musicality and the intrinsic motive pulse: Evidence from human psychobiology and infant communication. *Musicae Scientiae*, *3*(1, suppl), 155–215. doi:10.1177/10298649000030S109

Tronick, E. Z., Bruschweiler-Stern, N., Harrison, A. M., Lyons-Ruth, K., Morgan, A. C., Nahum, J. P., Sander, L., & Stern, D. N. (1998). Dyadically expanded states of consciousness and the process of therapeutic change. *Infant Mental Health Journal: Official Publication of The World Association for Infant Mental Health*, *19*(3), 290–299. doi:10.1002/(SICI)1097-0355(199823)19:3<290::AID-IMHJ4>3.0.CO;2-Q

Valenduc, G., & Vendramin, P. (2017). Digitalisation, between disruption and evolution. *Transfer: European Review of Labour and Research*, *23*(2), 121–134. doi:10.1177/1024258917701379

Valentine, K. A., Li, N. P., Meltzer, A. L., & Tsai, M. H. (2020). Mate preferences for warmth-trustworthiness predict romantic attraction in the early stages of mate selection and satisfaction in ongoing relationships. *Personality and Social Psychology Bulletin*, *46*(2), 298–311. doi:10.1177/0146167219855048 PMID:31184259

van Kleef, G. A., Heerdink, M. W., & Homan, A. C. (2017). Emotional influence in groups: The dynamic nexus of affect, cognition, and behavior. *Current Opinion in Psychology*, *17*, 156–161. doi:10.1016/j.copsyc.2017.07.017 PMID:28950964

Vicaria, I. M., & Dickens, L. (2016). Meta-analyses of the intra-and interpersonal outcomes of interpersonal coordination. *Journal of Nonverbal Behavior*, *40*(4), 335–361. doi:10.100710919-016-0238-8

Vink, R., Wijnants, M. L., Cillessen, A. H., & Bosman, A. M. (2017). *Cooperative learning and interpersonal synchrony*. Academic Press.

Von Scheve, C., & Ismer, S. (2013). Towards a theory of collective emotions. *Emotion Review*, *5*(4), 406–413. doi:10.1177/1754073913484170

Walther, J. B. (1996). Computer-mediated communication: Impersonal, interpersonal, and hyperpersonal interaction. *Communication Research*, *23*(1), 3–43. doi:10.1177/009365096023001001

Wegner, D. M. (1987). Transactive memory: A contemporary analysis of the group mind. In *Theories of group behavior* (pp. 185–208). Springer. doi:10.1007/978-1-4612-4634-3_9

Won, A. S., Bailenson, J. N., & Lanier, J. (2015). Homuncular flexibility: the human ability to inhabit nonhuman avatars. *Emerging Trends in the Social and Behavioral Sciences: An Interdisciplinary, Searchable, and Linkable Resource*, 1-16.

Wu, D. W. L., Chapman, C. S., Walker, E., Bischof, W. F., & Kingstone, A. (2013). Isolating the perceptual from the social: Tapping in shared space results in improved synchrony. *Journal of Experimental Psychology. Human Perception and Performance*, *39*(5), 1218–1223. doi:10.1037/a0033233 PMID:23750971

Zhang, Y., Meng, T., Hou, Y., Pan, Y., & Hu, Y. (2018). Interpersonal brain synchronization associated with working alliance during psychological counseling. *Psychiatry Research: Neuroimaging*, *282*, 103–109. doi:10.1016/j.pscychresns.2018.09.007 PMID:30292535

Zilcha-Mano, S., Shamay-Tsoory, S., Dolev-Amit, T., Zagoory-Sharon, O., & Feldman, R. (2020). Oxytocin as a biomarker of the formation of therapeutic alliance in psychotherapy and counseling psychology. *Journal of Counseling Psychology*, *67*(4), 523–535. doi:10.1037/cou0000386 PMID:32614232

Chapter 15
Building and Maintaining Trust in Virtual Teams

Colin Hughes
Technological University Dublin, Ireland

Mark N. K. Saunders
University of Birmingham, UK

ABSTRACT

The COVID-19 pandemic has led to widespread adoption of virtual teams (VTs), the prevalence of which had already been increasing steadily. However, studies show that VTs often fail to meet their potential, highlighting the centrality of trust to their success. While trust is important at the team member level and the focus of much of the extant research, it also underpins effective virtual leadership. Following a review of VT and trust literatures, research conducted within three global technology companies across Europe, Middle East, and Africa is used to provide insights into trust development in virtual leader-member dyads. These highlight leaders' behaviours that can both demonstrate their own trustworthiness to VT members and their trust of VT members. These behaviours are integrated into a framework for enabling high trust VT leadership which emphasises member-centricity.

INTRODUCTION

The advent of Covid-19 forced organizations and employees to adopt remote working and, for many, to work in virtual teams (VTs). This transition was facilitated by the experience of VTs developed over several decades and a large volume of research on their effectiveness. Within this research, scholars identified trust as an essential ingredient of VT success (Breuer et al., 2016; Romeike et al., 2016), research being focused predominantly at the team member level (Breuer et al., 2020; Cheng et al., 2016; Jarvenpaa & Leidner, 1999).

While trust between team members is important, VT leaders have an important role in creating, reinforcing, and maintaining such trust. As such, there is also a need to build trust between leaders and individual team members (Hacker et al., 2019). The importance of this has been highlighted in the trust

DOI: 10.4018/978-1-7998-6754-8.ch015

literature (Ferris et al., 2009; Jawahar et al., 2019; Knoll & Gill, 2011; Sue-Chan et al., 2012). However, studies have generally treated leader-member trust as unidirectional, focusing on members' trust in leaders, rather than treating trust as mutual or reciprocal (Jawahar et al., 2019; Nienaber et al., 2015). This is problematic as research suggests that trust levels between dyad members are not always mutual (Korsgaard et al., 2015) and the benefits of trust are only realized when the leader and member trust each other (De Jong & Dirks, 2012). In particular, there is limited research regarding how VT leaders effectively develop and maintain relationships with individual members (Liao, 2017); and consequentially we know little of the antecedents to trust development in virtual leader-member dyads. Such knowledge is important as trust may form differently in a virtual environment (Coppola et al., 2004), and by utilizing theories developed for the face-to-face context researchers risk ignoring variables that are particular to the virtual context (Breuer et al., 2020). This chapter therefore considers how leaders demonstrate both their own trustworthiness *to* members and their trust *of* members within virtual leader-member dyads, presenting findings from empirical field research conducted by the first author within three global technology companies.

The chapter commences with a consideration of the defining features of VTs and their growth within organizations. It then discusses both the benefits and challenges associated with VTs. Given its centrality to VT leadership effectiveness, trust is then defined, along with the factors which influence trust development and the various levels of trust possible within a dyadic relationship. Next the chapter focuses on the specific role of trust in VT leader-member dyads before introducing the empirical research study which reveals those behaviours which signal a leader's own trustworthiness to VT members and their trust of these members. Drawing on this, a framework for enabling high trust VT leadership is outlined and discussed highlighting the practical implications for organizations in a post-Covid world.

BACKGROUND

Virtual Teams: Form, Growth and Functioning

VTs have many forms. They can be fully virtual, where members never meet (Kimble, 2011), or semi-virtual/hybrid in nature, encompassing both virtual and co-located members (Webster & Wong, 2008). VTs may be established on a temporary basis, to accomplish a specific task or project, or on a more permanent basis, focussing on routine tasks (Alsharo et al., 2017). VT members may be remote workers, working from home or away from the office either some or all of the time, or they may work from offices in different locations. As such, members of virtual teams can be separated geographically, temporally and culturally (DeRosa et al., 2004; Hertel et al., 2005; Jarvenpaa & Leidner, 1999; Piccoli & Ives, 2003).

The one element common to most definitions is that VT members communicate primarily via technology, rather than in person (Breuer et al., 2020). However, given the increased use of technology by co-located teams, almost all teams can be considered at least partially virtual (Liao, 2017). Consequently, researchers have begun to consider all forms of team along a continuum of virtuality rather than contrasting virtual with co-located teams (Martins et al., 2004; Schaubroeck & Yu, 2017; Zigurs, 2003). VTs therefore encompass a wide variety of team types with labels such as transnational teams (Shapiro et al., 2002), global virtual teams (Kayworth & Leidner, 2000), computer-mediated teams (Wilson et al., 2006) and e-teams (Zaccaro & Bader, 2003). Given this, VTs are defined in this chapter as: teams whose members might be culturally, temporarily and/or geographically dispersed and who collaborate primarily via information and communication technologies in order to accomplish specific goals.

The growth of VTs prior to Covid-19 has been well documented. Initially adopted in the 1990s for short-term projects, they quickly became more mainstream. In 2009, 78% of European executives reported using VTs in their organization (Witchalls, 2009) and by 2014 90% of executives worldwide confirmed the use of VTs in their organizations, prompting the claim that VTs were the new normal and the team framework of the digital age (Dennis et al., 2014). Although it is difficult to determine the exact prevalence of VTs across specific organizations and in different countries prior to Covid-19, it is clear that usage rates were already high and that VTs were already considered commonplace (Hacker et al., 2019; Maes & Weldy, 2018; RW3 Culture Wizard, 2018).

Such growth is unsurprising given the range of benefits cited in the literature. Use of VTs allows organizations to recruit talented employees (Mysirlaki & Paraskeva, 2019) and to bring together teams with greater levels of diversity and experience (Greenberg et al., 2007; Hunsaker & Hunsaker, 2008 Kirkman et al., 2002) to work on problems and identify opportunities (Schaubroeck & Yu, 2017). VTs can be rapidly formed and disbanded (DeRosa et al., 2004), allowing organizations the flexibility to respond quickly to competition (Bell & Kozlowski, 2002). They also enable organizations to maintain a global presence (Monalisa et al., 2008) and provide enhanced levels of customer service and a closer connection to suppliers and customers (Hertel et al., 2005). Furthermore, the use of VTs can help reduce office expenses (Kayworth & Leidner, 2000), travel time and related costs (DeRosa et al., 2004; Mysirlaki & Paraskeva, 2019). From an employee perspective virtual working can reduce commuting time, allow for greater focus (EY, 2020) and better work-life balance (Ruiller et al., 2019); these benefits can in turn translate into greater job satisfaction, lower absenteeism and higher employee retention (Pattnaik & Jena, in press).

However, not all VTs live up to such expectations (Greenberg et al., 2007; Savolainen, 2014). Many face challenges associated with differences in geography, time zones, organizational and national cultures, language, work practices and technology (Dube & Robey, 2008; Ross, 2006). As a team becomes more virtual, greater geographical and temporal dispersion increases complexity, making effective functioning more difficult (Zigurs, 2003) with potential for isolation and disconnection from peers and supervisors (Ruiller et al., 2019). Workload and commitment issues associated with social loafing and absenteeism can be amplified (Hertel et al., 2005) and, where members are part of multiple teams, this can lead to role overload, misunderstanding and conflict (Jarvenpaa & Leidner, 1999; O'Hara et al., 1994). Technology-mediated interaction can exacerbate communication issues (Schaubroeck & Yu, 2017) hindering group cohesion, satisfaction (Warkentin et al., 1997) and knowledge sharing (Dube & Robey, 2008). Moreover, members may feel obligated to be connected always, negatively impacting work-life balance and damaging trust (Hacker et al., 2019).

While such issues have potential to reduce the advantages of VTs (Schaubroeck & Yu, 2017), researchers have identified trust as a possible solution. Regarded as an essential ingredient of VT success (Daim et al., 2012; Kanawattanachai & Yoo, 2002; Paul & McDaniel, 2004; Zaccaro & Bader, 2003), trust has become one of the most studied aspects in the VT literature (Gilson et al., 2015). It has been found to positively impact upon knowledge sharing and collaboration (Alsharo et al., 2017; Paul & McDaniel, 2004), team dynamics, proactiveness, optimism, frequency of communication and feedback, and task output (Jarvenpaa et al., 1998). A meta-analysis conducted by Breuer et al. (2016) found team trust to be positively related to team effectiveness, team satisfaction, team cohesion and team commitment. In other words, trust is the glue bonding physically isolated individuals together (Wilson et al. 2006), creating an emotional link which connects team members (Lipnack & Stamps, 1997) and helps prevent physical distance from creating a psychological distance (O'Hara et al., 1994).

Exploring Trust

Trust is a complex and multidimensional phenomenon (Lewis & Weigert, 1985), with multiple meanings (McKnight & Chervany, 2001), having been studied within a range of disciplinary lenses and filters such as psychology (e.g. Rotter, 1967), economics (e.g. Williamson, 1993), philosophy (e.g. Hosmer, 1995), sociology (e.g. Luhmann, 1979) and political science (e.g. Barber, 1983). Despite these differences, common characteristics can be identified. These comprise the willingness of one person (the trustor) to be vulnerable to another whom they rely on (the trustee) based on positive expectations of them, where a risk is present (Mayer et al., 1995; Rousseau et al., 1998).

Such trust decisions are shaped by a range of latent and overt influences (Dietz et al., 2010), being generated on the basis of good reasons and previous experiences, a trustor's decision being strongly influenced by their own propensity to trust along with their perception of the trustee's trustworthiness (Lewis & Weigert, 1985). Propensity to trust is therefore a characteristic of the trustor, and trustworthiness a quality of the trustee (Dietz & den Hartog, 2006). Mayer et al. (1995) summarise these trustee qualities in their integrative model of trust development in organizational settings as the components: ability, benevolence and integrity. Ability refers to the skills, competencies, and characteristics that have influence in the domain of interest (Knoll & Gill, 2011). For example, a potential trustee who has excellent communication skills is likely to be trusted to deliver an important sales presentation, even if their analytical skills are more limited. Benevolence refers to benign motives, kindness towards the trustee and a genuine concern for their welfare, often suggesting some form of attachment (Dietz & den Hartog, 2006). In contrast, integrity is a multifaceted factor which relates to a trustee's adherence to a set of principles which the trustor deems acceptable (Mayer et al., 1995) along with their behaviours and actions matching their words, referred to as their behavioural integrity (Whitener et al., 1998). All three components may be potentially significant as a trustor may decide not to trust if she or he considers any of the qualities both important and lacking in the trustee (Dietz & den Hartog, 2006). Alternatively, the trustor may overlook one component, if the trustee excels in another that is more important to the trustor; trustworthiness being context specific (Nooteboom, 2002).

Research suggests that different components of trustworthiness may be more or less important in different relationships. In their meta-analysis of trust studies Colquitt et al. (2007) found integrity to be the most important basis of leader trustworthiness, while other studies suggest that an employee's perceptions of a leader's trustworthiness may be based mainly on perceptions of benevolence (Meyerson et al., 1996; Knoll & Gill, 2011). In the majority of contexts, trust develops over time (Mayer et al., 1995; Lewicki & Bunker, 1996). Following Lewicki and Bunker's (1996) evolutionary model, a trusting relationship commences with the trustor weighing up costs and benefits rationally, focusing upon the cognitive components of competence and integrity. Within such calculus-based trust assessments, there is risk due to the information being incomplete and the need to focus upon proxies (Kramer 1999) and information from others (Burt & Knez, 1996). By suspending this uncertainty and being willing to make themselves vulnerable, the trustor makes an initial leap of faith to trust the trustee (Möllering, 2006). Lewicki and Bunker (1996) argue that, as the trustor gains more insights about the trustee and their actions, a deeper level of knowledge-based trust may develop. Where this relationship develops further, trust is based on a shared social orientation as well as knowledge, the affective component of benevolence gaining importance in what Lewicki and Bunker (1996) term identification-based trust.

As a willingness to be vulnerable, trust is regarded as an attitude (Robinson, 1996) or psychological state (Rousseau et al., 1998). Such trust is demonstrated usually through either reliance- or disclosure-related behaviours (Gillespie, 2003) whereby the trustor takes a 'leap of faith' (Möllering, 2001) and accepts risk (Dietz et al., 2010) in the expectation of a positive outcome. Such trusting behaviours can influence felt trustworthiness (Lester & Brower, 2003) on the part of the trustee, impacting upon their behaviour and their trust in the trustor (Gillespie, 2003). Each member of the dyad is both a trustor and a trustee, and each party's trust will be influenced by the other's trust in them (Ferrin et al., 2003). Therefore, when considering trust in VT leader-member relationships it is important to focus on both leader and member perspectives regarding trustworthy and trusting behaviours.

Leadership, Trust and Virtual Teams

Research has highlighted the role of leadership style in influencing followers' trust in their leaders (Fulmer and Gelfand, 2012), certain leadership styles having been linked clearly to trust building. Within this research has included work on leader behaviours and theories outlining transactional-, transformational- and authentic-leadership.

Transactional leadership takes place through a series of exchanges between leaders and followers. Leaders provide structure, establish rules and norms and specify the rewards or recognition the follower will receive for a specific level of performance – this being referred to as Contingent Reward. Using management by exception, either active or passive, leaders focus on mistakes, intervening when standards have not been met (Bass et al, 2003). Research suggests such leaders can be seen as trustworthy due to their perceived fairness, dependability and integrity (Dirks & Ferrin, 2002; MacKenzie et al., 2001).

While transactional leaders focus on employee rewards, transformational leaders seek to shift followers' attention from self-interest to a collective higher purpose, mission or vision (Kindarto *et al.,* 2020). Such leaders set out a clear and compelling vision and arouse a strong individual and team spirit (inspirational motivation). Putting followers' needs before their own they maintain consistency in relation to ethics and values (idealised influence). They encourage followers to question traditional ways of doing things, encouraging innovation and creativity (intellectual stimulation) whilst treating followers individually but equitably, showing concern and supporting their development through coaching or mentoring (individualised consideration) (Bass & Avolio, 1995; Bass et al., 2003). Such transformational leaders espouse trustworthy characteristics such as honesty, integrity and truthfulness (Bauman, 2013; Kouzes & Posner, 1987). They have been found to focus on ensuring care and concern are present and developing strong relationships with employees. A key feature of transformational leaders is their high moral and ethical standards (Bass & Avolio, 1995) and their focus on developing strong relationships with employees, gaining their trust, respect and admiration. Research suggests that a transformational style is more closely related to trust than a transactional leadership style (Dirks & Ferrin; 2002; Gillespie & Mann, 2004; Holtz & Harold, 2008).

Authentic leaders are "those who are deeply aware of how they think and behave and are perceived by others as being aware of their own and others' values/moral perspectives, knowledge, and strengths; aware of the context in which they operate and who are confident, hopeful, optimistic, resilient, and of high moral character" (Avolio, Luthans and Walumbwa, 2004, p.4). Such leadership involves demonstrating authentic behaviour despite external pressures (Gardner et al., 2005), it having attracted increased attention due to growing interest in leader morality and declining trust levels (Lyubovnikova *et al.*, 2017). Wong and Cummings (2009) argue that authentic leadership is essential for building trust because of its focus on honesty, integrity and high ethical standards, while Avolio and Gardner (2005) posit that all transformational leaders are in fact authentic.

A second strand of leadership theory focuses on leader-follower relationships, Leader-Member-Exchange (LMX) being one of the best-known theories. Proposed as an alternative to traditional theories focusing on leadership characteristics, situational features, or an interplay between the two (Gerstner and Day, 1995), LMX focuses on dyadic leader-follower relationships. Some authors make a link between LMX and both transactional and transformational leadership, arguing that low-quality LMX relationships are similar to transactional leadership, while high quality LMX relationships are analogous to transformational leadership (Graen and Uhl-Bien, 1995). There is general agreement amongst researchers that LMX is intertwined with mutual trust (Bauer and Green, 1996; Sue-Chan et al., 2012).

While studies of trust in traditional co-located environments have identified links between various leadership styles and trust, such traditional leadership styles and skills may not be suitable for virtual leadership (Pauleen, 2003). Research argues that VT leaders may need to place a greater emphasis on people and their interactions (Savolainen, 2014) and specifically on developing high trust relationships (Pauleen, 2003; Hacker et al., 2019), trust acting as a mediator between leadership style and VT performance (Sedrine et al. in press). However, despite research linking trust to the effectiveness of leader-member relationships (Dirks & Ferrin, 2002; Ferris et al., 2009; Hope-Hailey et al., 2012; Jawahar et al., 2019) VT trust scholars remain focused largely on trust at the team member level; with comparatively little focus on trust between individual VT leaders and members and limited guidance for VT leaders seeking to build high trust relationships with followers.

EXPLORING VT LEADER-MEMBER TRUST

To better understand VT leader-member trust development, research was conducted by the first author within three global technology companies. These organizations were chosen due to the growth of virtual teams in the technology sector (Daim et al., 2012), such multinational organizations being almost twice as likely to use virtual teams compared to organizations with domestic operations (SHRM, 2012). The study, conducted between 2017-2020, involved leaders and members in 20 dyads, based in various locations across Europe, Middle East and Africa (EMEA). Seeking perspectives of both leaders and members, the research addressed the question as to how leaders demonstrate both their own trustworthiness *to* members and their trust *of* members? A mono-method qualitative methodology was employed, involving some 40 separate in-depth interviews of approximately one hour's duration with leaders and members in VT dyads, 25 via videoconference and the rest in person. Thematic analysis (Braun & Clarke, 2006) of the transcripts revealed the importance of leaders' own trustworthiness (as trustees) and their trust (as trustors) of team members. It is these behaviours that provide the focus for the next section, being presented subsequently in the discussion as a framework for enabling high trust virtual leadership.

LEADERS' TRUST DEMONSTRATING BEHAVIOURS

Within VTs, leaders were, with very few exceptions, viewed by their members as being highly trustworthy, trust being knowledge- or identification-based. Within dyad trust was driven by two categories of leader behaviours: (1) the leader's demonstration of their own trustworthiness to members through their behaviours; and (2) the leader's demonstration of their trust of their team members; members' 'felt trustworthiness' in turn impacting positively on trust in the relationship.

Leader Behaviours Demonstrating their Trustworthiness to Members

Mayer et al.'s (1995) ABI bases of trustworthiness have been well supported in a range of studies (Breuer, et al., 2020; Jarvenpaa *et al.,* 1998; Robert *et al.*, 2009). This study, like others, found that benevolence and integrity were dominant influences on members' perceptions of leader trustworthiness. Members rarely mentioned the ability basis of trustworthiness, but their leaders were, for the most part, very experienced having significant responsibility in very large organizations. Members took for granted their leader's ability due to their experience and seniority within the organization. Reputation and third parties played a role in influencing these perceptions, with members referring to LinkedIn profiles and seeking insights from third parties.

While leader benevolence was found to influence members' perceptions of their trustworthiness, unlike in previous quantitative studies (e.g. Colquitt et al., 2007; Knoll & Gill, 2011) specific benevolent leader behaviours were identified. VT members wanted 'member-centric' leaders who supported them both personally and professionally. They trusted leaders who cared for them as people and were not solely focused on work tasks or targets, or on their own agenda. Members argued that leaders' care and concern for them and other team members was more important in virtual environments and that such benevolence had to be genuine, this also being recognised by VT leaders.

Supporting, Protecting and Being Fair

When asked about trusting their leader, members most frequently cited behaviours related to supporting, protecting and adding value; highlighting how trust was based on knowledge of the other. These comprised providing support in both personal and professional contexts, the latter of which helped members achieve their goals and thus was seen as adding value. Highly trusted leaders demonstrated general humanity towards others, with team members commenting on their benevolent behaviours towards the wider team noting: *"I trust him ... he cares about people..."*. Leaders emphasised the importance of offering personal support, their need to be aware of members' personal contexts and to be empathetic. Members mentioned the impact of specific incidences of personal support on their trust in the leader, for example: *"...but also on a personal level... I lost my parents a couple of years ago, they had cancer ... sometimes you just need some advice right... he gave me really good advice ... I really trust him..."*.

Instances of protecting included leaders' support of members' work-life balance. Such balance was particularly challenging where VT members had colleagues or customers in different countries and/or time zones, necessitating frequent travel and longer working days. Leaders respected members' personal time such as evenings and weekends by encouraging members to take a more balanced approach to their work commitments. This was appreciated considerably by members who recognised their leader's genuine concerns for their own and their families' welfare:

...when we (are) travelling a lot he says 'ye know guys I feel the same, I just want you to think about yourself ... so make sure you balance work and family'... that's the difference, some people expect regardless, even if they know that it's really tough but ... he always says 'if it's not possible just say so guys'... he definitely thinks about the welfare of everybody...

Within their professional context, members cited numerous instances in which leaders had supported them, showing benevolence in addressing issues or overcoming barriers to their career progress. They also mentioned how such support impacted positively on their trust of their leader, one noting: "*... I think the trust is, you know when you feel like your boss is going to back you up.*"

As in previous research, workload was potentially problematic for those members belonging to multiple virtual teams (O'Hara et al., 1994; Jarvenpaa & Leidner, 1999). In these instances, members particularly valued the support of their leaders when seeking to manage their workload. Leaders emphasised the need to be seen as fair in such situations, ensuring a balanced and manageable workload for the member, demonstrating their support and protection for their members.

Career Development and Coaching

The majority of leaders provided support through coaching and career development, such member-centric benevolent actions demonstrating their trustworthiness. Members spoke in general terms about how leaders' actions to develop them in their career engendered trust, one member typically commenting: "*...you trust your manager you know that he will guide you ... will let you grow in your career...this is what defines trust to me.*" Both leaders and members frequently emphasized the importance of coaching, leaders stressing that, as virtual leaders, they had to be coaches to members who were not physically co-located. This was particularly important for members who were new to virtual working. Coaching was viewed positively by team members, being seen as a clear example of leader benevolence, both in enabling their current role and in terms of their career progression. Typically, a team member noted: "*...it (coaching) made me feel that ... this person not only wants a success for his team, but he wants a success for the person in front of him ...so that made me feel more relaxed and comfortable to trust his opinion.*" Their leader commented: "*... the more we went with the coaching the more it (the relationship) improved... it's really about ... showing ... that you care about the people ...*"

A common focus of coaching conversations was member visibility. Leaders emphasised the need for members to be visible and be seen to contribute beyond their role description, in order to increase their chances of career progression but understood the challenges involved for virtual workers. To this end, leaders provided opportunities for members within their own networks, emphasising their members' abilities to other senior colleagues; their behaviours demonstrating their trust of members and impacting positively on reciprocal trust. Members and leaders cited instances whereby a leader actively helped a member to find a new role, despite not wanting to lose a highly performing employee. Such actions were deemed by members to be strongly member-centric demonstrating both integrity and benevolence, leaders placing their members' needs before their own.

Discussion thus far has focused on member-centric benevolent behaviours that demonstrate leader trustworthiness to members. However, a minority of leaders were viewed by members as focused on the tasks at hand and their own career, with little regard for member development or career advancement, demonstrating no real benevolence and often little integrity. The impact of such behaviours was noted by one member: "*It's not really a relationship I would say it's more based on 'so what is your target.*

When are you going to bring the numbers in … and can it not be higher?' nothing to do with eh personal … 'What are your goals in life or what do you want to achieve? Where do you see yourself next', it has nothing to do with that." In such situations, assessments of leaders' trustworthiness appeared to be more calculus-based.

Communicating Beyond the Agenda

VT leaders emphasized that a lack of face-to-face interaction could impede coaching and career development discussions. Both leaders and members bemoaned the agenda focused nature of virtual communication, and discussed the need to move "*beyond the agenda*" to support members, one leader highlighting the challenge by contrasting face-to-face and virtual teams:

…I think what is missing…it's on my leadership or maybe his own development plan…he can feel a bit alone for that …(member) deserves to grow in ORG C but I'm not giving him the time to do that… you know for example today I spend three hours with one of my guys in Barcelona in a room working on that. I haven't done that with him because you know it's by phone, so everything's been quicker you know with just a call…you're not sitting face-to-face talking about life or talking about the development plan… It's much more agenda focused.

There was ample evidence of leaders and members in trusting relationships making the effort to go 'beyond the agenda' when communicating virtually, resisting the urge to stick rigidly to business and ensure a level of personal connection. This involved learning more about members, their personal lives and their challenges, which in turn helped enable higher levels of support. Leaders also spoke of their efforts to still physically meet members, several highlighting the importance of face-to-face contact when coaching. Acknowledging the greater effort needed for virtual compared to co-located team leadership, all leaders emphasised the importance of demonstrating benevolence, their views being summarised by one: "*…when you're onsite, people can trust you because they see you care because of your body language, because eh you are smiling etcetera. That does not happen virtually. You need to be intentional in showing that you care."*

Ensuring Availability and Perceived Proximity

In demonstrating benevolence and integrity to members, leaders recognised the importance of leveraging multiple forms of communication to help ensure their availability and perceived virtual proximity to members. One explained:

It's not about physical presence, it's about me managing you and you have all my support so if an employee knows that his manager has his back whether he is in an office or the virtual world that will be a huge benefit so it's about the openness, it's about the availability, the trust … how you make sure that your employee sees you as if you are sitting next to them.

Support required by members varied, based on their experience levels and tenure in their current role. Many emphasised the benefit of face-to-face meetings for strategic conversations and brainstorming, the majority noting the need for timely access to the leader as required either *"many times of day, like*

1 minute - five minutes" or for *"very short 2-3 minute questions 2-3 times per day"*. The importance of such leader availability was mentioned by the majority of participants, including quite senior members with leadership responsibilities who spoke about needing to know their leader was available: *"...what's important is not that I spend an hour with him every week...for me what's important is when I send him a message or I call him that he calls me back within a few hours...just a minute, I need your brain on this thing [clicks fingers]."*

Being Open

The final leader behaviour demonstrating leader trustworthiness was being open to members. Identified in a variety of previous studies as a form of integrity (Gabarro, 1978; Jarvenpaa et al., 1998; Alsharo et al., 2017), this was highlighted by the majority of members in this study. Team members' open conversations with their leaders meant they felt the leader had all of their *"cards on the table"*. Some stated they trusted leaders who were honest and did not lie to them; others spoke about leaders being open about the members' strengths and weaknesses; these being seen as benevolent actions, helping members improve their performance and career prospects. Still others referred to leaders being open in letting the member know what they were thinking and being honest when discussing member ideas, whether they viewed them positively or negatively, one noting that this was important for knowledge-based trust: *"I relate trust a lot with two things. Right. That is with openness and integrity right... There's an aspect of his character let's say that attracted me as well that he was direct. Meaning he says what is on his mind, whether that would be positive or negative... In a small sense of we're not hiding stuff for each other."*

Leader openness from the outset of the relationship played a key role in ensuring alignment of expectations and goals. Leaders stressed the importance of this in virtual settings and its role in influencing their willingness to grant autonomy. In a number of dyads, open conversations helped ensure the development of knowledge- or identification-based trust, members' responses revealing these conversations as the key reason for a high trust relationship with their leaders. One compared this relationship with a manager where the alignment was not as strong: *"I think that is probably the big difference why there is a bigger or a big trust relationship between me and ([leader's name] and that's probably because my goals are much more aligned to the goals of [leader's name] than to the goals of my manager."* However, while openness was clearly linked to demonstrating their leader's trustworthiness, the majority of members also mentioned 'being open' when asked about leader behaviours demonstrating their trust of members. It is these behaviours that are considered next.

Leader Behaviours Demonstrating their Trust of Members

The vast majority of leaders highlighted the importance of their demonstrating trust of team members, emphasising the positive impact of doing so. Both leaders and members commented that the act of trusting could lead the other to be more trustworthy and result in reciprocal trust, one member noting: *"It immediately made me think well I need to succeed for him. He's trusting me to do this...I need to make sure I'm successful for him because he's putting his faith in me."* Three forms of leader behaviour demonstrating their trust of members were identified: being open, granting autonomy, and demonstrating value and respect.

Being Open

As well as demonstrating their own trustworthiness to members, being open also demonstrated leaders' trust of their VT members. Such openness was viewed as central to trust between leaders and members, being considered a form of disclosure-related trust (Gillespie, 2003). Members and leaders argued openness was more important in VTs due to the lack of face-to-face communication. Being open helped to bridge the virtual divide, building trust to levels which were sometimes considered higher than those with co-located leaders.

Most members cited their leader's openness as being critical in the positive development of their relationship. In particular, where leaders spoke openly about their objectives and their thoughts on certain confidential topics, including the sharing of privileged or confidential information, this helped to build trust: *"He told us our team, our group, what he wouldn't tell everyone else publicly so again that built the trust."* In divulging such information, leaders were taking risks and making themselves vulnerable, their actions offering a visible demonstration of trust. This was typified by one leader's explanation to a new team member outlining why he was unable to attend a meeting: the member commenting: *"I know a lot of managers who would never have told me that it was actually because of [personal issue]... But like I said, [leader's name] was very open ...so those are like little anecdotes that say okay I mean that confirmed let's say his openness and transparency."*

Granting Autonomy

Leaders cited their willingness to grant members autonomy and refrain from micromanagement as evidence of their trust in members, typically: *"So even if I believe that's not the best decision, I let him go for it. That's a way to demonstrate trust...so I'm not micromanaging him"*. Members clearly linked the granting of autonomy to trust, noting that they felt trusted when the leader didn't look to know all the detail of deals, when they were trusted to deliver to deadlines without being asked for progress updates, and when they were allowed to manage tricky situations by themselves. In the vast majority of dyads, some form of autonomy was granted from the very outset; the positive impact on trust being commented upon by members. One team member who was also a leader noted: *"From day one he gave me full autonomy and trust and allowed me to really do what I felt I had to do managing my team."*

Despite a strong dislike of micromanagement voiced by both members and leaders, it was recognised as necessary where, for example, competency gaps were evident, or a member was struggling in a certain area. In such instances, the lack of autonomy did not damage trust, providing an explanation was offered and the member believed it was a temporary measure. Where relationships began with micromanagement, being initially calculus based, and autonomy was granted over time, members felt an increased level of trust from the leader as their leaders' trust in them became more knowledge-based.

While autonomy was considered preferable to micromanagement, both members and leaders highlighted the responsibility of members to respect that autonomy. This highlighted the dyadic nature of trust; leaders bring willing to trust (take a risk) based on positive expectations but this was contingent on knowledge gained from their members demonstrating their trustworthiness on an ongoing basis.

Demonstrating Value and Respect

Alongside granting autonomy, leaders demonstrated their trust by respecting the advice and expertise members provided. A member commented: *"He won't question me at all, he won't ask me to go into it or show him evidence of what's happening as in why we're accepting this…he trusts what you're telling him."* Previous research suggests that leaders can enhance trust levels by involving members in decision making (Dirks & Ferrin, 2002; Gillespie & Mann, 2004) and those leaders active in seeking such member input, noted its importance in a virtual context given the lack of face-to-face visibility. One commented on the reciprocal nature of this: *"The thing is if I don't have [member's name] who tell(s) me that the policy I put in place or the direction I'm pushing on is wrong, I cannot be in Cairo every week… So, I need [member's name] to tell me I'm wrong, I need [member's name] to feel ok if I tell him that he needs to change something."*

Members commented positively about leaders who refrained from making decisions without firstly listening and consulting with members. Such behaviour was viewed by members as a sign that the leader trusted them, for example: *"I think, yes he trusts me; he listens to me, that's important, he takes into consideration my opinion. So, if I say: 'look for this and that reason I think this and that' he will consider that… and most of the time he will not move forward because we are not in agreement."*

Overcoming Difficulties to Trust Building in a Virtual Context

The findings presented above highlight some of the challenges of trust building in virtual relationships. It was evident that VT leaders needed to make a more conscious effort to build trust with team members. Leaders spoke about the difficulties in having coaching conversations and, in virtual communications, moving beyond an agenda focus to build connections. Furthermore, trust sometimes simply took longer to develop virtually due, in part, to the personalities involved and the type of communication platforms adopted by the organizations. These impacted upon the quality of support, perceptions of integrity (work ethic) and connection, and the building of trust. For some dyads, face-to-face communication had a transformational impact on trust, immediately benefitting relationships which had been slow to develop. Virtual working arrangements allowed for greater use of virtual reporting lines and for some these caused friction raising concerns about loyalty and trust. Team members' work experience also influenced trust development, some less experienced members simply needed more support and more regular communication; this not always being possible given the leader's other commitments. In some Occasionally, this led to members feeling that the leader lacked benevolence, this being most pronounced in those hybrid teams where a number of team members were co-located with the leader with others at other locations:

"… if I can imagine he's just sitting in the hub in Barcelona so everyone there can just run to him anytime. But for me I'm always like waiting for the reply or trying to send over a WhatsApp or call in his mobile and stuff like this to get replies…"

Notwithstanding these challenges, most leaders were successful in building high trust relationships with members. Discussion now turns to the leadership style most effective for building trust virtually.

DISCUSSION

Leadership Style Suited to Building VT Trust

Highly trusted VT leaders interviewed revealed many of the characteristics of transformational leaders. Drawing upon Bass et al.'s (2003) factors of transformational leadership, trusted leaders demonstrated idealised influence by considering members' needs above their own needs, supporting them personally and professionally and generally adding value. Specific examples of this include: leaders helping high performing members to find new roles despite the negative impact on team performance; protecting members from others in the organization, fighting their corner where required; encouraging members towards a greater work-life balance by allowing members to cancel travel plans or to push out deadlines where required; and negatively influencing their own work-life balance by travelling as often as possible to spend time with members in order to provide maximum support.

Members noted how highly trusted VT leaders demonstrated inspirational motivation (Bass et al., 2003) by outlining their vision for their team and setting clear expectations, often going to great efforts to ensure that member communication was open and beyond the agenda. Having leveraged openness to achieve alignment of expectations, virtual working was considered to be effective. Through seeking feedback from VT members, consulting before making decisions or taking actions, and encouraging members to question operational tactics or strategies or the way in which they worked, leaders demonstrated value and respect. Leaders also granted members autonomy, allowing them the space to make mistakes and to learn from experience. Invariably this required members to engage in problem solving and identify potential improvements, intellectual stimulation signifying further parallels with Bass et al.'s (2003) factors. Treating all followers equally and as individuals (Bass et al., 2003) was particularly challenging where some members were co-located with the leader and others were virtual. However, leaders were conscious of this issue working to ensure perceived proximity and availability for support when members needed. Furthermore, their efforts in coaching and developing members emphasised individual consideration.

Towards a Framework for Enabling High Trust VT Leadership

The specific leader behaviours identified in the research as enabling trust are summarised in figure 1 as a high trust VT leadership framework. This framework answers the two questions posed at the start of this chapter within the context of leader-member relationships in virtual teams.

Within the framework leaders' behaviours demonstrating their trustworthiness (as trustees) include supporting, protecting and adding value to virtual team members as trustors, developing individual career and coaching, communicating beyond the agenda, ensuring their own availability and perceived (albeit virtual) proximity and being open, especially in their communications. These behaviours affect members' perceptions of leader trustworthiness and, where positive, support the development of members' trust of their leader from calculus- to knowledge-based trust. Members' trust in their leader is demonstrated through a variety of their own trusting behaviours, providing an opportunity for leaders to further influence perceptions of their own trustworthiness, their behaviours potentially being influenced by felt trustworthiness and the need to reciprocate by rewarding the trust placed in them by the member.

Leaders' behaviours (as trustors) demonstrating their trust of members (as trustees) comprise being open, granting their members autonomy and demonstrating the value and respect they hold for them.

Members' behaviours subsequent to leaders' trusting behaviours further influence leaders' perceptions of members' trustworthiness, their trust in members and the trusting behaviours towards members; member trustworthy behaviours potentially being influenced by felt trustworthiness and the need to reward their leader's trust in them.

Figure 1. Framework for enabling high trust VT leadership

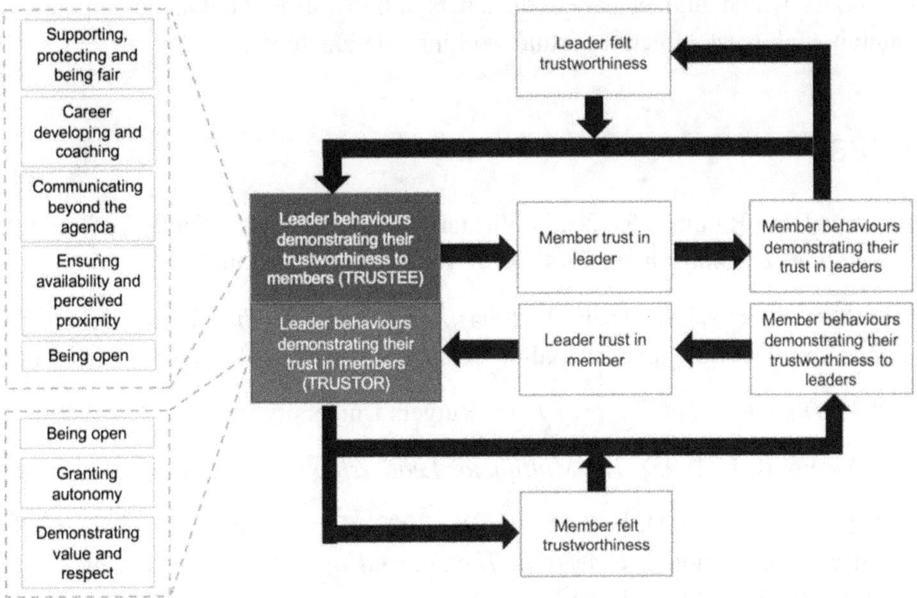

CONCLUSION

This chapter has presented the findings of empirical research into trust development in virtual leader-member dyads. This focus is important as despite existing research recognising the importance of trust in leader-member relationships, research on trust in VTs has been largely focused at the team member level, offering limited guidance for VT leaders seeking to build trust with members.

While the virtual context can present unique challenges to trust building, the findings of this study offer some comfort to those challenged by virtual leadership, revealing that trust is not only possible in virtual leader-member dyads but that it can in fact be stronger than in co-located relationships. These insights come at an important time as Covid-19 led to exponential growth in VT usage and high levels of virtual working are forecasted to continue post Covid-19 (EY, 2020). Given the centrality of trust to effective working relationships, and the likelihood that people managers will increasingly have to practice remote people management, the issue of how to build trust virtually should now be of primary concern for managers and organizations alike to leverage the well-established benefits of dyadic trust.

The framework offered presents VT leaders with a series of behaviours to help build high trust relationships with their members. It emphasises that virtual leaders could usefully consider adopting a member-centric leadership style, providing support for members in a personal context and supporting and protecting them to achieve their work goals. VT leaders might well also consider focussing upon coaching and developing members to enable their career development. In order to provide such high levels of support in a virtual context, leaders will need good communication skills, to be available to members when needed and take time to move 'beyond the agenda' when communicating. VT leaders could usefully seek to demonstrate openness, autonomy and respect from the outset of relationships, these helping members feel trusted and supporting trust reciprocation and a stronger relationship. In order to achieve high levels of trust with members, VT leaders are likely to need to spend more time reflecting on the needs of members and, where available, take advantage of opportunities for face-to-face coaching. Such behaviours, which align closely to the tenets of transformational leadership, are likely to help build and maintain high-trust, effective virtual working relationships.

REFERENCES

Alsharo, M., Gregg, D., & Ramirez, R. (2017). Virtual team effectiveness: The role of knowledge sharing and trust. *Information & Management, 54*(4), 479–490. doi:10.1016/j.im.2016.10.005

Avolio, B. J., Luthans, F., & Walumbwa, F. O. (2004). *Authentic leadership: Theory building for veritable sustained performance* [Working paper]. Gallup Leadership Institute, University of Nebraska-Lincoln.

Barber, B. (1983). *The Logic and Limits of Trust*. Rutgers University Press.

Bass, B. M., & Avolio, B. J. (1995). *The Multifactor Leadership Questionnaire*. Mind Garden.

Bass, B. M., Avolio, B. J., Jung, D. I., & Berson, Y. (2003). Predicting unit performance by assessing transformational and transactional leadership. *The Journal of Applied Psychology, 88*(2), 207–218. doi:10.1037/0021-9010.88.2.207 PMID:12731705

Bauman, D. C. (2013). The three faces of integrity. *The Leadership Quarterly, 24*(3), 414–426. doi:10.1016/j.leaqua.2013.01.005

Bell, B. S., & Kozlowski, S. W. J. (2002). A typology of virtual teams: Implications for effective leadership. *Group & Organization Management, 27*(1), 14–49. doi:10.1177/1059601102027001003

Braun, V., & Clarke, V. (2006). Using thematic analysis in psychology. *Qualitative Research in Psychology, 3*(2), 77–101. doi:10.1191/1478088706qp063oa

Breuer, C., Hüffmeier, J., & Hertel, G. (2016). Does trust matter more in virtual teams? A meta-analysis of trust and team effectiveness considering virtuality and documentation as moderators. *The Journal of Applied Psychology, 101*(8), 1151–1177. doi:10.1037/apl0000113 PMID:27228105

Breuer, C., Hüffmeier, J., Hibben, F., & Hertel, G. (2020). Trust in teams: A taxonomy of perceived trustworthiness factors and risk-taking behaviours in face-to-face and virtual teams. *Human Relations, 73*(1), 3–34. doi:10.1177/0018726718818721

Burt, R. S., & Knez, M. (1996). Trust and third party gossip. In R. M. Kramer & T. R. Tyler (Eds.), *Trust in organizations: Frontiers of Theory and Research* (pp. 68–89). Sage. doi:10.4135/9781452243610.n5

Cheng, X., Yin, G., Azadegan, A., & Kolfschoten, G. (2016). Trust evolvement in hybrid team collaboration: A longitudinal case study. *Group Decision and Negotiation*, *25*(2), 267–288. doi:10.100710726-015-9442-x

Colquitt, J. A., Scott, B. A., & LePine, J. A. (2007). Trust, trustworthiness, and trust propensity: A meta-analytic test of their unique relationships with risk taking and job performance. *The Journal of Applied Psychology*, *92*(4), 909–927. doi:10.1037/0021-9010.92.4.909 PMID:17638454

Coppola, N. W., Hiltz, S. R., & Rotter, N. G. (2004). Building trust in virtual teams. *IEE Transactions on Professional Communication*, *47*(2), 95–104. doi:10.1109/TPC.2004.828203

Daim, T. U., Ha, A., Reutiman, S., Hughes, B., Pathak, U., Bynum, W., & Bhatla, A. (2012). Exploring the communication breakdown in global virtual teams. *International Journal of Project Management*, *30*(2), 199–212. doi:10.1016/j.ijproman.2011.06.004

De Jong, B., & Dirks, K. (2012). Beyond shared perceptions of trust and monitoring in teams: Implications of asymmetry and dissensus. *The Journal of Applied Psychology*, *97*(2), 391–406. doi:10.1037/a0026483 PMID:22181679

Dennis, D., Overholt, M., & Vickers, M. (2014). The new dominance of virtual teams and leaders. *MWorld*, *13*(2), 18–21.

DeRosa, D. M., Hantula, D. A., Kock, N., & D'Arcy, J. (2004). Trust and leadership in virtual teamwork: A media naturalness perspective. *Human Resource Management*, *43*(2&3), 219–232. doi:10.1002/hrm.20016

Dietz, G., & Den Hartog, D. N. (2006). Measuring trust inside organizations. *Personnel Review*, *35*(5), 557–588. doi:10.1108/00483480610682299

Dietz, G., Gillespie, N., & Chao, G. T. (2010). Unravelling the complexities of trust and culture. In M. N. K. Saunders, D. Skinner, G. Dietz, N. Gillespie, & R. J. Lewicki (Eds.), *Organizational Trust: A Cultural Perspective* (pp. 3–41). Cambridge University Press. doi:10.1017/CBO9780511763106.002

Dirks, K. T., & Ferrin, D. L. (2002). Trust in leadership: Meta-analytic findings and implications for research and practice. *The Journal of Applied Psychology*, *87*(4), 611–628. doi:10.1037/0021-9010.87.4.611 PMID:12184567

Dube, L., & Robey, D. (2008). Surviving the paradoxes of virtual teamwork. *Information Systems Journal*, *19*(1), 3–30. doi:10.1111/j.1365-2575.2008.00313.x

EY. (2020). *Why remote working will be the new normal, even after COVID-19*. https://www.ey.com/en_be/covid-19/why-remote-working-will-be-the-new-normal-even-after-covid-19

Ferrin, D. L., Dirks, K. T., & Shah, P. P. (2003). *Many routes toward trust: A social network analysis of the determinants of interpersonal trust. Academy of Management Proceedings*. Research Collection Lee Kong Chian School of Business.

Ferris, G. R., Liden, R. C., Munyon, T. P., Summers, J. K., Basik, K. J., & Buckley, M. R. (2009). Relationships at work: Toward a multidimensional conceptualization of dyadic work relationships. *Journal of Management*, *35*(6), 1379–1403. doi:10.1177/0149206309344741

Fulmer, A., & Gelfand, M. J. (2012). At what level (and in whom) we trust: Trust across multiple organizational levels. *Journal of Management, 38*(4), 1167–1230. doi:10.1177/0149206312439327

Gabarro, J. J. (1978). The development of trust, influence, and expectations. In A. G. Athos & J. J. Gabarro (Eds.), *Interpersonal Behaviour: Communication and understanding in relationships* (pp. 290–303). Prentice-Hall.

Gardner, W. L., Avolio, B. J., Luthans, F., May, D. R., & Walumbwa, F. (2005). Can you see the real me? A self-based model of authentic leader and follower development. *The Leadership Quarterly, 16*(3), 343–372. doi:10.1016/j.leaqua.2005.03.003

Gerstner, C. R., & Day, D. V. (1995). *Putting leadership back into leader-member exchange: A meta-analytic review and extension* [Paper presentation]. Tenth Annual Conference of the Society of Industrial-Organizational Psychology, Orlando, FL, United States.

Gillespie, N. (2003). *Measuring trust in working relationships: The behavioural trust inventory* [Paper presentation]. Academy of Management Conference, Seattle, WA, United States.

Gillespie, N., & Mann, L. (2004). Transformational leadership and shared values: The building blocks of trust. *Journal of Managerial Psychology, 19*(6), 588–607. doi:10.1108/02683940410551507

Gilson, L. L., Maynard, M. T., Jones Young, N. C., Vartiainen, M., & Hakonen, M. (2015). Virtual teams research: 10 years, 10 themes, and 10 opportunities. *Journal of Management, 41*(5), 1313–1337. doi:10.1177/0149206314559946

Graen, G. B., & Uhl-Bien, M. (1995). Relationship-based approach to leadership: Development of leader-member exchange (LMX) theory of leadership over 25 years: Applying a multi-level multi-domain perspective. *The Leadership Quarterly, 6*(2), 219–247. doi:10.1016/1048-9843(95)90036-5

Greenberg, P. S., Greenberg, R. H., & Antonucci, Y. L. (2007). Creating and sustaining trust in virtual teams. *Business Horizons, 50*(4), 325–333. doi:10.1016/j.bushor.2007.02.005

Hacker, J., Johnson, M., Saunders, C., & Thayer, A. L. (2019). Trust in virtual teams: A multidisciplinary review and integration. *AJIS. Australasian Journal of Information Systems, 23*, 1–35. doi:10.3127/ajis.v23i0.1757

Hertel, G., Geister, S., & Konradt, U. (2005). Managing virtual teams: A review of current empirical research. *Human Resource Management Review, 15*(1), 69–95. doi:10.1016/j.hrmr.2005.01.002

Holtz, B. C., & Harold, C. M. (2008). When your boss says no! The effects of leadership style and trust on employee reactions to managerial explanations. *Journal of Occupational and Organizational Psychology, 81*(4), 777–802. doi:10.1348/096317907X251569

Hope-Hailey, V., Searle, R., & Dietz, G. (2012). *Where has all the trust gone?* https://www.cipd.co.uk/Images/where-has-all-the-trust-gone_2012-sop_tcm18-9644.pdf

Hosmer, L. T. (1995). Trust: The connecting link between organizational theory and philosophical ethics. *Academy of Management Review, 20*(2), 379–403. doi:10.5465/amr.1995.9507312923

Hunsaker, P. L., & Hunsaker, J. S. (2008). Virtual teams: A leader's guide. *Team Performance Management, 14*(1), 86–101. doi:10.1108/13527590810860221

Jarvenpaa, S. L., Knoll, K., & Leidner, D. E. (1998). Is anybody out there? Antecedents of trust in global virtual teams. *Journal of Management Information Systems, 14*(4), 29–64. doi:10.1080/07421222.1998.11518185

Jarvenpaa, S. L., & Leidner, D. E. (1999). Communication and trust in global virtual teams. *Organization Science, 10*(6), 791–815. doi:10.1287/orsc.10.6.791

Jawahar, I. M., Stone, T. H., & Kluemper, D. (2019). When and why leaders trust followers LMX as a mediator and empowerment as a moderator of the trustworthiness-trust relationship. *Career Development International, 24*(7), 702–716. doi:10.1108/CDI-03-2019-0078

Kanawattanachai, P., & Yoo, Y. (2002). Dynamic nature of trust in virtual teams. *The Journal of Strategic Information Systems, 11*(3-4), 187–213. doi:10.1016/S0963-8687(02)00019-7

Kayworth, T. R., & Leidner, D. (2000). The global virtual manager: A prescription for success. *European Management Journal, 18*(2), 183–194. doi:10.1016/S0263-2373(99)00090-0

Kimble, C. (2011). Building effective virtual teams: How to overcome the problems of trust and identity in virtual teams. *Global Business and Organizational Excellence, 30*(January/February), 6–15. doi:10.1002/joe.20364

Kirkman, B. L., Rosen, B., Gibson, C. B., Tesluk, P. E., & Pherson, S. O. (2002). Five challenges to virtual team success: Lessons from Sabre, Inc. *The Academy of Management Executive, 16*(3), 67–79. doi:10.5465/ame.2002.8540322

Knoll, D. L., & Gill, H. (2011). Antecedents of trust in supervisors, subordinates, and peers. *Journal of Managerial Psychology, 26*(4), 313–330. doi:10.1108/02683941111124845

Korsgaard, M. A., Brower, H. H., & Lester, S. W. (2015). It isn't always mutual: A critical review of dyadic trust. *Journal of Management, 41*(1), 47–70. doi:10.1177/0149206314547521

Kouzes, J. M., & Posner, B. Z. (1993). *Credibility: How Leaders Gain and Lose It. Why People Demand It*. Jossey-Bass.

Kramer, R. M. (1999). Trust and distrust in organizations: Emerging perspectives, enduring questions. *Annual Review of Psychology, 50*(1), 569–598. doi:10.1146/annurev.psych.50.1.569 PMID:15012464

Lester, S. W., & Brower, H. H. (2003). In the eyes of the beholder: The relationship between subordinates' felt trustworthiness and their work attitudes and behaviors. *Journal of Leadership & Organizational Studies, 10*(2), 17–33. doi:10.1177/107179190301000203

Lewicki, R. L., & Bunker, B. B. (1996). Developing and maintaining trust in work relationships. In R. M. Kramer & T. R. Tyler (Eds.), *Trust in organizations: Frontiers of theory and research* (pp. 114–139). Sage. doi:10.4135/9781452243610.n7

Lewis, J. D., & Weigert, A. (1985). Trust as a social reality. *Social Forces, 63*(4), 967–985. doi:10.2307/2578601

Liao, C. (2017). Leadership in virtual teams: A multilevel perspective. *Human Resource Management Review, 27*(4), 648–659. doi:10.1016/j.hrmr.2016.12.010

Lipnack, J., & Stamps, J. (1997). *Virtual teams: Reaching Across Space, Time and Organization with Technology*. Wiley.

Luhmann, N. (1979). *Trust and Power*. Wiley.

Lyubovnikova, J., Legood, A., Turner, N., & Mamakouka, A. (2017). How authentic leadership influences team performance: The mediating role of team reflexivity. *Journal of Business Ethics, 141*(1), 59–70. doi:10.100710551-015-2692-3

MacKenzie, S.B., Podsakoff, P.M. & Rich, G. (2001). Transformational and transactional leadership and salesperson performance. *Journal of the Academy of Marketing Science, 29*(Spring), 115-134.

Maes, J. D., & Weldy, T. G. (2018). Building effective virtual teams: Expanding OD research and practice. *Organization Development Journal, 36*(3), 83–90.

Martins, L. L., Gilson, L. L., & Maynard, M. T. (2004). Virtual teams: What do we know and where do we go from here? *Journal of Management, 30*(6), 805–835. doi:10.1016/j.jm.2004.05.002

Mayer, R. C., Davis, J. H., & Schoorman, D. F. (1995). An integrative model of organizational trust. *Academy of Management Review, 20*(3), 709–734. doi:10.5465/amr.1995.9508080335

McKnight, D. H., & Chervany, N. L. (2001). Trust and distrust definitions: One bite at a time. In R. Falcone, M. Singh, & Y. H. Tan (Eds.), *Trust in Cyber-societies* (pp. 22–46). Lecture Notes in Computer Science. Springer. doi:10.1007/3-540-45547-7_3

Meyerson, D., Weick, K. E., & Kramer, R. M. (1996). Swift trust in temporary groups. In R. M. Kramer & T. R. Tyler (Eds.), *Trust in Organizations: Frontiers of Theory and Research* (pp. 166–195). Sage. doi:10.4135/9781452243610.n9

Möllering, G. (2001). The nature of trust: From Georg Simmel to a theory of expectation, interpretation and suspension. *Sociology, 35*(2), 403–420. doi:10.1177/S0038038501000190

Möllering, G. (2006). Trust, institutions, agency: towards a neo-institutional theory of trust. In R. Bachmann & A. Zaheer (Eds.), *A Handbook of Trust Research* (pp. 355–376). Edward Elgar. doi:10.4337/9781847202819.00029

Monalisa, M., Daim, T., Mirani, F., Dash, P., Khamis, R., & Bhusari, V. (2008). Managing Global design teams. *Research Technology Management, 51*(4), 48–59. doi:10.1080/08956308.2008.11657514

Mysirlaki, S., & Paraskeva, F. (2019). Virtual team effectiveness: Insights from the virtual word teams of massively multiplayer online games. *The Journal of Leadership Studies, 13*(1), 36–55. doi:10.1002/jls.21608

Nienaber, A.-M., Romeike, P. D., Searle, R., & Schewe, G. (2015). A qualitative meta-analysis of trust in supervisor-subordinate relationships. *Journal of Managerial Psychology, 30*(5), 507–534. doi:10.1108/JMP-06-2013-0187

Nooteboom, B. (2002). *Trust: Forms, Foundations, Functions, Failures and Figures*. Edward Elgar. doi:10.4337/9781781950883

Nordback, E. S., & Espinosa, J. A. (2019). Effective coordination of shared leadership in global virtual teams. *Journal of Management Information Systems, 36*(1), 321–350. doi:10.1080/07421222.2018.1558943

O'Hara-Devereaux, M., & Johansen, R. (1994). *Global Work: Bridging Distance, Culture, and Time*. Jossey-Bass.

Oakley, J. G. (1998). Leadership processes in virtual teams and organizations. *The Journal of Leadership Studies, 5*(3), 3–18. doi:10.1177/107179199900500301

Pattnaik, L., & Jena, L. K. (in press). Mindfulness, remote engagement and employee morale: Conceptual analysis to address the "new normal". *The International Journal of Organizational Analysis*.

Paul, D. L., & McDaniel, R. R. (2004). A field study of the effect of interpersonal trust on virtual collaborative relationship performance. *Management Information Systems Quarterly, 28*(2), 183–227. doi:10.2307/25148633

Pauleen, D. J. (2003). An inductively derived model of leader-initiated relationship building with virtual team members. *Journal of Management Information Systems, 20*(3), 227–256. doi:10.1080/07421222.2003.11045771

Piccoli, G., & Ives, B. (2003). Trust and the unintended effects of behaviour control in virtual teams. *Management Information Systems Quarterly, 27*(3), 365–395. doi:10.2307/30036538

RW3 Culture Wizard. (2018). *Virtual Teams Survey 2018*. https://cdn2.hubspot.net/hubfs/466336/Virtual%20Teams%20Survey-Executive%20Summary--Final%20(2018).pdf

Robert, L. P. Jr, Dennis, A. R., & Hung, Y. C. (2009). Individual swift trust and knowledge-based trust in face-to-face and virtual team members. *Journal of Management Information Systems, 26*(2), 241–279. doi:10.2753/MIS0742-1222260210

Robinson, S. L. (1996). Trust and breach of the psychological contract. *Administrative Science Quarterly, 41*(4), 574–599. doi:10.2307/2393868

Romeike, P. D., Nienaber, A. M., & Schewe, G. (2016). How differences in perceptions of own and team performance impact trust and job satisfaction in virtual teams. *Human Performance, 29*(4), 291–309. doi:10.1080/08959285.2016.1165226

Ross, J. A. (2006). Trust makes the team go 'round. *Harvard Management Update*, (June), 3–6.

Rotter, J. B. (1967). A new scale for the measurement of interpersonal trust. *Journal of Personality, 35*(4), 651–665. doi:10.1111/j.1467-6494.1967.tb01454.x PMID:4865583

Rousseau, D. M., Sitkin, S. B., Burt, R. S., & Camerer, C. (1998). Not so different at all: A cross-discipline view of trust. *Academy of Management Review, 23*(3), 393–404. doi:10.5465/amr.1998.926617

Ruiller, C., van der Heijden, B., Chedotel, F., & Dumas, M. (2018). You have got a friend: The value of perceived proximity for teleworking success in dispersed teams. *Team Performance Management, 25*(1/2), 1352–7592.

Savolainen, T. (2014). Trust-building in e-leadership: A case study of leaders' challenges and skills in technology-mediated interaction. *The Journal of Global Business Issues*, *8*(2), 45–56.

Schaubroeck, J. M., & Yu, A. (2017). When does virtuality help or hinder teams? Core team characteristics as contingency factors. *Human Resource Management Review*, *27*(4), 635–647. doi:10.1016/j.hrmr.2016.12.009

Sedrine, S. B., Bouderbala, A., & Nasraoui, H. (in press). Leadership style effect on virtual team efficiency: Trust, operational cohesion and media richness roles. *Journal of Management Development*.

Shapiro, D. L., Furst, S. A., Spreitzer, G. M., & Von Glinow, M. A. (2002). Transnational teams in the electronic age: Are team identity and high performance at risk. *Journal of Organizational Behavior*, *23*(4), 455–467. doi:10.1002/job.149

SHRM. (2012). *SHRM survey findings: Virtual teams*. https://www.shrm.org/hr-today/trends-and-forecasting/research-and-surveys/pages/virtualteams.aspx

Sue-Chan, C., Au, A., & Hackett, R. (2012). Trust as a mediator of the relationship between leader/member behavior and leader-member-exchange quality. *Journal of World Business*, *47*(3), 459–468. doi:10.1016/j.jwb.2011.05.012

Walther, J. B. (1995). Relational aspects of computer-mediated communication: Experimental observations over time. *Organization Science*, *6*(2), 186–203. doi:10.1287/orsc.6.2.186

Warkentin, M. E., Sayeed, L., & Hightower, R. (1997). Virtual teams versus face-to-face teams: An exploratory study or a web-based conference system. *Decision Sciences*, *28*(4), 975–996. doi:10.1111/j.1540-5915.1997.tb01338.x

Webster, J., & Wong, W. K. P. (2008). Comparing traditional and virtual group forms: Identity, communication and trust in naturally occurring project teams. *International Journal of Human Resource Management*, *19*(1), 41–62. doi:10.1080/09585190701763883

Whitener, E. M., Brodt, S. E., Korsgaard, M. A., & Werner, J. M. (1998). Managers as initiators of trust: An exchange relationship framework for understanding managerial trustworthy behaviour. *Academy of Management Review*, *23*(3), 513–530. doi:10.5465/amr.1998.926624

Williamson, O. E. (1993). Calculativeness, trust and economic organization. *The Journal of Law & Economics*, *36*(1), 453–486. doi:10.1086/467284

Wilson, J. M., Straus, S. G., & McEvily, B. (2006). All in due time: The development of trust in computer-mediated and face-to-face teams. *Organizational Behavior and Human Decision Processes*, *99*(1), 16–33. doi:10.1016/j.obhdp.2005.08.001

Witchalls, C. (2009). *Managing virtual teams: Taking a more strategic approach*. The Economist Intelligence Unit.

Wong, C. A., & Cummings, G. G. (2009). The influence of authentic leadership behaviors on trust and work outcomes of health care staff. *The Journal of Leadership Studies*, *3*(2), 6–23. doi:10.1002/jls.20104

Zaccaro, S. J., & Bader, P. (2003). E-leadership and the challenges of leading E-teams: Minimizing the bad and maximising the good. *Organizational Dynamics*, *31*(4), 377–387. doi:10.1016/S0090-2616(02)00129-8

Zigurs, I. (2003). Leadership in virtual teams: Oxymoron or opportunity. *Organizational Dynamics*, *31*(4), 339–351. doi:10.1016/S0090-2616(02)00132-8

Zuofa, T., & Ochieng, E. G. (2017). 'Working separately but together: Appraising virtual project team challenges. *Team Performance Management*, *23*(5/6), 227–242. doi:10.1108/TPM-06-2016-0030

Chapter 16
Managing Social Distance in Geographically Distributed Teams

Vinita Seshadri
https://orcid.org/0000-0002-0552-1943
Christ University, India

Elangovan N.
https://orcid.org/0000-0002-4551-6081
Christ University, India

ABSTRACT

The chapter highlights the social distance, i.e. lack of emotional connection, formed among individuals working remotely in a geographically distributed team. The virtuality and cultural diversity of such teams creates limited opportunities for dispersed members to build social ties with remote team members leading to formation of 'us' versus 'them' attitudes which corrode team effectiveness. Based on a survey of 482 Indian IT professionals working in distributed teams, we find that social distance negatively impacts team effectiveness. Further, the results of the study show that practices such as task interdependence, inclusive communication, contextual information and shared identity can moderate the negative relationship between social distance and team effectiveness at varying levels of perceived status equality among individuals working in geographically distributed teams. The chapter provides recommendations for the effective management of geographically distributed teams whereby managers act as a bridge between the team members to overcome social distance.

INTRODUCTION

The COVID-19 pandemic has compelled businesses to transform their physical workplace into a digital one and a traditional co-located team into virtual or remote team making remote collaboration the new normal. A Future Workforce Survey conducted by Ozimek (2020) reveals that there is a steep increase

DOI: 10.4018/978-1-7998-6754-8.ch016

in the number of fully remote teams, from 2.3% pre-pandemic to 20% post-pandemic. This has generated a lot of interest among researchers to investigate the impact, advantages and challenges related to managing remote teams. In the COVID-19 era, working in remote teams is new for workforces in certain industries such as education, healthcare, banking and retail. However, accomplishing work away from a common physical workplace using information and communication technologies (ICTs) has been very much prevalent in the knowledge economy, including the IT sector (Felstead & Henseke, 2017). As such, studies related to the dynamics of virtual communication and collaboration in geographically distributed teams (GDT) or global virtual teams can provide important insights to understand and manage these newly formed remote teams.

A GDT is a remote team where members are dispersed across two or more locations collaborating virtually using computer mediated communication tools such as emails, audio-video conferencing, instant messaging, remote access systems, collaborating software etc. (Zimmermann, 2020). Distributed teams enable businesses to maximize their functional expertise by allowing them to access experts and professionals across the globe; running continuous 24/7 production taking advantage of time zone differences; eliminate travel, immigration, relocation and other overhead costs (Dulebohn & Hoch, 2017; Espinosa, Nan & Carmel, 2015). Professionals not bound by time or location to collaborate, can pool in a wide variety of ways, ideas, perspectives and opinions, which enhances organizational learning and maximises synergies of diversity (Berry, 2011). Geographically distributed teams (GDT) have been very widely used for open source software (OSS) projects, the main advantage being the flexibility of professionals to manage their work effectively, and 24hr work cycle enabling collaboration across the globe (Zhang, Hu & Li, 2016).

CONTEXT OF THE STUDY

Indian IT Companies hire a large number of software or IT professionals who work at remote (offshore) locations away from a client location (onsite or onshore) situated outside of India (Basant, 2006). The onsite and offshore teams respectively may themselves be co-located in a workplace or be distributed, e.g. working at home, with the latter being the case for many since the onset of the global pandemic. The onsite team defines the project requirements, transfer knowledge and information, coordinate and monitor offshore work, implement software and solutions, train the staff and provide rapid-reaction maintenance services. The offshore team in India provide technical and database design, software programming, testing, documentation and long-term maintenance services. Computer mediated communication tools such as emails, video and audio conferencing, instant messaging, collaboration software, document sharing software, remote access systems etc. allow dispersed team members to collaborate and concurrently execute IT projects remotely. This study reflects on the experiences of members of GDTs in India prior to the global pandemic, offers an insight into the practices that can moderate the negative relationship between social distance and team effectiveness, and methods for successful management of GDTs.

CHALLENGES OF REMOTE COLLABORATION

The three distances experienced in remote collaboration are geographic (location and time zone), operational (team size, bandwidth and skill levels), and affinity in terms of values, trust, and interdependency among dispersed members (Dhawan & Chamorro, Premuzic, 2018). Remote communication and collaboration have been plagued by issues like low level of engagement among individuals, difficulty in establishing trust and shared responsibility, feelings of isolation, formation of subgroups, low cohesion among members and challenges in monitoring performance (Bick, Chang, Wang & Yu, 2020; Dulebohn & Hoch, 2017; Ozimek, 2020). Despite of extensive usage of communication technology tools, virtuality and diversity in remote teams decreases the pace of collaboration and team productivity when compared to co-located teams (Ocker, Huang, Benbunan-Fich, & Hiltz, 2011). It also increases the chances of relational and task conflicts among dispersed team members (Armstrong & Cole, 2002; Hinds & Bailey, 2003; Hinds & Mortensen, 2005; Mortensen & Hinds, 2001). Individuals working in distributed teams often communicate less and thus share less information in comparison to co-located team members which negatively impact team performance (C. Cramton & Webber, 2005). Social isolation due to lack of opportunities to connect with colleagues in remote environments reduces sense of belongingness and can increase intention to leave (Larson, Vroman, & Makarius, 2020; Wang, Liu, Qian, & Parker, 2020).

In a cross culturally distributed team, virtual environments make it difficult to understand and connect with each other, and have personal interactions which facilitate sense of oneness and team spirit (Myungsuk, Park, & Lee, 2014). Thus individuals working remotely in a distributed teams exhibit less cohesive behaviour, distrust and reluctance to share information eventually leading to poor team performance (Shen, Gallivan, & Tang, 2016). The absence of face-to-face interaction and inability to observe a remote teammate's work can result in positive impressions about oneself and less favourable or hostile attitude towards others (Johri, 2012). Such biased behaviour has been attributed to be the main cause of strained relationships among distributed team members (Liao, 2017). This lack of emotional connection among members in GDT has been referred to as 'social distance' (Neeley, 2015). It is an 'invisible wall' that exists in a GDT whose members experience lack of closeness both physically and psychologically leading to 'us' vs 'them' attitudes (Boyraz, 2016). The 'us' versus 'them' attitude corrodes the effectiveness of GDT which is characterised as being dynamic, diverse, dispersed and digital in nature (Hass & Mark M, 2016). The main question this chapter addresses is 'how to mitigate social distance among distributed members? And what practices can alleviate 'us' vs 'them' attitudes and enhance GDT effectiveness?

SOCIAL DISTANCE IN GDT

Traditional co-located teams have individuals working together at the same place of work, they work side-by-side coordinating with each other, and engage in informal interactions e.g. coffee breaks which help in building social ties. Individuals when located remotely work virtually with each other which limits spontaneous interactions, they do not have opportunities to build personal relationships and thus can experience low team identity adversely affecting knowledge sharing and teamwork (Myungsuk et al., 2014). Individuals working in remote environments have difficulties in identifying whom to contact for specific tasks, are unable to reach common consensus for task priorities, can suffer from an absence of information about the availability and presence of remote colleagues, longer response times, difference in communication style, and lack of acknowledgment for their work leading to formation of 'us' versus ' them' attitudes (Privman, Hiltz, & Wang, 2013).

In a case study, which investigated the dynamics of GDT in IT offshoring work involving German and Indian software professionals, Zimmermann, Raab & Zanotelli (2013) found 'us' vs 'them' attitudes among the German team as they described the quality of software delivered by Indian colleagues below standard which they have to rework. The German team members expressed their inability to identify with the Indian offshore team thus exerted less effort in collaborating with them. They considered their Indian colleagues as service providers rather than fellow team members and also perceived them to be of lower status. Comparing the performance of GDT to co-located software development teams, it was revealed that GDT had low levels of performance compared to co-located teams, which was attributed to the communication and coordination issues between the dispersed members. As an outcome the quality of the outputs (software) was poor and task completion was slower (Colomo-Palacios, Casado-Lumbreras, Soto-Acosta, García-Peñalvo and Tovar, 2014). The remoteness due to geographic distance severely hinders formation of team trust, sharing of information and prompt communication between dispersed members ultimately lowering team effectiveness (Kaul, Pande & Ahuja, 2017).

Sources of Social Distance

Studies on the dynamics of virtual teams point out that social distance or an 'us' versus 'them' attitude is formed due to status differential, imbalanced communication, lack of awareness about the remote team's work context and cultural differences.

Status Differential

In an offshoring-outsourcing model, status differential is prominent between offshore and onshore teams due to their positions as vendors versus client, headquarters versus subsidiary or due to national boundaries (Marrewijk, 2011; Mattarelli & Gupta, 2009; Neeley, 2015; Zimmermann et al., 2013). Teams located at headquarters or close to clients have more access to financial resources, say in decision making, interact with clients directly and hold critical information about the project. Thus they are perceived to be of higher status in comparison to the others often leading to frictions in distributed teams which reduces team communication and identification. Individuals with higher status do not regard individuals of lower status equal, are not open to hear their suggestions and ignore their needs and contributions (Neeley, 2015; Wilson, O'Leary, Metiu, & Jett, 2005).

A case study analysis by Marrewijk (2011), examined collaborative practices between Indian and Dutch software teams, highlighted the fact that the Dutch team members directly dealt with customers and treated the Indian team as a back office which became a point of status inequality. Time zone difference can be another source of status inequality; due to the small common time window Indian members had to work unsocialable and long hours whereas the Dutch used to follow strict work rules of eight hours. The difference in status can also be based on skill and expertise of the team members. Boyraz (2016) identified that in distributed teams of software professionals located across Bulgaria and the US, the team members located in the US were perceived to be highly skilled and experienced hence considered to be of higher status than their Bulgarian team mates who were involved in less skilled work and perceived to be of lower status. Due to this American teams dominated the interactions most of the time and Bulgarian members did not have much opportunity to express their opinions and were hesitant to participate, resulting inteam social distance.

Imbalanced Communication

Uneven participation can be one of the challenges of working in a virtual environment (Zuofa & Ochieng, 2017). This is accentuated due to language differences in terms of fluency, accent and usage of English language which can lead to miscommunication resulting in weak social ties, low trust and absence of shared understanding among the distributed members (Pflügler, Wiesche, & Helmut, 2018). When English is not the first language for some members the fluent speakers often dominate the discussion and the less fluent speakers hesitate or withdraw from sharing their opinion and ideas in meetings (Huang, 2009; Neeley, 2015). Fuller, Vician, & Brown (2016), further, reported that in spite of using multiple computer mediated tools (email, video and audio conferencing etc.) for communications individual's anxiety i.e. fear or apprehension towards using computer mediation interactions, can render some individuals mute. Individuals who have high levels of anxiety send fewer work related messages, share few new ideas and participate less in conference calls leading to uneven or imbalanced communication.

Lack of Direct Experience

In a virtual environment, there are limited opportunities to observe remote colleagues working (Zuofa & Ochieng, 2017). Geographic distance and cultural differences impede formation of situational information about the environment in which a remote colleague is working. Delayed communication and short overlapping time zone windows can generate misunderstanding and mistrust among distributed members (Cramton, 2001; Johri, 2012; Koszegi, 2016; Mortensen & Neeley, 2012). Lack of understanding of cultural differences can also create misperception between team members (Neeley, 2015).

Inability to Identify

The physical proximity among colleagues makes them familiar about each other and how they work together. They get to know about each other's working style, communication style, personalities, roles and cultural context which builds personal ties. In virtual teams, where individuals are assigned specific tasks which they are supposed to do throughout the project, the limited frequency of communication or need to connect with each other lowers team identification (Lionel & You, 2018; Pflügler et al., 2018). This lack of affiliation can prompt "us" vs "them" dynamics, adversely impacting knowledge sharing (Eisenberg & Mattarelli, 2017).

Practices to Bridge Social Distance

Cramton & Hinds (2004) highlight the formation of location based subgroups in GDT and emergence of bias such as ethnocentrism. The study mentions The Intergroup Contact Hypothesis theory by Allport (1954) which proposes that cooperative interdependence, equal status, institutional or social support, inclusive communication and sharing of context can make remote team members motivated to engage and share information with each other, promoting cross national learning which can overcome intergroup bias. Neeley (2015) proposed the SPLIT framework to alleviate 'us' versus 'them' or social distance formed due to perceived status inequality in global virtual teams. The SPLIT framework stands for structure, process, language, identity and technology. It involves structuring of teams in terms of dispersion of members, setting up communication norms, and inclusion through participation in communication, fostering shared identity and usage of instant technology for spontaneous communication. In another study, Boyraz (2016) proved that communication and team identification can moderate the negative effect of subgroup formation on team innovation and member satisfaction in distributed teams. Hass & Mark (2016) based on their research about effectiveness of diverse, dispersed, digital and dynamic teams (also referred as 4D Teams) proposes that managers of such teams should offer clear articulation of goals and objectives of the team, ensure the correct number and mix of members, design and define each task and process, provide supportive resources such as access to information systems, training, technological assistance etc. and work on building common identity and understanding among team members. Based on the existing evidence we empirically test the extent to which four practices – task interdependence, inclusive communication, contextual information and shared identity – moderate the relationship between social distance and team effectiveness among GDT relative to perceived status equality (PSE) which refers to the relative interaction, appreciation and understanding between on-site and offshore team members.

Task Interdependence

Task interdependence is the degree to which individuals work closely and coordinate with a distant or remote member to complete tasks (Boyraz, 2016). Task interdependence dictates the amount of communication and coordination required between remote locations when work is globally distributed (Kumar, Van Fenema, & Von Glinow, 2009). It makes dispersed members communicate, attend meetings, share information and be accountable to each other (Joshi, Lazarova, & Liao, 2009). It prompts task driven interactions, frequent collaboration and coordination of activities among virtual team members (Robinson, 2015). In virtual teams goal, task and outcome interdependence were found to be positively related to team effectiveness (Staples & Webster, 2008). It involves closely working with onsite teams, frequent coordination, receiving information and feedback on work.

Inclusive Communication

Inclusive communication is the degree to which the individual participates and is involved in the communication process with the remote team (Shore et al., 2011). It can be practiced by encouraging participation from all members in discussions, making them contribute by expressing views, discouraging those fluent in language from dominating discussions and soliciting opinions from mute participants (Neeley, 2015). Setting clear expectations, prior information about meeting agendas, and sharing the minutes of meetings helps remote members to actively participate, stay involved and perform high quality work (Lerner, 2015; Zimmermann, 2020).

Contextual Information

Contextual information is the degree of awareness and understanding about the local situation and work environment in which the remote member works (Koszegi, 2016). It encompasses sharing information about work practices, availablity of remote members, holidays, work adjustment made by remote member due to time differences and understanding of cross cultural differences. Such information helps in avoiding misassumption about a remote colleague (Johri, 2012). Sharing of contextual information both through formal and informal interactions can improve interpersonal relationships among individuals in remote locations (Lionel & You, 2018).

Shared Identity

Shared identity is the degree to which the individual experiences similarity and oneness with remote colleagues. A sense of oneness can be developed by creating an open communication environment in which individuals are encouraged to speak their minds and openly share apprehensions (Koszegi, 2016). Fostering shared identity refers to developing a strong sense of common identity and making the remote team members aware of each others constraints and context which helps to overcome 'us' vs 'them' thinking (Hass & Mark, 2016). Studies have indicated that in virtual teams team identification can positively influence team cooperation which leads to higher team performance (Boyraz, 2016; Chieh Lin, He, Baruch, & Ashforth, 2017).

METHODOLOGY

Sample and Data Collection

Bengaluru, is known as the Silicon City of India which hosts more than 2,500 software companies and has 12 Special Economic Zones (SEZ) which produce software and electronics services for export. A multilevel random sampling was adopted with two IT SEZs, Pritech Park and Global Tech Village, were randomly selected. A survey was conducted among IT professionals working in multinational companies such as Accenture, Cognizant, Capgemini, Mindtree, NTT Data, Cisco, and IBM located in these SEZs. A cross-sectional study in a non-contrived organizational environment was conducted where concepts were measured by adapting established and validated scales. Data was collected from October 2019 to January 2020. A total of 2,000 respondents were invited to take the survey out of which 502 responses were received, making a response rate as 25%. All of the respondents were working remotely in collaboration with an onsite team. The questionnaires were checked for completeness and outliers were removed prior to statistical analysis. A total of 482 responses were used for statistical tests. Out of the 482 cases, 182 cases reported low PSE; 192 average PSE and 108 high PSE.

Variables

Independent Variable

Social Distance was measured by adapting a 17-item scale developed by Privman, Hiltz, & Wang (2013) assessed in terms of 'us' versus 'them' attitudes exhibited through trust, conflicts with respect to goals and tasks, and overall team spirit expressed by the individuals working at offshore towards their onsite team.

Dependent Variable

Team Effectiveness was assessed using a scale of 8 items adapted from the studies of Gibson, Zellmer-Bruhn & Schwab (2003); Chad Lin, Standing & Liu (2008); Zimmermann et al. (2013) with aspects like overall performance of the project team in terms of achievement of goals, quality, timeliness, cost, member satisfaction and intention to stay with the project team.

Moderating Variables

Task interdependence (M1) was assessed by how closely the individual works with an onsite colleague to complete tasks. This was assessed in terms of close coordination, frequent interactions, and exchange of information required with onsite colleague to finish the tasks. It was measured using 5-item scale adapted from Boyraz (2016). Inclusive communication (M2) is the extent an individual is encouraged to participate and is included in the communication process with the onsite team (Shore et al., 2011). This was assessed in terms of encouragement received by the respondent to participate and present views, express disagreements, reaching out to onsite colleagues, access to information and regular updates about project related information. It was measured with a scale of 10 items. Contextual information (M3) is the extent to which the individual is made aware of the remote location, understands the local situation and work environment in which his/her onsite colleague works. This was assessed in terms of information about availability of onsite members, work adjustment and pressure of onsite members, work processes followed onsite, work done by onsite teams and awareness of cultural differences. It was measured with a scale of 7 items. Shared Identity (M4) is the level of similarity and oneness experienced by the individual while working with the onsite colleague (Koszegi, 2016). This was assessed in terms of expressing concerns openly, approaching onsite members, similarity of goals and priorities. It was measured with a scale of 8 items.

Control Variable

Perceived Status Equality (PSE) was assessed in terms of the level of interest displayed by an onsite team member in interacting, appreciating and understanding the work practices of Indian offshore team (Mattarelli & Gupta, 2009). In this study perceived status equality with respect to onsite colleague has been considered as a control variable. The categories were 1- low PSE; 2-average PSE and 3-high PSE. The study investigated the interaction effect of moderating variables on the relationship between independent and dependent variables with perceived status equality as a control variable. Respondents indicated their response on a 5-point Likert scale with '1' as highly disagree and '5' as highly agree.

RESULTS

Demographic Profile of Respondents

Of the 482 respondents, 66.8% reported being team members and 33.2% team leaders, and 60.5% (291) are male. There are 12.2% respondents with less than 1 year of total work experience, 19.3% with 2 years to 4 years; 17.2% with 4 years to 6 years; 25.1% with 7 years to 10 years and 26.2% with more than 10 years of total experience in the IT industry. Around 61% of the respondents are engineers with a Bachelors of Technology or Bachelors of Engineering; 24.1% with a Master's in Business Management or Computer Applications; 6.6% have other qualifications at the undergraduate level and 8.3% are Masters in Technology. All respondents worked at Indian offshore locations in Bengaluru and collaborated with their distributed team located outside India (onsite) which included the US and Canada (62.7%); UK (13.5%); Europe (11.8%); Asia (6.8%); Australia (2.7%); Middle East (1.2%); South America (0.4%) and rest of the world (0.9%). This is consistent with the fact that maximum amount of software services from India being exported to North America and Europe (Electronic and Computer Software Promotion Council of India, 2019). Only 37.3% of the respondents in this study have visited the onsite location. Of all the respondents, 68.5% had their manager located with them in Bengaluru office, and 31.5% of them had a manager in a different location. It was found that 74% of respondents were working in project teams that were at the initial stages of development varying from 0 to 3 years.

Table 1 here depicts the mean and standard deviation values of all the variables in the study. The mean values, μ and standard deviation, σ of the variables are Team Effectiveness (μ=30.48; σ = 4.9); Task Interdependence (μ=15.70; σ = 2.5); Inclusive Communication (μ=38.49; σ = 6.8; Contextual Information (μ=26.52; σ = 5.06); Shared Identity (μ=30.4; σ=6.1); and Social Distance (μ=36.9; σ=9.2). For the test of normality, the skewness and kurtosis values of the variables, social distance, team effectiveness, task interdependence, inclusive communication, contextual information, shared identity and perceived status equality were examined. The values were found to be between -2 and +2, which is within the acceptable limits of normality (George & Mallery, 2010).

Table 1. Descriptive statistics

	Mean	Std. Deviation	Skewness		Kurtosis	
	Statistic	Statistic	Statistic	Std. Error	Statistic	Std. Error
Social Distance	36.9982	9.23786	-.314	.111	-.440	.222
Team Effectiveness	30.4845	4.97537	-.494	.111	.687	.222
Task Interdependence	15.7015	2.58886	-.584	.111	1.515	.222
Inclusive Communication	38.4927	6.85011	-.634	.111	1.301	.222
Contextual Information	26.5264	5.06727	-.489	.111	.484	.222
Shared Identity	30.4768	6.18523	-.702	.111	1.187	.222

For validation of scales, factor analysis using Principal Rotated Component was conducted. The results of the varimax rotation show the Kaiser-Meyer-Oklin (KMO) statistics which tests the sample adequacy, where a higher value (close to 1) indicates suitability for data analysis. The KMO statistics for each of the variables social distance, team effectiveness, inclusive communication, contextual information, shared identity and perceived status equality was found to be above 0.80, which is considered to be good for sample adequacy except for task interdependence which was found to be 0.670 which is moderate but acceptable. The Bartlett Test for Sphericity is an indication of the strength of the relationship among variables was found to be 0.00 (<0.05) for all the variables, indicating that the values are sufficiently related to each other. The loadings values on factors was more than 0.5 and no cross-loading was found in component matrix confirming convergent and discriminant validity of the variables. The Eigenvalues of all the variables were found to be more than 1 (see Annex A.1).

The responses for all the constructs were collected from the same respondent thus common method bias Harman's one-factor test was done using Principal Component factor analysis (Organ & Philip M.

Podsakoff, 1986). The results shows that maximum a factor explained a total variance of 33.85% only, which is less than the acceptable 50%. This shows that there is no apparent general factor. Therefore, the presence of common method bias is rejected. The Cronbach's alpha was calculated to determine the reliability of each variable. Table 2 presents the value of Cronbach's alpha for all the variable which was found to be above the acceptable value of 0.7 (George & Mallery, 2010).

Table 2. Reliability Statistics

S.no	Construct	No. of Items	Cronbach Alpha
1	Social Distance	17	.891
2.	Team Effectiveness	8	.849
3	Task Interdependence	4	.760
4.	Inclusive Communication	10	.901
5.	Contextual Information	7	.890
6.	Shared Identity	8	.912
7.	Perceived Status Equality	3	.789

The main effect with independent variable, social distance and dependent variable, team effectiveness was determined by a linear regression test calculated using SPSS version 21. The regression coefficient (B) with the standard error was found to be significantly negative (B=-0.29 (0.018), p=0.000), The R^2 value of 0.36 indicates that social distance explains 36% of the variance in team effectiveness. The model as a whole was significant with F=270.1, df= (1, 480); p=0.000, proving the negative impact of social distance on team effectiveness.

In the next stage, the moderating effect of task interdependence, inclusive communication, contextual information and shared identity was ascertained by first centering all the variables and then estimating the interaction effect (Dawson, 2014). The collinearity statistics showed the tolerance value to be more than .10 and VIF value less than 10, which rules out multicollinearity among the social distance and all the four moderating variables. The moderating effect of each variable was determined independently by examining the value of B, unstandardized coefficient of errors, standard error and p-value, at 95% confidence level ($p<0.05$) at each level of perceived status equality, PSE 1=low, 2=average and 3=high (Status_Cat) among respondents.

Interaction Effect of Task Interdependence

The results of interaction effect of task interdependence is depicted in Table 3. The effect was found to be insignificant at PSE1 (B=-0.22, p=0.980; R^2=14.3%,), but significant at PSE2 (B=-0.14), p=0.000; R^2=23.2%,) and PSE3 (B=-0.23, p=0.040; R^2=49.1%,). Task interdependence significantly ($p< 0.05$) reduces the negative effect of social distance on team effectiveness when PSE is average or high but not when it is low. The R^2 values explains the variance in team effectiveness due to the interaction effect which is significant at PSE 2 & 3. On examining the B value, a curvilinear effect of task interdependence depicting the interaction effect only dampens the negative effect of social distance when PSE is high but it weakens to a large extent when PSE is average.

Table 3. Interaction Effect of Task Interdependence

Unstandardized Coefficients	B (Standard Error); p value at 95%		
Perceived Status Equality	1=Low	2=Moderate	3=High
Social Distance	-.22(.04); p=0.000	-.14(.03); p=0.000	-.23(.03); p=0.000
Task Interdependence	.11(.16); p=0.501	.43(.11); p=0.000	.92(.20); p=0.000
Interaction Effect C_Social Distance x C_Task Interdependence	-.00(.01); p=0.980	.05(.01); p=0.000	.04(.01); p=0.004
R^2	14.3%	23.2%	49.1%
F value	9.86(p<0.000)	18.96(p<0.000)	33.38(p<0.000)
df	3,178	3,188	3,104

Interaction Effect of Inclusive Communication

The interaction effect of inclusive communication was found to be insignificant at PSE1 (B= -0.143; p=0.641, R^2=27.3%) but significantly moderating at PSE2 (B=-0.195; p=0.00, R^2=25.7%) and PSE3 (B=-0.276; p=0.00, R^2=49.4%) depicted in Table 4. Thus we conclude that inclusive communication significantly reduces the negative effect of social distance on team effectiveness when perceived status equality is average or high but not when it is low. On careful examination of the B value we find a curvilinear effect which shows that the moderating effect of inclusive communication is higher in cases of average PSE than high PSE.

Table 4. Interaction Effect of Inclusive Communication

Unstandardized Coefficients	B (Standard Error); p value at 95%		
Perceived Status Equality	1=Low	2=Moderate	3=High
Social Distance	-.14(.04); p=0.002	-.19(.03); p=0.000	-.28(.04); p=0.000
Inclusive Communication	.32(.06); p=0.000	.22(.05); p=0.000	.36(.08); p=0.000
Interaction Effect C_Social Distance x C_Inclusive Communication	-.00(.00); p=0.641	.02(.00); p=0.000	.01(.00); p=0.003
R^2	.27	.25	.49
F value	22.32 (p<0.000)	21.65(p<0.000)	33.82(p<0.000)
df	3,178	3,188	3,104

Interaction Effect of Contextual Information

Table 5 depicts the interaction effect of contextual information, which is found to be insignificant at PSE1 (B=-0.211, p=0.653; R^2=24.5%,) and PSE3 (B=-0.241, p=0.55; R^2=41%,) but significant at PSE 2 (B=-0.107), p=0.00; R^2=30.4%,). Again a curvilinear effect is found.

Table 5. Interaction Effect of Contextual Information

Unstandardized Coefficients	B (Standard Error); p value at 95%		
Perceived Status Equality	1=Low	2=Moderate	3=High
Social Distance	-.21(.04); p=0.000	-.10(.03); p=0.010	-.24(.04); p=0.000
Contextual Information	.37(.10); p=0.000	.49(.07); p=0.000	.16(.08); p=0.060
Interaction Effect C_Social Distance x C_Contextual Information	-.00(.00); p=0.651	.01(.00); p=0.010	.00(.00); p=0.560
R^2	.24	.30	.41
F value	19.22 (p<0.000)	27.39(p<0.000)	24.11(p<0.000)
df	3,178	3,188	3,104

Interaction Effect of Shared Identity

The results of the interaction effect of shared identity, depicted in Table 6, shows that at PSE1 (B=-0.16; p=0.513, R^2=22.3%) the effect is insignificant but at PSE2 (B=-0.09; p=0.010 R^2=27.3%) and PSE 3 (B=-0.21; p<0.000, R^2=50%) shared identity significantly reduces the negative effect of social distance on team effectiveness. We again observe a curvilinear effect.

Table 6. Interaction Effect of Shared Identity

Unstandardized Coefficients	B (Standard Error); p value at 95%		
Perceived Status Equality	1= Low	2=Moderate	3=High
Social Distance	-0.17(.04); p=0.000	-0.09(.03); p=0.010	-0.22(.04); p=0.000
Shared Identity	0.30(.07); p=0.000	0.35(.05); p=0.000	0.50(.10); p=0.000
Interaction Effect C_Social Distance x C_Shared Identity	-0.00(.00); p=0.510	0.01(.00); p=0.010	0.01(.00); p=0.000
R^2	.22	.27	.50
F value	17.02(p=0.000)	23.57(p=0.000)	34.62(p=0.000)
df	3,178	3,188	3,104

DISCUSSION

This empirical study examined the social distance in terms of 'us' vs 'them' attitudes among Indian off-shore IT professionals working in geographically distributed teams, thus their work involves collaborating with a remotely located onsite team. The responses from the Indian IT professionals shows that they do possess 'us' vs 'them' attitudes towards their onsite team which negatively influences their perception about the overall project team effectiveness. The results of this study are consistent with other research studies which revealed that in geographically distributed teams existence of 'us' vs 'them' thinking, characterised by level of distrust, conflict of goals and tasks and lack of awareness, adversely affects team effectiveness (Boyraz, 2016; Ocker, Huang, Benbunan-Fich & Hiltz, 2011; Pflügler et al., 2018; Privman et al., 2013; Zimmermann et al., 2013).

In an offshore-onsite model, the onsite team is either a client or the team located at client location or at headquarters. The onsite team often enjoys greater access to information about the business, software requirements and resource availability, and may also have a bigger say in decision making leaving the onsite team to be perceived of higher status in comparison to the offshore team. This creates perceived status inequality or differentials among distributed members which is accentuated when onsite members are restrictive in communication with offshore members, unaware about offshore work environments, and do not recognise or appreciate the work done by offshore colleagues (Boyraz, 2016; Mattarelli & Gupta, 2009; Neeley, 2015; A. Zimmermann et al., 2013). The finding of the interaction effects show the moderating effect of task interdependence, inclusive communication, contextual information and shared identity on the negative relationship between social distance and team effectiveness is significant when the individual working at offshore perceives themselves to be at equal status but not in cases when perceived status equality is low.

The moderating effect of task interdependence on the main effect in this study is consistent with other studies which proved that task interdependence promotes interaction and negates the negative impact of low team cohesion on team performance (Boyraz, 2016; Jong, Curşeu & Leenders, 2014). However, moderation is significant only when perceived status equality by offshore members is average to high and not when it is low (evidence in the curvelinear relationship reported), meaning creating interdependent tasks will fail to reduce negative impacts of 'us' versus 'them' thinking unless the onsite member makes an effort in communication and coordination with offshore member. Task interdependence is very essential in cross culturally distributed teams as it necessitate members to interact thereby making them familiar with each other and overcome the cultural differences, build trust and share knowledge thus dampening the adverse effects of subgroup formation on team performance (Boyraz, 2016; Ghosh, 2014; Pinjani & Palvia, 2013; Shen et al., 2016).

Secondly, the moderating effect of inclusive communication was found to be consistent with the Boyraz (2016) study which shows creating a psychologically safe communication climate (PSCC) improves the team identification when members perceive status equalities. Adopting inclusive communication practices in distributed teams which are culturally diverse can positively impact team innovation thus reaping the benefits of cultural diversity (Lisak, Erez, Sui & Lee, 2016). However, the sense of inclusion can only be built when onsite teams keep the line of communication open for all and displace status inequality. Increasing the frequency and depth of communication, sharing information, and open discussion about issues/challenges ensure all members are on the same page (Morgan, Paucar-Caceres & Wright, 2014).

Site visits builds in familiarity in distant work relationships (Hinds & Cramton, 2014). However, this can be an expensive affair for distributed teams. Sharing contextual information about the remote team member can help in creating the accurate image of the distant member, identify differences and similarities in distributed teams reducing intergroup bias (Cramton & Hinds, 2004). The results of the study show that contextual information did significantly moderate the negative relationship between social distance and team effectiveness in the case of average level of perceived status equality but did not moderate when status equality with onsite team was low or high. This may be true among lesser experienced team members, but as they gain experience and are aware of the nuances of working in a distributed team, such contextual information may not be very effective in reducing negative bias towards onsite team members.

The results shows that having a shared identity moderates the main effect significantly when perceived status inequality was average or high but not when it was low. This results are consistent with Voida, Bos, Olson, Olson and Dunning (2012) who also found shared identity to weaken the negative effect of location-based subgroups on team productivity. However, when the status equality is perceived to be low among the members of offshore and onshore teams, it is difficult to build a shared identity (Mattarelli & Gupta, 2009). Shared identity between subgroups is built by emphasising the importance of relying on each other for various skills and the overall team success (Hass & Mark M, 2016). But if the onsite is not very appreciative or do not recognise the work done by offshore team of much value in achieving team goals and objectives, then shared identity may be not be successful alleviating 'us' versus 'them' attitudes. Larson et al. (2020) highlighted video conferencing as an effective tool to reduce social isolation and facilitate exchange of non-verbal cues to understand the work environment of a remote colleague. In such situations managers could ensure that remote team members communicate with each other frequently and share information regularly. They should encourage or create events for social interactions such as informal talk about non-work topics among remote members to connect with each other at a personal level.

On the whole, findings of the study prove that practices like task interdependence, contextual information, inclusive communication and shared identity do weaken the negative impact of social distance on team effectiveness of a GDT but only when offshore members perceive themselves to have status equality with onsite colleagues. However, the onus of reducing social distance lies largely on the team with higher status i.e. onsite in this case. It is only when they believe that the work of members with lower status is important and treat them as equals (Mattarelli & Gupta, 2009; Neeley, 2015). Onsite members can bring in status equality by engaging in regular formal and informal interactions with the offshore team, visiting offshore locations, establishing rewards for offshore members and being culturally sensitive. Scheduling meetings on a rotating schedule where time zone difference is wide can further support effective GDTs (Dhawan & Chamorro, Premuzic, 2018).

MANAGERIAL IMPLICATIONS

The findings of the study suggest various implications for managers of distributed and remote teams. To understand the dynamics of distributed teams, role of group status or perception of power among members cannot be ignored. This status inequality creates interpersonal distance among remote members hampering team communication and cohesiveness leading to 'us' versus 'them' thinking.

Facilitating Communication Around Task

Communication is a vital skill for managers of distributed teams. GDT managers can ensure effective communication among distributed members by setting the standard, the expectations and the communication framework for the team. They should align task priorities of all the members with the overall project objectives and goal in order to control and manage team performance and effectiveness (Morgan et al., 2014). During the virtual interactions managers should encourage members to express their views and speak their mind to enable them to prepare by keeping them informed about the agenda of the meeting, updating them about the key decisions or any changes to bridge the knowledge gap which may exist between the distributed teams (Pazos, 2012; Robinson, 2015). Managers can maintain and monitor formation of team trust by keeping track of how often team members connect, respond to one another and share tasks. The remote members should also be trained on cross cultural differences and usage of communication technology tools. To boost interpersonal processes managers should set norms of communication, share information about onsite work regularly, be transparent in decision making and empower employees to participate in meetings. Managers should also regularly assess collaborative behaviours of remote members and strengthen it by highlighting the problem areas and hearing out employees concerns (Feitosa & Salas, 2020).

Fostering Shared Identity

Managers of dispersed teams can foster shared identity online through intranets and team homepages, encouraging key members to visit each other's location whenever opportunity arises and create collective activities (Johri, 2012). Creation of team names, logos, shared team goals and activities like designing team crests build shared similarity and enhance the group cohesion among remote members (Marlow & Dabbish, 2011). During meetings with team members, managers should emphasise the similarity in goals and priorities to build feelings of togetherness and 'oneness' among remote members. Shared identity can be nutured by managers through showing the team the bigger picture project's overall goals, financial targets to be achieved and how organization strategy will be executed by each member of the distributed team, uniting the team to a common goal and building togetherness (Knight, 2015).

Fostering Inclusiveness

Managers can bring inclusiveness in remote teams such as empowering remote workers to manage their communication and collaboration with the team, sharing a communication charter about the availability of members and managing time zone windows for conducting meetings and conference calls, increase the usage of video calls and encourage informal interactions between remote colleagues. In a remote team environment creating a psychologically safe communication environment where individuals are free to be themselves, can voice their opinions and ideas builds the feeling of inclusion (Boyraz, 2016; Erez et al., 2013; Zimmermann, 2020). Appreciating and acknowledging the work of remote team members makes them feel their efforts are noticed and visible in the virtual team environment. Managers can do that either by mentioning it in the team meeting or sending regular emails appreciating individual members for a job well done (Knight, 2015).

Sharing Contextual Information

The role of the manager in distributed teams is that of a liaison and hinge pin, who will share knowledge about team work practices, environment and social norms (Mattarelli & Gupta, 2009). Boyraz (2016) identified two roles of managers which can prove effective in building social ties among members of a distributed team, the one of a 'communication broker' and of a 'facilitator'. The manager should support in terms of communicating details of remote team members, sharing information about project work environment and create a sense of shared space which can lessen the negative effect of relationship conflicts on team performance in distributed teams (Wickramasinghe & Nandula, 2015). The manager should effectively use technology to store and share information among team members, emails, conference calls, video calls, chats, shared calendars and group folders, to get everyone on the same page (Gallagher, 2017). A manager should act as a multicultural broker, resolving culture-related misunderstanding, encouraging open communication and sharing of information between distributed teams (Eisenberg & Mattarelli, 2017).

Geographic and temporal distances are static in nature and cannot be changed with time, however distance-based perceptions and attitudes are dynamic in nature. Such distance can increase or decrease as individuals increase their frequency of interactions, involve themselves in communication process, familiarise themselves with each other's work environment and build consensus on common goals and objectives which ultimately leads to improved team performance and member satisfaction. Managers play a critical role in acting as a link to facilitate closeness and interpersonal relations in remote work settings.

LIMITATIONS AND FUTURE RESEARCH

This study was conducted prior to the COVID-19 global pandemic, and focuses on the experiences of workers in one sector, IT, working in geographically distributed teams in India and the US. Some of the findings here may, therefore, be less applicable to workers in other contexts. In addition, the specific case explored is not one of remote working at home, but has wider relevance in its focus on teams that are geographically distributed; something that existed prior to the pandemic and is certain to become a more common feature of work in many sectors and occupations in the post-pandemic era. As such, the findings from the study offer useful insight into the methods of managing teams, and promoting effective team working when teams are remotely distributed. Further research could explore the applicability of the recommendations generated from this study to applications of remote working in the COVID-19 post-pandemic context.

CONCLUSION

The results of this study shows reducing social distance is a two way process. The effort has to be made from both the onsite and offshore team members to communicate, collaborate and cooperate with each other for team success. Working in a cross cultural virtual team can be stressful to members, and status differential in teams can make it challenging to integrate distributed members into a coherent entity. Distributed teams are usually plagued with mistrust, conflicts and misunderstanding leading to an 'us' versus 'them' or social distance. In GDT, managers have an important role to act as a bridge to help onsite and offshore team members to overcome 'us' versus 'them' bias towards each other by encouraging frequency of interaction, involvement in communication processes, keep them updated about key information and decisions and emphasising the similarity of team goals. However, this is possible only when the team which has higher perceived status makes an attempt to involve in the communication process members of perceived lower status, the team members are culturally sensitive, and there is common appreciation of the work done by all remote team members.

The study conducted among remotely working IT professionals who collaborated across geographies, time zones and cultural diversity highlights the social distance experienced based on misperception or misunderstanding due to virtuality and cultural diversity among remote workers which can negatively impact team effectiveness. The results of the study highlight the role of task interdependence, inclusive communication practices, sharing contextual information and fostering shared identity in moderating the negative effects of social distance on team effectiveness in geographically distributed teams.

REFERENCES

Bick, R., Chang, M., Wang, K. W., & Yu, T. (2020). *A blueprint for remote working: lessons from China.* McKinsey & Company. Retrieved from https://www.mckinsey.com/business-functions/mckinsey-digital/our-insights/a-blueprint-for-remote-working-lessons-from-china

Boyraz, M. (2016). *How to break the "invisible walls" the role of communicative practices for overcoming challenges of subgroups in global teams.* The State University.

Colomo-Palacios, R., Casado-Lumbreras, C., Soto-Acosta, P., García-Peñalvo, F. J., & Tovar, E. (2014). Project managers in global software development teams: A study of the effects on productivity and performance. *Software Quality Journal, 22*(1), 3–19. doi:10.100711219-012-9191-x

Cramton, C. D. (2001). The Mutual Knowledge Problem and Its Consequences for Dispersed Collaboration. *Organization Science, 12*(3), 346–371. doi:10.1287/orsc.12.3.346.10098

Cramton, D., & Hinds, P. (2004). Subgroup Dynamics in Internationally Distributed Teams: Ethnocentrism or Cross-National Learning? *Research in Organizational Behavior, 26*(04), 231–263. doi:10.1016/S0191-3085(04)26006-3

Dawson, J. (2014). Moderation in management research: What, why, when and how. *Journal of Business and Psychology, 29*(1), 1–19. doi:10.100710869-013-9308-7

Dhawan, E., & Chamorro, Premuzic, T. (2018). How to Collaborate Effectively If Your Team Is Remote. *Harvard Business Review.*

Dulebohn, J. H., & Hoch, J. E. (2017). Virtual teams in organizations. *Human Resource Management Review, 27*(4), 569–574. doi:10.1016/j.hrmr.2016.12.004

Eisenberg, J., & Mattarelli, E. (2017). Building Bridges in Global Virtual Teams: The Role of Multicultural Brokers in Overcoming the Negative Effects of Identity Threats on Knowledge Sharing Across Subgroups. *Journal of International Management, 23*(4), 399–411. doi:10.1016/j.intman.2016.11.007

Electronic and Computer Software Promotion Council of India. (2019). *India's Computer Software Export Report.* Author.

Erez, M., Lisak, A., Harush, R., Glikson, E., Nouri, R., & Shokef, E. (2013). Going global: Developing management students' cultural intelligence and global identity in culturally diverse virtual teams. *Academy of Management Learning & Education, 12*(3), 330–355. doi:10.5465/amle.2012.0200

Feitosa, J., & Salas, E. (2020). Today's virtual teams: Adapting lessons learned to the pandemic context. *Organizational Dynamics*, (January), 19–21. PMID:32836509

Felstead, A., & Henseke, G. (2017). Assessing the growth of remote working and its consequences for effort, well-being and work-life balance. *New Technology, Work and Employment*, *32*(3), 195–212. doi:10.1111/ntwe.12097

Fuller, R. M., Vician, C. M., & Brown, S. A. (2016). *Longitudinal Effects of Computer-Mediated Communication Anxiety on Interaction in Virtual Teams* (Vol. 69). Accounting Faculty Publications., doi:10.1109/TPC.2016.2583318

Gallagher, B. D. (2017). *Overcoming Collaboration Obstacles in Globally Distributed Teams*. University of Oregon.

George, D., & Mallery, P. (2010). SPSS for Windows Step by Step: A Simple Guide and Reference 17.0 update (10th ed.). Boston: Pearson.

Ghosh, A. (2014). Culturally competent behaviors at workplace: An intergroup perspective for workplace diversity. *South Asian Journal of Management*, *21*(3), 73–95. http://proxy.cityu.edu/login?url=http://search.ebscohost.com/login.aspx?direct=true&db=bth&AN=99351505&site=ehost-live&scope=site

Gibson, Z.-B., Zellmer-Bruhn, M. E., & Schwab, D. P. (2003). Team effectiveness in multinational organizations: Development across contexts. *Group & Organization Management*, *28*(4), 444–474. doi:10.1177/1059601103251685

Hass, M., & Mark, M. (2016, June). The Secrets of Great Teamwork. *Harvard Business Review*, 1–11. PMID:27491197

Hinds, P., & Cramton, C. (2014). Situated Coworker Familiarity : How Site Visits Transform. *Organization Science*, *25*(3), 794–814. doi:10.1287/orsc.2013.0869

Huang, H. (2009). Globally distributed information technology work: A study of cross-cultural influences, communication, and management. *ProQuest Dissertations and Theses*, *275*(August). Advance online publication.

India Brand Equity Foundation. (2019). *IT & ITeS*. Retrieved from www.ibef.org

Johri, A. (2012). From a distance: Impression formation and impression accuracy among geographically distributed coworkers. *Computers in Human Behavior*, *28*(6), 1997–2006. doi:10.1016/j.chb.2012.06.038

Jong, J., Curşeu, P., & Leenders, R. (2014). When do bad apples not spoil the barrel? Negative relationships in teams, team performance, and buffering mechanisms. *The Journal of Applied Psychology*, *99*(3), 514–522. doi:10.1037/a0036284 PMID:24661274

Joshi, A., Lazarova, M. B., & Liao, H. (2009). Getting Everyone on Board: The Role of Inspirational Leadership in Geographically Dispersed Teams. *Organization Science*, *20*(1), 240–252. doi:10.1287/orsc.1080.0383

Kaul, S., Pande, N., & Ahuja, V. (2017). Virtual Team Effectiveness : An Empirical Study Using SEM. *Procedia Computer Science*, *122*, 33–41. doi:10.1016/j.procs.2017.11.338

Knight, R. (2015). How to manage remote direct reports. *Harvard Business Review*, 2–6. https://hbr.org/2015/02/how-to-manage-remote-direct-reports

Koszegi, S. T. (2016). *Building shared context and shared identity through communication*. Marshall Plan Foundation.

Kumar, K., Van Fenema, P. C., & Von Glinow, M. A. (2009). Offshoring and the global distribution of work: Implications for task interdependence theory and practice. *Journal of International Business Studies*, *40*(4), 642–667. doi:10.1057/jibs.2008.77

Larson, B. Z., Vroman, S. R., & Makarius, E. E. (2020, March 18). A Guide to Managing Your (Newly) Remote Workers. *Harvard Business Review*, 2–7.

Lerner, V. (2015). *Cultural Backgrounds Influencing Virtual Team Performance*. Walden University.

Liao, C. (2017). Leadership in virtual teams: A multilevel perspective. *Human Resource Management Review*, *27*(4), 648–659. doi:10.1016/j.hrmr.2016.12.010

Lin, C., He, H., Baruch, Y., & Ashforth, B. E. (2017). The Effect of Team Affective Tone on Team Performance: The Roles of Team Identification and Team Cooperation. *Human Resource Management*, *56*(6), 931–952. doi:10.1002/hrm.21810

Lin, C., Standing, C., & Liu, Y.-C. (2008). Standing, C., & Liu, Y. (2008). A model to develop effective virtual teams. *Decision Support Systems*, *45*(4), 1031–1045. doi:10.1016/j.dss.2008.04.002

Lionel, R., & You, S. (2018). Disaggregating the Impacts of Virtuality on Team Identification. In *GROUP'18*. ACM. doi:10.1145/3148330.3148337

Lisak, A., Erez, M., Sui, Y., & Lee, C. (2016). The positive role of global leaders in enhancing multicultural team innovation. *Journal of International Business Studies*, *47*(6), 655–673. doi:10.105741267-016-0002-7

Marlow, J., & Dabbish, L. (2011). Reducing psychological distance in globally distributed teams. *Chi*, *11*, 1–4. doi:10.1145/2141512.2141568

Marrewijk, A. (2011). Cross Cultural Management: Hybridization of Dutch — Indian Work Practices in Geographically Distributed IT Projects. *International Journal of Business Anthropology*, *2*(2), 15–35.

Mattarelli, E., & Gupta, A. (2009). Offshore-onsite subgroup dynamics in globally distributed teams. *Information Technology & People*, *22*(3), 242–269. doi:10.1108/09593840910981437

Morgan, L., Paucar-Caceres, A., & Wright, G. (2014). Leading Effective Global Virtual Teams: The Consequences of Methods of Communication. *Systemic Practice and Action Research*, *27*(6), 607–624. doi:10.100711213-014-9315-2

Mortensen, M., & Neeley, T. B. (2012). *Through the Looking Glass : Reflected Knowledge and Trust in Global Collaboration*. Faculty & Research., doi:10.2307/23359587

Myungsuk, C., Park, J.-G., & Lee, J. (2014). Effects of team member psychological proximity on teamwork performance. *Team Performance Management*, *20*(1/2), 81–96. doi:10.1108/TPM-03-2013-0007

Neeley, T. B. (2015). Global Teams That Work.pdf. *Harvard Business Review*, 74–81.

Ocker, R. J., Huang, H., Benbunan-Fich, R., & Hiltz, S. R. (2011). Leadership Dynamics in Partially Distributed teams: An Exploratory Study of the Effects of Configuration and Distance. *Group Decision and Negotiation*, *20*(3), 273–292. doi:10.100710726-009-9180-z

Organ & Podsakoff. (1986). Self-Report in Organizational Research. *Journal of Management*, *12*(4), 532–544. doi:10.1177/014920638601200408

OzimekA. (2020). The Future of Remote Work. doi:10.2139srn.3638597

Pazos, P. (2012). Conflict management and effectiveness in virtual teams. *Team Performance Management*, *18*(7), 401–417. doi:10.1108/13527591211281138

Pflügler, C., Wiesche, M., & Helmut, K. (2018). Subgroups in Agile and Traditional IT Project Teams. In *51st Hawaii International Conference on System Sciences* (pp. 5483–5492). 10.24251/HICSS.2018.683

Pinjani, P., & Palvia, P. (2013). Trust and Knowledge Sharing in Diverse Global Virtual Teams. *Information & Management*, *50*(4), 144–153. doi:10.1016/j.im.2012.10.002

Privman, R., Hiltz, S. R., & Wang, Y. (2013). In-Group (Us) versus out-group (Them) dynamics and effectiveness in partially distributed teams. *IEEE Transactions on Professional Communication*, *56*(1), 33–49. doi:10.1109/TPC.2012.2237253

Robinson, C. D. (2015). *Successful Virtual Teams: Collaboration and Influence As Drivers of Team Success*. University of Pennsylvania.

Shen, Y., Gallivan, M. J., & Tang, X. (2016). The Impact of Perceived Subgroup Formation on Transactive Memory Systems and Performance in Distributed Teams. *International Journal of e-Collaboration*, *12*(1), 44–66. doi:10.4018/ijec.2016010104

Shore, L. M., Randel, A. E., Chung, B. G., Dean, M. A., Ehrhart, K. H., & Singh, G. (2011). Inclusion and diversity in work groups: A review and model for future research. *Journal of Management*, *37*(4), 1262–1289. doi:10.1177/0149206310385943

Voida, A., Bos, N., Olson, J., Olson, G., & Dunning, L. (2012). Cross-Cutting Faultlines of Location and Shared Identity in the Intergroup Cooperation of Partially Distributed Groups. In Academy of Communication Management (pp. 1–10). doi:10.1145/2207676.2208724

Wang, B., Liu, Y., Qian, J., & Parker, S. K. (2020). Achieving Effective Remote Working During the COVID-19 Pandemic: A Work Design Perspective. *Applied Psychology*, *0*(0), 1–44. doi:10.1111/apps.12290 PMID:33230359

Wickramasinghe, V., & Nandula, S. (2015). Diversity in team composition, relationship conflict and team leader support on globally distributed virtual software development team performance. *Strategic Outsourcing*, *8*(2–3), 138–155. doi:10.1108/SO-02-2015-0007

Wilson, J. M., O'Leary, M. B., Metiu, A., & Jett, Q. R. (2005). Subjective distance in teams. *Global-Production.Com*. Retrieved from http://www.global-production.com/scoreboard/resources/wilson_2005_subjective-distance-in-teams.pdf

Zimmermann, A. (2020). Managing effective remote teams inclusively. *LSE Business Review*, 3–5. Retrieved from https://blogs.lse.ac.uk/businessreview/%0Ahttp://eprints.lse.ac.uk/104690/

Zimmermann, A., Raab, K., & Zanotelli, L. (2013). Vicious and virtuous circles of offshoring attitudes and relational behaviours: A configurational study of German IT developers. *Information Systems Journal*, *23*(1), 65–88. doi:10.1111/j.1365-2575.2012.00399.x

Zuofa, T., & Ochieng, E. G. (2017). Working separately but together: Appraising virtual project team challenges. *Team Performance Management*, *23*(5–6), 227–242. doi:10.1108/TPM-06-2016-0030

KEY TERMS AND DEFINITIONS

Contextual Information: Degree to which individual is aware and has understanding about the local situation and work environment in which remote member works.

Geographically Distributed Team (GDT): Team which comprises of members dispersed across two or more geographic locations, collaborating through computer mediated communication tools.

Inclusive Communication: Degree to which the individual participates and is involved in the communication process with the remote colleague.

Perceived Status Equality: Degree of interest displayed by individuals in interacting, appreciating and understanding the remote member.

Shared Identity: Degree to which the individual experiences the extent of similarity and oneness with the remote member.

Social Distance: Degree of 'us' vs 'them' attitude among the offshore member towards the onsite member.

Task Interdependence: Degree to which individual works closely and coordinate with the remote member to complete tasks.

Team Effectiveness: Degree to which project team is performing in terms of achievement of goals, quality, timelines, cost, member satisfaction and intention to stay in the team.

APPENDIX

Table 7. A.1 Results of Factor Analysis

Constructs	Items	Factor Loadings
Social Distance (Privman, Hiltz, and Wang, 2013) Eigen Value for Components & Variance % 1=4.5,26.69%; 2=3.12,45.08%; 3=1.93,56.47%	I am unsure of Onsite Team member's motives.	.65
	I feel Onsite team member will take unfair advantage of me.	.66
	Onsite Team avoid consulting us.	.73
	Onsite Team do not rely on us for support.	.53
	Onsite Team blame us for their mistakes.	.66
	Onsite Team Compete with us in unproductive ways.	.74
	Onsite team fails to share critical information.	.73
	Onsite Team have unfair advantages.	.75
	Onsite Team often do not give my work the priority I need.	.61
	Onsite team are overall trustworthy.	.63
	Onsite Team show a great deal of integrity.	.77
	Onsite Team members put a great deal of effort into their work.	.79
	Onsite Team member does their fair share of the work.	.72
	There is good team spirit among India site and Onsite team.	.70
	There are important differences concerning goals and tasks among the Onsite Team and India (Offshore) Team	.78
	Much disagreement exists between Onsite member and India Team about important issues	.68
	I am unsure of Onsite Team member's motives.	.71
Team Effectiveness (Lin, Standing and Liu, 2008; Zimmermann, A. Raab, K. and Zanotelli, 2013) Eigen Value 2.7; Variance 33%	The project team has achieved all the goals and objectives of the project.	.59
	The project team provides the deliverables (like product or services) on time.	.74
	The team has lower error rates.	.78
	The project team provide high quality work.	.71
	The project did not incur any unplanned cost.	.77
	I am satisfied with how my Onsite teammates and I work together.	.74
	I would want to work with this Onsite team in the future.	.85
	As a project team we have learned a lot from each other.	.85
Task Interdependence (Eigen Value 2.3; Variance 59%	I work closely with Onsite team in doing my work.	.87
	I frequently must coordinate my efforts with Onsite team.	.84
	My own performance is dependent on receiving accurate information from Onsite Team	.72
	The way I perform my job has a significant impact on Onsite Team.	.61
Inclusive Communication (Shore et al., 2011) Eigen Value 3.4; Variance 34%	I am encouraged to actively participate in the call meetings with Onsite Team.	.76
	I am informed about the agenda and the points of discussions before every call meeting with Onsite Team.	.67
	I am encouraged to present my views and opinions in discussions with Onsite Team.	.72
	I openly and honestly express my disagreements with Onsite Team.	.67
	I directly reach out to the concern person in Onsite Team for any clarification/doubts.	.83
	I frequently interact with the Onsite team members apart from the call meeting. (Through chat, email, skype etc.).	.70
	I have the access to same information as Onsite team members related to my tasks.	.80
	I am regularly updated with project information.	.87
	I am included in email distribution list for sharing key decisions taken affecting the project.	.87
	I am included in email distribution list for sharing key information related to project.	.85
Contextual Information Eigen Value: 4.2 Variance: 60.47%	I am informed about the unavailability of Onsite Team Member due to any public holiday and festive holidays.	.73
	I am aware when Onsite team members are available. (Either virtually or face-to-face).	.76
	I am aware of the work/personal adjustments Onsite Team member have to make due to time difference between Onsite and India Office.	.79
	I am aware about pressures Onsite team member face from the customers/business.	.78
	I am aware of the work processes followed by Onsite team member.	.83
	I am aware what Onsite team member is presently working on.	.80
	I am aware about the cultural differences that exist between us and the Onsite Team members.	.72
Shared Identity (Koszegi,2016) Eigen Value 4.97; Variance 62.17%	I can speak my mind and share if something is bothering me with the Onsite (Client) team member.	.79
	I feel comfortable approaching an Onsite (client) member for help.	.83
	I feel like we are working together as a team.	.87
	Onsite and our team have similar goals and objectives to achieve.	.82
	Onsite and our team have similar priorities to tasks.	.83
	When I talk about this project, I usually say "we" rather than "they".	.77
	This Project's success is my success.	.63
Perceived Status Equality (Mattarelli and Gupta, 2009) Eigen Value: 2.11 Variance 70.3%	I am proud to be part of this project.	.84
	Onsite Team member takes interest in understanding work practices followed in India	.85
	Onsite Team appreciates the work done by the India Team.	.81

Chapter 17
The Post-COVID-19 Era:
Impacts, Challenges, and Opportunities for Worker Representatives

Tatjana E. Byrne
Allianz, Germany

Rosa Maria Martins de Oliveira
Allianz, Germany

ABSTRACT

The repercussions of months of social distancing have affected workers and their representatives. Nearly 25% of workers in Europe had never teleworked before the pandemic. The accelerated adoption of digital technologies and continued remote working required workers' representatives to adapt their ways of working, as well as reassess priorities. By examining three key questions—1) What forms of governance were used to respond to the challenges of the COVID-19 crisis? 2) What topics will gain in importance and which ones may become less important? 3) How will the post-COVID-19 world affect the organization and ways of working of representative bodies?—the authors argue that post-COVID-19 it is imperative to revise governance arrangements to enable representatives to remain effective as the workers' voice. Normative considerations combined with practitioner insights also lead the authors to conclude that the pandemic has the potential to trigger a paradigm shift in organizational participation.

INTRODUCTION

The classification of the coronavirus outbreak as a pandemic in March 2020 (WHO, 2020) and subsequent nationwide lockdowns in many countries, led to the most extensive mass teleworking experiment in history (ILO, 2020). This immediately highlighted specific work-related issues, i.e. how to ensure health and safety standards when work no longer takes place in a physical business location where regulations can be addressed and monitored by workers' representatives. It also emphasised the need to update pre-pandemic proven practices, in order to be able to capture and convey workers' interests at

DOI: 10.4018/978-1-7998-6754-8.ch017

local, national and international levels, of particular interest being the need to safeguard workers' rights in accordance with prevailing legislation.

The chapter analyses the immediate reactions of workers' representatives to the challenges of the COVID-19 crisis. It investigates the effects of the pandemic on the ways of working in the context of a multinational financial services company operating across several European borders and with various forms of worker representation. The authors are workers' representatives themselves in the company and have used a systematic, descriptive approach to identify both short-term, explicit as well as longer term implicit consequences for the workers' representatives and their ways of working. The results presented in this chapter are derived from anonymous, qualitative interviews conducted with 15 colleagues working in different lines of business across Europe. The 15 interviewees are all worker representatives, based either in Germany as Works Council members of several group companies or as members of the company's European Works Council. Some interviewees are also Supervisory Board members of the various group companies. In their capacity as Worker Representatives some interviewees are full-time, whereas other colleagues fulfil this role on a part-time, voluntary basis, including the authors themselves.

The chapter assesses the roles and responsibilities of workers' representatives against a frame of reference that reflects the level, range and degree of organizational participation. Themes concerning the organization and management of work including the impact of digitalisation and specifically teleworking are also deliberated. In this context plural network organizations are discussed in more detail including the likely consequences of such organization forms on the role of workers' representatives. By bringing these various aspects together, the authors then assess the potential risks posed by the immediate crisis of the pandemic and those of longer-term economic trends on the ability of workers' representatives to remain effective in understanding and representing workers interests. Implicit in this is the view that a counterweight is needed to the trend towards greater centralisation of corporate control in a post-COVID-19 world of work. In the final part of the chapter the authors suggest a number of recommendations for further research intended to identify means by which the legitimacy of existing forms of workers' representation can be assured through the augmentation or enhancement of democratic rights in organizational participation.

BACKGROUND

Currently no unified or uniform European model defining workers' representation exists (IMU, 2019). The European reality is in fact characterised by a broad diversity of national legislations, practices, and traditions. However, workers' representation and workers' rights exist in all member states of the EU, despite notable differences between national systems (Hassel et al., 2018; Jevtić, 2012, 75). Labour Law legislation ranges from basic, i.e. Bulgaria, Romania, to forms that have strong, legally binding arrangements, as in Germany and the Netherlands (Vitols, 2018). Relations between social partners and the form of representation at board-level vary between EU states. In some countries, independent and autonomous representation by trade unions is predominant (Hassel et al., 2018). In others, in addition to collective bargaining, legally regulated works councils and board-level worker representation have long been established. In such cases collective bargaining can take place at workplace or at national level (Kluge et al., 2019).

However, at a European level the creation of European Works Councils (EWC) and SE Works Councils (SEWC) recognizes the trend towards transnational organizations, processes and hierarchies and the need for similar mechanisms to enable employee representatives to be able to operate effectively on behalf of the workforces in multinational enterprises. While EWCs address transnational matters the SE Works Council construct addresses the corporate traits of the European Company (SE), nevertheless both have similar roles, namely:

...a transnational works council comprises employee representatives who are elected or nominated by the national workforces or their representatives. As the collective interest representation of the European workforce, EWCs and SEWCs meet with company management, are provided with information, and formulate opinions that are to be taken into account in the company's decision-making process. (ETUI, 2020, 97)

The scale of the COVID-19 crisis has highlighted the complexities involved in managing responses at national and international level, particularly regarding the need to safeguard workers' rights in accordance with prevailing legislation. As the ETUC notes:

The consequences and management of the COVID-19 crisis are transnational issues to be dealt with also by EWCs. Since the COVID-19 pandemic crisis is sweeping across Europe, it is clearly impacting multinationals in complicated ways. This is where EWCs have a crucial role to play. (ETUC, 2020a, 2)

Since the early 1990s ideas encompassed in the legal framework for the German Works Council model have played a pivotal role in informing European legislation in this area. Although subsequent company-based forms of representation outside Germany were made possible by the European Works Council and the European Information and Consultation directives, nonetheless the German influence remains unmistakable (Whittall & Trinczek, 2019). In recognition of this the authors have chosen a multinational company with its headquarters in Germany and the German system of workers' representation to exemplify the analysis presented in this chapter.

An important aspect that will be discussed is the modified legislation that came into force in May 2020 in Germany allowing, at least until 30th June 2021, meetings and consultations to be held using audio and video conferencing technologies. This affects both national and European-level representation. Before the pandemic works council decisions in Germany were only legitimate if taken in face-to-face meetings. The change had a significant impact on the way of working for worker representatives. The expectation is that in the longer term this and other crisis-induced temporary measures may lead to further permanent changes in the laws governing the constitution of works councils and worker representation. Ultimately this may lead to changes to the forms of organizational participation.

Organizational participation as a research theme encompasses diverse perspectives regarding its scope and definition. In the context of this paper the authors apply a participation classification model based on two dimensions, i.e. organizational level and degree of control as posited by Child (2020). Furthermore, they reference Bernstein (1976) and Wilkinson et al. (2010) in considering the level of participation, e.g. localised tasks to company-wide strategy; the range of topics in which representatives are involved and the degree of control or influence on the governance of decision-making in terms of the so-called "escalator of participation". Here control is exercised as a progression from simple information provision, through communication, consultation, co-determination to control over decision-making.

The question of influence and control has been taken up by various research strands that emphasise the roles of different "organizational participants" in decision-making. These roles, according to Child

(2020), can be differentiated broadly in terms of the interests that workers have and those that reflect managerial objectives. Within the two-dimensional framework suggested by Child (2020), he identifies four types of control that workers or workers' representatives can exert: co-determination, joint consultation, workplace self-management and worker involvement. Of these the concept of co-determination describes the form of governance exhibited by worker presence on company boards, works councils, remuneration committees as well as co-operatives, and involves workers having a specified role in decision-making processes that affect an entire organization, e.g. strategic decisions involving investment, restructuring and relocation decisions. Joint consultation is more limited in its scope, usually focusing on information-sharing, policy implementation (as opposed to policy formulation), problem solving or productivity improvements. Workplace self-management and worker involvement were not considered by the authors as they are less relevant in the context of the analysis presented in this chapter. With respect to the findings the authors focus on the concept of co-determination as it is understood in the German model of worker representation, i.e. institutionalized through law and providing for a role in corporate decision-making. This definition covers all workers in Europe, a number of different institutional settings, such as plant, company and enterprise representatives as well as supervisor-level worker representation in large companies (Hassel et al., 2018).

Furthermore, it is important to clarify which aspects of organizational participation were specifically considered as part of the discussion on the impact of the COVID-19 pandemic. Hence, the responsibility of workers' representatives can be defined as the representation of workers' interests at the company- and/or the plant-level. Child's simplified classification of organizational participation is applied, which allows for more differentiation in terms of level by considering the types of issues covered when analysing the interview data. This was felt to be appropriate given that the interviewees represent not only a variety of different business units within the multinational, but also represent workers at different levels of the organization. These comprised colleagues operating at local as well as at supervisory board level. Consequently, the extent to which they are involved in different topics varies based on the following aspects:

- Level at which organizational participation occurs (e.g. task, departmental, company or corporate headquarters (HQ));
- Range of organizational participation (e.g. the nature or types of issues, i.e. non-strategic topics to ones of strategic importance);
- Degree of influence in organizational participation (e.g. information rights only through to control of the decision-making process)

These functions can be identified in different forms of representation, such as by trade unions, works councils, via collective bargaining and by representation at board-level. The authors used these categories to systematise the interview findings.

WORKER REPRESENTATION IN THE PANDEMIC

Findings From the Interviews with Workers' Representatives

In analysing the interviews the authors apply three dimensions to systematize the interview outcomes in relation to organizational participation involving workers' representatives: the level of representation, the range of participation, and the degree of participation. Furthermore, Table 1 summarizes the interviewees' primary roles as worker representatives and serves as a reference for quotations in the text.

Table 1. Worker representative interviewee identifier and primary role

Interviewee ID	Primary Role
F, H, J, N	Supervisory Board Worker Representative
A, I, M	European Worker Representative
B, C, D, E, G, K, L, O	German Worker Representative

Level of Organizational Representation: Expression of Workers' Interests

On March 23rd, 2020 the Federal Minister for Labour and Social Affairs for Germany, Hubertus Heil, resorted to an extraordinary measure to assure the operational viability of German Works Councils during the COVID-19 crisis. He published a "Ministerial Declaration" (BMAS, 2020a), which allows resolutions taken by Works Councils to be considered legally effective if taken in the form of on-line conference and/or video calls, i.e. when members are not all present in one room. The existing Works Constitution Act had no provision for virtual meetings and as such the call for workers to remain at home would have seriously impaired the ability of their representatives to perform their duties during the COVID-19 crisis. Following on from the ministerial declaration a temporary amendment to the Works Constitution Act was formally passed into law in May 2020, enabling the measure to be in force until June 30th, 2021. This, together with the imposition of a "lockdown" throughout Germany in March 2020, resulted in a situation where the entire workforce, including workers' representatives, were obliged to work from home for a period of approximately three months. Provisions were made to provide all workers with the necessary IT and ergonomic equipment to be able to telework for a sustained period from home. Although a partial return to office-based working was possible from the beginning of July 2020, in the form of controlled and phased utilisation of offices, there are no plans for a full return to office in the foreseeable future. This has been exacerbated by the second wave of the pandemic in late 2020 and the delays to the vaccination programme. Indeed, the relative success of the measures taken by the company in maintaining stable operations during the first and second lockdown periods has prompted an assessment of initiatives intended to radically extend teleworking as a permanent feature of work organization and management.

Against this background the German Government drafted a so-called Works Council Reinforcement Act (Betriebsrätestärkungsgesetz), which was published on 21st December 2020 (BMAS, 2020b). This act seeks to address the challenges arising from an increasing use of digital technologies and artificial intelligence in the world of work and to ensure that workers' representatives can continue to be effective in their roles. One of the main aims of the act is to introduce both an appropriate and sustainable legal provision for the participation in Works Council meetings using video and telephone conferencing technologies as well as to make a significant contribution to the digitalisation of the work of Works Councils generally (BMAS, 2020b. 2).

Most of the representatives interviewed stated that the enforced distancing from an office environment also significantly affected their ability to interact and communicate effectively with the workers whom they represent in their respective lines of business. This concern was most prevalent amongst the German representatives (Interviewees C, E, G, K, L, O). The ability to interact through various formal and informal channels is seen as essential to be able to capture and convey the so-called "Workers' Voice" effectively (i.e. quantity and quality of the communication). It was also noted that resorting to other forms of contact, e.g. telephone or e-mail was perceived as an inhibitor, partly because of its indirectness and partly because of the lack of spontaneity or indeed serendipitous nature of the exchange that occurs when colleagues are able to meet face-to-face in the office.

The interviewees considered personal, informal communication to be an important source of information about workers' thoughts, concerns and interests (Interviewees A, K). Informal communication takes place outside formal rules and hierarchies (Vaughan, 1999), and therefore has the potential to reveal the work "atmosphere", which comprises, e.g. underlying tendencies, rumours and insecurities that would most probably not be expressed in a formal exchange. Considered an inevitable part of organizational life, "idle talk" (Rosnow & Fine, 1976) in the workplace is often synonymous with the "watercooler effect," where people come together to make sense of their social worlds (DiFonzo, 2008) and observe as Kunda claims:

shared rules that govern cognitive and affective aspects of membership (as cited in Sobering, 2019, 413).

Another important opportunity for representatives to hear and understand the Workers' Voice is via formal meetings and assemblies, which are common in Germany where representation is carried out via works councils. Such meetings take place several times a year at plant or business unit-level. This format serves as a means of direct communication between the workforce, their representatives and the company. The company representative role is usually taken by the personnel department. The topics discussed are primarily related to collective bargaining arrangements and labour relations and provide an opportunity for both parties to ask questions and exchange views.

The interviews also revealed an additional issue regarding the quality of the information exchange between worker and representative. Teleworking, when used on a large scale, not only reduces the number of formal and informal contacts, which affects the quantity of information gained, but may also lead to one-sidedness or information bias. Here bias is taken to mean the result of communicating with a smaller group of trusted colleagues for an exchange of views and information than if there were no restrictions on meeting in person. Consequently, the information gained may reflect only the opinions of a relatively homogenous group, risking the development of blind spots, with potentially negative effects on the ability to understand and represent the true interests of the workers (Interviewee A). Some interviewees also expressed their concerns regarding a possible "inhibition threshold" on the part of workers in making contact, again related to the inability to meet in person, unless there was a specific reason for doing so.

Information deficits were also described as a particular issue by interview partners, because representative bodies are elected by the workforce and therefore a close relationship between both groups is needed to allow representatives to stay relevant and meaningful. A disconnect in the quality of information exchange may also affect the relationship with employer or management groups in the future, if the learning effect of the exchanges, as a prerequisite for being able to exert influence on decision-making, is impaired. This would be most detrimental for representative bodies, such as German Works Councils, that have been established for a long period of time, as they tend to have, according to Child (2020, 21):

a less adversarial relationship with management, greater influence in decision-making, and to be associated with higher productivity.

Range of Organizational Participation: Representation of Workers' Interests in the Company

The multinational, as the field of investigation in this paper, took immediate action when faced with the lockdown situation by closing premises and requesting that all work be done remotely. For the majority of workers this meant teleworking from home and was crucial to the company's operations. Prior to the crisis teleworking or "mobile working", the term the company used to describe non-office based working, was intermittent and depended very much on regional and business unit-specific circumstances. For Europe, where the majority of the multinational's staff are based, Eurostat research found that teleworking across the EU remained fairly constant in the decade between 2008 and 2018, with an average of 5.2% of workers usually working from home. Some large variations were noted with the Netherlands recording 14.0%, whilst Bulgaria recorded only 0.3%. In Germany a figure of 5% was recorded. Moreover, the number of workers occasionally working from home rose from 5.8% in 2008 to 8.3% in 2018 (Eurostat, 2018). The large-scale shift to so-called teleworking caused a re-ordering of the topics dealt with by workers representatives. Prior to the crisis the topics demanding the most attention were fairly constant. The analysis of a survey conducted in 2015 with over 4000 businesses with representation in Germany by the Institute of Social and Economic Analysis, summarised in Figure 1, illustrates these topics.

Figure 1. Summary based on WSI-Betriebsrätebefragung
Source: Baumann et al., 2017

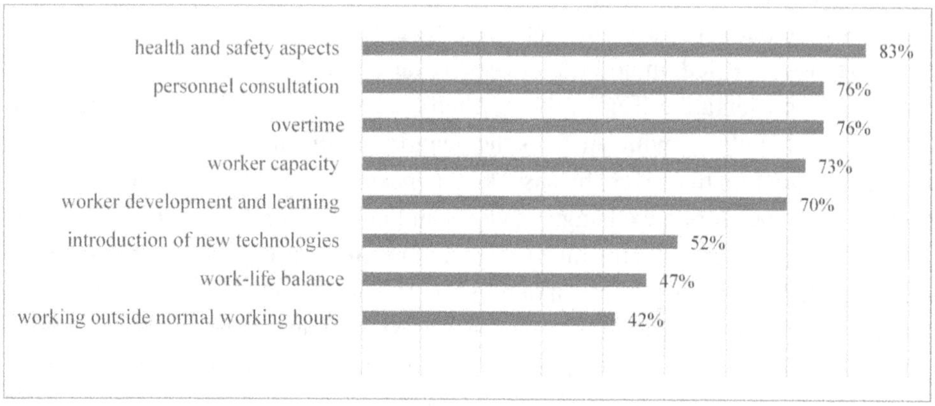

When governments introduced measures to bring the pandemic under control, teleworking became much more prevalent. An e-survey carried out by Eurofound across the EU in April and July 2020 indicated that in July nearly half of the respondents classified as 'worker' (48%) worked at home at least some of the time during the COVID-19-pandemic. Of these, over a third (34%) reported working exclusively from home (Eurofound, 2020). Furthermore, an average of 24% of workers in Europe who had never teleworked before started to work remotely for the first time (ILO, 2020, 3). The obligation to telework had a profound effect on refocusing priorities for workers' representatives. Not only were immediate health protection measures necessary, but as the lockdowns continued, other aspects emerged that revealed few arrangements were in place that governed extended teleworking. In common with other companies the first priority of the multinational was to protect its workforce, but within days it became the top priority for workers' representatives to make sure that the workforce was provided with appropriate technical equipment (hard and software) or ensure that they were suitably compensated when they bought their own.

However, as the weeks passed it became clear that there are both advantages and disadvantages associated with teleworking. Its almost ubiquitous use since March 2020 has drawn attention not only to the range of advanced enabling technologies, but also to the subsequent impact on other aspects of working conditions. Notably the implications of working outside an environment normally governed by extensive health and safety legislation raised concerns amongst workers representatives. In general employers have the same duty of care with respect to occupational health and safety arrangements in both office- and telework-based environments, but no formal agreements have yet been negotiated that sufficiently govern the latter. In the case of the multinational company in question, management and worker representatives from across Europe established "temporary" new working routines in accordance with health and safety at work requirements as well as labour law regulations such as working time directives.

Whilst teleworking can be beneficial, e.g. allowing workers to avoid long commuting times and to maintain a better work-life balance, there are risks associated with the physical isolation from the office and colleagues. The most widely recognized risks are psychosocial or related to ergonomics (ILO, 2020). Given the extraordinary circumstances arising from the pandemic and enforced lockdowns, observers have noted heightened levels of anxiety and stress, which in turn have been further exacerbated by uncertainty regarding the economic, social and health implications of the situation. A review of studies into the effects of enforced isolation or quarantine on a range of populations or participants highlighted symptoms such as burnout, depression and irritability associated with the impact of the COVID-19 crisis (Brooks et al., 2020). Other risks concern the increased use of monitoring software to track workflow and worker supervision in a teleworking context (ETUC, 2020b).

Work and working time management increasingly became a cause for concern during 2020 with the surge in teleworking. Findings from an IPPR report into the effects of the pandemic on working practices in both UK manufacturing and service businesses suggests that the latter have experienced significant adjustments due to the necessity of teleworking. Moreover, the IPPR report concluded that working hours had not decreased noticeably as a result of teleworking, rather that workers worked more flexibly with approximately one third of the interviewees falling into this category (Jung et al., 2020, 14). Another survey conducted by Liberty Games, during the lockdown in the UK indicated that concentration, mental health, breaks from work as well as working hours were adversely affected amongst people working from home (McCulley, 2020).

The impact of the COVID-19 crisis on working time management has also had a noticeable demographic and gender effect with women reducing their work times more in order to be able to take care of children (Böckler Impuls, 2020). A NAKO (German for national cohort) study conducted in May 2020 amongst 200,000 participants across Germany showed a marked decline in mental health, with the age group 20-49 most adversely affected (Steppat, 2020). For young women up to the age of 40 there was a pronounced decline in mental health with the burden of teleworking or home office work, care duties as well as household chores being the main causes. Against this background the multinational and its workers' representatives played a major role in addressing not only multiple business continuity and health and welfare concerns, but also in ensuring that the measures taken across Europe were consistent.

Here workers' representatives played an important role in co-determining effective plans and conveying consistent messages to workers, no matter where they were located.

The experience of the past several months has been used to develop crisis and Back-to-Office protocols that can be adapted as the COVID-19 situation changes. These have been developed and implemented in co-creation with workers' representatives, covering, for example, business trip policies, hygiene concepts for offices as well as precautions for the use of canteens and meeting rooms. Most of the issues tackled required co-determination and meant that there was a huge strain on the ability of workers' representatives to keep up with the pace of change across the entire organization.

Degree of Organizational Participation: Governance of Company Decision-making

Paradoxically the COVID-19 pandemic has had a certain equalizing effect on workers and management. As the pandemic affects more or less all workers in a similar way, no matter where they work in the multinational company or in what role, there is a need for a co-ordinated approach to prevent confusion and ensure that common measures do not impede the safety of the workforce or its ability to carry on working. Indeed, during the interviews the authors learned that the need for workers' representatives to align with the company on cross-border measures and to communicate consistently with workers was imperative to avoid unequal treatment.

Furthermore, all interviewees mentioned that the pandemic led to more ad hoc decisions, reflecting the pressure to act quickly. Also, interviewees stated that in the first weeks of the crisis, there was a clear consensus and very constructive collaboration between workers' representatives and management, focusing on what needed to be done to emerge from the crisis in a sustainable manner. The crisis mode of operation and the need to act consistently across the company resulted in a greater reliance on centralized decision-making (i.e. at group level) and consequently in less debate amongst representative bodies at a local, business and plant level. This was deemed justifiable in the interests of a group-wide, consistent approach. The authors asked the interviewees if and how the pandemic affected their ability to collaborate effectively as members of their respective representative bodies. These included local or plant, central, group and European-level representative bodies. They were also asked if they could see any difference in decision preparation and making, as a result of the impact of the COVID-19 crisis.

For one group of interviewees, mainly from the various German Works Councils, the use of teleconferencing tools for works council meetings was not possible prior to the pandemic as legislation required in-person meetings for legally binding decisions to be taken. With the shutdown this issue was immediately addressed and the law was temporarily changed to accommodate the extraordinary circumstances (since extended until 30th June 2021 and now subject to new draft legislation issued in December 2020). Whilst some representatives e.g. from Spain and the UK were already accustomed to operating in a virtual set-up, for German representatives the need to conduct meetings in this way represented a major change to their way of working. Some of the German interview partners confessed that it took them some time to get used to the different information tools and to define and establish new routines for their committee meetings. However, due to the large number of meetings conducted throughout the months since, the perception of many interviewees was that they had adapted to the new format successfully.

Although the virtual meetings enabled representatives to continue operating, the majority of the interviewees had reservations about this form of exchange. Before the crisis most of the participants were accustomed to a culture of debate that could be labelled as lively and temperamental, but deemed to be an essential part of the decision-making process. The difficulty of interpreting the mood of the participants or their attention levels was cited frequently as a concern. There was a general view that the (optional) use of Webcams was not sufficient to assess facial expressions used to signal non-verbal agreement and/or commitment (i.e. nod) or disagreement (frown, raise eyebrow). In terms of process the virtual meeting format also necessitated the introduction of specific disciplines, such as virtual hand-raising, to ensure that all participants had sufficient opportunity to engage in the discussions and express their opinions. However, it was stated that even with such rules in place, there were disadvantages to this approach with respect to an in-person meeting, including the unintentional silencing of less extrovert participants.

A combination of live and virtual meeting, or so-called "hybrid" meetings, was seen to be particularly problematic by several of the interviewees (Interviewees A, H, M). This format was introduced once some of the restrictions placed on gatherings had been partially lifted and a small number of participants were allowed to meet in person, following strict hygiene rules, whilst others joined virtually. The intention was to combine the two formats to eliminate the disadvantages of purely virtual meetings and to enable the attendance of participants who otherwise faced travel restrictions due to the pandemic. Several interviewees expressed concerns about the hybrid format such as fostering a feeling of exclusion for those attending on-line. There was also the perception that if only some colleagues could meet the employer representatives in person this would lead to a different dynamic in the discussions and the risk that not all contributions carried equal weight. One interviewee (E) also noted that facilitating virtual or hybrid meetings posed different challenges depending on whether or not the Works Council was a local, plant-level or a joint one. They expressed the view that local Councils have the advantage of more personal contact whereas the combined Councils often comprise geographically and organizationally distributed members who come together less frequently. Some interviewees also mentioned other effects of virtual meetings vs. in-person meetings including shorter, but more frequent appointments that focused on only a few topics. There was also a perception that more discussion occurred in pre-alignment meetings resulting in less debate during the formal sessions. The virtual format also inhibited more informal relationship building amongst attendees in the form of small talk or side conversations.

Despite acknowledgement that this crisis approach had helped the company and its workers remain operational, some interviewees shared concerns that going forward the management might want to use such fast-track collaboration to accelerate or promote other topics that normally would be dealt with in a more graduated manner. There was a sense that by referencing the pandemic other company priorities, such as proposed restructurings, would be carried out with an undue sense of urgency and subjected to a more centralized governance. The authors also found that in addition to management tendencies to centralize decision-making, there was evidence of a similar trend amongst the bodies representing workers at a national and European level. Although this trend was already visible before the pandemic, reflecting ongoing changes to business models and efforts to enhance the standardisation and automation of products and services, it now appears to be intensifying as a consequence of the pandemic. As Hamblin observes:

It is well-established that crisis legitimizes central authority, since in order for decisions to be taken quickly, decision-making levels may be circumscribed. (as cited in Janssen & van der Voort, 2020, 4)

Some interviewees clearly stated that such developments need to be carefully monitored and where appropriate also controlled, to ensure that potential information asymmetries and decision flows do not undermine the democratic process of participation at all levels of the organization. Furthermore, the view was expressed that decisions with long-term implications for the workforce should not be rushed through, but carefully prepared and analysed as they will have an impact well beyond the current crisis. Such a development would certainly be detrimental to representative democracy if provisions negotiated as a result of enterprise-specific exigencies were to lead to an erosion or lowering of national and/ or local, business-level standards. as per the observations of Child (2020, 10).

Normative Analysis of COVID-19 Effects on Workers' Representatives

The preceding analysis of the interview findings shows that the COVID-19 crisis required workers' representatives to mobilize or re-focus internal resources and co-ordinate cross-company activities with company management in a not hitherto seen manner. The rationale for taking this course was understood as the need to preserve the ability to convey the Worker's Voice, and to effectively exercise information and consultation rights on behalf of workers. In the following section the authors discuss these aspects in more detail using a normative approach and focus specifically on the German works council system.

In Germany the workers' representation system, especially works councils, is highly developed and has its origins in the 19th century. It is founded on the argument that the market economy and the organizations that participate in it do not operate in a perfectly rational manner. Perfect competition is not possible due to the information asymmetries that constrain the ability of market participants to optimize their behaviours. As Luhmann (2018) argues the task of resolving the issues caused by imperfect information is transferred to the organizations themselves who in turn respond with decision-making processes that are both autocratic and bureaucratic. Accordingly, the rights of workers to co-determination in Germany can only be represented satisfactorily if they are institutionalised in law and this continues to underpin the system to the present day and applies at all levels of the organization, i.e. at local or plant, company and at group level. As a result, the German system is characterised by frequent overlaps regarding the exercise of information and consultation rights by workers' representatives. This exercise of rights occurs predominantly at the local or plant level, because this is where the closest contact between worker and representative is to be found. This is also the level at which customised agreements between management and worker representatives are negotiated in order to accommodate localized, specific requirements. Depending on the history, the size and the organizational structure of the company this structure can become more complex. For example, where cross-company operations exist, and two or more organizational entities operate at the same premises there will be local works councils as well as a joint one intended to represent interests common to all constituent entities. In a holding company structure, there will also be a group-level works council and when a company has cross-border European operations there is likely to be a European Works Council (EWC) in place.

Specific forms of transnational representation, such as the EU or SE Works Council were created as vehicles for addressing the perceived shortcomings in existing legal and regulatory frameworks and contributing to good corporate governance in multinational companies. The role of such supranational bodies has been emphasized in tackling information asymmetries through the right to information and consultation as well as their links to supervisory bodies within the two-tier or dual board management system that have a system of co-determination in place (IMU, 2019).

However, case studies of EWCs, where the parent company is German, show it is often hard for worker representatives in these bodies to cooperate effectively. Benefits from joint planning, resource synergies and information exchange are often difficult to realise. There is also a need for a more detailed explanation of how the operation of such transnational bodies affects local forms of organizational participation when responding to economic and technological disruption with potentially significant social and economic implications for workforces across several regions or geographies.

Plural Network Organizations - Driving new Forms of Work Organization and Management

Discourses that seek to reinforce the Workers' Voice across Europe have articulated the importance of effective forms of organizational participation in mitigating potentially negative effects on the workforce arising from new ways of working and digitalisation. Network organizations are a particular manifestation of the underlying trend towards the externalisation of work. This occurs typically in the form of partnering with a "collective" of partner organizations who jointly contribute to delivering a product or service by leveraging resources and capabilities to create more value than any one partner could achieve on their own (Helfen & Wirth, 2020).

A characteristic of network organizations is the use of advanced technologies to erode the classical hierarchical forms of co-ordination of work and value creation. Examples of network organizations extend from businesses with multiple service providers in one location with the lead firm managing the co-ordination in a centralized manner through to service providers who are mainly remotely located and who work on a project-by-project basis. Helfen and Wirth (2020) draw attention to the fact that the consequences of the expansion of such forms of work organization and management are not clearly understood, but argue that this trend shares similar characteristics across geographies, contract forms and employment arrangements. Table 2 summarizes the work and employment modes that already exist in so-called plural network organizations and compares them to the traditional hierarchical model.

Table 2. Work and employment forms in plural networks (based on Helfen and Wirth, 2020)

Criterion	Work in a "normal" business	Multiple-employer establishments	Location-independent work	Platform work
Governance perspective	Hierarchy	Network in the form of a scaled hierarchy, often with a "lead firm"	(Project) network	Networks as markets
Network structure	Minor use of networks; focused on a single corporate venture	Heterogeneous businesses involved in the value chain	Numerous small businesses, primarily service providers	Platform operators broker between suppliers
Place of work	Plant	Plant, localized	Variable	Stable to variable
Workforce	Stable, long-term workforce; small peripheral workforce	Relatively stable core, fluid boundaries, small core workforce, large peripheral workforce	Segmented labour pools comprising legally independent undertakings	Profoundly unstable, heterogeneous labour pools
Form of employment	Employee	Employee, temporary contracts, service contracts	Employee, temporary contracts, service contracts, self-employment	(dependent) self-employment
Time horizon of employment	Long-term	Stable, flexible,	Short-term, selective, recurring	Normally short-term & temporary

Source: Helfen and Wirth, 2020

The increasing polarisation and segmentation of work and workers as organizations leverage digital capabilities presents existing forms of worker representation with several challenges. Firstly, the core population of workers associated with the organization shrinks as tasks are outsourced and distributed between multiple suppliers. This, for example, can lead to a reduction in the number of representatives as the outsourced workers are not eligible to be counted as part of the main workforce. Secondly, the profile of the workforce that remains as part of the core business is distributed more and more at either end of the skills spectrum as technology replaces the middle ground, making it more difficult for collective representation as inequalities in pay and prospects become more obvious. Thirdly, the displacement of the classical organizational set-up, as the main unit with which workers identify, in favour of highly individual and mobile forms of work organization brings with it the possibility that the intermediary role of the worker-representative as it is currently understood may become superfluous.

SOLUTIONS AND RECOMMENDATIONS

A common view emerged during the interviews centring on future ways of working for workers' representatives. Essentially, interviewees felt that the need to react and adapt to deal with future crises meant, for example, that current negotiation practices focusing on collective, one-size-fits all agreements would need to be adapted. Such negotiations are time-consuming for all parties and often reflect extensive compromise in order to achieve consensus. This makes it difficult to effectively accommodate the interests of an increasingly heterogeneous workforce and runs the risk of satisfying the "lowest common denominator" only.

At a European, multinational level it also became clear that current forms of governance will need to become more adaptive to enable workers' representatives at all levels to respond quickly and effectively in the interests of their workforces. In the current governance set-up in Europe representation is fragmented and focused on institutional rather than functionally equivalent representation, thus making it difficult to enforce uniform rights. The Workers' Voice European Governance project, initiated in 2015 is calling for workers' representation to be a core element of central management in major multinationals (IMU, 2019).

Two concepts that may help frame the discussion on how to develop the rights of workers to effective organizational participation in future are: Agile Governance and Adaptive Governance. In the context of the arguments laid out in this chapter, the term governance relates primarily to mechanisms and responsibilities through which authority is exercised, decisions are made, and strategy is coordinated and directed in organizations (Luna, et al., 2014, 123).

Agile Governance

Agile encompasses a variety of ways of responding to environmental changes that are volatile, uncertain in terms of outcomes, complex and where the responses are not determinable. The concept of agile governance is geared towards methods that reflect its roots in software engineering, and that were later extended to include organizational studies (Overby et al., 2006). In this context agility requires capabilities, such as flexibility, responsiveness and adaptability to be applied in combination with governance capabilities, such as strategic alignment ability, steering skills and dexterity to perform control, in order to achieve effective and responsive coordination of multiple levels of representation (Luna et al., 2014). Although the notion of agile governance may sound counter-intuitive, given that governance reflects mechanisms, control, accountability, and authority and agility conveys the idea of informality, simplicity, experimentation, both are dependent on each other in complex organizational settings when multilateral actions are required, that require consensus in order to be effective.

The interviews evidenced several examples of agile behaviours in response to the crisis. For example, round tables and daily crisis calls were immediately established across the organization to facilitate a co-ordinated response. Virtual meetings replaced on-site meetings and were scheduled more frequently, focusing on critical topics only. This development partly reflects the agile practice of a "Daily" where teams gather to discuss the status of their work, the topics they have prioritised for that day and any issues with which they need help. Another agile tool that could be adopted in future is the Kanban board. This is a tool that visualizes and monitors workflow and aims to prevent bottlenecks developing that would slow progress. Thus, it is useful in helping allocate time and effort to tasks more efficiently. Such a tool would be helpful in tracking the progress of negotiations for company agreements, or assisting working groups who are involved in complex projects such as business re-locations that encompass several aspects relevant to consultation and co-determination, including health and safety and workplace set-ups.

Agile methods are not, however, a panacea for existing constraints. Many representative bodies, such as German works councils, have a significant degree of autonomy and have working practices in place that accommodate the mainly voluntary participation of their members. Such representatives have other job responsibilities outside their role of workers' representative and so the introduction of new ways of working would need to take this into account. Another facet of agile that might benefit representatives in dealing not only with the workload, but also with the complex range of issues arising typically from crisis situations is in the fostering of an agile culture and mindset. This could be achieved by promoting multi-disciplinary learning and continuous improvement cycles using instruments such as regular debrief and retrospective sessions. Furthermore, it could be beneficial to offer job rotation to avoid blind spots and to engage workers' representatives on a broader scale in matters affecting them and their workforces.

However, a critical review of current ways of working of workers' representatives is needed, especially regarding the gathering and sharing of information. As discussed earlier, a major disadvantage of extensive teleworking is the limit that it places on personal, formal as well as informal, contact between representatives and workers. Consequently, the formerly more spontaneous and situational forms of interaction need to be replaced by a more proactive, systematic way of making contact and communicating with workers. This should be regular and more frequent to ensure that workers are constantly aware of the options available to them if they have need of advice, support or information.

The touchpoints that the workforce have with the organization need to be systematically identified and used to maintain relationships with a workforce that will become more remote due to teleworking and the reduced availability of office space in future. In response workers' representatives should develop, e.g. specific information packages for workers during their professional lifecycle, which can be supplied proactively and ideally by means of interactive channels of communication. Obvious individual touch points can be the onboarding and internal career moves, but also changes in the leadership team or overtime monitoring. Workers' representatives will also need to move from push to pull forms of communication, relying less on quarterly staff meetings and face-to-face conversations and more on social media and the internet or intranet to convey messages concisely and to engage with the workforce in a way that reflects their changing demographic profile. Video messaging and podcasts should also be examined and tested.

Adaptive Governance

Adaptive governance originates from evolutionary theory and draws widely on the ideas from political economy, resource and environmental economics, experimental economics, evolutionary game theory, organizational theory, ecology, systems theory, and complex systems science (Hatfield-Dodds, et al., 2007). It refers to the ability to deal with complex societal issues involving many stakeholders, diverging interests and uncertainty about the actions to be taken. (Bronen and Chapin as cited in Janssen & van der Voort, 2020, 1). Adaptivity is seen as essential when facing major, disruptive changes, such as the COVID-19 pandemic. Theories on adaptive governance therefore speak of "fitting" with changing and new environments and "learning" as central to governance efforts (Janssen & van der Voort, 2020).

The insights from this study suggest that the initially short-term measures taken by companies to deal with the COVID-19 crisis are likely to become more permanent features of work organization and management. The study also highlights the inherent tension between centralised decision-making, in the interests of rapid, reactive measures to ensure business continuity, and the diverse, decentralised groups who cede control to the central authority. The success of this approach was evident in the ability of the multinational company exemplified in this study to adapt successfully in a very short time to the situation.

However, if the crisis is also viewed in the context of complex technological, economic and demographic trends the need to adapt existing forms of worker representation governance in the long term becomes apparent. The increasingly heterogeneous forms of work organization and management, such as those exemplified by plural network organizations, will require highly specialised and localised responses. There will also be an impact on the range and level of topics that workers' representatives need to address in order to retain their role as the Workers' Voice. These should reflect the needs of an increasingly demographically as well as geographically diverse workforce. As a consequence, safeguards need to be put into place to ensure that the role of local workers' representatives remains relevant to the needs of the workforce by devolving responsibilities, rights and resources in an appropriate manner.

At a European level, the Workers' Voice initiative proposes harmonising workers' rights based on functional rather than institutional alignment. Instead of creating equivalent institutions in member states, existing bodies can serve the same purpose, assuming that common rights to worker consultation and co-determination are made legally binding across Europe. This is where representative bodies such as EWCs can bundle the interests of multiple workforces within an enterprise operating across several European borders. However, in order to deal with the complexity arising from the need to operate at multiple geographical and organizational levels there will be a need to consider alternative governance arrangements for worker representation. This will be necessary to ensure that external forces such as market competition and the increasing individualisation of worker interests are not displaced by:

The emergence of informal hierarchies and power structures that monopolize decision-making behind the scenes despite management's claims that there is transparency and participation. (Child, 2020, 9)

FUTURE RESEARCH DIRECTIONS

The study has provided an opportunity to explore the effect of a very specific phenomenon, i.e. the COVID-19 crisis, on various forms of worker representation in the context of a number of subsidiary companies belonging to a multinational organization. The study complements the literature emphasizing the need to augment legislation covering workers' rights at a European level. It illustrates how actors are struggling to respond to the limiting effects of the crisis on critical aspects of their own roles as workers' representatives whilst tackling issues affecting the well-being of colleagues arising from varying organizational and technological trends. In doing so the study focuses attention on the different forms of co-determination and consultation that exist in a multinational company operating across multiple European borders. In this respect the functional as opposed to the structural aspects of worker representation deserve further investigation, particularly regarding organizations that operate internationally and where different regulatory regimes govern workers' rights. Workers' representatives need guidelines on how to align in a democratic process with regard to the delegation of topics to a higher-level body. Principles used in federal political theories might pave the way to introducing concepts like subsidiarity, to clearly define roles and responsibilities, but also broaden deliberations about mechanisms of participation, feedback and control. Further consideration of the insights from the study indicates that workers' representatives may also need to challenge the way of doing things as well as the question of who does what in a complex organization. This could inform the current debate on the evaluation of the EWC Recast Directive and the need for further legislation or policy on the matter.

The study also draws attention to the demographic aspects of the pandemic's effect on workers and suggests that further analysis of the instruments available to workers' representatives such as collective agreements and the governance of negotiation rights may be helpful in determining future forms of co-determination and consultation. A further avenue of research that explores the relative effect of diversity amongst workers' representatives, both in terms of professional background as well as gender, opens up the possibility of providing more insight into their impact on the nature of the agreements that are negotiated on behalf of workers. Furthermore, the trend towards businesses operating as parts of network organizations with different employment terms and conditions and locations for workers suggests that it is unlikely that one-size-fits-all agreements will be sufficient to accommodate the growing diversity of participants in the future.

As this study only reports the findings from one organization, future studies could usefully focus on cases in multiple multinational companies, in which the balance between local or plant-based, national and European representative bodies can be further explored. Furthermore, longitudinal case studies could assess whether the hypotheses derived from the longer-term effect of trends such as centralisation and work externalisation are confirmed.

CONCLUSION

The sudden and profound impact of the COVID-19 pandemic provides an opportunity to examine how workers' representatives may need to adapt in the future to maintain their hard-earned role as guardians of workers' interests and rights. Topics that were important and subject to consultation and co-determination pre-COVID-19 have become an even greater priority as a result of the extensive lockdowns and the subsequent requirement for workers to substitute the office for their homes in the form of teleworking. The concerns resulting from mass teleworking, compounded by underlying trends in work and work organization have meant that workers' representatives have been confronted with challenges to the way they are involved in company decision-making, the prioritisation of matters affecting the workforce as well as to their internal ways of working.

The authors have argued that alternatives to the existing forms of consultation and co-determination, in the form of adaptive governance are necessary to ensure that representatives are able to accommodate the changes that have already occurred and organize accordingly for the future. Furthermore, they point out that this is essential to deal with other disruptive trends that have been accelerated by the pandemic such as digitalisation and that are rapidly altering the composition of the workforces and workplaces that they represent. Importantly, in order to harness the benefits as well as mitigate the disadvantages of such disruptive technological change Child & Loveridge argue that workers and their representatives must have a role in the decision-making processes related to these matters (as cited in Child, 2020, 15). At stake is the fundamental relevance of workers' representatives in the future, something which the authors maintain can only be secured through changes to organizational participation, not only at a pan-European level, but within the organizations themselves.

REFERENCES

Ahlers, E., & Zucco, A. (2020). *Homeoffice – Der positive zwang?* [Home Office – the positive necessity?]. https://www.boeckler.de/de/context.htm?page=wsi/blog-17857-homeoffice-der-positive-zwang-27498.htm

Baumann, H., Brehmer, W., & Klenner, C. (2017). *Frauen und Männer in Betriebsräten. Zur Umsetzung des Minderheitenschutzes bei Betriebsratswahlen* [Women and Men in works councils. Concerning the implementation of protection of minorities in works council elections]. https://www.boeckler.de/pdf/p_wsi_report_34_2017.pdf

Bernstein, P. (1976). Necessary Elements for Effective Worker Participation in Decision Making. *Journal of Economic Issues, 10*(2), 490–522. doi:10.1080/00213624.1976.11503358

BMAS. (2020a). *Sicherung der Arbeitsfähigkeit der Betriebsräte mit Blick auf Covid-19* [Securing the ability of works councils to operate in the face of Covid-19]. https://www.bmas.de/SharedDocs/Downloads/DE/PDF-Meldungen/2020/ministererklaerung-arbeit-der-betriebsraete-unterstuetzen.pdf?__blob=publicationFile&v=1

BMAS. (2020b). *Entwurf eines Gesetzes zur Förderung der Betriebsratswahlen und zur Stärkung der Betriebsräte (Betriebsrätestärkungsgesetz)* [Draft of a law to support works council resolutions (Works Council Reinforcement Act]. https://www.bmas.de/SharedDocs/Downloads/DE/PDF-Gesetze/Referentenentwuerfe/ref-entwurf-zur-foerderung-derbetriebsratswahlen-und-zur-staerkung-der-betriebsraete.pdf?__blob=publicationFile&v=2

Böckler Impuls. (2020). *Corona Krise verschärft soziale Ungleichheit* [Corona crisis is intensifying social inequality]. https://www.boeckler.de/de/boeckler-impuls-coronakrise-verscharft-soziale-ungleichheit-25092.htm

Brooks, S., Webster, R., Smith, L. Woodland, L., Wessely, S. Greenberg, N. & Rubin, G. (2020). *The psychological impact of quarantine and how to reduce it: rapid review of the evidence.* doi:10.1016/S0140-6736(20)30460-8

Child, J. (2018). Downward Accountability. *Corporate Governance in Contention*, 193.

Child, J. (2020). Organizational participation in post-covid society - its contributions and enabling conditions. *International Review of Applied Economics*. Advance online publication. doi:10.1080/02692171.2020.1774976

Child, J., & Loveridge, R. (1990). *New Technology in European Services*. Blackwell.

DiFonzo, N. (2008). *The watercooler effect: An indispensable guide to understanding and harnessing the power of rumors*. Avery.

Emmler, H., & Misterek, F. (2020). *Zahlen und Fakten zur Mitbestimmung* [Facts and Figures concerning co-determination]. Mitbestimmung der Zukunft. https://www.mitbestimmung.de

ETUC. (2020a). *Workers' information, consultation and participation*. https://www.etuc.org/en/publication/covid-19-watch-etuc-briefing-notes

ETUC. (2020b). *New Technologies allowing more surveillance at work*. https://www.etuc.org/en/publication/covid-19-watch-etuc-briefing-notes

ETUI Contributors. (2020, November 05). Benchmarking Working Europe 2014. In *ETUI, The European Trade Union Institute. Chapter 7, Chipping away at workers' participation rights*. https://www.etui.org/publications/books/benchmarking-working-europe-2014

Eurofound. (2020). *Living, working and COVID-19, COVID-19 series*. Publications Office of the European Union. https://www.eurofound.europa.eu/publications/report/2020/living-working-and-covid-19

Eurofound and ILO. (2017). *Working Anytime, Anywhere: The Effects on the World of Work*. Publications Office of the European Union and ILO.

Eurostat. (2018). *Working from home in the EU*. https://ec.europa.eu/eurostat/web/products-eurostat-news/-/DDN-20180620-1

Fine, G. A., & Rosnow, R. L. (1978). Gossip, gossipers, gossiping. *Personality and Social Psychology Bulletin*, *4*(1), 161–168.

Hassel, A., Helmerich, N., & von Verschuer, S. (2018). *Workers' Voice and Good Corporate Governance*. Hans-Böckler-Stiftung. https://www.boeckler.de/pdf/mbf_workers_voice_academical_final_report.pdf

Hatfield-Dodds, S., Nelson, R., & Cook, D. C. (2007). Adaptive governance: An introduction and implications for public policy (No. 418-2016-26492) [Paper presentation]. The 51st Australian and Resource Economics Society (AARES), Queenstown, New Zealand.

Helfen, M., & Wirth, C. (2020). *Management von Arbeit in pluralen Netzwerkorganisationen* [Management of work in plural network organizations]. https://www.boeckler.de/de/faust-detail.htm?sync_id=8922

ILO. (2020). *Teleworking during the COVID-19 pandemic and beyond A Practical Guide*. https://www.ilo.org/wcmsp5/groups/public/---ed_protect/---protrav/---travail/documents/publication/wcms_751232.pdf

IMU. (2019). *Workers' Voice in European corporate governance – an invitation to open new perspectives for participatory democracy*. Nr. 52, 08.2019.

IMU. (2020). *Mitbestimmung der Zukunft* [Co-determination in the future]. https://www.boeckler.de/pdf/p_mbf_report_2020_58.pdf

Janssen, M., & van der Voort, H. (2020). Agile and adaptive governance in crisis response: Lessons from the COVID-19 pandemic. *International Journal of Information Management*, *55*(102180). https://doi.org/10.1016/j.ijinfomgt.2020.102180

Jevtić, M. (2012). *The role of Works Councils and Trade Unions in representing interests of the employees in EU Member States (partnership or competition)*. Friedrich-Ebert-Stiftung, Regional Project for Labour Relations and Social Dialogue in South East Europe. https://library.fes.de/pdf-files/bueros/belgrad/08947.pdf

Jung, C., Statham, R., & Roberts, C. (2020). *How are working time and practices changing as a result of COVID-19? Institute for Public Policy Research*. IPPR.

Kluge, N., Leger, R., & Leuchters, M. (2019). *Workers' Voice: Die Stimme der Arbeitnehmer in der europäischen Corporate Governance– - eine Einladung, neue Perspektiven für die Mitbestimmung zu eröffnen* [Workers' Voice: The voice of workers in European corporate governance – an invitation to open up new perspectives on co-determination] (No. 52). https://www.boeckler.de/pdf/p_mbf_report_2019_52.pdf

Luhmann, N. (2018). *Schriften zur Organisation 1*. Die Wirklichkeit der Organisation., doi:10.1007/978-3-658-22503-2_15

Luna, A. J. H. de O., Kruchten, P., & Pedrosa, M. L. G. do E., Neto, H. R., & de Moura, H. P. (2014). State of the art of agile governance: a systematic review. *International Journal of Computer Science & Information Technology*, 6(5), 121-141. *arXiv preprint arXiv:1411.1922*

McCulley, L. (2020). *Lockdown: Homeworkers putting in extra hours – instant messaging up 1900%*. https://www.thehrdirector.com/business-news/the-workplace/new-data-over-a-third-38-admit-to-working-longer-hours-when-working-from-home/

Overby, E., Bharadwaj, A., & Sambamurthy, V. (2006). Enterprise agility and the enabling role of information technology. *European Journal of Information Systems*, *15*(2), 120–131.

Patmore, G. (2016). *Worker Voice: Worker Representation in the Workplace in Australia, Canada, Germany, the UK and the US 1914-1939*. Liverpool University Press.

Rosnow, R. L., & Fine, G. A. (1976). *Rumor and gossip: The social psychology of hearsay*. Elsevier.

Sobering, K. (2019). Watercooler democracy: Rumors and transparency in a cooperative workplace. *Work and Occupations*, *46*(4), 411–440.

Steppat, M. (2020, October 25). *Deutsche deutlich depressiver im Frühjahrs-Lockdown* [Germans markedly more depressed during spring lockdown]. FAZ. https://www.faz.net/aktuell/gesellschaft/gesundheit/coronavirus/wie-es-um-die-psychische-gesundheit-der-deutschen-steht-17017842.html

Vaughan, D. (1999). The dark side of organizations: Mistake, misconduct, and disaster. *Annual Review of Sociology*, *25*, 271–305.

Vitols, S. (2018). Kontinent vieler Geschwindigkeiten. Arbeitnehmer- und Bürgerbeteiligung in Europa [A continent of many speeds. Worker and citizen participation in Europe]. *WZB Mitteilungen, 160*, 30-32. bit.do/impuls1246V

Whittall, M., & Trinczek, R. (2020). Plant-Level Employee Representation in Germany: Is the German Works Council a Management Stooge or the Representative Voice of the Workforce? In International Comparative Employee Relations: The Role of Culture and Language. DOI doi:10.4337/9781788973229

WHO. (2020). https://www.who.int/director-general/speeches/detail/who-director-general-s-opening-remarks-at-the-media-briefing-on-covid-19---11-march-2020

Wilkinson, A., Gollan, P., Marchington, M., & Lewin, D. (2010). Conceptualizing Employee Participation in Organizations. In The Oxford Handbook of Participation in Organization. OUP.

ADDITIONAL READING

Batt, R., & Appelbaum, E. (2017). The networked organization: implications for jobs and inequality. In D. Grimshaw, C. Fagan, G. Hebson & I. Tavora (Eds.), Making work more equal (pp. 70-89). Manchester University Press.

Dobbins, T., & Dundon, T. (2020). Non-union employee representation. In A. Wilkinson, J. Donaghey, T. Dundon, & R. B. Freeman (Eds.), *Handbook of research on employee voice* (pp. 378–398). Edward Elgar Publishing. doi:10.4337/9781788971188.00030

Gumbrell-McCormick, R., & Hyman, R. (2010). Works councils: the European model of industrial democracy? In A. Wilkinson, P. J. Gollan, M. Marchington, & D. Lewin (Eds.), *The Oxford Handbook of Participation in Organizations. Oxford Handbooks in Business and Management* (pp. 286–314). Oxford University Press.

Haipeter, T., & Rosenbohm, S. (2020). Deutsche Betriebsräte in multinationalen Unternehmen: Befunde zur Artikulation von Interessen in Mehrebenensystemen [German works council members in multinational companies: Findings on the articulation of interests in plural level systems]. Industrielle Beziehungen. Zeitschrift für Arbeit. *Organisation und Management, 27*(3), 9–10.

Jirjahn, U., & Smith, S. C. (2018). Nonunion employee representation: theory and the German experience with mandated works councils. *Annals of Public and Cooperative Economics, 89*(1), 201–233. doi:10.1111/apce.12191

Nienhüser, W. (2020). Works councils. In A. Wilkinson, J. Donaghey, T. Dundon, & R. B. Freeman (Eds.), *Handbook of research on employee voice* (pp. 259–276). Edward Elgar Publishing. doi:10.4337/9781788971188.00023

Patmore, G. (2020). Employee voice and democracy: a critique of national and transnational laws. In A. Wilkinson, J. Donaghey, T. Dundon, & R. B. Freeman (Eds.), *Handbook of research on employee voice* (pp. 222–238). Edward Elgar Publishing. doi:10.4337/9781788971188.00020

Van der Brempt, O., Boone, C., van Witteloostuijn, A., & van den Berg, A. (2017). Toward a behavioural theory of cooperation between managers and employee representatives in works councils. *Economic and Industrial Democracy, 38*(2), 314–343. doi:10.1177/0143831X15578721

KEY TERMS AND DEFINITIONS

Co-Determination: The legally binding right of workers to participate in decisions that affect their workplace.

Company Agreement: A company agreement is a contract between the employer and the Works Council, which defines the rights and obligations of both parties with respect to a specific topic (e.g. introduction of new technology), but also formulates (similar to a law or a collective agreement) obligatory standards for all employees of a company.

EU Recast Directive: A 2009 update to the original legislative framework (2009/38/EC) from 1999 covering the role and remit of European Works Councils. The recast directive had two main goals: firstly, to improve the effectiveness of EWCs and secondly, to promote the increase in the number of EWCs operating in the European Union.

German Works Council Model: A form of worker representation specific to Germany, which provides for a range of legally enforceable employee rights including information provision, consultation, withholding of consent to employer proposals and enforceable co-determination.

Organizational Participation: A term used in multiple social science disciplines that deals with the ways in which worker and managerial or organizational interests are associated with each other.

Worker or Employee Involvement: Synonymous terms include worker or employee participation that describe the ways in which workers can participate in matters affecting their work and workplaces in the form of planning, decision-making and monitoring.

Worker Representation: Worker or employee representation can be defined as a worker's or employee's right to seek representation in negotiating with management on issues such as wages, hours, benefits and working conditions. The specific form this representation can take is rooted in individual national labour laws.

Worker's Rights: A comprehensive reference to the areas of workplace management where worker representatives have the right to participation in matters concerning, e.g. labour standards, diversity policies and programs, health and welfare, career development and employment opportunities, as well as dialogue on specific work-related issues.

Worker's Voice: A collective term referring to the articulation, representation, supervision and enforcement of workers' rights.

Workplace Self-Management: A form of work governance where employees have the autonomy to determine and carry out their work without direct intervention from management. It is exemplified by worker co-operatives and firms run by entrepreneurs.

Chapter 18

Work, Family, and Identity:
How Remote Work Will Challenge and Change Who We Are

Phil Lord
https://orcid.org/0000-0002-5097-4140
Faculty of Law, McGill University, Canada

ABSTRACT

The COVID-19 pandemic has accelerated the existing transition to remote work and, more broadly, flexible forms of work. Much energy and attention have been dedicated to analysing this transition and how governments and other actors can best respond to it. This chapter takes a step back and analyses the potential impacts of the transition to remote work on our individual and collective identities. Recognising that work is an important part of who we are and has historically been a microcosm and a catalyst of broader social change, this chapter analyses how remote work challenges gender roles, contemporary family structures, and our conceptualisation of the relationship between work and other commitments. The chapter admittedly offers more questions than it does answers. It complexifies our understanding of remote work and seeks to spark future discussions as to its consequences.

INTRODUCTION

Work is one of the most fundamental aspects in a person's life, providing the individual with a means of financial support and, as importantly, a contributory role in society. A person's employment is an essential component of his or her sense of identity, self-worth and emotional well-being.

- Former Chief Justice of the Supreme Court of Canada Brian Dickson (Reference Re Public Service Employee Relations Act, 1987, para. 91).

DOI: 10.4018/978-1-7998-6754-8.ch018

We've seen what can be accomplished when we use 50% of our human capacity. If you visualize what 100% can do, you'll join me as an unbridled optimist about America's future.

- Warren Buffett (on the participation of women in the workforce) (Brodock, 2013)

Work is an important part of who we are. We work in different ways and for different reasons (Knetz, 2016; Rosso et al., 2010). Many of us work to earn a living, to provide for ourselves and for those we love. Others work to contribute, to make a difference in the lives of those whose path they cross through their work. Yet others seek the apex in their profession as an intrinsically important aspiration, which defines their identity. Of course, these broad idea(l)s are neither exhaustive nor mutually exclusive. And regardless of our motivation, what we do for a sizeable portion of our days is bound to be an important part of who we are. It can provide us with a sense of belonging and contribution. As we earn a living and pay taxes, we also contribute to the shared aspirations of the society we form a part of. Work helps shape who we are, and the meaning we derive from life.

Over time, work has been both a microcosm[1] and a catalyst of broader social change. As a key part of who we are, it has witnessed and exemplified the struggles which have shaped our collective and individual identities. Work has also been a locus of these struggles. The various facets of work are intimately intertwined with broader social issues. Over time, much of the nature of work has changed: who works, who employs, how work is valued and remunerated, and how work is performed.

For millennia, human beings could be owned, sold and bought chiefly on the basis of the labour they could provide (Drescher, 2009). Just two centuries ago in the United States, the colour of one's skin still dictated whether one was free or owned, and whether one could reap the benefits of one's own labour (Berlin, 2015). More recently, work has been a significant locus in the transformation of the role of women in developed countries. Having fought for the right to vote and own property (which they could formerly only do through their spouse), women sought the possibility to enter the workforce and benefit from the same opportunities as men (Kirk, 1995; Lebsock, 1977; Punnett, 2016). Though this fight continues to this day, it has redefined the nature of work and of the workplace, and has been a significant driver of economic growth (S&P Global, 2017; Weinstein, 2018).

Today, the COVID-19 pandemic stands to permanently yet again redefine the nature of work. As we faced a generational public health threat, the only effective solution seemed to be broad lockdowns: the immediate and indefinite shutdown of broad sections of the economy (Lord, 2020a, p. 2). With these shutdowns, billions of people have had to work from home (Lord, in press). As we slowly emerge from the severest lockdown period, many companies have significantly expanded their remote work policies, allowing remote work through 2020 and beyond. The pandemic will therefore accelerate the existing transition to remote work and, more broadly, to more flexible forms of work.

I am a legal scholar who conducts principally doctrinal legal research. I have previously published on remote work: my research encouraged more sophisticated government responses to the increasing significance of remote work (Lord, 2020c; Lord, in press). This chapter adopts a different perspective. It is not concerned with legislative responses to remote work, and rather opts for a broader approach. Without adopting an explicitly favourable or unfavourable stance on remote work, it asks how remote work will redefine our identities. If the world indeed does move toward this mode of work, how will the transition reshape our individual and collective identities? Accepting work as a privileged locus in defining these identities, it analyses how remote work challenges gender roles, contemporary family structures, and our conceptualisation of the relationship between work and other commitments. This chapter admittedly offers more questions than it does answers. It complexifies our understanding of remote work, and seeks to spark future discussions as to its consequences.

The chapter proceeds in two sections, each anchored in North American labour and legal thought. The first section traces our historical understanding of the concept of work-life balance, as well as the various challenges which the evolution of contemporary societies has posed to its definition and relevance. It positions remote work within these broader challenges. The second section discusses the gendered consequences of work's foray into the home. It analyses how this foray challenges gender roles and family structures.

FROM BALANCE TO INTEGRATION?

Work is one locus where individual identities are defined. Individuals take on different roles in different physical and social loci, which jointly come to define their identities (Knetz, 2016). At work, we may project a different persona, which we find aligned with the nature of our work and our role within our organization. The nature of the work we do, and those we do it for, often plays a key role in defining this identity. Lawyers, including myself, routinely state: "I am a lawyer." In doing so, we seemingly conflate our work and our broader identity: we do not *work* as lawyers, we *are* lawyers. Prior to entering the profession in American states and Canadian provinces, I had to swear an oath which frames the nature of the profession in terms which transcend the nature of the work attorneys accomplish (see for instance Rules of professional conduct, 2009; Supreme Court of the State of New York Appellate Division (Second Judicial Department), 2006).[2] Attorneys should strive to serve justice in the work they undertake. In advocating zealously for their clients, they should nonetheless remember the duties they owe to the administration of justice, the judiciary, and their profession (Rules of professional conduct, 2009, rule 8.4). Attorneys, we are told, also need to, at least in part, bear the weight of the issues that exist in our justice systems. If the disadvantaged cannot access the justice system, or if organizations that cannot afford a lawyer wish to challenge important pieces of legislation, attorneys should heed the call to serve and provide services to these individuals and organizations for free (Rules of professional conduct, 2009, rule 6.1). To a lawyer, then, her profession transcends her work and defines her identity by setting core values which imbue her service to the disadvantaged and her participation in and contribution to the alleviation of societal problems which are not (at least strictly) juridical.

Yet if work, especially in certain professions, will inevitably be a key factor in the multiple and overlapping ones which define our identity, many of us seek to limit its influence in other areas of our lives. We often use the idiom that we *go to* work. There is, then, a break in physical location which facilitates that in our behaviour and identity. As we physically leave the home, we move to a different location, where we take on an identity which is related to the different role we occupy. Our social circle also changes, as we generally leave our family to join our work colleagues. This leads me to articulate and emphasise a nuance in my earlier claim that work is an important locus where our identity is defined. Even as we accept that our identity is the product of the multiple personas we adopt in the several significant loci where we spend most of our time (and which give meaning to our lives), we can compartmentalise these identities. Although we will be the product of these multiple personas, we can actively seek to make the boundaries which separate them more or less permeable. We can choose not to let our work (at least to the extent possible) penetrate our home. We can choose not to bring the physical tools relevant to our work, such as our computer, at home or choose never to work from home. Indeed, facilitating a break in these identities and in our roles, and declining to let our work penetrate the home, may be central to guarding our ability to dedicate time to the other key areas of our lives – and to finding balance and meaning (Golden & Wiens-Tuersb, 2006; Wang & Wong, 2014).

We have historically afforded much importance to the concept of "work-life balance" (Guest, 2002; Kanter, 1977; Lockwood, 2003).[3] Inherent to that concept, at least as it was initially construed, is the idea that the constituent parts (work and life) constitute distinct spheres of one's life, whose relative importance needs to be thoughtfully managed. Work-life balance is the process of apportioning one's time at and away from work, such that work interferes as little as possible with one's leisure time and responsibilities at home.

As the world changed, the relevance of that concept, at least as narrowly construed, has decreased. The twin products of industrialisation have been that people work harder and more intensely. I have previously described the impacts of industrialisation and globalisation as follows:

Over the past century, we have witnessed a remarkable and accelerating transition in how skills are valued and remunerated. Even as we went through decades of economic growth, the standing of the middle class has eroded, and our growth has disproportionately benefitted the wealthiest. With technology, the impact of the skills gap between the wealthy and the middle class has grown, and our economy increasingly values the skills of highly educated individuals.

There was a time where hard-working, middle-class North American workers could find jobs which required few skills. These jobs would not make them rich, but they would allow them to contribute and provide them with financial security. The salaries were reasonable, and workers who served a company for decades would have a pension they could retire on. Workers worked, and company owners profited. The stability of the relationship was underlain by its fairness: workers were fairly compensated for their work, and they did not need to worry about being laid off or funding their retirement.

Then we grew into service economies. Developed countries got exponentially wealthier. With globalisation, companies became able to take advantage of cheaper, overseas labour, which padded their bottom lines and concurrently reduced product prices for consumers. Developed countries rode and fed this wave by championing free trade agreements, which reduced national barriers to entry and further incentivised companies to outsource low-skilled labour to other countries.

As workers had to compete with those in other countries, their job security quickly vanished. Low-skilled jobs became low-paid ones, without pension and other benefits. […]

Then came a second wave of change, with the advent of companies such as Uber and the so-called gig economy. Companies found that they could further reduce their labour costs by reimagining the relationship which unites them and their workers. Not only could this relationship be stripped of its ancillary benefits, it could also be construed as something else entirely. Indeed, by making their workers independent contractors, companies could further shift the cost of the relationship to those who work for them. In doing so, companies no longer had to respect legislation regarding such things as work conditions, minimum wage, and overtime pay. (Lord, in press)

The plainest impact of the downward pressure on wages and devaluation of oversupplied skills has been a necessity for low-skilled workers to work longer hours to maintain their standard of living. Workers began to work overtime or juggle multiple part-time jobs just to make ends meet (Ehrenreich, 2011; Tilly, 1991; Valletta, Bengali & van der List, 2020). As they did, their ability to dedicate time to leisure and home responsibilities came under assault. Economic growth came as a result of productivity increases. While productivity increases can be affected by driving efficiencies in a number of ways, they at least in part resulted from workers accomplishing more in the same number of work hours (Baily, 1986; Jorgenson, Ho & Stiroh, 2008).

Technology has also made it harder for workers to guard the time they dedicate to leisure and home responsibilities. While technology drove efficiencies (and growth) (Baily, 1986; Jorgenson, Ho & Stiroh, 2008), it also changed that nature of work in many ways. The world became more interconnected; information began to be produced and consumed at an ever-faster pace (with individuals accepting this pace as the norm); and technological tools and devices revolutionised the ways in and pace at which we work (Fountain, 2004; Goldsby & Zinn, 2016; Morris & Ferguson, 1993).

Technology also marked a significant inflection point in the way we (can) conceive of work-life balance. Both metaphorically and literally, work made its way into the home. The previously significant physical separation between the locations where we work and don't, which had eased work-life balance and grounded its conceptualisation, was suddenly under siege. Through a somewhat analogous metaphor, Prof. Jeannie Suk discusses the criminal law's foray into the home (Suk, 2006). Historically, she argues, the home had been an intimate location, which existed beyond the reach of the criminal law. She states: " [the criminal law's] expansion has tended not only outward but inward. Traditionally, criminal law did not enter the intimate familial confines of the home. [...] The criminal law [did] not reach into this quintessentially private space" (Suk, 2006, p. 5). It is this intimacy and significance to conjugal relationships which justified the home's independence. The criminal law, with its stark punishments, did not belong in the home (Lord, 2020b).[4] Though the criminal law's foray into the home is contextualised by its broader expansion, both in scope and in the magnitude of the punishments it attributes, Prof. Suk notes that it is also singularly a product of the feminist movement. From a protection of intimacy, the home's independence was reconceptualised as anti-progressive and its consequences, as deeply gendered. She adds: "The idea that criminal law may not reach into this quintessentially private space has been rightly criticized for enabling the state's acquiescence in violence against women. During the period of over thirty years in which the criminalization of domestic violence has been in the making, feminists have sought to recast as 'public' matters previously considered 'private'" (Suk, 2006, p. 5).

Much like the criminal law's evolution we just considered, technology led work *into the home*. (This foray is analogously quite gendered, but that is addressed in the next section.) With technological devices, we became easily accessible, at all times and regardless of our location (Derks et al., 2015; Kreiner et al., 2009; Major & Germano, 2006). Technology bridged the physical divide between the workplace and the home. The workplace, admittedly in part as a result of client demands, evolved accordingly (Chesley et al., 2003; Derks et al., 2015; Galinsky et al., 2001). Suddenly, it became much harder to effect work-life balance. The locational boundaries between the two constitutive concepts became insignificant. Dedicating time to family and leisure would require significantly greater effort, and fully "disconnecting" from work, even when possible, could upset one's work – and the new expectations of the workplace. While work and other commitments had previously competed in time (i.e. in one's schedule), they now did so across locations and more intensely – and at *all* times.

The transition to remote work exists in these broader trends and transitions. While the COVID-19 pandemic has accelerated the transition to remote work, it was underway (and accelerating) much before (Lord, 2020c; Lord, in press). Indeed, remote work is intrinsically defined by technology. Although the shutdowns of broad sections of the economy were government ordered (Lord & Saad, in press, p.16), and public health related, these decisions to shut down parts of the economy would have been impossible (or, at least, would have involved carefully weighing more significant consequences) were it not for the assumption that much of the business world could survive with its employees working remotely (Helmore, 2020; NYC schools, 2020).[5]

Technology and remote work are mutually reinforcing. Technology empowers us to work from home, and remote work normalises the place already afforded to work within the home. To put it differently, remote work has consolidated and legitimised work's foray into the home. While technology forcefully defined our availability beyond the workplace and redefined the nature of work in a way that we may not have wanted, with remote work, we are *choosing* to invite work to play a greater role in the intimacy of the home. (As mentioned above, workers had been clamouring in favour of remote work much before the COVID-19 pandemic (Choudhury et al., 2019; Lord, 2020c; Owl Labs & Global Workplace Analytics, 2019).)[6]

Much of the public debate has lauded the great promise of remote work. The central claim has been that greater flexibility in the ways in, locations at, and times at which we work will make the workplace fairer (Lord, 2020c). By reducing commute times and allowing for more flexible work times, it will empower individuals to spend more time with their families – and achieve more at work or choose more demanding careers (Fox, 2020; Gelles, 2020; Powell, 2020). Companies will be able to compete globally for talent, regardless of a worker's location, which will ostensibly favour economic growth (Douglass & Edelstein, 2009; Ebersole, 2020; Florida, 2020). By being able to move away from expensive cities, workers will have more money to make ends meet (Fox, 2020; San Francisco, 2020).[7]

Yet, as mentioned, remote also fundamentally challenges the notion of work-life balance. More so than the emergence of technology, remote work challenges work-life balance at its core. It makes the boundaries between work and life permeable and elusive, arguably to such an extent that the concept loses most, if not all, of its significance. With remote work, work consistently happens in the home, a physical space where work and other aspects of life now compete with the same legitimacy.

This tension is exacerbated by the time flexibility which remote work imports. If work can take place at any time, then work and life compete at all times.[8] The home is fundamentally redefined, and the activities which take place within the home constantly compete with work. While, as mentioned above, remote work has been lauded for its potential to leave more time for non-work activities, it is also quite possible that remote work will instead make it easier for workers to work a greater number of hours (and for employers to adjust their expectations accordingly) and, with heterogeneous work schedules, further develop the expectation that workers will be available at all times. The COVID-19 shutdowns of sections of the economy happened among broader economic slowdowns caused by the pandemic. As such, workers may not have been able to fully assess the impact of remote work policies – whose impact on the behaviour of employers can only be assessed over time. Furthermore, employers were, at the time, likely grappling with a decrease in the volume of their business, which made it unnecessary to heighten their expectations regarding work hours or time flexibility.

This likely ratcheting up of expectations, combined with work time flexibility, makes it much harder for workers to disconnect from work and set boundaries between their work time and the time they dedicate to leisure and home responsibilities.

REMOTE WORK, GENDER AND THE FAMILY UNIT

In a previous article, I argued that the transition to remote work holds particular promise in that it could help alleviate structural issues in the nature of work which have had a disproportionate impact on women (Lord, 2020c). As women have historically borne a disproportionate share of household and family responsibilities, they have been, and remain, underrepresented in higher-paying, more senior roles (with correspondingly higher incomes). This has, in large part, caused the gender wage gap most developed countries continue to grapple with (Gangl & Ziefle, 2009; Lord, 2020c). By affording locational and time flexibility, and by reducing commute times, remote work has the potential to empower women to allocate more time, on more convenient schedules, to their work.

In this chapter, it is worth taking a further step back and reflecting upon how remote work more broadly challenges what happens *within* the home. Of course, the various issues and challenges discussed in the previous section apply to women as well. Yet the foray of work into the home is also defined by two operative characteristics which make its consequences somewhat gendered: the likely presence of both spouses within the home, and their consequent availability to engage in home and family responsibilities. These characteristics are likely to fundamentally upset the balance of power within the home, and also to alleviate the share of its burden which has historically fallen upon women.

From a broader conceptual standpoint, it is worth remembering the intrinsic tensions which define the home. I quoted above Prof. Jeannie Suk's assessment of the criminal law's expansion into the home. She states: "The idea that criminal law may not reach into this quintessentially private space has been rightly criticized for enabling the state's acquiescence in violence against women. During the period of over thirty years in which the criminalization of domestic violence has been in the making, feminists have sought to recast as 'public' matters previously considered 'private'" (Suk, 2006, p. 5). Prof. Suk's assessment is underlain by the implicit recognition that the home is defined by its occupants, traditionally a heterosexual couple, with or without children. It is further defined by the power relationship among these occupants, the man and woman, of differing physical strength and characteristics which make the woman more vulnerable to domestic violence and other crimes (Serra, 1993). Beyond this physical power dynamic, there is a converse power relationship in who heads the management of household and childrearing responsibilities – generally the woman, as discussed above (Cerrato & Cifre, 2018; Gangl & Ziefle, 2009; Lord, 2020c; Treas & Tai, 2012).

Remote work challenges this power dynamic. By securing the presence of both spouses within the home, it upsets the heterogeneous distribution of responsibilities and is likely to also help solidify the equality of both spouses. The presence of both spouses makes it easier for them to communicate and collaborate, and to allocate work. Without the locational boundaries between work and family, it will arguably be harder for men to elude their home responsibilities – and easier for women to keep them accountable.

Yet these are macroscopic aspects of the transition to remote work: they are likely long-term consequences of the reconceptualisation of work and the identities it bears upon. It would be myopic not to acknowledge that these long-term shifts may well take place only after converse short-term effects. To a large extent, these short-term effects can already be observed. I have, like many others, previously argued that the pandemic's consequences are intrinsically heterogeneous. The lockdowns ordered by governments to respond to the pandemic, and their economic consequences, have had a disproportionate impact on those who were already disadvantaged (DeLuca et al., 2020; Lord, 2020c, p. 64; Lord, in press). The first to lose their jobs were those in the primary and secondary sectors of the economy:

waiters, factory workers, and others in low-skilled, low-pay positions (Cortes & Forsythe, 2020; DeLuca et al., 2020; Nicola et al., 2020). Needless to say, it is these workers who could least bear the impact of the pandemic. More importantly, as minority and marginalised groups (including women) are overrepresented in these sectors of the economy, the brunt of the shock was borne by marginalised groups (Alon et al., 2020; Cortes & Forsythe, 2020; DeLuca et al., 2020; Keister, 2000). Absent government intervention to mitigate these heterogeneous impacts, for instance through taxation measures (Lord, in press), the pandemic risks entrenching and worsening existing inequality.

The impacts of the pandemic have been especially pronounced for women. As pandemic-related lockdowns led to school and daycare closures, couples have instinctively (and unsurprisingly) reverted to traditional gender roles (Alon et al., 2020; Arntz et al., 2020; Lord & Saad, in press; Modestino, 2020). Additional home and childrearing responsibilities have disproportionately fallen upon women. This compounded the impact of pandemic-related economic slowdowns. While typical recessions have a greater impact on marginalised groups, the pandemic-related shutdowns have (unlike prior recessions) also more acutely affected sectors of the economy where women are overrepresented (Alon et al., 2020; Arntz et al., 2020). The compounded effect of these slowdowns and school and daycare closures has made the pandemic's impact uniquely gendered.

The contrasting short- and long-term impacts of the transition to remote work are a testimony to the strength and malleability of the identities we forge through work. It is the strength of the gender-specific identities which existed at the time of the pandemic that led couples to revert to traditional gender roles, thereby exacerbating the pandemic's impact on already vulnerable women. Although they have been redefined over time, these identities are relics of a time when only men worked and, as a result, childrearing and household responsibilities were borne by women.

Nonetheless, gender roles, and the household, have evolved significantly since – in tandem with the nature of work. It is therefore not particularly bold to suggest that a fundamental transformation in the nature of work, the advent of remote work, will have a commensurate impact on our identities. In fact, early evidence suggests that we are at the crossroads of a fundamental change similar to that described in this section: a positive transformation of gender roles and of the household which will make the spouses closer to equal partners (Alon et al., 2020, pp. 4, 28, 38; Arntz et al., 2020, pp. 385-86). If that is any consolation, the pandemic's disproportionate impact on women will have paved the way to positive long-term change in the opposite direction – redefining the identities which have caused this disproportionate impact.

CONCLUSION

This chapter has analysed the transition to remote work, which the COVID-19 pandemic has accelerated. While much energy and attention have been dedicated to analysing this transition, and how governments and other actors can best respond to it, this chapter has taken a step back and analysed the potential impacts of the transition to remote work on our individual and collective identities. Accepting that work is an important part of who we are, and has historically been a microcosm and a catalyst of broader social change, this chapter has analysed how remote work challenges gender roles, contemporary family structures, and our conceptualisation of the relationship between work and other commitments. The first section positioned remote work within the broader challenges to the notion of work-life balance in contemporary societies. The second section analysed the gendered impact of remote work within the home and upon its family unit.

The chapter admittedly offered more questions, and food for thought, than it did answers. It complexifies our understanding of remote work, and seeks to spark future discussions as to its consequences. Its key takeaway may be that taking a few steps back is often helpful and insightful. Remote work may be neither good nor bad – or both. Regardless, a dichotomic understanding may not do it justice. Any such fundamental change in the things we do with most of our days is bound to be complex, nuanced, and elusive; fraught with both promise and peril.[9] In taking a few steps back, we find that remote work challenges, at their very core, the constitutive elements of our identity. Over time, work has been a uniquely fascinating and important locus in the definition of our individual and collective identities. It has witnessed the generational struggles which have redefined who works and who benefits from work, and enfranchised millions of us from legal objects to legal subjects. Remote work is a fundamental shift which will undoubtedly also define, in a significant way, the future of work, of the home, and of our conception of our identity.

ACKNOWLEDGMENT

I am grateful to Lydia Saad for thoughtful comments on earlier drafts.

This research was in part supported by a grant from Canada's Social Sciences and Humanities Research Council (grant not numbered).

REFERENCES

Agence France-Presse. (2020, September 13). San Francisco exodus as tech giants move towards remote work in COVID-19 era. *Agence France-Presse*. https://www.afp.com/

Alon, T., Doepke, M., Olmstead-Rumsey, J., & Tertilt, M. (2020). *This time it's different: The role of women's employment in a pandemic recession* (NBER Working Paper No 27660). https://www.nber.org/papers/w27660

Arntz, M., Ben Yahmed, S., & Berlingieri, F. (2020). Working from home and COVID-19: The chances and risks for gender gaps. *Inter Economics*, *55*, 381–386.

Baily, M. N. (1986). What has happened to productivity growth? *Science*, *234*(4775), 443–445.

Berlin, I. (2015). *The long emancipation: The demise of slavery in the United States*. Harvard University Press.

Brenan, M. (2020, April 3). U.S. Workers discovering affinity for remote work. *Gallup*. https://news.gallup.com/poll/306695/workers-discovering-affinity-remote-work.aspx

Brodock, K. (2013, May 6). Women in leadership as an economic imperative? *Forbes*. https://www.forbes.com/sites/katebrodock/2013/05/06/women-in-leadership-as-an-economic-imperative/#64f3f6a9c5a7

Cerrato, J., & Cifre, E. (2018). Gender inequality in household chores and work-family conflict. *Frontiers in Psychology*, 9.

Chesley, N., Moen, P., & Shore, R. P. (2003). The new technology climate. In P. Moen (Ed.), *It's about time: Couples and careers* (pp. 220–241). Cornell University Press.

Choudhury, P., Larson, B. Z., & Foroughi, C. (2019). Is it time to let employees work from anywhere? *Harvard Business Review*. https://hbr.org/2019/08/is-it-time-to-let-employees-work-from-anywhere

Cortes, G. M., & Forsythe, E. (2020). *The heterogeneous labor market impacts of the COVID-19 pandemic* (Upjohn Institute Working Paper 20-327). doi:10.17848/wp20-327

DeLuca, S., Papageorge, N., & Kalish, E. (2020). The unequal cost of social distancing. *Johns Hopkins University & Medicine*. https://coronavirus.jhu.edu/from-our-experts/the-unequal-cost-of-social-distancing

Derks, D., van Duin, D., Tims, M., & Bakker, A. B. (2015). Smartphone use and work–home interference: The moderating role of social norms and employee work engagement. *Journal of Occupational and Organizational Psychology*, *88*(1), 155–177.

Douglass, J. A., & Edelstein, R. (2009). *The global competition for talent: The rapidly changing market for international students and the need for a strategic approach in the US* (CSHE Paper No. 8.09). https://cshe.berkeley.edu/publications/global-competition-talent-rapidly-changing-market-internationalstudents-and-need

Drescher, S. (2009). *Abolition: A history of slavery and antislavery*. Cambridge University Press.

Ebersole, G. (2020, September 28). A post-pandemic paradigm shift is coming to the workplace. *Central Penn Business Journal*. https://www.cpbj.com/post-pandemic-paradigm-shift-coming-workplace/

Ehrenreich, B. (2011). *Nickel and dimed: On (not) getting by in America*. Picador.

Florida, R. (2020). The uncertain future of corporate HQs. *Harvard Business Review*. https://hbr.org/2020/09/the-uncertain-future-of-corporate-hqs

Fountain, J. E. (2004). Building the virtual state: Information technology and institutional change. Brookings.

Fox, M. (2020, September 21). With remote work flexibility, some people opt to relocate ahead of their retirement. *CNBC*. https://www.cnbc.com/2020/09/21/with-remote-work-options-people-opt-to-relocate-before-retirement-.html

Galinsky, E., Kim, S., & Bond, J. (2001). Feeling overworked: When work becomes too much [Paper presentation]. Conference Board/Families and Work Institute's Work-Life 2001 Conference, New York, NY, United States.

Gangl, M., & Ziefle, A. (2009). Motherhood, labor force behavior, and women's careers: An empirical assessment of the wage penalty for motherhood in Britain, Germany, and the United States. *Democracy (New York, N.Y.)*, *46*(2), 341–369.

Gelles, D. (2020, June 23). Are companies more productive in a pandemic? *The New York Times*. https://www.nytimes.com/2020/06/23/business/working-from-home-productivity.html

Golden, L., & Wiens-Tuersb, B. (2006). To your happiness? Extra hours of labor supply and worker well-being. *Journal of Socio-Economics*, *35*(2), 382–397.

Goldsby, T. J., & Zinn, W. (2016). Technology innovation and new business models: Can logistics and supply chain research accelerate the evolution? *Journal of Business Logistics*, *37*(2), 80–81.

Guest, D. E. (2002). Perspectives on the study of work-life balance. *Social Sciences Information. Information sur les Sciences Sociales*, *42*(2), 255–279.

Helmore, E. (2020, April 14). Business not as usual: WeWork tries to shrug off coronavirus despite upheaval. *The Guardian*. https://www.theguardian.com/business/2020/apr/14/wework-coronavirus-impact-business-not-as-usual

Jorgenson, D. W., Ho, M. S., & Stiroh, K. J. (2008). A retrospective look at the U.S. productivity growth resurgence. *The Journal of Economic Perspectives*, *22*(1), 3–24.

Kanter, L. M. (1977). *Work and family in the United States: A critical review and agenda for research and policy*. Russell Sage Foundation.

Keister, L. A. (2000). Race and wealth inequality: The impact of racial differences in asset ownership on the distribution of household wealth. *Social Science Research*, *29*(4), 477–502.

Kirk, L. J. (1995). Exclusion to emancipation: A comparative analysis of women's citizenship in Australia and the United States 1869-1921. *West Virginia Law Review*, *97*(3), 725–750.

Knetz, I. (2016). Toward a model of work-related self: A narrative review. *Frontiers in Psychology*, *7*, 331.

Kreiner, G. E., Hollensbe, E. C., & Sheep, M. L. (2009). Balancing borders and bridges: Negotiating the work-home interface via boundary work tactics. *Academy of Management Journal*, *52*(4), 704–730.

Lebsock, S. D. (1977). Radical reconstruction and the property rights of southern women. *The Journal of Southern History*, *43*(2), 195–216.

Lockwood, N. R. (2003). Work/Life: Balance Challenges and Solutions. *SHRM Research Quarterly*, 1-10.

Lord, P. (2020a). Incentivising employment during the COVID-19 pandemic. *The Theory and Practice of Legislation*, *8*(3), 355–372.

Lord, P. (2020b). "It doesn't work!": The symbolic aspect of law, from the criminal law to Bill 21. *Directions*, *9*(6), 1–18.

Lord, P. (2020c). The social perils and promise of remote work. *Journal of Behavioral Economics for Policy*, *4*(S), 63-67.

Lord, P. (in press). *COVID-19 and the future of work*. Denver Law Review Forum https://papers.ssrn.com/sol3/papers.cfm?abstract_id=3666588

Lord, P., & Saad, L. (in press). Tackling the COVID-19 pandemic. *Manitoba Law Journal, 43*. https://papers.ssrn.com/sol3/papers.cfm?abstract_id=3554436

Major, D. A., & Germano, L. M. (2006). The changing nature of work and its impact on the work-home interface. In F. Jones, R. J. Burke, & M. Westman (Eds.), *Work-life balance: A psychological perspective* (pp. 13–38). Psychology Press.

Modestino, A. S. (2020, July 29). Coronavirus child-care crisis will set women back a generation. *The Washington Post.* https://www.washingtonpost.com/us-policy/2020/07/29/childcare-remote-learning-women-employment/

Morris, C. R., & Ferguson, C. H. (1993). How architecture wins technology wars. *Harvard Business Review, 71*(2), 86–96.

NBC News. (2020, March 16). NYC schools close Monday, CT schools close Tuesday, NJ school shutdown "inevitable." *NBC News.* https://www.nbcnewyork.com/news/coronavirus/nyc-school-debate-continues-amid-coronavirus-pandemic-four-related-deaths-in-ny-nj/2327269/

Nicola, M., Alsafi, Z., Sohrabi, C., Kerwan, A., Al-Jabir, A., Iosifidis, C., Agha, M., & Agha, R. (n.d.). The socio-economic implications of the coronavirus pandemic (COVID-19): A review. *International Journal of Surgery, 78*, 185–193.

Owl Labs & Global Workplace Analytics. (2019). *State of Remote Work 2019.* K. Lister.

Powell, J. (2020, September 25). The rise of remote work can be unexpectedly liberating: What if you are better off without the office? *The New York Times.* https://www.nytimes.com/2020/09/25/opinion/remote-work-from-home-office.html

Punnett, B. J. (2016). Women in the workforce: A global snapshot. In M. L. Connerley & J. Wu (Eds.), *Handbook on well-being of working women* (pp. 579–602). Springer.

Reference Re Public Service Employee Relations Act, [1987] 1 S.C.R. 313.

Rosso, B. D., Dekas, K. H., & Wrzesniewskic, A. (2010). On the meaning of work: A theoretical integration and review. *Research in Organizational Behavior, 30*, 91–127.

Rules of professional conduct. (2009). New York Codes, Rules and Regulations, title 22, subtitle B, chapter IV, subchapter E, section 1200.

Serra, P. (1993). Physical violence in the couple relationship: A contribution toward the analysis of the context. *Family Process, 32*(1), 21–33.

S&P Global. (2017). *The key to unlocking U.S. GDP growth? Women.*

Suk, J. (2006). Criminal law comes home. *The Yale Law Journal, 116*(2), 2–70.

Supreme Court of the State of New York Appellate Division (Second Judicial Department). (2006). *Orientation to the profession.* http://www.courts.state.ny.us/courts/ad2/forms/law%20guardian%20handbook/orientationtotheprofessionprogrammaterials.pdf

Tilly, C. (1991). Reasons for the continuing growth of part-time employment. *Monthly Labor Review, 114*(3), 10–18.

Treas, J., & Tai, T. (2012). How couples manage the household: Work and power in cross-national perspective. *Journal of Family Issues, 33*(8), 1088–1116.

Valletta, R. G., Bengali, L., & van der List, C. (2020). Cyclical and market determinants of involuntary part-time employment. *Journal of Labor Economics, 38*(1), 67–93.

Wang, M., & Wong, M. C. S. (2014). Happiness and leisure across countries: Evidence from international survey data. *Journal of Happiness Studies, 15*, 85–118.

Weinstein, A. (2018). When more women join the workforce, wages rise – including for men. *Harvard Business Review*. https://hbr.org/2018/01/when-more-women-join-the-workforce-wages-rise-including-for-men

ENDNOTES

1 A microcosm is an illustrative example of the main characteristics of a broader situation.

2 Throughout the paragraph, I reference the rules mentioned with the New York Bar's rules on professional conduct.

3 Kanter's seminal work arguably introduced the concept into academic research and significantly solidified its continued centrality to research on labour, identity, and family.

4 As the cited article further details, the criminal law is unique in being both a public law tool (which is laid out and enforced by the state) and a tool with stark consequences, generally involving the loss of one's fundamental freedoms. While not strictly necessary for one not familiar with the law to understand my argument, understanding these distinctions can be enlightening. Unlike private law tools, which generally create rights between individuals, public law creates obligations of an ostensibly public nature, such as those imposed by the criminal law. It is thought that the responsibility to enforce public law therefore lies with the state. Preventing people from committing crimes protects the *public* interest by keeping us all safe. In keeping with this conception, the state bears the cost and responsibility of enforcing the criminal law (by prosecuting those who commit crimes), instead of leaving this responsibility to the victim who is directly affected by the crime. Conversely, private parties would need to avail themselves of private law recourses – and their decision to do so would be bounded by cost and other constraints.

5 The cited sources are examples.

6 For post-pandemic data, see Brenan (2020), which finds that a majority of U.S. workers now support working from home most of the time.

7 The news sources cited throughout the paragraph are examples.

8 This is especially so as the expectations regarding "normal" work hours change. In contrast, while technology made us available at all times, it did not challenge our assumptions regarding a normal work schedule.

9 And, perhaps, poetic possibility.

Compilation of References

ABS. (2020a). *Household Impacts of COVID-19 Survey*. https://www.abs.gov.au/statistics/people/people-and-communities/household-impacts-COVID-19-survey/latest-release#data-download

ABS. (2020b). *Labour Force*, May https://www.abs.gov.au/ausstats

Access Economics. (2010). Accessed 1 September, 2020. http://ict-industryreports.com.au/wp-content/uploads/sites/4/2010/07/2010-Impacts-of-Teleworking-under-the-NBN-July-2010.pdf

Achor, S., Kellerman, G. R., Reece, A., & Robichaux, A. (2018). America's loneliest workers, according to research. *Harvard Business Review*. https://hbr.org/2018/03/americas-loneliest-workers-according-to-research

Acun, V., & Yilmazer, S. (2018). A grounded theory approach to investigate the perceived soundscape of open-plan offices. *Applied Acoustics*, *131*, 28–37. doi:10.1016/j.apacoust.2017.09.018

Advancing Parental Leave Equality Network. (2019). *National working families report 2019*. https://aplen.pages.ontraport.net/WorkingFamiliesReport2019

Agence France-Presse. (2020, September 13). San Francisco exodus as tech giants move towards remote work in COVID-19 era. *Agence France-Presse*. https://www.afp.com/

Ahlers, E., & Zucco, A. (2020). *Homeoffice – Der positive zwang?* [Home Office – the positive necessity?]. https://www.boeckler.de/de/context.htm?page=wsi/blog-17857-homeoffice-der-positive-zwang-27498.htm

Ahn, S. J., Bostick, J., Ogle, E., Nowak, K. L., McGillicuddy, K. T., & Bailenson, J. N. (2016). Experiencing nature: Embodying animals in immersive virtual environments increases inclusion of nature in self and involvement with nature. *Journal of Computer-Mediated Communication*, *21*(6), 399–419. doi:10.1111/jcc4.12173

Aitken-Fox, E., Coffey, J., Dayaram, K., Fitzgerald, S., Gupta, C., McKenna, S. & Tian, A. (2020). COVID-19 has put trust front and centre in human resources management. *LSE Business Review*.

Akkirman, A. D., & Harris, D. L. (2005). Organizational communication satisfaction in the virtual workplace. *Journal of Management Development*, *24*(5), 397–409. doi:10.1108/02621710510598427

Al-Ani, B., Horspool, A., & Bligh, M. C. (2011). Collaborating with "virtual strangers": Towards developing a framework for leadership in distributed teams. *Leadership*, *7*(3), 219–249. doi:10.1177/1742715011407382

Aliyyah, R. R., Rachmadtullah, R., Samsudin, A., Syaodih, E., Nurtanto, M., & Tambunan, A. R. S. (2020). The perceptions of primary school teachers of online learning during the COVID-19 pandemic period: A case study in Indonesia. *Journal of Ethnic and Cultural Studies*, *7*(2), 90–109. doi:10.29333/ejecs/388

Allen, T. D., Golden, T. D., & Shockley, K. M. (2015). How effective is telecommuting? Assessing the status of our scientific findings. *Psychological Science in the Public Interest: A Journal of the American Psychological Society, 16,* 40-68.

Allen, M. (2007). Workplace surveillance and managing privacy boundaries. *Management Communication Quarterly*, *21*(2), 172–200. doi:10.1177/0893318907306033

Allen, T. D., Golden, T. D., & Shockley, K. M. (2015). How Effective Is Telecommuting? Assessing the Status of Our Scientific Findings. *Psychological Science in the Public Interest*, *16*(2), 40–68. doi:10.1177/1529100615593273 PMID:26403188

Allen, T. D., Johnson, R. C., Kiburz, K. M., & Shockley, K. M. (2013). Work–family conflict and flexible work arrangements: Deconstructing flexibility. *Personnel Psychology*, *66*(2), 345–376. doi:10.1111/peps.12012

Allgood, S., Walstad, W., & Siegfried, J. (2015). Research on Teaching Economics to Undergraduates. *Journal of Economic Literature*, *53*(2), 285–325. doi:10.1257/jel.53.2.285

Alloatti, M. (2014) *Una discusión sobre la técnica de bola de nieve a partir de la experiencia de investigación en migraciones internacionales*. Paper presented at IV Encuentro Latinoamericano de Metodología de las Ciencias Sociales, La Plata.

Alloatti, M., & Oliveira, A. L. M. (2021). *Deepening and widening the gap: the impacts of Covid-19 pandemic on gender and racial inequalities in the labor market, domestic work and domestic violence in Brazil*. Manuscript in preparation.

Allyn, B. (2020). *Your boss is watching you: Work from home boom leads to more surveillance*. NPR.org.

Alon, T., Doepke, M., Olmstead-Rumsey, J., & Tertilt, M. (2020). *This time it's different: The role of women's employment in a pandemic recession* (NBER Working Paper No 27660). https://www.nber.org/papers/w27660

Alsharo, M., Gregg, D., & Ramirez, R. (2017). Virtual team effectiveness: The role of knowledge sharing and trust. *Information & Management*, *54*(4), 479–490. doi:10.1016/j.im.2016.10.005

Alsup, J. (2006). *Teacher Identity Discourse. Negotiating Personal and Professional Spaces*. Lawrence Erlbaum Associates. doi:10.4324/9781410617286

Altig, D., Baker, S. R., Barrero, J. M., Bloom, N., Bunn, P., Chen, S., Mizen, P., Parker, N., Renault, T., Smietanka, P., & Thwaites, G. (2020). Economic uncertainty before and during the COVID-19 pandemic. *Journal of Public Economics*, *191*, 104274. doi:10.1016/j.jpubeco.2020.104274 PMID:32921841

Altman, I. (1975). *The Environment and Social Behavior: Privacy, Personal Space, Territory, Crowding*. Brooks/Cole.

Altman, I. (1990). Towards a transactional perspective: a personal journey. In I. Altman & K. Christensen (Eds.), *Environment and behavior studies: emergence of intellectual traditions* (pp. 335–355). Plenum. doi:10.1007/978-1-4684-7944-7_10

Amin, T. (2020, June 26). Laws related to sextortion. *Lawyered*. https://www.lawyered.in/legaldisrupt/articles/laws-related-sextortion/

Amis, M. (1995). *The Information*. Flamingo.

Anderson, A. J., Kaplan, S. A., & Vega, R. P. (2015). The impact of telework on emotional experience: When, and for whom, does telework improve daily affective well-being? *European Journal of Work and Organizational Psychology*, *24*(6), 882–897. doi:10.1080/1359432X.2014.966086

Anderson, A., Huttenlocher, D., Kleinberg, J., & Leskovec, J. (2013). Steering user behavior with badges. *Proceedings of the 22nd international conference on World Wide Web*, 95-106. 10.1145/2488388.2488398

Anderson, D. I., Magill, R. A., & Sekiya, H. (2001). Motor learning as a function of KR schedule and characteristics of task-intrinsic feedback. *Journal of Motor Behavior*, *33*(1), 59–66. doi:10.1080/00222890109601903 PMID:11265058

Arnetz, B., & Blomkvist, V. (2007). Leadership, Mental Health, and Organizational Efficacy in Health Care Organizations: Psychosocial Predictors of Healthy Organizational Development Based on Prospective Data from Four Different Organizations. *Psychotherapy and Psychosomatics*, *76*(4), 242–248. doi:10.1159/000101503 PMID:17570963

Arntz, M., Ben Yahmed, S., & Berlingieri, F. (2020). Working from home and COVID-19: The chances and risks for gender gaps. *Inter Economics*, *55*, 381–386.

Arthur, C. (2013). Yahoo chief bans working from home. *The Guardian*. Accessed 18 August 2020. https://www.theguardian.com/technology/2013/feb/25/yahoo-chief-bans-working-home

Arup. (2020). *Future of offices: in a post-pandemic world.* Arup.

Ashford, N., & Kallis, G. (2013). A Four-day Workweek: A Policy for Improving Employment and Environmental Conditions in Europe. *The European Financial Review*, 53–58.

Ashkanasy, N. M., Humphrey, R. H., & Huy, Q. N. (2017). Integrating emotions and affect in theories of management. *Academy of Management Review*, *42*(2), 175–189. doi:10.5465/amr.2016.0474

Aube, C., Rousseau, V., & Morin, E. M. (2007). Perceived organizational support and organizational commitment. *Journal of Managerial Psychology*, *22*(5), 479–495. doi:10.1108/02683940710757209

Austen, J. (1959). *Jane Austen's Letters to the Sister Cassandra and Others* (R. W. Chapman, Ed.). Oxford UP.

Australian Bureau of Statistics. (2017). *Childhood Education and Care, Australia.* Cat no. 4402.0.

Australian Council of Trade Unions (ACTU). (2020). *Working from Home Report.* ACTU.

Autor, D. H. (2019). Work of the Past, Work of the Future. *AEA Papers and Proceedings. American Economic Association*, *109*, 1–32. doi:10.1257/pandp.20191110

Avishai, B. (2020, June 21). The pandemic isn't a black swan but a portent of a more fragile global system, *The New Yorker*.

Avolio, B. J., Luthans, F., & Walumbwa, F. O. (2004). *Authentic leadership: Theory building for veritable sustained performance* [Working paper]. Gallup Leadership Institute, University of Nebraska-Lincoln.

Baard, P. P., Deci, E. L., & Ryan, R. M. (2004). Intrinsic Need Satisfaction: A Motivational Basis of Performance and Weil-Being in Two Work Settings. *Journal of Applied Social Psychology*, *34*(10), 2045–2068. doi:10.1111/j.1559-1816.2004.tb02690.x

Backhouse, A., & Drew, P. (1992). The design implications of social interaction in a workplace setting. *Environment & Planning B*, *19*(5), 573–584. doi:10.1068/b190573

Bailenson, J. N., & Yee, N. (2005). Digital chameleons: Automatic assimilation of nonverbal gestures in immersive virtual environments. *Psychological Science*, *16*(10), 814–819. doi:10.1111/j.1467-9280.2005.01619.x PMID:16181445

Bailenson, J. N., Yee, N., Patel, K., & Beall, A. C. (2008). Detecting digital chameleons. *Computers in Human Behavior*, *24*(1), 66–87. doi:10.1016/j.chb.2007.01.015

Bailey, D. E., & Kurland, N. B. (2002). A review of telework research: Findings, new directions, and lessons for the study of modern work. *Journal of Organizational Behavior*, *23*(4), 383–400. doi:10.1002/job.144

Baily, M. N. (1986). What has happened to productivity growth? *Science*, *234*(4775), 443–445.

Baird, M. (2011). The state, work and family in Australia. *International Journal of Human Resource Management*, *22*(18), 3742–3754. doi:10.1080/09585192.2011.622922

Baker, E., Avery, G. C., & Crawford, J. (2006). Home alone: The role of technology in telecommuting. *Information Resources Management Journal, 19*(4), 1–22. doi:10.4018/irmj.2006100101

Bakker, A. B., & Demerouti, E. (2017). Job Demands–Resources Theory: Taking Stock and Looking Forward. *Journal of Occupational Health Psychology, 22*(3), 273–285. doi:10.1037/ocp0000056 PMID:27732008

Bakker, A., & Demerouti, E. (2007). The job demands-resources model: State of the art. *Journal of Managerial Psychology, 22*(3), 309–328. doi:10.1108/02683940710733115

Balconi, M., Fronda, G., & Vanutelli, M. E. (2020). When gratitude and cooperation between friends affect inter-brain connectivity for EEG. *BMC Neuroscience, 21*(1), 1–12. doi:10.118612868-020-00563-7 PMID:32264825

Bal, M., Kordowicz, M., & Brookes, A. (2020). Workplace Dignity Perspective on Resilience: Moving Beyond Individualized Instrumentalization to Dignified Resilience. *Advances in Developing Human Resources, 22*(4), 453–466. doi:10.1177/1523422320946115

Baltar, C. T., Rolim, L. N., & Leone, E. T. (2020). The effects of the Brazilian recession on wage inequality between men and women. RBEST: Revista Brasileira de Economia Social e do Trabalho, 2.

Banakou, D., Kishore, S., & Slater, M. (2018). Virtually being einstein results in an improvement in cognitive task performance and a decrease in age bias. *Frontiers in Psychology, 9*, 917. doi:10.3389/fpsyg.2018.00917 PMID:29942270

Banerjee, I., Jacobsen, R., Krivkovich, A., Libotte, G., & Rambachan, I. (2020). *Shaping and safeguarding the banking workforce after COVID-19*. McKinsey & Company. https://www.mckinsey.com/industries/financial-services/our-insights/shaping-and-safeguarding-the-banking-workforce-after-covid-19#

Barak, A. (2005). Sexual harassment on the internet. *Social Science Computer Review, 23*(1), 77–92. doi:10.1177/0894439304271540

Barber, B. (1983). *The Logic and Limits of Trust*. Rutgers University Press.

Barbot, B., & Kaufman, J. C. (2020). What makes immersive virtual reality the ultimate empathy machine? Discerning the underlying mechanisms of change. *Computers in Human Behavior, 111*, 106431. doi:10.1016/j.chb.2020.106431

Barca, S. (2020). *Forces of Reproduction: Notes for a Counter-Hegemonic Anthropocene*. Cambridge University Press. doi:10.1017/9781108878371

Barsade, S. G., Coutifaris, C. G., & Pillemer, J. (2018). Emotional contagion in organizational life. *Research in Organizational Behavior, 38*, 137–151. doi:10.1016/j.riob.2018.11.005

Bartel, C. A., Wrzesniewski, A., & Wiesenfeld, B. M. (2012). Knowing Where You Stand: Physical Isolation, Perceived Respect, and Organizational Identification Among Virtual Employees. *Organization Science, 23*(3), 743–757. doi:10.1287/orsc.1110.0661

Bartunek, J. (2019). Contemplation and Organization Studies: Why contemplative activities are so crucial for our academic lives. *Organization Studies, 40*(10), 1463–1479. doi:10.1177/0170840619867717

Baruch, Y. (2000). Teleworking: Benefits and pitfalls as perceived by professionals and managers. *New Technology, Work and Employment, 15*(1), 34–49. doi:10.1111/1468-005X.00063

Baruch, Y. (2003). The status of research on teleworking and an agenda for future research. *International Journal of Management Reviews, 3*(2), 113–129. doi:10.1111/1468-2370.00058

Barzanò, G., Amenduni, F., Cutello, G., Lissoni, M., Pecorelli, C., Quarta, R., Raffio, L., Regazzini, C., Zacchilli, E., & Ligorio, M. B. (2020). When the place matters: Moving the classroom into a museum to re-design a public space. *Frontiers in Psychology, 11*, 943. doi:10.3389/fpsyg.2020.00943 PMID:32581905

Basketball. (2020). basketball-reference.com/contracts/players.html

Bass, B. M., & Avolio, B. J. (1995). *The Multifactor Leadership Questionnaire*. Mind Garden.

Bass, B. M., Avolio, B. J., Jung, D. I., & Berson, Y. (2003). Predicting unit performance by assessing transformational and transactional leadership. *The Journal of Applied Psychology, 88*(2), 207–218. doi:10.1037/0021-9010.88.2.207 PMID:12731705

Bateman, N., & Ross, M. (2020). *Why has COVID-19 been especially harmful for working women? Brookings Gender Equality Series*. The Brookings Institution.

Bauman, D. C. (2013). The three faces of integrity. *The Leadership Quarterly, 24*(3), 414–426. doi:10.1016/j.leaqua.2013.01.005

Baumann, H., Brehmer, W., & Klenner, C. (2017). *Frauen und Männer in Betriebsräten. Zur Umsetzung des Minderheitenschutzes bei Betriebsratswahlen* [Women and Men in works councils. Concerning the implementation of protection of minorities in works council elections]. https://www.boeckler.de/pdf/p_wsi_report_34_2017.pdf

Baumeister, R., & Leary, M. R. (1995). The need to belong: Desire for interpersonal attachments as a fundamental human motivation. *Psychological Bulletin, 117*(3), 497–529.

Baxter, P., & Jack, S. (2008). Qualitative case study methodology: Study design and implementation for novice researchers. *Qualitative Report, 13*(4), 544–559.

Bayram, A. B., & Ta, V. P. (2019). Diplomatic chameleons: Language style matching and agreement in international diplomatic negotiations. *Negotiation and Conflict Management Research, 12*(1), 23–40. doi:10.1111/ncmr.12142

BBC News. (2020, May 27). *Trump and Biden trade barbs over wearing a mask.* Retrieved from https://www.bbc.com/news/av/world-us-canada-52828602

Beach, E. (1938). Teaching Economics. *The American Economic Review, 28*(3), 515–515.

Beauregard, T., Canonico, E., & Basile, K. A. (2019). "The Fur-Lined Rut": Telework and Career Ambition. In C. Kelliher & J. Richardson (Eds.), Work, Working and Work Relationships in a Changing World (pp. 17-36). Routledge.

Becker, E. (1973). *The Denial of Death.* Free Press.

Becker, W. E. (2000). Teaching Economics in the 21st Century. *The Journal of Economic Perspectives, 14*(1), 109–119. doi:10.1257/jep.14.1.109

Becker, W., & Watts, M. (1999). How Departments of Economics Evaluate Teaching. *The American Economic Review, 89*(2), 344–349. doi:10.1257/aer.89.2.344

Bednar, P. M., & Welch, C. (2019). Socio-technical perspectives on smart working: Creating meaningful and sustainable systems. *Information Systems Frontiers*, 1–18. doi:10.100710796-019-09921-1

Beijaard, D., Meijer, P. C., & Verloop, N. (2004). Reconsidering research on teachers' professional identity. *Teaching and Teacher Education, 20*(2), 107–128. doi:10.1016/j.tate.2003.07.001

Beijaard, D., Verloop, N., & Vermunt, J. D. (2000). Teachers' perceptions of professional identity: An exploratory study from a personal knowledge perspective. *Teaching and Teacher Education, 16*(7), 749–764. doi:10.1016/S0742-051X(00)00023-8

Bélanger, F., & Allport, C. D. (2008). Collaborative technologies in knowledge telework: An exploratory study. *Information Systems Journal, 18*(1), 101–121. doi:10.1111/j.1365-2575.2007.00252.x

Bélanger, F., Watson-Manheim, M. B., & Swan, B. R. (2013). A multi-level socio-technical systems telecommuting framework. *Behaviour & Information Technology, 32*(12), 1257–1279. doi:10.1080/0144929X.2012.705894

Bell, B. S., & Kozlowski, S. W. J. (2002). A typology of virtual teams: Implications for effective leadership. *Group & Organization Management, 27*(1), 14–49. doi:10.1177/1059601102027001003

Bell, E., Bryman, A., & Harley, B. (2018). *Business Research Methods*. Oxford University Press.

Belojevic, G., Slepcevic, V., & Jakovljevic, B. (2001). Mental performance in noise: The role of introversion. *Journal of Environmental Psychology, 21*(2), 209–213. doi:10.1006/jevp.2000.0188

Bentham, J., Bowman, A., de la Cuesta, M., Ertürk, I., Folkman, P., Froud, J., Johal, S., Law, J., Leaver, A., Moran, M., & Williams, K. (2013) Manifesto for the Foundational Economy. Centre for Research on Socio-Cultural Change, University of Manchester.

Bentley, T., Teo, S., McLeod, L., Tan, F., & Bo, R. (2016). The role of organisational support in teleworker wellbeing: A sociotechnical systems approach. *Applied Ergonomics, 52*, 207–215. doi:10.1016/j.apergo.2015.07.019 PMID:26360212

Berg, M. (1988). Women's Work: Mechanization and the early phases of the industrialization of England. In On Work: Historical Comparative and Theoretical Approaches. Oxford: Blackwell.

Berg, J. M., Grant, A. M., & Johnson, V. (2010). When callings are calling: Crafting work and leisure in pursuit of unanswered occupational callings. *Organization Science, 21*(5), 973–994. doi:10.1287/orsc.1090.0497

Berg, J., Furrer, M., Harmon, E., Rani, U., & Six Silberman, M. (2018). *Digital labour platforms and the future of work Towards decent work in the online world*. International Labour Organization.

Berke, D. L. (2003). Coming home again: The challenges and rewards of home-based self employment. *Journal of Family Issues, 24*(4), 513–546. doi:10.1177/0192513X02250754

Berlin, I. (2015). *The long emancipation: The demise of slavery in the United States*. Harvard University Press.

Bernieri, F. J., & Rosenthal, R. (1991). *Interpersonal coordination: Behavior matching and interactional synchrony*. Academic Press.

Bernstein, E., Blunden, H., Brodsky, A., Sohn, W., & Waber, B. (2020, July 15). The Implications of Working Without an Office. *Harvard Business Review*. Retrieved from https://hbr.org/2020/07/the-implications-of-working-without-an-office

Bernstein, P. (1976). Necessary Elements for Effective Worker Participation in Decision Making. *Journal of Economic Issues, 10*(2), 490–522. doi:10.1080/00213624.1976.11503358

Bick, R., Chang, M., Wang, K. W., & Yu, T. (2020). *A blueprint for remote working: lessons from China*. McKinsey & Company. Retrieved from https://www.mckinsey.com/business-functions/mckinsey-digital/our-insights/a-blueprint-for-remote-working-lessons-from-china

BickA.BlandinA.MertensK. (2020). *Work from Home after the Covid-19 Outbreak*. CEPR Discussion Paper No. DP15000. https://ssrn.com/abstract=3650114

Bisbe, J., & Sivabalan, P. (2017). Management control and trust in virtual settings: A case study of a virtual new product development team. *Management Accounting Research, 37*, 12–29. doi:10.1016/j.mar.2017.02.001

Bitner, M. J. (1992). Servicescapes: The impact of physical surroundings on customers and employees. *Journal of Marketing, 56*(2), 57–71. doi:10.1177/002224299205600205

Bizzi, L. (2017). Network characteristics: When an individual's job crafting depend on the job of others. *Human Relations, 70*(4), 436–460. doi:10.1177/0018726716658963

Blackwell, L., Ellison, N., Elliot-Deflo, N, & Schwartz, R. (2019). Harassment in social virtual reality: challenges for platform governance. *PACM on Human-Computer Interaction, 3*(CSCW).

Blayney, S. (2017). Industrial fatigue and the productive body: the science of work in Britain, c. 1900–1918. *Social History of Medicine.*

Bliese, P. D., Edwards, J. R., & Sonnentag, S. (2017). Stress and well-being at work: A century of empirical trends reflecting theoretical and societal influences. *The Journal of Applied Psychology, 102*(3), 389–402. doi:10.1037/apl0000109 PMID:28125263

Bloom, N. (2020). *The Bright Future of Working From Home*. SIEPR, Stanford. siepr.stanford.edu/research/publications/bright-future-working-home

Bloom, N. (2020, June 29). Stanford research provides a snapshot of a new working from home economy, *Stanford News.*

Bloom, N. (2014). Fluctuations of uncertainty. *The Journal of Economic Perspectives, 28*(2), 153–175. doi:10.1257/jep.28.2.153

Bloom, N., Liang, J., Roberts, J., & Ying, Z. J. (2015). Does working from home work? evidence from a Chinese experiment. *The Quarterly Journal of Economics, 130*(1), 165–218. doi:10.1093/qje/qju032

Blume, C., Garbazza, C., & Spitschan, M. (2019). Effects of light on human circadian rhythms, sleep and mood. *Somnologie: Schlafforschung und Schlafmedizin, 23*(3), 147–156. doi:10.100711818-019-00215-x PMID:31534436

BMAS. (2020a). *Sicherung der Arbeitsfähigkeit der Betriebsräte mit Blick auf Covid-19* [Securing the ability of works councils to operate in the face of Covid-19]. https://www.bmas.de/SharedDocs/Downloads/DE/PDF-Meldungen/2020/ministererklaerung-arbeit-der-betriebsraete-unterstuetzen.pdf?__blob=publicationFile&v=1

BMAS. (2020b). *Entwurf eines Gesetzes zur Förderung der Betriebsratswahlen und zur Stärkung der Betriebsräte (Betriebsrätestärkungsgesetz)* [Draft of a law to support works council resolutions (Works Council Reinforcement Act]. https://www.bmas.de/SharedDocs/Downloads/DE/PDF-Gesetze/Referentenentwuerfe/ref-entwurf-zur-foerderung-derbetriebsratswahlen-und-zur-staerkung-der-betriebsraete.pdf?__blob=publicationFile&v=2

Boccaccio. (1995). *The Decameron* (G. H. McWilliam, Trans.). Penguin.

Böckler Impuls. (2020). *Corona Krise verschärft soziale Ungleichheit* [Corona crisis is intensifying social inequality]. https://www.boeckler.de/de/boeckler-impuls-coronakrise-verscharft-soziale-ungleichheit-25092.htm

Boddy, N. (2020). More stress, less trust: the truth about remote work. *Australian Financial Review*. https://www.afr.com/work-and-careers/careers/more-stress-less-trust-the-truth-about-remote-work-20200714-p55bv0

Bødker, K., Kensing, F., & Simonsen, J. (2009). *Participatory IT design: designing for business and workplace realities*. MIT Press.

Boland, B., De Smet, A., Palter, R., & Sanghvi, A. (2020). *Reimagining the office and work life after COVID-19*. McKinsey Report.

Boorsma, B., & Mitchell, S. (2011). *Work-life innovation smart work—A paradigm shift transforming how, where, and when work gets done.* Cisco IBSG Point of View. Accessed December 5th 2020 at https://www.cisco.com/c/dam/en_us/about/ac79/docs/ps/Work-Life_Innovation_Smart_Work.pdf

Borkovich, D. J., & Skovira, R. J. (2020). Working from home: Cybersecurity in the age of COVID-19. *Issues in Information Systems*, *21*(4), 234–246. doi:10.48009/4_iis_2020_234-246

Bosch-Sijtsema, P., Ruohomaki, V., & Vartianen, M. (2010). Multi-locational knowledge workers in the office: Navigation, disturbances and effectiveness. *New Technology, Work and Employment*, *25*(3), 183–195. doi:10.1111/j.1468-005X.2010.00247.x

Boskin, M. (1988). Observations on the Use of Textbooks in the Teaching of Principles of Economics. *The Journal of Economic Education*, *19*(2), 157–164. doi:10.1080/00220485.1988.10845254

Boston, N. B. C. (2020 May 4). *What to Know About Massachusetts' Mandatory Mask Order.* Retrieved from https://www.nbcboston.com/news/local/what-to-know-about-massachusetts-mandatory-mask-order/2117445/

Bosua, R., Gloet, M., Kurnia, S., Mendoza, A., & Yong, J. (2013). Telework, productivity and wellbeing: An Australian perspective. *Telecommunications Journal of Australia*, *63*(1), 11.1-11.12. doi:10.7790/tja.v63i1.390

Bosworth, G., & Venhorst, V. (2018). Economic linkages between urban and rural regions – what's in it for the rural? *Regional Studies*, *52*(8), 1075–1085. doi:10.1080/00343404.2017.1339868

Bowker. (2014). bowker.com/news/2014/Traditional-Print-Book-Production-Dipped-Slightly-in-2013.html

Bowlby, J. (1973). Attachment and loss: Volume II: Separation, anxiety and anger. London: The Hogarth Press and the Institute of Psycho-Analysis.

Bowlby, J. (1969). *Attachment and loss* (Vol. 3). Random House.

Bowles, S., & Carlin, W. (2020). What Students Learn in Economics 101: Time for a Change. *Journal of Economic Literature*, *58*(1), 176–214. doi:10.1257/jel.20191585

Bowling, N. A., Eschleman, K. J., & Wang, Q. (2010). A meta-analytic examination of the relationship between job satisfaction and subjective well-being. *Journal of Occupational and Organizational Psychology*, *83*(4), 915–934. doi:10.1348/096317909X478557

Boxall, P., & Purcell, J. (2016). *Strategy and Human Resource Management* (4th ed.). Palgrave Macmillan. doi:10.1007/978-1-137-40765-8

Boyraz, M. (2016). *How to break the "invisible walls" the role of communicative practices for overcoming challenges of subgroups in global teams.* The State University.

Brady, T. (1984) *New Technology and Skills in British Industry.* A report prepared for the Manpower Services Commission (Research and development series).

Brand, J. L. (2008). Office Ergonomics: A Review of Pertinent Research and Recent Developments. *Review of Human Factors and Ergonomics*, *4*(1), 245–282. doi:10.1518/155723408X342871

Bratteteig, T., & Wagner, I. (2016). Unpacking the notion of participation in participatory design. *Computer Supported Cooperative Work*, *25*(6), 425–475. doi:10.100710606-016-9259-4

Braun, V., & Clarke, V. (2006). Using thematic analysis in psychology. *Qualitative Research in Psychology*, *3*(2), 77–101. doi:10.1191/1478088706qp063oa

Braverman, B. (2020). The coronavirus is taking a huge toll on workers' mental health across America. *CNBC Online*.

Bray, M., Waring, P., Cooper, R., & Macneil, J. (2017). *Employment Relations: Theory and Practice*. McGraw Hill Education.

Breakwell, G. M., Hammond, S. M., & Fife-Schaw, C. (2000). *Research Methods in Psychology* (2nd ed.). Sage Publications.

Brenan, M. (2020, April 3). U.S. Workers discovering affinity for remote work. *Gallup*. https://news.gallup.com/poll/306695/workers-discovering-affinity-remote-work.aspx

Brenan, M. (2020, October 13). COVID-19 and remote work: an update. *Gallup*. https://news.gallup.com/poll/321800/covid-remote-work-update.aspx

Brennan, A., Chugh, J. S., & Kline, T. (2002). Traditional versus open office design: A longitudinal field study. *Environment and Behavior*, *34*(3), 279–299. doi:10.1177/001391650203400300l

Breuer, C., Hüffmeier, J., & Hertel, G. (2016). Does trust matter more in virtual teams? A meta-analysis of trust and team effectiveness considering virtuality and documentation as moderators. *The Journal of Applied Psychology*, *101*(8), 1151–1177. doi:10.1037/apl0000113 PMID:27228105

Breuer, C., Hüffmeier, J., Hibben, F., & Hertel, G. (2020). Trust in teams: A taxonomy of perceived trustworthiness factors and risk-taking behaviours in face-to-face and virtual teams. *Human Relations*, *73*(1), 3–34. doi:10.1177/0018726718818721

Bringslimark, T., Hartig, T., & Patil, G. G. (2007). Psychological benefits of indoor plants in workplaces: Putting experimental results into context. *HortScience*, *42*(3), 581–587. doi:10.21273/HORTSCI.42.3.581

Brodie, K. (2013). The power of professional learning communities. *Education as Change*, *17*(1), 5–18. doi:10.1080/16823206.2013.773929

Brodock, K. (2013, May 6). Women in leadership as an economic imperative? *Forbes*. https://www.forbes.com/sites/katebrodock/2013/05/06/women-in-leadership-as-an-economic-imperative/#64f3f6a9c5a7

Brooks, S., Webster, R., Smith, L. Woodland, L., Wessely, S. Greenberg, N. & Rubin, G. (2020). *The psychological impact of quarantine and how to reduce it: rapid review of the evidence*. doi:10.1016/S0140-6736(20)30460-8

Brown, A. (1995). *Organisational Culture*. Pitman Publishing.

Brown, G., & Robinson, S. L. (2011). Reactions to territorial infringement. *Organization Science*, *22*(1), 210–224. doi:10.1287/orsc.1090.0507

Brownlee, D. (2020). Twitter, square announce work from home forever option: What are the risks? *Forbes*. Retrieved from: https://www.forbes.com/sites/danabrownlee/2020/05/18/twitter-square-announce-work-from-home-forever-optionwhat-are-the-risks/?sh=437570402565

Brynjolfsson, E., Horton, J.J., Ozimek, A., Rock, D., Sharma, G., & TuYe, H.-Y. (2020). *COVID-19 and remote work: an early look at US data*. National Bureau of Economic Research Working Paper No. 27344. https://www.nber.org/papers/w27344

Bullinger, L. R., Carr, J., & Packham, A. (2020). *COVID-19 and crime: effects of stay-at-home orders on domestic violence*. National Bureau of Economic Research Working Paper No. 27667. doi:10.3386/w27667

Burt, R. S., & Knez, M. (1996). Trust and third party gossip. In R. M. Kramer & T. R. Tyler (Eds.), *Trust in organizations: Frontiers of Theory and Research* (pp. 68–89). Sage. doi:10.4135/9781452243610.n5

Butler, R., & Nisan, M. (1986). Effects of no feedback, task-related comments, and grades on intrinsic motivation and performance. *Journal of Educational Psychology*, *78*(3), 210–216. doi:10.1037/0022-0663.78.3.210

By, R. T. (2005). Organisational change management: A critical review. *Journal of Change Management*, *5*(4), 369–380. doi:10.1080/14697010500359250

Byrne, U. (2005). Work-life balance: Why are we talking about it at all? *Business Information Review*, *22*(1), 53–59. doi:10.1177/0266382105052268

Cairncross, F. (1997). *The Death of Distance: How the Communications Revolution Will Change Our Lives*. Harvard Business School.

Cairncross, F. (2001). *The Death of Distance: How the Communications Revolution is Changing our Lives*. Harvard Business Review Press.

Campbell, I., & Burgess, J. (2018). Patchy progress? Two decades of research on precariousness and precarious work in Australia. *Labour & Industry*, *28*(1), 48–67. doi:10.1080/10301763.2018.1427424

Campbell, J. B., & Hawley, C. W. (1982). Study habits and Eysenck's theory of extraversion–introversion. *Journal of Research in Personality*, *16*(2), 139–146. doi:10.1016/0092-6566(82)90070-8

Camus, A. (1948). *The Plague*. Hamish Hamilton.

Cantillon, B., Chzhen, Y., Sudhanshu, H., & Nolan, B. (2017). *Children of Austerity: Impact of the Great Recession on Child Poverty in Rich Countries*. Oxford University Press. doi:10.1093/oso/9780198797968.001.0001

Carillo, K., Cachat-Rosset, G., Marsan, J., Saba, T., & Klarsfeld, A. (2020). Adjusting to epidemic-induced telework: Empirical insights from teleworkers in France. *European Journal of Information Systems*, 1–20. doi:10.1080/0960085X.2020.1829512

Carmeli, A., Shalom, R., & Weisberg, J. (2007). Considerations in organizational career advancement: What really matters. *Personnel Review*, *36*(2), 190–205. doi:10.1108/00483480710726109

Carnevale, J. B., & Hatak, I. (2020). Employee adjustment and well-being in the era of COVID-19: Implications for human resource management. *Journal of Business Research*, *116*, 183–187. doi:10.1016/j.jbusres.2020.05.037 PMID:32501303

Carrillo, C., & Flores, M. A. (2020). COVID-19 and teacher education: A literature review of online teaching and learning practices. *European Journal of Teacher Education*, *43*(4), 466–487. doi:10.1080/02619768.2020.1821184

CBS. (2020 July 16). *Georgia governor bans cities from ordering people to wear face masks*. Retrieved from https://www.cbsnews.com/news/georgia-governor-brian-kemp-bans-city-face-mask-orders-coronavirus-pandemic/

Cederström, C., & Spicer, A. (2015). *The wellness syndrome*. John Wiley & Sons.

Center for Systems Science and Engineering. (2020). *COVID-19 Dashboard*. Johns Hopkins University.

Centre for Cities. (2020). *High streets recovery tracker: How are cities and large towns recovering from coronavirus?* Centre for Cities.

Centre for Cities. (2021). *Cities Outlook 2021*. Centre for Cities.

Cepeda Zorrilla, M. (2020, June 9). COVID-19 in the West Midlands: An opportunity for fostering urban micro-mobility. *West Midlands Economic Impact Monitor*.

Cerrato, J., & Cifre, E. (2018). Gender inequality in household chores and work-family conflict. *Frontiers in Psychology*, 9.

Chahine, S., Goergen, M., Wood, G. T., & Brewster, C. (2020). Context, governance, associational trust and HRM: Diversity and commonalities. *International Journal of Human Resource Management.*

Challenger, J. E. (1992). Telecommuters Risk Becoming Invisible Workers. *Management World, 20*(1), 8–10.

Champion, T., Cooke, T., & Shuttleworth, I. (2017). *Internal Migration in the Developed World: Are we becoming less mobile?* Routledge. doi:10.4324/9781315589282

Chang, A. M., Aeschbach, D., Duffy, J. F., & Czeisler, C. A. (2015). Evening use of light-emitting eReaders negatively affects sleep, circadian timing, and next-morning alertness. *Proceedings of the National Academy of Sciences of the United States of America, 112*(4), 1232–1237. doi:10.1073/pnas.1418490112 PMID:25535358

Chang-Arana, Á. M., Piispanen, M., Himberg, T., Surma-aho, A., Alho, J., Sams, M., & Hölttä-Otto, K. (2020). Empathic accuracy in design: Exploring design outcomes through empathic performance and physiology. *Design Science, 6.*

Cheng, X., Yin, G., Azadegan, A., & Kolfschoten, G. (2016). Trust evolvement in hybrid team collaboration: A longitudinal case study. *Group Decision and Negotiation, 25*(2), 267–288. doi:10.100710726-015-9442-x

Cherry, S. (2004). Edholm's Law of Bandwidth. *IEEE Spectrum, 41*(7), 58-60.

Cheshire, P., & Hilber, C. (2020). *COVID-19: Crashing the Economy so what will it do for the housing market?* Centre for Economic Performance, London School of Economics.

Chesley, N., Moen, P., & Shore, R. P. (2003). The new technology climate. In P. Moen (Ed.), *It's about time: Couples and careers* (pp. 220–241). Cornell University Press.

Chhabaria, R., & Tripathi, A. (2020, June 4). Prevention of Sexual Harassment at 'Online' Workplace. *The Leaflet.* https://www.theleaflet.in/prevention-of-sexual-harassment-at-online-workplace/#

Child, J. (2018). Downward Accountability. *Corporate Governance in Contention*, 193.

Child, J. (2020). Organizational participation in post-covid society - its contributions and enabling conditions. *International Review of Applied Economics.* Advance online publication. doi:10.1080/02692171.2020.1774976

Child, J., & Loveridge, R. (1990). *New Technology in European Services.* Blackwell.

Choudhury, P., Larson, B. Z., & Foroughi, C. (2019). Is it time to let employees work from anywhere? *Harvard Business Review.* https://hbr.org/2019/08/is-it-time-to-let-employees-work-from-anywhere

Choudhury, P. (2020). Our Work-from-Anywhere Future. *Harvard Business Review, 98*(6), 58.

Chung, H., & van der Lippe, T. (2020). Flexible Working, Work–Life Balance, and Gender Equality: Introduction. *Social Indicators Research, 151*(2), 365–381. doi:10.100711205-018-2025-x PMID:33029036

CIPD. (2011). *Developing resilience: An evidence-based guide for practitioners* [online]. Available at: https://www.cipd.co.uk/Images/developing-resilience_2011-evidence-based_tcm18-10079.pdf

Cirelli, L. K., Einarson, K. M., & Trainor, L. J. (2014). Interpersonal synchrony increases prosocial behavior in infants. *Developmental Science, 17*(6), 1003–1011. doi:10.1111/desc.12193 PMID:25513669

Clark, A. L., Karau, S. J., & Michalisin, M. D. (2012). Telecommuting Attitudes and the 'Big Five' Personality Dimensions. *Journal of Management Policy and Practice, 13*(3), 31–46.

Clark-Ibáñez, M., & Scott, M. (2008). Learning to Teach Online. *Teaching Sociology, 36*(1), 34–41. doi:10.1177/0092055X0803600105

Clark, M. A., Robertson, M. M., & Young, S. (2019). "I feel your pain": A critical review of organizational research on empathy. *Journal of Organizational Behavior, 40*(2), 166–192. doi:10.1002/job.2348

Coenen, M., & Kok, R. A. W. (2014). Workplace flexibility and new product development performance: The role of telework and flexible work schedules. *European Management Journal, 32*(4), 564–576. doi:10.1016/j.emj.2013.12.003

Cohn, E., Cohn, S., Balch, D., & Bradley, J. Jr. (2001). Do Graphs Promote Learning in Principles of Economics? *The Journal of Economic Education, 32*(4), 299–310. doi:10.1080/00220480109596110

Colenberg, S., Jylhä, T., & Arkesteijn, M. (2020). The relationship between interior office space and employee health and well-being–a literature review. *Building Research and Information*, 1–15. doi:10.1080/09613218.2019.1710098

Collins, A. M., Cartwright, S., & Hislop, D. (2013). Homeworking: Negotiating the psychological contract. *Human Resource Management Journal, 23*(2), 211–225. doi:10.1111/j.1748-8583.2012.00200.x

Collins, A. M., Hislop, D., & Cartwright, S. (2016). Social support in the workplace between teleworkers, office-based colleagues and supervisors. *New Technology, Work and Employment, 31*(2), 161–175. doi:10.1111/ntwe.12065

Colomo-Palacios, R., Casado-Lumbreras, C., Soto-Acosta, P., García-Peñalvo, F. J., & Tovar, E. (2014). Project managers in global software development teams: A study of the effects on productivity and performance. *Software Quality Journal, 22*(1), 3–19. doi:10.100711219-012-9191-x

Colquitt, J. A., Scott, B. A., & LePine, J. A. (2007). Trust, trustworthiness, and trust propensity: A meta-analytic test of their unique relationships with risk taking and job performance. *The Journal of Applied Psychology, 92*(4), 909–927. doi:10.1037/0021-9010.92.4.909 PMID:17638454

Colvile, R. (2016). *The Great Acceleration.* Bloomsbury.

Conrad, J. (2019). *How Much Does the Average Kindle Direct Publishing Book Make?* quora.com/How-much-does-the-average-Kindle-Direct-Publishing-book-make

Conservative Party Speeches. (2020). Available: https://conservative-speeches.sayit.mysociety.org/speech/601367

Cook. D. (2021, Jan. 5). How the pandemic will shape the workplace trends of 2021. *The Conversation.*

Cook, C. (2020). *Lost worker vs. tourism expenditure in the Central Activities Zone (CAZ).* Greater London Authority.

Cook, D. (2020). *The New Wilderness.* HarperCollins.

Cooke, T. J. (2011). It is not just the economy: Declining migration and the rise of secular rootedness. *Population Space and Place, 17*(3), 193–203. doi:10.1002/psp.670

Coombes, M., & Bond, S. (2008). *Travel-To-Work Areas: the 2007 Review.* Office of National Statistics.

Cooper, C. D., & Kurland, N. B. (2002). Telecommuting, professional isolation, and employee development in public and private organizations. *Journal of Organizational Behavior, 23*(4), 511–532. doi:10.1002/job.145

Cooper, C. L., & Marshall, J. (1976). Occupational sources of stress: A review of the literature relating to coronary heart disease and mental ill health. *Journal of Occupational Psychology, 49*(1), 11–28. doi:10.1111/j.2044-8325.1976.tb00325.x

Coppola, N. W., Hiltz, S. R., & Rotter, N. G. (2004). Building trust in virtual teams. *IEE Transactions on Professional Communication, 47*(2), 95–104. doi:10.1109/TPC.2004.828203

Corfe, S. (2020). *A new life for the high street.* Social Market Foundation.

Cortes, G. M., & Forsythe, E. (2020). *The heterogeneous labor market impacts of the COVID-19 pandemic* (Upjohn Institute Working Paper 20-327). doi:10.17848/wp20-327

Cortina, L. M., & Berdahal, J. L. (2008). Sexual harassment in organizations: a decade of research in review. In J. Barling & C. L. Cooper (Eds.), SAGE handbook of organizational behavior: volume 1 – micro approaches (pp. 469–497). SAGE Publications. doi:10.4135/9781849200448.n26

Costa, J. S., Pinheiro, L., Medeiros, M., & Queiroz, C. (2005). *A Face Feminina da Pobreza: Sobre-Representação e Feminização da Pobreza no Brasil* (TD 1137). Retrieved from https://www.ipea.gov.br/portal/index.php?option=com_content&view=article&id=4726

Coutinho, J., Oliveira-Silva, P., Fernandes, E., Gonçalves, O. F., Correia, D., Perrone Mc-Govern, K., & Tschacher, W. (2019). Psychophysiological synchrony during verbal interaction in romantic relationships. *Family Process*, *58*(3), 716–733. doi:10.1111/famp.12371 PMID:29888517

Covington, M. V., & Mueller, K. J. (2001). Intrinsic versus extrinsic motivation: An approach/avoidance reformulation. *Educational Psychology Review*, *13*(2), 157–182. doi:10.1023/A:1009009219144

Cramton, C. D. (2001). The Mutual Knowledge Problem and Its Consequences for Dispersed Collaboration. *Organization Science*, *12*(3), 346–371. doi:10.1287/orsc.12.3.346.10098

Cramton, D., & Hinds, P. (2004). Subgroup Dynamics in Internationally Distributed Teams: Ethnocentrism or Cross-National Learning? *Research in Organizational Behavior*, *26*(04), 231–263. doi:10.1016/S0191-3085(04)26006-3

Crawford, J. O., Maccalman, L., & Jackson, C. A. (2011). The health and well-being of remote and mobile workers. *Occupational Medicine*, *61*(6), 385–394. doi:10.1093/occmed/kqr071 PMID:21921124

Crescenzi, R., Nathan, M., & Rodríguez-Pose, A. (2016). Do inventors talk to strangers? On proximity and collaborative knowledge creation. *Research Policy*, *45*(1), 177–194. doi:10.1016/j.respol.2015.07.003

Creswell, J. W. (2014). *Research design: Qualitative, Quantitative, and Mixed Methods Approaches*. Sage publications.

Crosbie, T., & Moore, J. (2004). Work–life Balance and Working from Home. *Social Policy and Society*, *3*(3), 223–233. doi:10.1017/S1474746404001733

Csiksentmihalyi, M., Rathunde, K., & Whalen, S. (1993). *Talented teenagers: The roots of success and failure*. Cambridge University Press.

Cuccinello, H. C. (2019). World's Highest Paid Authors 2019. *Forbes*, *20*(December).

Cunha, J., Pianese, T., & Errichiello, L. (2020). *Paradoxes of Control in Remote Work Arrangements*. 4th RGCS symposium "Designing the Commons: Collaborative spaces, Open communities, Smart Cities", Lyon, France.

Czeisler, M. E., Lane, R. I., Petrosky, E., Wiley, J. F., Christensen, A., Njai, R., Weaver, M. D., Robbins, R., Facer-Childs, E. R., Barger, L. K., Czeisler, C. A., Howard, M. E., & Rajaratnam, S. (2020). Mental Health, Substance Use, and Suicidal Ideation During the COVID-19 Pandemic — United States, June 24–30, 2020. *Weekly*, *69*(32), 1049–1057. Retrieved from https://www.cdc.gov/mmwr/volumes/69/wr/mm6932a1.htm#suggestedcitation

Dahik, A., Lovich, D., Kreafle, C., Bailey, A., Kilmann, J., Kennedy, D., . . . Wenstrup, J. (2020). *What 12,000 Employees Have to Say About the Future of Remote Work*. Boston Consulting Group. Retrieved from https://www.bcg.com/publications/2020/valuable-productivity-gains-covid-19

Dahlstrom, T. R. (2013). Telecommuting and Leadership Style. *Public Personnel Management*, *42*(3), 438–451. doi:10.1177/0091026013495731

Daim, T. U., Ha, A., Reutiman, S., Hughes, B., Pathak, U., Bynum, W., & Bhatla, A. (2012). Exploring the communication breakdown in global virtual teams. *International Journal of Project Management, 30*(2), 199–212. doi:10.1016/j.ijproman.2011.06.004

Dai, Q., Huang, Y., Hao, L., Lin, Y., & Chen, K. (2018). Spatial and spectral illumination design for energy-efficient circadian lighting. *Building and Environment, 146*, 216–225. doi:10.1016/j.buildenv.2018.10.004

Damasio, A. R. (2006). *Descartes' error*. Random House.

Dambrin, C. (2004). How does telework influence the manager-employee relationship? *International Journal of Human Resources Development and Management, 4*(4), 358–374. doi:10.1504/IJHRDM.2004.005044

Darcy, O. (2020, November 11). Jeffrey Toobin fired from The New Yorker after exposing himself on a Zoom call. *CNN Business*. https://www.cnn.com/2020/11/11/media/jeffrey-toobin-fired-new-yorker/index.html

Darwall, S. (2011). Being with. *The Southern Journal of Philosophy, 49*, 4–24. doi:10.1111/j.2041-6962.2011.00054.x

Das, M., Das, A., & Mandal, A. (2020). Examining the impact of lockdown (due to COVID-19) on Domestic Violence (DV): An evidences from India. *Asian Journal of Psychiatry, 54*, 102335. doi:10.1016/j.ajp.2020.102335 PMID:32801078

Davies, B., & Harré, R. (2001). Positioning: the discursive production of selves. In M. Wetherell, S. Taylor, & S. Yates (Eds.), *Discourse theory and practice*. Sage.

Davis, M. C., Leach, D. J., & Clegg, C. W. (2011). The physical environment of the office: Contemporary and emerging issues. In G. P. Hodgkinson & J. K. Ford (Eds.), *International Review of Industrial and Organizational Psychology* (Vol. 26, pp. 193–237). Wiley Blackwell.

Davis, T. R. V. (1984). The influence of the physical environment in offices. *Academy of Management Review, 9*(2), 271–283. doi:10.5465/amr.1984.4277654 PMID:10266030

Dawson, J. (2014). Moderation in management research: What, why, when and how. *Journal of Business and Psychology, 29*(1), 1–19. doi:10.100710869-013-9308-7

Day, A., Paquet, S., Scott, N., & Hambley, L. (2012). Perceived Information and Communication Technology (ICT) Demands on Employee Outcomes: The Moderating Effect of Organizational ICT Support. *Journal of Occupational Health Psychology, 17*(4), 473–491. doi:10.1037/a0029837 PMID:23066697

Dayaram, K., Burgess, J., & Fitzgerald, S. (2020b). Workplace transmissions: a predictable result of the class divide in worker rights. *The Conversation*. https://theconversation.com/workplace-transmissions-a-predictable-result-of-the-class-divide-in-worker-rights-143896

Dayaram, K., Fitzgerald, S., & McKenna, S. (2020a). Working from home remains a select privilege: it's time to fix our national employment standards. *The Conversation*. https://theconversation.com/working-from-home-remains-a-select-privilege-its-time-to-fix-our-national-employment-standards-139472

Day, K. (2020). The impossible journey. *Public Finance*, (September/October), 37–40.

De Jong, B., & Dirks, K. (2012). Beyond shared perceptions of trust and monitoring in teams: Implications of asymmetry and dissensus. *The Journal of Applied Psychology, 97*(2), 391–406. doi:10.1037/a0026483 PMID:22181679

de Lucas Ancillo, A., del Val Núñez, M.T., & Gavrila, S.G. (2020). Workplace change within the COVID-19 context: a grounded theory approach. *Economic Research-Ekonomska Istraživanja*, 1-20.

de Macêdo, T., Cabral, E., Silva Castro, W. R., de Souza, C. C. Junior, da Costa, J. F. Junior, Pedrosa, F. M., da Silva, A. B., de Medeiros, V., de Souza, R. P., Cabral, M., & Másculo, F. S. (2020). Ergonomics and telework: A systematic review. *Work (Reading, Mass.)*, *66*(4), 777–778. doi:10.3233/WOR-203224 PMID:32925139

De Stefano, V. (2016). The Rise of the Just-in-Time Workforce: On-Demand Work, Crowdwork and Labor Protection in the Gig-Economy. *Comparative Labor Law & Policy Journal*, *37*, 471–504.

De Vos, A., Van der Heijden, B. I., & Akkermans, J. (2020). Sustainable careers: Towards a conceptual model. *Journal of Vocational Behavior*, *117*, 103196. Advance online publication. doi:10.1016/j.jvb.2018.06.011

Decety, J., & Meltzoff, A. N. (2011). Empathy, imitation, and the social brain. *Empathy: Philosophical and psychological perspectives*, 58-81.

Decety, J. (2010). The neurodevelopment of empathy in humans. *Developmental Neuroscience*, *32*(4), 257–267. doi:10.1159/000317771 PMID:20805682

Deci, E. L. (1971). Effects of externally mediated rewards on intrinsic motivation. *Journal of Personality and Social Psychology*, *18*(1), 105–115. doi:10.1037/h0030644

Deci, E. L., Connell, J. E., & Ryan, R. M. (1989). Self-determination in a work organization. *The Journal of Applied Psychology*, *74*(4), 580–590. doi:10.1037/0021-9010.74.4.580

Deci, E. L., Olafsen, A. H., & Ryan, R. M. (2017). Self-determination theory in work organizations: State of the science. *Annual Review of Organizational Psychology and Organizational Behavior*, *4*(1), 19–43. doi:10.1146/annurev-orgpsych-032516-113108

Deci, E. L., & Ryan, R. M. (2000). The "What" and "Why" of Goal Pursuits: Human Needs and the Self-Determination of Behavior. *Psychological Inquiry*, *11*(4), 227–268. doi:10.1207/S15327965PLI1104_01

DeConinck, J. B. (2010). The effect of organizational justice, perceived organizational support, and perceived supervisor support on marketing employees' level of trust. *Journal of Business Research*, *63*(12), 1349–1355. doi:10.1016/j.jbusres.2010.01.003

DeFilippis, E., Impink, S. M., Singell, M., Polzer, J. T., & Sadun, R. (2020). *Collaborating during coronavirus: the impact of COVID-19 on the nature of work*. Harvard Business School Organizational Behavior Unit Working Paper No. 21-006.

Defoe, D. (1719). *Robinson Crusoe*. Taylor.

Del Vicario, M., Bessi, A., Zollo, F., Petroni, F., Scala, A., Caldarelli, G., Stanley, H. E., & Quattrociocchi, W. (2016). The spreading of misinformation online. *Proceedings of the National Academy of Sciences of the United States of America*, *113*(3), 554–559. doi:10.1073/pnas.1517441113 PMID:26729863

DeLillo, D. (1986). White Noise. Penguin.

Deloitte. (2019). *Safe Space Survey Report*. Author.

DeLuca, S., Papageorge, N., & Kalish, E. (2020). The unequal cost of social distancing. *Johns Hopkins University & Medicine*. https://coronavirus.jhu.edu/from-our-experts/the-unequal-cost-of-social-distancing

Demarco, D., & Errichiello, L. (2021). Smart working, states of connectivity and work identities in transition Bridging philosophy and management research. *Research Trends in Humanities- Education & Philosophy*, *8*, 126-137.

Demerouti, E., Bakker, A. B., & Halbesleben, J. (2015). Productive and counterproductive job crafting: A daily diary study. *Journal of Occupational Health Psychology*, *20*(4), 457–469. doi:10.1037/a0039002 PMID:25798721

Demerouti, E., Hetland, J., Peeters, M. C. W., Petrou, P., & Schaufeli, W. B. (2012). Crafting a job on a daily basis: Contextual correlates and the link to work engagement. *Journal of Organizational Behavior*, *33*(8), 1120–1141. doi:10.1002/job.1783

Dennis, D., Overholt, M., & Vickers, M. (2014). The new dominance of virtual teams and leaders. *MWorld*, *13*(2), 18–21.

De, R., Pandey, N., & Pal, A. (2020). Impact of Digital Surge during Covid-19 Pandemic: A Viewpoint on Research and Practice. *International Journal of Information Management*, *55*, 102171. doi:10.1016/j.ijinfomgt.2020.102171 PMID:32836633

Derks, D., van Duin, D., Tims, M., & Bakker, A. B. (2015). Smartphone use and work–home interference: The moderating role of social norms and employee work engagement. *Journal of Occupational and Organizational Psychology*, *88*(1), 155–177.

DeRosa, D. M., Hantula, D. A., Kock, N., & D'Arcy, J. (2004). Trust and leadership in virtual teamwork: A media naturalness perspective. *Human Resource Management*, *43*(2&3), 219–232. doi:10.1002/hrm.20016

Deruyter, A., Browne, M., & Burgess, J. (2019). Gig Work and the Fouth Industrial Revolution: Conceptual and Regulatory Challenges. *Journal of International Affairs*, *72*(1), 37–50.

Desilver, D. (2020, March 20). Before the coronavirus, telework was an optional benefit, mostly for the affluent few. *Pew Research Center.* https://www.pewresearch.org/fact-tank/2020/03/20/before-the-coronavirus-telework-was-an-optional-benefit-mostly-for-the-affluent-few/

Determann, L., & Sprague, R. (2011). Intrusive monitoring: Employee privacy expectations are reasonable in Europe, destroyed in the United States. *Berkeley Technology Law*, *26*, 979–1036.

Dhawan, E., & Chamorro, Premuzic, T. (2018). How to Collaborate Effectively If Your Team Is Remote. *Harvard Business Review*.

Dietz, G., & Den Hartog, D. N. (2006). Measuring trust inside organizations. *Personnel Review*, *35*(5), 557–588. doi:10.1108/00483480610682299

Dietz, G., Gillespie, N., & Chao, G. T. (2010). Unravelling the complexities of trust and culture. In M. N. K. Saunders, D. Skinner, G. Dietz, N. Gillespie, & R. J. Lewicki (Eds.), *Organizational Trust: A Cultural Perspective* (pp. 3–41). Cambridge University Press. doi:10.1017/CBO9780511763106.002

DiFonzo, N. (2008). *The watercooler effect: An indispensable guide to understanding and harnessing the power of rumors*. Avery.

Digman, J. M. (1990). Personality structure: Emergence of the five-factor model. *Annual Review of Psychology*, *41*(1), 417–440. doi:10.1146/annurev.ps.41.020190.002221

Dingel, J. I., & Neiman, B. (2020). *How Many Jobs Can be Done at Home? NBER Working Paper Series: w26948.* National Bureau of Economic Research. Retrieved from https://www.nber.org/papers/w26948.pdf

Dingel, J. I., & Neiman, B. (2020). How many jobs can be done at home? *Journal of Public Economics*, *189*, 104235. doi:10.1016/j.jpubeco.2020.104235 PMID:32834177

Dirks, K. T., & Ferrin, D. L. (2002). Trust in leadership: Meta-analytic findings and implications for research and practice. *The Journal of Applied Psychology*, *87*(4), 611–628. doi:10.1037/0021-9010.87.4.611 PMID:12184567

Dittes, S., Richter, S., Richter, A., & Smolnik, S. (2019). Toward the workplace of the future: How organizations can facilitate digital work. *Business Horizons*, *62*(5), 649–661. doi:10.1016/j.bushor.2019.05.004

Dobbin, F. & Kalev, A. (2020, May). Why sexual harassment programs backfire. *Harvard Business Review Magazine.*

Dobbin, F., & Kalev, A. (2017, November 15). Training programs and reporting systems won't end sexual harassment. Promoting more women will. *Harvard Business Review*. https://hbr.org/2017/11/training-programs-and-reporting-systems-wont-end-sexual-harassment-promoting-more-women-will

Dobbin, F., & Kalev, A. (2019, June 18). The promise and peril of sexual harassment programs. *Proceedings of the National Academy of Sciences of the United States of America*, *116*(25), 12255–12260. doi:10.1073/pnas.1818477116 PMID:31160444

Dockery, A. M., & Bawa, S. (2014). Is working from home good work or bad work? Evidence from Australian employees. *Australian Journal of Labour Economics*, *17*(2), 163–190.

Donitsa-Schmidt, S., & Ramot, R. (2020). Opportunities and challenges: Teacher education in Israel in the Covid-19 pandemic. *Journal of Education for Teaching*, *46*(4), 1–10. doi:10.1080/02607476.2020.1799708

Douglass, J. A., & Edelstein, R. (2009). *The global competition for talent: The rapidly changing market for international students and the need for a strategic approach in the US* (CSHE Paper No. 8.09). https://cshe.berkeley.edu/publications/global-competition-talent-rapidly-changing-market-internationalstudents-and-need

Drescher, S. (2009). *Abolition: A history of slavery and antislavery*. Cambridge University Press.

Drouin, N., & Bourgault, M. (2013). How organizations support distributed project teams. *Journal of Management Development*, *32*(8), 865–885. doi:10.1108/JMD-07-2012-0091

Duan, H., Yang, T., Wang, X., Kan, Y., Zhao, H., Li, Y., & Hu, W. (2020). Is the creativity of lovers better? A behavioral and functional near-infrared spectroscopy hyperscanning study. *Current Psychology (New Brunswick, N.J.)*, 1–14. doi:10.100712144-020-01093-5

Dube, L., & Robey, D. (2008). Surviving the paradoxes of virtual teamwork. *Information Systems Journal*, *19*(1), 3–30. doi:10.1111/j.1365-2575.2008.00313.x

Dubrovsky, V. J., Kiesler, S., & Sethna, B. N. (1991). The equalization phenomenon: Status effects in computer-mediated and face-to-face decision-making groups. *Human-Computer Interaction*, *6*(2), 119–146. doi:10.120715327051hci0602_2

Ducar, D. M., & Cunningham, T. (2019). Honoring Life After Death: Mapping the Spread of the Pause. *The American Journal of Hospice & Palliative Care*, *36*(5), 429–435. Advance online publication. doi:10.1177/1049909118813553 PMID:30482027

Dugan, L., Nagin, D. S., & Rosenfeld, R. (2003). Exposure reduction or retaliation? The effects of domestic violence resources on intimate-partner homicide. *Law & Society Review*, *37*(1), 169–198. doi:10.1111/1540-5893.3701005

Duggan, M. (2017, July 11). Online harassment 2017. *Pew Research Center*. https://www.pewresearch.org/internet/2017/07/11/online-harassment-2017/

Dulebohn, J. H., & Hoch, J. E. (2017). Virtual teams in organizations. *Human Resource Management Review*, *27*(4), 569–574. doi:10.1016/j.hrmr.2016.12.004

Dumas, G. (2011). Towards a two-body neuroscience. *Communicative & Integrative Biology*, *4*(3), 349–352. doi:10.4161/cib.4.3.15110 PMID:21980578

Dunn, L. B., Iglewicz, A., & Moutier, C. (2008). A Conceptual Model of Medical Student Well-Being: Promoting Resilience and Preventing Burnout. *Academic Psychiatry*, *32*(1), 44–53. doi:10.1176/appi.ap.32.1.44 PMID:18270280

Duranton, G., & Puga, D. (2020). The economics of urban density. *The Journal of Economic Perspectives*, *34*(3), 3–26. doi:10.1257/jep.34.3.3

Durden, G., & Ellis, L. (1995). The Effects of Attendance on Student Learning in Principles of Economics. *The American Economic Review*, *85*(2), 343–346.

Durkheim, É. (1912). *Les formes élémentaires de la vie religieuse: le système totémique en Australie* (Vol. 4). Alcan.

Durlach, N., & Slater, M. (2000). Presence in shared virtual environments and virtual togetherness. *Presence (Cambridge, Mass.)*, *9*(2), 214–217. doi:10.1162/105474600566736

Duxbury, C. & Higgins, C. (2001). *The 2001 national work-life conflict study.* The Healthy Communities Division, Health Canada Report.

Duxbury, L., & Neufeld, D. (1999). An empirical evaluation of the impacts of telecommuting on intra-organizational communication. *Journal of Engineering and Technology Management*, *16*(1), 1–28. doi:10.1016/S0923-4748(98)00026-5

Dye, J. (2020, Sept. 20). NSW Workers get Pandemic Leave as state records first COVID-19 death in five weeks. *Sydney Morning Herald.*

Earle, J., Moran, C., Ward-Perkins, Z., & Haldane, A. (2017). Economics as indoctrination. In *The econocracy: The perils of leaving economics to the experts* (pp. 34–59). Manchester University Press.

Ebersole, G. (2020, September 28). A post-pandemic paradigm shift is coming to the workplace. *Central Penn Business Journal.* https://www.cpbj.com/post-pandemic-paradigm-shift-coming-workplace/

Echeburua, E., de Corral, P., & Amor, P. J. (2003). Evaluation of Psychological Harm in the Victims of Violent Crime. *Psychology in Spain*, *7*(1), 10–18.

Eclac. (2020). *América Latina y el Caribe ante la pandemia del COVID-19. Efectos económicos y sociales* (Informe Especial COVID-19 N1). Retrieved from: https://bit.ly/3gzeHWJ

Economist. (2011). *Pottering On, and On.* https://www.economist.com/blogs/dailychart/2011/07/film-franchises

Ehrenreich, B. (2011). *Nickel and dimed: On (not) getting by in America.* Picador.

Eisenberger, R., Armeli, S., Rexwinkel, B., Lynch, P. D., & Rhoades, L. (2001). Reciprocation of perceived organizational support. *The Journal of Applied Psychology*, *86*(1), 42–51. doi:10.1037/0021-9010.86.1.42 PMID:11302232

Eisenberg, J., & Mattarelli, E. (2017). Building Bridges in Global Virtual Teams: The Role of Multicultural Brokers in Overcoming the Negative Effects of Identity Threats on Knowledge Sharing Across Subgroups. *Journal of International Management*, *23*(4), 399–411. doi:10.1016/j.intman.2016.11.007

Eisenhardt, K. M. (1989). Building theories from case study research. *Academy of Management Review*, *14*(4), 532–550. doi:10.5465/amr.1989.4308385

Electronic and Computer Software Promotion Council of India. (2019). *India's Computer Software Export Report.* Author.

Elliot, A. J., & McGregor, H. A. (2001). A 2×2 achievement goal framework. *Journal of Personality and Social Psychology*, *80*(3), 501–519. doi:10.1037/0022-3514.80.3.501 PMID:11300582

Elliot, A. J., McGregor, H. A., & Thrash, T. M. (2002). The Need for Competence. In E. L. Deci & R. M. Ryan (Eds.), *Handbook of Self-Determination Research* (pp. 361–388). The University of Rochester Press.

Elliott, K. (2019). Negotiations between progressive and 'traditional' expressions of masculinity among young Australian men. *Journal of Sociology (Melbourne, Vic.)*, *55*(1), 108–123. doi:10.1177/1440783318802996

Elsbach, K. D. (2004). Interpreting workplace identities: The role of office décor. *Journal of Organizational Behavior, 25*(1), 99–128. doi:10.1002/job.233

Elsbach, K., & Pratt, M. G. (2007). The physical environment in organizations. *The Academy of Management Annals, 1*(1), 181–224. doi:10.5465/078559809

Emmler, H., & Misterek, F. (2020). *Zahlen und Fakten zur Mitbestimmung* [Facts and Figures concerning co-determination]. Mitbestimmung der Zukunft. https://www.mitbestimmung.de

Erez, M., Lisak, A., Harush, R., Glikson, E., Nouri, R., & Shokef, E. (2013). Going global: Developing management students' cultural intelligence and global identity in culturally diverse virtual teams. *Academy of Management Learning & Education, 12*(3), 330–355. doi:10.5465/amle.2012.0200

Errichiello, L., & Demarco, D. (2020). From social distancing to virtual connections. *TeMA Journal of Land Use, Mobility and Environment*, 151-164.

Errichiello, L., & Pianese, T. (2016). Organizational Control in the Context of Remote Work Arrangements: a Conceptual Framework. In Performance Measurement and Management Control: Contemporary Issues, vol. 31, Studies in Managerial and Financial Accounting, (pp. 273-305). Emerald Group Publishing.

Errichiello, L., & Pianese, T. (2016). Organizational control in the context of remote work arrangements: a conceptual framework. *Studies in Managerial and Financial Accounting, 31, 273-305.* doi:10.1108/S1479-351220160000031009

Errichiello, L., & Pianese, T. (2018). Smart Work Centers as "creative workspaces" for remote employees. *CERN ideaSquare Journal of Experimental Innovation, 2*, 14–21.

Errichiello, L., & Pianese, T. (2019). Toward a theory on workplaces for smart workers. *Facilities, 38*(3/4), 298–315. doi:10.1108/F-11-2018-0137

Esquivel, V., Faur, E., & Jelin, E. (2012). Hacia la conceptualización del cuidado: familia, mercado y estado. In Las lógicas del cuidado infantil. Entre las familias, el estado y el mercado (pp. 11-45). Buenos Aires: IDES, UNFPA, Unicef.

Esteves, T., & Lopes, M. P. (2017). Leading to crafting: The relation between leadership perception and nurses' job crafting. *Western Journal of Nursing Research, 39*(6), 763–783. doi:10.1177/0193945916659507 PMID:27432346

Estlund, C. (2003). *Working together: How workplace bonds strengthen a diverse democracy.* Oxford University Press.

ETUC. (2020a). *Workers' information, consultation and participation.* https://www.etuc.org/en/publication/covid-19-watch-etuc-briefing-notes

ETUC. (2020b). *New Technologies allowing more surveillance at work.* https://www.etuc.org/en/publication/covid-19-watch-etuc-briefing-notes

ETUI Contributors. (2020, November 05). Benchmarking Working Europe 2014. In *ETUI, The European Trade Union Institute. Chapter 7, Chipping away at workers' participation rights.* https://www.etui.org/publications/books/benchmarking-working-europe-2014

Eurofound and ILO. (2017). *Working Anytime, Anywhere: The Effects on the World of Work.* Publications Office of the European Union and ILO.

Eurofound and International Labour Organization. (2017). *Working anytime, anywhere: The effects on the world of work. WCMS_544138.* Publications Office of the European Union and the International Labour Office., doi:10.2806/372726

Eurofound and the International Labour Office. (2017). *Working anytime, anywhere: The effects on the world of work.* Publications Office of the European Union, Luxembourg, and the International Labour Office.

Eurofound. (2020). *Living, working and COVID-19, COVID-19 series*. Publications Office of the European Union. https://www.eurofound.europa.eu/publications/report/2020/living-working-and-covid-19

Eurofound. (2020). *Living, working and COVID-19*. Publications Office of the European Union. Retrieved from https://www.eurofound.europa.eu/sites/default/files/ef_publication/field_ef_document/ef20059en.pdf

European Commission. (2020). *What is Smart Specialisation?* https://s3platform.jrc.ec.europa.eu/what-is-smart-specialisation-

Eurostat. (2018). *Working from home in the EU*. https://ec.europa.eu/eurostat/web/products-eurostat-news/-/DDN-20180620-1

Evans, G. W., & Johnson, D. (2000). Stress and open-office noise. *The Journal of Applied Psychology*, *85*(5), 779–783. doi:10.1037/0021-9010.85.5.779 PMID:11055149

EY. (2020). *Why remote working will be the new normal, even after COVID-19*. https://www.ey.com/en_be/covid-19/why-remote-working-will-be-the-new-normal-even-after-covid-19

Fair Work Commission. (2020). *National Minimum Wage Order 2020*. https://www.fwc.gov.au/awards-and-agreements/minimum-wages-conditions/national-minimum-wage-orders

Fair Work Ombudsman. (2020a). *National Employment Standards*. https://www.fwc.gov.au/awards-and-agreements/minimum-wages-conditions/national-employment-standards

Fair Work Ombudsman. (2020b). *Alternative Working Arrangements During Coronavirus*. https://coronavirus.fairwork.gov.au/coronavirus-and-australian-workplace-laws/alternative-work-arrangements-during-coronavirus

Fairweather, N. (1999). Surveillance in employment – the case of teleworking. *Journal of Business Ethics*, *22*(2), 39–49. doi:10.1023/A:1006104017646

Fares, L. S.; Oliveira, A. L. M. (2020) Increasing inequality in working time: An international trend. *Revista da Sociedade Brasileira de Economia Política*, 57.

Farley, H., & Dahlgreen, W. (2020, November 17). *Working from home could lead to more prejudice, report warns*. BBC News. https://www.bbc.co.uk/news/uk-54937713

Farrer, L. (2020 May 12). The New Normal Isn't Remote Work. It's Better. *Forbes*. Retrieved from https://www.forbes.com/sites/laurelfarrer/2020/05/12/the-new-normal-isnt-remote-work-its-better/?sh=116d38c62405

Farrer, L. (2020). The new normal isn't remote work. It's better. *Forbes.com*.

Farruggia, F., Jones, P., & Siravo, J. (2020). The new normal: A blueprint for remote working. *Autonomy (Birmingham, England)*.

Fayard, A. L., & Weeks, J. (2007). Photocopiers and water-coolers: The affordances of informal interaction. *Organization Studies*, *28*(5), 605–634. doi:10.1177/0170840606068310

Feitosa, J., & Salas, E. (2020). Today's virtual teams: Adapting lessons learned to the pandemic context. *Organizational Dynamics*, (January), 19–21. PMID:32836509

Feldman, R. (2007). Parent–infant synchrony and the construction of shared timing; physiological precursors, developmental outcomes, and risk conditions. *Journal of Child Psychology and Psychiatry, and Allied Disciplines*, *48*(3-4), 329–354. doi:10.1111/j.1469-7610.2006.01701.x PMID:17355401

Felstead, A. (2012). Rapid change or slow evolution? Changing places of work and their consequences in the UK. *Journal of Transport Geography*, *21*(C), 31–38. doi:10.1016/j.jtrangeo.2011.10.002

Felstead, A., & Henseke, G. (2017). Assessing the growth of remote working and its consequences for effort, well-being and work-life balance. *New Technology, Work and Employment*, *32*(3), 195–202. doi:10.1111/ntwe.12097

Felstead, A., & Reuschke, D. (2020). *Homeworking in the UK: before and during the 2020 lockdown*. Wales Institute of Social and Economic Research.

Felstead, A., & Reuschke, D. (2020). *Homeworking in the UK: Before and During the 2020 Lockdown*. Wales Institute of Social and Economic Research.

Ferguson, K. (2020). *All in this together? The impact of COVID-19 on different places*. Local Government Information Unit.

Fernet, C., Austin, S., Trépanier, S.-G., & Dussault, M. (2013). How do job characteristics contribute to burnout? Exploring the distinct mediating roles of perceived autonomy, competence, and relatedness. *European Journal of Work and Organizational Psychology*, *22*(2), 123–137. doi:10.1080/1359432X.2011.632161

Ferrin, D. L., Dirks, K. T., & Shah, P. P. (2003). *Many routes toward trust: A social network analysis of the determinants of interpersonal trust. Academy of Management Proceedings*. Research Collection Lee Kong Chian School of Business.

Ferris, G. R., Liden, R. C., Munyon, T. P., Summers, J. K., Basik, K. J., & Buckley, M. R. (2009). Relationships at work: Toward a multidimensional conceptualization of dyadic work relationships. *Journal of Management*, *35*(6), 1379–1403. doi:10.1177/0149206309344741

Ferritti, M. (2021). *First evidence from the web survey: Closed Schools - Open Classes*. Speech by INAPP Public Policy Innovation, at the Convocation of the Council Commission "Education Culture Youth Communication."

Fielding, A. J. (1992). Migration and social mobility: South East England as an escalator region. *Regional Studies*, *26*(1), 1–15. doi:10.1080/00343409212331346741 PMID:12285048

Fine, G. A., & Rosnow, R. L. (1978). Gossip, gossipers, gossiping. *Personality and Social Psychology Bulletin*, *4*(1), 161–168.

Fisher, C. D. (2008). Experience sampling methodology in organizational psychology. In I. Glendon, B. Myors, & B. Thompson (Eds.), *Advances in organizational psychology: An Asia-Pacific perspective* (pp. 403–425). Australian Academic Press.

Flaherty, C. (2017). What are students rating when they rate instructors? *Inside Higher Ed*. Retrieved from https://www.insidehighered.com/news/2017/05/10/study-student-ratings-instructors-dependent-discipline-quantitative-fields-are-most

Fleming, P. (2019). Robots and organization studies: Why robots might not want to steal your job. *Organization Studies*, *40*(1), 23–38. doi:10.1177/0170840618765568

Florida, R. (2020). The uncertain future of corporate HQs. *Harvard Business Review*. https://hbr.org/2020/09/the-uncertain-future-of-corporate-hqs

Florida, R. (2002). *The Rise of the Creative Class*. Basic Books.

Florida, R. (2020). *Cities and the COVID-19 Crisis*. Centre for Cities.

Folbre, N. (2006, July). Measuring Care: Gender, Empowerment, and the Care Economy. *Journal of Human Development*, *7*(2), 183–199. Advance online publication. doi:10.1080/14649880600768512

Folbre, N., & Nelson, J. A. (2000). For love or money—Or both? *The Journal of Economic Perspectives, 14*(4), 123–140. doi:10.1257/jep.14.4.123

Folke, O., & Rickne, J. (2020). *Sexual harassment and gender inequality in the labor market.* Stockholm University, Swedish Institute for Social Research Working Paper Series.

Fonner, K. L., & Stache, L. C. (2012). All in a day's work, at home: Teleworkers' management of micro role transitions and the work–home boundary. *New Technology, Work and Employment, 27*(3), 242–257. doi:10.1111/j.1468-005X.2012.00290.x

Ford, M. T., Cerasoli, C. P., Higgins, J. A., & Decesare, A. L. (2011). Relationships between psychological, physical, and behavioural health and work performance: A review and meta-analysis. *Work and Stress, 25*(3), 185–204. doi:10.1080/02678373.2011.609035

Fortson, J., Hinson, L., Rajbhandari, B., & Bhalla, P. (2020, December 8). Technology facilitated gender-based violence in the time of Covid-19. *International Center for Research on Women.* https://www.icrw.org/technology-facilitated-gender-based-violence-in-the-time-of-covid-19/

Foss, N. J. (2020). The impact of The Covid-19 pandemic on firms' organizational designs. *Journal of Management Studies*, 57. doi:10.1111/joms.12643

Fotopoulou, A., & Tsakiris, M. (2017). Mentalizing homeostasis: The social origins of interoceptive inference. *Neuropsychoanalysis, 19*(1), 3–28. doi:10.1080/15294145.2017.1294031

Fountain, J. E. (2004). Building the virtual state: Information technology and institutional change. Brookings.

Fox, M. (2020, September 21). With remote work flexibility, some people opt to relocate ahead of their retirement. *CNBC.* https://www.cnbc.com/2020/09/21/with-remote-work-options-people-opt-to-relocate-before-retirement-.html

Franchini, R. (2020). *Una crisi da non sprecare. L'educativo digitale prima, durante e dopo il Coronavirus* [A crisis not to be wasted. Digital education before, during and after Coronavirus]. RASSEGNA CNOS.

Frank, R., & Cook, P. (1995). *The Winner-take-all Society.* Free Press.

Franks, M. A. (2012). Sexual harassment 2.0. *Maryland Law Review (Baltimore, Md.), 71*(3), 655–704.

Fraser, E. (2020). *Impact of COVID-19 pandemic on violence against women and girls.* VAWG Helpdesk Research Report No. 284.

Frayne, D. (2019). *The Work Cure: Critical Essays on Work and Wellness.* Monmouth: PCCS Books.

Fried, J., & Heinemeier-Hansson, D. (2013). *Remote: Office not required.* Random House.

Frith, U., & Happé, F. (1999). Theory of mind and self-consciousness: What is it like to be autistic? *Mind & Language, 14*(1), 1–22. doi:10.1111/1468-0017.00100

Fuhr, J. P., & Pociask, S. (2011). Broadband and telecommuting: Helping the U.S. environment and the economy. *Low Carbon Economy, 2*(01), 41–47. doi:10.4236/lce.2011.21007

Fuller, R. M., Vician, C. M., & Brown, S. A. (2016). *Longitudinal Effects of Computer-Mediated Communication Anxiety on Interaction in Virtual Teams* (Vol. 69). Accounting Faculty Publications., doi:10.1109/TPC.2016.2583318

Fulmer, A., & Gelfand, M. J. (2012). At what level (and in whom) we trust: Trust across multiple organizational levels. *Journal of Management, 38*(4), 1167–1230. doi:10.1177/0149206312439327

Furman, W., & Buhrmester, D. (2009). Methods and measures: The network of relationships inventory: Behavioral systems version. *International Journal of Behavioral Development, 33*, 470–478.

Gabarro, J. J. (1978). The development of trust, influence, and expectations. In A. G. Athos & J. J. Gabarro (Eds.), *Interpersonal Behaviour: Communication and understanding in relationships* (pp. 290–303). Prentice-Hall.

Gagliardi, P. (1990). *Symbols and artifacts: Views of the corporate landscape*. W. de Gruyter. doi:10.1515/9783110874143

Gagné, M., & Deci, E. L. (2005). Self-determination theory and work motivation. *Journal of Organizational Behavior, 26*(4), 331–362. doi:10.1002/job.322

Gagné, M., & Panaccio, A. (2014). The Motivational Power of Job Design. In M. Gagné (Ed.), *The Oxford Handbook of Work Engagement, Motivation, and Self-Determination Theory* (pp. 165–180). Oxford University Press.

Gajendran, R. S., & Harrison, D. A. (2007). The good, the bad, and the unknown about telecommuting: Meta-analysis of psychological mediators and individual consequences. *The Journal of Applied Psychology, 92*(6), 1524–1541. doi:10.1037/0021-9010.92.6.1524 PMID:18020794

Gajendran, R. S., Harrison, D. A., & Delaney-Klinger, K. (2015). Are telecommuters remotely good citizens? Unpacking telecommuting's effects on performance via i-deals and job resources. *Personnel Psychology, 68*(2), 353–393. doi:10.1111/peps.12082

Galbusera, L., Finn, M. T., Tschacher, W., & Kyselo, M. (2019). Interpersonal synchrony feels good but impedes self-regulation of affect. *Scientific Reports, 9*(1), 1–12. doi:10.103841598-019-50960-0 PMID:31604966

Galinsky, E., Kim, S., & Bond, J. (2001). Feeling overworked: When work becomes too much [Paper presentation]. Conference Board/Families and Work Institute's Work-Life 2001 Conference, New York, NY, United States.

Gallagher, B. D. (2017). *Overcoming Collaboration Obstacles in Globally Distributed Teams*. University of Oregon.

Ganczarek, J., Hünefeldt, T., & Belardinelli, M. O. (2018). From "Einfühlung" to empathy: exploring the relationship between aesthetic and interpersonal experience. In *The Effect of Media Richness on Transactive Memory System in Virtual Teams: the Moderating Role of Team Identity*. Academic Press.

Gangl, M., & Ziefle, A. (2009). Motherhood, labor force behavior, and women's careers: An empirical assessment of the wage penalty for motherhood in Britain, Germany, and the United States. *Democracy (New York, N.Y.), 46*(2), 341–369.

Ganster, D. C., Crain, T. L., & Brossoit, R. M. (2018). Physiological measurement in the organizational sciences: A review and recommendations for future use. *Annual Review of Organizational Psychology and Organizational Behavior, 5*(1), 267–293. doi:10.1146/annurev-orgpsych-032117-104613

Gardner, W. L., Avolio, B. J., Luthans, F., May, D. R., & Walumbwa, F. (2005). Can you see the real me? A self-based model of authentic leader and follower development. *The Leadership Quarterly, 16*(3), 343–372. doi:10.1016/j.leaqua.2005.03.003

Gartenberg, I., & Harikumar, N. (2019, October 2). How do we combat rampant sexual harassment in the workplace? *The Wire*. https://thewire.in/women/how-do-we-combat-rampant-sexual-harassment-in-the-workplace

Gartner Global Survey. (2020). *Gartner HR Survey Reveals 88% of Organizations Have Encouraged or Required Employees to Work From Home Due to Coronavirus*. https://www.gartner.com/en/newsroom/press-releases/2020-03-19-gartner-hr-survey-reveals-88--of-organizations-have-

Gartner. (2020, April 3). Gartner CFO Survey Reveals 74% Intend to Shift Some Employees to Remote Work Permanently. *Gartner.* Retrieved from https://www.gartner.com/en/newsroom/press-releases/2020-04-03-gartner-cfo-surey-reveals-74-percent-of-organizations-to-shift-some-employees-to-remote-work-permanently2

Gaspar, J. M., Christie, G. J., Prime, D. J., Jolicœur, P., & McDonald, J. J. (2016). Inability to suppress salient distractors predicts low visual working memory capacity. *Proceedings of the National Academy of Sciences of the United States of America, 113*(13), 3693–3698. doi:10.1073/pnas.1523471113 PMID:26903654

Gee, D. (2020a). An Uphill Battle. *Vancouver Sun, 1*(August), C1.

Gee, D. (2020b). A New Chapter. *Vancouver Sun, 5*(August), C1.

Geller, S. (2020). Cultivating online therapeutic presence: Strengthening therapeutic relationships in teletherapy sessions. *Counselling Psychology Quarterly*, 1–17. doi:10.1080/09515070.2020.1787348

Gelles, D. (2020, June 23). Are companies more productive in a pandemic? *The New York Times*. https://www.nytimes.com/2020/06/23/business/working-from-home-productivity.html

George, D., & Mallery, P. (2010). SPSS for Windows Step by Step: A Simple Guide and Reference 17.0 update (10th ed.). Boston: Pearson.

Gerdenitsch, C. (2017). New Ways of Working and Satisfaction of Psychological Needs. In C. Korunka & B. Kubicek (Eds.), *Job Demands in a Changing World of Work* (pp. 91–109). Springer., doi:10.1007/978-3-319-54678-0_6

Gerstner, C. R., & Day, D. V. (1995). *Putting leadership back into leader-member exchange: A meta-analytic review and extension* [Paper presentation]. Tenth Annual Conference of the Society of Industrial-Organizational Psychology, Orlando, FL, United States.

Ghosh, A., Puri, M., & Dewan, N. (2010, August 22). India inc Is waking up to the menace of sexual harassment. *The Economic Times*. https://economictimes.indiatimes.com/special-report/india-inc-is-waking-up-to-the-menace-of-sexual-harassment/articleshow/6389463.cms

Ghosh, A. (2014). Culturally competent behaviors at workplace: An intergroup perspective for workplace diversity. *South Asian Journal of Management, 21*(3), 73–95. http://proxy.cityu.edu/login?url=http://search.ebscohost.com/login.aspx?direct=true&db=bth&AN=99351505&site=ehost-live&scope=site

Gibb, L. S. F. (2017). *A tendência de despadronização da jornada de trabalho: configuração no brasil e impacto nas mulheres* [Unpublished PhD Thesis]. UNICAMP.

Gibb, L. S. F., & Oliveira, A. L. M. (2015) A Desigualdade na Distribuição do Trabalho Total no Brasil: A Quem Favorece? Pesquisa & Debate, 26, 87-104.

Gibson, J. W., Blackwell, C. W., Dominicis, P., & Demerath, N. (2002). Telecommuting in the 21st Century: Benefits, Issues, and a Leadership Model Which Will Work. *The Journal of Leadership Studies, 8*(4), 75–86. doi:10.1177/107179190200800407

Gibson, Z.-B., Zellmer-Bruhn, M. E., & Schwab, D. P. (2003). Team effectiveness in multinational organizations: Development across contexts. *Group & Organization Management, 28*(4), 444–474. doi:10.1177/1059601103251685

Gillespie, N. (2003). *Measuring trust in working relationships: The behavioural trust inventory* [Paper presentation]. Academy of Management Conference, Seattle, WA, United States.

Gillespie, N., & Mann, L. (2004). Transformational leadership and shared values: The building blocks of trust. *Journal of Managerial Psychology, 19*(6), 588–607. doi:10.1108/02683940410551507

Gilson, L. L., Maynard, M. T., Jones Young, N. C., Vartiainen, M., & Hakonen, M. (2015). Virtual teams research: 10 years, 10 themes, and 10 opportunities. *Journal of Management, 41*(5), 1313–1337. doi:10.1177/0149206314559946

Giovannella, C., Passarelli, M., & Persico, D. (2020). The effects of the Covid-19 pandemic on Italian learning ecosystems: The school teachers' Perspective at the steady state. *Interact. Des. Archit., 45*, 264–286.

Gissing, G. (1997). *New Grub Street*. J. M. Dent.

Gkorezis, P., Panagiotou, M., & Theodorou, M. (2016). Workplace ostracism and employee silence in nursing: The mediating role of organizational identification. *Journal of Advanced Nursing, 72*(10), 2381–2388. doi:10.1111/jan.12992 PMID:27113971

Glaeser, E. (2011). *Triumph of the City: How Our Greatest Invention Makes Us Richer, Smarter, Greener, Healthier, and Happier*. Penguin.

Global Workplace Analytics. (2020). Accessed 1 September 2020. https://globalworkplaceanalytics.com/telecommuting-statistics

Goergen, M., Chahine, S., Brewster, C., & Wood, G. T. (2012). Trust, owner rights, employees and firm performance. *Journal of Business Finance & Accounting, 40*(5-6), 589–619. doi:10.1111/jbfa.12033

Golden, L., & Wiens-Tuersb, B. (2006). To your happiness? Extra hours of labor supply and worker well-being. *Journal of Socio-Economics, 35*(2), 382–397.

Golden, T. D., & Gajendran, R. S. (2019). Unpacking the role of a telecommuter's job in their performance: Examining job complexity, problem solving, interdependence, and social support. *Journal of Business and Psychology, 34*(1), 55–69. doi:10.100710869-018-9530-4

Golden, T. D., & Veiga, J. F. (2008). The impact of superior–subordinate relationships on the commitment, job satisfaction, and performance of virtual workers. *The Leadership Quarterly, 19*(1), 77–88. doi:10.1016/j.leaqua.2007.12.009

Golden, T. D., Veiga, J. F., & Dino, R. N. (2008). The impact of professional isolation on teleworker job performance and turnover intentions: Does time spent teleworking, interacting face-to-face, or having access to communication-enhancing technology matter? *The Journal of Applied Psychology, 93*(6), 1412–1421. doi:10.1037/a0012722 PMID:19025257

Golding, W. (1954). *Lord of the Flies*. Faber & Faber.

Goldsby, T. J., & Zinn, W. (2016). Technology innovation and new business models: Can logistics and supply chain research accelerate the evolution? *Journal of Business Logistics, 37*(2), 80–81.

Gómez, S. M., Mendoza, O. E. O., Ramírez, J., & Olivas-Luján, M. R. (2020). Stress and myths related to the COVID-19 pandemic's effects on remote work. Management Research. *Journal of the Iberoamerican Academy of Management, 18*(4), 401–420.

Goodson, I. F. (2013). *Developing Narrative Theory, Developing Narrative Theory*. Routledge.

Goodson, I., & Schostak, J. (2020). Curriculum and coronavirus: New approaches to curriculum in the age of uncertainty. *Prospects*. PMID:33424039

Gottlieb, C., Grobovšek, J., & Poschke, M. (2020). Working from home across countries. *CEPR Covid Economics: Vetted and Real-Time Papers, 8*, 71-91. Retrieved from https://cepr.org/sites/default/files/news/CovidEconomics8.pdf

Gov, W. A. (2021). *COVID-19 coronavirus: Western Australia Government response*. https://www.wa.gov.au/organization/department-of-the-premier-and-cabinet/COVID-19-coronavirus-western-australian-government-response

Government of India. (2015). *Handbook on sexual harassment of women at workplace*. Ministry of Women and Child Development.

Government of Victoria. (2020). *Industrial Relations Framework for Managing the Coronavirus Pandemic*. https://www.vic.gov.au/victorian-public-sector-workforce-industrial-relations-framework-managing-coronavirus-pandemic

Government, N. S. W. (2005). *Workplace Surveillance Act 2005 No 47*. https://www.legislation.nsw.gov.au/view/html/inforce/current/act-2005-047#sec.19

Government, N. S. W. (2020), *What You Can and Can't do Under the Rules*. https://www.nsw.gov.au/COVID-19/what-you-can-and-cant-do-under-rules

Graeber, D. (2018). *Bullshit Jobs: a theory*. Simon and Schuster.

Graen, G. B., & Uhl-Bien, M. (1995). Relationship-based approach to leadership: Development of leader-member exchange (LMX) theory of leadership over 25 years: Applying a multi-level multi-domain perspective. *The Leadership Quarterly*, *6*(2), 219–247. doi:10.1016/1048-9843(95)90036-5

Grant, A. M., & Ashford, S. J. (2008). The dynamics of proactivity at work. *Research in Organizational Behavior*, *28*, 3–34. doi:10.1016/j.riob.2008.04.002

Grant, A. M., & Parker, S. K. (2009). Redesigning work design theories: The rise of relational and proactive perspectives. *The Academy of Management Annals*, *3*(1), 317–375. doi:10.5465/19416520903047327

Grant, S., & Betts, B. (2013). Encouraging user behaviour with achievements: An empirical study. *Proceedings of the 10th Working Conference on Mining Software Repositories*, 65-68 10.1109/MSR.2013.6624007

Green, A. E., Hogarth, T., & Shackleton, R. E. (1999). *Long Distance Living: Dual Location Households*. Policy Press.

Green, A. E., & Owen, D. W. (2006). *The geography of poor skills and access to work*. Joseph Rowntree Foundation.

Green, A., Froy, F., Kispeter, E., & Sissons, P. (2017). *How do cities lead an inclusive growth agenda*. Joseph Rowntree Foundation.

Greenberg, J., Ashton-James, C. E., & Ashkanasy, N. M. (2007). Social comparison processes in organizations. *Organizational Behavior and Human Decision Processes*, *102*(1), 22–41. doi:10.1016/j.obhdp.2006.09.006

Greenberg, P. S., Greenberg, R. H., & Antonucci, Y. L. (2007). Creating and sustaining trust in virtual teams. *Business Horizons*, *50*(4), 325–333. doi:10.1016/j.bushor.2007.02.005

Greenhaus, J. H., Parasuraman, S., & Wormley, W. M. (1990). Effects of Race on Organizational Experiences, Job Performance Evaluations, and Career Outcomes. *Academy of Management Journal*, *33*(1), 64–86. doi:10.2307/256352

Gregory, A. (2015). Work-life balance. In S. Edgell, H. Gottfried, & E. Granter (Eds.), *The Sage Handbook of Sociology of Work and Employment* (pp. 502–5519). Sage.

Group, N. P. D. (2021). *After a Slow Start, U.S. Print Book Sales Rose 8.2 % in 2020*. https://www.npd.com/wps/portal/npd/us/news/press-releases/2021/after-a-slow-start--u-s--print-book-sales-rose-8-2-%-in-2020--the-npd-group-says/

Grubb, T. (2007). Performance Appraisal Reappraised: It's Not All Positive. *Journal of Human Resource Education*, *1*(1), 1–22.

Grynszpan, O., Martin, J. C., & Fossati, P. (2017). Gaze leading is associated with liking. *Acta Psychologica*, *173*, 66–72. doi:10.1016/j.actpsy.2016.12.006 PMID:28013039

Guest, D. E. (2002). Perspectives on the study of work-life balance. *Social Sciences Information. Information sur les Sciences Sociales*, *42*(2), 255–279.

Guest, G., Bunce, A., & Johnson, L. (2006). How Many Interviews Are Enough?: An Experiment with Data Saturation and Variability. *Field Methods*, *18*(1), 59–82. doi:10.1177/1525822X05279903

Guimaraes, T., & Dallow, P. (1999). Empirically testing the benefits, problems, and success factors for telecommuting programmes. *European Journal of Information Systems*, *8*(1), 40–54. doi:10.1057/palgrave.ejis.3000317

Gundersen, L. (2001). Physician Burnout. *Annals of Internal Medicine*, *135*, 145–148. doi:10.7326/0003-4819-135-2-200107170-00023

Gunter, B. G., & van der Hoeven, R. (2004). The social dimension of globalization: A review of the literature. *International Labour Review*, *143*(1-2). Advance online publication. doi:10.1111/j.1564-913X.2004.tb00545.x

Haans, A., & IJsselsteijn, W. A. (2009). The virtual Midas touch: Helping behavior after a mediated social touch. *IEEE Transactions on Haptics*, *2*(3), 136–140. doi:10.1109/TOH.2009.20 PMID:27788077

Hacker, J., Johnson, M., Saunders, C., & Thayer, A. L. (2019). Trust in virtual teams: A multidisciplinary review and integration. *AJIS. Australasian Journal of Information Systems*, *23*, 1–35. doi:10.3127/ajis.v23i0.1757

Hackman, J. R., & Oldham, G. R. (1975). Development of the job diagnostic survey. *The Journal of Applied Psychology*, *60*(2), 159–170. doi:10.1037/h0076546

Haigh, G. (2012). *The office: A hardworking history*. The Miegunyah Press, Melbourne University Publishing.

Hakanen, J. J., & Bakker, A. B. (2017). Born and bred to burn out: A life-course view and reflections on job burnout. *Journal of Occupational Health Psychology*, *22*(3), 354–364. doi:10.1037/ocp0000053 PMID:27732007

Hakim, C. (1996). *Key issues in women's work: Female heterogeneity and the polarization of women's employment*. Oxford University Press.

Hale, J., & Hamilton, A. F. D. C. (2016). Cognitive mechanisms for responding to mimicry from others. *Neuroscience and Biobehavioral Reviews*, *63*, 106–123. doi:10.1016/j.neubiorev.2016.02.006 PMID:26877104

Halford, S. (2005). Hybrid workspace: Re-spatialisations of work, organization and management. *New Technology, Work and Employment*, *20*(1), 19–33. doi:10.1111/j.1468-005X.2005.00141.x

Hamari, J. Koivisto, J., & Sarsa, H. (2014). Does gamification work? A literature review of empirical studies on gamification. *System Sciences (HICSS)*, 3025-3034.

Hamel, G. (2007). *The future of management*. Harvard Business School Press.

Hamilton, B. A., & Scandura, T. A. (2003). E-mentoring: Implications for organizational learning and development in a wired world. *Organizational Dynamics*, *31*(4), 388–402. doi:10.1016/S0090-2616(02)00128-6

Hammond, G. (2021, Jan. 23). London Falling? *Financial Times*.

Han, G. (2006). Helping you out while Im away: Examining tenure diversity, leader support and ocb in global teams. *Academy of Management Proceedings: Knowledge, Action and the Public Concern*, 1-9.

Hardill, I., & Green, A. (2003). Remote working—Altering the spatial contours of work and home in the new economy. *New Technology, Work and Employment*, *18*(3), 212–222. doi:10.1111/1468-005X.00122

Harris, L. (2003). Home-based teleworking and the employment relationship managerial challenges and dilemmas. *Personnel Review*, *32*(4), 422–437. doi:10.1108/00483480310477515

Harvard Business Review Analytic Services. (2017). *How Collaboration Wins: Leadership, Benefits, and Best Practices.* Harvard Business School Publishing. Retrieved from https://hbr.org/resources/pdfs/comm/citrix/HowCollaborationWins.pdf

Harvey, D. (2005). *A Brief History of Neo-Liberalism.* OUP. doi:10.1093/oso/9780199283262.001.0001

Hasler, B. S., Hirschberger, G., Shani-Sherman, T., & Friedman, D. A. (2014). Virtual peacemakers: Mimicry increases empathy in simulated contact with virtual outgroup members. *Cyberpsychology, Behavior, and Social Networking, 17*(12), 766–771. doi:10.1089/cyber.2014.0213 PMID:25343577

Hassel, A., Helmerich, N., & von Verschuer, S. (2018). *Workers' Voice and Good Corporate Governance.* Hans-Böckler-Stiftung. https://www.boeckler.de/pdf/mbf_workers_voice_academical_final_report.pdf

Hass, M., & Mark, M. (2016, June). The Secrets of Great Teamwork. *Harvard Business Review*, 1–11. PMID:27491197

Hatayama, M., Viollaz, M., & Winkler, H. (2020). *Jobs' Amenability to Working from Home: Evidence from Skills Surveys for 53 Countries. Policy Research Working Paper 9241.* World Bank Group. Retrieved from https://openknowledge.worldbank.org/handle/10986/33753

Hatfield-Dodds, S., Nelson, R., & Cook, D. C. (2007). Adaptive governance: An introduction and implications for public policy (No. 418-2016-26492) [Paper presentation]. The 51st Australian and Resource Economics Society (AARES), Queenstown, New Zealand.

Hatfield, E., Cacioppo, J. T., & Rapson, R. L. (1993). Emotional contagion. *Current Directions in Psychological Science, 2*(3), 96–100. doi:10.1111/1467-8721.ep10770953

Hawisher, G. E., & Moran, C. (1993). Electronic mail and the writing instructor. *College English, 55*(6), 627–643. doi:10.2307/378699

Hedge, A. (1982). The open-plan office: A systematic investigation of employee reactions to their work environment. *Environment and Behavior, 14*(5), 519–542. doi:10.1177/0013916582145002

Helfen, M., & Wirth, C. (2020). *Management von Arbeit in pluralen Netzwerkorganisationen* [Management of work in plural network organizations]. https://www.boeckler.de/de/faust-detail.htm?sync_id=8922

Helmore, E. (2020, April 14). Business not as usual: WeWork tries to shrug off coronavirus despite upheaval. *The Guardian.* https://www.theguardian.com/business/2020/apr/14/wework-coronavirus-impact-business-not-as-usual

Henniger, A., & Papouscheck, U. (2008). Occupation matters – blurring work-life boundaries in mobile care and media industry. In C. Warhurst, D. R. Eikhof, & A. Huanschild (Eds.), *Work Less, Live More? Critical analysis of the work-life boundary* (pp. 153–177). Palgrave. doi:10.1007/978-1-137-11537-9_9

Hermans, H. (2001). The dialogical self: Toward a theory of personal and cultural positioning. *Culture and Psychology, 7*(3), 323–366. doi:10.1177/1354067X0173005

Hern, A. (2020). Covid19 could cause permanent shift towards home working. *The Guardian.* https://coronavirus.fairwork.gov.au/coronavirus-and-australian-workplace-laws/alternative-working-arrangements-during-coronavirus/working-from-home

Heron, R., & Unger, L. (1999). *Glossary of Labour Administration and Related Terms.* International Labour Organization. Retrieved from https://www.ilo.org/wcmsp5/groups/public/---ed_dialogue/---lab_admin/documents/publication/wcms_111331.pdf

Hersch, J. (2015). Sexual harassment in the workplace. *IZA World of Labor: Evidence-Based Policy Making, 188*, 1–10.

Hertel, G., Geister, S., & Konradt, U. (2005). Managing virtual teams: A review of current empirical research. *Human Resource Management Review*, *15*(1), 69–95. doi:10.1016/j.hrmr.2005.01.002

Herzberg, F., Mausner, B., & Snyderman, B. B. (2017). *The Motivation to Work*. Routledge. (Original work published 1959) doi:10.4324/9781315124827

Hess, A. (2017). *The science and design behind Apple's innovation obsessed new workplace*. Retrieved from https://www.cnbc.com/2017/09/13/the-science-and-design-behind-apples-innovation-obsessed-new-workspace.html

He, Y., Kraus, K., & Preece, J. (2013, July). You are not alone online: a case study of a long distance romantic relationship online community. In *International Conference on Online Communities and Social Computing* (pp. 23-32). Springer. 10.1007/978-3-642-39371-6_3

Heym, N., Kibowski, F., Bloxsom, C. A., Blanchard, A., Harper, A., Wallace, L., ... Sumich, A. (2020). The Dark Empath: Characterising dark traits in the presence of empathy. *Personality and Individual Differences*, 110172.

Hidalgo, A. (2020, Feb. 7). Paris mayor unveils '15 minute city' plan in re-election campaign. *The Guardian*.

Hill, K., & Fitzgerald, R. (2020). Student perspectives of the impact of COVID-19 on learning. *All Ireland Journal of Higher Education, 12*(2). Retrieved from https://ojs.aishe.org/index.php/aishe-j/article/view/459

Hill, E., Baird, M., Vromen, A., Cooper, R., Meers, Z., & Probyn, E. (2019). Young women and men: Imagined futures of work and family formation in Australia. *Journal of Sociology (Melbourne, Vic.)*, *55*(4), 778–798. doi:10.1177/1440783319877001

Hiltz, S. R., Johnson, K., & Turoff, M. (1986). Experiments in group decision making communication process and outcome in face-to-face versus computerized conferences. *Human Communication Research*, *13*(2), 225–252. doi:10.1111/j.1468-2958.1986.tb00104.x

Hinds, P., & Cramton, C. (2014). Situated Coworker Familiarity : How Site Visits Transform. *Organization Science*, *25*(3), 794–814. doi:10.1287/orsc.2013.0869

Hirschfeld. (2020). Coronavirus: How the world of work may change forever. *BBC*. Retrieved from https://www.bbc.com/worklife/article/20201023-coronavirus-how-will-the-pandemic-change-the-way-we-work

Hitachi Capital. (2020, July 29). *SME business cost savings from remote working*. Retrieved from https://www.hitachi-capital.co.uk/business-finance/invoice-finance/invoice-finance-blog/sme-business-cost-savings-from-remote-working/

Hoath, A., & Haslam McKenzie, F. (2013). *The socio-economic impacts of long distance commuting on source communities*. Co-operative Research Centre for Remote Economic Participation and Curtin Graduate School of Business.

Holland, P. J. (2017). Job and work design. In Human Resource Management (2nd ed). Palgrave Macmillan. doi:10.1057/978-1-137-52163-7_7

Holland, P., & Tham, T. L. (2019). Working under electronic monitoring and surveillance. In Contemporary Work and the Future of Employment in Developed Societies. Routledge.

Holland, P., Brewster, C., & Kougiannou, N. (2021). Employment, work and industrial revolutions: A Faustian deal. In The Changing Face of Globalisation and its Effects on Risk at Work. Routledge.

Holland, P., Ferrer, J. & Newman, A. (2020). *Impact of COVID-19 on the Working Lives of Business Academics in Australia and New Zealand*. Unpublished.

Holland, K. J., Cortina, L. M., Magley, V. J., Baker, A. L., & Benya, F. F. (2020, October 6). Do not let COVID-19 disrupt campus climate surveys of sexual harassment. *Proceedings of the National Academy of Sciences of the United States of America*, *117*(40), 24606–24608. doi:10.1073/pnas.2018098117 PMID:32948693

Holland, P., & Brewster, C. (Eds.). (2020). *Contemporary Work and the Future of Employment in Developed Countries*. Routledge. doi:10.4324/9781351034906

Holland, P., & Tham, T. L. (2020). Workplace biometric: Protecting employee privacy one fingerprint at a time. *Economic and Industrial Democracy*. doi:10.1177/0143831X20917453

Holstein, J. A., & Gubrium, J. F. (1995). *The active interview* (Vol. 37). Sage. doi:10.4135/9781412986120

Holt-Lunstad, J., Smith, T. B., Baker, M., Harris, T., & Stephenson, D. (2015). Loneliness and social isolation as risk factors for mortality: A meta-analytic review. *Perspectives on Psychological Science*, *10*(2), 227–237. doi:10.1177/1745691614568352 PMID:25910392

Holtz, B. C., & Harold, C. M. (2008). When your boss says no! The effects of leadership style and trust on employee reactions to managerial explanations. *Journal of Occupational and Organizational Psychology*, *81*(4), 777–802. doi:10.1348/096317907X251569

Hope-Hailey, V., Searle, R., & Dietz, G. (2012). *Where has all the trust gone?* https://www.cipd.co.uk/Images/where-has-all-the-trust-gone_2012-sop_tcm18-9644.pdf

Hoppe, M., Rossmy, B., Neumann, D. P., Streuber, S., Schmidt, A., & Machulla, T. K. (2020, April). A Human Touch: Social Touch Increases the Perceived Human-likeness of Agents in Virtual Reality. In *Proceedings of the 2020 CHI Conference on Human Factors in Computing Systems* (pp. 1-11). 10.1145/3313831.3376719

Hosmer, L. T. (1995). Trust: The connecting link between organizational theory and philosophical ethics. *Academy of Management Review*, *20*(2), 379–403. doi:10.5465/amr.1995.9507312923

Howard-Grenville, J. (2020). How to Sustain Your Organization's Culture When Everyone Is Remote. *MIT Sloan Management Review*, *61*(4), 1–4.

Hoyet, L., Argelaguet, F., Nicole, C., & Lécuyer, A. (2016). "Wow! i have six Fingers!": Would You accept structural changes of Your hand in Vr? *Frontiers in Robotics and AI*, *3*, 27. doi:10.3389/frobt.2016.00027

HSE. (2020). *Work-related Stress, Anxiety or Depression statistics in Great Britain*. Available: https://www.hse.gov.uk/statistics/causdis/stress.pdf

Huang, H. (2009). Globally distributed information technology work: A study of cross-cultural influences, communication, and management. *ProQuest Dissertations and Theses*, *275*(August). Advance online publication.

Hughes, R. (2020, May 31). Remote working: How cities might change if we worked at home more. *BBC*.

Humphrey, R. H., Burch, G. F., & Adams, L. L. (2016). The benefits of merging leadership research and emotions research. *Frontiers in Psychology*, *7*, 1022. doi:10.3389/fpsyg.2016.01022 PMID:27458415

Hu, N. C., Chen, J. D., & Cheng, T. J. (2016). The Associations Between Long Working Hours, Physical Inactivity, and Burnout. *Journal of Occupational and Environmental Medicine*, *58*(5), 514–518. doi:10.1097/JOM.0000000000000715

Hunsaker, P. L., & Hunsaker, J. S. (2008). Virtual teams: A leader's guide. *Team Performance Management*, *14*(1), 86–101. doi:10.1108/13527590810860221

Hunt, A. (2018). Pedagogical Techniques for Creating a Community of Inquiry in Online Learning Environments. In M. Kozimor-King & J. Chin (Eds.), *Learning from Each Other: Refining the Practice of Teaching in Higher Education* (pp. 27–39). University of California Press.

Huws, U., Podro, S., Gunnarsson, E., Weijers, T. A., & Trova, V. (1996). Teleworking and Gender. Institute for Employment Studies. Report 317. Sussex University.

Iachini, T., Coello, Y., Frassinetti, F., & Ruggiero, G. (2014). Body space in social interactions: A comparison of reaching and comfort distance in immersive virtual reality. *PLoS One*, *9*(11), e111511. doi:10.1371/journal.pone.0111511 PMID:25405344

Illegems, V., & Verbeke, A. (2004). Telework: What Does it Mean for Management? *Long Range Planning*, *37*(4), 319–334. doi:10.1016/j.lrp.2004.03.004

ILO. (2020). *Teleworking during the COVID-19 pandemic and beyond A Practical Guide*. https://www.ilo.org/wcmsp5/groups/public/---ed_protect/---protrav/---travail/documents/publication/wcms_751232.pdf

IMU. (2019). *Workers' Voice in European corporate governance – an invitation to open new perspectives for participatory democracy*. Nr. 52, 08.2019.

IMU. (2020). *Mitbestimmung der Zukunft* [Co-determination in the future]. https://www.boeckler.de/pdf/p_mbf_report_2020_58.pdf

India Brand Equity Foundation. (2019). *IT & ITeS*. Retrieved from www.ibef.org

Instituto Brasileiro de Geografia e Estatística (IBGE). (2020a) *Outras formas de trabalho: 2019*. Retrieved from https://biblioteca.ibge.gov.br/visualizacao/livros/liv101722_informativo.pdf

Instituto Brasileiro de Geografia e Estatística (IBGE). (2020b) *PNAD COVID-19*. Retrieved from https://covid19.ibge.gov.br/pnad-covid/trabalho.php

International Labour Organization (ILO). (2020a). *Teleworking during the COVID-19 pandemic and beyond: a Practical Guide*. Retrieved from https://www.ilo.org/wcmsp5/groups/public/---ed_protect/---protrav/---travail/documents/publication/wcms_751232.pdf

International Labour Organization (ILO). (2020b). *Working from Home: Estimating the worldwide potential* (Policy Brief April 2020). Retrieved from https://www.ilo.org/wcmsp5/groups/public/---ed_protect/---protrav/---travail/documents/briefingnote/wcms_743447.pdf

International Labour Organization. (2011). *New report highlights opportunities and challenges of expanding telework*. https://www.ilo.org/global/about-the-ilo/newsroom/news/WCMS_544108/lang--en/index.htm

International Labour Organization. (2013). *Preventing and responding to sexual harassment at work: guide to the Sexual Harassment of Women at Workplace (Prevention, Prohibition and Redressal) Act, 2013*. International Labour Organization. https://www.ilo.org/newdelhi/whatwedo/publications/WCMS_630227/lang--en/index.htm

International Labour Organization. (2020). *COVID-19 crisis and the informal economy Immediate responses and policy challenges*. International Labour Organization.

International Labour Organization. (2020). *Teleworking during the COVID-19 pandemic and beyond: A Practical Guide*. International Labour Office.

Iometrics and Global Workplace Analytics. (2020). *Global Work-from-Home Experience Survey*. Iometrics and Global Workplace Analytics.

Irish, L. A., Kline, C. E., Gunn, H. E., Buysse, D. J., & Hall, M. H. (2015). The role of sleep hygiene in promoting public health: A review of empirical evidence. *Sleep Medicine Reviews*, *22*, 23–36. doi:10.1016/j.smrv.2014.10.001 PMID:25454674

Ishida, H., Su, K.-H., & Spilerman, S. (2002). Models of Career Advancement in Organizations. *European Sociological Review*, *18*(2), 179–198. doi:10.1093/esr/18.2.179

Jacobson, B. H., Boolani, A., & Smith, D. B. (2009). Changes in back pain, sleep quality, and perceived stress after introduction of new bedding systems. *Journal of Chiropractic Medicine*, *8*(1), 1–8. doi:10.1016/j.jcm.2008.09.002 PMID:19646380

Jahncke, H., Hygge, S., Halin, N., Green, A. M., & Dimberg, K. (2011). Open-plan office noise: Cognitive performance and restoration. *Journal of Environmental Psychology*, *31*(4), 373–382. doi:10.1016/j.jenvp.2011.07.002

James, H. (2011). *The Art of the Novel: Critical Prefaces*. Chicago UP.

James, P. D. (1992). *The Children of Men*. Faber & Faber.

Janssen, M., & van der Voort, H. (2020). Agile and adaptive governance in crisis response: Lessons from the COVID-19 pandemic. *International Journal of Information Management*, *55*(102180). https://doi.org/10.1016/j.ijinfomgt.2020.102180

Jarvenpaa, S. L., Knoll, K., & Leidner, D. E. (1998). Is anybody out there? Antecedents of trust in global virtual teams. *Journal of Management Information Systems*, *14*(4), 29–64. doi:10.1080/07421222.1998.11518185

Jarvenpaa, S. L., & Leidner, D. E. (1999). Communication and trust in global virtual teams. *Organization Science*, *10*(6), 791–815. doi:10.1287/orsc.10.6.791

Jawahar, I. M., Stone, T. H., & Kluemper, D. (2019). When and why leaders trust followers LMX as a mediator and empowerment as a moderator of the trustworthiness-trust relationship. *Career Development International*, *24*(7), 702–716. doi:10.1108/CDI-03-2019-0078

Jelil Ladebo, O., Jacob Olaoye, O., & Oyekale Adamu, C. (2008). Extension personnel's self-esteem and workplace relationships: Implications for job satisfaction and affective organizational commitment foci. *Journal of Agricultural Education and Extension*, *14*(3), 249–263. doi:10.1080/13892240802207692

Jensen, R. H., Strengers, Y., Raptis, D., Nicholls, L., Kjeldskov, J., & Skov, M. B. (2018, June). Exploring Hygge as a desirable design vision for the sustainable smart home. In *Proceedings of the 2018 Designing Interactive Systems Conference* (pp. 355-360). 10.1145/3196709.3196804

Jervis, E. (2017). *Do Australians have a right to disconnect?* Legalvision. https://legalvision.com.au/do-australians-have-a-right-to-disconnect/

Jeske, D., & Holland, P. (2019). Employer and Employee Vetting: Reputation Management Challenges in the Information Age. In Contemporary HRM in the 21st Century. Emerald Publishing.

Jetelina, K. K., Knell, G., & Molsberry, R. J. (2020). Changes in intimate partner violence during the early stages of the COVID-19 pandemic in the USA. *Injury Prevention: Journal of the International Society for Child and Adolescent Injury Prevention*. Advance online publication.

Jevtić, M. (2012). *The role of Works Councils and Trade Unions in representing interests of the employees in EU Member States (partnership or competition)*. Friedrich-Ebert-Stiftung, Regional Project for Labour Relations and Social Dialogue in South East Europe. https://library.fes.de/pdf-files/bueros/belgrad/08947.pdf

Jin, L., Duan, K., & Tang, X. (2018). What Is the Relationship between Technological Innovation and Energy Consumption? Empirical Analysis Based on Provincial Panel Data from China. *Sustainability*, *10*(2), 145. doi:10.3390u10010145

Johlke, M. C., Stamper, C. L., & Shoemaker, M. E. (2001). Antecedents to boundary-spanner perceived organizational support. *Journal of Managerial Psychology*, *17*(2), 116–128. doi:10.1108/02683940210417049

Johri, A. (2012). From a distance: Impression formation and impression accuracy among geographically distributed coworkers. *Computers in Human Behavior*, *28*(6), 1997–2006. doi:10.1016/j.chb.2012.06.038

Jones, S. (2020 March 31). Coronavirus forced me to slow down and spend more time with my family — and I'm grateful | Solomon Jones. *The Philadelphia Inquirer*. Retrieved from https://www.inquirer.com/health/coronavirus/coronavirus-covid-19-family-isolation-20200331.html

Jones, P. S., & Green, A. E. (2009). The quantity and quality of jobs: Changes in UK regions. *Environment & Planning A, 41*(10), 2474–2495. doi:10.1068/a41228

Jong, J., Curşeu, P., & Leenders, R. (2014). When do bad apples not spoil the barrel? Negative relationships in teams, team performance, and buffering mechanisms. *The Journal of Applied Psychology, 99*(3), 514–522. doi:10.1037/a0036284 PMID:24661274

Jorgenson, D. W., Ho, M. S., & Stiroh, K. J. (2008). A retrospective look at the U.S. productivity growth resurgence. *The Journal of Economic Perspectives, 22*(1), 3–24.

Joshi, A., Lazarova, M. B., & Liao, H. (2009). Getting Everyone on Board: The Role of Inspirational Leadership in Geographically Dispersed Teams. *Organization Science, 20*(1), 240–252. doi:10.1287/orsc.1080.0383

Jospe, K., Genzer, S., Selle, N. K., Ong, D., Zaki, J., & Perry, A. (2020). The contribution of linguistic and visual cues to physiological synchrony and empathic accuracy. *Cortex, 132*, 296–308. doi:10.1016/j.cortex.2020.09.001 PMID:33010739

Judd, J., Rember, B. A., Pellegrini, T., Ludlow, B., & Meisner, J. (2020). *"This is Not Teaching": The Effects of COVID-19 on Teachers.* Accessed 05 February 2021. https://www.socialpublishersfoundation.org/ knowledge_base/this-is-not-teaching-the-effects-of-covid-19-on-teachers/

Jude, S., & Fuchs, N. (2020). The office is not dead. It's evolving. *Property Week, 87*(37), 26–27.

Judge, T. A., Thoresen, C. J., Bono, J. E., & Patton, G. K. (2001). The Job Satisfaction-Job Performance Relationship: A Qualitative and Quantitative Review. *Psychological Bulletin, 127*(3), 376–407. doi:10.1037/0033-2909.127.3.376 PMID:11393302

Jung, C., Statham, R., & Roberts, C. (2020). *How are working time and practices changing as a result of COVID-19? Institute for Public Policy Research*. IPPR.

Kallis, G., Kostakis, V., Lange, S., Muraca, B., Paulson, S., & Schmelzer, M. (2018). Research on degrowth. *Annual Review of Environment and Resources, 43*(1), 291–316. doi:10.1146/annurev-environ-102017-025941

Kanawattanachai, P., & Yoo, Y. (2002). Dynamic nature of trust in virtual teams. *The Journal of Strategic Information Systems, 11*(3-4), 187–213. doi:10.1016/S0963-8687(02)00019-7

Kanter, L. M. (1977). *Work and family in the United States: A critical review and agenda for research and policy*. Russell Sage Foundation.

Kaplan, S. (1995). The restorative benefits of nature: Toward an integrative framework. *Journal of Environmental Psychology, 15*(3), 169–182. doi:10.1016/0272-4944(95)90001-2

Karp, P. (2020), Unions Push for Better Protections as 80 Percent of Employees Say They Want to Keep Working from Home. *The Guardian*. https://www.theguardian.com/australia-news/2020/nov/04/unions-push-for-better-protections-as-80-of-employees-say-they-want-to-keep-working-from-home

Kaul, S., Pande, N., & Ahuja, V. (2017). Virtual Team Effectiveness : An Empirical Study Using SEM. *Procedia Computer Science, 122*, 33–41. doi:10.1016/j.procs.2017.11.338

Kayworth, T. R., & Leidner, D. (2000). The global virtual manager: A prescription for success. *European Management Journal, 18*(2), 183–194. doi:10.1016/S0263-2373(99)00090-0

Kearl, H., Johns, N. E., & Raj, A. (2019). *Measuring #MeToo: a national study on sexual harassment and assault.* UC San Diego Center on Gender Equity and Health.

Keister, L. A. (2000). Race and wealth inequality: The impact of racial differences in asset ownership on the distribution of household wealth. *Social Science Research, 29*(4), 477–502.

Kelliher, C., & Anderson, D. (2010). Doing more with less? Flexible working practices and the intensification of work. *Human Relations, 63*(1), 83–106. doi:10.1177/0018726709349199

Kello, J. E. (2015). The science and practice of workplace meetings. In J. A. Allen, N. Lehmann-Willenbrock, & S. G. Rogelberg (Eds.), *Cambridge handbooks in psychology. The Cambridge handbook of meeting science* (pp. 709–734). Cambridge University Press. doi:10.1017/CBO9781107589735.030

Kelly, A. (1977). Teaching Principles of Economics: The Joint Council Experimental Economics Course Project. *The American Economic Review, 67*(1), 105–109.

Kendon, A. (1970). Movement coordination in social interaction: Some examples described. *Acta Psychologica, 32*, 101–125. doi:10.1016/0001-6918(70)90094-6 PMID:5444439

Kennedy, R. (1978). *A Boy at the Hogarth Press*. Penguin.

Kimble, C. (2011). Building effective virtual teams: How to overcome the problems of trust and identity in virtual teams. *Global Business and Organizational Excellence, 30*(2), 6–15. doi:10.1002/joe.20364

Kim, J., Kim, H., Tay, B. K., Muniyandi, M., Srinivasan, M. A., Jordan, J., Mortensen, J., Oliveira, M., & Slater, M. (2004). Transatlantic touch: A study of haptic collaboration over long distance. *Presence (Cambridge, Mass.), 13*(3), 328–337. doi:10.1162/1054746041422370

Kingma, S., Dale, K., & Wasserman, V. (Eds.). (2018). *Organizational space and beyond: The significance of Henri Lefebvre for organization studies*. Routledge.

Kinreich, S., Djalovski, A., Kraus, L., Louzoun, Y., & Feldman, R. (2017). Brain-to-brain synchrony during naturalistic social interactions. *Scientific Reports, 7*(1), 17060. doi:10.103841598-017-17339-5 PMID:29213107

Kirk, L. J. (1995). Exclusion to emancipation: A comparative analysis of women's citizenship in Australia and the United States 1869-1921. *West Virginia Law Review, 97*(3), 725–750.

Kirkman, B. L., Rosen, B., Gibson, C. B., Tesluk, P. E., & Pherson, S. O. (2002). Five challenges to virtual team success: Lessons from Sabre, Inc. *The Academy of Management Executive, 16*(3), 67–79. doi:10.5465/ame.2002.8540322

Kirkman, B. L., Rosen, B., Tesluk, P. E., & Gibson, C. B. (2004). The impact of team empowerment on virtual team performance: The moderating role of face-to-face interaction. *Academy of Management Journal, 47*(2), 175–192.

Kleinman, M. (2020). Policy challenges for the post-pandemic city. *Environment and Planning. B, Urban Analytics and City Science, 47*(7), 1136–1139. doi:10.1177/2399808320950252

Kluge, N., Leger, R., & Leuchters, M. (2019). *Workers' Voice: Die Stimme der Arbeitnehmer in der europäischen Corporate Governance– - eine Einladung, neue Perspektiven für die Mitbestimmung zu eröffnen* [Workers' Voice: The voice of workers in European corporate governance – an invitation to open up new perspectives on co-determination] (No. 52). https://www.boeckler.de/pdf/p_mbf_report_2019_52.pdf

Knetz, I. (2016). Toward a model of work-related self: A narrative review. *Frontiers in Psychology, 7*, 331.

Kniffin, K. M., Narayanan, J., Anseel, F., Antonakis, J., Ashford, S. P., Bakker, A. B., Bamberger, P., Bapuji, H., Bhave, D. P., Choi, V. K., Creary, S. J., Demerouti, E., Flynn, F. J., Gelfand, M. J., Greer, L. L., Johns, G., Kesebir, S., Klein, P. G., Lee, S. Y., ... Vugt, M. V. (2021). COVID-19and the workplace: Implications, issues, and insights for future research and action. *The American Psychologist*, *76*(1), 63–77. doi:10.1037/amp0000716 PMID:32772537

Kniffin, K. M., Wansink, B., Devine, C. M., & Sobal, J. (2015). Eating together at the firehouse: How workplace commensality relates to the performance of firefighters. *Human Performance*, *28*(4), 281–306. doi:10.1080/08959285.2015.1021049 PMID:27226698

Knight, R. (2015). How to manage remote direct reports. *Harvard Business Review*, 2–6. https://hbr.org/2015/02/how-to-manage-remote-direct-reports

Knoll, D. L., & Gill, H. (2011). Antecedents of trust in supervisors, subordinates, and peers. *Journal of Managerial Psychology*, *26*(4), 313–330. doi:10.1108/02683941111124845

Koehne, S., Hatri, A., Cacioppo, J. T., & Dziobek, I. (2016). Perceived interpersonal synchrony increases empathy: Insights from autism spectrum disorder. *Cognition*, *146*, 8–15. doi:10.1016/j.cognition.2015.09.007 PMID:26398860

Kolomatsky. (2020). How Is the Pandemic Shaping Home Design? *New York Times*. https://www.nytimes.com/2020/10/22/realestate/pandemic-shaping-home-design.html

Kornberger, M., & Clegg, S. (2004). Bringing space back in: Organizing the generative building. *Organization Studies*, *25*(7), 1095–1114. doi:10.1177/0170840604046312

Korsgaard, M. A., Brower, H. H., & Lester, S. W. (2015). It isn't always mutual: A critical review of dyadic trust. *Journal of Management*, *41*(1), 47–70. doi:10.1177/0149206314547521

Kossek, E. E., Lautsch, B. A., & Eaton, S. C. (2006). Telecommuting, control, and boundary management: Correlates of policy use and practice, job control, and work–family effectiveness. *Journal of Vocational Behavior*, *68*(2), 347–367. doi:10.1016/j.jvb.2005.07.002

Koszegi, S. T. (2016). *Building shared context and shared identity through communication*. Marshall Plan Foundation.

Kotera, Y., Green, P., Rhodes, C., Williams, A., Chircop, J., Spink, R., Rawson, R., & Okere, U. (2020). Dealing With Isolation Using Online Morning Huddles for University Lecturers During Physical Distancing by COVID-19: Field Notes. *International Review of Research in Open and Distributed*, *21*(4), 238–244. doi:10.19173/irrodl.v21i4.4843

Kouzes, J. M., & Posner, B. Z. (1993). *Credibility: How Leaders Gain and Lose It. Why People Demand It*. Jossey-Bass.

Kowalski, K. B., & Swanson, J. A. (2005). Critical success factors in developing teleworking programs. *Benchmarking*, *12*(3), 236–249. doi:10.1108/14635770510600357

Kramer, R. M. (1999). Trust and distrust in organizations: Emerging perspectives, enduring questions. *Annual Review of Psychology*, *50*(1), 569–598. doi:10.1146/annurev.psych.50.1.569 PMID:15012464

Kram, K. E. (1983). Phases of the mentor relationship. *Academy of Management Journal*, *26*(4), 608–625. doi:10.2307/255910

Kraut, R. E., Fussell, S. R., Brennan, S. E., & Siegel, J. (2002). Understanding effects of proximity on collaboration: Implications for technologies to support remote collaborative work. *Distributed Work*, 137-162.

Kreiner, G. E., Hollensbe, E. C., & Sheep, M. L. (2009). Balancing borders and bridges: Negotiating the work-home interface via boundary work tactics. *Academy of Management Journal*, *52*(4), 704–730.

Kumar, S. (2018, September 22). What keeps women from the workforce: the invisible scourge of sexual harassment at informal workplaces. *Times of India*. https://timesofindia.indiatimes.com/blogs/toi-edit-page/what-keeps-women-from-the-workforce-the-invisible-scourge-of-sexual-harassment-at-informal-workplaces/?source=app

Kumar, K., Van Fenema, P. C., & Von Glinow, M. A. (2009). Offshoring and the global distribution of work: Implications for task interdependence theory and practice. *Journal of International Business Studies*, *40*(4), 642–667. doi:10.1057/jibs.2008.77

Kurland, N. B., & Bailey, D. E. (1999). Telework; The Advantages and Challenges of Working Here, There, Anywhere, and Anytime. *Organizational Dynamics*, *28*(2), 53–68. doi:10.1016/S0090-2616(00)80016-9

Kurland, N. B., & Cooper, C. D. (2002). Manager control and employee isolation in telecommuting environments. *The Journal of High Technology Management Research*, *13*(1), 107–126. doi:10.1016/S1047-8310(01)00051-7

Kurtessis, J. N., Eisenberger, R., Ford, M. T., Buffardi, L. C., Stewart, K. A., & Adis, C. S. (2017). Perceived organizational support: A meta-analytic evaluation of organizational support theory. *Journal of Management*, *43*(6), 1854–1884. doi:10.1177/0149206315575554

Kuvaas, B., Buch, R., Weibel, A., Dysvik, A., & Nerstad, C. G. (2017). Do intrinsic and extrinsic motivation relate differently to employee outcomes? *Journal of Economic Psychology*, *61*, 244–258. doi:10.1016/j.joep.2017.05.004

Lacey, A., Lester, K., Cartwright-Hatton, S., & Banerjee, R. (2020). *Coronavirus (COVID-19): Relationship, Emotional Well Being and Family Adjustment Study*. University of Sussex.

LaFrance, M. (1979). Nonverbal synchrony and rapport: Analysis by the cross-lag panel technique. *Social Psychology Quarterly*, *42*(1), 66–70. doi:10.2307/3033875

Lake, A. (2013). *Smart flexibility: Moving smart and flexible working from theory to practice*. Routledge.

Lakens, D. (2010). Movement synchrony and perceived entitativity. *Journal of Experimental Social Psychology*, *46*(5), 701–708. doi:10.1016/j.jesp.2010.03.015

Lakin, J. L., Jefferis, V. E., Cheng, C. M., & Chartrand, T. L. (2003). The chameleon effect as social glue: Evidence for the evolutionary significance of nonconscious mimicry. *Journal of Nonverbal Behavior*, *27*(3), 145–162. doi:10.1023/A:1025389814290

Lamond, D. (2000). Managerial Style and Telework. In K. Daniels, D. Lamond, & P. Standen (Eds.), *Managing Telework: Perspectives from Human Resource Management and Work Psychology* (1st ed., pp. 103–112). Thomson Learning.

Lapierre, L. M., Van Steenbergen, E. F., Peeters, M. C., & Kluwer, E. S. (2016). Juggling work and family responsibilities when involuntarily working more from home: A multiwave study of financial sales professionals. *Journal of Organizational Behavior*, *37*(6), 804–822. doi:10.1002/job.2075

Larson, B. Z., Vroman, S., & Makarius, E. R. (2020). A Guide to Managing Your (Newly) Remote Workers. *Harvard Business Review*. Retrieved 25 October 2020. https://hbr.org/2020/03/a-guide-to-managing-your-newly-remote-workers

Larson, B. Z., Vroman, S. R., & Makarius, E. E. (2020, March 18). A Guide to Managing Your (Newly) Remote Workers. *Harvard Business Review*, 2–7.

Larson, C. (2020). *The Profession of Author in the 21st Century*. The Authors Guild.

Lautsch, B. A., Kossek, E. E., & Eaton, S. C. (2009). Supervisory approaches and paradoxes in managing telecommuting implementation. *Human Relations*, *62*(6), 795–827. doi:10.1177/0018726709104543

Layard, R. (2006). *The Depression Report: A New Deal for Depression and Anxiety Disorders*. London School of Economics.

Le Bon, G. (1896). *Psychologie des foules*. F. Alcan.

Leana, C., Appelbaum, E., & Shevchuk, I. (2009). Work process and quality of care in early childhood education: The role of job crafting. *Academy of Management Journal*, *52*(6), 1169–1192. doi:10.5465/amj.2009.47084651

LeanIn.org & McKinsey & Company. (2019). *Women in the Workplace 2019 Report*. https://wiw-report.s3.amazonaws.com/Women_in_the_Workplace_2019.pdf

Leary, M. R. (1999). Making sense of self-esteem. *Current Directions in Psychological Science*, *8*(1), 32–35. doi:10.1111/1467-8721.00008

Lebsock, S. D. (1977). Radical reconstruction and the property rights of southern women. *The Journal of Southern History*, *43*(2), 195–216.

Lecchi, T., da Silva, K., Giommi, F., & Leong, V. (2019). *Using dual-EEG to explore therapist client interpersonal neural synchrony*. Academic Press.

Lederman, D. (2020). Evaluating Teaching During the Pandemic. *Inside HigherEd*. Retrieved from https://www.insidehighered.com/digital-learning/article/2020/04/08/many-colleges-are-abandoning-or-downgrading-student-evaluations

Lee, S. Y., & Brand, J. L. (2005). Effects of control over office workspace on perceptions of the work environment and work outcomes. *Journal of Environmental Psychology*, *25*(3), 323–333. doi:10.1016/j.jenvp.2005.08.001

Lefebvre, H. (1991). *The Production of Space* (D. Nicholson-Smith, Trans.). Blackwell.

Legault, L. (2017). Self-Determination Theory. In V. Zeigler-Hill & T. K. Shackelford (Eds.), *Encyclopedia of Personality and Individual Differences*. Springer. doi:10.1007/978-3-319-28099-8_1162-1

Legrottaglie, S., & Ligorio, M. B. (2017). The temporal dimension as a dialogical resource for teachers' professional development and fulfillment. *Teacher Development*, *21*(1), 57–80. doi:10.1080/13664530.2016.1190783

Lengel, R. H., & Daft, R. L. (1988). The Selection of Communication Media as an Executive Skill. *The Academy of Management Perspectives*, *2*(3), 225–232. doi:10.5465/ame.1988.4277259

Leonardi, P. M., Treem, J. W., & Jackson, M. H. (2010). The connectivity paradox: Using technology to both decrease and increase perceptions of distance in distributed work arrangements. *Journal of Applied Communication Research*, *38*(1), 85–105. doi:10.1080/00909880903483599

Lepak, D., & Snell, S. (2007) Employment subsystems and the 'HR architecture'. In The Oxford Handbook of Human Resource Management: A Critical Text. OUP.

LePine, J. A., Podsakoff, N. P., & LePine, M. A. (2005). A meta-analytic test of the challenge stressor-hindrance stressor framework: An explanation for inconsistent relationships among stressors and performance. *Academy of Management Journal*, *48*(5), 764–775. doi:10.5465/amj.2005.18803921

Lerner, V. (2015). *Cultural Backgrounds Influencing Virtual Team Performance*. Walden University.

Leshchinskaya, I., & Piani, C. (2020). *Student Evaluation of Teaching: COVID-19 Considerations for Validity and Fairness*. Liberal Education Blog. Association of American Colleges and Universities. Retrieved from https://www.aacu.org/blog/student-evaluation-teaching-covid-19-considerations-validity-and-fairness

Lester, S. W., & Brower, H. H. (2003). In the eyes of the beholder: The relationship between subordinates' felt trustworthiness and their work attitudes and behaviors. *Journal of Leadership & Organizational Studies*, *10*(2), 17–33. doi:10.1177/107179190301000203

Lewicki, R. L., & Bunker, B. B. (1996). Developing and maintaining trust in work relationships. In R. M. Kramer & T. R. Tyler (Eds.), *Trust in organizations: Frontiers of theory and research* (pp. 114–139). Sage. doi:10.4135/9781452243610.n7

Lewis, J. D., & Weigert, A. (1985). Trust as a social reality. *Social Forces*, *63*(4), 967–985. doi:10.2307/2578601

Liao, C. (2017). Leadership in virtual teams: A multilevel perspective. *Human Resource Management Review*, *27*(4), 648–659. doi:10.1016/j.hrmr.2016.12.010

Liao, E. Y., & Chun, H. (2016). Supervisor monitoring and subordinate innovation. *Journal of Organizational Behavior*, *37*(2), 168–192. doi:10.1002/job.2035

Limburg, D. O. (1998). Teleworking in managerial context. In R. Suomi, P. Jackson, L. Hollmen, & M. Aspnas (Eds.), *Teleworking Environments: Proceedings of the Third International Workshop of Telework. TUCS General Publication No. 8*, (pp. 93-106). Turku, Finland: Turku Center for Computer Science.

Limburg, D., & Jackson, P. J. (2007). Teleworkflow: Supporting remote control with Workflow Management Systems. *New Technology, Work and Employment*, *22*(2), 146–167. doi:10.1111/j.1468-005X.2007.00190.x

Lin, C., He, H., Baruch, Y., & Ashforth, B. E. (2017). The Effect of Team Affective Tone on Team Performance: The Roles of Team Identification and Team Cooperation. *Human Resource Management*, *56*(6), 931–952. doi:10.1002/hrm.21810

Lin, C., Standing, C., & Liu, Y.-C. (2008). Standing, C., & Liu, Y. (2008). A model to develop effective virtual teams. *Decision Support Systems*, *45*(4), 1031–1045. doi:10.1016/j.dss.2008.04.002

Lionel, R., & You, S. (2018). Disaggregating the Impacts of Virtuality on Team Identification. In *GROUP'18*. ACM. doi:10.1145/3148330.3148337

Lipnack, J., & Stamps, J. (1997). *Virtual teams: Reaching Across Space, Time and Organization with Technology*. Wiley.

Lisak, A., Erez, M., Sui, Y., & Lee, C. (2016). The positive role of global leaders in enhancing multicultural team innovation. *Journal of International Business Studies*, *47*(6), 655–673. doi:10.105741267-016-0002-7

Liveris, C. (2020, May 16). We proved we can work from home. Why do we need to go back to the office? *WA Today*.

Lockwood, N. R. (2003). Work/Life: Balance Challenges and Solutions. *SHRM Research Quarterly*, 1-10.

Longo, Y., Gunz, A., Curtis, G. J., & Farsides, T. (2016). Measuring Need Satisfaction and Frustration in Educational and Work Contexts: The Need Satisfaction and Frustration Scale (NSFS). *Journal of Happiness Studies*, *17*(1), 295–317. doi:10.100710902-014-9595-3

Lopez Valenzuela, A. (2020, Sept. 2). Can office workers save the day for local businesses ravaged by COVID-19? *City A.M.*

Lord, P. (2020c). The social perils and promise of remote work. *Journal of Behavioral Economics for Policy*, *4*(S), 63-67.

Lord, P. (in press). *COVID-19 and the future of work*. Denver Law Review Forum https://papers.ssrn.com/sol3/papers.cfm?abstract_id=3666588

Lord, P., & Saad, L. (in press). Tackling the COVID-19 pandemic. *Manitoba Law Journal, 43*. https://papers.ssrn.com/sol3/papers.cfm?abstract_id=3554436

Lord, P. (2020a). Incentivising employment during the COVID-19 pandemic. *The Theory and Practice of Legislation*, *8*(3), 355–372.

Lord, P. (2020b). "It doesn't work!": The symbolic aspect of law, from the criminal law to Bill 21. *Directions*, *9*(6), 1–18.

Lorenz, C. (2012). If you're so smart, why are you under surveillance? Universities, Neoliberalism, and New Public Management. *Critical Inquiry*, *38*(3), 599–629. doi:10.1086/664553

Lu, C., Wang, H., Lu, J., Du, D., & Bakker, A. (2014). Does work engagement increase person- job fit? The role of job crafting and job insecurity. *Journal of Vocational Behavior*, *84*(2), 142–152. doi:10.1016/j.jvb.2013.12.004

Luhmann, N. (1979). *Trust and Power*. Wiley.

Luhmann, N. (2018). *Schriften zur Organisation 1*. Die Wirklichkeit der Organisation., doi:10.1007/978-3-658-22503-2_15

Luna, A. J. H. de O., Kruchten, P., & Pedrosa, M. L. G. do E., Neto, H. R., & de Moura, H. P. (2014). State of the art of agile governance: a systematic review. *International Journal of Computer Science & Information Technology*, 6(5), 121-141. *arXiv preprint arXiv:1411.1922*

Lund, S., Madgavkar, A., Manyika, J., & Smit, S. (2020). *What's next for remote work: An analysis of 2,000 tasks, 800 jobs, and nine countries*. McKinsey Global Institute. Retrieved from https://www.mckinsey.com/featured-insights/future-of-work/whats-next-for-remote-work-an-analysis-of-2000-tasks-800-jobs-and-nine-countries

Lyttelton, T., Zang, E., & Musick, K. (n.d.). *Gender Differences in Telecommuting and Implications for Inequality at Home and Work*. 10.31235/ doi:osf.io/tdf8c

Lyubovnikova, J., Legood, A., Turner, N., & Mamakouka, A. (2017). How authentic leadership influences team performance: The mediating role of team reflexivity. *Journal of Business Ethics*, *141*(1), 59–70. doi:10.100710551-015-2692-3

MacDonald, W. (2003). The impact of job demands and workload on stress and fatigue. *Australian Psychologist*, *38*(2), 102–117. doi:10.1080/00050060310001707107

Mache, S., Servaty, R., & Harth, V. (2020). Flexible work arrangements in open workspaces and relations to occupational stress, need for recovery and psychological detachment from work. *Journal of Occupational Medicine and Toxicology (London, England)*, *15*(1), 1–11. doi:10.118612995-020-00258-z PMID:32206078

MacKenzie, S.B., Podsakoff, P.M. & Rich, G. (2001). Transformational and transactional leadership and salesperson performance. *Journal of the Academy of Marketing Science, 29*(Spring), 115-134.

MacNaughton, P., Satish, U., Laurent, J. G. C., Flanigan, S., Vallarino, J., Coull, B., Spengler, J. D., & Allen, J. G. (2017). The impact of working in a green certified building on cognitive function and health. *Building and Environment*, *114*, 178–186. doi:10.1016/j.buildenv.2016.11.041 PMID:28785124

Maddux, W. W., Mullen, E., & Galinsky, A. D. (2008). Chameleons bake bigger pies and take bigger pieces: Strategic behavioral mimicry facilitates negotiation outcomes. *Journal of Experimental Social Psychology*, *44*(2), 461–468. doi:10.1016/j.jesp.2007.02.003

Maes, J. D., & Weldy, T. G. (2018). Building effective virtual teams: Expanding OD research and practice. *Organization Development Journal*, *36*(3), 83–90.

Magnusson Hanson, L. L., Nyberg, A., Mittendorfer-Rutz, E., Bondestam, F., & Madsen, I. E. H. (2020). Work related sexual harassment and risk of suicide and suicide attempts: Prospective cohort study. *BMJ (Clinical Research Ed.)*, *2020*(370), m2984. doi:10.1136/bmj.m2984 PMID:32878868

Maister, L., Slater, M., Sanchez-Vives, M. V., & Tsakiris, M. (2015). Changing bodies changes minds: Owning another body affects social cognition. *Trends in Cognitive Sciences*, *19*(1), 6–12. doi:10.1016/j.tics.2014.11.001 PMID:25524273

Maitland, A., & Thomson, P. (2011). *Future Work*. Palgrave–Macmillan Hampshire. doi:10.1057/9780230354043

Major, D. A., & Germano, L. M. (2006). The changing nature of work and its impact on the work-home interface. In F. Jones, R. J. Burke, & M. Westman (Eds.), *Work-life balance: A psychological perspective* (pp. 13–38). Psychology Press.

Malhotra, A., Majchrzak, A., & Rosen, B. (2007). Leading virtual teams. *The Academy of Management Perspectives*, *21*(1), 60–70. doi:10.5465/amp.2007.24286164

Mancl, D., & Fraser, S. D. (2020). COVID-19's Influence on the Future of Agile. In M. Paasivaara & P. Kruchten (Eds.), *Agile Processes in Software Engineering and Extreme Programming – Workshops. XP 2020. Lecture Notes in Business Information Processing*. *396* (pp. 309–316). Springer. doi:10.1007/978-3-030-58858-8_32

Mandel, E. S. J. (2014). *Station Eleven*. Knopf.

Mani, D., & Tomar, S. (2020, March 30). Work from home in the time of COVID-19. *The Hindu*. https://www.thehindu.com/opinion/op-ed/work-from-home-in-the-time-of-covid-19/article31207008.ece

Mannix, L. (2020), Here comes the COVID-19 mental health surge. *Sydney Morning Herald*. https://www.smh.com.au/national/here-comes-the-COVID-19-mental-health-surge-20200614-p552g6.html

Manochehri, G., & Pinkerton, T. (2003). Managing telecommuters: Opportunities and challenges. *American Business Review*, *21*(1), 9–16.

Manzo, L. K. C., & Minello, A. (2020). Mothers, childcare duties, and remote working under COVID-19 lockdown in Italy: Cultivating communities of care. *Dialogues in Human Geography*, *10*(2), 120–123. doi:10.1177/2043820620934268

Maples, J. N., & Taylor, W. V. (2013). Writing Children's Books in Sociology Class: An Innovative Approach to Teaching Social Problems to Undergraduate Students. *International Journal on Teaching and Learning in Higher Education*, *25*(3), 1–11.

Maravelias, C. (2003). Post-bureaucracy – control through professional freedom. *Journal of Organizational Change Management*, *16*(5), 547–566. doi:10.1108/09534810310494937

Margulis, S. (2003). On the status and contribution of Westin's and Altman's theories of privacy. *Social Issues*, *59*(2), 411–429. doi:10.1111/1540-4560.00071

Markey, R. (2020). The Impact of the COVID-19 Virus on Industrial Relations. *Journal of Australian Political Economy*, *85*, 147–154.

Marlow, J., & Dabbish, L. (2011). Reducing psychological distance in globally distributed teams. *Chi*, *11*, 1–4. doi:10.1145/2141512.2141568

Marrewijk, A. (2011). Cross Cultural Management: Hybridization of Dutch — Indian Work Practices in Geographically Distributed IT Projects. *International Journal of Business Anthropology*, *2*(2), 15–35.

Marsh, K., & Musson, G. (2008). Men at work and at home: Managing emotion in telework. *Gender, Work and Organization*, *15*(1), 31–48.

Martin, B., & MacDonnell, R. (2012). Is telework effective for organizations? A meta-analysis of empirical research on perceptions of telework and organizational outcomes. *Management Research Review*, *35*(7), 602–616. doi:10.1108/01409171211238820

MartinD. (2021). https://www.perthnow.com.au/business/workplace-matters/is-the-boss-watching-your-every-wfh-moment-ng-b881722997z

Martínez Sánchez, A., Pérez Pérez, M., de Luis Carnicer, P., & José Vela Jiménez, M. (2007). Teleworking and workplace flexibility: A study of impact on firm performance. *Personnel Review*, *36*(1), 42–64. doi:10.1108/00483480710716713

Martin, S. L., Liao, H., & Campbell, E. M. (2013). Directive versus empowering leadership: A field experiment comparing impacts on task proficiency and proactivity. *Academy of Management Journal*, *56*(5), 1372–1395. doi:10.5465/amj.2011.0113

Martins, L. L., Gilson, L. L., & Maynard, M. T. (2004). Virtual teams: What do we know and where do we go from here? *Journal of Management*, *30*(6), 805–835. doi:10.1016/j.jm.2004.05.002

Martinuzzi, E. (2020, June 17). As work has moved home, so has harassment. *Bloomberg*. https://www.bloomberg.com/opinion/articles/2020-06-17/as-work-has-moved-home-so-has-online-bullying-harassment

Martinuzzi, E. (2020, June 17). As Work Has Moved Home, So Has Harassment. *Bloomberg*. https://www.bloomberg.com/opinion/articles/2020-06-17/as-work-has-moved-home-so-has-online-bullying-harassment

Maruyama, T., Hopkinson, P. G., & James, P. W. (2009). A multivariate analysis of work–life balance outcomes from a large-scale telework programme. *New Technology, Work and Employment*, *24*(1), 76–88. doi:10.1111/j.1468-005X.2008.00219.x

Maruyama, T., & Tietze, S. (2012). From anxiety to assurance: Concerns and outcomes of telework. *Personnel Review*, *41*(4), 450–469. doi:10.1108/00483481211229375

Maslach, C., & Leiter, M. P. (2016). Understanding the burnout experience: Recent research and its implications for psychiatry. *World Psychiatry; Official Journal of the World Psychiatric Association (WPA)*, *15*(2), 103–111. doi:10.1002/wps.20311 PMID:27265691

Masterson, V. A., Enqvist, J. P., Stedman, R. C., & Tengö, M. (2019). Sense of place in social–ecological systems: From theory to empirics. *Sustainability Science*, *14*(3), 555–564. doi:10.100711625-019-00695-8

Matheson, K., & Zanna, M. P. (1988). The impact of computer-mediated communication on self-awareness. *Computers in Human Behavior*, *4*(3), 221–233. doi:10.1016/0747-5632(88)90015-5

Mathews, J. (1989b). *Tools of Change: New Technology and the Democratisations of Work*. Pluto Press.

Mathieu, J. E., Heffner, T. S., Goodwin, G. F., Salas, E., & Cannon-Bowers, J. A. (2000). The influence of shared mental models on team process and performance. *The Journal of Applied Psychology*, *85*(2), 273–283. doi:10.1037/0021-9010.85.2.273 PMID:10783543

Matsui, T., Okada, A., & Kakuyama, T. (1982). Influence of achievement need on goal setting, performance, and feedback effectiveness. *The Journal of Applied Psychology*, *67*(5), 645–648. doi:10.1037/0021-9010.67.5.645

Matt, A. (2020, February 14). Know your rights: online harassment. *The Swaddle*. https://theswaddle.com/know-your-rights-protection-against-online-harassment/

Mattarelli, E., & Gupta, A. (2009). Offshore-onsite subgroup dynamics in globally distributed teams. *Information Technology & People*, *22*(3), 242–269. doi:10.1108/09593840910981437

Maurer, R. (2020, July 30). *Admin Jobs Projected to Stay Remote After COVID-19*. Retrieved from SHRM: Society for Human Resource Management: https://www.shrm.org/resourcesandtools/hr-topics/talent-acquisition/pages/admin-jobs-projected-stay-remote-covid19.aspx

Mayer, R. C., Davis, J. H., & Schoorman, D. F. (1995). An integrative model of organizational trust. *Academy of Management Review*, *20*(3), 709–734. doi:10.5465/amr.1995.9508080335

Mazmanian, M., Orlikowski, W. J., & Yates, J. (2013). The autonomy paradox: The implications of mobile email devices for knowledge professionals. *Organization Science*, *24*(5), 1337–1357. doi:10.1287/orsc.1120.0806

McCains, S., & Kastner, S. (2011). Interactions of top-down and bottom-up mechanisms in human visual cortex. *The Journal of Neuroscience: The Official Journal of the Society for Neuroscience, 312*(2), 587–597. doi:10.1523/JNEUROSCI.3766-10.2011 PMID:21228167

McCarthy, C. (2006). *The Road.* Knopf.

McCloskey, D. W., & Igbaria, M. (2003). Does "Out of Sight" Mean "Out of Mind"? An Empirical Investigation of the Career Advancement Prospects of Telecommuters. *Information Resources Management Journal, 16*(2), 19–34. doi:10.4018/irmj.2003040102

McConnell, C., & Lamphear, C. (1969). Teaching Principles of Economics without Lectures. *The Journal of Economic Education, 1*(1), 20–32. doi:10.1080/00220485.1969.10845293

McCoy, J. M., & Evans, G. W. (2002). The potential role of the physical environment in fostering creativity. *Creativity Research Journal, 14*(3-4), 409–426. doi:10.1207/S15326934CRJ1434_11

McCrindle Research. (2020). *Teleworking in Australia.* https://mccrindle.com.au/wp-content/uploads/2018/04/Teleworking-in-Australia_McCrindle-Research.pdf

McCulley, L. (2020). *Lockdown: Homeworkers putting in extra hours – instant messaging up 1900%.* https://www.thehrdirector.com/business-news/the-workplace/new-data-over-a-third-38-admit-to-working-longer-hours-when-working-from-home/

McEwan, A. (2013). *Smart working: Creating the next wave.* Routledge.

McKnight, D. H., & Chervany, N. L. (2001). Trust and distrust definitions: One bite at a time. In R. Falcone, M. Singh, & Y. H. Tan (Eds.), *Trust in Cyber-societies* (pp. 22–46). Lecture Notes in Computer Science. Springer. doi:10.1007/3-540-45547-7_3

McLaughlin, H., Uggen, C., & Blackstone, A. (2017). The economic and career effects of sexual harassment on working women. *Gender & Society, 31*(3), 333–358. doi:10.1177/0891243217704631 PMID:29056822

Mehrabian, A. (1972). *Nonverbal communication.* Aldine- Atherton.

Mello, J. A. (2007). Managing Telework Programs Effectively. *Employee Responsibilities and Rights Journal, 19*(4), 247–261. doi:10.100710672-007-9051-1

Mencl, J., Wefald, A. J., & van Ittersum, K. W. (2016). Transformational leader attributes: Interpersonal skills, engagement, and well-being. *Leadership and Organization Development Journal, 37*(5), 635–657. doi:10.1108/LODJ-09-2014-0178

Mendonca, J., & Pramanik, A. (2020, March 16). Covid-19 impact: IT firms seek client waivers so staff can work from home. *The Economic Times.* Retrieved from https://economictimes.indiatimes.com/tech/ites/covid-19-impact-it-firms-seek-client-waivers-so-staff-can-work-from-home/articleshow/74642447.cms

Metzger, R. O., & Von Glinow, M. A. (1988). Off-Site Workers: At Home and Abroad. *California Management Review, 30*(3), 101–111. doi:10.2307/41166517

Meyer, J. P., & Gagné, M. (2008). Employee Engagement From a Self-Determination Theory Perspective. *Industrial and Organizational Psychology: Perspectives on Science and Practice, 1*(1), 60–62. doi:10.1111/j.1754-9434.2007.00010.x

Meyerson, D., Weick, K. E., & Kramer, R. M. (1996). Swift trust in temporary groups. In R. M. Kramer & T. R. Tyler (Eds.), *Trust in Organizations: Frontiers of Theory and Research* (pp. 166–195). Sage. doi:10.4135/9781452243610.n9

Microsoft. (2020, September 22). *Work Trend Index: A pulse on employees' wellbeing, six months into the pandemic.* Retrieved from https://www.microsoft.com/en-us/microsoft-365/blog/2020/09/22/pulse-employees-wellbeing-six-months-pandemic/

Miller, A. R., Segal, C., & Spencer, M. K. (2020). *Effects of the COVID-19 pandemic on domestic violence in Los Angeles.* National Bureau of Economic Research Working Paper No. 28068. https://www.nber.org/papers/w28068

Miller, A. R., Segal, C., & Spencer, M. K. (2020). Effects of the COVID-19 Pandemic on Domestic Violence in Los Angeles. National Bureau of Economic Research, 28068.

Miller, C. (2020, July 31). Remote work isn't working? Maybe your company is doing it wrong. *The New York Times.* https://www.nytimes.com/2020/07/31/upshot/remote-work-tips.html

Miller, C. C. (2020, July 31). Remote Work Isn't Working? Maybe Your Company Is Doing It Wrong. *The New York Times.* https://www.nytimes.com/2020/07/31/upshot/remote-work-tips.html

Milliot, J. (2019, October). Number of Self-published Titles Jumped 40% in 2018. *Publishers Weekly*, 15.

Mills, G. (2003). *Action research: A guide for the teacher researcher* (2nd ed.). Merrill/Prentice Hall.

Mirchandani, K. (1998). Protecting the boundary: Teleworker insights on the expansive concept of "work". *Gender & Society, 12*(2), 168–187. doi:10.1177/089124398012002004

Mishori, R. (2020 August 29). Despite pandemic, some college students want to be on or near campus. Here are ways for them to reduce their risks. *The Washington Post.* Retrieved from https://www.washingtonpost.com/health/covid-going-to-college/2020/08/28/517f18a0-e6ee-11ea-97e0-94d2e46e759b_story.html

Mishra, M., & Ghosh, K. (2020). Supervisor monitoring and subordinate work attitudes: a need satisfaction and supervisory support perspective. Leadership & Organization Development Journal. doi:10.1108/LODJ-05-2019-0204

MMK. (2014). *Google offices around the world.* Retrieved from https://www.architecturendesign.net/google-offices-googleplex-around-the-world/

Modestino, A. S. (2020, July 29). Coronavirus child-care crisis will set women back a generation. *The Washington Post.* https://www.washingtonpost.com/us-policy/2020/07/29/childcare-remote-learning-women-employment/

Mohamed, Z. N. J. M. M. L., Newton, J. M., & McKenna, L. (2014). Belongingness in the workplace: A study of Malaysian nurses' experiences. *International Nursing Review, 61*(1), 124–130. doi:10.1111/inr.12078 PMID:24512262

Mokhtarian, P. L., Bagley, M. N., & Salomon, I. (1998). The impact of gender, occupation, and presence of children on telecommuting motivations and constraints. *Journal of the American Society for Information Science, 49*(12), 1115–1134. doi:10.1002/(SICI)1097-4571(1998)49:12<1115::AID-ASI7>3.0.CO;2-Y

Mokhtarian, P. L., & Salomon, I. (1996). Modeling the choice of telecommuting: 2. A case of the preferred impossible alternative. *Environment & Planning, 28*(10), 1859–1876. doi:10.1068/a281859

Molino, M., Ingusci, E., Signore, F., Manuti, A., Giancaspro, M. L., Russo, V., Zito, M., & Cortese, C. G. (2020). Well-being costs of technology use during covid-19 remote working: An investigation using the italian translation of the technostress creators scale. *Sustainability, 12*(15), 5911. doi:10.3390u12155911

Möllering, G. (2001). The nature of trust: From Georg Simmel to a theory of expectation, interpretation and suspension. *Sociology, 35*(2), 403–420. doi:10.1177/S0038038501000190

Möllering, G. (2006). Trust, institutions, agency: towards a neo-institutional theory of trust. In R. Bachmann & A. Zaheer (Eds.), *A Handbook of Trust Research* (pp. 355–376). Edward Elgar. doi:10.4337/9781847202819.00029

Monalisa, M., Daim, T., Mirani, F., Dash, P., Khamis, R., & Bhusari, V. (2008). Managing Global design teams. *Research Technology Management, 51*(4), 48–59. doi:10.1080/08956308.2008.11657514

Mongey, S., Pilossoph, L., & Weinberg, A. (2020). *Which workers share the burden of social distancing policies?* NBER Working Paper 27085, National Bureau of Economic Research.

Moore, P. (2017). *The quantified self in precarity: Work, technology and what counts.* Routledge. doi:10.4324/9781315561523

Moore, P. (2020). Who is the" smart worker"? Who should she be? *Global Labour Journal, 11*(2), 164–167. doi:10.15173/glj.v11i2.4313

Moretti, E. (2012). *The new geography of jobs.* Houghton Mifflin Harcourt.

Morgan, L., Paucar-Caceres, A., & Wright, G. (2014). Leading Effective Global Virtual Teams: The Consequences of Methods of Communication. *Systemic Practice and Action Research, 27*(6), 607–624. doi:10.100711213-014-9315-2

Morgan, P., & Gruber, J. E. (2010). Sexual harassment: violence against women at work and in schools. In C. M. Renzetti, J. L. Edleson, & R. K. Bergen (Eds.), *Sourcebook on Violence Against Women* (2nd ed.). SAGE Publications.

Morgenstern, S., Hodgson, R. J., & Law, L. (1974). Work efficiency and personality. *Ergonomics, 17*(2), 211–220. doi:10.1080/00140137408931340 PMID:4845889

Morris, C. R., & Ferguson, C. H. (1993). How architecture wins technology wars. *Harvard Business Review, 71*(2), 86–96.

Morrison, S. (2020, Apr. 2). Just because you are working from home doesn't mean your boss isn't watching. *Recode.*

Morrison, S. (2020, April 2). *Just because you're working from home doesn't mean your boss isn't watching you. Recode.* Retrieved from https://www.vox.com/recode/2020/4/2/21195584/coronavirus-remote-work-from-home-employee-monitoring

Morrison, R. L., & Macky, K. A. (2017). The demands and resources arising from shared office spaces. *Applied Ergonomics, 60*, 103–115. doi:10.1016/j.apergo.2016.11.007 PMID:28166868

Mortensen, M., & Neeley, T. B. (2012). *Through the Looking Glass : Reflected Knowledge and Trust in Global Collaboration.* Faculty & Research., doi:10.2307/23359587

Moseley, G. L., Gallace, A., & Spence, C. (2012). Bodily illusions in health and disease: Physiological and clinical perspectives and the concept of a cortical 'body matrix'. *Neuroscience and Biobehavioral Reviews, 36*(1), 34–46. doi:10.1016/j.neubiorev.2011.03.013 PMID:21477616

Mull, A. (2020, October). Generation Work-From-Home May Never Recover. *The Atlantic.* https://www.theatlantic.com/magazine/archive/2020/10/career-costs-working-from-home/615472/

Mull, A. (2021, January 21). The Pandemic Has Erased Entire Categories of Friendship. *The Atlantic.* https://www.theatlantic.com/health/archive/2021/01/pandemic-goodbye-casual-friends/617839/

Munir, Y., Sadiq, M., Ali, I., Hamdan, Y., & Munir, E. (2016). Workplace Isolation in Pharmaceutical Companies: Moderating Role of Self-Efficacy. *Social Indicators Research, 126*(3), 1157–1174. doi:10.100711205-015-0940-7 PMID:29563661

Muro, M. (2020). *Could Big Tech's move to permanent remote work save the American Heartland?* The Brookings Institution.

Murray, J. H. (2020). Virtual/reality: How to tell the difference. *Journal of Visual Culture, 19*(1), 11–27. doi:10.1177/1470412920906253

Mysirlaki, S., & Paraskeva, F. (2019). Virtual team effectiveness: Insights from the virtual word teams of massively multiplayer online games. *The Journal of Leadership Studies*, *13*(1), 36–55. doi:10.1002/jls.21608

Myungsuk, C., Park, J.-G., & Lee, J. (2014). Effects of team member psychological proximity on teamwork performance. *Team Performance Management*, *20*(1/2), 81–96. doi:10.1108/TPM-03-2013-0007

Nakamura, J., & Csikszentmihalyi, M. (2002). The concept of flow. In C. R. Snyder & S. J. Lopez (Eds.), *Handbook of positive psychology* (pp. 89–105). Oxford University Press.

Nakamura, L. (2020). Feeling good about feeling bad: Virtuous virtual reality and the automation of racial empathy. *Journal of Visual Culture*, *19*(1), 47–64. doi:10.1177/1470412920906259

Nandan, A. (2020, May 21). Is domestic violence the next pandemic in India? *The Times of India*. https://timesofindia.indiatimes.com/blogs/voices/is-domestic-violence-the-next-pandemic-in-india/

Nap Ministry. (2020). Available: https://www.instagram.com/thenapministry

Narayan, V. (2020, October 1). Mumbai second in cybercrimes for third consecutive year. *The Times of India*. https://timesofindia.indiatimes.com/city/mumbai/mumbai-second-in-cybercrimes-for-third-consecutive-year/articleshow/78419492.cms

Nardi, B. A., Whittaker, S. J., & Bradner, E. M. (2000). Interaction and outeraction: instant messaging in action. In *Proceedings of the 2000 ACM conference on Computer supported cooperative work* (pp. 79–88). Philadelphia, PA: Association for Computing Machinery. doi:10.1145/358916.358975

Nash, M., & Churchill, B. (2020). Caring during COVID-19: A gendered analysis of Australian university responses to managing remote working and caring responsibilities. *Gender, Work and Organization*, *27*(5), 833–846. Advance online publication. doi:10.1111/gwao.12484 PMID:32837013

Nathan, M. (2020). *The city and the virus*. https://maxnathan.medium.com/the-city-and-the-virus-db8f4a68e404

Nathan, M., & Overman, H. (2020). Will coronavirus cause a big city exodus? *Environment and Planning. B, Urban Analytics and City Science*, *47*(9), 1537–1542. doi:10.1177/2399808320971910

Natu, N., & Ram, S. G. (2020, July 26). As WFH employees start burning out, companies rejig leave policies. *The Times of India*. Retrieved from https://timesofindia.indiatimes.com/city/mumbai/as-wfh-employees-start-burning-out-companies-rejig-leave-policies/articleshow/77176631.cms

Naylor, M., Ridout, B., & Campbell, A. (2020). A Scoping Review Identifying the Need for Quality Research on the Use of Virtual Reality in Workplace Settings for Stress Management. *Cyberpsychology, Behavior, and Social Networking*, *23*(8), 506–518. doi:10.1089/cyber.2019.0287 PMID:32486836

NBC News. (2020, March 16). NYC schools close Monday, CT schools close Tuesday, NJ school shutdown "inevitable." *NBC News*. https://www.nbcnewyork.com/news/coronavirus/nyc-school-debate-continues-amid-coronavirus-pandemic-four-related-deaths-in-ny-nj/2327269/

Neeley, T. B. (2015). Global Teams That Work.pdf. *Harvard Business Review*, 74–81.

Newman, S. A., & Ford, R. C. (2020). Five Steps to Leading Your Team in the Virtual COVID-19 Workplace. *Organizational Dynamics*, 100802. doi:10.1016/j.orgdyn.2020.100802

News, A. B. C. (2020a). *Coronavirus have forced Australians to work from home, but what are the impacts on CBDs?* August 18. https://www.abc.net.au/news/2020-08-18/coronavirus-working-from-home-impact-on-australian-cities/12435248

News, A. B. C. (2020b). *Victoria to Pilot Sick and Carers Leave for Casual and Insecure Workers.* https://www.abc.net.au/news/2020-11-23/victorian-pilot-to-provide-sick-carers-leave-for-casual-workers/12910374

News, A. P. (2020, October 29). New workforce challenges emerge as remote work expands, according to new SAP SuccessFactors report. *AP News.* https://apnews.com/article/business-technology-lifestyle-virus-outbreak-government-business-and-finance-f1bf3e9e9d111088c0484aa8c92f9ded

Newton, A. (2020a). *Coronavirus Impact on Book Market – Part I.* K-lytics.com/coronavirus-impact-on-book-market-2020-part-1/

Newton, A. (2020b). *Coronavirus Impact on Book Market – Part #2.* K-lytics.com/coronavirus-impact-on-book-market-2020-part-2/

Newton, D. (2018). Study: Online College Classes Cost Less To Deliver Because They Are Larger, Hire Cheaper Teachers. *Forbes.* Retrieved from https://www.forbes.com/sites/dereknewton/2018/05/23/study-online-college-classes-cost-less-to-deliver-because-they-are-larger-hire-cheaper-teachers/?sh=8a394ad53797

Ng, C. F. (2010). Teleworker's home office: An extension of corporate office? *Facilities, 28*(3/4), 137–155. doi:10.1108/02632771011023113

Nguyen, T., Schleihauf, H., Kayhan, E., Matthes, D., Vrtička, P., & Hoehl, S. (2020). Neural synchrony in mother-child conversation: Exploring the role of conversation patterns. *Social Cognitive and Affective Neuroscience.* PMID:32591781

Nicola, M., Alsafi, Z., Sohrabi, C., Kerwan, A., Al-Jabir, A., Iosifidis, C., Agha, M., & Agha, R. (n.d.). The socio-economic implications of the coronavirus pandemic (COVID-19): A review. *International Journal of Surgery, 78*, 185–193.

Nienaber, A.-M., Romeike, P. D., Searle, R., & Schewe, G. (2015). A qualitative meta-analysis of trust in supervisor-subordinate relationships. *Journal of Managerial Psychology, 30*(5), 507–534. doi:10.1108/JMP-06-2013-0187

Nilles, J. M. (1997). Telework: Enabling distributed organizations. *Information Systems Management, 14*(4), 7–14. doi:10.1080/10580539708907069

Noblit, C. (2020). *KDP Global Fund Payouts* [November 2020 Update]. WrittenWord Media. writtenwordmedia.com/kdp-global-fund-payouts/

Noe, R. A. (1988). Women and Mentoring: A Review and Research Agenda. *Academy of Management Review, 13*(1), 65–78. doi:10.5465/amr.1988.4306784

Nooteboom, B. (2002). *Trust: Forms, Foundations, Functions, Failures and Figures.* Edward Elgar. doi:10.4337/9781781950883

Norah, J. (2019). *Where J. K. Rowling Wrote Harry Potter in Edinburgh.* independenttravelcats.com/cafes-where-jk-rowling-wrote-harry-potter-in-edinburgh/

Nordback, E. S., & Espinosa, J. A. (2019). Effective coordination of shared leadership in global virtual teams. *Journal of Management Information Systems, 36*(1), 321–350. doi:10.1080/07421222.2018.1558943

Novembre, G., Mitsopoulos, Z., & Keller, P. E. (2019). Empathic perspective taking promotes interpersonal coordination through music. *Scientific Reports, 9*(1), 1–12. doi:10.103841598-019-48556-9 PMID:31439866

Nowland, R., Necka, E. A., & Cacioppo, J. T. (2018). Loneliness and social internet use: Pathways to reconnection in a digital world? *Perspectives on Psychological Science, 13*(1), 70–87. doi:10.1177/1745691617713052 PMID:28937910

O'Connor, E. (2020 March 23). Yes, there is panic. But I'm embracing a slower life. *The Washington Post.* Retrieved from https://www.washingtonpost.com/lifestyle/2020/03/23/yes-there-is-panic-im-embracing-slower-life/

O'Hara-Devereaux, M., & Johansen, R. (1994). *Global Work: Bridging Distance, Culture, and Time*. Jossey-Bass.

O'Hara, J. (1969). The Doctor's Son. In *The O'Hara Generation*. Random House.

O'Neill, T. A., Hambley, L. A., Greidanus, N. S., MacDonnell, R., & Kline, T. J. B. (2009). Predicting teleworker success: An exploration of personality, motivational, situational, and job characteristics. *New Technology, Work and Employment*, *24*(2), 144–162. doi:10.1111/j.1468-005X.2009.00225.x

O'Reilly, J., & Robinson, S. L. (2009, August). The negative impact of ostracism on thwarted belongingness and workplace contributions. In Academy of management proceedings (Vol. 2009, No. 1, pp. 1-7). Briarcliff Manor, NY: Academy of Management. doi:10.5465/ambpp.2009.44243707

OAIC. (n.d.). *Workplace monitoring and surveillance.* Australian Government. Office of the Australian Information Commissioner, (Cth). Retrieved 3 November 2020. https://www.oaic.gov.au/privacy/your-privacy-rights/employment/workplace-surveillance/

Oakley, J. G. (1998). Leadership processes in virtual teams and organizations. *The Journal of Leadership Studies*, *5*(3), 3–18. doi:10.1177/107179199900500301

Ocker, R. J., Huang, H., Benbunan-Fich, R., & Hiltz, S. R. (2011). Leadership Dynamics in Partially Distributed teams: An Exploratory Study of the Effects of Configuration and Distance. *Group Decision and Negotiation*, *20*(3), 273–292. doi:10.100710726-009-9180-z

OECD. (2019). *Supporting and guiding novice teachers: Evidence from TALIS 2018, Teaching in Focus, No. 29*. OECD Publishing. doi:10.1787/fe6c9c0c-

Office for National Statistics. (2020). *Coronavirus and homeworking in the UK labour market.* https://www.ons.gov.uk/employmentandlabourmarket/peopleinwork/employmentandemployeetypes/articles/coronavirusandhomeworkingintheuklabourmarket/2019

Office for National Statistics. (2020). *What jobs can be done from home?* Office for National Statistics.

Okazaki, S., Hirotani, M., Koike, T., Bosch-Bayard, J., Takahashi, H. K., Hashiguchi, M., & Sadato, N. (2015). Unintentional interpersonal synchronization represented as a reciprocal visuo-postural feedback system: A multivariate autoregressive modeling approach. *PLoS One*, *10*(9), e0137126. doi:10.1371/journal.pone.0137126 PMID:26398768

O'Leary, M. B., Wilson, J. M., & Metiu, A. (2012). *Beyond being there: The symbolic role of communication and identification in the emergence of perceived proximity in geographically dispersed work.* Academic Press.

Oliveira, A. L. M. (2013). *Regulação estatal das relações de trabalho no capitalismo contemporâneo: uma crítica ao discurso da flexibilização e desregulamentação* [Unpublished Master Dissertation]. Unicamp.

Oliveira, A. L. M., & Emídio, A. P. (2021). *"The great equalizer"? The long-lasting effects of the COVID-19 pandemic on poverty and inequality in Latin America.* Manuscript in preparation.

Oliveira, A. L. M., Rolim, L. N., & Fares, L. S. (2021). *Who cares? Gender, unpaid domestic and care work in Brazil during the pandemic.* Manuscript in preparation.

Oppezzo, M., & Schwartz, D. L. (2014). Give your ideas some legs: The positive effect of walking on creative thinking. *Journal of Experimental Psychology. Learning, Memory, and Cognition*, *40*(4), 1142–1152. doi:10.1037/a0036577 PMID:24749966

Oprean, D., Simpson, M., & Klippel, A. (2017). Collaborating Remotely: An evaluation of immersive capabilities on spatial experiences and team membership. *International Journal of Digital Earth*, *11*(4), 1–17.

Organ & Podsakoff. (1986). Self-Report in Organizational Research. *Journal of Management, 12*(4), 532–544. doi:10.1177/014920638601200408

Orhan, M. A., Rijsman, J. B., & van Dijk, G. M. (2016). Invisible, therefore isolated: Comparative effects of team virtualitywith task virtuality on workplace isolation and work outcomes. *Journal of Work and Organizational Psychology, 32*(2), 109–122. doi:10.1016/j.rpto.2016.02.002

Orrico, A. (2019, January 3). An Official In Brazil's New Right-Wing Government Said "Boys Wear Blue And Girls Wear Pink". *BuzzFeed.* Retrieved from https://www.buzzfeednews.com/article/alexandreorrico/brazil-boys-wear-blue-girls-wear-pink-damares-alves

Orsini, C., & Rodrigues, V. (2020). Supporting motivation in teams working remotely: The role of basic psychological needs. *Medical Teacher, 42*(7), 828–829. Advance online publication. doi:10.1080/0142159X.2020.1758305 PMID:32366152

Overby, E., Bharadwaj, A., & Sambamurthy, V. (2006). Enterprise agility and the enabling role of information technology. *European Journal of Information Systems, 15*(2), 120–131.

Owl Labs & Global Workplace Analytics. (2019). *State of Remote Work 2019.* K. Lister.

Ozcelik, H., & Barsade, S. (2011). Work loneliness and employee performance. *Academy of Management Annual Meeting Proceedings*, 1-6.

OzimekA. (2020). The Future of Remote Work. doi:10.2139srn.3638597

Pacherie, E. (2014). How does it feel to act together? *Phenomenology and the Cognitive Sciences, 13*(1), 25–46. doi:10.100711097-013-9329-8

Paden, D., & Moyer, M. (1969). The Relative Effectiveness of Three Methods of Teaching Principles of Economics. *The Journal of Economic Education, 1*(1), 33–45. doi:10.1080/00220485.1969.10845294

Pahl, R. E. (1988). On Work: Historical Comparative and theoretical Approaches. Oxford: Blackwell.

Pakrasi, S. (2020, May 3). Significant' increase in cybercrime against women during lockdown: experts. *Hindustan Times.* https://www.hindustantimes.com/india-news/significant-increase-in-cybercrime-against-women-during-lockdown-experts/story-QNPwq5Jr1iAkAXzacLnc5K.html

Palermo, T. & Peterman, A. (2011). Undercounting, overcounting, and the longevity of flawed estimates: Statistics on sexual violence in conflict. *World Health Organization, 89*(853), 924-926.

Palmieri, A., Kleinbub, J. R., Calvo, V., Benelli, E., Messina, I., Sambin, M., & Voci, A. (2018). Attachment-security prime effect on skin-conductance synchronization in psychotherapists: An empirical study. *Journal of Counseling Psychology, 65*(4), 490–499. doi:10.1037/cou0000273 PMID:29494169

Panaccio, A., & Vandenberghe, C. (2009). Perceived organizational support, organizational commitment and psychological well-being: A longitudinal study. *Journal of Vocational Behavior, 75*(2), 224–236. doi:10.1016/j.jvb.2009.06.002

Pandit, A. (2020, June 2). Domestic violence accounts for over 47% complaints to NCW in lockdown. *The Times of India.* https://timesofindia.indiatimes.com/articleshow/76161829.cms?utm_source=contentofinterest&utm_medium=text&utm_campaign=cppst

Papagiannidis, S., & Davit, M. (2020). Smart offices: A productivity and well-being perspective. *International Journal of Information Management, 5*, 102027. doi:10.1016/j.ijinfomgt.2019.10.012

Papoutsaki, D., Buzzeo, J., Gray, H., Williams, M., Cockett, J., Akehurst, G., Alexander, K., Newton, B., & Pollard, E. (2020). *Moving out to move on: Understanding the link between migration, disadvantage and social mobility*. Social Mobility Commission.

Parker, P. A., & Kulik, J. A. (1995). Burnout, self-and supervisor-rated job performance, and absenteeism among nurses. *Journal of Behavioral Medicine*, *18*(6), 581–599. doi:10.1007/BF01857897 PMID:8749987

Parker, S. K., & Wall, T. B. (1998). *Job and work Design: Organizing Work to promote Well-being and Effectiveness*. Sage Publications.

Parliament of Western Australia. (2020). *Work Health and Safety Bill, 2020*. https://www.parliament.wa.gov.au/parliament/bills.nsf/BillProgressPopup?openForm&ParentUNID=8F320741B83643A8482584BF000CF89B

Patmore, G. (2016). *Worker Voice: Worker Representation in the Workplace in Australia, Canada, Germany, the UK and the US 1914-1939*. Liverpool University Press.

Pattnaik, L., & Jena, L. K. (in press). Mindfulness, remote engagement and employee morale: Conceptual analysis to address the "new normal". *The International Journal of Organizational Analysis*.

Patty, A. (2020). Employers prepare for return of mentally fragile workforce. *The Age Online*.

Paul, D. L., & McDaniel, R. R. (2004). A field study of the effect of interpersonal trust on virtual collaborative relationship performance. *Management Information Systems Quarterly*, *28*(2), 183–227. doi:10.2307/25148633

Pauleen, D. J. (2003). An inductively derived model of leader-initiated relationship building with virtual team members. *Journal of Management Information Systems*, *20*(3), 227–256. doi:10.1080/07421222.2003.11045771

Pazos, P. (2012). Conflict management and effectiveness in virtual teams. *Team Performance Management*, *18*(7), 401–417. doi:10.1108/13527591211281138

Pennington, A. (2020). *Working from home, once a novelty, is now wearing thin*. https://www.smh.com.au/business/workplace/-20201105-p56br1.html

Pérez, A., Dumas, G., Karadag, M., & Duñabeitia, J. A. (2019). Differential brain-to-brain entrainment while speaking and listening in native and foreign languages. *Cortex*, *111*, 303–315. doi:10.1016/j.cortex.2018.11.026 PMID:30598230

Pérez, M. P., Sánchez, A. M., de Luis Carnicer, P., & Jiménez, M. J. V. (2004). A technology acceptance model of innovation adoption: The case of teleworking. *European Journal of Innovation Management*, *7*(4), 280–291. doi:10.1108/14601060410565038

Pérez, M., Sánchez, A., & de Luis Carnicer, M. (2002). Benefits and barriers of telework: Perception differences of human resources managers according to company's operations strategy. *Technovation*, *22*(12), 775–783. doi:10.1016/S0166-4972(01)00069-4

Peterman, A., Potts, A., O'Donnell, M., Thompson, K., Shah, N., Oertelt-Prigione, S., & van Gelder, N. (2020). *Pandemics and violence against women and children*. Center for Global Development Working Paper 528. Washington, DC: Centre for Global Development.

Peters, P., & Heusinkveld, H. S. (2010). Institutional explanations for managers' attitudes towards telehomeworking. *Human Relations (New York)*, *63*(1), 107–135. doi:10.1177/0018726709336025

Petronio, S. (2002). *Boundary of Privacy: Dialectics of Disclosure*. SUNY Press.

Petronio, S., Ellemers, N., Giles, H., & Gallois, C. (1998). (Mis)communicating across boundaries. *Communication Research*, *61*, 101–113.

Petrou, P., Demerouti, E., & Schaufeli, W. B. (2015). Job crafting in changing organizations: Antecedents and implications for exhaustion and performance. *Journal of Occupational Health Psychology*, *20*(4), 470–480. doi:10.1037/a0039003 PMID:25798717

Pew Research Center (2015). *Raising Kids and Running a Household: How Working Parents Share the Load.* Technical Report.

Pflügler, C., Wiesche, M., & Helmut, K. (2018). Subgroups in Agile and Traditional IT Project Teams. In *51st Hawaii International Conference on System Sciences* (pp. 5483–5492). 10.24251/HICSS.2018.683

Phillips & Associates. (2020). Amid coronavirus quarantines, workplace sexual harassment in New York goes virtual. *New York Employment Attorney Blog*. https://www.newyorkemploymentattorney-blog.com/amid-coronavirus-quarantines-workplace-sexual-harassment-in-new-york-goes-virtual/

Piccoli, G., & Ives, B. (2003). Trust and the unintended effects of behaviour control in virtual teams. *Management Information Systems Quarterly*, *27*(3), 365–395. doi:10.2307/30036538

Piccolo, R., & Colquitt, J. (2006). Transformational leadership and job behaviors: The mMediating role of core job characteristics. *Academy of Management Journal*, *49*(2), 327–340. doi:10.5465/amj.2006.20786079

Pina, A., Gannon, T. A., & Saunders, B. (2009). An overview of the literature on sexual harassment: Perpetrator, theory, and treatment issues. *Aggression and Violent Behavior*, *14*(2), 126–138. doi:10.1016/j.avb.2009.01.002

Ping, C., Schellings, G., & Beijaard, D. (2020). Understanding What, How, and Why Teacher Educators Learn through Their Personal Examples of Learning. *Education Beyond Crisis*, •••, 249–276.

Pinjani, P., & Palvia, P. (2013). Trust and Knowledge Sharing in Diverse Global Virtual Teams. *Information & Management*, *50*(4), 144–153. doi:10.1016/j.im.2012.10.002

Piore, M., & Sabel, C. (1984). *The Second Industrial Divide: Possibilities for Prosperity*. Basic Books.

Pittman, T. S., Boggiano, A. K., & Ruble, D. N. (1983). Intrinsic and extrinsic motivational orientations: Limiting conditions on the undermining ad enhancing effects of reward on intrinsic motivation. In J. Levine & M. Wang (Eds.), *Teacher and student perceptions: Implications for learning* (pp. 319–340). Erlbaum.

Pochepan. (2018). 'Recharge Rooms' Are the Next Trend Your Employees Need in the Office and no, they're not for plugging in your tech. *Inc.* https://www.inc.com/jeff-pochepan/recharge-rooms-are-next-trend-your-employees-need-in-office.html

Pocock, B. (2003). *The Work-life Collision*. Federation Press.

Podsakoff, N. P., LePine, J. A., & LePine, M. A. (2007). Differential Challenge Stressor–Hindrance Stressor Relationships With Job Attitudes, Turnover Intentions, Turnover, and Withdrawal Behavior: A Meta-Analysis. *The Journal of Applied Psychology*, *92*(2), 438–454. doi:10.1037/0021-9010.92.2.438 PMID:17371090

Porter, K. A. (1939). *Pale Horse, Pale Rider*. Harcourt, Brace.

Postmes, T., Spears, R., & Lea, M. (1998). Breaching or building social boundaries? SIDE-effects of computer-mediated communication. *Communication Research*, *25*(6), 689–715. doi:10.1177/009365098025006006

Powell, J. (2020, September 25). The rise of remote work can be unexpectedly liberating: What if you are better off without the office? *The New York Times*. https://www.nytimes.com/2020/09/25/opinion/remote-work-from-home-office.html

Pozo, T. (2018). Queer games after empathy: Feminism and haptic game design aesthetics from consent to cuteness to the radically soft. *Game Studies, 18*(3).

Preece, J. (1999). Empathy online. *Virtual Reality (Waltham Cross)*, *4*(1), 74–84. doi:10.1007/BF01434996

Preissmann, D., Charbonnier, C., Chagué, S., Antonietti, J. P., Llobera, J., Ansermet, F., & Magistretti, P. J. (2016). A motion capture study to measure the feeling of synchrony in romantic couples and in professional musicians. *Frontiers in Psychology*, *7*, 1673. doi:10.3389/fpsyg.2016.01673 PMID:27833580

Primack, B. A., Shensa, A., Sidani, J. E., Colditz, J. B., Radovic, A., & Miller, E. (2017), Social Media Use and Perceived Social Isolation Among Young Adults in the U.S. *American Journal of Preventative Medicine*. Retrieved from https://www.ajpmonline.org/article/S0749-3797(17)30016-8/fulltext

Privman, R., Hiltz, S. R., & Wang, Y. (2013). In-Group (Us) versus out-group (Them) dynamics and effectiveness in partially distributed teams. *IEEE Transactions on Professional Communication*, *56*(1), 33–49. doi:10.1109/TPC.2012.2237253

Prizant-Passal, S., Shechner, T., & Aderka, I. M. (2016). Social anxiety and Internet use–A meta-analysis: What do we know? What are we missing? *Computers in Human Behavior*, *62*, 221–229. doi:10.1016/j.chb.2016.04.003

Productivity Commission. (2015). *Workplace Framework Inquiry Report*. Australian Government, Canberra. https://www.pc.gov.au/inquiries/completed/workplace-relations/report

Productivity Commission. (2020). *Mental Health, Report*. Australian Government, Canberra. https://www.pc.gov.au/inquiries/completed/mental-health#report

Punnett, B. J. (2016). Women in the workforce: A global snapshot. In M. L. Connerley & J. Wu (Eds.), *Handbook on well-being of working women* (pp. 579–602). Springer.

PWC. (2020). *The Economic Impact of Returning to the Office*. PWC.

Rae, A. (2017). The Geography of Travel to Work in England and Wales: Extracts from the 2011 Census. *Applied Spatial Analysis and Policy*, *10*(4), 457–473. doi:10.100712061-016-9196-0

Raghuram, S. (2014). Telecommuting in India: Pitfalls and Possibilities. *SA Journal of Human Resource Management*, *1*(2), 207–220. doi:10.1177/2322093714549108

Raghuram, S., London, M., & Larsen, H. H. (2001). Flexible employment practices in Europe: Country versus culture. *International Journal of Human Resource Management*, *12*(5), 738–753. doi:10.1080/09585190122083

Rai, A., & Sharma, N. (2016). Teaching versus research in higher education institutes: Revisiting the issue. *Current Science*, *111*(10), 1585–1586.

Raišienė, A. G., Rapuano, V., Varkulevičiūtė, K., & Stachová, K. (2020). Working from Home—Who Is Happy? A Survey of Lithuania's Employees during the COVID-19 Quarantine Period. *Sustainability*, *12*(13), 1-21. doi:10.3390u12135332

Ramsett, D., Johnson, J., & Adams, C. (1974). An Interinstitutional Study of Student Attitudes Towards Principles of Economics. *Journal of Experimental Education*, *42*(3), 78–85. doi:10.1080/00220973.1974.11011482

Ramseyer, F., & Tschacher, W. (2011). Nonverbal synchrony in psychotherapy: Coordinated body movement reflects relationship quality and outcome. *Journal of Consulting and Clinical Psychology*, *79*(3), 284–295. doi:10.1037/a0023419 PMID:21639608

Randall, M. L., Cropanzano, R., Bormann, C. A., & Birjulin, A. (1999). Organizational politics and organizational support as predictors of work attitudes, job performance, and organizational citizenship behavior. *Journal of Organizational Behavior*, *20*(2), 159–174. doi:10.1002/(SICI)1099-1379(199903)20:2<159::AID-JOB881>3.0.CO;2-7

Ransome, P. (2007). Conceptualizing boundaries between 'life' and 'work'. *International Journal of Human Resource Management*, *18*(3), 374–386. doi:10.1080/09585190601167425

Ratle, O., Robinson, S., Bristow, A., & Kerr, R. (2020). Mechanisms of micro-terror? Early career CMS academics' experiences of 'targets and terror' in contemporary business schools. *Management Learning, 51*(4), 452–471. doi:10.1177/1350507620913050

Read, S. & Espiner, T. (2020, Oct. 8). Lockdown city living 'wasn't the best idea'. *BBC.*

Reaney, P. (2012). About 20 percent of global workers telecommute: Poll. *Huff Post.* Retrieved from https://www.huffingtonpost.com/2012/01/24/workers-telecommute_n_1228004.html

Reference Re Public Service Employee Relations Act, [1987] 1 S.C.R. 313.

Reis, H. T. (2014). Responsiveness: Affective interdependence in close relationships. In M. Mikulincer & P. R. Shaver (Eds.), *The Herzliya series on personality and social psychology. Mechanisms of social connection: From brain to group* (pp. 255–271). American Psychological Association.

Reiss, S. (2012). Intrinsic and extrinsic motivation. *Teaching of Psychology, 39*(2), 152–156. doi:10.1177/0098628312437704

Rhoades, L., & Eisenberger, R. (2002). Perceived organizational support: A review of the literature. *The Journal of Applied Psychology, 87*(4), 698–714. doi:10.1037/0021-9010.87.4.698 PMID:12184574

Rhoades, L., Eisenberger, R., & Armeli, S. (2001). Affective commitment to the organization: The contribution of perceived organizational support. *The Journal of Applied Psychology, 86*(5), 825–836. doi:10.1037/0021-9010.86.5.825 PMID:11596800

Rhoads, M. (2010). Face-to-face and computer-mediated communication: What does theory tell us and what have we learned so far? *Journal of Planning Literature, 25*(2), 111–122. doi:10.1177/0885412210382984

Rice, R. E., & Love, G. (1987). Electronic emotion: Socioemotional content in a computer-mediated communication network. *Communication Research, 14*(1), 85–108. doi:10.1177/009365087014001005

Richter, A. (2020). Locked-down digital work. *International Journal of Information Management, 55*, 102157. doi:10.1016/j.ijinfomgt.2020.102157 PMID:32836629

Richter, A., Heinrich, P., Stocker, A., & Schwabe, G. (2018). Digital work design. *Business & Information Systems Engineering, 60*(3), 259–264. doi:10.100712599-018-0534-4

Richter, A., Tafvelin, S., & Sverke, M. (2018). The Mediated Relationship of Leadership on Job Insecurity. *Scandinavian Journal of Work and Organizational Psychology, 3*(1), 2. doi:10.16993jwop.43

Rifkin, J. (1995). *The End of Work.* Putnam's Sons.

Riggle, R. J., Edmondson, D. R., & Hansen, J. D. (2009). A meta-analysis of the relationship between perceived organizational support and job outcomes: 20 years of research. *Journal of Business Research, 62*(10), 1027–1030. doi:10.1016/j.jbusres.2008.05.003

Riley, R., Billing, C., Bramley, G., Green, A., Hoole, C., & Taylor, A. (2020). *Professional & Business Services Sector: Creating Further Demand and Growth Outside London.* BEIS Research Paper Number 2020/006.

Riva, G., & Wiederhold, B. K. (2020). *How Cyberpsychology and Virtual Reality Can Help Us to Overcome the Psychological Burden of Coronavirus.* Academic Press.

Riva, G., Wiederhold, B. K., & Mantovani, F. (2021). Surviving COVID-19: The Neuroscience of Smart Working and Distance Learning. *Cyberpsychology, Behavior, and Social Networking, 24*(2), 79–85. doi:10.1089/cyber.2021.0009 PMID:33577414

Robert, L. P. Jr, Dennis, A. R., & Hung, Y. C. (2009). Individual swift trust and knowledge-based trust in face-to-face and virtual team members. *Journal of Management Information Systems*, *26*(2), 241–279. doi:10.2753/MIS0742-1222260210

Robinson, C. D. (2015). *Successful Virtual Teams: Collaboration and Influence As Drivers of Team Success*. University of Pennsylvania.

Robinson, S. L. (1996). Trust and breach of the psychological contract. *Administrative Science Quarterly*, *41*(4), 574–599. doi:10.2307/2393868

Roche, W. K. (2014). HRM in the Recession: Managing People in the Private and Public Sectors. In *Strategic HRM Research and Practice in Ireland* (pp. 35–58). Open Press.

Roethlisberger, F. J., & Dickson, W. J. (1939). *Management and the worker*. Harvard Univ. Press.

Romeike, P. D., Nienaber, A. M., & Schewe, G. (2016). How differences in perceptions of own and team performance impact trust and job satisfaction in virtual teams. *Human Performance*, *29*(4), 291–309. doi:10.1080/08959285.2016.1165226

Romer, D. (1993). Do Students Go to Class? Should They? *The Journal of Economic Perspectives*, *7*(2), 167–174. doi:10.1257/jep.7.3.167

Rosen, L. D., Lim, A. F., Felt, J., Carrier, L. M., Cheever, N. A., Lara-Ruiz, J. M., Mendoza, J. S., & Rokkum, J. (2014). Media and technology use predict ill-being among children, preteens and teenagers independent of the negative health impacts of exercise and eating habits. *Computers in Human Behavior*, *35*, 364–375. doi:10.1016/j.chb.2014.01.036 PMID:25717216

Rosnow, R. L., & Fine, G. A. (1976). *Rumor and gossip: The social psychology of hearsay*. Elsevier.

Ross, J. A. (2006). Trust makes the team go 'round. *Harvard Management Update*, (June), 3–6.

Rosso, B. D., Dekas, K. H., & Wrzesniewskic, A. (2010). On the meaning of work: A theoretical integration and review. *Research in Organizational Behavior*, *30*, 91–127.

Rotter, J. B. (1967). A new scale for the measurement of interpersonal trust. *Journal of Personality*, *35*(4), 651–665. doi:10.1111/j.1467-6494.1967.tb01454.x PMID:4865583

Rousseau, D. M., Sitkin, S. B., Burt, R. S., & Camerer, C. (1998). Not so different at all: A cross-discipline view of trust. *Academy of Management Review*, *23*(3), 393–404. doi:10.5465/amr.1998.926617

Roy Chowdhury, J. (2014). Insecurities of the workers in the informal enterprises: A study of West Bengal in comparison to Kerala. *Research in Applied Economics*, *6*(3), 220–252. doi:10.5296/rae.v6i3.6005

Rueda, J., & Lara, F. (2020). Virtual Reality and Empathy Enhancement: Ethical Aspects. *Frontiers in Robotics and AI*, *7*, 160. doi:10.3389/frobt.2020.506984 PMID:33501297

Ruiller, C., van der Heijden, B., Chedotel, F., & Dumas, M. (2018). You have got a friend: The value of perceived proximity for teleworking success in dispersed teams. *Team Performance Management*, *25*(1/2), 1352–7592.

Rules of professional conduct. (2009). New York Codes, Rules and Regulations, title 22, subtitle B, chapter IV, subchapter E, section 1200.

Rupietta, K., & Beckmann, M. (2016). *Working from home: What is the effect on employees' effort?* University of Basel, Centre of Business and Economics.

Russell, S. (2019). Remote working could harm your mental health. *World Economic Forum and Conversation*. https://www.weforum.org/agenda/2019/10/remote-working-from-home-increase-stress-anxiety-mental-health/

Russell, D. W. (1996). The UCLA Loneliness Scale (Version 3): Reliability, validity, and factor structure. *Journal of Personality Assessment*, *66*(1), 20–40. doi:10.120715327752jpa6601_2 PMID:8576833

RW3 Culture Wizard. (2018). *Virtual Teams Survey 2018*. https://cdn2.hubspot.net/hubfs/466336/Virtual%20Teams%20Survey-Executive%20Summary--Final%20(2018).pdf

Ryan, R. M. (1993). Agency and organization: Intrinsic motivation, autonomy, and the self in psychological development. In J.E. Jacobs (Ed.), *Nebraska Symposium on Motivation: Developmental perspectives on motivation* (pp. 397-427). Academic Press.

Ryan, R. M., & Deci, E. L. (2000). Self-determination theory and the facilitation of intrinsic motivation, social development, and well-being. *The American Psychologist*, *55*(1), 68–78. doi:10.1037/0003-066X.55.1.68 PMID:11392867

Ryan, R. M., & Deci, E. L. (2000a). Intrinsic and Extrinsic Motivations: Classic Definitions and New Directions. *Contemporary Educational Psychology*, *25*(1), 54–67. doi:10.1006/ceps.1999.1020 PMID:10620381

Ryan, R. M., & Deci, E. L. (2017). *Self determination theory*. The Guildford Press.

Ryan, R. M., & Powelson, C. L. (1991). Autonomy and relatedness as fundamental to motivation and education. *Journal of Experimental Education*, *60*(1), 49–66. doi:10.1080/00220973.1991.10806579

S&P Global. (2017). *The key to unlocking U.S. GDP growth? Women.*

Saffioti, H. (2013). *A mulher na sociedade de classe: mito e realidade* (3rd ed.). Expressão Popular.

Sailer, M., Hense, J. U., Mayr, S. K., & Mandl, H. (2017). How gamification motivates: An experimental study of the effects of specific game design elements on psychological need satisfaction. *Computers in Human Behavior*, *69*, 371–380. doi:10.1016/j.chb.2016.12.033

Salancik, G. R., & Pfeffer, J. (1978). A social information processing approach to job attitudes and task design. *Administrative Science Quarterly*, *23*(2), 224–253. doi:10.2307/2392563 PMID:10307892

Samantrov, E., & Sarkar, K. (2020). Violence in times of COVID-19 lack of legal protection for women informal workers. *Economic and Political Weekly*.

Sander, E. L. J. (2019). The case for finally cleaning your desk. *Harvard Business Review*. Accessed 1 November 2020. https://hbr.org/2019/03/the-case-for-finally-cleaning-your-desk

Sander, L., & Bauman, O. (2020). Why Zoom Meetings are So Exhausting. In M. Glassey (Ed.). 2020: The year that changed us. Thames & Hudson.

Sander, E. L. J., Caza, A., & Jordan, P. J. (2019). Psychological perceptions matter: Developing the reactions to the physical work environment scale. *Building and Environment*, *148*, 338–347. doi:10.1016/j.buildenv.2018.11.020

Sandher, J., & Innes, D. (2020). *Storm ready - how to keep us afloat as unemployment hits*. Joseph Rowntree Foundation.

Sangani, P., & Chandrasekhar, A. (2020, April 22). IT campuses will never be the same: how India's 4 million IT workers shifted to working from home overnight. *The Economic Times*. https://economictimes.indiatimes.com/tech/ites/it-campuses-will-never-be-the-same-how-indias-4-million-it-workers-shifted-to-working-from-home-overnight/articleshow/75290054.cms

SangaS.McCraryJ. (2020). The impact of the coronavirus lockdown on domestic violence SSRN. https://ssrn.com/abstract=3612491 doi:10.2139srn.3612491

Sardeshmukh, S. R., Sharma, D., & Golden, T. D. (2012). Impact of telework on exhaustion and job engagement: A job demands and job resources model. *New Technology, Work and Employment*, *27*(3), 193–207. doi:10.1111/j.1468-005X.2012.00284.x

Sarkar, B. (2019, June 19). More than 50% women professionals believe sexual harassment at the workplace has increased over the years: survey. *The Economic Times.* https://economictimes.indiatimes.com/news/politics-and-nation/more-than-50-women-professionals-believe-sexual-harassment-at-the-workplace-has-increased-over-the-years-survey/articleshow/69855500.cms?utm_source=contentofinterest&utm_medium=text&utm_campaign=cppst

Sarkar, B., & Basu, S. (2020, August 26). Companies now look to check harassment during work from home. *The Economic Times*. https://economictimes.indiatimes.com/news/company/corporate-trends/companies-now-look-to-check-harassment-during-work-from-home/articleshow/77725397.cms?utm_source=contentofinterest&utm_medium=text&utm_campaign=cppst

Sarkar, U., Hemmat, S., & Linos, E. (2020). Sexual harassment and suicide. *BMJ (Clinical Research Ed.)*, *2020*(370), m3330. doi:10.1136/bmj.m3330 PMID:32878861

Satpodar, A. (2013). Sexual Harassment of Women: Reflections on the Private Sector. *Economic and Political Weekly*, 18–23.

Savolainen, T. (2014). Trust-building in e-leadership: A case study of leaders' challenges and skills in technology-mediated interaction. *The Journal of Global Business Issues*, *8*(2), 45–56.

Scandura, T., & Lankau, M. (1997). Relationships of Gender, Family Responsibility and Flexible Work Hours to Organizational Commitment and Job Satisfaction. *Journal of Organizational Behavior*, *18*(4), 377–391. doi:10.1002/(SICI)1099-1379(199707)18:4<377::AID-JOB807>3.0.CO;2-1

Schaefer, I. C. (2020, November 18). Rule 10: Don't be creepy. *The National Law Review*. https://www.natlawreview.com/article/rule-10-don-t-be-creepy

Schaubroeck, J. M., & Yu, A. (2017). When does virtuality help or hinder teams? Core team characteristics as contingency factors. *Human Resource Management Review*, *27*(4), 635–647. doi:10.1016/j.hrmr.2016.12.009

Schaufeli, W. B., & Bakker, A. B. (2004). Job demands, job resources, and their relationship with burnout and engagement: A multi-sample study. *Journal of Organizational Behavior*, *25*(3), 293–315. doi:10.1002/job.248

Schaufeli, W. B., & Taris, T. W. (2014). A Critical Review of the Job Demands-Resources Model: Implications for Improving Work and Health. In G. F. Bauer & O. Hämmig (Eds.), *Bridging occupational, organizational and public health: A transdisciplinary approach* (pp. 43–68). Springer. doi:10.1007/978-94-007-5640-3_4

Schein, E. H. (1990). Organizational culture. American Psychological Association, 45(2).

Schilbach, L., Timmermans, B., Reddy, V., Costall, A., Bente, G., Schlicht, T., & Vogeley, K. (2013). Toward a second-person neuroscience 1. *Behavioral and Brain Sciences*, *36*(4), 393–414. doi:10.1017/S0140525X12000660 PMID:23883742

Schmidt, R. M. (1983). Who Maximizes What? A Study in Student Time Allocation. *The American Economic Review*, *73*(2), 23–28.

Schon, J. B. (1991). *The Overworked American: The unexpected decline in leisure*. Basic Books.

Schumpeter, J. (1942). *Capitalism, Socialism and Democracy*. Routledge.

Scudellari, M. (2020 August, 5). How the pandemic might play out in 2021 and beyond. *Nature.* Retrieved from https://www.nature.com/articles/d41586-020-02278-5

Sedrine, S. B., Bouderbala, A., & Nasraoui, H. (in press). Leadership style effect on virtual team efficiency: Trust, operational cohesion and media richness roles. *Journal of Management Development.*

Seinfeld, S., Arroyo-Palacios, J., Iruretagoyena, G., Hortensius, R., Zapata, L. E., Borland, D., de Gelder, B., Slater, M., & Sanchez-Vives, M. V. (2018). Offenders become the victim in virtual reality: Impact of changing perspective in domestic violence. *Scientific Reports*, *8*(1), 2692. doi:10.103841598-018-19987-7 PMID:29426819

Sellick, J. (2020, July 27). Are more people looking to escape to the countryside? *Rural Services Network.*

Semin, G. R., & De Groot, J. H. (2013). The chemical bases of human sociality. *Trends in Cognitive Sciences*, *17*(9), 427–429. doi:10.1016/j.tics.2013.05.008 PMID:23796879

Serra, P. (1993). Physical violence in the couple relationship: A contribution toward the analysis of the context. *Family Process*, *32*(1), 21–33.

ServiceNow. (2020). *The Work Survey.* ServiceNow. Retrieved from https://www.servicenow.com/content/dam/servicenow-assets/public/en-us/doc-type/other-document/the-work-survey-by-servicenow-research-summary.pdf

Sewell, G., & Barker, J. R. (2006). Coercion versus care: Using irony to make sense of organizational surveillance. *Academy of Management Review*, *31*(4), 934–961. doi:10.5465/amr.2006.22527466

Shamir, B., & Salomon, I. (1985). Work-at-Home and the Quality of Working Life. *Academy of Management Review*, *10*(3), 455–464. doi:10.5465/amr.1985.4278957

Shapiro, D. L., Furst, S. A., Spreitzer, G. M., & Von Glinow, M. A. (2002). Transnational teams in the electronic age: Are team identity and high performance at risk. *Journal of Organizational Behavior*, *23*(4), 455–467. doi:10.1002/job.149

Sharma, H. (2020, April 9). Sexual harassment at workplace: a closer look at ILO Convention 190. *Intersectional Feminism.* https://feminisminindia.com/2020/04/09/sexual-harassment-workplace-ilo-convention-190/

Sharma, P. (2010). *India's first workplace sexual harassment survey reveals startling revelations.* http://www.release-news.com/

Shaw, E., Hegewisch, A. & Hess, C. (2018, October). *Sexual harassment and assault at work: understanding the costs.* Institute for Women's Policy Research, IWPR Briefing Paper #B376.

Shelton, B. A. (2006). Gender and Unpaid Work. In J. S. Chafetz (Ed.), *Handbook of the Sociology of Gender* (pp. 375–390). doi:10.1007/0-387-36218-5_17

Shen, Y., Gallivan, M. J., & Tang, X. (2016). The Impact of Perceived Subgroup Formation on Transactive Memory Systems and Performance in Distributed Teams. *International Journal of e-Collaboration*, *12*(1), 44–66. doi:10.4018/ijec.2016010104

Sheridan, B., Hoyt, G., & Imazeki, J. (2014). A Primer for New Teachers of Economics. *Southern Economic Journal*, *80*(3), 839–854. doi:10.4284/0038-4038-2013.054

Shin, Y., Hur, W., & Choi, W. (2018). Coworker support as a double-edged sword: A moderated mediation model of job crafting, work engagement, and job performance. *International Journal of Human Resource Management*, *31*(11), 1417–1438. doi:10.1080/09585192.2017.1407352

Shockley, K. M., & Allen, T. D. (2007). When flexibility helps: Another look at the availability of flexible work arrangements and work–family conflict. *Journal of Vocational Behavior*, *71*(3), 479–493. doi:10.1016/j.jvb.2007.08.006

Shore, L. M., Randel, A. E., Chung, B. G., Dean, M. A., Ehrhart, K. H., & Singh, G. (2011). Inclusion and diversity in work groups: A review and model for future research. *Journal of Management, 37*(4), 1262–1289. doi:10.1177/0149206310385943

Short, J., Williams, E., & Christie, B. (1976). *The social psychology of telecommunications*. John Wiley & Sons.

SHRM. (2012). *SHRM survey findings: Virtual teams*. https://www.shrm.org/hr-today/trends-and-forecasting/research-and-surveys/pages/virtualteams.aspx

Shukla, S. (2002, September 1). Indecent proposal. *Business Today*. http://archives.digitaltoday.in/businesstoday/20020901/cover1.html

Shute, N. (1957). *On the Beach*. Heinemann.

Silva, O., & Sousa, Á. (2020). Perception of teachers and students about teaching and learning in the period of Covid-19 pandemic. *Proceedings of ICERI2020 Conference*, 4832–4838.

Silverman, D. (2005). *Doing Qualitative Research: A Practical Handbook* (2nd ed.). Sage Publications.

Sinclair, R. R., Allen, T., Barber, L., Bergman, M., Britt, T., Butler, A., Ford, M., Hammer, L., Kath, L., Probst, T., & Yuan, Z. (2020). Occupational Health Science in the Time of COVID-19: Now more than Ever. *Occupational Health Science, 4*(1-2), 1–22. Advance online publication. doi:10.100741542-020-00064-3 PMID:32838031

Skinner, E. N., Hagood, M. C., & Provost, M. C. (2014). Creating a New Literacies Coaching Ethos. *Reading & Writing Quarterly, 30*(3), 215–232.

Slater, M. (2009). Place illusion and plausibility can lead to realistic behaviour in immersive virtual environments. *Philosophical Transactions of the Royal Society of London. Series B, Biological Sciences, 364*(1535), 3549–3557. doi:10.1098/rstb.2009.0138 PMID:19884149

Slater, M., Pérez Marcos, D., Ehrsson, H., & Sanchez-Vives, M. V. (2009). Inducing illusory ownership of a virtual body. *Frontiers in Neuroscience, 3*(2), 29. doi:10.3389/neuro.01.029.2009 PMID:20011144

Slemp, G. R. (2017). Job crafting. In The Wiley Blackwell Handbook of the Psychology of Positivity and Strengths-Based Approaches at Work. Hoboken, NJ: John Wiley & Sons, Ltd.

Smith, A. C. T., & Stewart, B. (2011). Organizational rituals: Features, functions and mechanisms: Organizational rituals. *International Journal of Management Reviews, 13*(2), 113–133. doi:10.1111/j.1468-2370.2010.00288.x

Smith, E. F., Gilmer, D. O., & Stockdale, M. S. (2019). Culture and support for workplace flexibility matter: An ecological framework for understanding flexibility support structures. *Business Horizons, 62*, 557–566. doi:10.1016/j.bushor.2019.04.002

Smith, S. A., Patmos, A., & Pitts, M. J. (2018). Communication and teleworking: A study of communication channel satisfaction, personality, and job satisfaction for teleworking employees. *International Journal of Business Communication, 55*(1), 44–68. doi:10.1177/2329488415589101

Snell, K. D. M. (2017). The rise of living alone and loneliness in history. *Social History (London), 42*(1), 2–28. doi:10.1080/03071022.2017.1256093

Sobering, K. (2019). Watercooler democracy: Rumors and transparency in a cooperative workplace. *Work and Occupations, 46*(4), 411–440.

Sokal, L., Trudel, L. E., & Babb, J. (2020). Canadian teachers' attitudes toward change, efficacy, and burnout during the COVID-19 pandemic. *International Journal of Educational Research Open*.

Solomon, S., Greenberg, J., & Pyszczynski, T. (2015). *The Worm at the Core: On the Role of Death in Life*. Random House.

Song, Y., & Gao, J. (2018). *Does telework stress employees out? A study on working at home and subjective well-being for wage/salary workers.* Institute of Labor Economics (IZA).

Song, Y. (2009). Unpaid Work at Home. *Industrial Relations, 48*(4), 578–588. doi:10.1111/j.1468-232X.2009.00576.x

SonicRim, L. S. (2001). Collective creativity. *Design, 6*(3), 1–6.

Sonnentag, S. (2012). Psychological detachment from work during leisure time: The benefits of mentally disengaging from work. *Current Directions in Psychological Science, 21*(2), 114–118. doi:10.1177/0963721411434979

Sonnentag, S., & Bayer, U. V. (2005). Switching off mentally: Predictors and consequences of psychological detachment from work during off-job time. *Journal of Occupational Health Psychology, 10*(4), 393–414. doi:10.1037/1076-8998.10.4.393 PMID:16248688

Sonnentag, S., Binnewies, C., & Mojza, E. J. (2010). Staying well and engaged when demands are high: The role of psychological detachment. *The Journal of Applied Psychology, 95*(5), 965–976. doi:10.1037/a0020032 PMID:20718528

Sowndhararajan, K., & Kim, S. (2016). Influence of Fragrances on Human Psychophysiological Activity: With Special Reference to Human Electroencephalographic Response. *Scientia Pharmaceutica, 84*(4), 724–752. doi:10.3390cipharm84040724 PMID:27916830

Sparrow, J. (2020). Working from home has a long history – be careful what you wish for in not wanting to go back to the office. *The Guardian Online.*

Spatz, S. (2018). *3 Self-Published Authors Who Went On to Have Mainstream Success – And How They Did It.* https://writingcooperative.com/3-self-published-authors-who-went-on-to-have-mainstream-success-and-how-they-did-it-36ce6dc4512f

Spicer, A. (2020). *Finding endless video calls exhausting? You're not along*. The Conversation.

Spicer, A. (2020). Organizational Culture and COVID-19. *Journal of Management Studies, 57*(8), 1737–1740. doi:10.1111/joms.12625

Spielmann, S. S., MacDonald, G., & Tackett, J. L. (2012). Social threat, social reward, and regulation of investment in romantic relationships. *Personal Relationships, 19*(4), 601–622. doi:10.1111/j.1475-6811.2011.01377.x

Spreeuwenberg, P. (2018). Reassessing the Global Mortality Burden of the 1918 Influenza Pandemic. *American Journal of Epidemiology, 187*(2), 2561-2567.

Staff SurveysN. H. S. (2019). Available: https://www.nhsstaffsurveys.com/Page/1085/Latest-Results/NHS-Staff-Survey-Results/

Standing, L., Lynn, D., & Moxness, K. (1990). Effects of noise upon introverts and extroverts. *Bulletin of the Psychonomic Society, 28*(2), 138–140. doi:10.3758/BF03333987

Stanford, J. (2017). The resurgence of gig work: Historical and theoretical perspectives. *Economic and Labour Relations Review, 28*(3), 382–401.

Stansfeld, S., & Candy, B. (2006). Psychosocial work environment and mental health-a meta-analytic review. *Scandinavian Journal of Work, Environment & Health, 32*(6), 443–462. doi:10.5271jweh.1050 PMID:17173201

Steers, R. M., & Spencer, D. G. (1977). The role of achievement motivation in job design. *The Journal of Applied Psychology, 62*(4), 472–479. doi:10.1037/0021-9010.62.4.472

Steiner, G. (1995). Interview. *Paris Review, 137.*

Stephens, J. (2020). *The Psychologist Letters.* Available: https://thepsychologist.bps.org.uk/volume-34/january-2021/want-and-buy-less

Stephenson, K. A., Kuismin, A., Putnam, L. L., & Sivunen, A. (2020). Process Studies of Organizational Space. *The Academy of Management Annals, 14*(2), 797–827. doi:10.5465/annals.2018.0146

Stephenson, K. A., Putnam, L. L., Kuismin, A., & Sivunen, A. (2018). Spacing and organizing: Process approaches to the study of organizational space. *Academy of Management Proceedings, 2018*(1), 18025. doi:10.5465/AMBPP.2018.18025abstract

Steppat, M. (2020, October 25). *Deutsche deutlich depressiver im Frühjahrs-Lockdown* [Germans markedly more depressed during spring lockdown]. FAZ. https://www.faz.net/aktuell/gesellschaft/gesundheit/coronavirus/wie-es-um-die-psychische-gesundheit-der-deutschen-steht-17017842.html

Stewart, A. (2020). *COVID-19 and the Future of Australian Industrial Relations.* CCEP-Labour-2020-Andrew-Stewart-Industrial-Relations.pdf

Stewart, G. R. (1949). *Earth Abides.* Random House.

Stop Street Harassment. (2018). *Study on sexual harassment and assault: the facts behind the #MeToo movement: A national study on sexual harassment and assault.* http://www.stopstreetharassment.org/resources/2018-national-sexual-abuse-report/

Strenio, J. (2019). Economic considerations of intimate partner violence. In R. Geffner, J. W. White, L. K. Hamberger, A. Rosenbaum, V. Vaughan-Eden, & V. I. Vieth (Eds.), *Handbook of interpersonal violence and abuse across the lifespan: a project of the National Partnership to End Interpersonal Violence Across the Lifespan (NPEIV).* Springer Nature. doi:10.1007/978-3-319-62122-7_167-1

Studemann, F. (2020, May 23). Brave New World for the Bookfests. *Financial Times.*

Sue-Chan, C., Au, A., & Hackett, R. (2012). Trust as a mediator of the relationship between leader/member behavior and leader-member-exchange quality. *Journal of World Business, 47*(3), 459–468. doi:10.1016/j.jwb.2011.05.012

Suemo, J. (2020). 12 most asked questions on Australian employee monitoring laws. *Work Time.* Retrieved 3 November 2020. https://www.worktime.com/12-most-asked-questions-on-australian-employee-monitoring-laws

Suk, J. (2006). Criminal law comes home. *The Yale Law Journal, 116*(2), 2–70.

Sundstrom, E., Bell, P. A., Busby, P. L., & Asmus, C. (1996). Environmental psychology 1989–1994. *Annual Review of Psychology, 47*(1), 485–512. doi:10.1146/annurev.psych.47.1.485 PMID:8624141

Supreme Court of the State of New York Appellate Division (Second Judicial Department). (2006). *Orientation to the profession.* http://www.courts.state.ny.us/courts/ad2/forms/law%20guardian%20handbook/orientationtotheprofession-programmaterials.pdf

Surman, E. (2002). Dialectics of dualism: The symbolic importance of the home/work divide. *Ephemera, 2*(3), 209–223.

Swinney, P. (2020). Why our city centres will survive COVID. *New Statesman Spotlight – Regional Development: "Levelling Up" Post-COVID,* 16-17.

Sytch, M., & Greer, L. I. (2020). Is your organization ready for permanent WFH? *Harvard Business Review.* https://hbr.org/2020/08/is-your-organization-ready-for-permanent-wfh

Tait, A. (2020, September 9). You met them on Zoom, now they're in the office freaking everyone out. *Wired*. https://www.wired.co.uk/article/meeting-colleagues-zoom-second-first-impressions

Tangen, S. (2005). Demystifying productivity and performance. *International Journal of Productivity and Performance Management*, *54*(1), 34–46. doi:10.1108/17410400510571437

Tansky, J. W., & Cohen, D. J. (2001). The relationship between organizational support, employee development, and organizational commitment: An empirical study. *Human Resource Development Quarterly*, *12*(3), 285–300. doi:10.1002/hrdq.15

Taparia, H. (2020 March 25). The Future of College Is Online, and It's Cheaper. *The New York Times*. Retrieved from https://www.nytimes.com/2020/05/25/opinion/online-college-coronavirus.html

Taris, T. W., & Schreurs, P. J. G. (2009). Well-being and organizational performance: An organizational-level test of the happy-productive worker hypothesis. *Work and Stress*, *23*(2), 120–136. doi:10.1080/02678370903072555

Tarr, B., Launay, J., & Dunbar, R. I. (2014). Music and social bonding:"self-other" merging and neurohormonal mechanisms. *Frontiers in Psychology*, *5*, 1096. doi:10.3389/fpsyg.2014.01096 PMID:25324805

Taylor, M. (2017). *Good Work: The Taylor Review of Modern Working Practices*. Available: https://www.gov.uk/government/publications/good-work-the-taylor-review-of-modern-working-practices

Taylor, F. W. (1911). *The Principles of Scientific Management*. W.W. Norton & Company.

TechGig. (2020, July 6). *Stress-free WFH: Accenture implements new rules for employees. TechGig*. Retrieved from https://content.techgig.com/stress-free-wfh-accenture-implements-new-rules-for-employees/articleshow/76810872.cms

TechRepublic. (2020). Transitioning Asia-Pacific to a New Normal of Work. *Microsoft*. Retrieved 25 October 2020. https://news.microsoft.com/wp-content/uploads/prod/sites/43/2020/07/Whitepaper-Transitioning-Asia-to-a-New-Normal-of-Work.pdf

Thacher & Reinheimer. (2015). https://www.stlawu.edu/news/student-faculty-sleep-research-published-presented

Tharenou, P. (1997). Explanations of Managerial Career Advancement. *Australian Psychologist*, *32*(1), 19–28. doi:10.1080/00050069708259614

Thayer, J. F., Verkuil, B., Brosschot, J. F., Kampschroer, K., West, A., Sterling, C., ... Sternberg, E. M. (2010). Effects of the physical work environment on physiological measures of stress. *European Journal of Cardiovascular Prevention and Rehabilitation*, *17*(4), 431–439. doi:10.1097/HJR.0b013e328336923a PMID:20404733

The Economist. (2020, December 3). How the pandemic is forcing managers to work harder. *The Economist*. Retrieved from https://www.economist.com/business/2020/12/03/how-the-pandemic-is-forcing-managers-to-work-harder

The Economist. (2020, November 24). People are working longer hours during the pandemic. *The Economist*. https://www.economist.com/graphic-detail/2020/11/24/people-are-working-longer-hours-during-the-pandemic

The World Bank. (2020). *COVID-19 to Add as Many as 150 Million Extreme Poor by 2021*. Available: https://www.worldbank.org/en/news/press-release/2020/10/07/covid-19-to-add-as-many-as-150-million-extreme-poor-by-2021

Tichavsky, L., Hunt, A. N., Jicha, K., & Driscoll, A. (2015). It's Just Nice Having a Real Teacher: Student Perceptions of Online Versus Face-to-face Instruction. *International Journal for the Scholarship of Teaching and Learning*, *9*(2). Advance online publication. doi:10.20429/ijsotl.2015.090202

Tietze, S., & Musson, G. (2005). Recasting the home-work relationship: A case of mutual adjustment? *Organization Studies*, *26*(9), 1331–1352. doi:10.1177/0170840605054619

Tilly, C. (1991). Reasons for the continuing growth of part-time employment. *Monthly Labor Review*, *114*(3), 10–18.

Times of India. (2020, May 18). Domestic violence cases in India on the rise during lockdown. *Times of India*. https://timesofindia.indiatimes.com/life-style/relationships/love-sex/domestic-violence-cases-in-india-on-the-rise-during-lockdown-says-report/articleshow/75801752.cms

Timms, C., Brough, P., O'Driscoll, M., Kalliath, T., Siu, O. L., Sit, C., & Lo, D. (2015). Flexible work arrangements, work engagement, turnover intentions and psychological health. *Asia Pacific Journal of Human Resources*, *53*(1), 83–103. doi:10.1111/1744-7941.12030

Tims, M., Bakker, A. B., & Derks, D. (2011). Development and validation of the job crafting scale. *Journal of Vocational Behavior*, *80*(1), 173–186. doi:10.1016/j.jvb.2011.05.009

Tims, M., & Parker, S. (2020). How co-workers attribute, react to, and shape job crafting. *Organizational Psychology Review*, *10*(1), 29–54. doi:10.1177/2041386619896087

Toffler, A. (1980). *The Third Wave*. Pan Books Ltd.

Toniolo-Barrios, M., & Pitt, L. (2020). Mindfulness and the challenges of working from home in times of crisis. *Business Horizons*. Advance online publication. doi:10.1016/j.bushor.2020.09.004 PMID:33041346

Tosini, G., Ferguson, I., & Tsubota, K. (2016). Effects of blue light on the circadian system and eye physiology. *Molecular Vision: Biology and Genetics in Vision Research*, *22*, 61–72. PMID:26900325

Townsend, A. M., DeMarie, S. M., & Hendrickson, A. R. (1998). Virtual Teams: Technology and the Workplace of the Future. *The Academy of Management Executive*, *12*(3), 17–29. doi:10.5465/ame.1998.1109047

Trahan, T., Durant, S., Müllensiefen, D., & Williamson, V. (2018). The music that helps people sleep and the reasons they believe it works: A mixed methods analysis of online survey reports. *PLoS One*, *13*(11), e0206531. doi:10.1371/journal.pone.0206531 PMID:30427881

Treas, J., & Tai, T. (2012). How couples manage the household: Work and power in cross-national perspective. *Journal of Family Issues*, *33*(8), 1088–1116.

Trevarthen, C. (1999). Musicality and the intrinsic motive pulse: Evidence from human psychobiology and infant communication. *Musicae Scientiae*, *3*(1, suppl), 155–215. doi:10.1177/10298649000030S109

Trollope, A. (1861). *Framley Parsonage*. George Smith.

Tronco-Hernandez, Y. (2020). Remote Workers During the COVID-19 Lockdown. What Are We Missing and Why Is Important. *JOEM*, *62*(11).

Tronick, E. Z., Bruschweiler-Stern, N., Harrison, A. M., Lyons-Ruth, K., Morgan, A. C., Nahum, J. P., Sander, L., & Stern, D. N. (1998). Dyadically expanded states of consciousness and the process of therapeutic change. *Infant Mental Health Journal: Official Publication of The World Association for Infant Mental Health*, *19*(3), 290–299. doi:10.1002/(SICI)1097-0355(199823)19:3<290::AID-IMHJ4>3.0.CO;2-Q

Troup, C., & Rose, J. (2012). Working from home: Do formal or informal telework arrangements provide better work-family outcomes? *Community Work & Family*, *15*(4), 471–486. doi:10.1080/13668803.2012.724220

TUC. (2015). *Report: The Price of Austerity*. Available: https://www.tuc.org.uk/sites/default/files/ThePriceofAusterity.pdf

Turner, R. H. (1960). Sponsored and Contest Mobility and the School System. *American Sociological Review*, *25*(6), 855–867. doi:10.2307/2089982

U.S. Equal Employment Opportunity Commission. (1997). *Facts about sexual harassment.* Retrieved from: https://www.eeoc.gov/publications/facts-about-sexual-harassment

U.S. Merit Systems Protection Board. (1995). *Sexual harassment in the federal workplace: trends, progress, continuing challenges.* U.S. Merits System Protection Board.

United Nations Department of Economic and Social Affairs. (2019). *World Urbanization Prospects: The 2018 Revision.* Author.

United Nations Working Group on Discrimination Against Women and Girls. (2020) *Discrimination against women and girls: women's human rights in the changing world of work (A/HRC/44/51).* https://unworkinggroupwomenandgirls.org/wp-context/uploads/2020/07/G2009480.pdf

United Nations. (2020). *Policy Brief: The Impact of COVID-19 on Women.* United Nations. Retrieved from http://digitallibrary.in.one.un.org/TempPdfFiles/4896_1.pdf

Urban Developer. (2020). Accessed November, 2020. https://theurbandeveloper.com/articles/commsec-abs-australian-houses-largest-world

Vachris, M. (1999). Teaching Principles of Economics without "Chalk and Talk": The Experience of CNU Online. *The Journal of Economic Education, 30*(3), 292–303.

Valenduc, G., & Vendramin, P. (2017). Digitalisation, between disruption and evolution. *Transfer: European Review of Labour and Research, 23*(2), 121–134. doi:10.1177/1024258917701379

Valentine, K. A., Li, N. P., Meltzer, A. L., & Tsai, M. H. (2020). Mate preferences for warmth-trustworthiness predict romantic attraction in the early stages of mate selection and satisfaction in ongoing relationships. *Personality and Social Psychology Bulletin, 46*(2), 298–311. doi:10.1177/0146167219855048 PMID:31184259

Valletta, R. G., Bengali, L., & van der List, C. (2020). Cyclical and market determinants of involuntary part-time employment. *Journal of Labor Economics, 38*(1), 67–93.

Van den Broeck, A., De Cuyper, N., De Witte, H., & Vansteenkiste, M. (2010). Not all job demands are equal: Differentiating job hindrances and job challenges in the Job Demands-Resources model. *European Journal of Work and Organizational Psychology, 19*(6), 735–759. doi:10.1080/13594320903223839

Van den Broeck, A., Vansteenkiste, M., De Witte, H., Soenens, B., & Lens, W. (2010). Capturing autonomy, competence, and relatedness at work: Construction and initial validation of the Work-related Basic Need Satisfaction scale. *Journal of Occupational and Organizational Psychology, 83*(4), 981–1002. doi:10.1348/096317909X481382

Van der Heijden, B. I., & De Vos, A. (2015). Sustainable careers: introductory chapter. In A. De Vos & B. I. Van der Heijden (Eds.), *Handbook of Research on Sustainable Careers* (pp. 1–19). Edward Elgar., doi:10.4337/9781782547037.00006

Van Eck, D., & Jammaers, E. (2020). Chronicles of conflicting care in confinement: Documenting the work experiences of seven 'patient zeros'. *Gender, Work and Organization, 2020*, 1–14. doi:10.1111/gwao.12532

van Kleef, G. A., Heerdink, M. W., & Homan, A. C. (2017). Emotional influence in groups: The dynamic nexus of affect, cognition, and behavior. *Current Opinion in Psychology, 17*, 156–161. doi:10.1016/j.copsyc.2017.07.017 PMID:28950964

Van Wingerden, J., Derks, D., & Bakker, A. B. (2017). The impact of personal resources and job crafting interventions on work engagement and performance. *Human Resource Management, 56*(1), 51–67. doi:10.1002/hrm.21758

Van Yperen, N. W., Rietzschel, E. F., & De Jonge, K. M. (2014). Blended working: For whom it may (not) work. *PLoS One, 9*(7), e102921. doi:10.1371/journal.pone.0102921 PMID:25033202

Vanden Abeele, M. M. (2020). Digital Well-being as a Dynamic Construct. *Communication Theory*, qtaa024. doi:10.1093/ct/qtaa024

Varma, A. (2020, April 22). Dealing with sexual harassment in the virtual workplace. *The Hindu Business Line*. https://www.thehindubusinessline.com/opinion/dealing-with-sexual-harassment-in-the-virtual-workplace/article31403719.ece

Vaughan, D. (1999). The dark side of organizations: Mistake, misconduct, and disaster. *Annual Review of Sociology*, *25*, 271–305.

Vegas, E., & Winthrop, E. (2020). Beyond reopening school: How education can emerge stronger than before COVID-19. *Brookings*. Retrieved from https://www.brookings.edu/research/beyond-reopening-schools-how-education-can-emerge-stronger-than-before-covid-19/

Vera, D., Samba, C., Kong, D. T., & Maldonado, T. (2020). Resilience as thriving: The role of positive leadership practices. *Organizational Dynamics*, 100784. doi:10.1016/j.orgdyn.2020.100784 PMID:32836512

Vergallito, A., Mattavelli, G., Gerfo, E. L., Anzani, S., Rovagnati, V., Speciale, M., Vinai, P., Vinai, P., Vinai, L., & Lauro, L. (2020). Explicit and Implicit Responses of Seeing Own vs. Others' Emotions: An Electromyographic Study on the Neurophysiological and Cognitive Basis of the Self-Mirroring Technique. *Frontiers in Psychology*, *11*, 433. doi:10.3389/fpsyg.2020.00433 PMID:32296363

Vermooten, N., Boonzaier, B., & Kidd, M. (2019). Job crafting, proactive personality and meaningful work: Implications for employee engagement and turnover intention. *SA Journal of Industrial Psychology*, *45*, a1567. doi:10.4102ajip.v45i0.1567

Vicaria, I. M., & Dickens, L. (2016). Meta-analyses of the intra-and interpersonal outcomes of interpersonal coordination. *Journal of Nonverbal Behavior*, *40*(4), 335–361. doi:10.100710919-016-0238-8

Vink, R., Wijnants, M. L., Cillessen, A. H., & Bosman, A. M. (2017). *Cooperative learning and interpersonal synchrony*. Academic Press.

Virick, M., DaSilva, N., & Arrington, K. (2010). Moderators of the curvilinear relation between extent of telecommuting and job and life satisfaction: The role of performance outcome orientation and worker type. *Human Relations*, *63*(1), 137–154. doi:10.1177/0018726709349198

Vitols, S. (2018). Kontinent vieler Geschwindigkeiten. Arbeitnehmer- und Bürgerbeteiligung in Europa [A continent of many speeds. Worker and citizen participation in Europe]. *WZB Mitteilungen*, *160*, 30-32. bit.do/impuls1246V

Voida, A., Bos, N., Olson, J., Olson, G., & Dunning, L. (2012). Cross-Cutting Faultlines of Location and Shared Identity in the Intergroup Cooperation of Partially Distributed Groups. In Academy of Communication Management (pp. 1–10). doi:10.1145/2207676.2208724

Von Scheve, C., & Ismer, S. (2013). Towards a theory of collective emotions. *Emotion Review*, *5*(4), 406–413. doi:10.1177/1754073913484170

Waber, Magnolfi, & Lindsay. (2014). Work spaces that move people. *Harvard Business Review*. Accessed 21 August 2020. https://hbr.org/2014/10/workspaces-that-move-people

Wajcman, J., & Rose, E. (2011). Constant connectivity: Rethinking interruptions at work. *Organization Studies*, *32*(7), 941–961. doi:10.1177/0170840611410829

Walker, J., Brewster, C. & Fontina. (2020). *Consultation on the Impact of Covid-19 on the working lives of business, management and economics' academics in UK – 2020*. International Business & Strategy, Henley Business School at the University of Reading.

Walker, L. D. (2020). The COVID-19 office in transition: Cost, efficiency and the social responsibility business case. *Accounting, Auditing & Accountability Journal, 33*(8), 1943–1967. doi:10.1108/AAAJ-06-2020-4609

Walther, J. B. (1995). Relational aspects of computer-mediated communication: Experimental observations over time. *Organization Science, 6*(2), 186–203. doi:10.1287/orsc.6.2.186

Walther, J. B. (1996). Computer-mediated communication: Impersonal, interpersonal, and hyperpersonal interaction. *Communication Research, 23*(1), 3–43. doi:10.1177/009365096023001001

Wang, B., Liu, Y., Qian, J., & Parker, S. K. (2020). Achieving Effective Remote Working During the COVID-19 Pandemic: A Work Design Perspective. *Applied psychology = Psychologie appliquee*. doi:10.1111/apps.12290

Wang, B., Lui, Y., & Parker, S. (2020). How does the use of information communication technology affect individuals? A work design perspective. *The Academy of Management Annals, 14*(2), 695–725. doi:10.5465/annals.2018.0127

Wang, H.-J., Demerouti, E., & LeBlanc, P. (2017). Transformational leadership, adaptability, and job crafting: The moderating role of organizational identification. *Journal of Vocational Behavior, 100*, 185–195. doi:10.1016/j.jvb.2017.03.009

Wang, M., & Wong, M. C. S. (2014). Happiness and leisure across countries: Evidence from international survey data. *Journal of Happiness Studies, 15*, 85–118.

Wapshott, R., & Mallett, O. (2012). The spatial implications of homeworking: A Lefebvrian approach to the rewards and challenges of home-based work. *Organization, 19*(1), 63–79. doi:10.1177/1350508411405376

Warkentin, M. E., Sayeed, L., & Hightower, R. (1997). Virtual teams versus face-to-face teams: An exploratory study or a web-based conference system. *Decision Sciences, 28*(4), 975–996. doi:10.1111/j.1540-5915.1997.tb01338.x

Watson, T. J. (2008). Managing Identity: Identity Work, Personal Predicaments and Structural Circumstances. *Organization, 15*(1), 121–143. doi:10.1177/1350508407084488

Waugh, I. M. (2010). Examining the sexual harassment experiences of Mexican immigrant farmworking women. *Violence Against Women, 16*(3), 237–261. doi:10.1177/1077801209360857 PMID:20093433

Wayne, S. J., Shore, L. M., & Liden, R. C. (1997). Perceived organizational support and leader-member exchange: A social exchange perspective. *Academy of Management Journal, 40*(1), 82–111.

Webster, J., & Wong, W. K. P. (2008). Comparing traditional and virtual group forms: Identity, communication and trust in naturally occurring project teams. *International Journal of Human Resource Management, 19*(1), 41–62. doi:10.1080/09585190701763883

Wegner, D. M. (1987). Transactive memory: A contemporary analysis of the group mind. In *Theories of group behavior* (pp. 185–208). Springer. doi:10.1007/978-1-4612-4634-3_9

Weinstein, A. (2018). When more women join the workforce, wages rise – including for men. *Harvard Business Review*. https://hbr.org/2018/01/when-more-women-join-the-workforce-wages-rise-including-for-men

Wellman, B., Salaff, J., Dimitrova, D., Garton, L., Gulia, M., & Haythornthwaite, C. (1996). Computer Networks as Social Networks: Collaborative Work, Telework, and Virtual Community. *Annual Review of Sociology, 22*(1), 213–238. doi:10.1146/annurev.soc.22.1.213

Westin, A. F. (1967). *Privacy and Freedom*. Athenaeum Press.

Wheatley, D. (2020). Changing places of work. In Contemporary Work: The Future of Employment in Developed Countries. Routledge. doi:10.4324/9781351034906-8

Wheatley, D. (2012). Good to be home? Time use and satisfaction levels among home-based teleworkers. *New Technology, Work and Employment*, *27*(3), 224–241. doi:10.1111/j.1468-005X.2012.00289.x

White, M. (2017). IBM Tells Its Remote Employees to Get Back to the Office. *ABC News*. Retrieved at https://www.nbcnews.com/business/business-news/ibm-tells-its-remote-employees-get-back-office-n763441

Whitener, E. M., Brodt, S. E., Korsgaard, M. A., & Werner, J. M. (1998). Managers as initiators of trust: An exchange relationship framework for understanding managerial trustworthy behaviour. *Academy of Management Review*, *23*(3), 513–530. doi:10.5465/amr.1998.926624

White, R. W. (1959). Motivation reconsidered: The concept of competence. *Psychological Review*, *66*(5), 297–333. doi:10.1037/h0040934 PMID:13844397

Whittall, M., & Trinczek, R. (2020). Plant-Level Employee Representation in Germany: Is the German Works Council a Management Stooge or the Representative Voice of the Workforce? In International Comparative Employee Relations: The Role of Culture and Language. DOI doi:10.4337/9781788973229

WHO. (2019). *Burn out an 'occupational phenomenon.'* Available: https://www.who.int/news/item/28-05-2019-burn-out-an-occupational-phenomenon-international-classification-of-diseases

WHO. (2020). https://www.who.int/director-general/speeches/detail/who-director-general-s-opening-remarks-at-the-media-briefing-on-covid-19---11-march-2020

Wickramasinghe, V., & Nandula, S. (2015). Diversity in team composition, relationship conflict and team leader support on globally distributed virtual software development team performance. *Strategic Outsourcing*, *8*(2–3), 138–155. doi:10.1108/SO-02-2015-0007

Wicks, S. (2020). High street heart beat (regenerating town centres). *The Planner*, (August), 20–24.

Wiesenfeld, B. M., Raghuram, S., & Garud, R. (2001). Organizational identification among virtual workers: The role of need for affiliation and perceived work-based social support. *Journal of Management*, *27*(2), 213–229. doi:10.1177/014920630102700205

Wilder, D. A., & Thompson, J. E. (1980). Intergroup contact with independent manipulations of in-group and out-group interaction. *Journal of Personality and Social Psychology*, *38*(4), 589–603. doi:10.1037/0022-3514.38.4.589

Wiles, F. (2013). 'Not easily put into a box': Constructing professional identity. *Social Work Education*, *32*(7), 854–866. doi:10.1080/02615479.2012.705273

Wilkinson, A., Gollan, P., Marchington, M., & Lewin, D. (2010). Conceptualizing Employee Participation in Organizations. In The Oxford Handbook of Participation in Organization. OUP.

Williamson, O. E. (1993). Calculativeness, trust and economic organization. *The Journal of Law & Economics*, *36*(1), 453–486. doi:10.1086/467284

Williamson, S., Colley, L., & Hanna-Osborne, S. (2020). Will working from home become the 'new normal' in the public sector? *Australian Journal of Public Administration*, *2020*(4), 1–7. doi:10.1111/1467-8500.12444

Wilson, J. M., O'Leary, M. B., Metiu, A., & Jett, Q. R. (2005). Subjective distance in teams. *Global-Production.Com*. Retrieved from http://www.global-production.com/scoreboard/resources/wilson_2005_subjective-distance-in-teams.pdf

Wilson, J. M., Straus, S. G., & McEvily, B. (2006). All in due time: The development of trust in computer-mediated and face-to-face teams. *Organizational Behavior and Human Decision Processes*, *99*(1), 16–33. doi:10.1016/j.obhdp.2005.08.001

Windle, G. (1999). Critical conceptual and measurement issues in the study of resilience. In M. Glantz & J. L. Johnston (Eds.), *Resilience and Development: Positive Life Adaptations.* Kluwer Academic/Plenum Publishers.

Wire, I. T. (2020). Employee Monitoring Software Relevance in All Working Environments. *IT Wire.* Retrieved 2 November 2020. https://www.itwire.com/sponsored-announcements/employee-monitoring-software-relevance-in-all-working-environments.html

Witchalls, C. (2009). *Managing virtual teams: Taking a more strategic approach.* The Economist Intelligence Unit.

Wittenberg, A. (2020). *The Economics of Remote Work.* Bloomberg CityLab.

Wogahn, D. (2019). *Bowker Self-Publishing Report Analysis – 5 Surprising Findings for 2019.* authorimprints.com/bowker-self-publishing-report/

Women, U. N. (2020, July 21). Take five: Why we should take online violence against women and girls seriously during and beyond COVID-19. *UN Women.* https://www.unwomen.org/en/news/stories/2020/7/take-five-cecilia-mwende-maundu-online-violence

Won, A. S., Bailenson, J. N., & Lanier, J. (2015). Homuncular flexibility: the human ability to inhabit nonhuman avatars. *Emerging Trends in the Social and Behavioral Sciences: An Interdisciplinary, Searchable, and Linkable Resource*, 1-16.

Wong, C. A., & Cummings, G. G. (2009). The influence of authentic leadership behaviors on trust and work outcomes of health care staff. *The Journal of Leadership Studies*, *3*(2), 6–23. doi:10.1002/jls.20104

Wood, P. (2020). *Employee monitoring software surges as companies send staff home.* Retrieved 18 November 2020. https://www.abc.net.au/news/2020-05-22/working-from-home-employee-monitoring-software-boom-coronavirus/12258198

Woolf, L. (1964). *Beginning Again: An Autobiography of the Years 1911-1918.* Hogarth Press.

Woolf, V. (1925). *Mrs Dalloway.* Hogarth Press.

Woolf, V. (1929). *A Room of One's Own.* Hogarth Press.

Worldometers. (2020). https://www.worldometers.info/coronavirus/

Wrzesniewski, A., & Dutton, J. E. (2001). Crafting a job: Revisioning employees as active crafters of their work. *Academy of Management Review*, *26*(2), 179–201. doi:10.5465/amr.2001.4378011

Wu, D. W. L., Chapman, C. S., Walker, E., Bischof, W. F., & Kingstone, A. (2013). Isolating the perceptual from the social: Tapping in shared space results in improved synchrony. *Journal of Experimental Psychology. Human Perception and Performance*, *39*(5), 1218–1223. doi:10.1037/a0033233 PMID:23750971

Xiao, L., & Rahman, S. (2017). Predicting learning styles based on students' learning behaviour using correlation analysis. *Current Science*, *113*(11), 2090–2096. doi:10.18520/cs/v113/i11/2090-2096

Yadav, M., Kim, J., Cabrera, D., & de Dear, R. (2017). Auditory distraction in open-plan office environments: The effect of multi-talker acoustics. *Applied Acoustics*, *126*, 68–80. doi:10.1016/j.apacoust.2017.05.011

Yin, R. K. (2003). *Case Study Research: Design and Methods.* Sage Publications.

Zaccaro, S. J., & Bader, P. (2003). E-leadership and the challenges of leading E-teams: Minimizing the bad and maximising the good. *Organizational Dynamics*, *31*(4), 377–387. doi:10.1016/S0090-2616(02)00129-8

Zaglauer, M., Drotleff, H., & Liebl, A. (2017). Background babble in open-plan offices: A natural masker of disruptive speech? *Applied Acoustics*, *118*, 1–7. doi:10.1016/j.apacoust.2016.11.004

Zalesny, M. D., & Farace, R. V. (1987). Traditional versus open offices: A comparison of sociotechnical, social relations, and symbolic meaning perspectives. *Academy of Management Journal, 30*(2), 240–259.

Zhang, C., & Ramse, J. (2021). Teaching economics behind the global COVID-19 pandemic. *International Review of Economics Education, 36*, 1–10. doi:10.1016/j.iree.2020.100206

Zhang, Wang, Yang, & Wang. (2020). Suspending Classes without Stopping Learning: China's Education Emergency Management Policy in the COVID-10 Outbreak. *Journal of Risk and Financial Management, 13*(58), 1–6.

Zhang, Y., Meng, T., Hou, Y., Pan, Y., & Hu, Y. (2018). Interpersonal brain synchronization associated with working alliance during psychological counseling. *Psychiatry Research: Neuroimaging, 282*, 103–109. doi:10.1016/j.pscychresns.2018.09.007 PMID:30292535

Zhong, C. B., & House, J. (2012). Hawthorne revisited: Organizational implications of the physical work environment. *Research in Organizational Behavior, 32*, 3–22. doi:10.1016/j.riob.2012.10.004

Ziffer, D. (2020). Coronavirus work from home might become work done overseas. *ABC News*. Retrieved from: https://www.abc.net.au/news/2020-08-11/covid-work-from-home-might-become-work-done-overseas/12542354

Zigurs, I. (2003). Leadership in virtual teams: Oxymoron or opportunity. *Organizational Dynamics, 31*(4), 339–351. doi:10.1016/S0090-2616(02)00132-8

Zilcha-Mano, S., Shamay-Tsoory, S., Dolev-Amit, T., Zagoory-Sharon, O., & Feldman, R. (2020). Oxytocin as a biomarker of the formation of therapeutic alliance in psychotherapy and counseling psychology. *Journal of Counseling Psychology, 67*(4), 523–535. doi:10.1037/cou0000386 PMID:32614232

Zimmermann, A. (2020). Managing effective remote teams inclusively. *LSE Business Review*, 3–5. Retrieved from https://blogs.lse.ac.uk/businessreview/%0Ahttp://eprints.lse.ac.uk/104690/

Zimmermann, A., Raab, K., & Zanotelli, L. (2013). Vicious and virtuous circles of offshoring attitudes and relational behaviours: A configurational study of German IT developers. *Information Systems Journal, 23*(1), 65–88. doi:10.1111/j.1365-2575.2012.00399.x

Zuboff, S. (2019). *The Age of Surveillance Capitalism: The Fight for a Human Future at the Frontier of Power*. Profile Books Limited.

Zucker, R. (2019, December). How to stop thinking about work at 3am. *Harvard Business Review, 20*. https://hbr.org/2019/12/how-to-stop-thinking-about-work-at-3am

Zuofa, T., & Ochieng, E. G. (2017). 'Working separately but together: Appraising virtual project team challenges. *Team Performance Management, 23*(5/6), 227–242. doi:10.1108/TPM-06-2016-0030

About the Contributors

Daniel Wheatley (http://orcid.org/0000-0002-6753-2867) is Reader in Business and Labour Economics at University of Birmingham, UK. His research focuses on work and well-being including job quality, work-life balance and flexible working arrangements, spatial dimensions of work including work-related travel, and other aspects of time-use including leisure time and the household division of labour. Daniel is author of Time Well Spent: Subjective Well-being and the Organization of Time and editor of the Edward Elgar Handbook of Research Methods on the Quality of Working Lives. His work has appeared in a number of edited volumes, and in peer reviewed journals.

Irene Hardill (https://orcid.org/0000-0003-1287-0647) FAcSS is Professor of Public Policy, Northumbria University, UK. Her research explores the changing world of work through the many meanings of work, paid and unpaid in the home and the community. Irene has long held a commitment to feminist methods, especially from a lifecourse perspective. She is leading a UK-wide study of the impact of the COVID-19 on the role of voluntary action in the pandemic which is funded by the UK Economic and Social Research Council (ESRC) rapid response call for projects which contribute to understanding of, and response to, the COVID-19 pandemic and its impacts.

Sarah Buglass (https://orcid.org/0000-0002-1079-8461) is a Principal Lecturer in Psychology at Nottingham Trent University, where she leads on departmental initiatives related to digital skills development and curriculum enhancement. Her main research interests span the domains of social and cyber psychology, where her work explores the psycho-social motivations and outcomes of engaging with contextually collapsed online social networking applications.

* * *

Swati Alok is an Assistant Professor with five years of experience in industry and twelve years in academics. Her research domain includes Human Resource Management & Organizational Behaviour. She has published in and acts as an ad-hoc reviewer for many peer-reviewed international journals.

Francesca Amenduni is Senior Researcher and Project Manager at SFIVET (Swiss Federal Institute for Vocational Education and Training). She is a member of the SC of the EDEN Network of Academic and Professionals. She has a PhD in Experimental Pedagogy with a research on semi-automated assessment of Critical Thinking in essays and open-ended answers (AES) carried out at Roma Tre University.

Julia Ayache is a PhD candidate at Nottingham Trent University, conducting research investigating togetherness in virtual spaces. Graduated by a Master in Cognitive Psychology from Paris Descartes University and by a Bachelor in Communication from Cesacom Paris, she worked as a project manager and user experience designer in IT companies from 2008 until 2017. Before moving in the UK to conduct her PhD, she has been involved in several research projects, investigating the use of new technologies such as virtual reality or mobile applications to improve patient well-being and implement new research methods.

Oliver Bauman is an Assistant Professor in the School of Psychology at Bond University. He received his Master of Psychology from the Carl von Ossietzky University Oldenburg (Germany) and his PhD from the University of Regensburg (Germany). He is a member of the Australian Psychological Society (APS) and the Australasian Cognitive Neuroscience Society (ACNS). Dr Baumann's research focusses on human perception, memory, and emotion, and employs a combination of behavioural, psychophysiological and neuroimaging methods.

Chris Brewster is now a part-time Professor of International Human Resource Management at Vaasa University in Finland; Henley Business School, University of Reading in the UK; and Radboud University in the Netherlands, specializing in international and comparative HRM. He had substantial industrial experience and got his doctorate from the London School of Economics before becoming an academic He been in involved as author or editor in the publication of more than 30 books, more than 100 chapters in other books and well over 200 articles.

John Burgess is Conjoint Professor at Torrens University, Adelaide. Research interests include the future of work; the ageing workforce; the development and regulatory implications of gig working; HRM practices of multinational enterprises; and human resource development in the rural regions of emerging economies.

Tatjana Byrne has a BA Honours degree in Engineering Science from Oxford University. In 2005 she completed an MSc in International Business and in 2014 she was awarded her PhD in Organization Studies (both from Birkbeck, University of London). Her research interests have included the socio-economic implications of cultural policy and she has contributed to a number of conference papers that consider the impact on organizations and individuals in fields dependent on public sector subsidies. Her work has also been published, most recently in 2010, in the anthology Dance and Politics (Peter Lang). Since 2014 she has worked for a global financial services company in Munich and is currently professionally active as an Agile Coach there.

Maria Grazia Chillemi is a high school teacher of Latin and Greek, now seconded at the Department of Curriculum and Evaluation, Ministry of Education (Italy) and member of the management team of various study groups. She is part of the steering committee of the international school network "Rete Dialogues", where she is involved in planning action-research activities, and facilitating online conferences and webinars.

Andrew Connor is an Associate Professor in the Department of Creative Technologies at Auckland University of Technology (AUT). His undergraduate training is in mechanical engineering and he holds a PhD in mechatronics. Following a number of years of commercial experience as a Software Engineer and a Systems Engineering Consultant, Andy emigrated from the UK to New Zealand and has held a number of positions at AUT. His research interests include evolutionary computation, interactive technologies and tangible interaction, and the current state and future of the tertiary education.

Kantha Dayaram is an Associate Professor in employment relations and global human resource management at Curtin University. She teaches and consults in the areas of international regulatory frameworks that support equitable employment. Her research interests include remote and flexible work arrangements, work and well-being and mature age employment. Her most recent research on Work Strain and Health Consequences and, International Industrial Relations have been published in leading Industrial Relations journals and various professional and media outlets.

Paul Delany is a professor emeritus of English at Simon Fraser University, Vancouver. He co-edited with George Landow two collections on the impact of computing on the humanities: Hypermedia and Literary Studies (MIT Press, 1991) and The Digital Word: Text-based Computing in the Humanities (MIT, 1994). He has written on the economics of literature in Literature, Money and the Market from Trollope to Amis (Palgrave, 2002). He has also written biographies of D. H. Lawrence, of the photographer Bill Brandt, of George Gissing, and of Rupert Brooke.

Luisa Errichiello is Researcher at the Institute for Studies on the Mediterranean (ISMed) of the National Research Council (CNR), Italy. She obtained a Master Degree in Management Engineering and a PhD in Engineering and Economics of Innovation. Her research interests are related to organizational innovation and change, the interplay between technology and organizing, the organization of remote work arrangements and new work practices in collaborative spaces.

Patrizia Giaveri is school principal of ITCTS Vittorio Emanuele II in Bergamo, Italy.

Anne Green is Professor of Regional Economic Development at City-REDI, University of Birmingham. Her research interests span employment, non-employment, regional and local labour market issues, skills strategies, urban and rural development, migration and commuting, associated policy issues and evaluation. She has published in high profile journals and has written numerous reports for UK Government Departments and agencies and international organisations.

Nadja Heym is a Senior Lecturer in Psychology at Nottingham Trent University since 2014. Dr Heym was awarded her PhD in 2009 from the University of Nottingham, and was employed there as a Research Coordinator on the IMAGEN project in the Brain and Body Centre and later Teaching Fellow before she moved to NTU. Her main research interests are within the area of individual differences, psychopathology and forensic mental health. She is an expert in reinforcement sensitivity, threat perception and empathy as (neuro-)psychological mechanisms underpinning maladaptive behaviours (e.g., aggression) and psychopathology (e.g., personality disorders, depression, anxiety). Her research focuses on the specific roles of affective and cognitive empathy deficits in the associations between personality traits and pro-/antisocial behaviour tendencies.

Peter Holland is a Professor of Human Resource Management and Director of the Executive MBA at Swinburne University of Technology, Melbourne. His current research interests include employee voice and silence and workplace and electronic monitoring and surveillance. He has authored/co-authored 12 books and over 150 journal articles, monographs, and book chapters on a variety of human resource management and employee relations issues.

Colin Hughes is Head of the Graduate Business School at Technological University Dublin. Colin completed his PhD at the University of Birmingham. His main research interests include leadership, trust, and virtual teams.

Peter Jordan is a Professor of Organizational Behavior and Acting Director of the Work Organization and Wellbeing Research Centre at the Griffith Business School, Griffith University, Australia. Peter's current research interests include emotional intelligence, discrete emotions in organizations and employee entitlement in organizations. Prior to working at Griffith University, he worked for the Federal Government doing strategic and operational planning.

Maria Kordowicz is a Chartered Psychologist and Senior Lecturer in Business Psychology at the Lincoln International Business School, University of Lincoln. Maria holds visiting fellowships in health services research at London South Bank and Birmingham universities and King's College London, where she was formerly a Quality Improvement Research Fellow and Master's in Public Health Programme Lead. Maria is an ethnographer whose research interests lie in the qualitative evaluation of quality improvement in public sector. Maria has been carrying out independent organisational development, management and research consultancy work on behalf of public, private and third sector clients for over 15 years. Since joining Lincoln International Business School, where she was formerly the Founding Director of the new Centre for Organisational Resilience, Maria has become interested in reconceptualising labour and productivity for meaningful working lives and sustainable futures.

Navya Kumar is currently pursuing a doctoral degree. She holds more than a decade of work experience at premier organizations, including as a research professional supporting internal strategy, consulting, and business development.

M. Beatrice Ligorio is Full Professor in Educational Psychology at the University of Bari, where she teaches Educational Psychology and E-learning. Her research interests concern educational technologies and new theoretical approaches to learning such as dialogic and trialogical approach. She is the Department delegate for E-learning. She is vice-president of the inter-university Collaborative Knowledge Building Group (CKBG; www.ckbg.org/) and since 2006 she has been the main editor of the interdisciplinary journal called Qwerty (indexed on Scopus) (www.ckbg.org/qwerty/index.php/ qwerty). She is in the scientific committee of many journals of the field. She has more than 200 publications among national and international journals, chapters and edited texts.

Phil Lord conducts research at McGill University's Faculty of Law. His research concerns public law, behavioural economics, and law and religion. He has authored more than twenty academic articles.

Stefan Marks is a researcher and senior lecturer of Creative Technologies in the School of Future Environments at Auckland University of Technology. His main areas of research are collaborative extended reality (XR) and data visualisation. He combines these interests in his function as director of Sentience Lab, a facility for the development of immersive, multimodal and multisensory data visualisation and interaction. Stefan has eight years of industry experience as a hardware and software developer, a Diplom of Microinformatics and a Master's Degree in Human-Computer Interaction from the Westfälische Hochschule, Germany and a PhD from The University of Auckland.

Dena Markudova is a PhD student in Electrical, Electronics and Communications Engineering at the Polytechnic University of Turin. Her research focuses on Data science applied to Computer Networking – analysis of Network traffic and application of Machine learning algorithms for better Network management. She did her Bachelor studies in Telecommunications at "Ss. Cyril and Methodius" University in Skopje, North Macedonia and her Master studies in ICT for Smart Societies at Politecnico di Torino.

Rosa Martins de Oliveira studied Economics in Germany and Spain, and she holds a Phd. in Health Care Economics from the University of Nuremberg. She joined the Allianz Group in 2002, holding positions in various roles and line of businesses, i.e. Executive Assistant, Sales and Project Manager, as well as Researcher and Learning Expert. In 2018, Rosa got elected to represent workers in Allianz SE, the headquarter of Allianz. In this role, she is member of the executive and the economic committee. Her main areas of interest are New Work and Learning & Development.

Ana Luíza Matos de Oliveira is an economist and PhD in Economic Development, Visiting Professor at FLACSO - Brazil, Coordinator of the Executive Secretary of the Parliamentary Caucus in Defense of Public Service (Frente Servir Brasil), researcher and consultant. Member of the International Association for Feminist Economics (IAFFE)'s Membership Committee. She was a visiting scholar at Zakir Husain Centre for Educational Studies (Jawaharlal Nehru University, India), Lateinamerika-Institut (Freie Universität Berlin, Germany) and Université de Genève (Switzerland). Her areas of interest are labour relations, working conditions in the health care sector, public and social policy, austerity, inclusion in higher education, feminist economics, social economic and 4.0 industry.

Elangovan N. is an Associate Professor in the School of Business and Management at Christ (Deemed to be University), Bangalore, India. He also coordinates the PhD Programme at the School. He was earlier the Director of National Institute of Fashion Technology (NIFT), Kannur Campus. He comes to academics after a long experience in running a textile business. He earned a PhD in Management Science from Anna University, Chennai, India. He holds an MBA from Pondicherry University and an MSc in Psychology. He also holds a BE in Mechanical from Bharathiar University and a BA in psychology from Madras University. He has published in journals including International Journal of enterprise resource planning, and International Journal of Innovation and Technology Management. His research interest is in the areas of Strategic Information Systems, Entrepreneurship, Design and innovation, Consumer behaviour studies.

Lílian Nogueira Rolim is a Ph.D. candidate in Economics at the University of Campinas, in Brazil. She holds a MA in Economics from the University of Campinas and a MA in International Macroeconomics and Finance from the University of Paris 13, in France. Her research covers topics related to gender, income distribution, economic activity, and macroeconomic models.

Tommasina Pianese is Researcher at the Institute for Studies on the Mediterranean (ISMed) of the National Research Council (CNR), Italy. Her researches focus on organizational innovation, namely a) remote working (i.e. telework, virtual work, smart working) enabled by progress in ICT; b) Smart Work Centers, innovative corporate workplaces whose layout inspired to collaborative spaces. The focus is on understanding changes in organizational processes, managerial practices and individual behaviors because of these innovations in work arrangements and workplace design. She is coordinator of #RGCSRoma, Italian Chapter of #RGCS Research Group on Collaborative Spaces, an interdisciplinary research group on collaborative spaces.

Alannah Rafferty is an Associate Professor in the School of Employment Relations and Human Resources at Griffith Business School, Griffith University, Brisbane, Australia. Her research interests include attitudes to organizational change (e.g., change readiness, commitment to change, resistance to change), leadership (transformational leadership, abusive supervision), and stress and coping during organizational change.

Lorenzo Raffio is a Project Manager at the Tony Blair Institute for Global Change. He is specialised in leading the development of large-scale learning platforms for education and in the monitoring and evaluation of digital activities designed for young people. He is interested in research concerning experiences in education involving innovative technological tools that leverage the power of the internet to create opportunities for dialogue and intercultural exchange.

Rebecca Riley is Business Development Director at City-REDI at the University of Birmingham and Head of the Office of Data Analytics at West Midlands Combined Authority. She has wide-ranging expertise in undertaking research and consultancy projects and in partnership development. She has experience in the higher education, local government and national policy sectors. Previously she has been Head of Research at the Northwest Regional Development Agency and led a regional economic observatory, providing the evidence base for regional, local and policy specific strategies and programmes.

Joyita Roy Chowdhury is an Assistant Professor of Economics at FLAME University. She holds a Ph.D. degree and an M.S. in Economics from the University of Utah, USA. She holds an M.Phil. degree in Development Studies and Economics, an MSc degree in Economics, a BSc degree in Economics (Honors), all from the University of Calcutta, Kolkata. Before joining FLAME, she was a Visiting Assistant Professor of Economics at Hobart and William Smith Colleges, Geneva, New York. Her research interests lie in the areas of applied microeconomics with a particular focus on the role of institutions in addressing resource and environmental issues. She applies different research methods and uses multiple perspectives of economics to study micro-development issues. She collects survey data and conducts behavioral experiments in rural villages with real-world subjects. Also, she analyzes longitudinal data on current economic problems and uses it to contribute to social and economic change.

Lygia Sabbag Fares is core faculty at the Brooklyn Institute for Social Research. PhD on Development Economics: Social and Labor Economics, from the University of Campinas (UNICAMP) (Brazil), was a visiting scholar at York University (Canada). Master of Arts in Labor Policies and Globalization at Kassel University (Germany), Certificate degree in Labor Economics, and Bachelor of Arts in International Relations. Organizer of the Gender working group of the Young Scholars Initiative (YSI) - Institute for New Economic Thinking. Member of a multidisciplinary research group on development studies at the University of São Paulo, and representative of the Young Scholars member committee of the International Association for Feminist Economics (IAFFE). Areas of interest: Development Economics, Labor Economics, Feminist Economics, Political Economy, Macroeconomics, Brazilian Economics.

Elizabeth (Libby) Sander is an Assistant Professor of Organizational Behavior at the Bond University Business School, a TEDx speaker and an Agenda Contributor at the World Economic Forum. Libby's research centres on the physical work environment and its effects on cognition, emotions, relational behavior and performance. She is leading several funded grant projects and her multi-disciplinary research on the physical work environment spans organizational behavior, neuroscience, architecture, psychology, mixed reality, entrepreneurship, and urban design.

Mark N. K. Saunders is Professor of Business Research Methods at the Birmingham Business School, University of Birmingham where he is Director of Global Engagement. Mark currently holds visiting professorships at the Universities of London (Birkbeck), Surrey and Worcester. He was awarded a fellowship of the Academy of Social Sciences in 2019 in recognition of his contribution to methods and human resource management research and social science researcher development. He was elected to Fellow of the British Academy of Management in 2014 and in 2017 was awarded their Medal for Leadership in recognition of prolonged contribution to doctoral capacity building. Mark's research interests include research methods, human resource aspects of the management of change, in particular trust. He has co-authored and edited over 30 books including 'Research Methods for Business Students' (currently in its 8th edition) and 'How to Keep Your Doctorate on Track'. He has published over 100 research articles and book chapters including papers in journals such as British Journal of Management, Field Methods, Human Performance, Human Relations, Journal of Small Business Management, Management Learning, R&D Management, Social Science and Medicine and Annals of Tourism Research.

Vinita Seshadri is an Assistant Professor in School of Business and Management at Christ (Deemed to be University), Bangalore, India. She holds Masters in Business Administration from Pune University. She started her career as a faculty in School of Business and Management in the year 2010 after working for a while in the industry. Her research interest is in the areas of Strategy, Organisational Behaviours and Human Resource Management. She has travelled and stayed in countries like United States of America, United Kingdom and Canada.

Jacqueline Strenio is an Assistant Professor of Economics at Southern Oregon University and affiliated faculty in Gender, Sexuality, and Women's Studies and Healthcare Administration. Her research interests are in health and feminist economics. Her current research focuses on violence against women, including sexual harassment and intimate partner violence. Her research emphasizes that such violence is not only a substantial violation of a person's right to a life free from violence, but also results in other significant unfreedoms, including reducing the capability to achieve economic empowerment. Her recent publications on these topics have appeared in the journal Feminist Economics and the Handbook of Interpersonal Violence and Abuse Across the Lifespan. She earned her M.S. and Ph.D. in Economics from the University of Utah, USA and a B.A. in Economics from the University of Colorado at Boulder, USA.

Alexander Sumich completed his PhD at Kings College London in 2009, and joined Nottingham Trent University in 2010, where he holds an Associate Professor post in Psychology.

Index

F

G

H

I

J

K

L

M

N

O

P

Q

R

S

T

U

V

W

Premier Reference Source
Emerging GIS Applications for Emergency and Disaster Management

Premier Reference Source
Managerial Strategies and Green Solutions for Project Sustainability

Premier Reference Source
Comparative Approaches to Using R and Python for Statistical Data Analysis

Premier Reference Source
Solutions for High-Touch Communications in a High-Tech World

www.ingramcontent.com/pod-product-compliance
Lightning Source LLC
LaVergne TN
LVHW060357300926
849162LV00006B/1288